THE PRITCHETT CENTURY

Sir Victor Sawdon Pritchett was born above a toy-shop in Ipswich, Suffolk in 1900. His family moved constantly during his childhood and he left school at sixteen to work in the leather trade in London. In the 1920s he became a journalist, first during the Irish Civil War and later in Spain: his first book, *Marching Spain*, was published in 1928. From that time on, although he held several academic posts, he was first and foremost a writer, achieving fame for his short stories and wide admiration for his journalism and his criticism, particularly his weekly column 'Books in General' for the *New Statesman* in the 1950s, in which he surveyed the whole range of European literature. He became President of the Society of Authors, was a foreign member of the American Academy of Arts and Letters and the Academy of Arts and Sciences, and also President of the International P.E.N. He became C.B.E. in 1968, was knighted in 1975, and was made Companion of Honour in 1993.
He died in London, in March 1997.

ALSO BY V.S. PRITCHETT

Short Stories

The Spanish Virgin
You Make Your Own Life
It May Never Happen
Collected Stories (1956)
*Sailor, Sense of Humour and
Other Stories*
When My Girl Comes Home
The Key to My Heart
Blind Love and Other Stories
*The Camberwell Beauty and
Other Stories*
Selected Stories
On the Edge of the Cliff
Collected Stories (1982)
More Collected Stories
*A Careless Widow and
Other Stories*
The Complete Short Stories
The Lady from Guatemala

Novels

Clare Drummer
Shirley Sanz
Nothing Like Leather
Dead Man Leading
Mr Beluncle

Memoirs

A Cab at the Door
Midnight Oil

Literary Criticism

In My Good Books
*The Living Novel and
Later Appreciations*
Books in General
The Working Novelist
*George Meredith and the
English Comedy*
The Myth Makers
The Tale Bearers
A Man of Letters
Lasting Impressions

Travel

Marching Spain
The Spanish Temper
London Perceived
(with photographs by Evelyn Hofer)
Foreign Faces
New York Proclaimed
(with photographs by Evelyn Hofer)
Dublin: A Portrait
(with photographs by Evelyn Hofer)
At Home and Abroad

Biography

Balzac
*The Gentle Barbarian:
The Life and Work of Turgenev*
Chekhov: A Spirit Set Free

V.S. Pritchett

THE PRITCHETT CENTURY

The Selected Writings
of V.S. Pritchett

VINTAGE

Published by Vintage 1999

2 4 6 8 10 9 7 5 3 1

Jacket photograph of V.S. Pritchett as a young man
courtesy of the author
Jacket photograph of V. S. Pritchett © Jane Bown

For Acknowledgments, please see pxxi

First published in Great Britain in 1998 by
Chatto & Windus

First published in the USA in 1997 by
Random House, Inc., New York

Vintage
Random House, 20 Vauxhall Bridge Road,
London SW1V 2SA

Random House Australia (Pty) Limited
20 Alfred Street, Milsons Point, Sydney
New South Wales 2061, Australia

Random House New Zealand Limited
18 Poland Road, Glenfield, Auckland 10,
New Zealand

Random House South Africa (Pty) Limited
Endulini, 5A Jubilee Road, Parktown 2193,
South Africa

The Random House Group Limited Reg. No. 954009
www.randomhouse.co.uk

A CIP catalogue record for this book
is available from the British Library

ISBN 0 09 975541 6

Printed and bound in Great Britain by
Cox & Wyman Limited, Reading, Berkshire

V. S. PRITCHETT

Victor Sawdon Pritchett, the extraordinarily prolific and versatile man of letters widely regarded as one of the greatest stylists in the English language, was born in Ipswich, Suffolk, on December 16, 1900. His father, whom he recalled in the enchanting memoir *A Cab at the Door* (1968), was a boundlessly optimistic but chronically unsuccessful businessman whose series of failed ventures necessitated frequent moves to elude creditors. These repeated uprootings interrupted Pritchett's formal education, yet he was a voracious reader from an early age, devouring the novels of Charles Dickens and Thomas Hardy as well as the complete works of Shakespeare. Apprenticed in the leather trade at fifteen, Pritchett alleviated the boredom of a menial clerical job by delving extensively into the classics. At twenty he left for Paris, vowing to become a writer. He later reflected on his experiences there in *Midnight Oil* (1971), a second volume of autobiography that endures as an intimate and precise record of an artist's self-discovery.

Pritchett began his writing career as a foreign correspondent for *The Christian Science Monitor*, which sent him on assignments in Ireland and Spain. *Marching Spain* (1928), his first book, recounts impressions of a country that held a lifelong fascination for Pritchett. His other travel writing includes *The Spanish Temper* (1954), *The Offensive Traveller* (1964; published in the U.K. as *Foreign Faces*), and *At Home and Abroad* (1989). In addition, he collaborated with photographer Evelyn Hofer on three acclaimed metropolitan profiles: *London Perceived* (1962), *New York Proclaimed* (1964), and *Dublin: A Portrait* (1967).

After his career as a roving journalist, Pritchett returned to London and started writing fiction. *Clare Drummer* (1929), the first of his five novels, draws on his travels in Ireland, while *Elopement into Exile* (1932; published in the U.K. as *Shirley Sanz*) again reflects his enthrallment with Spain. During this period he also completed *Nothing Like Leather* (1935), a compelling saga about the rise and fall of an English businessman, and *Dead Man Leading* (1937), an allegorical tale of a journey into darkness that is reminiscent of Conrad. Pritchett's best-known novel, *Mr. Beluncle* (1951), is a work of Dickensian scope featuring an endearing scoundrel-hero modeled after his own father.

Yet it is widely acknowledged that Pritchett's genius as a storyteller came to full fruition in his short fiction. "Pritchett's literary achievement is enormous, but his short stories are his greatest triumph," said Paul Theroux. Beginning with *The Spanish Virgin and Other Stories* (1930) right up through *Complete Collected Stories* (1991), Pritchett published fourteen volumes filled with masterful tales that chronicle the lives of ordinary people through a flood of details and humorous, kindhearted observations. His other collections include: *You Make Your Own Life* (1938), *It May Never Happen* (1945), *The Sailor, Sense of Humor, and Other Stories* (1956), *When My Girl Comes Home* (1961), *The Key to My Heart* (1964), *Blind Love* (1970), *The Camberwell Beauty* (1974), *Selected Stories* (1978), *On the Edge of the Cliff* (1980), *Collected Stories* (1982), *More Collected Stories* (1983), and *A Careless Widow* (1989).

"We read Pritchett's stories, comic or tragic, with an elation that stems from their intensity," observed Eudora Welty. "Life goes on in them without flagging. The characters that fill them—erratic, unsure, unsafe, devious, stubborn, restless and desirous, absurd and passionate, all peculiar unto themselves—hold a claim on us that is not to be denied. They demand and get our rapt attention, for in their revelation of their lives, the secrets of our own lives come into view." And Reynolds Price noted: "An extended view of his short fiction reveals a chameleonic power of invention, sympathy and selfless transformation that sends one back as far as Chekhov for a near-parallel."

The acclaim lavished on Pritchett for his short stories has been matched by that accorded his literary criticism. "Pritchett is not only our best short story writer but also our best literary critic," stated Anthony Burgess. *In My Good Books* (1942), *The Living Novel* (1946), *Books in General* (1953), and *The Working Novelist* (1965) contain essays written during his long association with the *New Statesman*. Pritchett continued his exploration of world literature in *George Meredith and English Comedy* (1970), *The Myth Makers* (1979), *The Tale Bearers* (1980), *A Man of Letters* (1985), and *Lasting Impressions* (1990). His magnum opus of literary criticism, *Complete Collected Essays*, was issued in 1992. In addition he produced three masterful works that artfully meld criticism with biography: *Balzac* (1974), *The Gentle Barbarian: The Life and Work of Turgenev* (1977), and *Chekhov: A Spirit Set Free* (1988).

"Pritchett is the supreme contemporary virtuoso of the short literary essay," said *The New York Times Book Review.* "His essays are sketches of an author's life, times and works. Always the short-story writer, he is fascinated by people, by characters. He has the lower-middle-class Londoner's quick eye and sharp tongue and appetite for comedy. He's quick to spot pride, the cover-up, flummery, snobbery, cant. From his work he appears to be an emotional, intensely curious man—plucky, blunt, generous.... Pritchett is informal but never clubby, witty but never snide or snobbish, precise and always full of gusto." And Gore Vidal, who deemed him "our greatest English-language critic," remarked: "It would be very nice for literature if he lived forever."

"If, as they say, I am a Man of Letters I come, like my fellows, at the tail-end of a long and once esteemed tradition in English and American writing," Pritchett once said. "We have no captive audience. We do not teach. We write to be readable and to engage the interest of what Virginia Woolf called 'the common reader.' We do not lay down the law, but we do make a stand for the reflective values of a humane culture. We care for the printed word in a world that nowadays is dominated by the camera and by scientific, technological, sociological doctrine.... I was not a product of Eng. Lit. I had never been taught and, even now, I am shocked to hear that literature is 'taught.' I found myself less a critic than an imaginative traveller or explorer ... I was travelling in literature."

Knighted in 1975 for his services to literature and made a Companion of Honour in 1993, Sir Victor Pritchett died in London on March 20, 1997. As novelist Margaret Drabble noted before his death: "Pritchett has lived as a man of letters must, by his pen, and he has done it with a freshness of interest and an infectious curiosity that have never waned."

FOREWORD

BY

OLIVER PRITCHETT

It never struck me as odd, when I was growing up, that I had a father who was generally known by a set of initials. At lunchtime, my mother would stand in the hall and call out "V.S.P." No response. She would try again two or three times, then sometimes she would change the call to "Voospie."

If there was still no answer, my sister, Josephine, or I would be sent to fetch him. The pipe smoke got thicker as I approached and when I opened the door he would be seated in an old armchair, surrounded by a sprinkling of used matches, with his legs crossed and his old pastry board propped on his lap.

Over the years the pastry board had turned as dark as mahogany and there were sometimes doodles round the side of it—usually of faces with wavy furrowed brows. The paper was fastened to the board with a Bulldog clip, and V.S.P. wrote in fountain pen and terrible handwriting.

As I first peeped round the door he looked frightening. He wore a terrible frown and his bottom jaw jutted fiercely in his struggle to order the words on the page. It was a battle. Sometimes he held his head away from the board, as if he expected those words to rise up from the page and fight back.

Then he would look up and see me and immediately become his welcoming, smiling self again, coming to lunch, leaving some of his thoughts behind in his study, sometimes rehearsing his ideas at the table.

"The extraordinary thing about Henry James. . . "

"Can I have another potato, please?"

I was never a very satisfactory audience.

We were in a word factory. My sister and I learned quickly that we had to be quiet in the house when V.S.P. was working. No shouting, no barging into his study. It seemed quite normal to us. When my sister was very small, she would wait in ambush outside his study, and he would have to climb out of the window and creep round the outside of the house when he wanted to go to the lavatory.

The handwritten pages, covered in revisions, crossings out, second and third thoughts, and sideways writing in the margins, were given to my mother to type. They would be revised and typed again and again. The Imperial typewriter was a sacred object. Nobody else was allowed to touch it. I was nervous of even standing too close to it.

My mother typed with such speed and force that it was not like mere machine gun fire. She seemed to be at the keyboard playing tremendous major chords, producing a whole paragraph at once.

Her ability to decipher V.S.P.'s handwriting must have been the result of some sort of brilliant telepathy. When he was abroad a five-line postcard from him would take me two days to work out and a letter could last for a week or more.

And what an output there has been from this word factory! Selecting a fraction of it for this volume has been difficult, of course, but it has also been a huge pleasure—re-reading the autobiography, the short stories, and the novels, recognising incidents from our life which have been smuggled into the stories, feeling a sort of thrill at a brilliant phrase or a daring generalisation in the literary criticism.

I soon realised that I could not make an entirely logical or even sensible selection, or anything that could be taken as the last word. So I have tried to give an idea of the extraordinary range of my father's work, the amazing breadth of his reading, the variety of his subjects.

Some of the choices are based on our conversations. Sometimes, in recent years, when we talked at the table after dinner, he would wave his hand in the direction of the imposing ranks of Walter Scott novels in the bookshelf and say, "Nobody reads Scott anymore" and then speak about him so amusingly that those volumes no longer seemed so daunting.

That is the reason I have included his essay on Scott from *The Living Novel*. I have chosen other essays simply for the pleasure they have given me and for the way he has always made literature unintimidating.

He often talked about his misery at being taken away from school and being made to work in the leather trade when he wanted to go to university, and about how valuable the experience turned out to be, so I have included the section from his autobiography about that time. Years ago, he and I took a walk in Bermondsey, in South London, and found the building where he first went to work.

The early chapters of his novel *Mr. Beluncle* are included because they are very funny, but also give another perspective on V.S.P.'s childhood with his Christian Scientist father.

He many times talked to me about the short story "Sense of Humour," about how he re-wrote it again and again, thinking of different ways of telling the story and how, when it was finally published, it suddenly made his reputation. When he recalled this success he put on that particular expression of his, a mixture of puzzlement, amusement, and pleasure, which he always had when somebody paid him a compliment.

Spain had to have a prominent place, so you will find a chapter from *Marching Spain*, first published in 1928, as well as extracts from *The Spanish Temper* and a more recent essay on Gerald Brenan, his great friend and another interpreter of that country.

There are also sections of my father's books on Chekhov and Turgenev. I have tried to find passages from these books, and also from the two volumes of autobiography and the novels, which are self-contained. They can only provide a glimpse of the work, but I hope they may encourage people to read the whole thing.

There is also a chapter here from the novel *Dead Man Leading*, first published in 1937, written when V.S.P. had never been to South America but had just made a model of the Amazon in the garden with matches and bits of string to help him. He went to South America about twenty years later to write travel articles, and I thought it would be interesting to include his piece on Amazonia, as he eventually found it—and also a later short story "The Vice Consul," which is set in South America.

In deciding which short stories to include, I have indulged myself and picked some of my own favourites, added my father's favourite, "When My Girl Comes Home," and my mother's choice, "The Fig Tree," and the one he wrote specially for my mother, "The Marvellous Girl."

Cocky Olly was a game my sister and I used to play with other children when we lived in the country and visited nearby families. Years later it re-appeared in a V.S.P. short story of the same name, which is in this collection. It surprised me, because I had not really believed he had noticed our game or had not expected he would remember it. I should have known better. He has always had a way of sharply observing while appearing not to be paying much attention, and the stories are full of odd details that have been stored for years.

In *The Turn of the Years*, V.S.P. wrote of his feelings at reaching the age of eighty, of being as old as the century, having been born at the end of 1900. This collection includes work written in the early part of this century and in its last decades. It is only a small fraction of all he wrote. When I consider the output of that word factory, I am still filled with admiration and astonishment.

In Memoriam: V. S. Pritchett

by

John Bayley

It's often said that the short story today goes with poetry. But the trouble with bringing poetry in is not only that the "poetic" is a bad thing in prose but that it implies a degree of consciousness and concentration which the very best stories don't seem to have. William Gass rationally observed that the story "is a poem grafted onto a sturdier stock" but Borges decreed that "unlike the novel, it may be essential." That has an ominous sound.

None of these suggestions seems to fit the way in which V. S. Pritchett wrote his novels and stories. Many are absolute masterpieces, no doubt about that: but the master who wrote them did not think his own process deserved any extended comment. Never had a great craftsman, and one who was universally admitted to be such, so unpretending a persona. Nothing in him needed to build himself up. There seem to be no stories about him, no legend, no special atmosphere or locality which an admirer can feel that he haunts. Everyone knows what "Chekhovian" means, or has come to mean, but "Pritchettian," or "Pritchett-like"? No, one cannot imagine that becoming part of the literary vocabulary. So was there a style, and what was it, and how did it succeed so well?

It is here that the idea of poetry, the poetry of the short story, does give the necessary clue: and yet it must be obtained without any suggestion of the poetic, which is what Pritchett contrived. Elizabeth Bowen sometimes obtained the same sort of effect by different means. In one of her stories a married woman and a younger man, who know in their heart of hearts that their affair will soon break up, have spent Sunday afternoon on a common in Metroland, and as they make for the bus-stop they see a photographer taking a picture of a girl across a pond. Elizabeth Bowen moves her "atmosphere" briefly into that of the photograph's ambience: the picture will be called "Autumn Evening," and will appear in a professional magazine as an art study in mood, symbolising the sadness of ending, and romance and the time of year. This, too, is how the lovers have seen themselves, and how the real pathos of their relation is merged into the kind of plangent sadness they can cope with, and the reader can recognise.

The probable source of this particular effect is *Dubliners,* in which Pritchett had once found even more inspiration than had Elizabeth Bowen. Such settings-up of poetry must be meticulously done, though seeming casual. If too casual they become jarringly offhand, sometimes a feature of the Kingsley Amis technique: "He noticed that the various lights of the High Street were reflected on the wet pavements in not too bad a way at all." The complex effect aimed at here—this "he" has sensibility which the reader will recognise as that of the author, who is quite capable of that sensibility even as he frames it and sends it up—draws so much attention to itself that it becomes portentous instead of light-handed. The masters of this kind of narrative draw no attention to it all. In Chekhov's "The Lady with the Dog" the pair have met, found themselves making love, and then taken a cab along the sea-front and sat on a bench together in the dawn.

Yalta was barely visible through the dawn mist; white clouds hung motionless on the mountain peaks. Not a leaf stirred on the trees, cicadas chirped. Borne up from below, the sea's monotonous muffled boom spoke of peace, of the everlasting sleep awaiting us. Before Yalta or Oreanda yet existed that surf had been thundering down there; it was roaring away now, and it will continue its dull booming with the same unconcern when we are no more. This persistence, this utter aloofness from all our lives and deaths ... do they perhaps hold the secret pledge of our eternal salvation, of life's perpetual motion on earth, of its uninterrupted progress? As he sat there, lulled and entranced by the magic panorama—sea, mountains, clouds, broad sky—beside a young woman who looked so beautiful in the dawn, Gurov reflected that everything on earth is beautiful, really, when you consider it— everything except what we think and do ourselves when we forget the lofty goals of being, and our human dignity.

Someone—a watchman no doubt—came up, looked at them, went away. Even this incident seemed mysterious—beautiful, too. In the dawn they saw a steamer arrive from Feodosia, its lights already extinguished.

'There's dew on the grass,' Anne said after a pause.

'Yes, time to go home.'

They went back to town.

In the friendliness and anonymity of his best tales Pritchett is often just like this: the same style of uninsistent genius. His admirable study of Chekhov, and particularly of "The Lady with the Dog," does not actually mention this passage: but one can feel his sense of it, and the meaning it had for him, not only throughout the book, which is eminently compressed and factual, but throughout the whole span of his own narrative art. What he learned from Chekhov was not in the least how to be "Chekhovian," but something much more precise and at the same time invisible: the art of blending, as author, into the sensibility of his characters without seeming to distinguish between that sensibility and the writing itself; to glide imperceptibly in and out of another's sensibility; and invariably to put the objective detail at the correct spot, as Chekhov puts the watchman who comes up, looks at the lovers, goes away.

This mastery is present throughout all his narratives, short or long. An illustration of quite a different kind, but showing the same inseparable flow of character, narrator and situation, can be taken from Pritchett's story called "The Diver." The youthful narrator, an Englishman, is working for a small firm in Paris, but his ambition is precisely to write stories.

> And what were these stories? Impossible to say. I would set off in the morning and see the grey, ill-painted buildings of the older quarters leaning together like people, their shutters thrown back, so that the open windows looked like black and empty eyes. In the mornings the bedding was thrown over the sills to air, and hung out, wagging like tongues about what goes on in the night between men and women. The houses looked sunken-shouldered, exhausted, by what they told; and crowning the city was the church of Sacré-Coeur, very white, standing like some dry Byzantine bird, to my mind hollow-eyed and without conscience, presiding over the habits of the flesh and—to judge by what I read in newspapers—its crime also; its murders, rapes, its shootings for jealousy and robbery. As my French improved, the secrets of Paris grew worse. It amazed me that the crowds I saw on the street had survived the night, and many indeed looked as sleepless as the houses.

Pritchett contrives to blend the "story" elements simmering inside the young narrator ("black and empty eyes", "wagging like tongues") with a more deep and comprehensive sense of town and people. The story is in some ways a reworking of Pritchett's early novel, *Nothing like Leather*, drawing on his experiences as a young man in the trade. "After I had been a little more than a year in Paris—14 months in fact—a drama broke in the monotonous life of our office. A consignment of dressed skins had been sent to us from Rouen. It had been sent to us by barge—not the usual method in our business." The narrator is both the young businessman with a proper sense of precision and a pride of professional decorum, and the literary aspirant coining phrases about Paris. The barge sinks near the warehouse and a diver is sent down to rescue the skins. In the course of the operation the young man is accidentally knocked into the water, fished out, and befriended by the colleague—probably mistress—of the boss, who runs a cleaning and mending shop nearby. In the course of lending him dry clothes she makes a heavy pass at him, and in the attempt to keep his end up he invents a story of having found a nude strangled woman when, at the age of twelve, he was sent by his parents on an errand. A true Parisienne, the woman is fascinated, and in seducing him has the thrill of imagining he will strangle her. "Have you seen his hands?" she says to the boss, who puts on a shrewd look.

Pritchett has a delicate sense of the way people live inside clichés, and only come out to give them a fresh emphasis. Gurov, in "The Lady with the Dog," reflects on the beauty of life in the peaceful aftermath of a successful seduction, and Chekhov contrives not to "place" him in the course of those reflections but to merge them into the space and meaning of the tale. In "The Diver" Pritchett performs a similar operation, mingling cliché with symbol—on two national levels—to produce a work which dives almost involuntarily into the texture of different lives.

He once said about Hemingway, whom he much admired, that he discovered other people in his stories by a process of stylisation based on a single unitary fantasy: the Hemingway version of living. Pritchett himself learnt how to be stylish without drawing attention to it—making style an observed indication of other people. In Hemingway's story "Indian Camp," a traumatic birth and suicide, preceded and ended by an evening and dawn voyage across water, leave the narrator knowing that he "would never die." Other people have that effect on the hero of the "eternal moment," as fixed in such a tale. Pritchett, by contrast, leaves a plurality of existences to run on apart, after they have come together for the duration of his story.

Pritchett was an admirable critic as well as a superb novelist: novels like *Mr Beluncle* and the studies of Balzac and Turgenev are made to last. But the stories are of a wholly superior and indeed a unique manufacture. Like Kipling and Chekhov, he was interested in how people do their jobs, and what they think about them, but unlike the other two, he never drew attention to the fact. He was an expert at showing how love and obsession usually go with the nature of a job, or the daily grind; and his characters, like Mr and Mrs Fulmino in "When My Girl Comes Home," never have to be displayed in the standardised light of emotion. Poetry is an invisible asset, suffusing lives which have no sense of it, and no conscious knowledge of what gives to living a space and a relish; but at the same time Pritchett never paraded oddities for our inspection—as a showman like Dickens does—or gave the impression of seeking out the "colourful" aspects of human nature. On the contrary: his great gift is a beautiful accuracy and sobriety, as much in relation to people as to the events which determine their essentiality. Even Chekhov manipulates—the specifications of "The Lady with the Dog" are openly unconvincing if we pay a strict attention to them; and they are set up as arbitrarily as a magazine scenario. Isaac Babel, whom Pritchett admired and on whom he wrote a shrewd critique, can be shameless in his exploitation of consciousness in relation to event. As Pritchett pointed out, the peasant's goose whom the narrator ruthlessly kills in one of his most famous tales of the Red Cossack cavalry, is in its context a wholly implausible and indeed merely literary property, for why have the narrator's murderous companions, who mock him for his lingering bourgeois scruples, not devoured the bird themselves already? Pritchett had a sharp eye, both as critic and as craftsman, for the giveaway device in a seemingly stark and brutal narrative sequence—the kind of story that had come increasingly into fashion in his own time. He never cooked his own goose by giving way to it.

And he wrote his stories over a very long period. The earliest of them came out in England in the early twenties, published in monthlies like the *Cornhill,* and in the then civilised and cultivated pages of the *New Statesman.* Respected periodicals at that time, even if their policies were largely directed towards ideology and politics, carried short stories as a matter of course. One imagines that it was some little while before these stories were recognised as having a special quality and character of their own. And it was some years before he brought out his first collection. *The Spanish Virgin and Other Stories* came out in 1930; a novel, *Clare Drummer,* had been published the previous year. There was rather a fashion at the time for novels with women's names as the title—a leftover from realism: *Germinie Lacerteux, Thérèse Raquin* and, in England, George Moore's *Esther Waters*—and Pritchett followed in the realists' wake, his novel having no great individuality of its own. But the short stories were all the better for the lack of an author who put himself forward, and in time were recognised as coming from a master craftsman's hand. His reputation was confirmed by succeeding volumes. *You Make Your Own Life* came out just before the Second World War (the title again has the mildly anonymous flavour of the period) and twenty and thirty years later came further collections—*When My Girl Comes Home* and *The Camberwell Beauty. Collected Short Stories,* and *More Collected Short Stories,* were published both in England and in America in 1982 and 1983.

Interspersed between were novels, memoirs, biographies of other authors, literary criticism, books of travel. Nothing if not prolific, Sir Victor's achievement had begun already to look like that of a Victorian polycreator, a grand old man of letters. And it will be noticed, too, that his achievement begins now to take on a timeless quality, an air of belonging everywhere over a seventy-year timespan, but nowhere in particular. The manner and the subject-matter seem irrespective of age, or local taste, or the whims of the moment: there is no trademark, no logo to win immediate recognition. "No one alive writes a better English sentence," observed Irving Howe, and there is something peculiarly just about that, for no one could be less narrowly and definably English in outlook and manner than Pritchett. Howe's verdict suggests a time when English, as such, was well-written as a matter of course by a large number of people: before authors and poets, and the language itself, hived off into doing and being their respective things. His fellow story-writer Elizabeth Bowen, whose skills he greatly admired, is apt to invoke the notion of the good sentence too openly, to obtain an atmosphere: brilliant as they are, her stories do not perhaps in the final analysis wear as well as his, for they depend too much on a bravura felicity of style which announces that the narrative has outsoared the simple business of storytelling.

Pritchett's stories never do that. His style is always wholly subordinated to the tale; even its economy is unobtrusive. The poetry is entirely a matter of density of reference, a deft helping of the reader to inference, imagining whole lives and personalities in a single turn of phrase or scrap of dialogue. In this way a story like "A Trip to the Seaside," from the 1989 collection *A Careless Widow*, has the redolence of a Pinter play, or a poem by Betjeman, but with these suggestions metamorphosed into the absolute originality of a short story creation. Gertrude Stein famously said of Oakland, California, that there was "no there, there." In Pritchett's tales there is always a "there," all the more haunting and uncompromising for being so contingent.

"A Trip to the Seaside" is a gem. From the first word to the last—and the tale is only a few pages long—the reader is gripped conclusively, compelled to participate in the experience. A widower visits a small seaside town to see his former secretary, with a view to negotiating a possible second marriage. What happens is unexpected, and yet in some way inevitable. Pritchett's mastery of the milieu, its thought and speech patterns, crowds out any need for explanation or description. A seaside setting was one of Elizabeth Bowen's favourite locales, but she would not have resisted the lure of a few vivid paragraphs, transfixing the scene as a visual impression. Pritchett has no need for that: the whole place is there with barely a word said, just as the "consciousness" of the secretary is made for ever visible by the note of pride in her voice when she tells her suitor that she got married to her new husband "when the divorce came through." It is a staggering blow—the widower was hoping for a convenient marital follow-up with a docile former employee—but she has attracted another man enough to make him divorce his wife for her! No wonder when the widower leaves the resort by train in the last sentence he sees that the boats in the estuary "were flying no pennants and no flags."

Pritchett was fascinated by trades, and the habits they engender. The hairdresser in *A Careless Widow* sees his customers as "tousled and complaining," but leaving him "transfigured, equipped for the hunt again." "They were simply topknots to him. When they got up he was always surprised to see they had arms and legs and could walk. He sometimes, though not often, admired the opposite end of them: their shoes." That sentence has the kind of perfection which Irving Howe had in mind: but like the notes in a late Beethoven quartet it in no way parades such perfection. The stories in *A Careless Widow* originally appeared in magazines—*The New Yorker, Ladies' Home Journal, Vanity Fair*—but there is never a hint in them of the magazine short story formula, the telling phrase, the situation worked up.

He is a master of the odd and secretive vagaries of human nature, which emerge at defenceless or vulnerable moments. The careless widow's eyes fill with tears when she enlarges not on the virtues of her husband but on a minor bit of irresponsibility she has long and loyally concealed. Pritchett never lost his humble passion for what occurs, a passion which makes his tales the reverse of Kipling's. All his books are marked by a mute disinclination to present a world of his own that affects to be the real world. His Spain is not a personal fantasy, as Hemingway's is. For the same reason he never claimed—explicitly or implicitly—to be telling the truth, as so many tellers of tales have done. He merely got on with the business of doing it. His reputation grew gradually, increasing with each book. He was not the kind of author who becomes famous overnight; and when his work became well-known it never identified or placed him. Now his stories speak for him, but they still do not claim a name for the remarkable man who wrote them.

CONTENTS

Acknowledgments

Portions of this work were originally published in *At Home and Abroad, New York Proclaimed, Dublin: A Portrait*, and *Mr. Beluncle.*

Grateful acknowledgment is made to the following for permission to reprint previously published material:

PETERS FRASER & DUNLOP GROUP LTD.: Chapters 1 and 5 from *The Spanish Temper* by V. S. Pritchett; Chapter 10 from *Marching Spain* by V. S. Pritchett; Chapter 8 from *Foreign Faces* by V. S. Pritchett; "Sense of Humour," "The Evils of Spain," "The Oedipus Complex," "Things as They Are," "When My Girl Comes Home," "The Liars," "The Camberwell Beauty," "Did You Invite Me?" "The Marvellous Girl," "The Vice-Consul," "The Fig Tree," "Cocky Olly," and "The Image Trade" from *The Complete Short Stories of V. S. Pritchett;* Chapter 10 from *Dead Man Leading* by V. S. Pritchett. All essays reprinted by permission of Peters Fraser & Dunlop Group Ltd.

The New York Times: "Looking Back at Eighty" by V. S. Pritchett from the December 14, 1980 issue of *The New York Times.* Copyright © 1980 by the New York Times Co. Reprinted by permission.

RANDOM HOUSE, INC.: "The American Puritan," "Clarissa," "Scott," "Edwin Drood," "The Living Novel," "Poor Relations," "The Russian Day," "The Notebooks of Henry James," "Boswell's London," "The Unhappy Traveller," "The Performing Lynx," "Meredith's Brainstuff," "Quixote's Translators," "The Despot," "The Myth Makers," "The Con-Man's Shadow," "Jumbos," "The Sayings of Don Geraldo," "Irish Behaviour," "A Better Class of Person," and "Midnight's Children" from *The Complete Collected Essays* by V. S. Pritchett, copyright © 1992 by V. S. Pritchett; Chapter 3 from *The Gentle Barbarian* by V. S. Pritchett, copyright

As Old as the Century:
V. S. Pritchett at Eighty

Since my boyhood I have been vain of being born just before the end of 1900 and at every birthday thinking of myself as pretty well as old as the century. I was at ease with its assumptions for fourteen years: after that, two dreadful wars, huge social changes, technological revolution, the disappearance of British power, the rise of the Welfare State, a decade or two of "peace" in the world abroad, dramatic threats once more.

Now I am eighty I see I have been shaken up like a dice in a box, if not as brutally as people born ten years earlier than myself. Many are still alive and in voice. I am abashed by my survival rather than proud of it; there is no merit in it. The credit goes to those secretive gamblers we call the genes.

I come of long-lived forebears among whom there were few defaulters on the Yorkshire side. Also, because of the great advances of medical science and hygiene, the average expectation of life in Great Britain has enormously increased in the past fifty years or more. The old are no longer revered curiosities; on the contrary, often a social problem. We swarm in cities and resorts, ancient mariners who square our shoulders as we pick one another out at a glance in the pubs, the shops, the park seats, the planes and the tourist buses. Our skins do not yet give off the eerie smell of senility. That glance of ours is often frisky, conspiratorial and threatening, warning you that we could a tale unfold if we should happen to get a grip on your wrist.

Not a day's illness—we boast—except a winter cough or a twinge of arthritis or gout; we speak of these twitches as medals we have won. Smoke like fish (we go on), drink like a chimney, pity people who do not work a twelve-hour day, who have not ducked their heads through two world wars or known the good old hard times. And as for this new thing called sex ...!

As our tongues wag and our metaphors mix we turn into actors on our conspicuous stage. We are good at pretending to be modest; we refuse to acknowledge we are ever in the wrong or incompetent. A brisk eighty-year-old electrician came to do a job at my house six years ago and serenely drove his drill clean through a hidden water pipe I had warned him of. He turned accusingly on me as the water spouted over us. Like all us oldies he congratulated himself and boasted he had never done such a thing to a water pipe. He and I still greet each other as we rush by in the street, equals in conceit and folly, and say how young we feel.

Our acting is, of course, a defence against our fear of senility and death. What shall we be like in our nineties? Are we for the old folks' home? We have seen so many of our friends paralysed, collapsing in mind and physically humiliated. Shall we escape? Yet, behind our acting there is also the knowledge that age does not march mathematically year by year with the calendar. One's real age stands still for large blocks of time.

My hair is now white and veins stand out on my temples, I have dark brown spots on my hands, my arms shrink, but to my mind I seem to be much what I was at fifty: at fifty-seven I looked despairingly bleak, ill and flaccid, to judge from a photograph, less brisk than I became in my sixties, seventies or today. Middle age was more agonising and trying than the later years have been, but perhaps my age has always gone up and down because I am one of those who "live on their nerves." I know one thing for certain: I was far, far younger in my thirties than I had been in my twenties, because my heart was fuller at thirty, my energies knew their direction, chiefly due to a happy marriage. It has lasted forty-four years. There is nothing like a *coup de foudre* and absorption in family responsibility for maturing the male and pulling his scattered wits together. I became physically stronger after years of bad health. Yet I had not lost what I valued in my twenties: living for the liberation of the moment.

Today I still go fast up the four flights of steep stairs to my study in our tall late-Nash house, every day of the week, at nine o'clock in the morning, Saturdays and Sundays included, cursing the Inland Revenue and inflation, groaning at the work I have to do, crying out dishonestly for leisure, thinking of this year's holiday and the ten-mile walks on the cliffs of North Cornwall, complaining that surely at my age I should be able to get some time off.

Why, even when I travel, do I still have to work? But the moment I've cleaned my pipe and put pen to paper the groans stop. I am under the spell of language which has ruled me since I was ten. A few minutes later—four hours' writing have washed out all sense of time—my wife calls me down to a delicious lunch. She has spent the morning typing what I wrote the day before, laughing at my bad spelling, inserting sportive words when she can't read my insectile hand—that has got smaller—and knowing she'll have to do the whole damn thing over again two or three times because I cover each page with an ant's colony of corrections; she is a perfectionist too. We enjoy working together; she has a better memory than I have and I depend on her criticism. It is she who charms away the swarms of people who telephone, the speculators who think I exist for reading their theses and books, for more and more reviews, for giving interviews or lectures or signing their applications for grants. She has also driven off the droppers-in, the Mormons and Jehovah's Witnesses and other enemies of a writer's life. She is much younger and more decisive than I am.

After lunch I have a nap for an hour, do some household shopping in Camden Town where I pass as an old pensioner called Pritchard—very suited to a writer's double life—and return to take up tea and then back to work about four until seven and then a couple of Martinis, eat, try to catch up with letters and bills or in good weather go out and work in the garden. Unless we are going out we are in bed by ten. I sleep pretty well, dream wildly; the bad nights are those when I go on writing in my sleep, in English mostly but often, out of vanity, in Spanish, French or in dog-German which I stopped learning when I left school at fifteen. For Latin I have to rely on my wife.

I am a very lucky man, of course. If our pleasant house among the old trees of the quiet terrace is too large for us now our family have grown up, after twenty-five years here where else could we go with thousands of books? Would that frozen Buddha—the freezer that has changed our lives—fit in a new kitchen? Moving would betray our furniture and new draughts often kill old men.

I am lucky to be able to work at home, to commute upstairs instead of by train or bus. It is lucky I am still able to earn my living as a writer which I dreamed of when I was a boy. Thomas Hardy, in his old age, told Virginia Woolf that to write poetry was simply a matter of physical strength. So is writing prose. And that energy I was given by my parents: my Kentish Town mother's energy was nervous, my father's had the obdurate Yorkshire self-will. I cannot claim credit as an heir to this enlivening mixture of fortune which has generated in me a mixture of fantasy and wry common sense.

I am fortunate in these times which are hard for many workers—especially the pensioned-off or redundant—to be "in work." Many a pensioner, forced to be idle against his will, has greater reserves of character than I have. I do have my occasional days of leisure, but for the most part I have to carry what Keats called the indispensable sense of "negative capability" about with me and then, as he also said, work makes "the disagreeables evaporate."

I look back now at my "evaporations" with astonishment. If I spent my boyhood in the low Kippsian regions of Edwardian Britain, the British assurance and locality had given an elegance to British comedy. The "man of letters" I aspired to be was pre-eminent, if poor, in English periodical writing. Also modest families like mine were beneficiaries of the Education Act of the 1870s. Disagreeable to have education cut short at fifteen, but there had been a brief evaporation into foreign languages at a grammar school, language of any kind being my obsession.

It was disagreeable at first to be put into the malodorous leather trade, but the animality of skins fascinated me and so did the Bermondsey leather dressers and fellmongers. The smell of that London of my boyhood and bowler-hatted youth is still with me. I coughed my way through a city stinking, rather excitingly, of coal smoke, gas escapes, tanyards, breweries, horse manure and urine. Flies swarmed, people scratched their fleas. The streets smelled of beer; men and boys reeked of hair oil, vaseline, strong tobacco, powerful boot polish, mackintoshes and things like my father's voluptuous cachous.

The smell of women was racy and scented. Clothes were heavy; utterances—in all classes—were sententious whether witty or not. Music hall songs were epigrammatic stories. "Lurve" had not yet killed them. Artful euphemism hid a secret archive of bad language. If a "bloody" broke through, people would say "Language, I hear," disapproving as they admired. Hypocrisy was a native fruit, if then overripe.

By 1918 the skirts of the liberated girls who had worked in ammunition factories and offices were shortened a few inches. One now saw their erotic ankles and sex broke out; not as yet in plain Anglo-Saxon, but soon Latinised as copulation in the classier Twenties, for youths like myself who had moved on to Aldous Huxley. I had read enormously, most of Scott, Dickens, most of the Victorian novelists, caught up with Chesterton and Bennett and was heading for *Anna Karenina* and *Madame Bovary*.

I might have stuck in leather all my life but 1918 liberated me. Travel was cheap; I "evaporated" to Paris, earned my living in the shellac and glue trade and discovered I could write sketches. I became the autodidact abroad and education was open to me at last.

It was even good luck to grow up among non-intellectual people, all in trades; better luck, to have a vocation fixed in my mind—so few boys have—to grow up in a period when the printed language was the dominant teacher and pleasure-giver. Good luck to escape, by going abroad, the perpetual British "no" to the new boy; good luck to meet the American "yes" to my first bits of writing. France, Ireland, Spain were for six years my universities. They taught me European history and the conflicts of cultures and quickly got me clear of the hurdles of the then sticky English class system. Once they have made their bid, all kinds of artists—writers, painters, sculptors, musicians, educated or not—are free of that. It is also half-native in our tribe that we can talk and listen to anyone in his language. Among writers Kipling is an exemplar of what travel does for this faculty.

Since the wilful Twenties, the committals of the Thirties, it seems to me that my life as a man and as a writer has been spent on crossing and recrossing frontiers and that is at the heart of any talent I have. It cheers me that I live on the frontier of Camden Town and Regent's Park. Frontier life has been nourishing to me. Throwing something of oneself away is a way of becoming, for the moment, other people, and I have always thought that unselfing oneself, speaking for others, justifying those who cannot speak, giving importance to the fact that they live, is especially the privilege of the storyteller, and even the critic—who is also an artist.

And here, at the age of forty when the Second World War seemed that it would ruin my life as a short story writer, novelist and critic, I found that my early life in trade was an advantage: it prepared me for another evaporation. I had to divide my time between serious criticism in the *New Statesman* every week and studies of factories, mines, shipyards, railway sidings and industrial towns. I did my literary work in trains. I have always been wary of what used to be called "committal" to the social and political ideologies which numbers of my contemporaries preached and now in war my foreignness abated: I began to know once more how my own people lived: that abstraction called The People dissolved as I saw real people living lives in conditions unlike my own but with passions like mine and as proud of something unique in them.

The decisive books of the period about English life for me were Jack Common's *The Freedom of the Streets* and—on the Spanish war—Borkenau's *The Spanish Cockpit*. I found my own *raison d'être* in some words of Dostoevsky's that "without art a man might find his life on earth unliveable."

If as a storyteller I have had an ear for how people speak and my travelling, bookish nature turned me into that now fading type, a man of letters, how do I see the changes that have slowly come about in the past forty years? In a searching way these changes were predicted in the late Thirties by Louis Mumford in his absorbing book *The Culture of Cities*. My London has become a megalopolis. It has turned into a fantastic foreign bazaar. The Third World is replacing the traditional European immigrants.

Mumford argued that social betterment has been outstripped every decade by technology. We have become, or feel we have become, anonymous items in a mass society at once neutral and bizarre. As for technology the printed word no longer predominates in popular taste and, as Auden said, literature is now turning into "a cottage industry." The descendants of ordinary people who read their Dickens and the Victorian and Edwardian periodicals have given up the printed word for the instant sensation of sight and sound, for pictures on the screen.

One can tell this, if by nothing else, from popular speech in which half the vowels and consonants are missing, and in which a sentence becomes like one slurred word, a telegraphic message. The schools have turned out a large number of grown men and women who cannot read or write, for machines have made this unnecessary for them. I suppose the small core of addicted readers will remain, just as Latin remained for the medieval clerks, but the outlook for prose is not good. The new generation faces the attack of spoken and visual drama which cuts out our prose.

No professional writer becomes famous until his work has been televised or filmed: the rest of us may have to live in the conceit of being like the lamenting figures in the chorus of the Greek drama. That chorus was, in its tedious, humble way, the indispensable gang of prosing human moralists chanting the general dismay as they watched the impersonal and violent passions murderously at work on a stage without backcloth. We may of course become Aristophanic fabulists mocking the ruling cliques of a State Machine. Anthony Burgess and Angus Wilson are revelling in this at the moment.

There is another danger to literary culture: it comes from the technological habits of academic criticism. Scholars have been for ages the traditional conservers of literary tradition, but under the powerful influences of technology and the sciences, linguistics, psychology, sociology, philosophy, they are now using a new and portentous verbiage. They detach themselves from life and reduce it to an esoteric game or treat it as a kind of engineering. Their commentaries are full of self-important and comic irrelevancies. Their specialised ironmongery may be good training for engineers, scientists and spacemen, but it has little relation to imaginative literature.

I speak from experience for—to my astonishment as one who had never been inside any university until I was turned fifty—I have found myself teaching at Princeton, Berkeley, Columbia and the delightful Smith College, in the United States. I suppose to give their tormented Faculties a rest while I unloaded a chattering mind that has always read for delight. I like teaching because it wakes me up and teaches me and I am grateful to those institutions for giving me the free time an imaginative writer needs and which I get little of in England.

From my earliest days I have liked the natural readiness and openness of the American temperament and I had been brought up in childhood a good deal on the classic American writers and their direct response to the world they lived in. If American seriousness is often exhausting, the spontaneous image-making vernacular and wit are excellent. American short stories have often an archaic directness more striking than our own. I must also say that some of the most illuminating and helpful remarks about my own writing have come from American critics who, unlike so many of our own, are not out to display themselves rather than the authors they are dealing with. As for the American student—naive and earnest he may sometimes be, as I was when young; but he is continuously expectant and is without the European sneer.

At eighty I look at the horrible state of our civilisation. It seems to be breaking up and returning to the bloody world of Shakespeare's Histories which we thought we had outgrown. But public, like private life, proceeds in circles. The Third World is reliving history we have forgotten and indeed brings its violence to our cities. I am a humanist but I do not think human beings are rational: their greeds and passions are not quickly outgrown. We have now to school ourselves to deal with danger and tragedy.

I have some stoicism but I have often thought lately of a courageous friend of mine, now dead, an adventurous explorer, mountaineer and rather reckless yachtsman. He was one of those born to test his fears. I once sailed in a wild gale with him—much against my will—and was terrified, for I am afraid of the sea and have never learned to swim more than ten yards. He was not afraid. Or, if he feared, his fears exhilarated him and, in fact, vanished in danger because (he said) he was always "thinking of the next thing to do." (I suppose this is what I do, when I leave land for the perils of writing prose in which there have been so many shipwrecks.) In physical danger I am capable only of identifying myself with my evil: not as good a recourse as his, but it helps.

I have another friend, eighty-six years old, who has lately been hit by a tragedy in his family. He said he wanted to die at once—but not, he added, until he had seen what happened next in Poland and after that in Iran. At eighty I find myself on the lookout expectantly for the unexpected and am more than half allured by it.

Am I wiser in my old age? I don't know. I am not yet old enough to know loneliness and that puts one to the tests of folly and rage. But I am more tolerant than when I was young. I was not an affectionate young man and indeed I was thought of as fierce—a bolting pony, someone once said. But passionate love made me affectionate. I am deeply touched by the affection I now receive. It is one of the rewards of old age. I suppose I am slowly growing up. I am not a man's man for I owe much to women since my boyhood when my mother fascinated me by the whirligig of her humour and her emotions. And what about serenity? I see that many old women have it. In men it is more often torpor and I am drawn to activity and using myself. And to laughter, which wakes up the mind.

Strangely, laughter seems to me like the sexual act which is perhaps the laughter of two bodies. Whatever there is to be said for serenity there is not much opportunity for it in the modern world; and indeed I know by watching myself that old people are liable to fantasies of sadistic vengeance. The old should not look at the news on television at night.

The pleasures of old age are of the lingering kind, love itself becomes more mysterious, tender and lasting. The great distress of old age is the death of friends, the thinning ranks of one's generation. The air grows cold in the gaps. Something of oneself is drained away when friends go, though in mourning for them we learn to revalue a past we had more than half forgotten, and to bring them walking back to keener life in our memory. We have been members of one another. In old age we increasingly feel we are strangers and we warm to those who treat us as if we are not.

The new sensation is that living people are a wonder. Have you noticed how old people stare at groups of talkers, as if secretly or discreetly joining them silently at a distance? This does not happen to me much for I am always on the move, but I am aware of it. I used to sit long over my beer in pubs and clubs; now I swallow a double gin and run. I don't know why. Trying to pack more into the day? No: I just want to get home.

A sign of old age in myself is that, knowing my time is limited, I find myself looking at streets and their architecture much longer and more intensely and at Nature and landscape. I gaze at the plane tree at the end of the garden, studying its branches and its leaves. I look a long time at flowers. And I am always on the watch for the dramatic changes in the London sky. I have always liked to sketch formations of clouds. I store up the procession of headlands and terrifying ravines of North Cornwall and of all the landscapes that have formed me: the shapes of the Yorkshire Fells and the Downs in Sussex and Wiltshire, the tableland of Castile.

I have no religious faith. I am no pantheist or sentimentalist in my love of Nature but simply an idolater of leaf, hill, stream and stone. I came across a line of Camus which drily describes people like myself:

"One of our contemporaries is cured of his torment simply by contemplating a landscape."

That, and lately falling into the habit of reading Gibbon's *Decline and Fall* on Sunday evenings, "evaporates the disagreeables" of history that now advance on us: the irony of the learned Gibbon excites the sense of tragi-comedy and is, except for its lack of poetic sense, close to the feeling I have about the present and the past.

(1980)

FROM

A Cab at the Door

CHAPTER THREE

Such was the family I was born into. There was this cock-sparrow, my father, now a commercial traveller, dressy and expansive with optimism, walking in and out of jobs with the bumptiousness of a god. And there was our sulky moody mother, either laughing or in tears, playing *The Maiden's Prayer* on the piano—she could "cross hands" too—and also *The Mocking Bird* which was closer to her nature. She would sink into mournful tales of illnesses and funerals, brood on railway accidents and ships lost at sea. She loved a short cry, easily went pink on her cheek-bones with jealousy or flew out into a fishwife's tempers. She was a hard-working woman. We were in a small villa of damp red brick in Woodford. I had a brother now, Cyril, eighteen months younger than myself. My parents' bedroom contained a large lithograph called *Wedded*. A Roman-looking couple are walking languorously along a city wall. The man had strong hairy legs and, I believe, wore a tiger skin. I confused him with my hairy father. In the twenties I met an Italian who had sat for the legs of this figure, one more blow to my sense of the uniqueness of our family. There was another lithograph called *The Soul's Awakening*, a girl with her nightgown falling off in the wind as she was swept up to heaven. On the washstand there was yellow chinaware which had a pattern of Dutch girls and boys. Hidden behind the chamber-pot in the cupboard was a small copy of Aristotle's "masterpiece" on gynaecology with startling pictures of the moronic foetus in the womb. In another cupboard were my father's leather top-hat boxes; already he was buying clothes for himself in notable quantities. There were "words" if mother had not washed and ironed his underclothes or starched his cuffs and collars as well as his mother had done.

In the small dining-room there was red and blue linoleum of floral pattern. There was a small palm in a pot. There were ornaments with mottoes on them. "Dinna trouble trouble till trouble troubles you" and "Don't Worry It May Never Happen." Also a picture which gave me my first lesson in the "who" and "whom" difficulty. Two old men in red robes with their backs to each other, but looking with medieval grumpiness over their shoulders, held an antique parchment in their hands on which the following words were printed:

> *In Men Whom Men Condemn as Ill*
> *I find so much goodness still,*
> *In Men whom Men pronounce divine*
> *I find so much of sin and blot*
> *I hesitate to draw the line*
> *Between the two where God has not.*

This poem was often bandied about and pointed at when Granda Pritchett came down to London and denounced my father's latest religion, for Father was continually going one better in the matter of faith. The other picture showed simply an envelope on which was written:

> Messrs Sell and Repent,
> Prosperous Place,
> The Earth.

This was the spirit of the early 1900's. Things, as Father said, were beginning to hum.

My parents rarely stayed in one house for as long as a year. After Woodford there is a dash to Derby where Father hoped to do well with a Canadian Insurance Company, and where, in north-country fashion, we had a pump beside the sink; in a month or so we are back. We had various London addresses: Woodford again, Palmers Green, Balham, Uxbridge, Acton, Ealing, Hammersmith, Camberwell are some of them; then back to Ipswich again, on to Dulwich and Bromley. By the time I was twelve, Mother was saying we had moved fourteen times and Father went fat in the face with offence and said she exaggerated. At this, she counted up on her fingers and said she now made it eighteen.

We moved mainly to small red-brick villas, the rents running from 9s. and even to 12s. a week, once or twice to poor flats. It seemed to us that Father had genius. By the time there were four children—three boys and a girl—Father seemed as sumptuous as a millionaire and my mother was worn down. It was like a marriage of the rich and the poor. She cooked, cleaned, made our clothes and her own, rarely had the money to pay for a girl to help her and went about a lot of the day with a coarse apron on, her blouse undone and her hair down her back. Patently genius was lacking in her. For it was he who came home in the evenings or at week-ends from places like Glasgow, Bournemouth or Torquay, having stayed in hotels with names like Queens, Royal or Majestic, palaces of luxury. We learned to wait at the door and to open it for him when he came home, because he was affronted if he had to let himself in with his own key. We would often wait for an hour. When he got in he walked into the front room where we ate, sat down in an armchair and, without a word, put out his foot. Mother's duty was to kneel and unbutton his boots until laced boots came in, when she unlaced them; eventually we squabbled for this honour. "Ease the sock" Father would say with regal self-pity. And he would tell her about the orders he had taken that week. His little order books were full of neat figures and smelled warmly of scent.

And then—the magic of the man!—without warning we would, as I say, get up one morning to find my mother in her fawn rain-coat (her only coat), and hat, ourselves being pulled into coats too. A cabby and his horse would be coughing together outside the house and the next thing we knew we were driving to an underground station and to a new house in a new part of London, to the smell of new paint, new mice dirts, new cupboards, and to race out into a new garden to see if there were any trees and start, in our fashion to wreck the garden and make it the byword of the neighbourhood. The aggravating thing was that my mother was always crying in the cabs we took; and then my father would begin to sing in his moving bass voice:

> *Oh dry those tears*
> *Oh calm those fears*
> *Life will be brighter tomorrow.*

Or, if he was exasperated with her, it would be

> *Tell me the old, old story*
> *For I forget so soon.*

I look back on these early years and chiefly remember how crowded and dark these houses were and that, after Uxbridge, there is always a nasty smell, generally of sour breadcrumbs at the edges of the seats of chairs, the disgusting smell of young children, after my sister and youngest brother were born. And there was the continual talk of rudeness. It was rooted in our very name for we soon learned that Pritchett was the same as Breeches for other children; one polite little boy called my mother Mrs Trousers because he had gathered that "breeches" was rude. Mother—and especially her mother, Gran—were the sources of a mysterious prurience. Gran liked chamber-pot humour and was almost reverent about po's, mentioning that Aunt Short said that the best thing for the complexion was to wash one's face in "it"—and good for rheumatism too. The bottom was the most rude thing we had, and, in consequence, the Double U. Rudeness became almost mystical if we caught Gran on the Double U when she left the door unlocked. Girls were rude because of their drawers; women, because of their long skirts, and more rude than men because they had so much more to cover. To crawl under a table and lift the hem of a skirt was convulsively rude. At certain times Mother and Father were rude—not when she was in bed and her astonishing titty-bottles slipped out of her nightdress, like a pair of follies; but when she and Father went for a walk together and we walked behind them. We felt that it was rude to see a marriage walking about in front of the neighbours. Granda and Grandma Pritchett were never rude; but Mother was rude in herself—she wore "bloomers" and often "showed" them—but Father, on his own, never. I was ashamed for years of a photograph of us children. The corner of my sister's silk dress had lodged on my knee as I sat next to her. I was rude.

One thing became noticeable in our removals. Very often my father and mother went to different destinations—she to the new house while my father and I would find ourselves at Euston station in the middle of the night. I was off by the midnight train to my grandfather's in Repton and later to Sedbergh, to be away in the north for weeks or even months. My brother, it seemed, was off to Ipswich to stay with my mother's sister, Ada. My sister and baby brother were at home. At one time I found myself sitting on the carrier of my father's bicycle travelling from Nottingham to Derby. Another time I remember travelling in a hansom to Paddington and yet again standing one winter's morning beside the driver of a horse tram down Tooley Street on a roundabout journey via Tower Bridge to King's Cross. So began my love of change, journeys and new places. As many London children do, I skilfully lost myself in the streets and was twice picked up by the police. Most of these journeys which my father thoughtfully provided were, as I say, to the north. Repton I scarcely remember; but to Sedbergh, Kirbymoorside and Appleton-le-Moors I went again and again. We would get out of the night train, my father and I, at a junction near Kendal, at the gateway through the mountains to the Scottish border, cross the lines and take the little train to Sedbergh, that neat town of grey stone lying under the bald mountain I thought was called the Berg. The horse brake would take us up the main street, following a herd of cows. By the Manse and chapel, Granda was waiting. In the distance, on her whitened doorstep and close to a monkey-puzzle tree, stood Grandma in her starched white apron, her little pale iced-cake face and her glasses glittering. I remember an arrival when I was six. My grandmother would not let me into her clean house until she looked me over.

"Eeh Walter, for shame, t'lad's buttons are off his jersey, his breeches have a hole in them. I'm raight vexed with your Beatie, letting a son of hers come up with his stockings in holes and his shoes worn through. Eeh, he looks nowt but a poor little gutter boy. For shame, Walter. For shame, Victor. I lay you've been playing in the London muck. I dassn't show you to the neighbours. Nay, look at his breeches, Willyum."

"Mother made them." I stuck up for Mother, not for her sake but because of the astonishing material she used—mostly curtains from our house. Nothing covering a window, a table or a sofa was safe from my mother's scissors when the sewing fit was on her. "I'll get those old curtains down." She was an impatient woman.

My grandmother took me inside, undressed me in the hall and held the breeches up and looked at them.

"Eeh Willyum, come here. They're not stitched. They're just tacked. T'lad'll be naked in 't street."

It was true. Mother's slapdash tacking often let us down.

On these visits, the minister would be having a sarcastic argument with his son about the particular God of the moment, for Father had left the Congregationalists, the Baptists, the Wesleyans, the Methodists in turn, being less and less of a Jehovah man and pushing his way—it turned out—towards the Infinite. He was emerging from that pessimism which ate at his Victorian elders. The afternoon bus came and he went. Up the back step of the station brake he skipped, to pick up a couple of hampers of traveller's samples in Manchester. I was glad to be rid of the family and scarcely thought of my mother or my brother and sister for weeks. Here was what I was made for: new clothes, new shirts, new places, the new life, jam tarts, Eccles cakes, seed-cakes, apple puffs and Yorkshire pudding. My grandparents looked at each other and then at me with concern for my character. I did not know that almost every time we moved house Father had lost his job or was swinging dangerously between an old disaster and a new enterprise, that he was being pursued by people to whom he owed money, that furniture had "gone back" or new unpaid-for furniture had "come in." I did not know that my mother wept because of this, even as she slyly concealed, clenched in her fingers a half sovereign that some kind neighbour had given her. And I remember now how many times, when my father left in the morning for his work, she barred his way at the door or screamed at him from the gate, "Walt, Walt, where's my money?" But I did see that here in Sedbergh there was domestic peace.

It is a small old town smelling of sheep and cows, with a pretty trout beck running through it under wooded banks. The fells, cropped close by sheep, smelling of thyme and on sunny days played on by the shadows of the clouds, rise steeply behind the town and from the top of them one sees the austere system of these lonely mountains running westward to the Pikes of the Lake District and north to the border. One is almost in Westmorland and, not far off, one sees the sheepwalks of Scott's *The Two Drovers*, the shepherd's road to Scotland. The climate is wet and cold in winter; the town is not much sheltered and day after day there will be a light, fine drizzle blowing over from Westmorland and the Irish Sea. When it begins people say "Ay, it's dampening on." These people are dour but kindly.

Yorkshire is the most loved of all the many places of my childhood. I was sent to my first school, the village school at the top of the town, up the lane from the Manse garden—it is just as it was when I was a child sixty years ago. The school sat in two classes and, I suppose, each class had about forty or fifty boys and girls, the girls in pinafores and long black or tan stockings. Douthwaite, Louthwaite, Thistlethwaite, Braithwaite, Branthwaite were the common surnames. The children spoke a dialect that was hard to understand. They came from farms and cottages, both sexes brisk and strenuous. We sat in three tiers in the class-room, the upper one for bigger children. While I was doing pothooks and capital D's from a script, the others were taught sums. Being a London child with a strange accent I began to swank, particularly to the girls. One who sat with me in the front offered to show me her belly if I lowered my own breeches. I did so, being anxious to show her my speciality—a blind navel, for the cord had been so cut that my navel was closed. In her opinion—and that of others—this was "wrong" and foretold an early death because no air could get inside me. This distinction made me swank more. She did not keep her part of the bargain, neither did any of the other girls in Sedbergh. She put up her hand and told teacher. This was the first of many painful lessons, for I instantly loved girls.

This incident was reported to the Manse. Also a scuffle or two in the school yard, being caught peeing over a wall to see how far we could go, with a lot of village lads, and a small burglary I got into with a village boy who persuaded me to slip into an old woman's cottage and steal some Halma pieces from her desk. We lied about this. My grandfather, waiting to catch me naked in the bath tub, gave me a spanking that stung for hours. I screamed at him and said that I hoped he would be run over by the London express at the level-crossing the next time he crossed the line at the Junction. More spanking. I was removed from the school because the neighbours were talking. I was surprised for I was a pious little boy, packed with the Ten Commandments and spotless on Sundays: the farmers' boys, the blacksmiths' sons and all the old wheelwrights, tree fellers, shepherds thought I was a townee and a softie. I would never be able to herd sheep, shoe or ride a horse, use a pickaxe or even work in a woollen mill. My secret was that I was going to be a preacher like my grandfather; he had begun teaching me Latin, pointing out the Latin words on a penny—*fidei defensor.* I was to be defender (with spears and guns if necessary) of the faith, "prepared to receive cavalry." For years I thought this and Calvary were the same thing.

The Manse at Sedbergh smelled of fruit and was as silent as church and had even churchy furniture in yellow oak, most of it made by country craftsmen, who in a fit of fancy, might carve, say, acorns or leaves all round the edge of a table. There was no sound but the tick tock of the grandfather clock. Everything was polished, still and clean. One slept in a soft feather bed and woke to see the mist low down on the waist of the Berg. On the old brick wall of the garden my grandfather grew his plums and pears, and in the flower-beds his carnations, his stock, his roses and his sweet-williams; and under the wall flowed a little stream from the mountains.

It was a kind, grave house. My grandparents were in their early fifties. For my grandmother cleanliness was the first passion. Whenever I stayed in my first years with her she bathed me in a zinc tub before the kitchen fire and was always scrubbing me. Once she tried to remove a mole from my nose, thinking it was a speck of tar. For two days, on and off, she worked at it with soap, soda, pumice and grit and hard brushes, exclaiming all the time like Lady Macbeth; while my grandfather growled "Let it bide, you're spreading his nose all over his face." He had a genial sadistic touch, for he loved to point to a scar on the tip of my nose which seemed to shine like a lamp and make me ridiculous; and also to say that my nose was the nearest thing to an elephant's foot he had ever seen. He enjoyed making me angry. It was Yorkshire training.

Grandma always kept her white hair in curlers until a late hour in the afternoon, when she changed into one of her spotted blue dresses. The only day on which she looked less than neat was Monday. On this terrible day she pinned a man's cloth cap to her hair, kirtled a rough skirt above her knees, put on a pair of wooden clogs and went out to the scullery to start the great weekly wash of sheets, pillow-cases, towels, table-cloths and clothes. They were first boiled in a copper, then she moved out to a wash-tub by the pump in the cobbled yard and she turned the linen round and round with the three-legged wooden "dolly"—as tall as myself—every so often remarking for her neighbours to hear that her linen was of better quality, better washed, whiter and cleaner than the linen of any other woman in the town; that the sight of her washing hanging on the line—where my grandfather had to peg and prop it—would shame the rest of the world and the final ironing be a blow to all rivals. The house smelled of suds and ironing. Her clogs clattered in the yard. But, sharp at five o'clock she changed as usual and sat down to read the *British Weekly*.

On Tuesday, she made her first baking of the week. This consisted of different kinds of bread and I watched it rise in its pans to its full beauty before the fire; on Thursday, she made her second baking, concentrating less on bread than on pies, her Madeira cake, her seed-cake, her Eccles cakes, her puffs, her lemon-curd or jam tarts and tarts of egg "custard," operations that lasted from seven in the morning until five in the afternoon once more. The "bake" included, of course, the scouring of pans and saucepans which a rough village girl would help her with. At the end, the little creature showed no sign of being tired, but would "lay" there was no better cook in the town than herself and pitied the cooking of her sisters.

On Wednesdays she turned out the house. This cleaning was ferocious. The carpets were all taken up and hung on a line, my grandfather got out a heavy stick to beat them while she stood beside him saying things like "Eeh Willyum, I can't abide dirt." There was some nasty talk among the Congregationalists in Sedbergh about my grandfather's carpet-beating; they got their own back for the boasting of my grandma and some said out loud that he was obviously not the class of man to be teaching the word of God in that town. (Forty years later when I went back to the town after his death, one or two old people still spoke in a shocked way of their working-class minister who was under the thumb of his "stuck-up" wife. That came of a man's marrying above himself.)

After the carpets, the linoleum was taken up and Grandma was down on her knees scrubbing the floor boards. Then came hours of dusting and polishing.

"Woman," Granda often said on Wednesdays, standing very still and thundery and glaring at her, "lay not up your treasure on earth where moth and dust doth corrupt."

"Eeh Willyum," she would reply, "wipe your boots outside. Ah can't abide a dirty doormat. Mrs So-and-so hasn't whitened her step since Monday."

And once more she would settle down as pretty as a picture to an evening, making another rag rug or perhaps crocheting more and more lace for her dresses, her table-centres and her doilies. By the time she was eighty years old she had stored away several thousand of these doilies, chests full of them; and of course they were superior to the work of any other woman in the country. In old age, she sent boxes of them to her younger son who had emigrated to Canada, thinking he might be "in want."

I remember a tea for Sunday-school teachers at the Manse. They came, excited young men and bouncing young women who went out in the fields and trees along the beck to see who could collect and name the largest number of different species of wild flower in an hour. An older woman won with fifty-seven different kinds. We got back to my grandmother's parlour where the sun shone through the little square lights of her windows, to see one of my grandmother's masterpieces, a state tea laid on the table. The scones, the tea-cakes, Eccles cakes, jam tarts, iced tarts, her three or four different kinds of cake, sultana, Madeira, seed and jammed sponge, her puffs and her turn-overs were set out in all their yellows, browns, pinks and, as usual, in her triumph, my grandmother was making a pettish little mouth, "laying" that "nowt like it" would be seen on any table in the town. The company stood reverently by their chairs and then, to my disgust, they broke out into a sung grace, conducted by the eldest of the teachers, each taking parts, bass and tenor, soprano and contralto, repeating their variations for what seemed to me a good twenty minutes before setting to. To my wonder—for I had been nicely brought up by my grandmother— the eldest teacher who was a very old man with the big hands of a labourer, tipped his tea into his saucer, blew on it and drank.

"Look at the man," I shouted. "He's being rude."

There was a silence. The old man was angry. Grandma was vexed. There was a dispute about whether I should be told to leave the room. One of the girls saved me. But the old man kept coming back to it and it was the whole subject of the tea-party, and for days the minister and his wife had the matter over with me. If that was "London manners," the old man growled when he left, he didn't want owt of them. Such slights are never forgotten in the north; they go all round the town and add to its obdurate wars. The story was reported to my father in London and was brought up indignantly year after year. To think that a boy, a relation of the minister's, too, and already known to have exposed himself in school, should say a thing like that. One experience I feared to tell them. That day of the flower hunt, I had found a beautiful white flower like a star growing near the river. I had never seen a white flower so silky and star-like, in its petals, and so exquisite. I picked it, smelled it and dropped it at once. It stank. The smell was not only rank, it suggested rottenness and a deep evil. It was sin itself. And I hurried away, frightened, from the river, not daring to mention it and I never walked through that field again. For many years I thought of this deceit. I did not know this flower was the wild garlic, the most evocative of our aphrodisiacs, the male to the female musk.

The general portrait of the country people of Haworth which is given by Mrs Gaskell in her life of Charlotte Brontë, very closely fitted the character of my Yorkshire relations if one allows for the taming effects of lower middle-class gentility. Haworth-like tales were common among the Sawdons. They were proud, violent, egotistical. They had—according to your view—either a strong belief in the plain virtues or a rock-like moral conceit. Everything was black or white to them. They were blunt to your face, practical and unimaginative, kind yet iron-minded, homely and very hospitable; but they suspected good manners, they flayed you with their hard and ironical eyes. They were also frugal, close and calculating about money—they were always talking about "brass"—and they looked on outsiders with scorn. They were monosyllabic talkers but their silences concealed strong passions that (as Mrs Gaskell said) lasted for life, whether that passion was of love or hatred. Their friendship or their enmity was for ever. To listen to their talk was like listening to a fire crackling. They had no heroes. They were cautious and their irony was laconic. I was in the city of York soon after it was bombed in the last war and I said to a railway worker,

"Well they didn't destroy the Minster."

"Ay, they say as how Hitler says he's going to be married there next May. But ah doan't know . . ."

With that last phrase dryly uttered he gave me a look as hard as steel.

Year after year I went to Sedbergh to sit on the stool by my grandmother's fire, staring at the pots that hung simmering on their shining chains over the coals, smelling the green country bacon and the rising bread. One day a boy from the famous Public School at Sedbergh was called in to tell me how many years it would be before I reached the verb "sum" in Latin and could enter the school and go for their terrible fifteen mile "runs" across the fells, the toughest schoolboy run in England. I often saw the boys slogging along near the ravine. This was one of the many schools I never went to.

My grandfather's home life was laborious and thrifty. Coals were bargained for in the summer and sacked down, carefully counted piece by piece, in a heap near the stone shed. He would then grade the pieces in sizes and (reverting to his brick-laying days), he would build them into a wall inside the shed. Each day he would collect, one by one, the various sizes of coal needed for an economical fire. They were small, slow burning fires, often damped down in order to save, but in the winters of valley fog or snow, we were thickly clad in Yorkshire wool and I remembered no cold. After his work in the house he had work to do in his garden also. He had to dig all of it. There were his vegetables and his raspberries which, in the ripe season, he sold at twopence a cup to the town. Notices saying, Thou Shalt Not Steal were placed on sticks on the wall by the school lane. He had little time or peace for his ministry; or opportunity for his secret vice: cigar smoking. The Congregationalists would not have tolerated tobacco smoking in their minister, any more than they would have stood for drinking, but I've known him drink a glass of strong home-brewed ale at an isolated farm and, as for the cigar, his habit was to sneak off to the petty or earth closet at the end of the garden, latch himself in with Bible and writing-paper, light up, take his ease and write his sermon. My grandmother was always frantic when he was out of her sight for a minute—she did her best to stop him going on his parish visits, for she would "lay" the men would be out at work and he would have to see the women, which raised her instant jealousy—and on his cigar days her delicate nose would sometimes catch the smell coming out of the top of the petty door. She would run down the garden and beat on the door with a yard-broom, shouting.

"Willyum, Willyum, come out of that, you dirty man."

Sunday was his day. On this day my grandmother respected him and herself withdrew into a silent self-complacency as her Willyum prepared for the Christian rites. He had an early and a late service in the mornings, another in the afternoon and one in the evening. He prepared for the day in soldierly way, as for battle. He shaved so closely that there was generally a spot of blood on his chin and his cheeks were pale. His surplice was a disappointing, cotton affair, like a barber's sheet—poor quality I came to think, shop-shoddy—as he set off across the gravel path to the chapel which made one side of his garden cold and damp. I was put into my Sunday best—sailor collar, vest that choked me, linen breeches that sawed at the crotch and cut me above the knees when I sat, legs dangling, swelling and aching in the pew; and my grandmother had on her best bonnet and costume. We smelled of new cloth, but she relieved this by soaking her handkerchief in Lily of the Valley and gave me a sniff of it. She also took smelling salts. Then comes the agony of sitting in those oaken pews and keeping my eyes fixed on Grandfather. What he says I never understand but he goes on and on for a long time. So do the hymns. There is the cheerful break when the plate goes round, the happiness of putting in a penny; and then there is the moment which makes me giggle—and at times (when my brother was with me), the joke was too much. My grandfather would give out notices and announce the sum of last Sunday's collection, a sum like eight shillings and three pence halfpenny. (His living, by the way.) His voice is harsh, but what convulses me is his way of pronouncing the word halfpenny; he calls it, in curt northern fashion ha'penny with the broad "a"—"hah-pny." I often tell my father of this later in London who points out I have no call to complain when, in pure Cockney I talk of a boy who lives "dahn ahr wy."

Back we go to cold beef for it is wicked to cook anything on Sundays—except Yorkshire pudding. This is sacred. Light as an omelette yet crisp in the outer foliations of what it would be indelicate to call crust, it has no resemblance to any of that heavy soggy fatty stuff known all over England and America by the name. Into it is poured a little gravy made of meat and not from some packaged concoction. One might be eating butterflies, so lightly does it float down; it is my grandmother's form of poetry. Grandfather asks if I would like "a small bortion more" for Non-conformists often affected small changes of consonant, "p" becoming "b" and an "s" becoming a "z," and then asks his wife what she thought of the sermon. The faithful always called themselves "uz," the "z" separating them from sinners. Her reply is to ask if he noticed Mrs Somebody's terrible new hat and to add that she didn't think owt to the material of the new coat Mrs Somebody Else had dressed herself up in.

The afternoon is more serious. I had no toys or games at my grandfather's—nor did my father when he was a boy—and I did not miss them. There was enough in garden, country or the simple sight of things to keep me occupied and, for years, in my parents' house the smell of toys seemed unpleasant and their disasters too distressing. One always thought of the money they cost. On Sundays at Sedbergh I was allowed into my grandfather's study. It was a small room with a few hundred books in it, almost all sermons, and he would read to me some pious tale about, perhaps, a homeless orphan, driven to sleep on straw, in some shed in Manchester, surrounded by evil-doers. The boy resists starvation, and after a long illness, is rescued by benevolent middle-class people.

When I tried to read these tales I found the words were too long and so I gazed at the green Berg, watched the cloud shadows make grey or blue faces on the grass, and the sheep nibbling there. The quiet and loneliness were exquisite to me; and it was pleasant to smell the print of my grandfather's paper and hear him turn over the pages in such a silence. When I grew up the Christian God ceased to mean anything to me; I was sick of Him by the twenties; but if I think of a possible God some image of the Berg comes at once to my mind now, or of certain stones I remember in the ravine. To such things the heathen in his wisdom always bowed.

I did not understand my grandfather's sermons. My mother who had sat through many told me his manner was hard and monotonous and that he was one to whom hatred and the love of truth were very much the same thing, his belief being that truth is afflicting and unpleasant. He argued people into hell, not in the florid manner of the melodramatic hell-fire preachers who set the flames dancing so that in the end they became like theatre flames to the self-indulgent. My grandfather's method was to send people to hell rationally, contemptuously and intellectually. He made hell curtly unattractive; he even made it boring. This was an error; later on, his congregations dwindled, for he offered no beanos of remorse, salvation or luxuriant ruin. He could not see that sin is attractive and that therefore its condemnation must be more voluptuous.

Frankly the congregations expected an artist and they discovered instead a critic. They were puzzled. That enormous success in the Free Trade Hall at Manchester was not repeated. Grandfather was essentially an intellectual and some said—my parents among them—that his marriage to a vain, houseproud and jealous girl who never read anything in her life except the love serial in the British Weekly and who upset the ladies of his many chapels by her envies and boastings, was a disaster for an intellectual man. The Congregationalists invite their ministers and the news of her character got round. But how can one judge the marriages of others? There are families that are claustrophobic, that live intensely for themselves and are indifferent to the existence of other people and are even painfully astonished by it. His truculence in the Army was a symptom of solitary independence.

The pious story of the Manchester orphan had one importance: for the first time I heard of the industrial revolution. This was real to the north-country people. We knew nothing about it in the commercial south. There were little mills in the valleys where my grandfather took me to see the mill girls at their machines. There were the tall chimneys of Leeds and York. One spoke of people, not by who they were, but by what they did. Their work defined them. Men who met at street corners in Sedbergh knew of strikes and labour wars; and my grandfather told me of masters and men with war-like relish. These stories were not told in terms of rights and wrongs very much, though my grandfather was radical enough; Carlyle's *Past and Present* fitted his view. The stories were told with a pride in conflict itself. Hard masters were as much admired as recalcitrant workmen; the quarrel, the fight, was the thing. The fight was good because it was a fight. Granda's youth was speaking when he told of this.

The Ten Commandments, of course, came into my grandfather's stories, particularly the commands to honour one's parents—though of mine he clearly had a poor opinion—because that led to obedience; then stealing the old lady's Halma pieces, the allure of apples, raspberries and Victoria plums. Finally murder. About murder he was vehement. It attracted him; he seemed to be close to it. I felt I must be close to it too. I had a younger brother whose goodness (I jealously knew) was palpable. How easily I could become Cain. To the question "Cain, where is thy brother Abel?" how glad I was that I could honestly reply "Uxbridge, near the canal," though I had once tried to push him into it. Granda kept on year after year about murder. When I was nine or ten and the famous Crippen cut up his wife and buried her in his cellar, Granda made me study the case thoroughly. He drew a plan of the house and the bloody cellar, for me to reflect on. He had a dramatic mind.

In the summer my grandparents took a holiday, paying for it out of a few preaching engagements. We took the train across Yorkshire to the North

Riding. For the first week we would stay with my Great Uncle Arthur and his wife Sarah, who was my grandmother's sister. After the placid small town life of Sedbergh, York was a shock. We were in an aristocratic yet industrial city. The relations were working-class people. The daughters of the tailor in Kirbymoorside were expectant heiresses in a small way, but both had married beneath them. Very contentedly too: the difference cannot have been very great and was bridged by the relative classlessness of the north—relative, I mean, to life in the south.

We arrived at one of an ugly row of workers' houses, with their doors on the street, close to the gas works, and the industrial traffic grinding by. A child could see that the minister and his wife thought themselves many cuts above their York relations. Great Uncle Arthur was a cabinet-maker in a furniture factory. The minister glittered blandly at him and Uncle Arthur looked as though he was going to give a spit on the floor near the minister with a manual worker's scorn.

Great Uncle Arthur was a stunted and bandy man, with a dark, sallow and strong boned face. He looked very yellow. He had a heavy head of wiry hair as black as coals, ragged eyebrows and a horrible long black beard like a crinkled mat of pubic hair. A reek of tobacco, varnish and wood-shavings come off him; he had large fingers with split unclean nails. The first thing he did when he got home from work was to put on a white apron, strap a pair of carpet knee-pads to his trousers, pick up a hammer or screw-driver and start on odd jobs round the house. He was always hammering something and was often up a ladder. His great yellow teeth gave me the idea he had a machine of some kind in his mouth, and that they were fit to bite nails; in fact, he often pulled a nail or two out of his mouth. He seemed to chew them.

Uncle Arthur's wife was Grandma's eldest sister and in every way unlike her. She was tall, big boned, very white faced and hollow-eyed and had large, loose, laughing teeth like a horse's or a skeleton's which have ever since seemed to me the signs of hilarious good nature in a woman. Though she looked ill—breathing those fumes of the gas works which filled the house cannot have been very good for her—she was jolly, hard-working and affectionate. She and Uncle Arthur were notorious (in the family) for the incredible folly of adoring each other. She doted on her dark, scowling, argumentative, hammering little gnome: it seemed that two extraordinary sets of teeth had fallen in love with each other.

For myself, Uncle Arthur's parlour, Aunt Sarah's kitchen and the small back yard were the attractions. The back yard was only a few feet square but he grew calceolarias there. It gave on to an alley, one wall of which was part of the encircling wall of the city. Its "Bars" or city gates, its Minster are the grandest in England and to Uncle Arthur who knew every stone in the place

I owe my knowledge and love of it. One could go up the steps, only a few feet and walk along the battlements and shoot imaginary arrows from the very spot where the Yorkists had shot them in the Wars of the Roses; and one could look down on the white roses of York in the gardens near the Minster and look up to those towers where the deep bells talked out their phenomenal words over the roofs of the city. They moved me then; they move me still.

Uncle Arthur's house had a stuffy smell—the smell of the gas works and the railway beyond it was mixed with the odour of camphor and camphor wax. The rooms were poorly lit by gas jets burning under grubby white globes; air did not move easily, for there were heavy curtains in the narrow passage-way to the stairs. But the pinched little place contained Uncle's genius and the smell of camphor indicated it. The cabinet-maker was a naturalist—he used to speak of Nature as some loud fancy woman he went about with and whom his wife had got used to. On the walls of his kitchen hung pretty cases of butterflies and also of insects with hard little bubble bodies of vermilion and green—creatures he had caught, killed and mounted himself. In the lower half of the kitchen window he had fixed a large glass case of ferns in which he kept a pet toad. You put a worm on the toad's table—one of Uncle's collection of fossils—and the spotted creature came out and snapped it up.

The smell of camphor was strongest in the small front parlour. A lot of space in the window corner was taken up by another large glass case containing a stuffed swan. This enormous white bird, its neck a little crooked and sooty, was sitting on a nest of sticks and seemed to be alive, for every time a lorry or a train passed, it shook and—by it's stony eye—with indignation. In two other corners there were cabinets containing Uncle's collection of birds' eggs; and on the mantelpiece was a photograph of Uncle being let down by a rope from the cliffs of Whitby where he was collecting eggs under a cloud of screaming gulls.

Granda was the sedentary and believing man; Uncle was the sceptic and man of knowledge. He had been born very poor and had had next to no schooling. He told me he could not read or write until he was a grown man. A passion for education took him. He took to learning for its own sake and not in order to rise in the world. He belonged—I now see—to the dying race of craftsmen. So he looked for a book that was suited to his energetic, yet melancholy and quasi-scientific temperament. At last, he found it: he taught himself to read by using Burton's *Anatomy of Melancholy*. This rambling and eccentric compendium of the illnesses of the brain and heart was exactly suited to his curious mind. He revelled in it.

"Look it up in Burton, lad," he'd say when I was older. "What's old Burton say?"

He would quote it all round the house. Burton came into every argument. And he would add, from his own experience, a favourite sentence:

"Circumstances alter cases."

Burton was Uncle Arthur's emancipation: it set him free of the tyranny of the Bible in chapel-going circles. There were all his relations—especially the minister—shooting texts at one another while Uncle Arthur sat back, pulled a nail or two out of his mouth and put his relatives off target with bits of the *Anatomy*. He had had to pick up odds and ends of Latin and Greek because of the innumerable notes in those languages, and a look of devilry came into his eyes under their shaggy black brows. On top of this he was an antiquarian, a geologist, a bicyclist and an atheist. He claimed to have eaten sandwiches on the site of every ruined castle and abbey in Yorkshire. He worshipped the Minster and was a pest to curators of museums and to librarians.

In short, Uncle Arthur was a crank. When the minister and he sat down in the parlour they looked each other over warily. The swan shook irritably in its glass case as they argued and there they were: the man of God and the humanist, the believer and the sceptic; the workman who had left his class and the workman who scorned to leave it. The minister said Uncle Arthur was naïve and a joke; Uncle Arthur regarded the minister as a snob, a manual worker who had gone soft and who was hardly more than his wife's domestic servant. The minister was prone to petty gossip as the clergy are apt to be. Uncle Arthur said "Let's stop the tittle tattle." He wanted a serious row. He puffed out his chest and grinned sarcastically at his brother-in-law; the minister responded with a bland clerical snort. They were united in one thing: they had both subscribed to the saying, often heard in Yorkshire: "Don't tha' marry money, go where money is." They had married heiresses.

I fancy Uncle Arthur's atheism was weakening in these days, and that he may have been moving already towards spiritualism, theosophy and the wisdom of the East—the philosopher's melancholy. There was a ruinous drift to religion in these northerners. I did not know that, in this room, there was to occur before very long, an event that would have a calamitous influence on my family but one that would play a part in starting my career as a writer. Uncle Arthur had two sons and a daughter. She was a brisk, jolly Yorkshire girl who was having a struggle with her parents. She was about to be married and, after coming home from work her idea was to go round to the house she and her fiancé had found a few streets away. He would be painting and papering it and she would have more things like fire-irons, or a coal-bucket, to take there. Uncle Arthur and Aunt Sarah thought this might lead to familiarities before marriage and would not allow her to go unless she had one of her brothers with her, but they were rarely at home.

The clever girl saw that I was the answer and petted me so that I was delighted to go with her. I was the seven-year-old chaperon and I fell in love with her. It piqued me that when we got to the house, her young man would spring out at her from the front door and start kissing and cuddling her. "Oh, give over," she cried out and said "I'm going to marry him," pointing to me. I did not leave them alone for a minute. A bed had come to the house and the excited young man soon had us all bouncing up and down on it, rumpling my hair with one hand while he tickled her with the other, till she was red as a berry. At last the wedding day came and I was sad. I longed to be with them and wanted to be their child and was sad that I was left out of it. Aunt Sarah teased me afterwards and said that since I was in the photograph of the wedding group, I was married too. This cured me of my passion. For at home in London we had a book, bought by my father, called *Marriage on Two Hundred a Year* which, like my mother's song "At Trinity Church I met me doom" caused words between my father and mother. I was beginning to form a glum opinion about married life. Why did these tall, adult animals go in for what—it seemed—was nothing but worry?

Uncle Arthur's eldest son was a tall, sad young man, with puffy cheeks. Whenever I was in York and he was at home he took me out rowing on the Ouse. He was a hero to me for he was a post office sorter who worked on the night mail train to London. He had the superb job of putting out the mail-bags into the pick-up nets beside the line, as the train screamed through at sixty miles an hour.

It was the other son, a lithographer whom I saw only once, who made the strongest and most disturbing impression on me. There are certain pictures that remain with one all one's life and feed disquieting thoughts. I was taken to a poorish house in the winter one evening and there he sat, a pallid and ailing man, with blue circles under his eyes, with medicine bottles beside him. Several young children were playing on the floor: the mother was giving the bottle to a new baby. There was—to me—the sickly smell of young children which I hated, for being the eldest of my family, I had often to look after my brothers and sisters when they were tiny. This second cousin of mine was very ill, he had lost his job as a lithographer because of his illness, and looked as if he were dying. In fact, he was no more than a nervous sickly dyspeptic, one of the victims of the Yorkshire diet of pastry, cakes and strong tea; and my grandfather said with disapproval that he was an artist. One was shown a lot of people in Yorkshire who were "warnings": after the picture of Crippen the murderer in the papers, there was the town drunk of Sedbergh, the town fighter, the town gambler. This cousin of mine was the warning against the miseries of art, unwise marriage and failure. (When I was eighteen I wanted to be a painter and the sick smell, above all the sensation of defeat and apathy in that room worried me.) Years passed. I must have been about eleven when father brought home the news that the dying Cousin Dick had been suddenly and miraculously cured by Christian Science.

It was on one of these stays in York that my grandfather took me along the walls to the Minster and showed me the Lincoln green glass. I had already had many pernickety tours with Uncle Arthur, who pointed out bits of joinery and stone masonry, and explained every historical detail. He was a connoisseur of carving and especially of tombs. His was a craftsman's attitude. It was a sight to see him standing, bandy, threatening and bearded in the aisle, with bicycle clips on his trousers—for he rarely took them off—and looking up to the vault of the aisles with an appraising eye. He often had a ruler sticking out of his jacket pocket and on my first visit I really thought he was going to pull it out and start measuring up. He didn't go so far as to say he could have built the place himself, but once we got to the choir stalls and started on the hinges and dove-tailing, he looked dangerously near getting to work on them. The choir stalls appealed to him because there are often pot-bellied and impish bits of lewd carving under a seat or on the curl of an arm, and he always gave me a pagan wink or nudge when he found one. Once he said "That'd vex t'minister." Uncle Arthur behaved as if he owned the place and would get into arguments with vergers and even bewilder a clergyman by a technical question.

My grandfather's attitude was different. The grandeur, height and spaciousness of the place moved him. He was enraptured by it. But, pointing down at the choir, he said that it was sad to know that this lovely place was in the possession of the rich and ungodly and a witness not to the Truth but to a corrupt and irrelevant theology.

The Minster was scarcely the house of God any more but the house of a class.

"And you cannot," he said severely, "worship God freely here. You have to pay for your pews." The clergy, he said, were like the Pharisees in the Bible.

We left the cathedral and went up to the steps to the walls once more at the point where the railway runs under an arch into the old York station where Stephenson's Rocket stands; and we sat in one of the niches of the battlements and looked down on the shunting trains, the express to Edinburgh coming in, the Flying Scotsman moving out to London, under their boiling white smoke. And there he told me about the wrongs of England and of a great man like Carlyle and of another, John Ruskin, who had hated the railways.

"Great men," he said. "God-fearing men."

The granite walls, the overpowering weight of English history seemed to weigh on us. To choose to be a great man was necessary; but to be one one must take on an enormous burden of labour and goodness. He seemed to convey that I would be a poor thing if I didn't set to work at once, and although the idea appealed to me, the labour of becoming one was too much. I wasn't born for it. How could I get out of it? In the south fortunately we were feebler and did not have to take on these tasks. I loved the north but I was nervous of its frown; and even of the kindly laughter I heard there.

After York we used to take the train to see the remaining sister of my grandmother, the third heiress. She lived upon the edge of the moors above Kirbymoorside where my grandmother came from, in a hamlet called Appleton. This was wild and lonely country. You drove up five or six miles in the carrier's gig; if it was raining, the passengers all sat under one enormous umbrella. There was a long climb to the common, with the horse snorting and puffing, and then you were in the wide single street of the hamlet, with wide grass verges on either side and you were escorted in by platoons of the fine Appleton geese. You passed the half-dozen pumps where girls were getting water for the cottages and arrived at a low flint cottage where my Great Aunt Lax lived.

The frown went off Grandfather's face when he left his York relations. His preaching was over. He was free. He was back in his wife's country. Aunt Lax had a farm and land that she now let off. The industrial revolution, the grim days of Hull and Nottingham and Bradford were forgotten, we were in true country and had gone back a century and Granda forgot his respectability and took off his clerical collar.

At first sight Aunt Lax looked hard. She was a tallish and skinny woman with iron-grey hair which she kept in curlers all the week except Sundays. She had a long thin nose, a startling pair of black eyebrows like charcoal marks, wore steel spectacles and was moustached and bearded like a man. Not only that, like a man, she was always heaving things about—great pails of milk in her dairy—churning butter, clattering about on clogs, shouting across the street; and her skirts were half the time kirtled to her knees. Her arms were long and strong and bony. On a second look you saw that her lizard-like face had been beautiful; it was of a dark Scandinavian beauty. But the amusing thing about this spinsterish creature—and perhaps it was what made her so gay and tolerant—was that she had been married three times. The rumour was that there had been a fourth. These marriages were a shock to the family, but Lax in name, Lax in nature, this indefatigable Wesleyan did well out of her weddings and funerals and had a long stocking.

When I was six I met the last Mr Lax. He was a dumb giant who sat on a chair outside the cottage in the sun. He was very old and had a frightening glass eye. Since there were many ploughs, carts and traps and gigs in her farmyard, I came to think he was a moorland farmer, but this was not so. A few years ago, sitting in a pub at Lastingham near by, I found an old shepherd who had known him well.

"Nay, he was nobbut t'old watchman up at t'lead mine," he told me. If Aunt Lax had done well out of her two previous husbands, the third was obviously a folly. And a strange one. The chimney of the lead mine—now abandoned—stands up like a gaunt warning finger in the middle of the heather that rolls away from Lastingham, and when she was a girl she was locked in the house, as all the village girls were, when the miners came down on Saturday nights to the village pub. North-country love is very sudden. There it was: a miner got her in the end.

Year after year I went to Appleton, sometimes alone, sometimes with Cyril, the brother who was a year or so younger than I. Aunt Lax had no children of her own so that there was nothing possessive or spoiling in her affections. We hauled water for her at the pump and, for the rest, she let us run wild with the jolly daughters of the blacksmith and anyone we came across. We scarcely ever went to chapel. The smell of bacon woke us in the morning and we went down from our pretty room which contained a chest of drawers made by Uncle Arthur, to the large kitchen where the pots hung on the chains over the fire and where she sometimes cooked on a spit. Her baking days were less fanatical than my grandma's and her washing days were pleasanter. Even the suds smelt better and there were always the big girls to chase round with us when the washing was brought in from the line or the hedges when the day was over.

When her third husband died, it was thought that amorous or calculating Great Aunt Lax would take a fourth. She had picked her second and third at the funeral feasts at which dozens of local farmers could form a sound opinion of her as a caterer and housekeeper. They had a good look round at her stables when they came, knew her acres and her fame as the leading Wesleyan for miles around. Instead, she took in a female friend, a Miss Smith. She, too, died and on the very day my brother and I arrived at the cottage. We arrived in a storm and were taken at once to one of the outer sculleries where a village girl came in, stripped us, scrubbed off the London dirt and swore to us she'd let us see the body upstairs. We longed to see it, but the girl took us off to the blacksmith's where we had to stay. More promises were made but we never saw the body. But we were allowed to play in a barn and watch the country people coming to the funeral feast. We avenged ourselves by opening six or seven bales of rag strips which Aunt Lax used for her winter occupation: making rag hearth-rugs. We threw them all over her orchard.

She was not very vexed. There was a lot of questioning of us afterwards in York and in London about who had come to the funeral, for Aunt Lax was supposed to have added to her wealth by Miss Smith's death, and everyone was trying to guess if there would be a fourth or whether other relations were on the prowl. She grew to be rather witch-like.

The moorland life was eventless. Every so often Aunt Lax would dress up in a heavy grey tweed costume, put on her hat and go off to Kirbymoorside Market, sitting by the carrier. It was a state visit. She would go there to buy cloth, or stones of flour and other things for her bins, and to see her lawyer. Once a week a pedlar would come round or a man selling herrings from Whitby and she gossiped with them. She understood boys. She told us of all the local crimes and knew the sites of one or two murders. She sent us down to the mill because a man had murdered his wife there years before. One year when I was nine I came up from London terrified with street tales about Jack the Ripper and I tried to get her to tell me he did not exist or had at any rate died long ago.

"Nay," she said. "He's still alive. He's been up here. I saw him myself at 'Utton-le-'Ole last market day." (None of our Sawdons had "an aitch to their names.")

This cured me of my terror of the Ripper: the fears of childhood are solitary and are lasting in the solitariness of cities. But in villages everyone knows everything that goes on, all the horrors real or imaginary; people come back from prison and settle down comfortably again; known rapists drink their beer in the public house in the evenings; everyone knows the thieves. The knowledge melts peacefully into the general novel of village life.

But one alarming thing occurred when I was five or six, in Appleton. It had the Haworth touch and it showed the dour, dangerous testing humour of the moorland people. We all set out one afternoon in a gig, my grandparents, Aunt Lax and myself, to a farm, a lonely stone place with geese, ducks and chickens fluttering in the yard. A few dark-leafed trees bent by the gales were standing close to it. We had tea in the low ceilinged kitchen and the farmer noticed that I was gazing at a gun which hung over the mantelpiece.

"T'lad is looking at yon gun of yours, Feyther," said his wife.

"Ay," said the farmer. "Dost know what this is lad?"

"A gun. It shoots."

"Ay. And what does it shoot?"

"I don't know."

"Would 'ee like to see it?"

"Eeh. He'd be fair capped to touch it," said my grandmother. The farmer got the gun down and let me touch it, then (helping me, for it was heavy), he let me hold it.

"Dost know how it works?"

I murmured.

The farmer broke the gun, showed me where the cartridges went, closed it, clicked the safety catch and the trigger. He gave it to me again and allowed me to do this. I was amazed.

"Would 'ee like to see the cartridges?"

"Yes."

"Yes please," said my grandmother.

"Please," I said.

He got a couple of cartridges from a drawer and loaded the gun.

"There you are. It can shoot now. Hold it."

"Ready! Present! Fire!" said my grandfather. "You can shoot a rabbit now."

The farmer steadied the gun which swayed in my small hands.

"Ay," said the farmer. "Take offt' safety catch. Now if you pull t' trigger now it'll fire."

I trembled.

"Would it kill rabbits?" I asked.

"Ay," laughed the farmer. "And people. Come, Mother, come Grandma and Mrs Lax, stand over against the wall, t'lad wants to shoot you."

"No," I said.

"Ay he does," said the excited farmer, waving them to the dresser and there they stood laughing and the gun swung in my aching hand.

"Eeh t'little lad wouldn't shoot his grandma as makes him those custard pies," Grandma said.

"Safety catch off. Now if you pull t' trigger—has 'e got his finger on it?— they'll all be dead."

"No," I said with tears in my eyes and nearly dropped the gun. The farmer caught it.

"Eeh well, it's a lesson," said the farmer hanging the gun back on the wall.

"Old Tom likes a joke," they said, going home, but Aunt Lax said the kitchen was small and that was the way Mr Robinson shot his wife down 't Mill, no accident that was. But all the way my grandma moaned:

"Eeh, who would have thought our Victor would want to shoot his grandma. Eeh. Eeh, well."

I sulked with misery and, after a couple of miles, she said to me: "He's got a monkey on his back," a sentence that always roused my temper for I felt at my back for the monkey and screamed "I haven't. I haven't."

That was the night I told my grandfather again I hoped he'd be knocked down by a train at the Junction when he crossed the line and I got my second spanking.

I came home from these Yorkshire visits sadly to whatever London house we were living in and would see in my mind's eye the white road going across the moors, like a path across a swollen sea, grey in most seasons but purple in the summer, rising and disappearing, a road that I longed to walk on, mile after mile. I was never to see one that moved me so strangely until, in my twenties, I saw another such in Castile. It brought back my childhood and this was the cause of my walking across Spain. So, when one falls in love with a face, the reason may be that one saw such a face, perhaps of an old woman, that excited one in childhood. I always give a second look at any woman with Aunt Lax's eyebrows and her lizard-like face.

CHAPTER TEN

Why the leather trade? Father had met a man who belonged to the Chamber of Commerce and who had said he knew a firm of Leather Factors that had an opening for an office boy. Begin (he said) at the bottom of the ladder, like Henry Ford. I shall not forget that spiritless January morning when Father took me to a place in the Bermondsey district of London. The one pleasant but intimidating thing was that for the first time I sat with Father in a corner seat of a First Class compartment of the train on the old South Eastern and Chatham railway. I was wearing a new suit, a stiff collar that choked me, a bowler hat which bit hard into my forehead and kept slipping over my ears. I felt sick. There were two or three city gentlemen in the compartment, smoking pipes; my father presented me with a copy of the *Christian Science Sentinel* and told me to read it while he closed his eyes and prayed for me. I disliked being seen with this paper. He prayed as far as Hither Green—I opened my eyes for a glance at a house which had been torn in half by a bomb in the autumn raids—and then he leaned across to me and, not as quietly as I would have liked, for the city gentlemen were staring at us, he reminded me of the story of the infant Samuel. Father was becoming emotional. To me the situation was once more like the sacrifice of Isaac.

"When he heard the voice of God calling, Samuel answered 'Speak Lord, they servant heareth.' When the manager sends for you, I want you to remember that. Say to yourself 'Speak Lord . . .' as Samuel did and go at once. It's just an idea. You will find it helpful. I always do that when I go to see the Buyer at Harrods."

I had thought of myself as growing up fast at school. Now, under my bowler hat, I felt I was sinking back into infancy. At London Bridge, where we got out, a yellow fog was coating the rain as we went down the long flights of sour stone stairs into the malodorous yet lively air peculiar to the river of Bermondsey. We passed the long road tunnels under the railway tracks, tunnels which are used as vaults and warehouses convenient to the Pool of London. There was always fog hanging like sour breath in these tunnels. There was a daylight gloom in this district of London. One breathed the heavy, drugging, beer smell of hops and there was another smell of boots and dog dung: this came from the leather which had been steeped a month in puer or dog dung before the process of tanning. There was also—I seemed to be haunted by it at the critical moments of my childhood—the stinging smell of vinegar from a pickle factory; and smoke blew down from an emery mill. Weston Street was a street of leather and hide merchants, leather dressers and fell-mongers. Out of each brass-plated doorway came either that oppressive odour of new boots; or, from the occasional little slum houses, the sharp stink of London poverty. It was impossible to talk for the noise of dray horses striking the cobbles.

We arrived at a large old-fashioned building and walked into a big office where the clerks sat on high stools at tilted desks. The green-shaded lamps were lit. A hard bell struck over an inner door. "Speak Lord," I instantly murmured—and a smart office boy who had given a wisp of vaseline to his forelock took us to the office of the head of the firm.

This ancient gentleman was like God himself—Grandfather and all Victorians would have recognized him. He was a tall, massive, hump-shouldered man in his late seventies, with a waving mat of long thick white hair which had a yellow streak in it, and a white beard. He had pale-blue eyes, very sharp, a wily smile and an alert but quavering voice. He was the complete City gentleman of the old school. My father and he were courtly with each other; the old man was soon on to the slump of the 1870's when his uncle had sent him to Vienna for the firm and where (he slyly said) he had got the better of a competitor because of his knowledge of German. He said he was glad to hear I was a church-goer, for he himself held a Bible class every Sunday; and his secretary, an old woman like my grandmother, taught in Sunday School too. He mentioned his eleven children, four of the sons being in the business. My father said I was good at French. The old gentleman suddenly snapped at me:

"Assez pour tirer d'affaires?"

I was bowled out and could not speak. The old gentleman grinned kindly. We were interrupted by a sugary, languid tinkle on the old-fashioned telephone that stood in the middle of his large desk. It was really two desks joined; it had spawned some odd side-tables and was covered with papers, letters and periodicals. I watched the bent knees of the old man rise, then his back heave up, then the hump elongate itself and finally a long arm with a powerful and shaking hand on it stretched across the wide desk and reached the telephone. The quavering voice changed now to a virile, barking note, the mild blue eyes became avid, the teeth looked the teeth of a lynx. His talk was brisk and commanding: when it was over he sank back in his chair and gazed at us as if he had never seen us before and, panting a little, said:

"The *Arabic* has docked with 4,000 bales."

His knees went up and down under his desk feeling for a concealed bell, and the office boy came pelting in.

The room, I saw, was like a studio under a dirty glass roof, and was supported by iron pillars here and there. In two corners of it were two more crowded desks and against one of the walls was a large Victorian fireplace. The smoke of the coal fire mingled with the fog that had entered the room.

I worked for four years, until I was nearly twenty, at the leather factors, starting at 12s. 6d. a week and finishing at 18s. 6d. The firm was one of the most important factors in the trade. Other factors, it was said, were merchants on the side, a lack of probity which the firm denounced: we—as I quickly learned to say—sold on commission only. We—it turned out— were the agents of a very large number of English tanners and fell-mongers, also of large sheepskin tanners in Australia, of hide merchants in general and dealt also in dry-salted South American hides. More rarely, and reluctantly "we" dealt in Moroccan and India dressed leather and woolled sheepskins. There was more money in the raw material. A large part of this stock was stored in the warehouse attached to the office, but also in the docks, in the wharves of the Pool of London and in the cold storages. The firm also dealt in tanning materials: oak bark, shumac, myrobalams and tanning extracts. The correspondence came from all over the world and was heavy; the size of the cheques the firm paid out astonished me; they ran often into the thousands; all of them bearing the large, spidery, childishly clear signature of the old gentleman. It was incredible that a firm in such shabby, old-fashioned offices should be so rich.

The premises were opened at 7:30 in the morning by an old clerk called Haylett who wobbled in fast, lame and gouty, but always wearing a flower in his buttonhole. He was one of those gardeners of *The Waste Land*. He was satiny pink, fat and very bald and went about singing bits of music-hall songs or making up words. He then went over to the warehouse and let the workmen into the warehouse. One of these, a young, feeble-minded man, cross-eyed and strong, would lumber down to the safes and carry up a load of heavy ledgers which he set out on the various desks. Dust flew out of them. His name was Paul—he, like one of the carmen, who was known as Ninety, because it was the number of the house where he lived—had no surname. Paul lived with his mother and was very religious. When he had put down his ledgers, Paul would advance upon Mr Haylett and say his usual morning greeting in a toneless voice and unsmiling:

"Well, my venereal friend."

To this the gay old Mr Haylett replied:

"Good morrow, good morrow, good morrow." And add one of his made-up words: "Hyjorico," and shake with laughter. Paul, who wore a heavy leather apron, lowered his head and looked murder at Mr Haylett, and went off on his bandy legs, waving his clenched fists dangerously.

At eight we office boys arrived and often saw this scene. The other boy whose name was Les Daulton had to teach me my job. He was a weak-voiced, fair creature, as simple as Paul and also famous for his comic mis-pronunciations. Offices—like my mother's shop in Kentish Town of the earlier generation—depend for their life on repeated jokes. Goods were often collected from Thameside quays: Daulton always called them "Kways" and the clerks concentrated on getting him to say it. Daulton gave a simple smile. He knew he was a success. Once we had arrived Mr Haylett went to the W.C. in the basement where he sat smoking his first cigar and reading the paper; Daulton and I followed him down, taking with us the packs of rubber sheets which were used in the copying of letters in the letter presses, and soaked them in the wash-basins. This done, the boy took me out with the local letters that had to be delivered by hand. We went down to the hide market, to the tanners and leather dressing firms and then came back to our main job: answering the Chairman's bell. This bell was fixed outside Mr Kenneth's door, in the main office, and snapped in startling, rusty and panicky agitation.

"Boy. Bell," Mr Haylett would call out in panic, too.

"Speak Lord, Thy servant heareth," I murmured. One of us would jump off our stools and go in to see what the old gentleman wanted. Sometimes he handed us an urgent letter which had to be copied, but often his knee had pressed the bell by mistake; or he had forgotten he had called us and he gazed at us blankly with the lost, other-worldly eyes of an old man.

Occasionally the bell was rung from another desk in Mr Kenneth's office. This was the desk of another old man, Mr James, Mr Kenneth's brother, well-known to be the fool of the business and never trusted with any serious matters. He wandered in to "work" at eleven or so, wrote a private letter to Lord This or Lady That—for he was vain of aristocratic acquaintance—and would then shuffle out into the main office, calling out "I'm going to get me hair cut" in a foggy, husky voice. Sometimes he would wander into the warehouse and watch the bales of leather swinging on the crane.

"Coming in or going out?" he would ask, putting on as much of a commanding air as he could manage, considering his voice and the absurd angle of his pince-nez glasses which were held lop-sided on his nose by a piece of black ribbon.

Under his foolishness Mr James concealed the character of an old Victorian rip and he was terrified of his pious brother Kenneth. Mr James's only work was to hand us our wages every Saturday in a sealed envelope. I was warned that he would slyly pay me too much the first time—another Victorian trick—to test my honesty. Sure enough he did; he gave me fifteen shillings instead of the agreed 12s. 6d. and I had to go through the farce of explaining there had been a mistake. The expression on his face was one of immense self-congratulation at his cleverness. We liked Mr James because his daily hair-cut took place at a smart Bar near London Bridge. Everyone envied his life of folly. We indexed the letter books, putting the number of the previous letter written to the firm at the top of the flimsy page in blue chalk. This indexing took us a large part of the day, for we, as well, had to see the customers at the counter, answer the bell, and begin copying the next crop of out-going letters. Late in the morning, Mr Haylett, our boss, would go off on a round of messages in the City, carrying shipping documents, contracts, cheques and so on, and would return about 3:30, rosy in the face, smelling of cigars and scent.

"Where's he been, the dirty old man. Up Leicester Square. Lounging in the Leicester Lounge," the other clerks would greet him enviously.

Les and I, in the meantime, went out to lunch together into the Boro' to someone's Dining Rooms, a good pull-up for carmen, near the Hop Exchange. Upstairs we ate the same food for the next year, every day; either steak and kidney pudding followed by date or fig pudding, or steak and kidney pie followed by the same. The helpings were heavy; the whole cost 8d. but went up to 10d. the following year. I was afraid of London and especially of the price of things and it was pretty well a year before I had the courage to go into the Express Dairy Café under the arches at London Bridge Station. We walked back to the office past Guy's Hospital. The clock crawled from 2 to 2:05, from 2:05 to 2:10 in the tedious afternoon. At four we had a quarter of an hour's break for tea up in the housekeeper's kitchen, I having been sent across to a little cake and tobacco shop for sugared buns. Relays of clerks came up for tea. We sat at a kitchen table looked after by a cross woman called Mrs Dunkley or—as she sometimes wrote it—Mrs Dunkerley. The clerks munched their buns and made sly remarks about how much she stole, about her corset, her bottom, what she did with her lodger, and built up fantasies about her sexual life. She (like Daulton) could be cornered into saying one of her classic sentences such as the one made to Mr Elkins, the dispatch clerk:

"Ho, Mr Helkins, I dropped the Heggs."

Among the clerks there was the weedy, lewd and sarcastic Mr Drake, a sandy-haired man who invented the day's dirty jokes and backed horses. At a desk under the long iron-barred windows, sat a respectable puffing middle-aged man with a dirty collar, the shipping clerk, his desk a confusion of bills of lading, delivery orders, weight slips. An inaccurate and over-worked man, he was always losing important documents and was often blown up by one of the angry partners, the sons of Mr Kenneth. There was Mr Clark, a dark, drawling defiant figure who looked like a boxer. He was the invoice clerk. He would stand warming himself by the fire, unmoving, even if the head cashier arrived, until the clock struck nine. If the cashier glared at him, Mr Clark stood his ground and said: "Nine o'clock is my time."

The arrival of the head cashier set the office in motion and something like a chapel service began. He was a tall, grizzled, melancholy man who stood at his desk calling over figures to an assistant, like a preacher at a burial. He was famous for his sigh. It was a dull noise coming from low down in his body. "Um ha ha," he said. And sometimes he would call to an idling clerk:

"Press on, Mr Drake."

"Press on what?" Mr Drake would mutter.

"Your old woman," from Mr Clark.

"I did that last night," sniggered Mr Drake. "The air raid upset her."

"Sit on her head," called Mr Clark.

Conversations that were carried across the office in penetrating mutters. The head cashier's stomach noise pleased everyone. If he left the office for a moment, it was ten to one that Mr Haylett would mimic it and bang his desk lid up and down, like a schoolboy.

About nine arrived the only two women employed in the main office—there were five sacred typists upstairs. These two women were quarrelling sisters. Women were in the post-corset, pre-brassiere period and it was the joy of the office to exclaim at the jumpings, bobbings and swingings of a pair of breasts. One lady combined a heavy white blouseful with an air of swan-like disdain.

"Things are swinging free this morning, do you not observe, Mr Clark?" Drake would say.

"Do you fancy fish for lunch?" Mr Clark would reply, nodding to the prettier sister.

The elder girl raised her nose, the pretty one shrugged her shoulders and pouted.

Hour after hour, the cashier and the swan carried on their duet.

"Feb. 2 By Goods. Cash £872 11. 4."

And the swan answered:

"£872 11. 4."

"Comm. and dis. £96 16. 2," intoned the cashier. "Um, ha, ha." The mournful sing-song enchanted us.

At 9:30 the "lady secretaries" arrived. They were the secretaries of the partners, their little breasts jumping too and their high heels clattering. These girls were always late.

"The troops stay so late," sniggered Mr Drake. "How can a working girl get to work?"

As the day's work went on, the foremen in leather aprons would come over to the office from the warehouse. They were responsible for different kinds of leather and they usually came over to settle matters arising from the chief problem of the leather trade. Most of it is sold by weight, but leather can gain or lose weight, depending upon the season and the weather. The men in the warehouse despised the "shiny arsed clerks with their four ten a week." Sometimes Bermondsey life would break in on us. The kids would climb up the wall and, hanging on to the bars of the office windows, would jeer at us. A clerk would be sent to drive them off, but they picked up stones and threw them at him or spattered our windows with horse manure. But often the clerk could not get out because they had tied up the door with rope. If a boy was caught and got his ears boxed, the mother would be round in a minute, standing in the office and shouting she wanted "the bleeding fucker" who had hit her Ernie. The mothers were often hanging about in the pub next door, feeding their babies stout or a drop of port to keep them sleepy.

We worked until seven in the evening. On Saturdays we left between two and four, this depending on the mail. In the evenings I went home from London Bridge Station. In *The Waste Land* T. S. Eliot wrote of the strange morning and evening sight of those thousands of men, all wearing bowlers and carrying umbrellas, crossing London Bridge in long, dull regiments and pouring into that ugly, but to me most affecting, railway station which for years I used. I was captivated by it as I suppose every office worker is by the station in the great city that rules his life. Penn Station in New York, St Lazare in Paris, Waterloo, Paddington and Liverpool Street, are printed on the pages of a lifetime's grind at the office desk. Each is a quotidian frontier, splitting a life, a temple of the inexorable. The distinction of London Bridge Station, on the Chatham side, is that it is not a terminus but a junction where lives begin to fade and then blossom again as they swap trains in the rush hours and make for all the regions of South London and the towns of Kent. The trains come in and go out over those miles of rolling brick arches that run across South London like a massive Roman wall. There were no indicators on the platforms in my day and the confusion had to be sorted out by stentorian porters who called out the long litanies of stations in a hoarse London bawl and with a style of their own. They stood on the crowded platform edge, detected the identifying lights on the incoming engine and then sang out. To myself, at that age, all places I did not know seemed romantic and the lists of names were, if not Miltonic, at any rate as evocative as those names with which the Georgian poets filled up their lines. I would stare admiringly, even enviously, at the porter who would have to chant the long line to Bexley Heath; or the man who, beginning with the blunt and challenging football names of Charlton and Woolwich would go on to comic Plumstead and then flow forward over his long list till his voice fell to the finality of Greenhythe, Northfleet and Gravesend; or the softer tones of St Johns, Lewisham and Blackheath. And to stir us up were the powerful trains—travelling to distances that seemed as remote as Istanbul to me—expresses that went to Margate, Herne Bay, Rochester and Chatham. I saw nothing dingy in this. The pleasure of my life as an office boy lay in being one of the London crowd and I actually enjoyed standing in a compartment packed with fifteen people on my way to Bromley North. How pleasant it was, in the war years, to stop dead outside Tower Bridge and to see a maroon go off in an air-raid warning and, even better, for a sentimentalist, to be stuck in one of those curry powder fogs that came up from the river and squashed London flat in its windless marsh. One listened to the fog signals and saw the fires of the watchmen; there was a sinister quiet as the train stood outside the Surrey Docks. And when, very late, the train got to Bromley North and one groped one's way home, seeing the conductors with flares in their hands walking ahead of the buses, or cars lost and askew on the wrong side of the road, and heard footsteps but saw no person until he was upon you and asking where he was, one swanked to oneself that at last one had had a load of the traditional muck on one's chest.

The thing I liked best was being sent on errands in Bermondsey. They became explorations, and I made every excuse to lengthen them. I pushed down south to the Dun Cow in the Old Kent Road, eastward by side streets and alleyways to Tower Bridge. I had a special pleasure in the rank places like those tunnels and vaults under the railway: the smells above all made me feel importantly a part of this working London. Names like Wilde's Rents, Cherry Garden Street, Jamaica Road, Dockhead and Pickle Herring Street excited and my journeys were not simply street journeys to me: they were like crossing the desert, finding the source of the Niger. London was not a city; it was a foreign country as strange as India and even though I knew the Thames is a small river compared with the great ones of the world, I would patriotically make it wider and wider in my mind. I liked the Hide Market where groups of old women and children hung about the hide men who would occasionally flick off a bit of flesh from the hides: the children like little vultures snatched at these bits and put them in their mothers' bags. We thought the children were going to eat these scraps, but in fact it is more likely—money being urgent to all Londoners—they were going to sell them to the glue merchants. The glue trade haunted many busy Cockney minds. Owing to the loop of the river, Bermondsey has remained the most clannish and isolated part of London; people there were deeply native for generations. Their manner was unemotional but behind the dryness, there was the suggestion of the Cockney sob.

"What'll y'ave? Lovin' mem'ry or deepest sympathy?" the woman in the shop asked when I went to buy a mourning card for one of our office cleaners.

I would pass the Tanners Arms and wonder at the peculiar fact that the owner had a piece of tanned human skin "jes like pigskin." The evenings came on and a procession of women and children would be wheeling their mattresses up to the railway tunnels or the deep tube station to be safe from the occasional raids. I would see other office boys wearing their bowler hats as I wore mine: we were a self-important, cracked-voice little race, sheepish, yet cocky, regarding our firms with childish awe.

But my work was dull. The terrible thing was that it was simple and mechanical; far, far less difficult than work at school. This was a humiliation and, even now, the simplicity of most of the work in offices, factories and warehouses depresses me. It is also all trite child's play and repetition and the correcting of an infinitude of silly mistakes, compared with intellectual or professional labour. Most people seemed to me, then, and even now, chained to a dulling routine of systematized and tolerated carelessness and error. Whatever was going to happen to me, I knew I must escape from this easy, unthinking world and I understood my father's dogged efforts to be on his own, and his own master. In difficulty lay the only escape, from what for me seemed to be deterioration of faculty.

The dullness, the long hours, the bad food, the low pay, the paring away of pleasure to a few hours late on Saturday afternoon, the tedious Sundays brightened only by that brief hour at the Sunday School—all these soon stunned and stunted me in my real life however much they moved me to live in my imagination. I accepted, with the native London masochism, that these were hard times and that this was to be my life. London has always preferred experience to satisfaction. I saw myself a junior clerk turning into a senior clerk comfortable in my train, enjoying the characters of my fellow travellers, talking sententiously of the state of affairs in France, Hong Kong and Singapore and, with profound judiciousness, of the government. Over the years one would know these season ticket holders—perhaps not speaking to them—as well as the characters in a novel. Sometimes there was an oddity—the man who read Virgil as he travelled up and down. And there was always, for diversity, the girls who knitted for the soldiers and read novels. There was also the pride I felt in being enslaved in a city so world-famous, in being submerged in its brick, in being smoked and kippered by it. There was the curious satisfaction, in these months, of a settled fate and the feeling that here was good sense and, under the reserve, humour and decency.

But the office was brutalizing me. One morning I arrived and began teasing Daulton, the other office boy. He was slow and childish. I was trying to make him say: Parson's Kway. He would take that from a clerk but not from an equal. He saw an enemy and flew at me. It was delightful: it was like being at school again. We were soon rolling on the floor and I was laughing, but he, I saw, was savage. Old Haylett wobbling up from the W.C. found us dishevelled in the dust. He put a stop to it and Daulton, trembling, began to cry. What had I done to him? He was afraid of getting the sack. Haylett took his side. So did the clerks. Daulton was their joke and treasure. I was spoiling it. When the cashier came he called me over and I said we were only "having a game." "You have upset Daulton," the cashier said gravely. "I am surprised at a boy like you wrestling with a boy of that type. You went to a better school than he did." And I who had thought that Daulton and I were fellow victims! Daulton gave me a look of pompous disapproval and wistful reproach after this. The matter went on being debated by the cashier and the clerks, and I saw that I was in serious trouble. It was discussed with one of the partners. I became scared when he sent for me and came away incredulous. I was to be promoted. I was to go into the warehouse and learn the trade.

My life became freer and more interesting at once and I scarcely spoke to Daulton after that.

The firm was run by Mr Kenneth whose chauffeur brought him up from the country at ten. Mr Kenneth came in burdened like Abraham and went, knees bent, in a fast aged shuffle, like a man stalking, to his office where he was soon ringing his bell. About the same time his four sons arrived, four quarrelling men between thirty-seven and fifty years old. The firm was a working model of that father-dominated life which has been typical of England since the Elizabethan age and perhaps always, for we must have got it from the Saxons and the Danes. In the Victorian age, with the great increase in wealth, the war between fathers and sons, between older brothers and younger, became violent, though rather fiercer in the middle-class than among manual workers where the mother held the wage packet. Until 1918 England was a club of energetic and determined parricides; in the last generation the club appears to have vanished altogether. So, in their various ways, Mr James, Mr Frederick, Mr William and Mr John, active and enterprising City men, were at war with each other and attacking Father when one or other of them was in favour. Mr John, the youngest and most genial, was the only one to regard the fray with grinning detachment. He sat on the opposite side of his father's desk, unperturbed.

Mr James was the eldest, a precisionist and cultivated and intelligent man; he dealt in heavy leather. Mr Frederick, handsome, dashing and hot-tempered, whose eyes and teeth flashed operatically, was in foreign hides, a very speculative market; he lived in a fine house in Regent's Park; Mr John drawled a shrewd and lazy life among fell-mongers and raw pelts; Mr William, to whom I fell, had an office on the warehouse floor and dealt in basils and skivers, i.e., tanned sheepskins. On this subject, under his teaching, I was to become an expert.

The British merchant has the reputation of being a deep and reserved, untalkative fellow, slow to act until he is certain, not easily deceived and a shade lazy. The four brothers entirely contradicted this legend, except in one respect: they were not easily deceived. Reserve they had none. They talked and shouted their heads off, they exposed their passions, they were headlong in action, as keen and excitable as flies and worked hard. Mr William was the most emotionally self-exposing of the brothers. He was a sportsman who had played hockey for England, a rather too ardent and too reminiscent golfer and extrovert. Owing to a damaged knee he was rejected for the Army during the war. His emotionalism annoyed his brothers. He would come into the office crying out: "Father hates me. James has been telling Fred ..." and so on, a wounded and sulky man. What their differences were I don't know; but they were strong enough to break up the firm when the old man died.

I had often known the chapel-like groans of the main office to be interrupted by a pair of these storming brothers who pranced in a hot-tempered ballet. There had to be a peacemaker or catalyst and there was.

When I described the arrivals at our office there was one figure I did not mention: a dandy called Hobbs. For some reason he was not called *Mr* Hobbs and these were the days before people called anyone but a servant or a workman by Christian or nickname. The voice in which Hobbs was addressed was reverent; it might have been used to a duke who had, for some reason, condescended to slum with us all; it was a tone of intimacy, even of awe. He was on simple, equal terms with everyone from the old gentleman down to the boys. One finds his type more often in the north of England than in the south, and indeed he came from Leeds and had a faint, flat weary Yorkshire accent. His speech was plain but caressing. He had walked into the business, in his deceptively idle way, some years before and discreetly appointed himself to be the brains of the firm. To everybody and to me especially, he was the only person to whom I could talk. He was a man of about thirty.

One saw him, a tall thin figure, a sort of bent straw, but paddling down Weston Street early in the winter mornings, in his patent leather shoes, his fur-lined overcoat reaching to his ankles, his bowler hat tipped back from a lined forehead and resting, because of the long shape of his head, upon a pair of the ugliest ears I have ever seen. His little remaining hair rose in carefully barbered streaks over the long, egg-like head. A cigarette wagged in his mouth, his face was pale, seamed, ill and amused. Hobbs was a rake and his manner and appearance suggested days at the races and evenings at the stage door of the Gaiety, and the small hours at the card table. He looked as if he were dying—and he was—the skull grinned at one and the clothes fluttered about a walking skeleton.

Eyes bloodshot, breath still smoking gin or whisky of the night before, he arrived almost as early as the office boys in order to get at the office mail before anyone else saw it. He memorized it; he was now equipped to deal with all the intrigue, quarrels and projects. By some nervous intimation he knew whenever a girl came into the office and he smiled at them all and his large serious eyes put them into a state. To all, at some time or other, he said "Darling, I'd like to bite your pretty shoulders." Except to the dragon, the old man's secretary, who often handed out religious tracts. She saw in Hobbs, no doubt, an opportunity for rescue and he deferred to her and started reading a line or two of the tracts at once while she was there and making expert comments on a passage in Exodus or Kings, so that the old lady began to blush victoriously. Girls liked to be caught in the warehouse lift with him for he instantly kissed their necks and looked their clothes over. His good manners overwhelmed Mrs Dunkley-Dunkerley in her kitchen. All office work stopped, even the cashier stopped his call-over of the accounts, when Hobbs went to the telephone and smiling at it, as if it were a very old raffish crony, ordered a chauffeur-driven Rolls to collect him in the evening and pick up one of his girls to take them to dinner at the Ritz. The partners listened to him in fright, wondering aloud about his debts, but would soon be confiding in him, as everyone else did and be angling for his advice.

"Look what Father has done. James has told Father that Fred . . ." — Hobbs who always wore his bowler hat in the office and was the only one who was allowed to smoke, nodded and listened with religious attentiveness. The appearance of physical weakness and dissipation was a delusion. The firm chin, strong coarse mouth, the rapidity of mind, were signs of great nervous strength. The partners were gentlemen of the cheerfully snobbish kind. Hobbs was an intellectual from a provincial university who had read a lot and was a dilettante. His brain was in a continuous and efficient fever. If trade was slack and he had no business or customers to deal with, he'd go round the office and, with a smile that they could not resist, would take the clerks' pens from them with a "By your leave, laddie" and do all their accounts and calculations in a few minutes while they gaped at him. Their lives were ruled by having to work out exasperating sums as, for example, 3 cwt. 2 quarters 9 lbs. at 3s. 4½d. per lb. less commission and discount of 3½ per cent. He could do scores of sums like these in a few minutes. Or, for amusement, he would tot up the head cashier's ledgers so fast that this sorrowing and very pious man would look over his glasses with admiration and momentarily forgive Hobbs his obvious debauches. With the workmen he was the same; he got them out of the labourious messes they made of their weighing slips, gave them racing tips, was knowing about prize fights and once in a while would buy them a drink in the pub next door where he was well known. Where was he not well known!

"Out of the great kindness of your heart, duckie," I've heard him say to the barmaid of a discreet hide-out near London Bridge, "would you give me a rather large gin and French?"

I had to work with Hobbs and soon, infatuated, I dressed exactly as he in white coat and bowler hat, pushing it back over my ears in helpless admiration of him. I had to sit with him and keep the Epitome Book, a summary of the hundreds of letters that came in. I have always been prone to intellectual disaster. For years I thought this book was called the Opitomy Book, for I used to think of Epitome as a three syllable word.

I was enraptured by Hobbs. For a boy of sixteen is there anything like his first sight of a man of the world? I was enraptured by London Bridge, Bermondsey and the leather trade. I liked its pungent smell. I liked watching the sickly green pelts come slopping out of the pits at the leather dresser's down the street, I liked paddling among the rank and bloody hides of the market; I would cadge the job of cutting the maggots of the warble fly out of a hide in our hide shed. I liked the dirty jobs. I wanted to know everything I could about leather. Gradually, literature went out of the window: to be a leather factor, or, better still, a country tanner was my dream. I spent my days on the seven floors of the warehouse, turning over dozens of calf skins with the men, measuring sheepskins and skivers and choking myself with the (to me) aromatic shumac dust. At home the family edged away from me: I stank of the trade. With my father and me it was a war between Araby and the tanpit.

The leather trade is an interesting trade, for skins and hides are as variable as nature. At certain seasons, in the breeding season, for example, the skin will be hard and "cockled"; heavily woolled sheep like the merinos drag the surface of the leather into ridges so that the body of some old man seemed to lie under my measuring ruler. Some skins are unaccountably greasy and have to be degreased; others may have heated in the hold of a ship; yet others may have been over-salted by a tanner who perhaps hopes when the temperature rises, that they will pick up moisture and weight. After a time one could tell from which town and county of England any skin came and from which tannery, for each tanner had his own methods, his peculiar waters and style. The names were cheerful: skivers and basils, shoulders, bellies, split-hide bellies and butts—the animals seemed to lie ba-aaing and lowing, as one looked at the grain of the skins for their quality or their defects; to see which could be dyed in red or green, say, or which— owing to the flaws in the grain, would have to be dyed in the cheaper black. There was change in every bale that the crane lifted off the vans and heaved into the "gaps" where the men chalked the tally on the walls. And change in the human scene too. On market days, many of the tanners came to the office. They came mainly from the small towns of England and the variety of character fascinated me. A brash bearded fellow in a cowboy hat who came roaring in and shouting that we were "a lot of stuckup London snobs" and his money was as good as ours; the trembling pair of elderly black-bearded brothers from Dorset who stood together, shoulders touching, like Siamese twins and had the suspicious and dour look of conspiring lay preachers; the flash Welshman; the famous sole leather man from Cumberland; the sad country gentleman tanner from Suffolk; the devastating fashionable tycoon who was making a fortune, wore a monocle, was something to do with Covent Garden Opera and introduced me to the name of Flaubert.

In due time I was sent down to the wharves of Pickle Herring Street or the docks, to make reports on damaged skins that had been dropped into the river, or on thousands of bales which had come in from Australia. A literary job: as the bales were opened for me in these warehouses that smelled of camphor or the mutton-fat smell of wool or rancid furs, I wrote in my large book, an estimate and a description. It was curious to open a bale from the ship or barge alongside and to see, as one got to the centre of it, that it was blackening with heat and at the centre, charred and cindery. When I grew up and read Defoe's Complete English Tradesman I knew the pleasure he felt in the knowledge of a trade, its persons and its ways. If I knew nothing else, at the end of four years I was proud of my knowledge of leather. It was a gratifying knowledge. During the last war I had to spend some time in shipyards on the Tyne and the Clyde and the passionate interest in a craft came back to me; and although I was then an established writer, I half wished I had spent my life in an industry. The sight of skill and of traditional expertness is irresistible to me.

My absorption in the leather trade went to comical lengths. Father had bought a fat encyclopaedia, second hand, and dated 1853; I discovered in it a full technical account of the tanning process. I decided to tan a skin myself. I got a small tank, brought home some shumac and then considered the process. First I had to get an animal and then skin it; then, either by pasting it on the flesh side with a depilatory, or letting it heat to the point of decay that is not injurious to the skin, I would have to scrape off the hair. There were superficial skins to remove. I would then have to place it in the proper liquids, having first transferred it for a time to a tank of fermented dog dung in order to soften it. And so on. The difficulty was to find an animal small enough. Our dog? Our cat? One of our rabbits? The thought sickened me. A mouse? There were plenty in the house. I set a trap and caught one. But it was pretty and the prospect of letting its skin sweat and removing the fur with my fingers repelled me. I gave up the idea.

In my second year in the trade, in the summer holiday, I hired a bicycle and went up to Ipswich, stopping at a country tannery on the way. It belonged to the sad gentleman farmer. He gave me lunch and I showed off to his pretty daughter. After lunch he took me round the tannery. This was the life, I thought, as I walked round the pits: to be a country gentleman, marry this nice girl and become a tanner. There might be some interesting erotic social difficulties of the kind that occurred in *John Halifax, Gentleman* by Mrs Craik, a novel that fed my daydreams at this time. The pits were laid out like a chequer board and we walked between them. I was in the midst of this daydream when I slipped and I fell up to the neck into the cold filthy ooze of the pit. A workman hooked me out on his pit pole before I went under, for these pits are deep; I was rushed to a shed, stripped and hosed down. Stinking, I was taken back to the house, and dressed up in an assortment of clothes, including a shooting jacket much too large and a pair of football shorts belonging to the tanner's ten-year-old son. The nice girl had left to laugh in her room.

This was my baptism into the trade; now I think of it, the only baptism I have ever had.

I was happier in my hours in the leather trade than I was at home; and strangely, I believe, the encouragement to think again of being a writer came from people in the trade. One or two of the customers saw the books I was reading on my desk and I discovered that many of these businessmen knew far more about literature than I did. There was the tycoon with his Flaubert—whom I did not read for years—there was Beale, the leather dresser, who recited Shakespeare at length, as we went through the skivers on the top floor; there was Egan, our foreman, a middle-aged and gentle man with a soft voice who, in between calling orders to the men and going over his weighing slips, would chat to me about Dickens and Thackeray. Once a month he would get blind drunk for a few days and then return, otherworldly and innocent, to have a bookish talk. There was a leather belting manufacturer who introduced me to literary criticism. They were amused by my naïvety; but when they got down to their business affairs with Mr William and the watching of the market, I realized that although I knew a lot about leather, I knew nothing about trade and money, and that the ability or taste for making it was missing in me. Beale, the Shakespearean, showed that to me. He was a man of fifty who had inherited his business and was always in straits and was rather contemptuously treated in the trade because of his incompetence. He took me round his works and looked miserably at the rollers that came down from their arms, striking the skins, with a racket that he could not stand. "Keep out of it," he said. "Unless you know how to make money, it is no good."

Hobbs sat or dangled from his high stool and said "Journalism's the life, laddie. You read too many classics. You ought to read modern stuff.

Journalists are the bright lads. What about W. J. Locke?"

I saw it at once when I read *The Beloved Vagabond*, *The Morals of Marcus Ordeyne* and *Septimus*, that Hobbs had modelled himself on Locke's gentlemanly, Frenchified Bohemianism. A bottle of wine, a French mistress was his ideal—often realized; at any rate he had soon established one of the new women who came to the firm, the widow of a French soldier, in his flat. There was Thomas Hardy, too, he said, and Arnold Bennett. So I threw up the classics and took to the open (French) road with Locke as a successor to Stevenson; and a precursor to Belloc. I had discovered the writers I really admired: the travellers. I bought most of the books I read, and had done so at school too, by spending my food money on them. I gave up the Dining Rooms and the Express Dairy; instead in the lunch-hour I bought a bar of chocolate or a packet of biscuits and a book for a few pence at a shop near the arches at the station, walked across London Bridge and went on lunch-hour tours of the Wren churches—to the organ recitals at St Stephen's in Walbrook and St Dunstan's in the East and to St Magnus the Martyr in Billingsgate. I knew I should admire the Wren churches but they bored me. The classical Italian beauty of St Stephen's in Walbrook seemed cold to the clerkly follower of Ruskin; cold and also—to a dissenter—moneyed and even immoral. The elegant St Mary Woolnoth and even St Magnus the Martyr and its carvings, seemed to me as "worldly" as the boardrooms of banks. And in Southwark Cathedral I had an experience of the "mechanical" worship of the Church of England. A young clergyman sitting at a harmonium in one of the aisles was teaching another the correct intonation of

"The Lord be with you"

and the response

"And with Thy spirit"

which they repeated dozens of times, trying to get it right. Now I could admire; then I scowled like a Bunyan at "vain repetitions."

The one real church, for me, was St Bartholomew's. I visited these churches as a stern cultural duty, but also out of a growing piety towards the London past. The pleasure was in the organ recitals held in the lunch-hour. Lately introduced by our neighbour to Sibelius and Rachmaninoff, I now was entranced by Bach's fugues. This taste was literary and due to Browning; all my tastes were conventionally Victorian. The monocled tycoon who had revolutionized the tanning of sheep-skins, heard with horror of my unfashionable ideas. I seemed irredeemably backward and lower class and the cry of the autodidact and snob broke out in me in agony "Shall I never catch up?"

I soon knew the alley ways of the city and intrigued to be sent to Ministries in Westminster. I ventured into Fleet Street and stared longingly at newspaper offices. Often I longed to be in love; but I was already in love with London, and although too shy to go into pubs—and hating anyway the taste of beer—I would listen to the rattle of dominoes among the coffee tables of the Mecca as far north as Moorgate, and obscurely feel my passion. I even walked from Bermondsey to Westminster. To love, travel is almost the complete alternative; it is lonely, it is exhausting, but one has lived completely by one's eyes and ears and is immolated in the world one is discovering. When, at last, I did find a girl, all we did was dumbly walk and walk round London Streets till I dropped her at her office door. When I read books of the glamour-of-London kind, I was disappointed with myself and tried to whip myself up into a glamorized state, for I could not see or know what the writer knew; but a London of my own was seeping into me without my knowing it and, of course, was despised because it was "every day experience."

One summer morning when I was on the heavy leather floor of our building, I heard the impudent whistle of Atterbury, the foreman of the floor. He was a cross-eyed, jeering little fly, known to everyone as Ankleberg.

"I got a nice birthday present this morning," he shouted. "My old woman give it me. Somethink I coulda done without. Same as last time, same as time afore that—nine bleeding times! Another bleeding kid. And no lie either."

He had an accusing manner.

"Know what the woman next to her in hospital said to the doctor? 'E's never off me.' "

Ankleberg stared and, then, he shouted with laughter and went off looking like the devil. He was the man who let me have a go at cutting maggots out of some cow-hides in return for loading a van with them.

"Here Ankle," said his mate but coming over to me and opening a wallet. "This is what you want." And showed him a packet of French letters.

"Dirty bastard," said Ankleberg. "You'll get some poor girl into trouble."

Our talk was stopped by a curious sound of pumping and hammering going on in the sky and we went over to the gap. The sound was gunfire.

"Stone me, it's bleeding Fritz," said Ankleberg.

Up we went in the warehouse lift.

"Nine little hungry mouths," said Ankleberg on the way up. "What d'you make of that, son?"

We got on to the roof. Not far off, high in the sky over the Tower of London and coming westward were a dozen German aircraft. They looked like summer gnats in the clear sky and around them hundreds of little cherub-like bursts of anti-aircraft fire were pocking the blue. Sudden bursts of bomb smoke came stepping along the Thames towards St Paul's, where black and green clouds went up from the roofs: and then, down our way the aircraft came. In the street people were watching the planes, most of our staff were there and they ran indoors when a bomb fell; some said on a printing works in Newcomen Street near by, or in the Boro.'

In a minute or two the raid was over. I was looking at the fires near St Paul's. I tried to ring my father. There was no answer. I got permission to go and see if he was all right; but in fact I was longing to see the damage. It was, for those days, startling. A flight of aircraft had bombed London for the first time by day. Over London Bridge I went down the steps by St Magnus the Martyr into Billingsgate and saw the street walls of several houses and wharves had been stripped off, carts were overturned and horses lay dead among the crowds. The pubs in Bermondsey had filled with women pouring drink into themselves and their babies as I left; it was the same in Billingsgate. Outside a pub at the Monument, on the very spot where the old fire of London had started, one of those ragged and wild-looking women street singers with enormous plumes in her coster hat was skirling out a song, luscious with Cockney sentiment and melodrama: "Cit-ee of larfter, Cit-ee of tears." I kicked my way through little streets of broken glass in Little Britain and, passing the stink of burning chemical works, reached my father's office. The flames of the fire were so hot that he and I could not stay on his roof.

(1968)

FROM

Midnight Oil

CHAPTER ONE

I started work on a misty morning. The shop was in an arcade and was the Paris branch of an English manufacturer of photographic plates and papers. At first I had thought the boss was French, for he had the black long curly moustache and frisked-up hair of a French barber of the period and wore a tight little jacket and boots with high heels. In fact, he was a London sparrow brought up in Marseilles. His sallow skin looked as though it had been painted with walnut stain and he spoke French fast but with an entirely English pronunciation. His "combiangs" and "ker voolay voos" raced through the tongue of Molière like a rusty lawn mower. He pointed out that on the small salary he was paying me I should have to leave my hotel and find a cheaper room.

That morning, I saw that my job was a come-down after the leather trade. First of all, the situation of the shop was wrong. Du Maurier, Murger and W. J. Locke and Anatole France would have dropped me if they had known I was earning my living on the Right Bank within five minutes of Thomas Cook and the American Express: that I was in Paree and not Paris. My mind split: here I was copying, in pencil, lists of stock on half sheets of flimsy paper, hour after hour, in the dark back office of the shop, but my other self was across the river among the artists. The other people working in the shop were, first, the salesman: he was a heavy, black-haired, scowling young Highland Scot, a handsome man with grey threatening eyes and a very soft voice. He had run away from home at fifteen and, disguising his age, he had fought in the artillery in the 1914 war. He was a broken-nosed Army boxer, too. Towards the end of the war he had been blown off his horse and received a chunk of high explosive in his bottom and spoke of this with gravity. He had married a French woman and I imagined a pert little midinette: but one day she stood in the arcade outside making signs to him and I saw she was a plain, short woman, middle-aged and enormously fat. They lived in Montmartre and he spoke of her cooking reverently. He was a magnet to all the women who came to the shop. They became helpless or frantic at the sight of him; he would stand close to them and look down into their eyes, unsmiling, and speak in a low voice, with slow, pedantic deliberation.

The rest of the staff were a nimble little guttersnipe from Montmartre called Pierre, and a gangling, hot-faced Breton. I was the clerk: they were messengers and packers. I checked the stock in a store-room opposite the shop and packed as well. After a month, when suddenly my awkward French became fluent, I had to serve the customers and deal with the dozens of Cash on Delivery forms at the Post Office. By this time, if the boss had left, I had to type out short letters to the customers, on an old English typewriter. I bought a book on French commercial correspondence. I was the hero of Pierre, the Montmartre boy, who jumped about as he watched me type with three fingers and helped me salt and pepper the letters with the proper French accents.

The customers were mainly from firms of photographers in Paris, but many came up from the provinces bringing with them—to my mind—all that one thought of as the provincial bourgeois. Madame Bovarys came in to see the Scot. Their voices—and his—would drop to murmurs. Sometimes the two would disappear into the street together and the Scot would be away for half an hour; the office boys, particularly the Breton, danced about him when he came back trying to get details out of him. What was she like in bed? The male photographers had an artistic appearance which I admired. They wore hard-crowned black hats with wide brims and a loose black bow dangling from the collar. I longed to dress as they did, but the artistic dress was beyond my income.

For some time I was the office joke. The French boys could not pronounce my name. I became Monsieur Shwep or Machin-Shwep, occasionally M. Victor and their clown. We all got on well. There is that picture of me standing by the counter of the shop, wearing the tweed jacket and flannel trousers—a uniform unknown to the French in the twenties for most Frenchmen wore black then—and my juvenile grin. I grinned most of the time for I was careless of the future, living from day to day, free to do as I pleased. I became finally acceptable to the French boys when in the evenings we left the shop and all walked arm in arm along the Boulevard practising the girl auction invented by the Breton.

"How much to sleep with this one? A thousand, five hundred, a hundred, twenty, ten?" they shouted as the girls came towards us.

One day I had a triumph.

"M. Shwep—how much?"

"Twenty-two francs fifty," I said.

They were ravished by this superb office joke. Twenty-two francs fifty was the well-known price of one of the photographic papers we sold. How easily the office humorist is born.

But the Scot was the hero of the shop. It was he who was worshipped as we trailed after him to the bistro round the corner. His unsmiling face imposed. His drinking amazed. His betting at Auteuil and Longchamps was famous. We marched back to the shop after lunch, the Montmartre boy singing:

> O, O, O, O, O!
> Monsieur Mac boit pas d'eau.

The boss was frightened of the Scot, who towered over him. Mac's gestures were as slow as his speech. His arm came up as if judging for an uppercut when he talked to the boss, whose eyes began to flutter and his feet to edge back. Sometimes, when one of the Madame Bovarys came in to the shop and the magnetizing stares and monosyllabic invitations began, the boss would come out to stop them, but his courage always failed; and with ceremonious impudence Mac would say that in view of the importance of the lady as their best customer from Lille or Dijon, he thought he would go out for half an hour with her for a drink. One lunch time when we were at the bistro and he was talking to the barman about some horse-race or other, one of his women (who could not get a word in), became annoyed. She made a dart at his flies and pulled his cock out. The Scot turned slowly to her with admiration. He buttoned up and our procession marched back to the shop; Mac went straight to the boss and in the sad manner of some old Scots preacher he told the boss what had happened.

"I thought it might be advisable to warn you about the bistro," he said, "in case you should find yourself in a similar situation."

—

I left my room on the *cinquième* at the hotel. I now lived in a cheap room at Auteuil, a fashionable quarter, but my room was in the poorer part of it, where servants, shop assistants and small employees lived. I had given up trying the Latin Quarter, for thousands of Americans had swarmed in and put up the prices. I had been forced to reject a tiny room in the Mont St Geneviève because the place stank. In Auteuil I found a good cheap room on the ground floor in the flat of a war widow who went out to work every day as a charwoman. She was a sad women in her thirties who came from

Tours, and she was very religious, a strong Catholic, and very proud of the pâtés of her region. A priest used to bring her little boy back from school at the weekends: nuns visited her. The flat had two rooms. Mine was nearly filled by a large bed and a washstand and looked out on a yard and dirty wall.

When she was at home Mme Chapin wore a black overall from chin to feet and felt slippers. She had a lamenting voice and sounded like one of the Fates. On Sunday mornings, usually when I was naked and washing in cold water, for there was no bathroom, she would come in with my laundry and stand there telling me bits of her life.

"Oh, that filthy war," she would say again and again. "My husband would have been the chief mechanic at the garage if he had not been killed."

Paris was a wicked city of heartless people, she would groan, as I tried to cover myself with the little wet towel. And there was a good deal of "Such is life," in my mother's fashion. Madame Chapin worked for a rich cocotte up the street.

"A life of luxury—but with women like that, a false step, a suspicion, and the man who keeps them throws them into the gutter."

On Sundays she dressed in her best black and now her face would seem rounder and her yellowish eyes would become warm and seductive. Her pale, dressed-up little boy would stare at me.

"Ah, my son," she often said to him. "Look at the gentleman. He works. Work—follow his example, my son."

And they would go off to Mass. I got to know Madame Chapin very well.

"I feel safe with you," she said after a month. "It was not the same with my Polish lodger. I never felt any confidence with him, but with you it is different."

I was hurt. One Sunday, when Christmas came, she came in dressed up in her black as usual with her boy. She was going on her annual visit to her sister who had come to stay at the Ritz. This sister was a kept woman and lived with a motor car manufacturer. The rich sister gave her discarded dresses to sell and the boy was given a book or a toy. When Madame Chapin came back she fell back on her stock epitaph, standing still as stone in the doorway, in her mournful voice:

"With those women, one false step . . ." She seemed more like a man than a woman to me.

It did not occur to me until forty years later that this annual visit would make a good story. I moved the two sisters to London and, in the manner of writers, changed or added to what I could guess of their characters. I gave Madame Chapin a husband. I think that what prevented me from writing the story before was my knowledge of her real life. It was not until I had given her an imaginary husband and transferred her to another place that she took on the reality of a fiction that I think dignified her. It is part of the function of the novelist to speak for people, to make them say or reveal what they are unable to say, to give them a dignity, even the distinction of being comical though she was not comical in my story. But in those Paris days I could not easily think of what to write about, and I did not know that the creative impulse is often ignited when scenes and people from the almost forgotten past are struck like a flint against something from the present. Her one happiness was knowing the "saintly Brothers" who took charge of her son.

———

At lunch-time I usually ate a crusty roll and butter, and by six o'clock, after the long wait in the queue at the Post Office with the parcels, I was torn between hunger and the whole of Paris. I walked down to the Tuileries, crossed the Pont des Arts into the Latin Quarter and then began a torturing study of the grocers, the butchers and the menus of restaurants. I was reading Rabelais by now and his joy in the belly, his lists of sausages and pâtés and his cries of "*A boire*," half fed me. The sight of snails, cheeses, garlic sausages and the oily *filet d'hareng*, worked on me until I had to give in. In the next two years I ate my way through the cheap streets of Paris. I sat alone, read or watched people. I was no longer a shop assistant when I left at six o'clock. I became a gifted student, a writer, a painter "studying life." The noise of these restaurants made me happy. I had no friends, but the crowd seemed to be my friends. There was a stout, shouting fellow in a place in the Rue de Seine whose voice was rich and greedy: he had a peg-leg and when he came in he used to unstrap it and hand it to the waitress who stood it in the corner. Now where in London, I thought, would you see a sight like that? Afterwards I sat in cafés in the Boulevard St Michel and watched the students at their game of squirting soda water at one another and joined in their singing:

> Ton honneur sera perdu
> Commes les autres
> Tu feras ma pauvre fille
> Comme les autres font.

One day a sewage cart passed and the students rushed from the café, took off their hats, and with bowed heads walked in funeral procession behind it.

I discovered that the artists met in the *Rotonde* and *Dôme* at Montparnasse, and there I sat over a glass of coffee or beer for the rest of the evening, hoping that some of their genius would rub off on me. Once, there was a violent thunderstorm. I had switched from Rabelais to Plato. What with the lightning, and the wine inside me, I was exalted. After these speechless evenings I would walk across that part of Paris, through Grenelle, to the room in Auteuil, and I would either go exhausted to bed or sit up trying to write, while my landlady groaned in her sleep in the room next door.

—

Most writers begin by imitation. I had the examples of Stevenson, Chesterton, Belloc, and—for his practical hints—the clever short sketches of Barrie. In French there were the essay-like writings of Anatole France. Naïvely I supposed that these writers were all learned men who had read enormously at the university and that until I had read pretty well as much, I would not be able or even entitled to write at all. I passed my Saturdays looking over the bookshops of the Boulevard St Michel or the boxes of the bouquinistes. I saw that I had not only English literature but the whole of French literature standing between me and the act of writing. Books were cheap. I was used to going without a meal, if necessary, to buy them. I bought indiscriminately. I had got a history of French literature; then the Rabelais; Balzac with his gluttonous appetite for the names of pieces of furniture, door knockers, lamps, the names of trades and products, pushed me to the dictionaries, but the *Contes Drolatiques* were cheerfully licentious; at any rate, in print, I would be a sexual adventurer. I read Lamartine, Vigny and witty Beaumarchais: out of duty to my dead cousin Hilda I read Victor Hugo *and* the Pléiade; I mixed the sermons of Boileau with the titillations of *Manon Lescaut*; Chateaubriand was given up for the adulteries and seductions of Maupassant, or the ballads of Villon. What could I possibly get out of such chaotic reading? How far did my understanding reach? Not far at all, but I did seize the nature of these writers in some of their pages, for something stuck in the confusion of my mind as I sat reading by the light of Madame Chapin's oil lamp. The row of books along the high fly-blown mirror over the marble mantelpiece in my room got longer and longer and the smell of the lamp was made aromatic by the smoke of Gauloises.

There was another reason for hesitating to write: a love of painting, the old hang-over from Bartlett's days at Rosendale Road School, and *Modern Painters*. I spent afternoons in the galleries and stood unnerved by the pictures of the Post-Impressionists in the shops. The smell of paint itself excited my senses. I gazed with desire at the nudes. The attraction of painting was that a work could be instantly seen—no turning of the page— and each brush stroke "told" to the eye. I lived by the eye: the miles I walked in Paris fed the appetite of the eye above all, so that I could imagine everything in the city was printed or painted on me. One warm Saturday I took my water colours to St Cloud and sat down to paint a group of trees. Other painters, stout men with beards, were painting Cézanne-like pictures of Prussian blue avenues. I squeezed and dabbed my paints and after a couple of hours got up to study the running muddle I had made. I was angry with my incompetence. I sneezed. The grass was damp and within an hour

I was down in a café trying to kill a heavy cold with hot rum and lemon. It lasted a dreadful fortnight in which I moved to Russia and read *Anna Karenina*. My career as a painter was over; but, all the more, pictures seemed to tell me how I ought to write.

The question was—what to write about? I found I simply wanted to write anything. I used to go and look at the Sorbonne: obviously I was not a man of learning. I gazed at Racine's face: dramatic verse was beyond me. I had read that one writes because one has something to say. I could not see that I had anything to say except that I was alive. I simply wanted to write two or three sentences, even as banal as the advertisement on a sauce bottle, and see them in print with my name beneath them. I was at the bottom rung.

—

Suddenly I had a stroke of luck. I saw in the Paris *New York Herald* a note asking their readers to send in jokes. I realized I had been giggling for some weeks over one. After an hour or so of struggle I wrote it out. I had been standing outside the Opera with a young Englishman I had met, studying the playbills. He said: "Let's go there tomorrow night." I said: "We can't. There's nothing on." He pointed to the notice. "Yes, there is," he said, "they're doing Relâche." I sent this to the paper. The next day it was published with my full name and address underneath it. (I resented that they put in my address, exposing me as an amateur.) They did not pay me. This was my first published work. I kept it a long time. It taught me one thing. If one had nothing to say one could at any rate write what other people said.

I was unable to progress from this point. I went back to the English writers I then admired: the Georgian poets, people like Stevenson, Chesterton, Belloc, Max Beerbohm. What was their common characteristic? It was obvious. They walked. Even Max Beerbohm had walked one morning. Walking started the engine inside them and soon came the words: but they walked on the "open road," not simply about city streets.

So, when the weekend was fine I took to the road. Paris was small in 1921. It ended at the fortification where the Metro stopped. There were not a great many cars about and I often walked out to Saint-Cloud, to Saint-Germain, to Versailles, and to Marly; and once, on a longer holiday, to Chartres, to see the blue glass and the withered kings. I came back white with dust and with a full notebook. I was being Stevenson without the donkey, or *The Beloved Vagabond*, with knapsack, garlic sausage to eat in a field by the roadside or at some cheap restaurant where, sweating and tired, I found my head spinning with the wine I drank. (*A boire!*) I think I was never happier. On longer journeys—to Pontoise and Poissy—I came back by train. Later on I found a young Englishman who came into the shop one day and talked about a writer called Lytton Strachey. My friend worked at the

Bourse; we went on a tramp in the Bellocian tradition. We made a vow. We vowed we'd cross the Loire. We walked to Orléans and crossed the river. The country was dull, the pavé roads were straight and monotonous, the villages were not pretty: in the nights the bullfrogs barked in the pools of the plain; the wide river bed of the Loire, when we came to it, was all stones and the water had dwindled to little pools between them. We were twice pulled up by astounded gendarmes who thought we were tramps and asked us why we didn't take a train. We said it was "*pour le sport,*" a phrase that was just coming in. "You are mad," they said as they got back on their bikes, with that heavy swing of belts and leggings, and continued the interminable moralizing of the gendarmerie.

This young man was intelligent. He too felt liberated by being in Paris and hated that he had to go back into the family stockbroking business in London. He was a more sensible reader than I: he introduced me to the works of the new writers: Keynes, Roger Fry and Clive Bell. I envied him because he had been to an English Public School; he envied me for wanting to be a writer. I said if I could not manage to be a writer I would still not return to England. He said I was right. He added he had an uncle who owned a mine in Morocco and that the uncle might give me a job as a Labour Manager there. On and off, after that, I would see myself dressed in breeches, gaiters and open-necked shirts by the lift of some rattling mine. I was always weather-beaten in these pictures. This dream became so real to us that he wrote to his uncle who wrote back and said, alas, he had sold his mine. Another fantasy of ours arose because he had acted in *A Midsummer Night's Dream* at school: we called ourselves Pyramus and Thisbe, a joke that seemed side-splitting to us. When he laughed his wide mouth curved up almost from ear to ear and his eyes closed into long curving slits. He was very shocked by the screaming greedy frenzy of the brokers at the Bourse, a noise that could be heard streets away, even in the Boulevard des Italiens. After we had been friends for some time, an American at the Christian Science Meeting said:

"I suppose you know he is Jewish? I thought I ought to warn you."

This was my first meeting with anti-semitism. I did not know he was Jewish; but it made me reflect that, especially in my school life, the only boys who took my desire to write seriously were Jewish.

—

But what was I to write about? My collected works were on the little bamboo table at Madame Chapin's. There was my major work, done three or four years back: three pages on the Reformation and Renaissance meeting in the works of Milton. There was half a page describing the clock in our dining-room at home. There were two more half-pages on my brother's hairy friend and another two on a man in the leather trade who was always quoting Shakespeare as we turned over the sheepskins on the warehouse table. And there was my latest work: the joke. I must hurry. I have already told how I had read in Barrie's *When a Man's Single*, that the thing to do was to write on the smallest things and those near to you. There is a straw caught on the window ledge. Will it fall or will it stay? There was an essay, he said, in things like that. What was nearest to me? My room, Madame Chapin groaning next door. Nothing there. And then, by a trick of memory, my mind went back to my first room in Paris. There was a barracks near my new room and at night I would hear the bugle, as I used to hear the bugle at the Champ de Mars. The beautiful word *cinquième* sounded at once in my head. My nights there came back to me. I set about evoking the rough blue cloth on the table, the attic window, the carpet worn by so many predecessors till it was as thin as a slice of ham, the bugle call, even the notices on the door: "No strangers in the room after eleven," and "After eleven a supplement for electricity will be charged:" and how the light flicked off at that hour. I began to write. Madame Chapin's groans supplied a tenant for the room next door at my old hotel. I wrote for two hours. On other nights I re-wrote several times. I added some sentimental moralizings.

At the photographers I stayed late and typed the thing. I sent it to a London paper and not to lose time I finished two more and sent them. They went to two weekly reviews—the *Saturday Westminster* and *Time and Tide*—and to the Christian Science Monitor. There were weeks of iron silence. Then, within a month or two of each other, the three papers accepted them. There! It was easy to be a writer. Outwardly cool and with a curious sense of being naked and exposed, I hummed inside with the giddiness of my genius.

—

I cannot describe my shame-faced pride. There was no more "I want to be a writer." I was a writer. Editors thought so, I told the boys and the Scot at the shop. The Scot had his nation's regard for the written word. The wet-mouthed Breton gaped and punched me in the back. Pierre astonished me. He was always picking up Montmartre songs and about this time his favourites were one about the rising price of Camembert, and a topical one about Deschanel, the Prime Minister who had fallen out of the train on his way to the lavatory, a song with a chorus of innuendo:

> Il n'a pas abîmé ses pyjamas
> c'était épatant, mais c'était comme ça.

He stopped and put on a small act:

"M. Shwep, the great Balzac," he sang and danced around me. He had picked up the name from the street. At this age boys knew everything.

I told Madame Chapin. She congratulated me, but hers was a face of little expression. Mournfully, after reflection, she said the man who kept the woman for whom she worked was a journalist. I could not tell her how her groans had helped me to write and I felt, when I saw her, how strange it was when she stood bringing in my shirts, that part of her led a ghost life in what I had written. She asked to borrow the first article. She wanted to show it to the priest who came on Saturdays with her boy.

A week later the priest returned it.

"Ah," he moralized. "At that time you were on the cinquième. Now you are on the ground floor."

There was, to judge by the amusement in his eyes, another meaning to this sentence; like every Frenchman he loved a nuance. I read and re-read this article again and again and then, as happens to writers, I was impatient with it and disliked it. I had my first experience of the depression and sense of nothingness that comes when a piece of work is done. The satisfaction is in the act itself; when it is over there is relief, but the satisfaction is gone. After fifty years I still find this to be so and that with every new piece of writing I have to make that terrifying break with my real life and learn to write again, from the beginning.

CHAPTER SIX

On a misleading sunny day on the first of February, 1923, I took the train from London to Holyhead. In a heavy leather suitcase I carried a volume of Yeats's poems, an anthology of Irish poetry, Boyd's *Irish Literary Renaissance*, Synge's *Plays* and a fanatical book called *Priests and People in Ireland* by McCabe, lent to me by a malign Irish stationer in Streatham who told me I would get on all right in Ireland so long as I did not talk religion or politics to anyone and kept the book out of sight. Unknown to myself I was headed for the seventeenth century.

The Irish Sea was calm—thank God—and I saw at last that unearthly sight of the Dublin mountains rising from the water, with that beautiful false innocence in their violets, greens and golden rust of grasses and bracken, with heavy rain clouds leaning like a huge umbrella over the northern end of them. My breath went thin: I was feeling again the first symptoms of my liability to spells. I remember wondering, as young men do, whether somewhere in this city was walking a girl with whom I would fall in love: the harbours of Denmark gave way to Dublin Bay and the Wicklow Hills. The French had planted a little of their sense of limits and reason in me, but already I could feel these vanishing.

Once through the Customs I was frisked for guns by a Free State soldier with a pink face and mackerel-coloured eyes. I got out of the local train at Westland Row, into that smell of horse-manure and stout which were the ruling Dublin odours, and was driven on an outside car with a smart little pony to (of all things, in Ireland!) a temperance hotel in Harcourt Street. It was on this first trot across the city that I had my first experience of things in Ireland not being what they seem. I have described this in a book on Dublin which I wrote a few years ago. The jarvey whipped along, talking his head off about the state of the "unfortunate country," in a cloud of Bedads, Begobs, God-help-us-es, but turned out to be a Cockney. The Cockney and Dublin accents are united by adenoids. Cab drivers are, perhaps, the same everywhere.

It was now dark and I went out into the wet streets. Troops were patrolling them and I was soon stopped by a patrol and frisked once more. More friskings followed as I got to the Liffey. It was enjoyable. I didn't realize that my green velour hat from the Boulevard des Italiens with its wide, turned-down brim, was an item of the uniform of the I.R.A. I went straight to the Abbey Theatre. In the shabby foyer, a small middle-aged woman with grey hair and looking like a cottage loaf, was talking to a very tall man. He was unbelievably thin. He seemed to be more elongated by having a very long nose with a cherry red tip to it. The woman's voice was quiet and decided. His fell from his height as waveringly as a snow-flake. The pair were Lady Gregory and Lennox Robinson. He took me to his office for an hour and then we went into the theatre. To an audience of a dozen or so people (for the Civil War kept people away), the company were going through the last act of The Countess Cathleen, in sorrowing voices. They went on to the horse-play of The Shewing-Up of Blanco Posnet. Both plays had caused riots years before when they were first put on. Now the little audience was apathetic.

Soot came down the chimney in my room at the hotel when a bomb or two went off that night.

—

The spell got a decisive hold of me in the next two days as I walked about the comfortable little Georgian and early Victorian city, where the red brick and the brown were fresher and less circumspect than the brick of London. The place seemed to be inhabited only by lawyers and doctors. The mists of the bog on which it is built softened the air. Complexions were delicate, eyes were alive with questions. As you passed people in the street they seemed to pause with expectation, hoping for company, and with the passing gaiety of hail and farewell, with the emphasis particularly on the latter. There was a longing for passing acquaintance; and an even stronger longing for your back to be turned, to give a bit of malice a chance.

The Civil War was moving to the south west; now de Valera's men—

called with beautiful verbal logic the "Irregulars"—had been driven out of Dublin. I had seen the sandbags and barbed wire round the Government offices and the ruins of O'Connell Street; now I took a morning train in cold wet weather to Cork from Kingsbridge, the best of Dublin's monumental railway stations, a station that indeed looked like a fantastic chateau. A journey that normally takes two or three hours, took close on fourteen, for at Maryborough (now called Port Laoise), we stopped for the middle of the day, while they got an armoured engine and troops to escort us. I had seen pictures of these extraordinary engines in books about the Boer War: I suppose the British had dumped a lot of them in Ireland. One of the exquisite pleasures of the Irish (I was soon to find out) is pedantry: a few of us, including a priest, left the train and went into the town for a drink, sure of finding the train still there after a couple of hours. It was. It gave a jolt. "Are we starting?" someone asked.

"Sure, we haven't started starting yet," the porter said.

The afternoon faded as we went across the bogland; at Mallow it was dark, and there we got into cars to join another train across the valley. The viaduct had been blown up. We eventually arrived in Cork in a racket of machine-gun fire. I hesitated. But the passengers took it for granted and a barefooted urchin who took my case said: " 'Tis only the boys from the hills." The firing went on, from time to time, into the small hours, and patrol lorries drove up and down. One stopped at the hotel and after a lot of shouting and banging of doors, a posse of soldiers came into my room, got me out of bed and searched the bedding and my luggage. They looked respectfully at my books and one of them started reading a poem of Yeats and said if I kept to that I would be all right.

Cork is a pretty city, particularly in the dappled buildings of its riverside quays and estuaries. By this time my mind was singing with Irish poetry. I went out into the countryside to see how Blarney was surviving the revolution. It was surviving in the best of its tradition. I plodded round with a farmer whose chief ejaculation was a shout of "Blood and hounds," when his narrative needed it. It often did. Back in Cork, I went to the theatre where Doran's touring company were playing a different Shakespeare tragedy every night: my earliest experience of *Macbeth*, *Othello* and *Hamlet*. Doran's company had been slogging away in England and Ireland for years. He himself was a sturdy man with a huge voice. He hogged the plays of course, and put such a stamp on his roles that it was pretty well impossible to distinguish Hamlet from Macbeth, or Macbeth from Othello. The theatre was always packed. When Hamlet said his line about everyone being mad in England, the whole house cheered. I had gone with a commercial traveller from Kerry, who came back to the hotel and then he and one or two other commercials recited Shakespeare to one another for the rest of the evening. I couldn't understand a word the torrential Kerryman said, but Shakespeare was tempestuously Elizabethan in a Kerry accent.

I travelled across Tipperary to Limerick, arriving there in one of those long soft brown and yellow sunsets of the West, with the white mists rising from the Shannon. The Celtic twilight was working on me. I sat up drinking with a satanic engineer; and, thinking it was about time, I tried that night to write one of my articles. I found that after two or three whiskies my pen swept across the paper. When I read the thing in the morning, I saw it was chaotic and I tore it up. That is the last time I ever wrote on alcohol.

Limerick was in an edgy state. It had just been relieved of a siege and there was still a crack or two of sniping at night. There was a strike on at the bacon factories; and there was an attempt to start a Soviet. I went to see the committee and politely took my hat off and made a small French bow when I went into their room. The leader told me to put my hat on: they had finished, he said, with bourgeois manners. We had a wrangle about this because, although I am shy, I am touchy and argued back. We had a rapid duel of sarcasms. He was one of those "black" Irishmen one occasionally comes across; there was another, a waiter at the hotel in Limerick who threw a plate of bacon and eggs at a customer. He was a big fellow who looked murderous every time he came into the dining room with a plate.

There occurred in Limerick one of those encounters which—looking back on it—I see as a portent. I found there a very serious young Englishman, in fact a Quaker, who took me to a house inside the town. As we climbed up on an outside car, he whispered to me not to talk on the long ride out because, he said, his situation was delicate. He had caught the Irish love of conspiracy, even the whisper. When we got to his house he told me he had been in the fighting against the Sinn Feiners, but had lately married an Irish girl. I think he had been in the Auxiliary Police. Except for having his tennis court shot up now and then, he said, when he and his wife were playing in the afternoons, there was not much trouble now. The English have stubborn natures but, I saw, could get light-headed in Ireland. Into the sitting room, which was furnished in faded Victorian style, with pictures of lakes and vegetation on the walls and the general Irish smell of rising damp, came an elderly woman wearing a wig of black curls and with a sharp, painted face; and with her a pale little girl of twelve—I thought—one of those fey, unreal Irish children with empty blue eyes and untidy russet hair. She looked as if she had been blown down from the sky, as, in her tiny skirt, she sat bare-legged on the floor in front of the fire. She was *not* a child of twelve; she was the Quaker's wife, and very excitable. The shooting, she said, livened up the tennis and they were afraid for the strings of their rackets, because in these times you might have to send them to Dublin to be re-strung. A brother-in-law came in, a man who sat in silence breathing sociably, as Guinness after Guinness went down. I gazed from the old lady to the girl, from brother-in-law to the ascetic looking young Quaker soldier, and could not see how they could be together in the same house. In how many Irish families was it to seem to me that the people had all appeared accidentally from the wheel of fortune, rather than in the course of nature. The old lady chattered about balls and parties, about Lord this and Lady that, about the stage—was she an actress? In her wig, paint and her rings, bracelets and necklace, and her old-fashioned dress of twenty years before, she was nimble and witch-like. Indeed, she got out a pack of cards and told my fortune. I dropped the Queen of Spades. She sprang on it with glee:

"You will be surrounded by women who intend to harm you."

I walked back to Limerick late, feeling, as I was so often to do in Ireland, that I had stepped into a chapter of a Russian novel. The smell of turf smoke curled among the river fogs and I was not sure of the way in the dark. I waited for a shot or two, for the Irregulars liked to loose off at night to keep the feeling of war alive, from behind a friendly hedge. There were no shots that night. It was an eerie and pleasant walk, like a ghost story told in the dark.

I went on to Enniskillen, the border town, all drapers, hardware stores and useful shops, brisker in trade than the towns of the south, a place half Orange, half Catholic. The Town Clerk, a twentieth-century man, was the kind who enjoyed the comedies of fanaticism, but the jokes rippled over the surface of the incurable seventeenth-century bitterness. It is often said that Irish laughter is without mirth, but rather a guerrilla activity of the mind. I was stuck in Enniskillen for another cold wet Sunday when the only other guest in the hotel was a glum commercial traveller from the English Midlands, a man with one of the flattest minds I had met up to then. Careful with his money, too; his father was an undertaker and the son used the motor hearse at the weekends to give his girl a ride. He was to be—from my point of view as a writer—the most important man I met in Ireland, but it took me ten years to realize this. I wrote down every word of his I could remember.

—

I look back upon this Irish expedition with an embarrassed but forgiving eye. I see the empty mountains, the bog and the succulent marshy valleys, the thin, awkward roads, through a steam of strong tea. The sun came and went, the rain dripped and dried on my hat. I stuffed with fried cod, potatoes, potato cakes, scones and butter as I read my Yeats and Synge; the air, even when cold, was lazy and I couldn't get up until eleven in the morning. I was thick in the head, with no idea of what to write about until, in despair, I was driven to write flatly everything I saw and heard. The "everything" was a torture for I discovered that places overwhelmed me.

Every movement of light, every turn of leaf, every person, seemed to occupy me physically, so that I had no self left. But perhaps this means I was all self. It was with a conviction of failure that I sent my first four articles to the paper and sat staring into a "jar" of Guinness. I was dumbfounded to get a telegram from London saying my articles were excellent.

Alas, I have seen them since. They are very small beer. They are thin and sentimental; but here and there is a sentence that shows I was moved and had an eye. They were signed by my initials and that is why from then on people dropped my Christian name—to my relief—and I was called V.S.P. or R.S.V.P. My literary name developed from this. I preferred the impersonal, and to have added the "t" of Victor to a name that already had three, and was made more fidgety by a crush of consonants and two short vowels, seemed ridiculous.

In this short trip I had easily rid myself of the common English idea that Ireland was a piece of England that for some reason or other would not settle down and had run to seed. I had heard at school of "the curse of Cromwell." I ardently identified Irish freedom with my own personal freedom which had been hard to come by. A revolutionary break? I was for it. Until you are free you do not know who you are. It was a basic belief of the twenties, it permeated all young minds and though we became puritanically drastic, gauche and insensitive in our rebellions against everything we called Victorianism, we were elated.

I became the Irish correspondent. It was momentous. I had a career. This was no time for living the dilapidated day to day life I had lived in Paris. And there was the religious question: I had lapsed in Paris where I had been the average sensual young man. Now I found myself employed by the paper from whose religion I had lapsed. It seemed to be my duty to reform. The shadiness of Puritans! I threw my last cigarette into the Liffey, gave up drinking wine, beer and whiskey, though my tastes there were youthfully moderate. I was really more austerely the Romantic idealist than Puritan for I soon found the Calvinism of Ireland—scarcely buried under Irish high spirits—distasteful and indeed dull; my nature rebelled against it.

I lived in Dublin in two periods and I write now mostly of my first year there when, far more than in Paris, I lived in my imagination. When I re-read nowadays the German court episode in Meredith's *Harry Richmond* and of the ordeal through which Meredith's young romantic passes, I recognize something close to my Irish experience and indeed to other experience in my youth; like Stendhal, Meredith is outstanding in his observation of easily inflamed young men.

If Ireland moved me, it also instructed me. As a political education, the experience was excellent. One was observing a revolution: a country set free, a new young state, the first modern defeat of colonialism. Sitting in the

Press Gallery of the Dail day after day, listening to the laughing, fighting voice of Cosgrave, the irony of Kevin O'Higgins or the tirades of the old defeated Redmond was like being at school taking a course in the foundation of states. I realized what a social revolution was, although I was (inevitably as an Englishman and Protestant), much more in the old Anglo-Irish society, the majority of whom reluctantly accepted the new regime, than among the rising Catholic middle class. I did not really know them until many years later. I was carried away by Irish sociability and nervous scorn of England into thinking I was in the contemporary European world. I was not, but there was the beguiling insinuation that Ireland was in temperamental contact with Paris and Italy and had by-passed the complex social preoccupations of industrial England. (Joyce's flight from Dublin to the Continent was an example of the Irish tradition.) The snobberies of the Ascendancy were very Colonial—as I now see—though not as loud as the Anglo-Indian, nor as prime as the Bostonian: they came closer to those of the American southern states. (There is a bond between Anglo-Irish writing and the literature of the American south.) In Ireland, shortage of capital and decaying estates had given these snobberies a lazy but acid quality; in many people there was a suggestion of concealed and bloodless spiritual superiority. English snobbery was based firmly on vulgar wealth; and a class system energized by contention and very mobile; the Irish was based on kinship, without wealth. The subject is perfectly displayed—though in an earlier generation—in *The Real Charlotte* by Somerville and Ross. Noses were kept raised by boisterous and tenuous claims to cousinage.

Ireland is really a collection of secret societies; for a rootless young man like myself, this had a strong allure. I was slow to see that I was meeting an upper class in decay and at the point when it was disappearing in boatloads, from Dun Laoghaire every day; and that I was really living in a world far more like that of Mrs Gaskell's novels in the prim and genteel England of, say, 1840 to 1860 (except that old ladies had been using the word "bloody" in company freely for a couple of hundred years). Genealogy, as one could tell from the Libraries and the number of societies given to it, was the national passion.

The easy-going life in this Victorian lagoon was delightful to me. It is often said that in Ireland there is an excess of genius unsustained by talent; but there is talent in the tongues and Irish manners are engaging. I sat in my office in St Stephens Green, a cheerful outsider in Irish quarrels, turning myself into the idlest of newspaper correspondents. I lodged with two Protestant spinsters in a sedate early Victorian terrace house in Waterloo Road, where they left me cold meat and pickles and a pot of strong tea for my supper; they popped up every quarter of an hour, if I had a young woman to visit me, to see that nothing was "going on." Dublin was a city so gregariously domestic that the sexes did not care to meet without other company. The English were deplored as coarse sensualists who ate too much, were sex-mad and conventional.

The pleasant wide eighteenth-century streets of Georgian Dublin were easing to the mind, and the wild mountains over which the weather changed every hour, excited the fancy. And there was Dublin Bay, so often enamelled and Italianate. More and more, I was idling at Blackrock or Dalkey, with a crowd of young men and girls, watching the sea or walking across the mountains as far as Glendalough or the Vale of Avoca or scooping a kettle of water out of a stream in the heather, for a picnic.

My mind fed on scenery. The sight of lakes, slatey in the rain, or like blue eyes looking out of the earth in the changing Irish light; the Atlantic wind always silvering the leaves of beech and oak and elm on the road to Galway, empty except for a turf cart or a long funeral; the Twelve Pins in Connemara now gleaming like glass in the drizzle, now bald, green and dazzling; the long sea inlets that on hot days burn their way deeply inland beyond Clifden where the sands are white and the kelp burns on them; the Atlantic coming in stormily below the high cliffs of Moher; and the curious tropic of Kerry. My brother came over from England and with two girls we borrowed a horse and cart and went slowly across to the West and back; and in Clare, which was still in a disorganized state, we attracted the "boys from the hills" who kept us up dancing half-sets, singing all the rebel songs and finishing up with "Nancy Hogan's Goose." Two young Englishmen with two unmarried girls! The scandal of it! There was a lot of talk in Dublin. I do not think only of landscape but of the wide disheartening streets of the long villages and the ruined farms of the West; and the elaborately disguised curiosity of the impulsively kind but guarded people, looking into your eyes for a chance of capping your fantasy with one of theirs, in long ceremonies of well-mannered evasion, craving for the guesswork of acquaintance and diversion.

The darker side of this was blurred and muddied and stinking; the dramatic character of the misery. In Dublin, the tenements were shocking; the women still wore the long black shawl, the children were often barefooted. You picked up lice and fleas in the warm weather in the Dublin trams as you went to the North side to the wrecked mansions of the eighteenth century. The poor looked not simply poor, but savagely poor, though they were rich in speech and temperament. There were always ragged processions of protesters, on the general Irish ground that one must keep on screaming against life itself. There were nasty sights: a man led down a mountain road with his wrists tied behind his back, by a couple of soldiers.

I think of the story of the house close to a lonely cottage I had in my second Irish period at the sea's edge near Clifden. It was no more than a two-roomed cabin with a loft and, with the Irish love of grand names, was called Mount Freer and had once belonged to an English painter. (A pensioned-off sailor owned it.) Near it was the Manor or farm, a ruinous place of rusty gates and scarcely habitable, occupied by a bank manager from some inland town. He was very ill and was still suffering from the shock of having been badly beaten up in a raid on his bank in the Civil War. He was not alone at this time. His brother, a cropped Australian ex-soldier, had come over to look after him for a while. I used to go shooting rabbits with the Australian in a deserted graveyard. It had belonged, the Australian said, to the ferocious O'Flahertys, from whom the people in Galway had in the far past called on God to protect them. He was trying to persuade his dim sick brother to go back with him. If the sick man saw anyone in the road he would climb gingerly over the stone wall and dodge away in a wide, lonely circle across the rocky fields to the house. I knew the Australian well. He was a good fisherman. We used to go out and spear plaice in the sands and catch mackerel. Many a fry we had. Often I walked, as night fell, to look at the wink of light on Slyne Head, America the next parish. He told me the brother refused to go near anyone.

"The poor bloody brother, he has the idea he stinks. He thinks he's got a bloody smell on him. He'll never come near you." His house had almost no furniture—simply a couple of beds, a table and two chairs—and if I went there, the sick man slipped away and hid in another room. Eventually the Australian had to leave and when he did the "mad feller" as he was called cut his throat or hanged himself. Thank God I'd left before that happened.

It has been said that the Irish live in a state of perplexity. The poet Patrick Kavanagh has written that the newborn child screams because it cannot bear the light of the real world. Yet, from Shaw onwards one finds the Irish saying they are not dreamers, but are realists. Not in the literary sense of the word "realism," but in the sense of seeing with cold detachment where exact practical advantage lies. I would have said their instincts are tribal. They evade the moral worries of settled societies and there is a strain of anarchy in them: they can be charitable and cruel at the same time. It is self-indulgent to generalize like this and, anyway, the Irish do that more coolly than we English do. But one has to make something of the way they turn tragedy to farce and farce back into tragedy; and when in the thirties I wrote a story called *Sense of Humour*, a piece of premature black comedy, which was set going by the meeting with that glum commercial traveller I had met in Enniskillen, it expressed something of the effect of an Irish experience on myself.

One of my acquaintances among the gentry class—how naturally one associates the word "gentry" with the same class in old Russia rather than with an English equivalent—took me down to a mansion he had inherited together with a title he detested. He was not one of the raffish, shooting kind, and he was too simple and plain a fellow to care much about the brilliant group of Anglo-Irish intellectuals who still dominated Irish life. He was a bit deaf and was thought dull—"I hear he's a decent kind of feller." He was by way of being a gentleman socialist, and the "good society," in that sense, interested few Irishmen. The decent fellow had a social conscience and had to bear the curse of land-owning. It had fallen on him by accident. As a poor boy he had been sent off to Canada where he became a Mountie; in the war he had been one of the early flying men. Suddenly he came into "the place"; he married a beauty whom he bickered with, because he refused to have anything to do with fashionable life in Ireland, London or Italy. His real taste—but as a social reformer—was for low life on the Dublin quays. After I left Ireland I heard he had sold his mansion to the nuns, as many Irish landlords did in the end (the Irish Church having a shrewd eye for property) and cleared off, at a moment's notice, without telling a soul, to America. He is now dead.

This week-end was my only experience of Irish country house life in the Civil War. It was still sputtering away when we drove off in a little French racing car with planks strapped to the side of it. This was to outwit "the clowns" on his estate who had burned down the mill he had built—part of his practical socialism—and had dug trenches across the key roads to prevent him getting home. A true Irishman, he was more than half on their side. At each new trench we got out, put down the planks and drove across. He loved the comedy.

We drove into a large demesne. The mansion stood empty above its lake; he had built himself an efficient little villa near it. When we got in, we found the house had been invaded by "Irregulars," who had come searching for guns and ammunition. The servants were hysterical and a parrot imitated them, calling out "Glory be to God." He went up to his bedroom, slid back a panel in the wardrobe: there was a good supply of untouched weapons, but girls among the raiders had gone off with his wife's riding clothes, and one of the men had emptied a gallon jar of ink over the drawing-room carpet. The raiders had found a safe in the estate office, but could not open it. So they dumped it in the middle of the lake. My host rang up the local military who put on an offensive.

"We'll send down the Terrorizer," the officer said. The Terrorizer and his men rowed about the large lake very happily. It was a lovely afternoon. Her ladyship came down in the evening. She was a slender and handsome, dark-haired woman with fine features and an amused sparkle in her eyes and a despairing voice. She treated me very kindly, but firmly, as the social peculiarity I was, because I had not changed into a dinner jacket. (I hadn't got one.) Still, despite her high-class groans, she was an amusing and witty woman. The more snobbish she became, the rougher her husband.

"She's talking a lot of rot," he'd say down the table, jerking his thumb at his wife. I felt, like another Pip, one of my moods of Miss Havisham worship coming on, for a caustic, mocking tongue and beauty combined were irresistible. I put on dog and burst out with a long speech about a new book of D. H. Lawrence's.

"What extraordinary things are going on," she said. "How very unpleasant."

The next two days I was put through a short course in Irish country house life. We went out fox-cubbing in the rain with a lot of wind-reddened country neighbours. We got very muddy. I was never one for the sporting life. We went for a drink to a large dark house where the family portraits looked like kippers. A man was dumbstruck when I told him I didn't hunt, shoot or fish. "What do you do?" he asked coldly. I naturally supposed this was directed at my employment. I told him I was a journalist. He looked shocked and had never heard of the paper. Trying to think of a comparable English paper, I said, "It's like the *Manchester Guardian.*"

He stepped away making a few short sarcasms about that traitorous "Sinn Fein rag." In Ireland, it is nowadays, I believe, called "The Niggers' Gazette."

The following afternoon we went riding. I had never been on a horse before. To me the animal smelt of the leather trade. I was surprised to find that horses are warm. I gripped the reins as if they were a life line; I was jellied and bumped by its extraordinary movement. The party began to canter and I was tossed in the air and I got a fixed smile on my face. We arrived in a field to try some jumps. A wicked old trainer shouted bits of advice. I went over one or two gaps and arrived, surprised and askew, but still up. So they tried some more difficult jumps. The party hung about waiting for the slaughter. The animal rose, I fell on its neck, but I did not come off. The stakes were raised; at the next jump the horse and I went to different parts of the sky. I was in the mud. I got up and apologized to the horse, which turned its head away. Afterwards we walked and trotted home; it seemed to take hours. Back in the house, I felt someone had put planks on my legs and turned my buttocks into wooden boxes. So my life as an Irish sportsman and country gentleman came to an end. Still, I had stayed with a baronet. I was snobbish enough to be pleased by that.

I like curious clothes. Back in Dublin I stayed in my riding breeches, bought at a cheap shop in Dublin, and wore them for weeks after, as an enjoyable symbol of the Irish habit of life, until someone tactfully suggested I looked like a stable boy.

—

There was one seminal and lasting gain in my time in Dublin. The Irish revel in words and phrases. Their talk is vivid and inventive. They live for the story. I had no idea of what kind of writer I wanted to be, but there were many, in the flesh, to offer me a new example, and who woke something in me.

In their twilight, the Anglo-Irish, especially, had discovered their genius. Yeats was in Merrion Square, A.E. was editing the *Irish Statesman* next door but one; James Stephens, Lennox Robinson, Lady Gregory were there. And so was the young Liam O'Flaherty—not Anglo-Irish—and Sean O'Casey was working in his slum room on the North Side. There were other good dramatists and there were the gifted actors and actresses of the Abbey Theatre where I went every week. There one could see not only the plays of Synge and writers of the Revival, but masters of tragic form like the unjustly forgotten T. C. Murray, and Shaw, Ibsen and Strindberg. Literature was not to be studied or something to be caught up with, but to be practised and at once. In writing, the stories of Liam O'Flaherty excited me for he had the Irish gift of writing close to the skin of life. The best Irish writers have always had a fine surface. They have always had élan. The writing is clear and sensuous and catches every tremor of movement in the skin of the human animal and of landscape. The prose is athletic and flies along untroubled as if language were their life. Then, the Dublin bookshops were excellent. It was in Dublin that I read Katherine Mansfield, Chekhov and D. H. Lawrence, and Joyce's Dubliners and hoped to catch his sense of epiphany. In 1923 the short story, like the one act play, had a prestige. I wrote my first stories in Ireland and Spain.

Living among writers who were still at their good moment added to my desire to emulate them. I had the—to me—incredible sight of the beautiful Mrs W. B. Yeats riding a bicycle at St Stephens Green; and of A.E. (George Russell), also riding a bicycle and carrying a bunch of flowers. I had tea with James Stephens one Sunday at that hotel at Dun Laoghaire where people go to day-dream at the sight of the mail-boat coming in from England, that flashing messenger to and from the modern world. This gnome-like talker sparkled so recklessly that one half-dreaded he might fall into his teacup and drown. One afternoon I took tea with Yeats himself in his house in Merrion Square.

It was a Georgian house, as unlike a hut of wattle in a bee-loud glade as one could imagine. To begin with, the door opened on a chain and the muzzle of a rifle stuck through the gap. A pink-faced Free State soldier asked me if I had an "appointment." I was shown in to what must have been a dining-room but now it was a guard room with soldiers smoking among the Blake drawings on the wall. Yeats was a Senator and he had already been shot at by gunmen. Upstairs I was to see the bullethole in the drawing-room window. Presently the poet came down the stairs to meet me.

It is a choking and confusing experience to meet one's first great man when one is young. These beings come from another world and Yeats studiously created that effect. Tall, with grey hair finely rumpled, a dandy with negligence in collar and tie and with the black ribbon dangling from the glasses on a short, pale and prescient nose—not long enough to be Roman yet not sharp enough to be a beak—Yeats came down the stairs towards me, and the nearer he came the further away he seemed. His air was bird-like, suggesting one of the milder swans of Coole and an exalted sort of blindness. I had been warned that he would not shake hands. I have heard it said—but mainly by the snobbish Anglo-Irish—that Yeats was a snob. I would have said that he was a man who was translated into a loftier world the moment his soft voice throbbed. He was the only man I have known whose natural speech sounded like verse.

He sat me in the fine first floor of his house. After the years all that remains with me is a memory of candles, books, woodcuts, the feeling that here was Art. And conversation. But what about? I cannot remember. The exalted voice flowed over me. The tall figure, in uncommonly delicate tweed, walked up and down, the voice becoming more resonant, as if he were on a stage. At the climax of some point about the Gaelic revival, he suddenly remembered he must make tea, in fact a new pot, because he had already been drinking tea. The problem was one of emptying out the old tea pot. It was a beautiful pot and he walked the room with the short steps of the aesthete, carrying it in his hand. He came towards me. He receded to the bookcase. He swung round the sofa. Suddenly with Irish practicality he went straight to one of the two splendid Georgian windows of the room, opened it, and out went those barren leaves with a swoosh, into Merrion Square—for all I know on to the heads of Lady Gregory, Oliver St John Gogarty and A.E. They were leaves of Lapsang tea.

I can remember only one thing he said. We had got on to Shaw whom he disliked. I murmured—showing off—something about Shaw's socialist principles. The effect on Yeats was fine. He stood now, with a tea pot full of tea in his hands, saying that Shaw had no principles. Shaw was a destroyer. Like lightning, Shaw flashed in hilarious indifference, and what the lightning briefly revealed was interesting but meaningless. This has always stuck in my mind, but of the rest I remember nothing except that with solemnity he pointed to the inner door of the room and said that, sitting in this room, he had experimented in thought transference with Mrs Yeats who sat in her room next door. As I say, I had seen her out on her bicycle and I have often wondered, as the eloquent mind expelled its thoughts to the wall, whether Mrs Yeats was always next door at the time. He was kind enough to walk with me to the Irish Senate near by, and I was overcome when he leant on my shoulder while he lifted a foot, took off his shoe and shook out a stone. I noticed he had a pretty blue ring on one of his fingers.

I went to see A.E. in the office of the *Irish Statesman*, the weekly review that preached cooperative farming. He was a large tweedy bunch of a man with a beard, a talker who drowned me in beautiful phrases of a mystical, theosophical kind. The walls of his office were an extension of his mind, for they were covered with golden murals of ethereal beings. He must have been the kindest and most innocent man in Ireland, for he was a slave to the encouragement of young writers. When I wrote my first story, he took it at once, kept it for two years, and almost with tears of apology sent it back saying it was crowded out. This was inevitable. A.E.'s talking overflowed into print and occupied nearly the whole paper. I sat again with both Yeats and A.E. at Yeats's house, while Yeats praised D'Annunzio and A.E. tried to argue him out of the admiration. I watched on Yeats's fireplace, for A.E. distracted himself during Yeats's long utterances by making designs in the soot with Yeats's poker.

The only playwright I knew a little was Sean O'Casey. He was still living in his tenement on the North Side, a smashed fanlight over the door. His room was bare and contained only an iron bed, a table and a couple of poor chairs. He always wore a cloth cap in the house. A fire of cheap coal dust was smouldering on the fire where a kettle was singing—a true sign of the old Ireland. On the shabby wall was a notice he had printed:

GET ON WITH THE BLOODY PLAY.

He was writing The Plough and the Stars at this time. Again, only one thing remains of his conversation: he was angry because he said that the "authorities" were trying to keep the poor from using the Public Libraries, on the grounds that the poor would spread their diseases through the books. I'd been angered myself by the argument when I was ten, and I had read it in a book by Marie Corelli.

(1971)

TRAVEL WRITING

The Appalachian Mountains

OVERTURE TO A MOUNTAIN THEME

The southern train had cannoned me loudly over Virginia into Tennessee. And after an eventless waiting at a junction there, I was tugged under difficult steam up a light railway into the mountains of the North Carolina border. I had seen the blue lips of these mountains before, briefly arched over and beyond nearer hills.

To live in blue mountains, I began to think; to alight in that horizon unawares and extravagantly to plunge one's body in it! And then I was drawn over narrow steel into those very mountains. They circled by as we trudged. We invaded their gorges, serpenting through them, striking arcs into their townships, outlining their bases. And as we passed, echoes like unleashed dogs ran barking up the mountain sides and were lost in the woods.

The hills were at times huddled like sheep, at times scattered and grouped like herds. The sunlight was golden on them, the gold of laden furnaces, but the deep shades sunken between the ridges had the winding, varying blue of turf smoke. The processional hills trended back and down and away; new ones came before old ones had been grasped or regretted. I wished for the power of a king to halt them; and for the gifted hands of a poet to grasp them and pull them into myself. For a mountain is something high and blue within one.

We pelted into N——, galloped in like mountaineer horsemen and reined in sharply at Jenkins's store. N—— is highly set, like a pool on a mountain summit. There is a low, surrounding ridge of woods and the village itself has twenty timber shacks of all kinds, and about fifty-three inhabitants, including children. Of these, all the men sit on the platform of Jenkins's store, accompanied by "Zeb" Jenkins, and wait for the daily train to arrive.

I remember the men, fifteen of them, taller than corn, but scarcely stouter, wearing blue overalls and wide black hats, with brims flapped this way and that with the challenging nonchalance of raven's wings. There were no exceptions; each man wore blue overalls and a black hat. Each man was thin and nasal, drawling to canny length, with a startling amount of bone, with a reach as long as the dawn.

Each man had blue eyes and fair hair. It was as though these mountaineers were wearing a uniform, and my sensations were like those of Rip Van Winkle when he came upon the Dutchmen. As I watched these fifteen men, long and thin as turnpikes, looking wordlessly at me, and with their idle lengths of leg hung over the platform of the store, a fear seized me that by a general conspiracy of men, trains and blue mountains I had been thrown into an outlaw stronghold, and that the outlaws were just taking their time.

I found myself listening for their thoughts, trying to meet their spare blue gaze. But impossible. The main thoroughfare of N—— was the railway track, by which stood a few shacks and a sawmill, and as I turned back to escape this way I could feel that fifteen black hats, cocked at all angles of defiance, had turned with me, that thirty blue eyes turned and perforated me; and that the silence was refining to its ultimate frigidity. Oh, for a stout man!

As though answering, a rotund fellow came from behind a wagon and smiled at me, seized me and undertook my defense, strode over railway tracks and fields, gave me a bed for the night, and fed me on corn bread and chunks of salt bacon, and dippers of spring water. The strangeness of blue mountains departed and they attended my walk that night with so warm a familiarity that I did not even think about them. It was dark, and as I reconnoitered the tracks and the store, there was not a man of that lanky band to be seen.

The world had been blackened out by the heavy charcoal of night. There was no moon. But the sky was vaguely luminous, a dome of light in which the stars swung, and their keen votive smoke brought involuntary tears to the eyes and dimmed them, as wood smoke will. The white stars burned at a far, heatless distance. On that sky they might have been the white-hot and minute cinders of diamonds, which the wind had raked down, blown and scattered.

The hills which had waited with heads raised, like lowing cattle, during the day, were now straightened and flattened into a one-dimensional rim circling the world, and bluntly standing out against the light of void thrown up from beyond it. The earth was like a black caldron swinging over the reflected glow of the night fires of space.

I found a dimmed road and followed it to the liquid pulsations of the crickets. There were shrill encampments of these insects blotted in the fields and hills. Their notes were the sizzling of the caldron. Over the floor of silence ricocheted the sudden barking of dogs. A fan of yellow light opened across the fields, from the porch of a house, and in the porch two men were talking.

I heard solitary words drop on to the air and eddying briefly down, extinguish into the dark. I passed closed doors, and windows in which oil lamps burned sparingly and laid a film of yellow light on the heads of talking people. A hand moving the light would start a whirligig of shadows over the walls, like the wings of big moths; and settling would cast and fix a new fantasy.

I passed a shack on a hill, and out of its window was hopping the skirl of a gramophone. But the trees broke up and subdued the noise, and the black silence crept closely in as though it had been the breathing of the earth. I blotted myself into the woods, led on by a light which I discovered to be the lamp of a white frame church standing up naïvely like a child's toy.

In the church a wide voice was preaching, and words of the sermon jumped out of the open door into its funnel of light and fell out of the light to earth like the turning leaves. There was singing, a reverent monody. After, a deep silence, and I expected to see the lights put out. But a long silence of vacant dark. A chestnut aimed to earth.

The lights clicked out. The preacher came out of the church and by the light of a storm lantern walked with a dozen men and women between the trees. The preacher, seeing the star smoke above, sang out courageously the tune of a hymn, till a woman's voice stopped him with,

"Right smart o' chestnuts bin fallin', Mr. Cooper. Last night one fell and hit Doc McDowell plum' on the head."

The high nasal comment from Doc:

"Yes. And I hain't never seen no chestnut the size o' that-a-one. Seemed like it kind o' fell searchin' for me."

Then the moon rose, yellow as candle light, and I could see the group by the boles of the columnar trees. The men were wearing black hats and blue overalls.

AN ASIDE ON THE MOUNTAINEERS

After hearing Doc McDowell's widely drawling voice tell how the bursting chestnut hit him "plumb on the head," I hurried home, feeling the ice of mountain strangeness had been cracked by this small wedge of overheard speech. But I awoke the next morning to see the immutable highlands waiting for me. They seemed to be mirrored in the air, like glass, to resist anything but a surface acquaintance.

North Carolina is proud. Proud of having less than 1 percent of foreign blood in its stock. Proud of its pure Scottish, Irish and English blood. There you hear a strange dialect, not an acquired twang, but a traditional, custom-hewn brogue, something which hovers naïvely between a Devonshire accent and the Oxford manner.

In these border mountains of western North Carolina, in the Unakas and Blue Ridge, it is said you may hear the English of Shakespeare and Chaucer; though in my wanderings to the remote parts of these mountains I did not experience the happiness of noting anything so rare, except the name Leander.

Sitting in his storm-thinned and weather-split shack in one of the highest ranges, fifteen miles from a railway and eight miles from any road but a rough wagon trail, was Leander, tall, shaggy, unkempt as a furze bush; and his brother Beaumont. They could neither read nor write. Beaumont and Leander Wiggins, who gave us apples and asked, "Now is you-uns kin to ol' Uncle Moses P—— on the yon side o' Little Rock Creek?" That is as near to Shakespeare as we ever got!

The mountaineers are perhaps America's only peasantry. These men and women have been shut up in their loved mountains since the coming of the first settlers, and have conserved their rough, antique modes of living. The mountains still hold more of mysterious life than a stranger can quickly penetrate.

The scattered huts shelter men almost startled by their own voices. Their speech has the intonation of solitude. Within the last two or three years roads have been carved into the mountains, and it is possible for the avid to "do" them at anything up to forty miles an hour. But the mountaineers accept the change suspiciously, keep to where one can travel only on horseback, and often only on foot.

One sees the tall blue figures, with narrow heads looking to the ground, with hands in pockets, and gun laid across their arms, behind their backs— one sees them stalking along in depths of thought beyond the length of our conventional-sounding chains.

Is it as grim as it appears to be? What does this brooding betoken? The thoughts of the mountaineer flow in deep, evasive channels. One is warned of the suspicious nature and lawless tendencies of these men. But I am safely back in New York to testify that a more hospitable and genial people does not exist, that they have what Pío Baroja—who would have been enthusiastic about them—would call a "dynamic" sense of freedom, the unconfiding, unadministered freedom of bears and squirrels, and that like the rest of us they do not want outsiders to meddle in their affairs.

I became involved in no feuds. I discovered no stills—about which hearsay has brought forth a vast brood of exaggerations, though there was vague evidence of both feuds and stills. But, even in these desperate matters, I prefer to remember these men are living according to the customs of 150 or 200 years ago. Better education and roads have only begun to penetrate their retreats. They have been a law unto themselves, have lived as clansmen and hunters, shot, hewn and eaten for their own bare needs in solitudes where even the echo of an ordered society has not been heard.

Knowing only the stark changes of life, the unexplained varying of sun, wind, rain, the diurnal infusions of light and darkness, and the sporadic labor of the open air, the mountaineer obeys instinct without discriminating. Though unconsciously he carries within him, as he breaks into the laurel, that primal instinct of all, the instinct for law.

The mountaineer fights hard for his liquor yet, and will do so until his adventurous impulses and his active mind are given occupations measuring up to his powers. Meanwhile, he is shrewd enough to let his children take advantage of the better opportunities for education which are now offering.

I heard of one aged mountaineer, whose wild career had become a byword in the country, but who fell upon hard times and was forced to live in the corner of a sawmill shed throughout a severe winter. When strangers commiserated and asked how he spent the long, bare evenings, he said he taught his two grandchildren to read and write. "Thar never hain't bin no ignorant Perkinses," he said proudly.

All this and "a right smart piece" more—as they say—I have discovered since that morning when, hesitating before the start, I saw the mountains indifferently, signlessly waiting like furred animals with the casual, upward forest marked on them. The moist, alluring blue had gone from them. They were gray-green, real, ponderous. They exhaled odors, the humid odors of sap and clay.

The noon heat swayed over their hollows. Chords of wind moved in white vibration over their ridges. There were the short, warm smell of fields and the smell of damp earth under trees. There were the tang of thickets, the hanging odor of laurel or rhododendron, the flavor of stripped bark. The torches of corn rattled dryly like paper. The air weighed like the air of a warm barn, the rafterless barn of the sky to which the steep fields of corn and rye reached and attained.

Blue rainclouds, sagging and weighty spheres of vapor, were forced over the ridges and, listing heavily, rolled over upon us with staring, electric clarity. Their enormous movements were defined powerfully in white curves and blue bodies of polished thunder. They bulked in silence.

"Hit hain't rained since the spring o' the year. What way was it whaur ye came from?" commented and asked the first man we met on our way. Large and single circles of rain, slate blue, tapped the dust; and as we turned up our first creek, we heard ahead of us, lumbering wagons of thunder jolting stolidly down from the gaps.

ON THE TRAIL OF ALISON

Unknowingly we were on the trail of Alison, the grandiloquent Alison.

Vagrant unshapely audiences of cloud moved before the sun, broke up, obscured and then released the main force of his light, giving the earth an inconstant, vaporous glaze. We walked through a valley for miles and miles, among sumac, goldenrod and Michaelmas daisies.

Finding the mountains now built into ranges of loftiness, like green naves; the hills like chapels and chapters around them; and the ranges themselves supported by flying buttresses, ridges; and windows of light shining with the soft restraint of sun-wakened hills, the scene changed for us. We turned up one of the least habited creeks, as though it were the aisle of a cathedral. We climbed, as it were, turret, stairs, ridding ourselves of the weighty valley sun, and breathing a more agile air.

A man getting corn out of his barn told us we could spend the night at his sister's house. He had a grandiloquent figure, filling his overalls to an ample blue like a bombastic sky, wearing his black hat—through which his hair stuck like ears of wheat at the side of the crown—more as a tilted and permanent gesture of expatiation than as headgear.

He was delighted with life. As we walked with him toward his sister's solitary shack poked onto the brow of a hill, he pointed out to us high lifts of land and askew triangles of corn and rye and pasturage which he owned on the ridge.

"Nat Pearcy is my name. Yessir. I didn't catch yours. Oh, yes. Why, right smart of them folk living in Gap Creek over Cloudland. There's Ned, and Doc, and Tom, and Commodore. Would you-uns be like kin to them? Well, no, I guess not, because you-uns comes over the waters. Whaur did you-uns come from? Are you married? So am I. Well, well! My wife went over to Linville to pick galax for a week. If she was here I'd have ye lodge with us. That's my house. No, thata one, thar. Them's my fields, way up to the yan side of thata wood and then yan ways down the creek. Hit's a right pretty piece.

"And how old did you-uns say you-uns is? Why, and jes kinda hikin' round? That's what ol' man Alison did. He came over the waters too. He jes went sportin' roun' peddlin'. I hain't seed the like o' thata one. He was an Irishman. He jes went snoopin' aroun' like you-uns, peddlin' things, toting 'em on his back, and gettin' folk to take him in o' nights. He sure was the workingest man I ever seed. He used to tell us about Canady and Jerusalem. Sight in the world o' peddlers comes thisa way and they all says what Alison says: 'Thar hain't better water nor the mountain water in the world.' Hit's plumb pure."

On the air was the odor of fallen apples. On the highest ranges of the mountains drawn back in gray austerity white clouds were curtaining. A blue gauze of thundercloud shone in a low gap. The sky, burdened for hours, and tiring of its pulling sacks of vapor, seemed to pause, look around helplessly. Unable to hold out, it released those blue sacks and the white hail grain streamed and channeled down. And dull balls of thunder bumped over the gap and rolled cannoning down the creek.

"That sure is a pretty sight," shouted Mr. Pearcy as we ran. "Hit's fallin' right hard."

Mr. Pearcy's sister, Mrs. Ayres, lived in a shack of two small rooms, each containing two wide beds. The walls and roof had slits of open air between the cracks in the beams and boards. There was no ceiling. The walls were partly papered by tailors' catalogues and newspapers. There was a fireless iron stove in the middle of the room. Mrs. Ayres had a pale earthen countenance, and a chin which levered forth her words resonantly.

But Mr. Pearcy's gusty eloquence silenced all by its heartiness. He picked up a newspaper three months old and began reading about Mustafa Kemal. "That's what ol' man Alison used to say. He waur the travelingest man I know'd. Hit's dangerous, he told me. If that thar Mustafa goes on a 'fiscatin' o' everything, that'll get the Greco-Japanese alliance plumb tore up. Was you-uns ever in Jerusalem? No? Alison was. Thar hain't nowhaur Alison hain't bin."

Mrs. Ayres, allied with the smell of dinner, silenced her brother. As we took our places on the benches she shouted, "Now you-uns jes help yourselves, like hit was your own homes, and jes reach what you-uns wants. Here, Ned"—to her husband, sliding some chunks of salt-encrusted bacon to him off the dish. Then to us, explaining, "I help him first, like he was kind o' handier."

Everyone ate with great gesticulation, Mrs. Ayres standing on the bridge, as it were, commanding as the conversation continued scrappily.

"Have ye fed the hogs, Ned?"

"Zeb Vance says he's got pretty smart o' honey, this month."

"Thar's sights o' wagons on the pike goin' up and Tom McKinney's got his mules."

"If only this rain had fallen in the summer. When I seed them clouds fallin' over the gap, I thought, Hit sure is goin' to rain at last. An' hit come, plumb hard."

"Hit's real mean haulin' water from the spring, because our'n dried up."

After a pause, a thin piping voice from the end of the table: "Whaur does you-uns 'spectation to end, like whaur is you-all goin'?"

I had scarcely noticed him before, Mrs. Ayres's husband. He had sat against the wall with his small flat head against a string of drying peppers. His skin was pink and fair, and was tightly stretched over his face making his eyes peer out in two small, hard balls, inquisitively, birdlike. As he sat there, his head barely above the table, he seemed ephemeral, like a slice of thundercloud with a pink sunset flush to it, which might melt into colored waters and disappear if the sun became too strong. He was but the cloud. His brother-in-law was the thunder.

After dinner a neighboring mountaineer and his wife stopped and came in, slowly and gravely, smiling appropriately like a diplomatic corps. The conversation of the men drifted strangely to the subject of courthouses and trials, and Mr. Pearcy expatiated on the rights of juries, and by a suspicious association of ideas began to talk freely about "hit," and how difficult it was to make "hit," but how, in spite of the "revenue," some assumed the risk.

I was surprised at these confidences, but an apologetic, quizzical expression on the face of the grave neighbor led me to believe that Nat Pearcy, having found an audience, was remembering "with advantages." Talk waned to the subject of postage stamps, and then Nat Pearcy picked up the newspaper again and brought us back to Mustafa Kemal. Mr. Ayres, cloud pale, said shyly:

"Nat sure is the readingest man in the world."

But Nat demurred modestly:

"The readingest man and the travelingest man I ever know'd waur Gashry Alison. I hain't seed him for a right smart bit. Mebbe he has quit peddlin' and built him a house somewhaur."

The strangers went. Mr. and Mrs. Ayres and their three children blew out the lamp and got into the two beds, with all their clothes on. We were given the other bed. Through the wide cracks and holes in the walls and roof we could see the wet, vague hills and hear the shrill scissoring of the crickets. Once in the night, rain drummed down and splashed at us. The wide air pushed in. All night the room was loud with the squeaking, creaking and scampering of little feet on the floors and beds, and with the tearing of paper and the overturning of tins, in minute pandemonium. Gashry Alison—what a name, I thought. And he had slept under that very roof.

A MOUNTAIN SHERIFF

Broken in to the mountains now, we assaulted new heights, took unknown trails and saw with little wonder the mounting contours and abrupt dropping of the ridges. The leaves of the rhododendrons were long, dew-weighted arcs. The massed and intricate undergrowth of the woods drooped with condensing vapors. Infinitesimal spheres of water lay in dim rind over bark and foliage. Early forms of mist floated like curled leaves in the pools of morning in the valleys.

Clouds were low like motionless surf, poised forever without falling. There were the wet odors of fallen and decaying leaves, of new-cut timber, of sodden fibrous soil, the green dankness of the woods, the rude smell of bruised leaves and of moss-grown tree wreckage, the tang of broken ramage of fir, balsam, spruce, of chestnut, hickory, walnut, oak and maple. The morning vapors sucked strong flavors from the earth, and the tepid gray of coming rain seemed to draw out of the mountain floor a bitter, green exhalation of sap.

We climbed over miles of mist-choked woodland, passing no one except an occasional black-hatted mountaineer with his gun, swinging out of the laurel and jumping onto the track, hiding his suspicions with a parrying "Howdy." Clay and ocher leaves were matted on the boots of these men, and moss stains were on their overalls, and their black hats were faded to lichen and verdigris.

Violet smoke spiraled cannily heavenward from dingles where women were boiling water and washing clothes near the springs. They boiled the clothes in huge brass caldrons. The greeting was always the smiling, "Howdy," masking a quick scrutiny. But the polite hospitality always shone through: "If you-uns is tired, get ye chairs up at t'house and rest up a spell, an' take some apples. The spring done dried up so I hauled the clothes down to thisa one and lit me a fire here to save fetchin' water to bile. Has thar bin no rain whaur you-uns come fro'? Wall they claim hit's the same in all the world."

The shacks were one- or two-roomed, with a bending porch and a barn, the timber charred and flaked with age, like warped black wafers. Trays of sliced apples would be drying on the roofs, strings of peppers hanging in the windows, and a drying sheepskin in the barn. Lines of rain were traveling down the creek toward us, a dense warp taut from the looms of cloud. Scarlet birds pitched out of the laurel with the tumbling flights of bats.

"Hit's clar over Cloudland," said a youth, gathering apples. "But them weather birds means rain."

Crossing the stepping-stones of a river we met in midstream an oldish man carrying a bag. He was gentler than the usual mountaineer. He wore a frayed but neat black suit, and a newish black hat with a crown unsullied by defiant bulge or hollow. He wore no collar. His eyes were pale as watery sunlight and the lineaments of his face were penciled with a natural irony and obstinacy. He spoke in reedy falsetto. He twinkled half gayly, half superciliously before us and said:

"Howdy. Pretty day! Yessir! What's your name? Where do you all come from? Waal. That your wife? Where are ye going? My name's Sam Robinson. I am a preacher. I go everywhere. I belong to no one. No one belongs to me. I belong to myself. Kinda strange to think of a man not belonging to himself! Mighty glad to know ye and if you're over the Tennessee side ye'll find my folk on the hills. They've got farms, and cows and hogs and sheep. Sam Robinson, and remember I don't belong to no one."

Leaving it at that he left us abruptly, jumped to the next stone in the river and turned up the mountain; and the woof of haze rising in the rain's warp wove him into the gray-green blur of wet.

We entered the trees again and still climbing, we heard the rain clattering on the roof of the forest and leaking in crackling channels and spouts. We went for miles up the green forest caverns, and the close, spindling tree trunks, distancing to a blur of silver, seemed to pour like cold and noiseless torrents from the sky. Gashry Alison must have taken that trail a score of times, we imagined, silently trudging, absorbing from the still air of the solitary acres of woodland, new currents of eloquence.

At a break in the trail we hit a creek and there was a high barnlike store there propped up high on a platform. Posters of sales, wanted men, and advertisements were pasted on the planks, and were tearing limply from them. The storekeeper was sitting at the door reading a large Bible. His gun stood beside him. It turned out he was the sheriff, and from his conversation and girth we perceived he played a gigantic part in the scattered community of ten farms and a white church tiptoed on a knoll.

A yellow beard, like a corn shuck, spouted from the sheriff's chin. His voice had the nasal pitch of the village dialectician. He denounced Darwin partly as a nincompoop, partly as an ill-equipped emissary from Avernus. He told us of the theological disputes of the creek, the public debates about the Scriptures, in which he had downed many an opponent amid the applause of one side and the groans of the other.

"The last time waur wan I defended ol' Sam Robinson. Does you-uns know him? Waal, he hain't no debater and waur kinda 'fused like by a feller from Roarin' Creek. He allowed he waur a right smart feller, but he looked a purty mean sort o' popskull wan I'd finished. 'I suspicioned hit all 'long,' I said opening the Bible. 'Ye can't 'scape Holy Writ. Ye hain't even got your tex' c'rrect!' "

For days afterward I confess I was merely amused by this muscular Christian, who the next moment was describing how he had repulsed a "shootin' up fray" from over the state line, roped his prisoners to chairs, and read the New Testament to them. But a mountaineer took me to task and showed me that men like the sheriff had done a lot, after their fashion, to destroy much of the superstition and emotionalism to be found in the creeks.

"Sky's gettin' clar," said the sheriff as we walked to the door. I asked if he had ever heard of Gashry Alison, the peddler.

"Why, reckon I did. He used to come in here, peddlin' things—clothes, spectacles, brooches. He tol' me he was born in Jerusalem. That's in Turkey. Waal, pretty smart o' peddlers and sich comes thisa way. But thar hain't one like ol' Gash Alison. He's bin sportin' 'roun' the whole of Americky on foot. He's a quare man. He's got a quare furrin name too. He tol' me, 'I'm the only Gash in the world. My mother said wan I was born—' "

A horseman jumping down at the door looked in, up, about and around, and stopped when he saw us. He then picked up a sack of flour and laid it, behind the saddle. Mounting, he leaned over and smiled at the sheriff, and called:

"Doc says the apples is all picked and the firs' waggon is way up on the yan side o' Ripshin Ridge."

"Jinks," exclaimed the sheriff. "Must be plumb on the Pike."

And locking up the store, he walked off lankily with his gun and his Bible.

WHAT THE VOICE SAID

He looked at us tolerantly. He turned and pointed up the creek, saying: "I disremember 'xackly, but mebbe hit's ten miles an' terrible rough. Does you-uns 'spectation to get to the top? Waal, it sure is a wunnerful place. They say ye can see—"

"It's burning. Keep a-stirrin' it," threw in his wife, a dry, cane-colored woman, crisp and lined like a corn shuck. His little rapture fell like a cut stalk. He turned to the steam and the smoke and went on stirring the apple butter in the huge black caldron. He was stirring with a heavy wooden pole six feet long.

The caldron was standing on a stick fire in the field, and at a distance from the heat of it his barefooted wife and his barefooted daughters were slicing apples and throwing them into the caldron. The eyes of this family seen through the keen haze of cobalt smoke had a wildness in them. This might have been the witch scene in *Macbeth*.

"Hit's awful mean stirrin', stirrin'—" apologized the man.

The range we were to cross against his advice was nearly seven thousand feet high. It was forest-covered from base to summit, and a rocky trail, once used by ox wagons in fetching lumber but now altogether disused, tackled the slope abruptly and looped the contours.

When the trail reached the high gap it fizzled out into a wide "bald," a bare dome of mountain where the gales had cleared away the trees and cropped the turf almost to the roots. The skeleton gray stumps of cut or uprooted trees stared oddly, vacantly, like forgotten milestones. The earth was windstripped and seemed to be lighted only by the gaze of the fog as it moved over.

It is simple thus in a few lines to indicate hours of struggle, for comparatively low as the range was, it takes large effort to haul oneself up such slopes. The filtering underworld gloom of the forest is something to fight through. After plodding and hard breathing without any apparent gain, we would see through a gap in the trees that already we were head and shoulders out of the lower valley ocean where the choppy hillocks swirled minutely and crumbled into green surf.

Then we would turn and dive again into the submarine forest verdure and feel its fluid air. The spindling gray trunks of millions of trees packed like threads of water into a blurred torrent of distance, poured and splashed down in immense silence about us. We had the sensation of walking in flooded vaults of touchless sap-distilled water.

The earth drew the noise out of our feet as we strode from silence to silence, while the multitudinous forest waited. In cities silence is negative, is the absence of sound. But on that vast shield of mountain forest the silence was positive. One felt its presence, breathed it in tangible, inaudible drafts.

At times we felt there was no air; only this greenish, glassy quiet in which the falling of the crisp body of a leaf hit distinctly, deliberately, with the ring of event.

For hours we pushed, pushed, pushed back the air, pressed back the trees, stamped the earth, toed the rocks, shouldered all our forces to the ascent. After the first ridge I vowed I would never climb a mountain again. But which is worse, to climb a mountain or to be in a valley wanting to climb one?

The thought of Gashry Alison comforted me. It was the constant mention of him among the mountaineers, and the spur which the unknown gives to the imagination, that made this lonely and unknown figure a companion. His pack must have been heavier than mine, what with his clothes, spectacles and peddling staff.

How did he find the ascent? Did this quiet solidify against him? Seize him like deep pervading water? Or did his warm nature melt and release the mountain forces, till leaves fell from the trees like the crash of cymbals, and springs sang out, and partridges rattled up from cover like country people cluttering out of church, and till winds mounted and swelled a manifold diapason through the forest's mighty register of pipes?

How was it with Alison? Did he sing? Did he muse? Did he tire? Did he rush his hills? Or did he sink back into his own pace and lug his body up glumly, while the forest, always ahead and standing in thin, silver battalions, ordered him up and up, in its inescapable routine?

Perhaps traveling is a mundane thing. All our giants are windmills, all our armies are sheep, if we go forth with the rhetorical expectations of Don Quixote. Gashry Alison must have had something the Spanish gentleman missed.

It takes more than a pair of legs to make a man climb mountains and live on salt bacon and pastry among strangers in order to peddle brooches, clothes and spectacles. I believe all Alison's windmills must have been giants.

There was always some news of Alison to be got at a mountaineer's hut. Sitting on the porch while leading the lanky, genial but suspicious "Doc" or "Pete" onto the subject, one would eventually hear something like this:

"Thar hain't no one the like o' Gash Alison. He's the travelin'est man I ever seed. Seemed like as though he waur always footin' it over the worl'. 'Wan will I build me a house an' settle?' he says, the last night he waur here. 'Boys,' he says, 'I fit in three wars and seen a sight o' frays and places, and guess I'll jes be shacklin' 'round till I'm as ol' as you-uns is, grandf'er.' "

Before dusk we reached the "bald" and were as high as we ever climbed in our wanderings. Over the gale-cropped dome of the "bald," the gritty gray clouds passed low like enormous buzzards. Scarves of cloud moved down from the banks, and looking below them as through a half-covered window, we could see the sun-honeycombed forest cast distantly away into the ultimate hollows of the world.

The clouds rolled like a surge over the spruce and balsam, smudging the indigo masses with fog. But westward we could see the tidal summits of an ocean of hills; varying, pellucid ranges over which passed squalls of green, ultramarine and gray. The long fields swept up obliquely to where the summits broke or rolled over, throwing up calls of spray to the inaccessible sky.

This was crisis. Alison must have stood where we were standing, many a time, a wind-dark speck pausing on the dome of the "bald." Now I should find him, hear all about him. Or this would be the end.

But life and mountains do not have our dramatic sense. I heard of Alison again that night and again the day following, when, like a falling star, his golden course burned suddenly out halfway up in the heavens, unfinished. But this night we slept in a shack in the upper branch. The grandfather, father, mother, daughter and son of the house slept in one room and we in the other. The mountaineers will give anything up for a stranger, do anything for them. In fact, the conversation turned that way as we sat before the fire.

"We-uns niver turns away no one wan they asks for shelter an' a meal's victuals. Thar's always someone comin' through the gap, peddlers and sich. Gash Alison uster come reg'lar."

The father broke in with high-up voice:

"Does you-uns know Gash Alison? Waal, he were a furriner and him comin' over the waters. He 'llows he's the only Gash in the worl'. He says the day he waur born his mother didn't know how to call him till one night, like it would be ol' man Alison had a dream, and a v'ice said, plumb loud, so hit woke him, 'Gashry!!' That's a right quare name. 'How d'ye spell it?' I asks. 'I couldn't rightly denote,' says Gash. 'Like the v'ice kinda didn't say nathong more'n that.'"

THE WOMAN WHO SMILED

I sat on the porch of the shack of the woman who smiled.

Everyone on the creek was related to everyone else. There had been intensive intermarriage for generations. The wit who said a man might be his own grandmother and not know it, erred more in lack of tact than he erred in exaggeration. The Ayreses, the Ingrams and the Vances brooded in their lofty hollows far from call of man or beast from the plains.

The blue smoke of the caldrons scratched the air, the bare, damp feet of the women and children were marked by the basket patterning of the field grass. These earth-held families raised corn, sliced apples, made honey, shot in the woods, and brought sacks of flour on horseback to their shacks.

The Ayreses, the Ingrams and the Vances brooded and fattened turkeys, and nothing ever happened except a great gale or a spell of drought. The boys tried the settlement school for a while, grew up and felt their legs getting too long for them, took guns and went up into the woods alone to live, till inclement weather or weariness of excitement drove them down to the creek again.

The wind is clever, the rain is sharp, and earth clings to boots and body; and something of the wind, the rain and the clay, something careless, dynamic, stolid, entered the ways of these boys, these Ulstermen, these Scotsmen, these English whom the mountains held.

These boys had never seen the sea, or cities, or Negroes. One of them told me he first saw a Negro when he was eighteen, and that he ran home frightened, shouting, "I've seen the boogeyman!" Horace Kephart, in his book on the mountains, tells almost the same tale.

Skies are fair today, but tomorrow gray gullies of water may spurt down, or winds hiss arrowing through the air. So one night Ed Ingram—I naturally never give the real names of these mountaineers—who was eighteen, ran off with Rose Vance, who was fourteen. It was not exactly an elopement because nearly everyone knew about it.

The couple ran over into Tennessee, where the marriage laws are easier; and the magistrate in one of the creeks married them. The ceremony was brief. Mountain ceremonies always are brief. A tale is current that one magistrate boasted his marriage ceremony to be only four words: "Stand up. Jine. Hitched." I understand it is longer nowadays.

At news of the elopement the parents were scandalized, having done exactly the same themselves; then resigned; then relieved. As old McCoy Vance said, "Wan a woman takes an idee into her head hit hain't no good obstructioning. I've got twelve daughters and seven sons, an' I know summat about it."

Ed Ingram worked a bit, loafed a bit and went for days and days on end shooting in the woods. He could never resist the cool, lengthy woods, free and clear to him as spring water. He didn't harm anyone. He didn't interfere with anyone. The mountains are wide as the wind. Why should anyone want to interfere with him? Isn't there room enough and to spare for all in the mountains?

It is good enough to enjoy one's own happiness. It is bad enough to suffer one's own wretchedness. What business is it all of strangers, of educators, officers, of the monotonous, organized people of the plains, where the water is so poor and warm with lying in lead pipes that the townspeople have to put ice in it! Fancy putting ice in water!

Rose Ingram may have five, ten, fifteen children by now. Besides there are turkeys to fatten, fruit to preserve, food to cook, and that man to wait on hand and foot; and water to carry from the springs, and clothes to mend, taxes to pay, and apples to sell.

Once in a while she washes clothes, not often, though; and complains of the clouds of flies that fill her bedroom-cum-kitchen-cum-parlor. If she and Ed were to read this they would probably resent the implication of poverty, for a mountaineer will admit himself to be everything except poor.

"Wan has you-uns ever lacked a meal's victuals or a bed in the mountains?" I can hear them asking. But it is not that kind of poverty. If hospitality is riches, then the mountaineers are the richest people in the world. I remember the rebuke I received from a man whom I had offered to pay for a service:

"Pore folks haster work. But we don't hafter work. We hain't pore."

All this I thought while sitting on the porch of the hut of the woman who smiled. Gray parallelograms of rain shadowed the creek, and soaking scarves of white cloud surf flew from the wet blue and madder mountains. The water haze was over the creek, a web of flat vapor. The sky was hoofed and rutted with botched cloud traveling and thrown up in heavy clods.

Runnels of bright clay water were richly pouring with the note of clear cattle bells, and a stocky rain tapped like drumsticks on the roof of the hut. Escaping from the collapse of rain, we rushed to the porch of the woman's house. It was little more than a shed propped up high on four piles of rock.

A semicircle of beehives made of pipes and tin cans with rocks for lids stood in the clearing before the house. A lambskin was stretched over the wall to dry.

The woman was sitting on the floor in the doorway of the hut. She was scantily clothed in a coarse dress, and her legs and feet were bare. Her straw-colored hair was drawn from her forehead and fell in limp tails down her back. Ten ragged and contented children were crawling over her as she nursed a young baby, and sat curled on the floor like a gentle animal, uncomplainingly.

She was as pale as water, pale as sap, pale as a cane of rye, and her faint, narrow eyes shone with an idling light. She looked at us dreamily; and her lips, weirdly thin and colorless (from wind and rain and not from poverty, we felt), construed a little changeless smile. It was always there. She seemed to look at us and smile at us through water from another world. It was the smile of Mona Lisa.

Questions dawdled from between her lifted lips:

"Whar does you-uns come from? What did you-uns say you-uns was called? Is you-all man and wife? Uh, huh. How old are ye? An' you-uns comes over the waters? That'd be a scandalous long ways, yander, I reckon. Would you-all like some apples? If you-uns wants any, jes get ye them. Thar's more apples this y'ar nor any y'ar I ever seed."

This reads absurdly, for every sentence loafed between linked pauses in that drooping intonation which is of the soil. She said she had been married when she was fifteen and was now twenty-nine. She said she had eight children, and had three sisters younger than her own eldest daughter. She herself had been one of a family of twenty-one.

She smiled continuously her faint pearl smile.

"Las' night the moon was travelin' north," she said. "Hit'll rain a right smart piece more and get cold. I mind the time wan our spring friz plumb up on the first of September."

I laughed at this and she looked at the feathering rain. And her lips lifted and her constant smiles moved lightly like a single ripple of water.

A break in the thicket showed two men coming to the house. Lanky figures with hands in pockets, and a gun apiece laid horizontally between their arms behind their backs. They stopped when they saw us, then jumped onto the porch and smiled a doubtful "Howdy" and scanned the dimly greeting lips of the woman for information about us.

They went inside the house and studied us from behind the curtains, evidently very suspicious. "I know whar ye've bin, daddy," cried out one of the children, but the father came out genially and clapped his hand over the child's mouth. He introduced himself: "I'm Tom McKinney, yours truly. I didn't catch yourn?"

He went inside and fell to whispering with his companion. A lot of mysterious operations went on inside the room. We noticed signaling with fingers, chins and lips. Turning sharply, I caught the woman scrutinizing us closely with awakened clear eyes, but when she saw me turn they fell back subtly to the underwater idling gaze.

The man walked up and down impatiently inside the house, and, muttering, stepped to the window to peer at us. We were obviously not wanted, and they were all greatly relieved when we rose to go, although they pressed us politely to stay. I remember seeing the lifted lips of the woman. A pale, queer smile has been dawdling after me ever since.

IN THE SMOKIES

It was the last house in the creek, and we stayed the night there. Beyond was a heaped wall of enmeshing forest, and mountains, retreating ridge by ridge and outflanking valley by valley into Tennessee: virgin forest, pathless, uninhabited except by shy bears and other wild animals. The last house, after that nothing, smudges of dull green, cold, dark.

The house was a half-roofless shack hidden by a palisade of tall corn. There were two bedrooms with sacks nailed over the windows for lack of glass. And a kitchen with only three walls, the fourth being the forest. Another room and the kitchen were roofless.

It was vague blue dark when we asked for shelter, but the tall shrill woman of the house took us in pleasantly enough, but in an impersonal way as though we entered by the right of nature, like the wind and the rain.

She intoned her welcome in a voice that was neither melancholy nor joyful, but like a bodyless voice, a thing soughing from the trees or talking over the soil.

We groped in by the yellow light of the lamp, sat, and so fixed our shadows on the walls; and talked with the family. There were a man, the woman, her daughter and her son, and an older woman who must have been the boy's grandmother.

They asked us the usual questions. They had always lived in the mountains until two years before when they migrated to South Carolina to work in the cotton mills. But owing to the changes in trade the family had returned to the mountains, and were now ten miles away from the nearest store, five miles away from a wagon road, with two rivers to ford and steep land, steep as clouds, to till. Well may they speak of a man falling out of his field.

As we talked, bats flew into the room and dodged around. Bars of heavy blue night lay solidly between the rafters. All we could get to eat was cold pastry and molasses; but the white stars, like drooping small wells of white water, hung closely above us. There was not a flake of moon.

The shrill woman lamented her inhospitality: "I hain't handy at all with me stove all tore up from jolting in the wagon."

Conversation dropped, and there were stark silences. There were glances, and the grandmother said, "I'm a going to bed now," and climbed into bed with all her clothes on. The girl shouted to her brother, "Get ye to your pallet."

We sorted ourselves out. The father slept in our room in the other bed, snored all night and talked to himself, while the wind blew at the sacking nailed over the window, and the crickets scissored their monody of high notes.

Early in the morning, while it was still empty and dark and all sound but the creeping of water in the stream had stopped, the man got out of bed and tapped on the wall. He was answered, and later met his wife in the kitchen where they began to prepare breakfast. It seemed to us it could hardly be much past midnight, and we dragged ourselves dismally to a meal of hot pastry, salt bacon, blackberries and buttermilk; with the shrill woman urging, arguing and persuading all the time. She said it was six o'clock.

Came a thump and scuffling from the other room and in ran the grandmother shouting, "Does you-uns know what the time is? Waal, hit's three o'clock!" Protests were in vain. It was only three o'clock. I had felt it in my bones. It turned out the man had only guessed the time when he knocked on the wall, and that his wife had looked at her clock without lighting a match, and had thought it was half past five!

We all stood there, gray and vacant forms, with a yellow film of lamplight cast limply without enthusiasm upon us. At last when the shrill debate had ended the woman said, "Waal, reckon I'll hafter make an extry meal today to make up. And you-uns will be able to get the bursted chestnuts before the squirr'ls gets them."

But we went back to bed.

The man set off on foot—he had no horse—down the creek on his ten-mile journey to the nearest store, to bring back a sack of flour.

Later that morning we discovered where the woman had bought her molasses of the night before. A man was standing in a field supervising the crushing of rye cane between two revolving rollers set in a frame to which was attached a pole ten feet long. A mule was harnessed to the pole and as he walked round and round, the rollers turned, the cane was crushed and the syrup oozed down a gully pipe and was strained through sacking into a tub.

"Today's 'll be a right smart piece cl'arer than what you-uns had las' night," said the man.

His son, a sinewy fellow, was chopping at a stump of tree: "I'm hewin' me a block for my corn mill," he said. He had already built a large wooden wheel, and a race propped high in the air on stilts. All the grinding in the mountains is done by these old watermills and the corn is crushed between two enormous millstones.

After miles and miles of climbing we prepared to assault one of the flanking ridges and so descend into a far creek, where there was a lumber camp. The distance was varyingly given as between two and ten miles. It turned out to be over fifteen miles, and the hardest fifteen, the roughest and the steepest, I have ever done. Eight miles of it was done in heavy rain and cloud. We took a mountain youth to guide us to the top of the ridge.

He was as silent and as expressionless as a leaf. He had carved blue eyes. He strode easily where we struggled. And the more I tried to get conversation out of him, the more laconic and defensive he became, replying "Uh huh" to nearly everything I said. We went on something like this:

"Hot," I said, feeling very blown.

"Warm," he replied.

"You're used to it"—from me.

"Uh huh."

"Do you often go this way?"

"Uh huh."

"Is it far?"

"Uh huh."

"Have you always lived in that creek?"

"Uh huh."

The only time he became eloquent was when we passed a deserted farm lying in a boulder-strewn clearing in the mountain forest.

"Beaumont Starr's farm," he drawled. "He left las' spring. Hit was too hard. Siles gone old and wore out, an' nothin' 'll grow in that thar."

Tremendous chestnut trees shot like isolated gray columns out of the green ruin of thickets. Beaumont Starr had lived there with his brother, and their ancestors before them, tilling granite.

We climbed for three hours through steep woods of pine, balsam, chestnut and hickory; of bellwood, maple, walnut and oak—a struggle in green monotone. On the summit, which seemed unattainable, we finally flung ourselves down on the hard earth utterly exhausted; with a faint ocean of blue ranges palely washing and lapping in noiseless surge and foam of cloud-capped summits, below us.

The air was still. Not a sound. Not even the motion of one leaf touching another. It seemed that the world had stopped: that we lay supine at a point beyond all sound and effort, that we lay closely beneath the flawless and level ceiling of the world.

We saw sturdy and extraordinary foreshortened clouds and ethereal territories of mountains, range after range, merging into a haze of moth silver. The mountains were strips of water modeled by the air. Ranks of solidifying ether. Anything but mountains. Anything.

From our "Necket" we could see our ridge slung like a firm hammock of green from knob to knob, a blue-green causeway crossing the water of sky, or broad and churned with green and choppy light like the wake of a steamer. Distantly was Clingman's Dome, with the other gray hosts, while a wide surf cloud lay fixedly, mazedly upon them. From their highest elevation bannered a stilly chrome wash of startled light.

We descended alone. Rain collapsed on the roof of the trees and spouted through. We shattered the forest silence as a rod splits emerald ice. We hurtled down, deeper at every jump, into the high and bare cold cavern of frigid trees. A shot suddenly was fired somewhere before us and below, and its staccato echoes ricocheted on the polished walls of green. Were we at last mistaken for revenue officers as had been prophesied? But life lacks our sense of the dramatic. We soon came upon three hunters standing in a ditch and they smiled ironically at our little excitement.

When at last we came out under the open sky it was torn into rags of mist and vapors which drifted, a soaking tatterdemalion, across the knobs and creeks; and entering a valley, whose form was quite smudged out by rain and night, we splashed through sodden miles of clay, eight miles to the lumber camp, and found bed there.

SITTING IN A MOUNTAIN TOWN

In the morning I crossed the river and walked into the town. It had a railway station, four churches, a bank, a main street, two side turnings and no "movie," among other things, for the distraction of its eight hundred or more inhabitants.

An automobile road looping through the mountains from the center of North Carolina was just nearing completion, and during the day one might occasionally see gangs of colored men throbbing by on trucks to the excavations and quarries, and an odd white-bearded mountaineer of the old school riding horseback and sidling and prancing about as though he were conducting a daring military operation.

The main street of the town was shaded by an avenue of maples, and poplars with dull green and silver leaves. The wide almost motionless river was rust yellow and cloudy dense with clay flood water, on which lay the heavy cobalt and sepia shadows of trees.

In the street the sunlight opened in grotesque and formless gapes between rare shadows. Men in blue overalls and monstrous black hats were sitting on walls, fences and benches in the sun.

These men were spare, long and springy as whips. Some walked with guns behind their backs, or sat with their long ungainly legs propped up or pulled out across the pavement. They had lengthy, calculating noses, and judicious deprecatory chins. They rarely moved. But they saw everything.

One knew this by the sensitive jerking of the crowns of their hats, if a Ford car clattered by or if a cannonade of blasting pealed on the new road, or if a stranger crossed brazenly into the sun, and had his boots cleaned. Wind blew in casually, as everything else did.

The only thing to do in the town was to find a foot of unoccupied bench and sit on it. I sat. I sat for hours and watched better men than I—also sitting.

I sat on the wall of the bridge first of all, and soon another sitter there began to edge toward me. We inspected each other from under the brims of our hats. Our eyes reconnoitered. We tried to give our inevitable, approaching acquaintanceship a strategic casualness, as though it were an accident and not a matter of passionate curiosity.

The man was an Indian half-caste. His eyes were thick, cloudy and red hot. He pulled at his yellow, twiggy mustache and stared at the river. He said ultimately: "Thar's right smart o' fish in th' river. Catfish. Yellow catfish and blue uns. An' a redfeller—red horse like we call him."

The sun wheeling like a white stream filled in the hollow of broken silence, leveled it up and flowed over as though nothing had happened. The half-caste pulled in his belt and let his length of leg dangle forward, and so stepped away as it were on tiptoe, like a marionette.

"Reckon I'll turn aroun' and seek arter a bit o' grub," he said. And he went to the barber's doorstep and sat there in the shade.

The mountains lay in masterful elevation around the town and descended into it. Their ardent slopes, green-pored and filigreed, rose to every touch of sun. There were cool smoky blue forms of shadows modeled into the body of the ranges. A bare heat, like the look in an animal's eyes, and a prolific coarseness and toughness, as of a bullock's hide, were in the mountains. They stood like herds of green bison. The little town seemed within the casual print of a great mountain hoof.

I climbed up a stairway into the shade, and shortly a man came up and sat on the stair below me. He was oldish, agile, with stringy red skin, and a fistful of mustache stuffed under his nose like straw. He wore one brown boot and one black boot. We fell into conversation.

He had lived in the mountains all his life and knew every creek of them. He was very scornful of the "ol' fellers" of the previous generation, and especially of their queer ways, speech and customs. And he fed his scorn on the constant reading of a book describing the amusing life of the mountaineers. He referred to them as "ol' crackters."

"Wan he came hyur and writ thata book he writ the truth. Hit's jes the way the ol' fellers uster speak. They was a quare c'llection. He's a right smart boy, and the travelin'est man I knowed. He's seed the whole worl' except two states and now he jes stays foolin' aroun' writin'."

His reference was to that noted writer on the mountains, Horace Kephart.

I led him gently to reminiscence.

"I've bin four times over Clingman's Dome. Thar hain't no trail, but twen'y y'ars ago a feller cut a wagon trail, figgerin' he waur going to haul lumber along the top. But I reckon that'd be covered plumb up with laurel an' trees, the way nobody wouldn't never know it.

"I've done purty smart o' b'ar huntin', sometimes with the snow that high. B'ars is harmless an' is jes as afeered of you as you is o' them. Thar hain't no real reason fer huntin' up so, either. Rattlesnakes is the same. Reckon all animals is like that. Don't harm them an' they won't touch ye.

"Waal, hit's mighty dense up thar and terrible rough. If ye get up on top of the Dome and shins up a tree a man could see everywhars in the worl' almos' till—till his eyes was a-tired o' lookin', an' he come down an' go away. But ye hafter climb. The Dome's too coverdly wi' trees to see without.

"Yeh, I've had many experiments with b'ars," he continued. "Pete Hughes was the real boy fer b'ars, though. He fell into a b'ar wallow on the Dome one day an' lit plum' on top o' the greates' ol' b'ar he'd ever seed, and kinda got into a reg'lar spat with him. Reckon that's in the book, too. Wane'er the ol' boy heered summat good like that he made a note of it so's not to disremember.

"Nat'rally thar's a sight o' things bin writ that hain't never occurred. Like ol' Uncle Durham uster say that every time a story crossed water it doubled itself.

"Did you-uns ever hear o' Phil Morris's defeat? That's a true un. Phil, like the rest o' us, was in a kinda o' mixed-up business. Hit'd be hard to say what kinda business it'd be with one thing an' another an' nothin' reg'lar.

"Waal, we was up in the woods and thar was snow on the ground and the country 'most friz up. We lit a fire and Phil sits him down and offs with his boots to kinda rest up his feet like.

"Waal, durin' the night one of them boots gets pushed into the fire and burned up. An' in the mornin' Phil sent up a great hollerin', and had to make him moccasins out of his leggins and walk back sixteen miles in 'em. And ever since they have called that place Phil Morris's defeat."

A rending explosion of dynamite on the new road shook the town, and there was a short brushing of wind in the trees and the tossing up of a few birds.

"That's the deefeninest n'ise," said the man. "Muster bin like that in France. Was you-uns ever in France? Uh huh. French is heathians."

"It's hot in the sun," I said.

"Waal now, I'll tell ye, I hain't bin out in the sun yet today. Reckon I'll be broguin' round a bit."

And he backed obliquely down the stairs, brown boot first.

(1925, 1989)

FROM

Marching Spain

THE VENTA DE LA SEGURA

It was important to attain the next hill, to advance upon the retiring ranges, to attack them, strike through them, and see what lay beyond. To sit and rest by the wayside was to let precious excitement of living and diamond minutes pour through the fingers wastefully. Instead of resting during the heat of the day I marched through it. And it was heat: a vertical wall of cerulean throwing out a fire that branded the skin, throbbed in the ears and immersed the earth in a brilliant presence weighing upon everything and silencing it. I would cross the Sierra de San Pedro rising before Caceres, and teased myself with the idea of reaching that town itself, thirty-nine miles from my starting-place.

I knew such a march to be beyond my powers, but who does not play the hero and exaggerate the magnitude and ardours of his task? I walked savagely in those early days, and men jogging high on bulging mules and donkeys up the long, red loops of road, stared at me in stupefaction and remembered only as an afterthought to say "Vaya usted con Dios," the eternal "Walk with God" of Spain. I struck trees with my stick, splitting bark, bruising nettles. I sang loudly everything I could think of, and imagined so many adventures that my heart was beating loudly with the rotund excitement. I was leading a glorious invisible army, and each swoop of the road before me rose brassily like a heralding bugle challenge.

In the unheroic moments when I made my imagination admit I could not reach Caceres that night, I decided that in the pass of the Sierra I could stay at the Venta de Clavin, of which a carter had told me. There was not an inch of shade on the road. The sun was riding on my shoulders. Around me camped the wilderness hills, dark as gypsies and, in the great distances, wild ranges waved and crinkled like intense licking flames at the summits. It was as if the earth were a huge pan frying between the curled, violet flames of the mountains.

I was marching through one of those immense uninhabited wildernesses, the despoplados of Extremadura. The sunlight crackled and split and splintered among the oak scrub and blazed spurting like blinding gas flare from the great boulders. Lizards leapt up in vivid rain from my feet, and there were the cries of frightened birds breaking like rods of fountain water among the trees. At the feet of the trees was the common multitude of spring grass, and on it the trees stood in their tilted pools of shadow. One passed walking from pool to pool quietly in the grass like a leaf gliding over the dabbled pebbles of a clear stream.

After some miles I heard the familiar aqueous talking of sheep bells in the wilderness, and at last overtook the outskirts of an enormous flock of sheep babbling northward. There were four huge dogs, like mastiffs, with them, and I saw the shepherd, a weird man clothed in fantastic bits of sheepskin and cowhide, lichened with age, walking high on wooden clogs over the turf and carrying besides a crook and a leathern botero of wine.

We greeted each other, and I walked with him among the trees. He told me he was driving sheep twenty-five miles, and would do half the distance that day. His master then sent the sheep northward for the summer by train to Leon, so he had only to put them on the train, for which he said he was grateful, as he used to have to drive them northward all the way, on foot.

"And you are walking to Caceres?" said he. "If you walk well and if the sun does not get too hot," he said, looking up appraisingly at that enemy, "you will arrive before midnight. Another eight leagues. And you have no beasts!"

A man bent up and straddling with the gait of an olive tree. Forty miles was nothing to him!

He was one of that great number of itinerant shepherds who twice yearly drive their huge flocks across Spain, spearing the night-black hills with their red fires and sleeping in huts made of mud and branches. Creatures solitary and silent as animals. The flocks spend their winter in the south, where the climate is mild and the pasturage fresh; but in May, when the sun empowers himself of the south, they are driven over Extremadura and La Mancha to the northern provinces. The custom is an ancient one, and came to be called La Mesta, and there was an authoritative Council of the Mesta which looked after the rights and privileges of the wanderers. Although the Council has been abolished this hundred years, the cañada de paso or sheepwalk, ninety paces wide, is still left on either side of the great roads.

It has always been assumed that the custom of La Mesta originated in the days when the victorious Spaniards drove the Moors out of Extremadura, razed and devastated until the region became so depopulated by the sword and the plagues that vast territories, at one time as many as fifty districts, were left unclaimed. It was to these the highland shepherds descended with their flocks and the long seasonal migration began. Some flocks travelled between two and four leagues a day. There were endless disputes between the shepherds and the surviving resident farmers, but the Council of the Mesta was powerful enough to protect the shepherds. The Council no longer exists, but as my shepherd showed, the custom survives, and although he was taking his flock to the train, most of the shepherds I met thereafter were proceeding on foot, for it was early May and the northward trek of two or three hundred miles had begun. It was one of those dust-raising armies of sheep that deceived Don Quixote. Northward, as I walked, swelled that lake of bells.

At six in the evening I completed my twenty-three miles at the Venta, a disappointing hovel in a clearing of the red hills. The sun banged down like a hot bell. Men in the woods were loading cork bark on to carts. They gave me water in the Venta, and asked me the usual questions. Who was I? Where had I come from? Where was I going? What was my trade? Was I married?

To tell the peasants I was an author would have meant nothing to them. They would have considered authorship a suspicious kind of crime. I told them I was an itinerant photographer, and that I took photographs of interesting sights and sold these photographs in England. But why was I walking? A train journey across Spain costs!—ay, what it costs! The beardy, gravelly voiced innkeeper pulled a piece of bread and garlic out of his waistband. He knew how much things could cost!

I sat with the family in the yard. I gleaned there was another inn with the promising name of Venta de la Segura, less than a league away they said, in the plain on the other side of the pass. I felt that Venta could not be quite so filthy as this one, and after an hour's rest, the sun being lower and the cool lengthening with the shadows which now pierced the road, I descended to the plain in which the Venta lay.

A miraculous floor of emerald that plain was with the road now white—for in the hills it had been grinding red—breaking it like a sensitive vein in marble, or a slight line of spent foam in a calm sea. Young, brief crops of beryl rippled in it. I breathed the evening ecstasying fields, slender exhalations of serenity and paradise. Before my eyes the level swathes of the Vega lay back to the pale beams of the hills of Caceres, fifteen miles away.

The devil take those cork-gathering innkeepers at the Venta de Clavin, for there was no sign of another inn for some miles. Night came quickly; dark, moonless night and cold. There were no trees, no landmarks, only the grey dimming sea of plain on either side of the road in which my feet churned up a great foam of dust. My spirits began to fall. I had walked twenty-seven miles. My feet were sore, my body was aching, and the straps of my haversack cut my shoulders. Where was the bombast, where was the pace of the burning, golden daytime when I had ridden early over the red Sierra like a gay boat over a sea? The stroke of my heels was now muffled by the dust. I was walking upon a cloud-white path of silence.

Out of the darkness a man tapped by on a donkey. He stopped singing to stare at me, and, when I hailed him, said the Segura was a league away, and that I should know it when I saw it because there were three trees—the only trees for miles and miles—and a ruined tower which people called the Torre del Moro.

At nine o'clock I saw a light scratching the darkness like a pin, but I seemed to get no nearer to it. Left, right. Left, right. Hunger pulling and biting at one like a pack of wolves. Feet burning. I was the only sound in that plain. At last I saw the three trees and the tower, tower and trees, tower and trees, and the forms of the buildings. The light had gone, perhaps it had never been there. The place appeared to be abandoned. There were no windows, no doors. No sound but the crackling chorus of frogs in some pond. Opaque night. Nothing.

The ruined tower delivered its muffled blow of darkness in the face of the star-populated heavens. Not a very cheerful destination for one who had walked about thirty miles out of the frying-pan of the Sierra into the fire of the plain; and talking of frying-pans, oh, for some food. My eyes groped the darkness for sight of door or light, and as I stood there the air was suddenly twisted into the spiralling caterwaul of a peacock. A vulgar, gaudy cry. Where there are peacocks there are men, I argued. (There is nothing so comforting as poor logic.) I felt my way across a mass of rock, turf, and cart tracks, towards the smallest of the buildings, and was rewarded by an open door.

The building was a small stone hut. I stepped inside. The place was in darkness, but I heard voices from a room within. I might have been in a stable or a workshop, for I knocked into a bench with an iron vice on it and came to a couple of stone steps rising to an inner room. A man came out of the inner to the outer darkness and asked me what I wanted.

"There is no Venta here," he said. "Though they call this the Segura, because we sell brandy to carriers and to the labourers in the fields. I am the blacksmith. There is no Venta between here and Caceres, three leagues away. We certainly cannot give you a bed for the good reason that we have none. We can give you something to eat, yes. If you don't want much, because we are poor people."

A woman now appeared from the passage with a yellow oil-flare in her hand smoking, hungering green fumes of burning olive oil, that struck the room and splintered it with shadows, like a window starred by a stone. I was in the smithy itself. She set the flare down on a bench and I saw a twitching forge, the shaking stacks of iron, the benches jumping in the light.

"No, there is nothing here," said she.

She was small, stout, and young with large calf-like gaping eyes, and she wore over her shoulders a pink and green embroidered shawl, knotted so tightly at the waist that it seemed to make a humpback of her. Her candle-pale face was framed in her braided hair, and her earrings jingled and jumped like two grotesque, gilt animals, from her ears.

I took off my pack and sat down on the floor exhausted. The man and his wife watched me anxiously. I asked for water. She brought this. Water cold as swords piercing me. I shivered. Then I told the smith who I was, where I had come from, where I was going to, what my trade was, how my family was, and that I was not a Portuguese. He became very interested and friendly, and was amazed at the distance I had walked, and was very worried at not having a bed to offer me. He told the woman, his wife, to get me something to eat—eggs, sausage, something or other. He sat on the anvil, and his block of shadow wobbled like a fantastic black cloud over the walls. He said perhaps I could sleep with the labourers in the tower. He asked me had I been to Madrid, where the traffic was tremendous, passing, he said, like a flight of parrots?

The smithy was roofed with boughs of trees. The floor was of earth and cobbles. I smelled frying, and in time the woman brought me a fine plate of eggs fried in oil, and gave me a round of bread as hard as a rock and some water in a tin. We sat talking.

A carter came in. A man whitened with dust, and with curly black hair tumbled in bushes over his eyes, which bloomed wildly through them. He called hoarsely for brandy, and his voice was garlic and crumbled like earth as though speaking were too much for it. He wore corduroy, and leather, brass-studded facing to his trousers. He sat down on the floor and stared at me, biting bits off his whip. He could contain his curiosity no longer. He asked me, "Has the friend any gold or silver?"

I was mystified.

"Has he any gold or silver, the companion?" he asked again.

"Money?" I ventured.

"I thought the friend might have brought some gold with him," said the carter, watching my face.

"Ah," said the smith, "what he means is, have you any contraband? He thinks you are a Portuguese smuggler, and that you have smuggled gold earrings and ornaments across the frontier, which is so near."

The smith explained all about me, but the carter was not convinced.

"Many people come over the border at night—it is not too far—and bring gold and silver," he said doubtfully.

"Yes," said the smith, and explained again what I did, but the carter only glared, and said it struck him as fantastic that a man should travel from his own country and on foot from Badajoz and not bring contraband. All the Portuguese brought contraband.

We talked and argued till nearly midnight. Then the smith went out with the carter, and left his wife and me sitting on the doorstep.

A taut, clear wind was stretched across the darkness, and the stars were scattered from horizon to horizon, like the night fires of a myriad shepherd camps on an immense plain. Fires like a multitude of jewels, and when one raised one's arms to the heavens the stars shone like rings upon the fingers. One had the sense of omnipotence and of the incalculable riches of the heart, and again the sense of blackest loneliness. The tower was crowned like a king with a diadem of stars.

The woman sat at the door. She was pretty and tired. Her voice was slow and weary. Again and again she sighed, "Ay! Ay!"

"Are you married?" she asked.

"Yes," I said.

"Have you any children?"

"No."

"Ay. No children either. No children. How lonely life is without children. Seven years I have been married and I have no children," she said blankly. "Ay! And your wife is alone? Ay! Poor creature, to be alone. And you wander alone? Like the shepherds who never see their families. What a life for them. Ay, poor creatures. And is your wife older than you? I am older than my husband. I am two years older. It is better for the woman to be older. Ay, it is better, much better. Ay de mi! It is better, because thus there is more confidence in the house," she said. "Ay de mi! I travelled twenty miles to-day on a donkey to the market and I am tired out. It is wonderful to go to the city."

Her husband came back with two big sacks of straw. "Antonio," she said, "he is married and he has no children either." She looked blankly at him like a pretty cow.

"I am sorry," he said to me. "God has given us no children either," he said.

He then presented me with two sacks of straw. "I am sorry to have to ask you to sleep here, but we have no bed," he said. We laid the sacks on the floor. He turned out his two greyhounds and bolted the door.

An old man appeared tottering with a stick at the inner door and walked across to what was evidently a bedroom on the opposite side of the smithy. He looked like the smith's father. The smith and his wife and two younger brothers followed him in, shut the door, and left me in darkness, with polite "good-nights," to make the best of a bad job on the sacks, having previously covered me with two vivid red and yellow mule blankets which smelled strongly of their owners. I slept under a boarded-up window near the door. The night was very cold. My limbs stiffened quickly and every turn was agony.

I dozed for a while, but the smithy and its surroundings, which had been so quiet a few hours before, now became as lively as the tuning-up of an orchestra. A flock of sheep, their bells babbling loudly, were penned at the back of the smithy; and near-by was a pen of goats, with bells too, but on a higher, shriller note. The bells of yoked oxen nodded tolling by the tower. Country dogs began barking like artillery, or solitarily howling; and the smith's greyhounds spent hours jumping up at the door and sniffling and whining around. Little pittering ballets of mice ran about the thatch and the benches tearing up paper—the heavens rending like calico—and once or twice the creatures chased across me as though I were nothing but a mountain range on the floor. To add to this minute uproar and dancing, the peacock gouged the air with his twisty cry. I lay musing. The floor had begun to make itself felt through the sack, and a host of insects advanced from the straw and took possession of me like Lilliputians.

At four o'clock I was awakened most dramatically out of my stupor by one of the greyhounds, which, in fury and despair, had leaped at the boarded window above my head, burst the boards in, and landed plumb on top of me. In the confusion the beast became entangled with my legs, and though I kicked him savagely and sent him away yelping, he insisted on coming back and licking my face. He then curled himself up on my feet and slept. He kept me warm. At five o'clock the bedroom latch clicked up and out stepped the smith. Obviously he had slept in all his clothes.

"And how did he sleep, the companion?" asked he.

"Beautifully," I said.

He opened the door and let in a freezing, dawnless wind, lit the forge fire, and began to hammer out a ploughshare. Four wild, unshaven men with tousled hair and bloodshot eyes rushed in and called for brandy. They had slept in the tower.

"More!" they cried.

They drank four glasses each, and then ran for their lives down the road to the team they had let wander on its own.

Labourers came in and brought ploughshares and pieces of wheel to be mended. The smith and his brother fell to the clang-cling tap of the anvil. The little hovel was showered with sparks and raftered with blows. The woman did not appear. There was no talk of food. The sun was cast into the sky, but the wind was steel cold. The plains were as pale as frost lain to the blue mountains from which, the night before, I had struggled. I saw the buildings and the tower, cold, tarnished blocks of stone.

After a couple of hours a stout, unshaven fellow, a bailiff, for he was not dressed in the peasant leather and corduroy, came to have his horse shod. He was a greasy, yellow man, with a face like a football, almost featureless, and he wandered about complaining about prices, weather, women, horses, everything, with a stained stump of cigarette stuck to his loose lower lip, and his hat planted on the back of his head. The young smith took no notice of him, but sent hard swinging blows arching down upon the anvil. The place rang like a belfry.

A boy brought a bullock to be shod, for the bullocks are yoked for drawing big loads. The beast was put into a kind of stocks outside the smithy, roped down by the horns, and lifted bodily almost off the ground by two straps under its belly, and with its feet trussed by ropes. Two small half-moons of steel were nailed to its hoofs.

Then the woman came out and boiled me a couple of eggs and some coffee, and charged me only two reales—about fourpence—for my food and lodging. I made long speeches and protestations of farewell and, looking up at my enemy the sun, wondered if I could get to Caceres before he conquered that country of rock and pink furrows and besieged the town itself.

(1928, 1988)

FROM

The Spanish Temper

CHAPTER 1

I make these notes during those two hours of impatience which begin in the early morning when the electric train clatters out of Biarritz Ville. One is hungry and queasy, one has slept badly and begins smoking nervously and too soon. In the corridor no one wants to talk after this night. Women are patching up their faces, combing their hair, men stand outside rubbing the night's growth of beard. The lavatory smells. One watches the long shadows of the rising sun in the pines; one sees the dust, the dewy greenness, the dry, heavily tiled houses, the fruitful green of a kind climate, a candid sky, and the sedate life. Yesterday's sun is still warm in these villa towns of terracotta. Here one would be glad to have a doll's house and count one's pension and rentes thirty times a day like a Frenchman and rest one's nervous northern mind in conversation consisting so largely of abstract nouns, to parcel out one's sous, one's pleasures and permissions.

But the prolonged sight of France annoys; one is impatient for the drama of the frontier and for the violent contrasts, the discontent and indifference of Spain. One is anxious to fill out that famous text of Galdós, so often quoted from the Episodios Nacionales: "O Spain, how thou art the same into whatsoever part of thy history one may look! And there is no disguise to cover thee, no mask to hide thy face, no fard to disfigure thee, for wherever thou appearest, thou art recognized at once from a hundred miles away, one half of thy face—fiesta; and the other misery; one hand bearing laurels and the other scratching thy leprous sores."

To know what we are up against we ought to go to Spain by aeroplane and fly to the centre of it. Beneath us England is packed with little houses, if the earth is visible at all through the haze; France lies clearly like green linoleum broken into a small busy pattern, a place of thriving little fields; but cross the dark blot of the Pyrenees, and Spain is reddish brown, yellow, and black, like some dusty bull restive in the rock and the sand and (we would guess) uninhabited. The river-beds are wide and bleached and dry. After Switzerland this is the highest country in Europe. The centre is a tableland torn open by gorges, and on the table the mountain ranges are spaciously disposed. There is little green, except on the seaboard; or rather the green is the dark gloss of ilex, olive, and pine, which from the height at which we are flying appear in lake-like and purple blobs. For the most part we are looking down at steppe which is iced in the long winter and cindery like a furnace floor in the short summer. Fortified desert—and yet the animal image returns again and again in this metalled and rocky scene, for occasionally some peak will give a sudden upward thrust, like the twist of a bull's horns, at the wings of the plane. Flying over Spain, we wonder at the torture that time had put upon the earth's crust and how human beings can live there. In Soria, the terrible province, below the wicked mountains of Aragón I remember picking up an old woman who had fallen off her donkey and carrying her to the side of the road and wiping the blood off her nose. She was a figure carved in wood, as light as a husk. It was like having starvation in one's hands.

But it is better, I think, to go the slow way to Spain and to feel the break with Europe at the land frontiers. It is true that at Irún one is not in Spain but in the Basque provinces, among people of mysterious race and language who are an anomaly in Europe; and that, at the other end of the Pyrenees, one is in Catalonia, where the people are really Provençal, speak their own tongue, and scornfully alter the Spanish proverb: "Africa begins at the Pyrenees," into "Africa begins at the Ebro." But the stamp of Spain is on these provinces and the Spanish stain runs over the frontiers. One finds it in Montpellier; on the Atlantic side it reaches into Biarritz, Saint-Jean-de-Luz, and Bayonne. And in these towns one meets something profoundly and disturbingly Spanish, which goes down to the roots of the Spanish nature: one meets the exiles. For, long before the Europe of the 1930's or the Russia of the early nineteenth century, Spain is the great producer of exiles, a country unable to tolerate its own people. The Moors, the Jews, the Protestants, the reformers—out with them; and out, at different periods, with the liberals, the atheists, the priests, the kings, the presidents, the generals, the socialists, the anarchists, fascists, and communists; out with the Right, out with the Left, out with every government. The fact recalls that cruel roar of abuse that goes up in the ring when the bullfighter misses a trick; out with him. Hendaye and Bayonne are there to remind us that before the dictatorships and police states and witch-hunters of contemporary history, Spain has been imperial in the trade of producing exiles. And the exiles go out over the bridge at Hendaye into France, the country that has tolerated all, and at the windows of the French hotel the new exile stands, looking across the bight of sea at the gloomy belfries of his native country, hears their harsh bells across the water, and hates the France which has given him sanctuary. He is proud of his hatred, sinks into fatalism, apathy, intrigue, quarrels with all the other exiles, and says with pride: "We are the impossible people."

Hendaye: the train dies in the customs. One gets a whiff of Spanish impossibility here. A young Spaniard is at the carriage window talking to a friend who is on the platform. The friend is not allowed on the platform; what mightn't he be smuggling? The gendarme tells him to go. The Spaniard notes this and says what he has to say to his friend. It is a simple matter.

"If you go over to see them on Wednesday tell them I have arrived and will come at the end of the week." But if a bossy French gendarme thinks that is how a Spaniard proceeds, he is wrong. The simple idea comes out in this fashion:

"Suppose you see them, tell them I am here, but if not, not; you may not actually see them, but talk to them, on the telephone perhaps, or send a message by someone else and if not on Wednesday, well then Tuesday or Monday, if you have the car you could run over and choose your day and say you saw me, you met me on the station, and I said, if you had some means of sending them a message or you saw them, that I might come over, on Friday, say, or Saturday at the end of the week, say Sunday. Or not. If I come there I come, but if not, we shall see, so that supposing you see them ..." Two Spaniards can keep up this kind of thing for an hour; one has only to read their newspapers to see they are wrapped in a cocoon of prolixity. The French gendarme repeats that the Spaniard must leave. The Spaniard on the platform turns his whole body, not merely his head, and looks without rancour at the gendarme. The Spaniard is considering a most difficult notion—the existence of a personality other than his own. He turns back, for he has failed to be aware of anything more than a blur of opposition. It is not resented. Simply, he is incapable of doing more than one thing at a time. Turning to the speaker in the train, he goes over the same idea from his point of view, in the same detail, adding personal provisos and subclauses, until a kind of impenetrable web has been woven round both parties. They are aware of nothing but their individual selves, and the very detail of their talk is a method of defeating any awareness of each other. They are lost in the sound of their own humming, monotonous egos and only a bullet could wake them out of it. Spanish prolixity, the passion for self-perpetuating detail, is noticeable even in some of their considerable writers—in the novels of Galdós, for example: in the passage I have quoted there are three images to describe "disguise"—and it creates a soft impenetrable world of its own. Yet they have a laconic language, the third-person form of address is abrupt and economical, their poetry even at its most decorative is compressed in its phrases and cut down to the lapidary and proverbial, and they can be as reserved and silent as the English; and yet when, in their habit of going to extremes, they settle down to talk, one feels one is watching someone knitting, so fine is the detail, so repetitious the method. The fact is that they are people of excess: excessive in silence and reserve, excessive in speech when they suddenly fly into it. It is absurd of course to generalize about a nation from the sight of two people on a railway platform; but we are travellers—let us correct one generalization by adding a great many more. There will be time to reflect on the variety of human nature, and the sameness of its types, afterwards. Let us consider the other Spaniards on the train.

It was easy to pick them out from the French when they got on the train in Paris; not quite so easy to pick them out from the Italians. The Spanish men were better dressed than the other Latins, and this was true of all classes. Their clothes fitted them at the waist and the shoulders, they carried themselves with reserve and dignity. Their gestures were restrained, their farewells were quiet and manly, they did not talk much and what they said was dry, composed, and indifferent. They behaved with ease as people who live by custom do; and they gave an impression of an aristocratic detachment. This is true of all classes from the rich to the poor, who have the same speech and the same manners. There are no class accents in Spain worth mentioning; there are only the regional variants of speech. This man is an Andalusian, this a Gallego; you can only guess his class from his clothes. One is markedly among gentlemen, and even the "señorito," the bouncing little mister, falls back on that when he has exhausted his tricks. The word "gentleman" is not altogether complimentary, for it implies a continual conscious restraint on part of the human personality, and it carries a narrow connotation of class. In this narrow sense a Spaniard cannot be a "gentleman," for though he has a sense of fitness in his quiescent mood, he is unrestrained when he wakes up. His conduct is ruled by his personal pride, not by his category; and it is natural for him to be proud. His pride may be a nuisance, but it fits him and it cannot be removed. He is, he has always been, a hidalgo—*a hijo de algo*—a person of some consideration. And upon this consideration, however impalpable it may be, the very beggar in the streets reposes. A point not to forget is that in the sixteenth and seventeenth centuries the Spaniards were the master-race of the world, the founders of the first great empire to succeed the Roman Empire, more permanent in their conquest and administration than the French, who followed them, successful where the Germans have never yet succeeded, the true predecessors of the British empire-makers of the eighteenth and nineteenth centuries. The Spaniards in the train had the simplicity of people who had once had the imperial role. One could suppose them to be looking back on it with philosophical resignation. The place of those who have ceased to rule is to teach.

There was no conceit or vanity in these travellers. The nervous pushing bustle of the European was not in them. The quick vanity and sharp-mindedness of the French, their speed in isolating and abstracting a problem, were not there. Nor were there the naïve vivacity and affectability which electrify the agreeable Italians. These races care to attract or please continuously; the Spaniard cares very little and leaves to us to discover him. He gives us time to breathe by his very negligence. "*Nada*—nothing," he says restfully before every subject that is broached.

They stood in the corridor of the train and they gazed at the fields of France. These fields are richer and better cultivated than a good deal—though not all—of the Spanish land. The Spaniard does not deny this, though he will think of the province of olives in Jaén, the vega of Granada, the vines of Rioja and Valdepeñas, and the long rich cultivations of Valencia and say, with that exaggeration which is natural to local pride, that these are "the richest places in the whole world"; and about Valencia he will be right. But Spain on the whole is a poor country, and he does not deny it. He is simply not interested in what is outside of Spain; because he has no feeling for the foreign thing and even regards its existence as inimical and an affront. He turns his back. His lack of curiosity amounts to a religion.

When I first crossed the frontier at Irún nearly thirty years ago, I remember listening to a declamation by a Spaniard against his own country. At the time I thought the protest was a sign of some specific political unrest, but I have heard that speech dozens of times since. Again and again: "It is one of the evils of Spain. We are decadent, priest-ridden, backward, barbarous, corrupt, ungovernable," etc., etc. Spain is either hell or heaven, a place for fury or ecstasy. Like Russians in the nineteenth century, the Spaniards are in the habit of breaking into denunciations of their country, and between 1898 and 1936 these denunciations culminated in a puritan renaissance. There had been two savage civil wars in that century and, among intellectuals, these wars presented themselves as a conflict between reactionary Catholicism and liberal Catholicism, between Africa and Europe, tradition and progress. In the writings of Ganivet, in Ortega y Gasset, Unamuno, the early Azorín, in Maeztu, in Ayala and Baroja—a brilliant school which has had no successors and which was contemporary with the effective efforts of Giner de los Ríos to create an educated minority—the examination of the Spanish sickness was made without rhetoric. Wherever one finds a superior mind in Spain it is certain to have been formed by this tragic generation, many of whom died of broken hearts in the Civil War, were executed, or are in exile. Possibly some of these train travellers have been influenced by them, possibly they are hostile or indifferent; if we are to find some common ground on which they stand we shall have to look beyond the accidents of opinion. That common ground is not their nationality.

For the Spaniards are not Spaniards first, if they are Spaniards in the end. The peninsula is a piece of rocky geography. It is the subject of Spanish rhetoric, the occasion for their talk about Spanishness, for chauvinism and rebellion—and they know from experience in every generation how those things end: they end in *nada*, nothing, resignation. The ground these travellers rest their lives on is something smaller than Spain. They are rooted in their region, even nowadays, after the Civil War, which has mixed up the population and broken so many ardently maintained barriers. They are Basques, Catalans, Galicians, Castilians, Andalusians, Valencians, Murcians, and so on, before they are Spaniards; and before they are men of these regions they are men of some town or village; and in that place, small or large, they think perfection lies—even the self-castigating people of Murcia, who say of themselves: "Between earth and sky nothing good in Murcia." One thinks of that little play of the Quintero brothers called *The Lady from Alfaqueque*. A lady in this lost little Andalusian town, who was so in love with it that she could be cajoled and swindled into any folly by anyone who said he came from that place. I remember a woman in Madrid who had spent the last ten years in political exile saying: "We had a much better life abroad when we were in exile, but I could never forget the water of Madrid and the craving for the taste of it became a torture."

This provinciality of the Spaniard is his true ground and passion. And with it runs a psychological parallel. His town is not like any other town. It is the only town. And he too is not like any other human being; he is indeed the only human being. If he is brought to the test, there is only himself in the world, himself and, at the other extreme, the Universe. Nothing between man and the Universe. For ourselves, the Westerners, there is something else besides man and the ultimate, or universal; there is civilization, or what Spaniards call despairingly "ambiente"; and it is their continual argument that nothing can be done in Spain because of this "lack of *ambiente*" or lack of a favourable atmosphere; how can anything as mundane as a "favourable atmosphere" exist where people do not feel related to each other, but only to some remote personal extremity. The pious belong to God, not even to the city of God, but to some deeply felt invisible figure; the impious to some individual vision. In the end they are anarchists.

—

Irún. Holiday-makers on the French side of the river that divides the two sides of the Basque country watched the fighting begin in the Civil War here and saw men swim the river to safety. The town of Irún is famous in the history of Pyrenean smuggling. There have been two traditional kinds of smuggling on this frontier: the mule loaded with tobacco coming over the mountain paths at night, and the smuggling organized by high-up officials from Madrid, which is part of the bribery system that never dies in Spain. It is described in the Galdós novel *La de Bringas*. In all classes the personal approach through "influence" is preferred to the direct one; without "influence" one cannot "get in." A foreign official told me that after many years living in Spain he had come to the conclusion that there are two kinds of Spaniards: those who have "influence" and those too poor to have any; for the former, life is "normal," for the latter it is hell. The pursuit of "influence" is partly due to economic causes. In poor countries a job of some slight importance is a phenomenon and attracts a court of parasites. The fortunate slave at the desk is besieged by a crowd of less fortunate slaves; the fortunate slave himself is the unfortunate slave of one more fortunate. Like the Russian bureaucracy in Gogol's time, the Spanish is a huge collection of poor men. One has only to buy a motor-car or make a contract to be surrounded by people consumed by the anxiety to "facilitate" the deal, register the papers, put the thing through with the right officials, for a small commission. The affair would be lost in the ordinary and proper channels. Weeks and months would go by and nothing would happen. Fatal to take the normal course; indispensable to have an introduction in the right quarter. Watch the fortunate Spaniard at the railway office. Discreetly he inquires about a ticket, does not boldly ask for it. A significant rubbing together of thumb and forefinger takes place, a furtive flicker comes into the eyes. A little personal deal is starting: unfortunate Spaniards without "influence" will not get the seat, but he will. It is an unjust system, but one unjust flea has other unjust fleas on his back; the method introduces elaboration, sociability, a sea of acquaintance, into ordinary action: "I will give you a card to my uncle, who will arrange everything." Everyone in Spain, down to the extremely poor, to whom so little is possible, is waiting for someone else, for a "combination," or arrangement, of some kind, and since time is no object, they make a lot of friends. If time is an object, if it is a matter of life and death, then a black figure which all Spaniards understand, rises up and interposes her immovable hand—the great croupier, Fate. "*Ay, señor, que triste es la vida.*"

The railway station at Irún is as shabby as it was thirty years ago. The place is glum, thinly painted, and grubby. The eye notices how many ordinary things—things like pipes, trolleys, door handles—are broken. The grass grows out of the rusting tracks, the decaying old-fashioned coaches and wagons rot in the sidings, the woodwork exposed to a destructive climate. The railways were half ruined by the Civil War, but, except for the electric trains of the Basque provinces, they were always shabby and went from bad to worse as one travelled southwards or got off the main lines. After France this material deterioration is sudden except in one respect; in the last two years the Spaniards have built a new train, called the Talgo, which runs three days a week to Madrid and has shortened the thirteen-hour journey across Castile by two or three hours. This Talgo is a luxury, Pullman train, low in build like the London tube coaches, and each coach has a concertina-like section in the middle which enables it to bend at the alarming mountain curves in the Basque mountains. Its motion is, however, violent. One cracks one's head, or bruises one's stomach against the handrails; but it is a change from the slow, dusty, bumping caravan of coaches that crawl to Madrid on other days of the week. Spanish locomotives are always breaking down. There is still not a complete double track from the frontier to Madrid, or from Madrid to Seville.

Nothing else has changed at Irún. One has heard Spanish garrulity; now one meets for the first time Spanish silence, disdain and reserve on its own soil. Those superb Spanish customs officers, young, handsome, wearing the tropical uniforms of naval officers, stroll up and down in a quiet ecstasy of satisfaction, talking and aristocratically ignoring the crowd. Their leisure is lovely to gaze at. The inferior officers who examine your luggage wearing white gloves—it is possible to refuse examination until the gloves are put on, but I have never seen a Spanish customs official without them—are poor devils and they get to work suspiciously and tragically. They fumble with listless dignity in the midst of some private wretchedness. The tragedy is the habit of work, perhaps. They have the melancholy of people who go through this monotonous life with nothing on their minds, and not very much—at the present cost of living—in their stomachs. They look as though they are thinking of some other world, and possibly about death. More likely, until something dramatic happens, they are extinct. Our suitcases might be coffins.

Sombreness is so much the dominant aspect of these people that one is puzzled to know how the notion of a romantic and coloured Spain has come about.

What shall we declare at the customs? Almost everything will be opprobrious to them. We are English—and we have Gibraltar. We defeated the Germans and Italians; the Franco government supported them actively, and has in a large number of ways copied their regime. We are not Christians. By that the official means we are not Roman Catholics; if you are Protestant you are not a Christian. You are, for him and historically speaking, a Moor or a Jew. Or if we are Roman Catholics, Spanish Catholics will be quick to point out improprieties in our Catholicism. And then suppose you are on the Right politically, that will not help you. Are you a Carlist from Navarre, a descendant of those who supported the pretender to the Spanish throne in the two civil wars of the nineteenth century and who professed feudalism in politics and the ultramontane in religion? Or are you a monarchist, an old conservative, a clerical, a supporter of the Jesuits or the Army; are you for the Church without the Jesuits, or for Franco's Falange, which Franco himself does not much care for or, at any rate, plays down so that he can keep his balance between them, the higher Army officers, and the bishops? The Pope can be left out of it; the Spanish Catholics have always treated as equals with the Italian Pope. Or do you declare you are on the Left? Well, privately the customs officer is on the Left, or half his relations are. If you are on the Left you are a Red. But what kind of Red? Are you an old liberal republican, liberal monarchist, liberal anticlerical? One of several kinds of socialist? Which kind of anarchist? Which kind of Communist—Trotskyite, Titoist, Leninist, Stalinist? Though against the Church, are you a non-practising Catholic? A mystic? An atheist, a new atheist? The Spaniards are not allowed by government decree to discuss Party politics; there is only one Party. They do, of course, discuss them, but without much energy: that energy was exhausted in the Civil War, but the political look burns in the sad eye, a spark inviting to be blown on. And we have not exhausted the parties: for where do you stand on Basque and Catalan autonomy? Are you a centralist or a federalist?

These silent questions are rhetorical, for, as I say, no political matters may be publicly discussed in Spain today. There is only one Party, General Franco is the conductor of a fractious political monologue. So exhausted is the nation by the Civil War that people have little desire to talk about politics. They have fallen back on a few jokes. And suppose that, hoping to curry favour, you declared that you were in favour of the state of vertical syndicates, the military conquest of Gibraltar and Portugal, the renewal of the Spanish Empire, the ecclesiastical control of all ideas, and a return to the glories of Fernando and Isabella, there would be an appalled suspicious silence. People would step back a yard or two from you and say: "Yes, yes, of course," and leave you firmly alone in your abnormal orthodoxy. For you would have declared something no Spaniard can possibly think: that the Spanish government is good.

But one does not make any of the foregoing declarations. One declares simply that, being a foreigner, one is inevitably the enemy; occasionally, in remote places, I have had showers of stones thrown at me when I walked into a village. I have been asked also whether I was a Portuguese jewel-smuggler in a place outside Badajoz. And, crossing the Tagus once, whether I was a Frenchman "making plans"—the tradition of the Napoleonic invasion still alive, handed down from father to son for a hundred and fifty years. And many times if I was a Christian, suggesting not that I was an atheist, but a Moor or a Jew. A Protestant is not a *"cristiano."*

I do not mean that enmity means open hostility; one meets that open, suspicious antagonism in France and Italy, but not in Spain, where manly welcome and maternal kindness, simple and generous, are always given to the traveller without desire for reward or wish to exploit. The poorer and simpler the people, the more sincere the welcome. In some lonely inn, a venta of Extremadura, where there are never beds to sleep in, but men sleep on the floor in the outer stables, while their mules and donkeys sleep inside, just as they did in the time of Cervantes, they will ask you if you have brought your sack and your straw, and if you have not brought them, they will get them for you. The suspicion common in industrial society, the rudeness of prosperous people, have not touched the Spaniards; one is treated like a noble among nobles. There is never avarice. One sits before the hearth, the brushwood blazes up, the iron pan splutters on the fire, and conversation goes on as it has always gone on. The enmity I speak of is part historical inheritance and part an unbridgeable difference of type. A very large number of the beliefs of people brought up in modern, urban, industrial civilization make no contact even with the urban Spaniard. As for the historical inheritance, an Englishman thinks of the life-and-death struggle with Spain in the Elizabethan age. Spain threatened our life as a nation, our Protestant faith, the idea of freedom on which, for economic and spiritual reasons, our life during the last four hundred years has prospered. A Dutchman would make the same reflection. To Protestants, Spain was what Protestants have hated most: the totalitarian enemy. To Spanish Catholics, the Protestant attack upon the Church was their supreme stimulus to action in the Counter-Reformation. They were the first people in Europe to put into practice ideals which liberal societies have always resisted: the ferocious doctrine of racial purity or *"limpieza,"* revived by the Nazis; the paralysing idea of ideological rightness, the party line, supervised by the Inquisition, which, for all the excuses that are made on its behalf, remains the notorious model of contemporary persecution in Russia and in America. It was a Spaniard who founded the first order of Commissars in Europe, the Society of Jesus. Time has softened, abolished, or transformed these things in Spain; but they were, in spite, models which the enemies of liberal civilization have copied. The Spanish mind invented them and made them intolerably powerful. They represent something which is permanent, still potential, if not always powerful in Spanish life. One may be a foreign Catholic and still be on one's guard against them; many great Spaniards have fought their country's tendency and suffered from its authoritarianism.

Spanish fanaticism has sown fanaticism on the other side of its frontiers.

It has its comedies. How many foreigners, especially the English-speaking countries, are Ruskinians about Spain. In his autobiography *Et Præterita*, Ruskin describes his own ludicrous meeting with the daughters of his father's Spanish partner in the sherry trade, the Domecqs. He behaved with all the gaucheness and absurdity of a Protestant youth.

". . . my own shyness and unpresentableness were further stiffened, or rather sanded by a patriotic and Protestant conceit, which was tempered neither by politeness nor sympathy. . . . I endeavoured to entertain my Spanish-born, Paris-bred and Catholic-hearted mistress with my views upon the subjects of the Spanish Armada, the Battle of Waterloo and the doctrine of Transubstantiation."

The young ladies from Jérez de la Frontera would have only noticed his "shyness": shyness is incomprehensible to anyone born in Spain.

On their side, the Spaniards might reply, and many have: We are not an industrialized society, but look at the sickness of industrial man! We have little social conscience, but look at the self-mutilation of countries that have it. If we are mediæval, the latest communities, and, most of all, the Communists, indicate a return to a mediæval conception of society. Whom would you sooner have, the Commissars or the Jesuits? We have digested all that long ago. Spanish scepticism is inseparable from Spanish faith, and though we have a large population of illiterate serfs, we have not a population of industrial slaves. We present to you a people who have rejected the modern world and have preserved freedoms that you have lost. We have preserved personality.

This silent dialogue in the Customs House is a dialogue of half-truths. It indicates only one thing: we have already been infected by the Spanish compulsion to see things in black and white. We are entering the country of "*todo o nada*"—all or nothing.

And change is slow. In the Customs House at Irún there is still that finger-marked hole in the station wall through which you push your passport; still that thin, sallow-faced man with the sick eyes, the shrunken chest, the poor bureaucrat's jacket, writing slowly in the large useless book, in silence. Thirty, twenty, fifteen, two years ago he was there. He wears a black shirt now, a dirty white shirt no longer—that is the only difference. He sits like a prisoner. His hands can only do one thing at a time. It is impossible for him to write in his book, blot his paper, and hand you your passport in a single continuous action. He certainly cannot hold passport in one hand and pen in the other. Each action is separate and he does not speak.

The Talgo fills up at San Sebastián with rich Madrid people returning from their summer holidays. There are dressed-up children in the care of nurses. Everyone very well dressed. In the whole journey, little conversation. A Brazilian like a little dragonfly tries to make people talk by extravagant South American means. He stands up in the passageway, but has few words of Spanish and only a phrase or two of atrocious French. So he suddenly begins snapping his thumbs above his head and dancing.

"Carmen Miranda," he sings out.

People turn their heads.

"Spain," he says. "Dance."

"Ta rara! Tarra," he sings dramatically.

People turn away and look understandingly at one another. "Brazilian," they say. Two distinguished Spanish ladies resume reading their two books on Court Life in the Reign of Louis XIV.

"Spain," sings out the Brazilian. "Bullfights." He begins to play an imaginary bull. The performance is a failure. This is the most decorous train in Europe. He sits down behind me and taps me on the shoulder.

"Commercial traveller?" he says.

"Almost," I say. "Journalist."

"Me, the same. Novelist. Forty-seven novels. How many?"

"Three or four," I say.

"Come and see me at the Ritz." (He was unknown at the Ritz.)

This happy little waterfly had a demure wife who laughed quietly into her handkerchief all the time, in her pleasure with this exquisite husband. But the middle-class Spaniards—no. ("One does not know what class of person," etc., etc.) Anyway, it was impossible to talk to him, but one could have sung, I suppose.

The train drops through the Basque provinces into the province of Álava. It is Welsh-looking country of grey hills, glossy woods, and sparkling, brawling brown trout streams. The haycocks are small in the steep fields, the villages are neat and are packed round their churches. One sees the pelota court, and sometimes the game is played by the church wall. Pelota is a fast game, and the great players are a delight to watch as they hit the white ball and send it in a lovely long flight and with an entrancing snap to the wall. It is a game that brings out the character of the players and, although the Basques are reserved in most things, they show their feelings of rage, disgust, resentment, and shame when they fail in a stroke. Their audience does the same. Sometimes an excited shout of praise comes from the spectators, often shouts of bitter mockery, which are answered by glares of hatred from the silent player. There is loud betting on the games. The bookmakers stand shouting the odds on the side of the court and throw their betting slips in balls to the audience. There is pandemonium, cigarette smoke, the beautiful leaping and running of the white-trousered players, the tremendous swing of the shoulders as the arm flies back for the full force of the stroke.

The Basques are the oldest settled race in Europe. They are locked in their language. Are they a pocket of the original Iberians caught in the mountains? No one knows. Their language is like the code of a secret society and has been very useful to them in smuggling. Racial generalizations are pleasant to make but they rarely fit the case. One would suppose, for example, that the French and the Spanish Basques are alike, but in fact the French Basques are a poor and backward race of peasants and fishermen; the Spanish Basques are prosperous and those in the cities are active, well off, and progressive in the material sense. To a northerner they are more "progressive" than the people of Barcelona. When we notice that deterioration at Irún, what we are really looking at is not the Basque provinces, but the negligent stain of bureaucratic Spain seeping up by the railway from Castile.

The traditional fanaticism of the Spanish Catholic is the expression of a people who are naturally prone to scepticism: they go from one extreme to the other. Spanish atheism is as violent and intolerant as Spanish piety. The Basques have a different character. Their Catholicism is solid in all classes and is not in the least fanatical. They have little religious superstition and have little regard—perhaps because they are poor in imagination and poetry—for the image-loving and decorative forms of Catholicism. Their religion is plain; their faith is immovable—*Qui dit Basque, dit Catholique*—and is married to the sense of tradition which rules them. In this they have the integration of primitive societies. That is to say their religion is racial and dispenses with both the aggressive and the mystical feeling of other kinds of Catholicism. In the Spanish Civil War the Basque Catholics fought for their autonomy beside the Republicans—the so-called "Reds," who were commonly anticlerical, when they were not irreligious—presumably because the Basques knew their religion could not be endangered. The Basque Christianity is closer to the Old Testament than to the New and is even a little Protestant in its plain, practical simplicity. The Basque novelist Pío Baroja, who speaks of himself as an anarchist and an atheist, goes as far as to question both the traditionalism and the religiosity of his people. He recalls the testimony of mediæval missionaries who found the Basques at that time completely pagan, and Ortega y Gasset has pointed out that in the Basque language there was no word for God. For this conception the Basques used a circumlocution: *el señor de lo alto*, the feudal lord higher up, the chief or the laird, a simple idea springing from their tribal organization and not from the religious imagination. The religious spirit of the Basques is exemplified by Saint Ignatius Loyola, the founder of the Jesuit order. Whatever may have been the visionary experiences of the saint, he thought of his mission in the practical terms of soldiery: the militant company obeying orders from someone "higher up." Elsewhere in Spain the Church has become separated from the people; in the Basque provinces it is united with them.

The Basques, like the Asturians and the people of Navarre, live in one of the satisfied areas of Spain—those coastal provinces of mild climate where the rainfall is regular and plentiful. They are either farmers on the family community system in which the property belongs to the family and the head of the family council decides on his successors among his children, or they are sharecroppers—and the success of this system lies in the liberal and reasonable spirit in which it has been worked. Yet every statement one makes about Spain has to be modified immediately. Navarre is a Basque province that has lost its language, and the Navarrese, shut up in their mountains, are in fact fanatical in religion and they are the main source of the ultramontane form of conservatism, called Carlism. Navarrese economy, too, is successful and prospers. But as the train travels south, the rainfall dwindles in Castile, the peasant farmer becomes poor; money, not crops, becomes the landowner's reward, the religious quarrel begins. We are among a different race of more dramatic, more egotistical, less reasonable men.

In the rest of Spain the Basque is thought of as insular, obstinate, reserved, and glum, a pedestrian and energetic fatalist, working in his fields, putting his steel-pointed goad into the oxen that plough his land, making the wines of Rioja and Bilbao, and smelting his iron ore; or he is thought of as a sardine fisherman and packer in those reeking little fishing towns of the coast where they stack the tins. These sea towns are clean, prim, dour places. There is a narrow gap between the headlands through which the Biscayan tide races into a scooped-out haven or lagoon—all harbours of the Bay of Biscay are like this, from Pasajes, near the frontier, to the mountain-bound harbours of Corunna. It is a coast that smells of Atlantic fish, the sky is billowy white and blue, or the soft sea rain comes out of it. Basques who can afford it drive out of the grey, warm, glum days towards Álava and Castile, to breathe dry air and feel the sun, which reigns over the rest of Spain like a visible and ferocious god. There the Basque in his dark blue beret, which sits square on his stolid forehead, is thought of as an oddity. His family is matriarchal. The breaking of the marriage bond is forbidden. Even the second marriages of widows or widowers is disliked. Rodney Gallop, in his scholarly book, *The Book of the Basques*, describes the wedding night of a widow. The mockery was kept up with the beating of tin cans, the ringing of bells, and blowing of horns until sunrise. This custom is called the *galarrotza* (night noise). It occurs, of course, in many peasant countries.

My own collection of Basques contains indeed one dour character: a man who ran a bar in France, one of the exiles. He was a municipal employee and fought against Franco in Bilbao. He was also obstinately determined to visit his family there and did so twice secretly. But money affairs cropped up. It was necessary to go to Bilbao openly. The matter proceeded in the usual manner of the peninsula. First his relatives used what "influence" they could find, working through the relatives of relatives. He was told to come. This was about five years ago and required courage, for at that time there were tens of thousands of political prisoners; but in addition to courage this man had the insurmountable Basque conscience. He fought (he told the authorities) because his conscience told him to do so; not necessarily for Basque autonomy, but simply because it was the duty of municipal employees to obey the lawful government. Such a conscience must have maddened and annoyed the Falange who had done just the opposite, but, for all their revengefulness and intolerance, the Spaniards recognize the man in their enemies, and when passions have fallen, maintain their dignity and seek for the modus vivendi in the same glance.

The other Basques I have known were Unamuno and Pío Baroja, the novelist. In Unamuno one saw the combativeness, the mischief and pugnacious humour of the Basques. A brief light of unforgettable charm, delicacy, and drollery touches their set faces. In Pío Baroja it is the same. I sat in his dark flat in Madrid and listened to the gentle, tired, clear voice of the very old man talking very much in the diffident, terse way of his books, watched the shy, sharp smile that never becomes a laugh, and the sly naïve manner.

"But who else painted your portrait, Don Pío?"

"Many people. Picasso, I believe, did one once."

"Picasso! Where is it?"

"Oh, I don't know. It may exist. Perhaps it got lost. It had no value."

As evasive as a peasant, but say anything against the Pope or the Jesuits and he is joking at once. I asked about the puritanical Archbishop of Seville.

"Never trust a Spanish archbishop when he behaves like an Englishman," Baroja says.

Baroja once signed the visitors' book in some place and where he was expected to add his profession, rank, or titles, wrote: A humble man and a tramp.

He sat at his plain oak table in an upright chair, in needy clothes and the same blue beret on his grey hair—it seemed to me—that he had worn twenty years ago when I first saw him. His eyes were pale blue, his face very white—one can imagine the baker's flour still on it, for he once ran a bakery with his brother. It is a sad sight, the old age of a writer who, in addition to the usual burdens, has to bear the affront of the Franco censorship, which refused to allow him to publish his book on the Civil War.

"They said it showed the Spanish character in a bad light. And that is true. We see now we are a nation of barbarians."

Baroja and Unamuno were broken by the Civil War. Baroja has fallen into melancholy. Unamuno, who came out on Franco's side as a good many liberals did, heard of the atrocities and rushed out into the streets of Salamanca screaming curses on Franco, the Falange, and his country, and went out of his mind.

Baroja is an exceptional Basque in his hostility to the Church and in his anarchism; he has lived chiefly in Madrid. But he is thoroughly Basque in his obstinacy and his tenacity and his droll humour. Unamuno had the same obstinacy. His book *Del Sentimiento Trágico de la Vida—The Tragic Sense of Life*—is one of the most important works in the last fifty years of Spanish literature. He was the outstanding figure in the movement towards Europeanization, which began after the loss of Cuba in 1898, and he was all the more important because he embodied the ambiguity of the Spanish attitude to the modern world. The Basques live in prosperous and liberal-minded community; the rhetorical exaggerations and the desuetude of the rest of Spain are alien to them. They are, in fact, "modern" to a degree of modernity which not even the Catalans have attained. All the more, therefore, was Unamuno conscious of the need of Europe, all the more of the price. His life became a battleground for the quarrel between Reason and Faith, between the European consciousness and the mediæval soul. *The Tragic Sense of Life* sets out the essence of a profound conflict in the Spanish mind on its opening page, where he describes the subject of his book: not man in the abstract, but "the man of flesh and bone, who is born, suffers and dies—who, above all, dies and who does not wish to die."

Unamuno's book is a search for the solution to the problem which cannot be solved: man's agonized desire to be assured of personal immortality. We cannot have this assurance, but out of the agony our soul must found its energy. With its pugnacious egoism, and its Quixotic quality, Unamuno's philosophy described the positive side of the Spanish spirit, and came closer to the positive spirit of the Spaniards in the Counter-Reformation than their reactionary successors have done. There was more than a touch of the Protestant preacher in Unamuno, and the great figures of the Counter-Reformation were, in fact, counter-protestors who had not yet dulled and hardened into an oligarchy. Unamuno's energy and truculence, his non-conformity before the Castilian mind and authority, were very Basque.

CHAPTER 5

In the mornings in Madrid we used to go to the Prado. The slow walk was like a swim through the sunlight, and it was a preparation for the intense life we should see there. The Spanish streets prepare one for the unabashed records of Spanish painting—a dwarf, an idiot, a deaf and dumb couple laughing, a pair of blind lovers, a beggar or two have their picaresque place in the unpreoccupied crowds. We used to go, for a moment and mainly to get out of the heat for a minute or two, into any church on our way, and we used to notice the difference of worship between Spanish and Italian custom. For whereas in Italy the churches were places for wandering in and camping in, places used by life, which continually flowed into them from outside, and God's familiar market places, the Spanish churches were used by people with a strong sense of purpose and *tenue*. It was on our way to the Prado that I saw an old man kneeling before the crucified Christ in one of the Jesuit churches, a figure splashed by blood specks and with raw wounds, gaping as they would upon the mortuary slab, the face torn by physical pain, the muscles and tendons stretched. One imagined that the sculptor must have copied a crucified model to be so inflexible an anatomist and that the thought of *imagining* the agony of Christ had been beyond him. Before this figure kneeled an old man, and tears ran down his cheeks like the real-seeming tears glazed on the cheeks of the Christ; and, as he prayed, the old man kissed and caressed the toes, the calves, the knees of the figure and held them also with his hands. What grief, what dread or longing the old man was thus transposing one could not know, but one saw how his prayer depended utterly upon the communication of the senses, that he worshipped carnally and conceived of his acquaintance with God as a physical thing. If he described his God, the description would be physical, and the nature of his God would be a minute copy of his own or, if not a copy, a detailed response in the man's own terms.

I am not an art critic, but since I live chiefly by the eye, I get more pleasure out of painting and sculpture than any other arts. I have a purely literary point of view; that is to say, when I see a picture I find myself turning it into writing about human nature, habits of mind, the delight of the senses—all that is meant to me by "the pride of life." As one looks at the paintings of the Spanish, sombre as so many of them are whether they are earthly or religious, one sees what a great volume of emotion these minutely watched figures contain. How closely the great Spanish painters watch, sometimes for every detail, always for the key dramatic detail, the clue to a character, the spring of action! The faces and the bodies are caught at the moment of movement from one state of mind or feeling to another. The painters are not copyists from a still model; they are readers of nature; their view of nature might be described as the view of creative criticism. At the first acquaintance, with Velásquez's portraits of the court of Philip IV, even with that enchanting picture of the naughty Princess, Las Meninas, or with the picture of those arrogant and stubborn dwarfs, one sees the infinitely patient copyist who never conveys more than the visual scene before him; but presently we observe he is a painter of light, a critic of reflections. We see that he has caught the trance of human watchfulness, as if he had caught a few hard grains of time itself. Life is something pinned down by light and time. He has frozen a moment, yet we shall feel that it is a moment at its extreme point: that is, on the point of becoming another moment. If he is the most minute observer in the world, notice how his subjects are caught, themselves also minutely watching the world, with all the concentration the hard human ego is capable of. This is what living is to the human animal: it is to look. To look is to be. We see in Velásquez, as in all the Spaniards, the marriage of mind and eye. No painting could be, in the northern sense, less suggestive of a life without other accoutrement than the body and the habit of the hour.

The sensibility, the pride, the sensuous weakness of the court of Philip IV, where the decadence put out its first flowers in Spanish life, before the fruit formed and rotted, are seen in the realism of Velásquez. In an earlier painter like Zurbarán, in Greco, even in Murillo, and finally in Goya, the same basic, psychological dramatic realism can be seen. We cannot doubt that thus life was, was seen and felt to be. And it is part of the genius of such exact penetration to horrify us with the tacit questions: What for? To what end? Behind such certainty is the certainty of death. The mad pride of the Duchess of Alba, her eccentric vanity! The homely foolishness of Charles IV, the total crookedness of Fernando VII! Goya caught the lowness of his world, its surrender of all style, its survival by a sort of ape-like impudence and by the shamelessness of Spanish vitality. The court did not object to these blistering portraits, but having no idea of themselves and no idea by which they lived, were grossly contented with the sight of their own likenesses.

Goya's savage anticlerical pictures are not now shown in the Prado, but they are well known. The satire of Goya is savage, but this distortion—like the very different distortions of El Greco—does not lessen his realism. This realism in Spaniards proceeds out of hot blood, not coolness. When Goya draws scenes of war, he feels the madness of action, its giddy and swooning movement, the natural boiling up of all human feeling towards crisis and excess, and it is in this state of mind that his eye becomes receptive to detail. Once again: psychological realism is not psychological analysis or speculation after the event, but the observation of the event in the tremor and heat of occurrence. Goya does not draw torture, rape, murder, hangings, the sadism of guerrilla warfare rhetorically, patriotically, or with a desire to teach, but he is as savage in his realism or his satire as the war itself. He is identified with it, and eventually he was driven out of his mind by acts which he could not forget. The nightmares themselves are horrible in their animality.

The terrifying quality of Goya's *Disasters of the War* springs, in part, from the comeliness and vanity of the human victims, from their complacency.

There are no standard figures, but a great gallery of diverse characters whose ruling passion is clear in their faces. Each one palpably lives in his senses and, in the moment of death, their horrified eyes see the loss of the body. Goya's realism marries fury, insanity, corruption, whatever the state or passion is, to the body; it gives body to the sadism, the venom, the thieving, the filthy-mindedness, the smugness, the appalled pity of massacre.

Goya lived in a revolutionary age and turned from the traditional obsessions of the Spanish, with their religion and their lordliness, to the life of the populace of Madrid. There were three cults of the people in his time; some members of the upper classes took pleasure in following popular fashions in dress and put on the exaggerated, bold finery of the dandy or majo. The Duchess of Alba's picture in the Prado shows her in the costume of the maja—the full yellow dress, the black mantilla. There was a taste for fantasy and vulgarity in behaviour, ornament and exhibitionism in speech. The celebrated Spanish oath Caramba is taken from the stage name of a singer of *tonadilla* or one-act comic opera popular at the time. Goya drew her portrait, too. Goya's picture of the royal family represents them as ordinary people without kingliness or pride. Maria Luisa looks like a washerwoman, Fernando like a lackey. The cult of the people also had its political aspect and derived from the welcome given by the liberal-minded to the ideas of the French Revolution, but here "the People" is one of those alien political abstractions which Spaniards always, in the end, reject. The Spanish populace rose in Goya's time—but against the Revolution and the invader. The emotion was primitive, chauvinist, and patriotic. It was spontaneous, brave, and wild. The men who are being shot down in Goya's *Dos de Mayo* are ordinary Spaniards off the street.

This popular spirit has always existed in Spain; it is the bottomless well of Spanish vitality and exuberance, so that where there is deadness and corruption in the higher levels of society, there is always this creative energy underneath. It shows itself in the vitality of the popular arts. The Spaniards have a genius for popular display: the bullfight, the religious procession, and the fiesta. They have a genius for dancing and for the popular song. In the past thirty years there has been a slight decline in the typical regional character of this popular culture, but it remains easily the strongest and most lively in Europe. Even the decline, which is due to industrialism and better communications from one region to another, is less dangerous than it might seem. Spanish vitality is so great that it can digest the most awkward extraneous elements. The Spaniards have a genius for adapting everything to their own life; their indolence, the obstinate, individual refusal to break easily with custom, has given them enormous, natural power of resistance.

The radio blares from every street corner, but it is not often blaring the last American songs and dance tunes. Almost always the tune is *flamenco*, or *cante hondo*, a song from a popular zarzuela or musical comedy, a Spanish march. Once one is across the frontier, one is aware of being outside of Europe musically. One hears a new cadence, haunting, monotonous, yet also of pronounced dramatic rhythm. It is the rhetoric of music, sometimes tragic and grave, sometimes swanking and feverish with a swirl of skirts in it, sometimes Oriental and gypsy-like, lyrical and sad. The ear catches the strange notes of the cadence at once—la, sol, fa, mi—in the singing voice or in the guitar.

After midnight in Madrid, when one has just finished dinner one goes off into those packed, narrow streets lying off the Puerta del Sol in the middle of the city. They are streets of small bars crowded with men roaring away at each other, drinking their small glasses of beer or wine, tearing shellfish to bits and scattering their refuse and the sugar-papers of their coffee on the floors. The walls are tiled and in gaudy colours. The head of a bull will hang there, or some bloody painting of a scene at the bullfight. Through the door at the back of the bar one makes one's way into a private room, tiled again, like a bathhouse, and furnished only with a table and a dozen chairs. There one can invite a guitarist and singers and listen to *cante flamenco*.

Less respectably, one can find some cellar in the same quarter, some thieves' kitchen which will probably be closed by the police in a week or two, and there one may hear *cante flamenco* and, even better, the true *cante hondo*, or deep song, brought up in the last thirty years from the south, and sung not for the traveller's special entertainment but, as it were, privately, for the singer's own consolation. For, despite its howling, it is also an intimate music, perhaps for a singer and a couple of friends only. It can be sung in a mere whisper. The dirty room, lit by one weak and naked electric-light bulb, is full of wretched, ill-looking men; the proprietor wanders round with a bottle of white wine in his hand filling up glasses. In one corner four men are sitting, with their heads close together, and one notices that one of them is strumming quietly on the table and another is murmuring to himself, occasionally glancing up at his friends, who gravely nod. The finger strumming increases and at last the murmurer breaks into one low word, singing it under the breath in the falsetto voice of the gypsies. "Ay," he sings. Or "Leli, Leli," prolonging the note like a drawn-out sigh, and when he stops, the strumming of the fingers becomes more rapid, building up emotion and tension and obsession, until at last the low voice cries out a few words that are like an exclamation suddenly coming from some unknown person in the dark. What are the words? They are difficult to understand because the gypsies and, indeed, the Andalusians, drop so many consonants from their words that the speech sounds like a mouthful of small pebbles rubbed against one another:

> *Cada vez que considero*
> *Que me tengo que mori*

the voice declaims:

> *"Whenever I remember that I must die—"*

wavering on its words and then suddenly ending; and the strumming begins again until the rapid climax of the song,

> *Tiendo la capa en el suelo*
> *Y me jarto de dormi*

> "I spread my cloak on the ground
> And fling myself to sleep."

The manners of the thieves' kitchen are correct and unmarred by familiarity. A yellow-haired and drunken prostitute may be annoying a man by rumpling his hair, but otherwise the dejected customers at three in the morning are sober. One night, in a place like this in the middle of Madrid, we sat next to one of these private artists who was murmuring away to his friends. When we nodded our admiration to the whispering singer, he sang a polite love song of delightful conceit to the lady in our party and asked afterwards for "the loan of a cigarette until next Thursday." He became obviously impatient of a gypsy singer and guitarist who had smelt us out. He objected, on the usual Spanish grounds, that the young singer—who also danced—was not keeping to the rigid requirements of his art, and was introducing unclassical extravagance and stunts in order to show off to foreigners. The criticism was audible. The gypsy, egged on by criticism, scornfully tried to surpass himself. He had a weak chest and was inclined to be wild and raucous on his top notes, but he was not bad. Finding himself still mocked by the quiet man in the corner, the gypsy decided to silence him by a crushing performance, which meant a display of whirling fury. He moved one or two chairs, to make room to dance in: the customers murmured at this move. They were prepared to put up with it and hold their hand. But when the gypsy started taking off his jacket—the supreme symbol of male respectability in Spain—there was that alarming and general shout of "¡Eso no!"—"None of that!"—from everyone in the room, and half the men stood up. The proprietor rushed out at him. The gypsy put back his jacket. He knew he had gone too far.

Performances of this kind, in which some players fasten themselves on the tourist and give their performance, are usually paid for with a bottle of brandy and a cigarette or two; or, in smarter surroundings when there is a special invitation, by money. One pays up and hopes for the best, but we had a large, quiet Yorkshireman in our party whose air of Saxon shyness concealed a deep knowledge of the Spanish vernacular and an obstinate respect for correct procedure. Our young gypsy made the error of asking the Yorkshireman a special fee because he was a professional artist giving an unusual performance, and when this was refused there was a characteristic row. It began on the doorstep of the cellar, continued in the street, trailed down to the middle of the Puerta del Sol. It was a hot night; the clock on the Ministry of the Interior coldly struck four, while the gypsy shouted, the Yorkshireman argued back. The gypsy called for witnesses. At four in the morning the recognized authority of the streets is the night watchmen. They came out one by one from their doorways like the Watch of Fielding's London, and with them the strange night population who sleep out in doorways or the streets. The gypsy stuck out his chest, produced his official papers. The crowd listened. A woman, a lottery-ticket seller, recommended going to the police station, and on the whole the crowd were against us, until the gypsy made a fatal mistake of overplaying his hand. From his papers he picked out some document.

"I am an artist," he cried. They nodded sympathetically.

"I was a soldier of Franco," he added, showing more papers. They stepped back from him at once.

"None of that," someone said politely.

Among the common people of Madrid one is not likely to get very far with being a soldier of Franco.

The dispute now left the chest-baring, chest-thumping, and paper-showing stage, to insults like:

"You are boring me. Go away."

"On the contrary, it is you who are boring me."

The quarrel trailed off to the police station, but within sight of it the gypsy gave in. It was not the time for face-saving. The gypsy said he had no wish to quarrel. The Yorkshireman said he loved the greatness of the Spanish nation. The gypsy said he loved the greatness of the English nation. A year later I was astonished to see my friends had engaged this gypsy to sing again. He had a young wife now. The gypsy was not at all surprised. Such rows are common in Spain.

"It is better," he said, "to begin a friendship with a little aversion."

His wife, a little round thing of sixteen, eight months pregnant and with pretty eyes as dark as linseed, sat with the dignity of a little duchess on her chair. She sang with the wit and grace of an angel one moment, and the next could let out the gutter howl of her race and the distorted vowels of her tongue, with the resonance of a hammer on the anvil. Strong, good-humoured and quick to catch the slightest allusion in talk, she had already acquired that matriarchal force, militancy, and content characteristic of Spanish women, and her young husband, ill from the grim night-life of the streets and bars, anxious and excitable, seemed superior to her only in his power of indifference.

As the singer of *cante flamenco* proceeds, his friends nod and wait for him to reach the few difficult ornamental notes of the little song, which has been sung entirely for this short crisis of virtuosity. It breaks suddenly, and then the voice flows cleverly away, to the murmurs of Olé, Olé, by his friends. After a long interval, in which all seem to be savouring the satisfaction the song has given them, one of the others takes his turn and so, in this low whispering, like musing aloud or like grief and sobs, they will pass their evenings.

Cante hondo or *cante flamenco* is not commonly heard in this quiet fashion. The Spaniards love noise, and the singing is usually done at the top of the voice, but the same collusive demeanour of the party will be observed. They listen, nodding, seeming to be waiting for some unknown, intimate moment; an audience will go on talking with indifference, at the beginning of a song, for they are interested only in the few bars that test the singer. They react to every syllable of that passage and when the singer has reached it, when the most tortured ornament the voice can utter is before him, they fall dead silent as they do at some high moment of the bullfight. The peculiarity of a *cante hondo* is that it is sung within "a compass which rarely exceeds the limits of a sixth, which is not composed solely of nine semitones" (I quote from Trend's translation of Falla's work on the subject) "as is the case with our tempered scale. By the employment of the enharmonic genus, there is a considerable increase in the number of tones which the singer can produce." Metrical feeling is often destroyed and one seems to be listening to a sudden, lyrical or passionate statement or exclamation, torn out of the heart of the singer.

Cante hondo is the name given to this kind of singing in its pure form. *Cante flamenco* is the modern popular name for it and covers its more florid variations. The word "*flamenco*" is a mysterious word, literally meaning Flemish, which has come to mean popular, vulgar, exuberant. A loud and free behaviour—for Spaniards usually comport themselves with gravity and reserve—is called "muy flamenco." The word is half abusive, half indulgent, and is thought to have come in when Charles V brought his Flemish court to Spain. The Spaniard, who has always derided foreigners and blamed all his misfortunes on them, thought of the Flemings as outlandish. *Flamenco* singing has been despised in the past and it has only become common all over Spain since Falla held a congress of *flamenco* singers in Granada in 1922, when he was exploring the history and growth of Spanish folk music.

What the world outside of Spain regards as "typically Spanish music" was fixed in the 1880's of the last century by *Carmen*, a manifestation of the romantic view of Spain fostered by Gautier and Mérimée and other French writers. It really has its roots in the eighteenth century. There is a good deal of street music and the barrel organ in it, but in fact *Carmen* has one or two indigenous Spanish things to say, as Trend points out. The Spanish idiom came out in the *zarzuelas* or musical comedies of the century; there are traces of it in the seventeenth century and there are motifs that have been traced back to the songs sung by the shepherds of Castile in the fifteenth century. The interesting thing is that one of the orchestral interludes from *Carmen* is really an Andalusian polo, and a polo is really *cante hondo*.

But *cante hondo* is not like the rest of Spanish folk music, which recalls the gay, gracious, tinkling folk songs of Russia, and indeed of all European countries. The words often amusingly convey a purely Spanish foible. *Cante hondo* is Andalusian, but it is not Andalusian folk music which has felt the influence of the Byzantine liturgy and of the Moors. *Cante hondo* is gypsy; it has a lot in common with Indian singing. It contains the melancholy, the fury, the lyrical and tragic feeling of that wandering race. Though it may be sung at some gypsy feast, with the old gypsy gripping the bars of his chair outside his cave dwelling, as he mouths his way towards the notes, the prolonged and tortured "a's" and "o's," the "l" turned into an "r," the effect is of soliloquy, an utterance out of loneliness, an utterance of tragic memory, hate, vengeance, or derision. Some are, indeed, called soleares (the Spanish word "*soledades*" in the gypsy pronunciation), songs of solitude:

> *Le dijo er tiempo ar quere:*
> *Esa soberbia que tienes*
> *Yo te la castigare*

> Let me tell you now we are making love—
> I will punish this pride of yours

Some, simply coplas, or verses:

Er tambo es tu retrato;
Que mete mucho ruio
Y si se mira por dentro
S'ecuentra qu'esta basio

> This drum is just like you:
> It makes a loud noise.
> But look inside—it is empty!

> *Si la Inquisicion supiera*
> *Lo mucho que t'he querio*
> *Y er mai pago que m'has dao*
> *Te quemaban por judio*

> If the Inquisition had known
> How much I loved you
> And the bad coin in which you paid me for it
> They would have burned you for a Jew.

Falla organized his congress in Granada thirty years ago in order to preserve *cante hondo*, and spoke of its "grave, hieratic melody." Hieratic it is; in another form, the *saeta*, it is sung to convey the agony of religious desire and remorse, as the images of the Christ or the Virgin are borne round the white-walled streets of Seville in the nights of Holy Week. But the modern tendency has been to get away from the severe, classical design of this pattern of sound which seems to cut the southern night like a knife, to stir in one animal feelings of fear, cruelty, and pity. The more florid, rasping, less inhibited *flamenco* versions are replacing the older form. One hears a good deal too much of the nasal howl let out in a voice that whines and strains the blood vessels. The Spanish voice is harsh, powerful, and dry, as if there were sand in the singer's throat, in any case. Impatient of restraint, the Spanish popular arts are quickly spoiled by exuberance. Spanish fury, when it is aroused in life or simulated in art, is terrifying, for it is carried to the limit of frenzy. Nothing grips the Spaniards so much as the dancer whirling herself into a state of mad, dishevelled passion, and the gypsies are unsurpassed in these transports and climaxes of abandon.

One has only to go to the theatre or to any display of dancing in Spain to see how actors and dancers come onto the stage, not as artists—even though they may be good artists—but as persons. They recognize friends in the audience, wave to them or smile to them indiscreetly in the middle of their performance, with a slackness and an indolence towards the discipline of their art which is provincial and amateur. It is hard for them to sink the person in the artist; they are incurable and obstinate human beings. Yet the opposite tendency is there—an exact, indeed pedantic knowledge of the *castizo* or classical canon, and if the singer or the dancer fails in one single particular of what he ought to do, the audience rises at once—and I mean rises—they get to their feet and shout "*No*" and cry abuse and irony, as they do at the bullfight when the bullfighter makes even a minor error.

(1954)

FROM

Foreign Faces

SEVILLE

Take a blind man out of Castile in the spring, put him on the Tierra de María Santissima, the plain of short green corn and rye grass outside Seville and he will know at once he is in Andalusia and on the way to that city. He will know by the smell of the air. The harsh and stinging odours of lavender and thyme have gone. Now he is walking or riding no longer, but is being lifted or wafted towards the city on air that has ceased to be air and has become a languid melting of the oils and essences of orange blossom and the rose, of jasmine and the myrtle. And although in the city itself he will meet again the strong native reeks of Spanish life—something compounded of olive oil, charcoal, cigar smoke, urine, horse dung, incense and coffee—the flowers of Andalusia will powerfully and voluptuously overrule them, the rose and the orange blossom will blow hotly upon his face from walls and street corners, until he reels with the nose-knowledge of Seville.

It is even more dizzying to the eyes. As we come across the hedgeless flat country we see a low-built, oriental city of roof gardens rising innocently like a tray of white china, chipped here and there by tender ochres. We see the tops of the palms sprouting like pashas in the squares. Inside the city white walls are buried in bougainvillea and wistaria and all climbing flowers, geraniums hanging from thousands of white balconies, great lilies in windows, carnations at street corners, and roses climbing up the walls and even the trees so that all the gasps and hyperbole of pleasure are on our lips. In a minute we are voluptuaries. In two minutes our walk slackens. In three minutes we are looking for a foot of cool shade. And gazing at the oranges on the trees by the trolley bus stop, we ask ourselves how it is that, in a city like this, people do not pick them as they go by, how trains can be got out of the lazy station, lorries unload at the port on the Quadalquivir where ships have come up seventy miles from the sea, or how any of the inhabitants do anything but sigh, sit down or sleep.

Andalusia is the home of Spanish lyrical poetry. Delight, enchantment, all the words suggested by little fountains playing in cool courtyards come almost monotonously to the poets. George Borrow, who saw the Inquisition at every corner of this city, confessed as he stood by the rose walls of the Alcazar that he burst into tears of rapture. His rage had gone. But we need other words than delight, rapture and enchantment to define the city. What is there in the spirit of the Sevillano that breaks the burden of so much sensual beauty and saves him from oriental torpor? Certainly he sleeps in the afternoon and talks half the night, but he is notoriously the liveliest, most sparkling creature, the cleverest monkey, his enemies would say, in Spain. Ask the enemies of Seville to define it. They reply at once: "A city of actors." Seville is theatre. It is totally and intimately a stage. Lope de Vega, the greatest of the Spanish dramatists, called it "the proud theatre of the world" and in its greatest days when Columbus came back from his first voyage to America and before its 16,000 silk looms had been silenced by the wool trade of Castile and the glut of Pizarro's gold, there was nothing bombastic in the phrase.

The legendary figures by whom we know Seville are all theatrical: it is the city of Don Juan, of Figaro and Carmen—but we must say this discreetly because it annoys Sevillanos; they have had enough of Carmen. Cervantes, not a native of the city, was in trouble there—as elsewhere—and caught enough of the spirit of the place to get himself thrown out of the cathedral for protesting against a statue. A place—he saw—for gestures, like Don Juan's. The painters who were born or lived there—Velazquez and Zurbarán—were respectable; and Murillo, the true painter of the women of the city, caught the softer aspect of it: the flowered, moonlit sweetness. But the legendary figures like Peter the Cruel and Don Miguel de Mañara come straight from the stage. The monstrosities committed by Peter the Cruel are as sordid as any in history; the interesting thing is what the dramatic instinct of the Sevillano did with them. One of his notorious murders occurred at night in a silent street of the labyrinth called Santa Cruz. There was only one witness—an old woman who went to her window, candle in hand, and saw his face for a second. That street is still called the street of the Candlestick—Candillejo. But Mañara comes even closer to our notions of the emotional extremity to which the Sevillian character can run and illustrates how it tends to give men a single purpose which utterly absorbs them for a time and may, at a shock, turn with equal singleness into the opposite direction.

Don Miguel de Mañara was once thought to be the original of Don Juan. The idea was mistaken. He was not born when the original play portraying the character was written. Mañara was a rake who repented but, in truly Sevillian fashion, he was not content with an ordinary act of remorse. He had to make the exorbitant gesture and enact the awful scene. From wealth, lust and riot he turned suddenly to the contemplation of death. Pursuing a veiled woman in the street at night, he pulled the veil off her face and a death's head stared at him. He encountered a funeral in the street and, lifting the cloth of the bier, saw that the corpse was himself. When he came to repentance, it was in the great manner. He built a splendid Charity Hospital for the Poor which still exists and there at the entrance one can see the stone of a Sevillano who was an actor for ever. The inscription reads: "Here lies the body of the worst man who ever lived." The worst! Nothing less would satisfy him as a curtain line.

It would be fanciful to see Seville only through its past fantasies, its amorous brawlers, its thousands of witty barbers and its dangerous cigarette girls and its penitents; it was once a Roman capital and, after the discovery of America, Seville produced also that reserved and grave masculine character, the Empire-builder; so that often in Seville one sees examples of those reserved, dignified and grave Roman types, excellent in the saddle, family-proud and conscious of occasion, who look like southern forerunners of the imperial kind of Englishman turned out by Dr. Arnold. Even the clubs of Seville recall those of London, except that the windows are wide open, so that the members are in the front row of the stalls. No one ever reads a book in these clubs, twice as many members are fast asleep as in any club in Pall Mall and the waistline is more abandoned. Trousers have to be cut high and wide to accommodate the great globe below; a belt would expose all that owning bull farms and olive estates can do to the figure. But even these men, stunned by the blessings and martyrdoms of obesity, will get to their feet about midday, proceed like slowed-down planets to the barbers to be clipped, shaved and oiled, to hear what rascalities Figaro has to tell them; or will stand in the Sierpes where no traffic ever runs, and argue dramatically with their friends. Roman Seville is full of the old Andalusian Adam. A street scene, in the perpetual play, is what they love to enact or watch. The last time I was in Sierpes I saw a small procession of youths and children and a couple of police moving towards me. Its centre was a young drunken American who, happily, spoke some Spanish, for he was able to put on quite a show for the crowd who were teasing him. A little girl of ten was having a battle of wits with him. He stood up to them all so well that they accompanied him like an admiring and mischievous court. Reluctantly the police gave up; they had to keep a point with their sergeant elsewhere. All occurrences are revered, the small and the very great.

So it is fitting that at Corpus Christi, the choirboys should dance their medieval dance before the high altar of the Cathedral; it is fitting that when this cathedral was built to celebrate the triumph of Spain in freeing Western Europe from Islam it was made the largest Gothic cathedral in the world. And today it is natural that the processions of Holy Week should have been the most extraordinary religious spectacles to be seen in Europe since the fourteenth century. Thousands of foreigners come to see it, but they are swallowed up by the whole population of the city, nearly 400,000 people, who are out in the streets for a week, living and acting the whole display. Spectacle is in the blood. What the State occasion is to the British, what the historical pageant is to the Germans, and the parade to Americans, the religious pageant is to the Spaniards and to the Sevillano most of all.

The first distinctive quality of Holy Week in Seville lies in the Sevillano and the Sevillana themselves. They do not think of themselves as simply natives of the place or as a number of separate creatures who happen to live and work there. Each one feels himself to be the whole city. All Spaniards feel this about their native place, but the Sevillano carries it to a point at once exquisite and absurd. His feeling is rhetorical, yet, even more, his sense of the city is intimate and domestic. All Seville is his house. The streets are the living quarters, the squares are where he meets his friends, the little baroque churches are his gilded drawing-rooms. It is extraordinary, if one happens to visit or stay in one, how silent and empty-seeming the houses are. A face at a window, a servant going upstairs, a figure alone in rooms darkened to keep out the sun—there is not much more sense of habitation than that. People eat there and sleep there, they water flowers on the balcony—but not there, one supposes, do they live. And so, when the processions of Holy Week begin, the Sevillano is no spectator; he is of them. They are part of his personal drama.

Even if we go only by the number, length, duration and membership of the processions, we see how completely they pervade. Are all Sevillanos passionately religious? No. Has the Church enemies after the Civil War? Yes, very many. Do some people deplore the processions, pointing to the enormous amount of convent, church and religious monument building of the last twenty years in a poor country that lacks the will or the talent to do more than nibble lazily at its worst social problems? Many do so deplore. Yet, because the processions are theatre, eyes brighten and the arguments vanish. In each parish church there is a *cofradia* or brotherhood—they are exclusively male institutions—which maintains the elaborate and beautifully carved and golden floats on which the image of the Virgin patroness or the Christ is carried. Some *cofradias* maintain two or even three of these floats. They are objects of pride, for some of the figures are by the great Spanish sculptors—Montañes, Hito del Castillo, the Roldans, Alonso Cano, are among them—who excelled in the dramatic realism of their work. One or two are masterpieces and, listening to the crowd, one sees that, whether they respond to the religious meaning or not, they respond totally to the work of art and to the expressiveness of the figures in the scenes of the Crucifixion.

There are something like fifty of these *cofradias* in Seville. Their membership is large. It is not always easy to become a member. Parents are known to put their sons' names down for them at birth. Some of the *cofradias* originate in the guilds of the Middle Ages and their popular trade names have stuck to them: cigarette-makers, bankers, bakers, roadmakers and so on. Beginning on the Monday before Easter, the *cofradias* in turn bear the floats through the streets from their parish and then along a set route in the centre to the Cathedral; the procession pauses there, and then the return journey begins. Some of the processions are eight or eleven hours on their route and they go on through the night—first a posse of the municipal guard, then barefoot penitents carrying their lighted torches, the standard S.P.Q.R., banners, acolytes swinging the smoking censers and then the image at last, followed by a band. For half a mile the members of the *cofradia* precede the image, in their conical hats with eye-slits and in robes, carrying their candles. After a week of this the streets are glazed with candle grease. The making of the show is its slowness, for each float is borne on the shoulders of thirty-six men concealed beneath the velvet curtains below. They shuffle forward in the heat only fifty to a hundred yards at a time. They work like galley slaves. The very slowness of the progress means that they effectually occupy the main part of the city and entirely close its centre. The crowds hang about and then suddenly someone shouts "Here comes San Vicente" or "Here comes Santa Cruz" and the neighbourhood of the Cathedral is packed and impenetrable. On Good Friday the climax is reached. Famous images like the Macarena, which excites an extraordinary fervour in the crowd, or the Jesus del Gran Poder, which draws out its admiration, pass into the Cathedral. The *Miserere* of the composer Eslava is sung in a last orgy of theatrical magnificence and to crown all, a peal of artificial thunder booms and rebounds in the enormous edifice.

There is nothing more to be said of the stage management of Holy Week; it is the play that counts, its peculiar quality of penetrating into the daily life of the people. The Sevillano, like all other Spaniards, is addicted to the repetitious and monotonous; he wakes up only at the high moments. There, as in the dance, in the bullfights, in his songs, he is taut and silent and most critical. He is the man of the crisis. In singing or the dance, the guitar mutters away monotonously, playing on the nerves, slackening off in order with dramatic suddenness to deceive and to enhance until the torpor of the audience is broken down and the singer or dancer can electrify him by wit or take him by storm. Something like that occurs in the processions. The high moments occur when the image leaves its church, when it enters the Cathedral, when it leaves and, finally, when, in an uproar of enthusiasm, it returns to the family possession of its parish. That moment of the return, if it should happen, as it often does, to be at two or three in the morning, is superb.

You have been hanging about in some bar drinking beer in the heat of the night and presently in the crowd outside there is pushing and scrambling and flurry: the sound of drum taps is coming nearer. The streets are narrow—in some of them there is only room for a carriage, many are only alleys—the houses are chalk-white, the starlit sky is black. The breath of the flowers is cool and oily. The street lights are put out and the walls are lit only by the candles of the hundreds of penitents in their hoods and robes and by the scores of candles on the image. The windows are crowded. People stand along the roof gardens. The simple façade of the church, with its baroque scroll, looks like a strong gracious face, for, though they may be like drawing-rooms inside, the churches of Seville have those well-found and noble walls which Spaniards still have the custom and art of building. The candles round the Virgin flutter and her affecting, doll's face shines out of her headdress and her jewelled velvet robes. She stands, certainly like a Queen, under her canopy. Eyes sparkle in the crowd. The prettiness, the peep-show prettiness, delights the Sevillano. They have an almost childish excitement before pretty things. And now, before the image is carried in, there is sudden silence. The small voice of a singer rises. He is singing a *saeta*, one of those weird and traditional "deep songs" which seem to be the music of a man in complete solitude, a personal cry of strangled passion and loneliness, and whose words are a naïve mingling of self and religion, Arab lyricism and the love of the city. The falsetto voice, whinnying and gulping its minutely broken syllables, is half Arab but also half gypsy, for the final vowel is drawn out into that curious grunting "aun" of the gypsy singing. The pauses in the song are there so that we shall be astonished by a sudden cruel heightening of crisis which breaks at last into the downhill rush of fulfilment. The words are not hard to catch. They are essentially declarations of love: the singer is singing his personal praise of the Virgin, saying that she is the prettiest of all and the pride of the proudest and most beautiful city on earth. It is said that in recent years the *saetas* have become more extravagant and have travelled a long way from traditional simplicity. The tendency in all Spain in the last twenty years is to "pile it on" in a manner one can't but think decadent. (I notice old bullfight fans complain that whereas the crowd in Seville was once unique in Spain, in freezing into contemptuous silence—no whistles, no catcalls—when the torero made some ghastly mistake or lost his nerve, now it has lost the classical dignity and shouts with the worst.) Even so, if the modern Spanish tendency is to overdo things and run into vulgarity, there is no doubt that dramatic extravagance is in the Sevillian nature.

But the high moments of the processions that pervade the city in this week are few. The night scene before the Cathedral is magnificent. Flood-lighting turns this tremendous domed, buttressed and towered building, where the stained glass blazes at night, into something fabulous. The smoking incense and the candlelight transform the crowd. All this is high drama. But when one looks at the whole thing, hour by hour, one notices that the normal character of the processions is slack, dawdling and familiar. An American will be shocked by the slowness, a German by the lack of precision, an Englishman by the absence of dignity. There is nothing of the rehearsed occasion. The penitents lounge, their candles and hoods at all angles, the bands play popular waltzing marches—I noticed again and again that they play a slow military version of the *Maiden's Prayer*—the crowd pushes through the ranks. Even in the Cathedral, where an inured Protestant like myself expects a certain *tenue*, I have seen one or two penitents get and answer messages from the congregation: "See you at So-and-so later on"; and in bars I have seen a thirsty young penitent pull off his hood, gulp down a beer and rush back to his place. Occasionally young boys appear in the processions and one will see an anxious mother and a father on his dignity go up to their son and put his hood straight. And when the image is set down for a rest the sweating bearers beneath naturally lift the curtains and squat on the ground getting a breath of air. The water-sellers crowd round them with jars, people give them cigarettes and wives or sisters will rush up to give them sandwiches or a cup of coffee. In the meantime the bearers are grinning and cursing and making wisecracks at the crowd, for the Sevillano does not miss an opportunity in this game. This easy familiarity is not only delightful but it is of the very essence of the *popular* spirit which the Spanish have preserved to an extent I have seen nowhere else in the world. The proudest of all people, they are the most at ease with each other and quite classless—in the ordinary relations of life the most classless people I know.

And this ease of theirs in the great occasion comes out in another way. They know at what points a procession will be prettiest or most dramatic. They know the procession of Santa Cruz is exquisite after it has turned off the boulevard just above Carmen's tobacco factory—now the university—and passes under the rich trees of the gardens beyond the rose walls of the Alcazar, its candlelight glittering and its incense smoking under the acacias, its music diffused in the gardens. Others know that at points in Sierpes or some other narrow street barely wide enough for the float, it will be set momentarily like a shrine; or that in the square called San Salvador it will stand against the huge dwarfing walls of great churches. They know where the most curious of all, the Silent procession, is best seen. This familiar knowledge of what is felicitous, where the charming moments are, is a sign of how they own their city street by street, knowing the character of each part of it. Once more, we see the Sevillano's talent and taste for the small pleasures of life, and for thinking the local thing is the one to be cherished most. Smallness is important to them. One can tell that by their speech— wherever they can they use a diminutive: not a glass of wine, but a *little* glass; not a snack of fried squid, shrimps, sausage or tiny silver eels from the north, with their glass of manzanilla, but a *little snack*; and if they want more than that, a dish of it, then the dish becomes a *little* dish, flowers become *little* flowers, birds singing in their cages on the walls of the patio become *little* birds; even bulls become *little* bulls. Smaller and smaller things become in their minds, until they have reached the imaginary tinyness of childish delight.

Yet, as I said earlier, the people of Seville are not awed spectators of their show; they are part of it. If you go into any of the churches when a particular procession is over, on any of the days following, you will find scores of people coming to admire the floats and particularly those famous as works of art. These churches all have something of the family house about them; there is always something going on and, anyone, any passing stranger, will eagerly show you its curiosities. One morning in the Triana—the gypsy quarter on the other bank of the Quadalquivir—in the Santa Anna, the oldest church in the city, they had put a ladder over the altar and were changing the Virgin's clothes, tying on her many bodices and petticoats and getting her ready for an ordination service in the afternoon. This church looks like a picture shop. Its choir and organ carvings are good; but it also has the usual haphazard collection of antique oddities. One of the strangest was an image of the Virgin presented in the nineteenth century by the Duc de Montpensier, the patron and friend of Alexandre Dumas. The Spaniards do not care much for French importations and this one embarrasses. The Virgin is portrayed in the fashionable clothes of a society woman at a reception or the races. The verger looked dubiously at it but, a true Sevillano, he had an eye for the bizarre. By the altar stood a fine grandfather's clock. Rich Spaniards had a craze for collecting fine English clocks at the end of the eighteenth century and their families have dumped these curiosities on the nearest church. One finds them everywhere. Once more one sees that the churches are one more room in the family life of the city.

On Thursday of Holy Week, the shops close and now the whole of the city is out and crowds swarm in on the country buses. At five in the afternoon the popular *paseo* begins, the ritual of walking up and down. Until now the women had been present but inconspicuous. The Sevillana is small and plump and pale, inclined to roundness and heaviness in the face and, until she talks, without light in her eyes. Beside the male, whether of the grave Roman type or the jumping cracker, the lady is placid and demure. But on Thursday the sex suddenly grows a foot taller. They have taken off their flat slippers and shoes—so convenient for the cobbles of this cobbled place—and have put on their high heels, their high combs and their black mantillas. One blinks. Women who were unnoticeable the day before have suddenly become beauties, coolly conscious of a part to play. A hidden pride has come out. They rarely, one notices, deign to talk to their escorts. After Holy Week, in the excitement of the *Feria*, they will change again. They will be clapping hands, snapping thumbs and fingers, clacking the castanets in the night-long dances that go on in the *casetas*, the family marquees and avenues by the Park. It will be a new play of whirling and stamping pleasure.

The civilisation that Seville has inherited is a good deal Arab. Almost all the older things in Seville were built by Arab craftsmen and although modern blocks of flats have gone up, the main domestic part of the city is based on the Arab patio or courtyard. There is a strong white wall, and the rooms open on to a central court. The streets of Santa Cruz wind and tangle. They are built to catch only glancing blows of the terrible Spanish sun, to be channels of cool air, and the names of these streets are set out in the large black classical letters of centuries ago, and are dramatic in their direct and simple evocations. Streets are called, quite plainly: Air, Water, Bread, Straw, the Dead Moor, Glory, Barrabas, Mosque, Jewry and Pepper. No fantastications in that heroic age. The Spaniards of the Reconquest were simple men. In the gypsy quarter of the Triana, the traditional home of bullfighters, dancers and singers, the main street is called Pureza—Purity. It is one of the clues to the character of the Sevillano that even in modern streets he has not changed his lettering. It is superior to that of any city in the world and it emphasises how important place and locality are to the Sevillian temperament. No search for identity here; he is a man and, as Don Juan said when he posted his name on a wall, if anyone wants anything of him, here he is. The streets of Seville are clean; even the poor streets are clean. There is no filth in the Triana. One breathes flower-borne air, as one passes the grilled windows and gates of the houses and looks into the courtyards. From the modest patios to those of the greater houses, the cool ferns stand there on the tiles and the flowers are massed. These patios are really open rooms, often with chairs and tables in them and under the gallery in the house of some well-off lawyer or family who do well out of the olive oil or the sherry trade, one sees the best pictures of the house and the finest furniture standing virtually in the open. Silent always, mysterious and as if entranced by their own flowers, the patios are little stage sets, little peep-shows in themselves. They display the pride of the family as well as its natural pleasure in living in the open air.

In the *Feria*, those who can afford it hire or build "casetas," wooden booths or marquees near the Park. The caseta has a "living room" in the front and a kitchen concealed behind it; the living room is separated from the street by a low rail and there many families move elegant pieces of furniture from their houses—armoires, sideboards, handsome dining tables. Pictures hang on the wall. Publicly, with some air of consequence, the family lives in the open for the Fair and takes enormous family pride in keeping open house, inviting the passing stranger as well as their friends to drink with them. There is no rough-and-ready camping about this. They are here to be seen at their best and in abandoned gaiety, drinking and dancing all through the night. In the Feria, there is the procession of carriages to watch. Remarkable and luxurious equipages go by, drawn by their teams of fine horses. The great families own them; the less great hire them. At this time one sees the parade of riders, formally dressed in the Andalusian style—the low-crowned Cordoba hat, the short jacket that sets off the waist of the rider, the tight trousers with the florid leather facings and, behind the riders, the girls in their long red-and-white dresses, their combs and the roses or carnations in the hair.

So well known is this, that when the foreigner thinks of Spain, he thinks of this Sevillian scene, hears the castanets and the tambourines and the speed of the tossing music of the Sevillana. Spain is, of course, quite unlike this. It is a purely Sevillian scene and it has spread abroad that legend of romantic Spain which has infuriated so many Spanish writers. There is, one has to say, something very provincial in this city. Its habits and manners are set. The stranger must not get the impression that the gaiety he sees will pass the bounds of formality, even when it appears at its wildest. The very wildness has its rules. Spanish life is profoundly unromantic. Overwhelmingly it is ruled—as the theatre is ruled—by the strict sense of genre and local style. Things change, of course. Seville has become an important river port. The Vespas roar in the streets, the old grinding yellow trams have gone and have been replaced by the trolley bus. Young girls go in for blonde hair dips. And lovers, sitting among the roses in the park, are bolder. It is now permissible for them to hold hands or put an arm round a waist. Many of those lovely houses in Santa Cruz are let out in flats. The bullfights after Holy Week are rarely good, for this spectacle has its terrible periods of boredom, when the bulls are bad or the torero incompetent. There are plenty of people in the crowd coming away from the bull ring complaining of the enormous prices charged, the commercialisation of the show and the decline of its quality. Foreigners who used not often to go now swarm in and there is a good deal more of showiness than the rigour of the game. Foreign writers who have become fans of the bullfight have a lot to answer for.

But, in defence of the provinciality of Seville and its contented incuriosity towards the outside world, this must be said. Provinciality has preserved the Sevillano and enhances his local genius. He is incurably an actor and a mocker. "Come on, gypsy," calls out one gypsy, derisively, to another in the street. He loves to shout a compliment to a woman and prides himself on the neatness of it. To a very tall woman a workman shouted, "Come by tomorrow so that we can see the other half." The *piropo*, or public compliment, is now supposedly illegal—it annoyed foreigners—but it has not entirely vanished. Wit, the invention of conceits, are irrepressible in the Sevillano; he loves riposte and fantasy. At the height of Holy Week, when the crowds are thickest and the café tables almost filled one little square, I heard two rival shrimp and crab sellers shouting at each other from their stalls on opposite sides of the square. One was making up fantastic eulogies, full of astute local references, of his shrimps that came from Cadiz; his opponent listened, carefully, the crowd was almost silent and then burst into admiring laughter. Then it was the turn of the other, a man from Alicante, who let fly with his own fantasy. The crowd were entranced. The act went on for half an hour, a real battle of comical words between two cities. I wish I had written it down, but it was going too fast for me and both parties were helpless with laughter. Make a light passing remark to any inhabitant of this place and he will outstrip you in a flash. "How are you this morning?" you say to the cab driver expecting a mild little "Very well, thank you" or a conventional "Fine." That's too dull for the cabman. Skinnily he stands up and looks down at his skinny horse which is soon for the bull ring, "Stupendous!" he says.

Seville is theatre. Great theatre, yet with thousands of little turns and scenes going on its stage. Its vanity is to be the city of Don Juan; it is in fact far more the city of Figaro, mocking, playing practical jokes and then dropping off into a self-absorbed yet blank-minded doze, until the next wicked or childish opportunity occurs. A place of dignity—and yet I have seen an old gentleman of the gravest kind pick up a sugar castor and, leaning out of the café window where he was sitting, sprinkle another old gentleman's hair with it. I suppose people use the telephone there out of simple respect for the instrument; for their real business they send a boy out with a note to the favourite bar or café of the person it is addressed to. It is a paradise of hangers-on, of doorstep characters who know everything, of people who stop to talk; but do not suppose it is happy-go-lucky and unbusiness-like. The slowest action in the blissfully slow life of Andalusia is the action of letting money pass out of one's hand. Seville put up a considerable struggle to keep the South American gold.

The regions of Spain and their cities have an extreme independence of temperament and, even in the levelling of modern civilisation, some of this survives in the attacks of ridicule they jealously make upon one another. When one uses this word "theatre" of Seville, the citizens of other cities read it in the pejorative sense of shallowness, showiness, rhetoric and the arts of the mountebank. It must be admitted that modern Seville, beyond the Park, is either pretentious or ugly. It reached the depths of decadence at the time of the Exhibition in the thirties. Seville has no need of rhetoric about its past. In that enormous historical show the city put on in the fifteenth and sixteenth centuries, there were no rhetoricians; it was the time of men of action. All the cities of Europe have great historical claims on our imagination, until we are choked with history. The claim of Seville is truly colossal and world-changing. I do not know whether many people visit the Archives of the Indies, but in that not very interesting building, near the Cathedral, one has the shock of knowing what it must have been like to be discoverers and colonists of America. It meant, above all, the work of men of action: explorers, sailors, soldiers, governors, architects, builders, judges. Here, in thousands of white boxes, are their documents: their plans for cities like Buenos Aires, for the forts at Cartagena, for the avenues of Montevideo and the government houses of Peru; the drawings, the leases, the law suits, the certificates of governorship, the trials, the executions. Here we can read the report of Hernan Cortés, the letters of Columbus. And of a failure, too: the long letter of Cervantes, the imprisoned tax collector, failed author, unwanted soldier, and cathedral brawler—applying vainly for a job overseas. Seville played out the great roles; and now history has passed beyond it, it amuses itself with the little ones, the magic that passes the tedious hours of life.

THE OFFENSIVE TRAVELLER

I am an offensive traveller. I do not mean that I arrive in a foreign country in a state of arrogance and start complaining about the beds, the plumbing, the food, the transport, the prices. I do not refuse to drink the water; I do not see bacteria everywhere. I do not say: "The country is wonderful, but you can have the people." I do not suspect everyone who speaks a foreign language of being a thief. I do not scream that I cannot get a good steak in Morocco—steak travellers are the hypochondriacs of motion—a decent haggis in Naples, or an edible chop suey on Ascension Island. I do not complain of the lack of Night Life in English villages or of the absence of thatch in Ohio. One thing, of course, does annoy me: other tourists. Clear the Americans out of Paris; throw the Germans out of Venice; rid Majorca and the Costa Brava of the British. I say that loudly. If I had lived in

Canterbury in the Middle Ages, I would have said the same about those palfrey-loads of pilgrims. To the inhabitants I am as obliging as a Portuguese. By "being offensive" I mean that I travel, therefore I offend.

I represent that ancient enemy of all communities: the stranger. Neapolitan girls have crossed themselves to avert the evil eye at the sight of me. (And of you, too, hypocrite lecteur.) And rightly: We are looking on the private life of another people, a life which is entirely their business, with an eye that, however friendly it may be, is alien. We are seeing people as they do not see themselves. I say "we," but I do worse than this. I not only look. I make notes. I write.

Forty years ago I wrote my first impressions of a country not my own and began my career as a traveller who causes offence in print. I began to be paid for insulting others. I remember the first occasion. There was—perhaps there still is—a local train that runs from Cork to Blarney (significant destination!) and the country people piled in bringing their chickens with them. I mentioned the fact because the journey was a jolly one in a country then torn apart by Civil War. I was accused of bringing the new Irish nation into ridicule. No Irish man or woman ever brought a chicken into a train. If he or she did, a foreigner ought not to mention it. I was playing up the Victorian charm of a nation determined to be Victorian no longer. I moved on to Spain, where I was accused of saying there would shortly be a vacant throne: there was, but in this my offence was without distinction. Everyone was saying it. Who were my friends? Abominable intellectuals like Unamuno, Ortega y Gasset, Baroja—people who were notorious Europeanizers and objectors to bullfighting and were kindly disposed to education, parliaments, football, and walking in the mountains. I migrated to the United States; my talent developed. One summer evening I was sitting on the jetty of a small New England town listening to the distant voices of some old fellows jawing and whittling away. I could not hear what they said, but on that peaceful evening the sound was like one of the pleasantest sounds in nature: the cawing of returning rooks. I was a fanciful youth. I mentioned the sound in print. Uproar. I had conveyed that New Englanders, among all human animals, had not yet evolved the power of speech, forgetting in my smug British way that English speech has been compared to the hissing of geese.

With this incident, I realized that I had been born with a remarkable gift. I exploited it. There were the Swiss, for example; I praised them for their domestic contentment. They objected at once: did I not know that their family life was as awful as that of any other people? Was I insinuating that they lacked a capacity to suffer? A young Swiss came to my office in London to assure me that a Swiss could suffer, if he got half a chance, as much as any man on earth. I praised Scandinavian architecture. These Nordics were indignant that I had not mentioned their high suicide rate. In time, the Germans spoke out. When I said that the Germans loved flowers I was clearly insinuating that they were "sissies" and one reader got in a nasty dig at me. "Don't the British love flowers too?" The mayor of a town in South America said I obviously intended an affront when I said they had just installed traffic lights. My gift was developing fast—so fast that I was invited to a discussion on the Welsh character in a small Welsh town and there I made the sort of mistake that comes from overconfidence. I was asked to insult the Welsh, because the meeting had fallen into the doldrums of self-praise. The meeting took place in a small room; indeed one of the company, a learned shepherd, had to lie on the floor at my feet. He stared expectantly, waiting to spring. My speech was brief, even trivial. All I said was that the Welsh were touchy, hot-tempered, hypocritical, and given to lying. No more. The shepherd sprang—but not at me. He sprang at the audience and in a beautiful lamenting voice, as if he were declaiming from Jeremiah, he shouted: "What this Englishman has just said is true! We are liars, we are hypocrites..."

You observe my error. I learned the lesson and, as a result, reached the peak of my offensive career. It was during the war. I had written a film script showing that the ordinary Englishman and the ordinary Frenchman were natural allies and friends. I presented a flighty and talkative Englishman, keen on beer and girls, and a silent, industrious, abstemious Frenchman, dignified and scrupulous. You notice my cunning? I had reversed a sacred myth. The film was banned as anti-Allied propaganda and insulting to both parties. I could go no higher.

As an offender of foreigners, I recognize that my place in a long tradition is a humble one. Unlike Shakespeare, I have not made fun of foreign accents. I have not made fun of Frogs, Taffys, Wops, or Polacks. The nonchalance of Mark Twain and the insinuations of Henry Adams are far beyond me. Mrs. Trollope being rude to Americans, Nathaniel Hawthorne being rude about the British, Bernard Shaw making a laughingstock of both, are far above my level. I could not equal Bemelmans on Ecuador, though I did get a broadside from a politician in that country—the eighty volcanoes of the lovely place have, perhaps, contributed to the sensibility of its public men—and I have not debunked Spain like that brilliant Italian scholar Mario Praz in Unromantic Spain. None of these great offenders can, of course, vie with Tobias Smollett, whose Travels Through France and Italy is the supreme classic of offence. Smollett had the fine art of excusing a vice by substituting a worse one. Of the French he wrote:

> If their acts of generosity are rare, we ought to ascribe that rarity not so much to
> a deficiency of generous sentiments, as to their vanity and ostentation, which,

engrossing all their funds, utterly disable them from exerting the virtues of beneficence.

Taine's view of the British seems to have been that they were a kind of brute cattle with addled heads and censorious habits, living in steam. I say nothing of Dr. Johnson and the Scots. He spoke it at a time when half the inns of northern England had "Scots go home" chalked on their walls.

I must not claim too much for my gift for offence. I could not have been born at a luckier moment. In the eighteenth century it was impossible to offend anyone. Today, more people are offendable than at any other time in the history of the world. The number increases. There are two reasons for this, one of them practical: the other harder to define precisely. The first is that more people travel and annoy one another. People whose blood boiled only once in a lifetime can now have it brought to the boil every night of their lives in books, on television, or in the cinema. Why are they offended? They are rightly offended by errors of fact. But why are personal descriptions and interpretations offensive to them? I think the tendency of modern society is to make us think there ought to be only one view, that there is a mysterious standard eye or opinion like the standard inch. That very unobjective word called "objective" is constantly used. This is natural: we, the offended, are fed on the single view of propaganda, advertising, and myths.

But the second reason for the increase in the number of the offended is more important. More people are offended because more are insecure. More people in the world are uprooted and unsure of themselves. There are more chips on more shoulders. It began with the Industrial Revolution, the break-up of long-settled patterns of life in which people felt so settled that they did not care what was said about them, good or bad. In some countries the Industrial Revolution has only just begun. If I want to stir up chauvinism or hysteria and tickle an inferiority complex, I go to the big cities; the countryman or the man of the small town which has no new buildings cannot easily be moved. A fisherman, a Spanish shepherd, a German woodcutter, a man working in the fields, regards the people who write about him or interpret him with amusement, contentment, and even pity. He is strong in his own world and often better educated, in the true sense of being able to draw on stored experience, than those who have merely new knowledge. But in the new countries and new towns it is not so. Doubt is much stronger. "What do you think of our new telegraph poles?" a Japanese student asked an English poet who was teaching him Gray's "Elegy." The greatest tact was required in the poet's reply. It is offensive in such places not to mention the latest thing. The enormously high buildings shooting up in some unlikely parts of the world may be monuments to modern art, hope, and endeavour; they are also monuments to an inferiority complex. The newer the country the more noticeable the chip, the more certain the aggression. Even when the assured do not condescend to the ill-assured, it is resented that the assured do not know that they are assured. If two assured well-rooted peoples meet—the French and the Spaniards, for example—the comedy has the most delicate dryness, though as far as offence is concerned the French easily win. I have found mayors the most ready of all people to take offence, if their towns are small. A new country or regime regards interpretation or criticism—anything except the official view—as anti-social. And some countries are not as old as they think they are. The Germans are an ancient race; their influence on European institutions has been enormous from the time of the Roman Empire. They are pre-eminent in modern science. They have great vitality and often combine an extraordinary precision in work with a powerful, if not always determinable, emotional force. Everyone has observed this. But as a nation, the Germans are very young. They are, like the young, affronted if their estimate of themselves is questioned. And when Germans, or British, or Italians, or any other people become racial minorities in other countries, they become more chauvinist, more resentful of criticism or interpretation, than their relatives in the homeland. The Italians in Buenos Aires, the British in Chile, the Irish in Sydney or New York, are far thinner-skinned than the people they have left behind. Self-criticism is the beginning of maturity. One of the harshest books ever written by a foreigner about another country was George Borrow's *The Bible in Spain*. It was translated into Spanish about thirty years ago, and was praised by most of the Spanish critics because they recognized in Borrow a fanatical enemy, a man who, they said, might have been one of themselves and not a Bible-punching heretic. They disagreed with every word he wrote. What they admired was his intolerance.

More offence is caused by praise than blame. The Spaniards hate being called romantic by the French, the Irish hate being called fanciful, the British hate being called solid, the French hate being called volatile, the Italians hate being called clever, and the Portuguese dislike being praised for anything at all and quickly tell you how all "your" things are better than theirs. What really offends is the destruction of a myth. I remember Alberto Moravia saying that a young Neapolitan saves up enough money to buy a Vespa in order to dash across Europe to Scandinavia, where (he has been told) passionate, aristocratic girls of surpassing intelligence and beauty are dedicated to free love; while at the same moment, young love-starved Scandinavians are dashing south to Naples, where (they understand) the dark beauties of the South will come out of palaces into their arms. Both parties would clearly be happier in puritan London, where—Billy Graham tells us—the parks are one vast bedroom. It is hard to decide here who are the offended parties. The best thing to do is to declare all parties undersexed. That causes enormous offence. Northern Italians have been saying this successfully of Southern Italians for generations. There are other myths: that Americans talk of nothing but dollars, that the British are strangled by their class system, that the Germans don't laugh, that every Frenchman keeps a mistress, that the South Americans are always shooting each other.

Being an offender, I am myself easily offended. Where is my weak spot? There is no single place. I am a weak spot all over. I just dislike being looked at. As the coachload of tourists passes me with their cameras in my own country, I feel myself swelling into one fevered wound. Has it come to this, I say, as their cameras click, that I have degenerated into a native, a local character daubed with racial characteristics, liable to remind people of what they have read, interesting for my folk customs, my peculiar diet, my curious clothes? Am I being taken for a Dickensian porter, a lord, Mrs. Grundy's husband, a slippery pickpocket, a town crier, a folk dancer, a decayed Empire builder? Or much worse, the supreme insult in fact: am I being studied as an example of the typical? Is someone going home to write about my habits and deduce from them the unlucky attributes of my nation? If you catch me, I am tempted to say, I shall have my revenge. I shall do as I have been done by in many, many countries. I shall be a most misleading guide.

(1964)

FROM

New York Proclaimed

ONE

One comes as a fortune hunter with looting eyes, the latest innocent of a greedy procession. It began with Hudson, the English captain who sold himself to the Dutch. A cosmopolite, foreign to his crew, his loyalty questioned, he was attacked by mutineers two years later and left to freeze to death in the Arctic: it is the standard story of the Age of Discovery. His kind of foreignness was basic to the city from the beginning. It has never really changed. New York is the metropolis of the United States because it is the most European city in the country; that is to say, it reproduces in miniature the fundamental foreignness of Europe, where we are all foreign to one another. That lonely Statue of Liberty, standing in the bay with tourists clambering round it, is French, La France in person.

These are a stranger's sensations; but even in the handful of New Yorkers who have been native for generations, they must still have some echo. A raw arriving ancestor must once have felt them and handed down some memory of panic—and the cure for it: activity, harshness, drama, change. New York is not the only Atlantic city to convey this. One hears it in the aggressive voice of Buenos Aires and the soft voice of Rio. On the Pacific Coast, another three thousand miles on, one catches what the inhabitants call "the Pacific sadness." New York has none of that; it is never sad. It has hardened the human shell. It offers that dramatic, rhapsodic self-consciousness which sets the American tone. It instills the spirit of the tallest of the tall stories. For generations the American landscape was seen (and perhaps still is) as a backdrop against which it is inevitable for a man to turn actor and, again and again, in his talk to adopt the historic present. The show is always going on.

The chart has been read: 40°42′ North, 74°01′ West. About thirteen thousand vessels a year come in to this seaport, placed well inside its enormous bay. They say, as they always say of things, that it is the world's largest. This time they are right. They say that there are fifteen hundred square miles of land and water—exuberantly reckoning the port to extend to a twenty-five-mile radius of the city—and that a ship goes through the Narrows every twenty minutes. Greedy and innocent, one waits—if one comes by ship—for the curtain of sea haze to go up and reveal the stage. Vessels unseen for days now slant towards a harbor as yet out of sight. The bell buoy clangs along the Ambrose channel. The foghorns grunt and breathe out their profoundly mortal moans. And then the curtain rises on a shore that is mildly hilled and wooded, which in summer looks steamy, tropical, and ill-used and which presently rises to the rock Palisades of the Hudson. And there in the middle of the scene, Manhattan stands tall and narrow, even more like a ship than a city, a structure of tiered decks, glassed in like a liner's, growing taller and taller until, if one were anchored, the thing looks as though it would run one down. Life in a city like that, we guess, will be ship life, confined, briskly run to order and signals. Somewhere among those millions of windows will be one's cabin. Small, it will be buzzing with noises overhead. There will be long journeys down corridors. There will be depths of solid machinery and wire. And here the fortune hunter, caught by his inability to grasp it all, finds his mind awash with metaphors. We have called Manhattan a ship and we shall think of a hundred more likenesses before we have done. This city has situation, as London and Paris have not; as Rio de Janeiro and Istanbul have, but Buenos Aires has not. Whatever happens, New York will always have that.

In a couple of pages of his *The American Scene,* written at the time when Manhattan was at the beginning of building high, Henry James was soon splashing about in metaphor as extravagantly as all who have followed him. The sight from the Battery to Twenty-third Street is compared to a pincushion already overplanted with extravagant pins; it turns immediately into a "loose nosegay of architectural flowers," the flower being the "American beauty, the rose of interminable stem," a non-lasting blossom, for it has "confessedly" risen to be nipped off by the shears "as soon as 'science' applied to gain has put upon the table [we are now in some gaming saloon] from far up its sleeve, some more winning card." We move to music. The skyscrapers become "the most piercing notes in that concert of the expensively provisional into which your supreme sense of New York resolves itself." Exhausted, we fade "into the consciousness of the finite, the menaced, the essentially invented state." The last phrase tells; "invented"— we shall never hit upon a word as exact and pregnant; but the Master has given us a license for intoxication in a city which is clearly celebrating.

And one also that invites conquest—but this Dick Whittington complex, I fancy, is far stronger in the Americans coming in ambitiously from other states. Thomas Wolfe, of course, felt it; when was he not feeling "the beat . . . of the pulse of Tamerlaine . . . riding in triumph through Persepolis"? He looked down over the city from the roof of the Hotel St. George in Brooklyn and, as he wrote in *Of Time and the River*:

> . . . for the first time his vision phrased it as it had never done before. It was a cruel city, but it was a lively one, a savage city, yet it had such tenderness; a bitter, harsh and violent catacomb of stone and steel and tunneled rock, slashed savagely with light, and roaring, fighting a constant ceaseless warfare of men and of machinery; and yet it was so sweetly and so delicately pulsed, as full of warmth, of passion and of love as it was as full of hate. . . .

That describes nothing, but Wolfe, too, has his license.

We foreigners also have our moods. In some of these daytime arrivals, in summer and in winter, I have been struck by the stereoscopic hardness, the unblending, hazeless, hostile separateness of the skyscrapers. Their columns of windows have not suggested a closer connection with human life than one sees in the columns of other people's bank accounts. These buildings are, one feels, only computable. The first signs of a familiar New York madness come on: one starts counting and reckoning windows and, later indeed, one will meet taxi drivers who know only numbers and not places. One gets madder: one realizes that this supposedly vertical city is dominated by horizontal lines. At other times of day, if the sky is hard and clear, one is surrounded by tall fungi which by tomorrow will be replaced by growths that have the look of things that know their own mortality. The vision of a petrified forest thousands of years old comes to mind, the now invincible newness of the buildings looks like the rigid newness of death. Yet, suddenly, this gives way to sensations of decorous gaiety, as the boat steams up. These buildings are beings, and they move. The Chrysler glides northward and the Empire State moves graciously south; soon all are changing places in a millionaire's waltz, slow and silent, male and female, exchanging the light in their eyes, the touch of roof and penthouse like the touch of passing hands. All cities move, but none so strangely as the steel figures of the New York ball. You had noticed that few of the buildings in themselves are beautiful, but that most are amazing. They are plain, ugly, and useful in a way that makes one wonder at the city's dramatic sense of use; their real beauty lies in the movements of their grouping, their continually changing juxtapositions, and—when you and they are still— above all in the movements of light upon them. The hours of the day are never dead and play upon Manhattan like changing thought.

But it is at the Battery that the New York ship raises its bows at you. The fortune hunter arriving by freighter at Brooklyn has a finer sight of the city than you get by taking the head-on punch and entering the Hudson. The time to take that punch is at night, when the downtown buildings are blocked by darkness into a sentineled medieval keep of enormous height and unscalable defense. The blackness of the whole hulk is all the more sinister for the few lights that occasionally signal from it. Dead kings, not recent bankers, might then inhabit it. The dull Babylonian clatter with its appalling overtone of what Henry James called "the vocabulary of thrift" is gone. Downtown, even Wall Street, can look mysterious and noble and timeless.

Island cities that are built up close from shore to shore are explicit. In no way does Manhattan hide. To the eye the varying heights of the high and the middling high are as diverting as the human mixture, the long, the short, and the tall. James was depressed by the commerce, but in fact the mercantile spirit makes for variety; there are big fortunes and small. In this aspect the sight of Manhattan is a comment on the giddiness of the market: the shapes that have been cut out of the sky are jumbled, for if there are a lot of glass cases, fake cathedrals, and brick packing cases, there are also many smaller, zoned buildings that look like little stepladders, ambitious to climb, but having run short of financial breath architecturally. One is looking at the sharp rectangles, often aborted, of a flat abstract painting— where else has one seen them? On the Greek islands; in Byzantium.

The beauty of your arrival in Manhattan is that your ship can dock in deep water right inside the city. Your liner is moored amidships against the greatest liner of all. That is, as sensations go, superb. It keys you up, you are in tune with the place at once. Even before the city built high and when it was, in fact, a slightly humped plain, peppered all over by the spires of its innumerable churches, the Irish immigrant could tumble straight off the quay into his lodgings, his tavern, and, above all, his church. He needed to walk with his boxes no more than a hundred yards and by that time had probably been able to sell his vote. This arrival amidships has other charms. You are discharged, it is true, in confusion upon cobbles and you may, if you are not careful, be re-exported at once in a consignment of packing cases going off in the ship next door. But, for the inhabitants, the advantage is that they hear the blast of the sirens all over the island, detonating in Fifth Avenue, shaking the place at night, ripping the heart out, arousing a general pride in the contact with places across the sea. And where there is blasting, there are echoes. This place, dedicated far more to the demigod Activity, even more than to Thrift and Mammon, echoes all day and all night. The blast ricochets from building to building like speech, so that one might say that the buildings are shouting at one another with the sort of authority that repeated messages have and yet with that touch of snap and folly which is also in the genius of the place.

One has had the pleasure of being borne up the splendid Hudson. The idle eye has been diverted by the classical, embossed green columns and ironwork of the shabby dock sheds. I hope someone will save these façades when they are torn down and put a stretch or two in some pleasant spot, for they are one of the minor heirlooms of the place. If I could afford to start a waterside theater or dance hall, I would buy a Manhattan dock on the Hudson side. But the midtown arrival is nothing compared to the arrival at Brooklyn, and I put it above the sight—except at night—from Hoboken, too. The view of downtown and midtown New York from Brooklyn Heights beats all. The air is better here. I have no objection to poisoned cities: I live in one. But it is striking, in a salt-water island with the ocean close to its windows, that you do not smell the sea till you disembark at Brooklyn and stand on the Heights. Across water which was usually blue, if filthy, when I was there, you felt you had only to stretch out your hands across the East River to put your fingers into the tills of the Chase Manhattan Bank, so clear was the dry air. Across the water downtown cliffs spread and display themselves in separate pieces. The shapes are still abstract art but here one appreciates the subtle variety of colors. New Yorkers exaggerate nearly everything; but nothing so much as the dirt of their city. No doubt it is dirty, and dirtier than it was—before the motorcar its stone must have been almost in a state of primeval chastity—and we know that Americans have an odd fear of dirt. But how is it that these buildings preserve their whites, their cool grays, their fair yellows and their ochers, their crimsons, their dark grays, and their browns? How freshly the slim-seeming red building at the end of Wall Street stares. From this vantage point Manhattan does not huddle, nor would I have said that it menaced, except as those columns in the account book menace; it displays itself serenely, and Brooklyn Bridge with its stone arches and its harp of steel wire makes the view orderly and momentous. Brooklyn Bridge tethers an island to reality, an island which otherwise has the terrible explicitness of a phantom. Or perhaps, because in the United States one is always thinking of elsewhere, one should say that it tethers reality to a phantom. Hart Crane's line says this: "*Thy cables breathe the North Atlantic still*," and he, too, sees the bridge as a harp:

> *O harp and altar, of the fury fused,*
> *(How could mere toil align thy choiring strings!)*
> *Terrific threshold of the prophet's pledge,*
> *Prayer of pariah, and the lover's cry . . .*

For all the bridges in America—and architecturally it is the bridges rather than the buildings or even the way of life that are the supreme American achievement—that second line is the forgotten tribute.

But there are other means of invasion. The native American would come in years ago across the continent to Hoboken and take the ferry where Hudson once had moored. They were fortunate: the Hoboken ferry, still running for commuters, is a fine specimen of nineteenth-century art, seemly in its lines, spacious in its curving deck, nicely foliated and unfunctional in its ironwork, and calming to the nerves. Speculators on the verge of breakdown should be prescribed a daily voyage on it and a diet of clams on the Hoboken side on the way back home. The remarkable water beetle docks downtown, there is a therapeutic noise of ratchets: one is released. Not here that long hysteria of the tiled white tunnels that connect Manhattan to the mainland and Long Island by a prolonged madhouse scream.

The foreigner coming into the John F. Kennedy International Airport has to endure one of these high-class sewers after about seven hours at thirty thousand feet of being closer to God than he could have wished. His plane, humming itself to sleep in the long suspense from life over the Atlantic, suddenly wakes up, sights the million puddles of Labrador, turns south at Gander over forested tracts, estuaries, and the little American lakes which were formed when the Ice Age melted away and the ice scoured the rock all the way beyond the palisades of jointed sandstone on the Hudson at Manhattan, and beyond it. The air traveler grasps, at least, the scale, the emptiness of the continent of which New York was and still is the key. The harbor of Halifax, like New York's, can also hold a fleet and did so during the war. We drone south with America burning, sun-shot, under its cloud-smoke. We gaze down on the rich pathway of New England. We strain our necks trying to pick out the features of the hinterland and to name a town, to see Thoreau by his pond, Hawthorne shoveling manure at Brook Farm, those old men whittling by little harbors, or the schoolboys at Andover. We bucket over one of Boston's frequent storms where the dear placid Christian Science ladies are praying to protect the pineapple on top of Mother Church from lightning. (How characteristically American: they call prayer "Doing their work.") Jammed in with over one hundred other human sacks, our ears dulled, our heads splitting, our ankles swollen, our bladders arrested, and our brains reduced to the state of broken typewriters, we are tipped headfirst towards the marshy geography of Long Island, see with unpleasant exactness the ripples of the lagoons, hit some lucky stretch of tarmac, and slump back into the grateful smell of overheated rubber. We are led, mindless bodies that we are, in startling silence to what appears to be a glass hospital for forcing ailing plants.

Still, one recovers. Up in the air, when the first New York roads came into sight, one was aware of mysterious blue, green, and yellow beetles in winding procession; to this infestation one now belongs, but those beetles were rats. One is on the rat race of the American highway. In all countries of the world is there anything more dreadful than the road from the airport? It is the modern nightmare. It has been designed to shock the sky visitor with the full visual horror of the life of industrial man fighting for his place in the dormitory, choked by products. The sea is free of these indecencies.

What one wants is the city. And here, as one comes in from the airport, is another startling view, one that is palatial, ethereal, and also macabre. For coming across the hills of Queens one enters the huge estates of the city's cemeteries. Their stones are black. A few miles away, beyond the hills falling to the East River, is the desired apparition of Manhattan, floating low in the air, rising through squalls of thundercloud, wraithlike in the winter snow, a string of faraway diamonds in the summer; but before one gets there, there is this glum, black parody of its life. The black stones are arranged in sizes, in rigid avenues and even streets on the pattern of the Manhattan grid. They extend on all sides to the skyline. Only monotonous lives or organizational existences could—one moralizes—have been so plain-spoken about the monotony, the treadmill probability of a money-conscious Hereafter. It is the occupational ill-luck of cemetery makers everywhere, if they are in the mass business, to mar the scene. What strikes one here is the barrenness of memory, the lack of piety, the absence of grotesque, the lack of family distinctiveness: instead, neutrality. The cemetery establishes and multiplies a fact. Yet, conscious or unconscious as the makers of this place may have been, and of what they were contributing to arrival, they did something immensely dramatic, and in some moods I find this the most impressive approach to the city. For one is taken through this deep and rigid region of peopled blackness, through the Shades, as it were, to see Manhattan set out in all its gaiety of line. From the Battery to Harlem, one sees the towers rise, fall away, rise again for miles in whatever disguise the weather is giving them for the hour of day: and if it is at night, one comes out of a double darkness to see the city like a collection of lighted lanterns hanging from the sky and not rising from the earth at all.

There remains one more major assault upon the eyes in Manhattan: the sight of it from above. As you came gravely into the wide harbor and that short distance to your berth you saw small colored insects buzzing over you in the skies. These little stingers are the helicopters. In your new life the vertical dimension is certain to prevail over the horizontal; you will be going up and down oftener than you are going along. In fact, suppose you could remove all the buildings from Manhattan but leave the people exactly where they were, you would see the fantastic sight of people sitting high up in the air or whizzing upwards and downwards; very few would be on the earth. It is cheerfully reckoned that in the new Pan American Building, 150,000 people whiz up and down per day at speeds of up to seventeen hundred feet a minute. The physical course of a New Yorker's daily life is a preoccupation with right angles: he is a man conditioned to an automatic process of anxiously going along and inevitably going up. He returns to earth to go along and, at right angles, to cross on the flat. This is a drastically mathematical life, a training in precision that leaves a mark on his life, leaving him to think of his interests and his psyche geometrically. But once you have got into the bubble cabin of your helicopter, on the top of, say, the Port of New York Authority Building, once the windmill begins to roar and the thing to shake your bones and teeth—to your vast relief, for nothing would be more terrifying than a flight in unenthusiastic silence over the city—once the bubble rises and then takes that sickening dip over the edge into space and pitches you like some suicide going down from the fiftieth floor counting windows for the last time, you find yourself floating and joining the foolish life of the skyscraper tops, which makes the geometry below look endurable. Now those tall things stand up like sugar sticks. All the confections, all the follies of Manhattan (in the English sense of a rich man's whim), occur at the tops of buildings. Or rather, they used to, before the flat-roof glass-case engineers started spoiling the game a few years ago. You rattle round these giddy banks and lightheaded corporations: you see the light change from white to blue, from pink to purple down the long slabs: at sunrise or sunset, you see the flush and the shadow. You fly out over the bay and go carefully round the cheeks and nostrils of the Statue of Liberty—rather sphinxlike at close quarters, staring from her great bland stone eyes and answering no questions; you see the beetles coming in from Newark; you turn back to resume your dance over the city that is roped by its East River bridges. You see the torn shapes of water high on the horizon, sad in the evening on the flattish eastern side, and the salty Hudson coming down, nobler than the Rhine, to freshen the concrete island with its water and green banks. From this height how poor Manhattan is in greenery, compared with other cities. There are little patches in Union and Madison Squares and around Gramercy Park, oases to the thirsty eye. Not until the enormous rectangle of Central Park, uptown, is the eye assuaged. That park saved the place from madness. For down below your feet you see that New York's dramatic pride has deceived you. It has shown you its high buildings, but in fact it is a lowish city like any other. Only thirty years ago, Mumford says, at the height of the high period, eighty-five per cent of its millions of buildings were not more than eight stories high; the average number of stories was lower than in Paris. No doubt the average is rising. As it is, the stranger can be recognized anywhere by his fixed upward gaze and his look of one with an aching neck.

But now from the helicopter, and indeed from any high building, you look and see the real Manhattan. It is at first a shocking sight. One is looking down into the pitted jawbone of some Megatherium, into the rotting stumps and cavities of the giant sloth. No doubt this is the morbid reaction to your immaterial altitude. When it passes, you look with some affection on the lower roofs, with increasing affection at roofs still lower, and then with a positive yearning for the little cracks between them which are evidently streets. In any case, the taste for the View is out of date, Ruskinian, a hangover from German Romanticism and, going further back, from Rousseau and the cult of the high mountain. Good-by to all that. For myself, the middling altitudes of New York, with their sociable ups and downs, their surprising revelations of the hardware of other people's rooftops and the minor follies of the penthouse are more enjoyable. There with some point—New York life being what it is at night—one can ponder those lines from *Macbeth*.

> *Sleep shall neither night nor day*
> *Hang upon his penthouse lid.*

The nearer ground level one is in this city the more one feels the intimacies of a place which are all the more intense for having so much that is unintimate to contend with.

You come down and down in your bubble. You see a collection of approaching rooftops: they are discarded by the pilot-fly; you waggle your way towards others. Somewhere here the landing is, surely? And then, to your horror, you see it. The yellow target circle, the size of a dartboard. You are now in the agonizing process of reversing your suicide, of praying for accuracy, of returning plumb in the middle of the sill you jumped from. My God, the fly has made it! How often in your right-angular New York life, going up and down, along and across, in elevators, at street corners, you will say that: after a few months the anxiety to "make it," the absolute necessity of "making it" will have become an accustomed undertone in your life.

And that is what you are now entitled to say about your arrival on that shiplike, daggerlike, targetlike island, nearly thirteen and a half miles long and only two and a quarter miles across at its widest point, of a city that with four other boroughs across the waters has 7,781,984 inhabitants. In Manhattan alone, they are stacked, shelved, slotted to a density of seventy-five thousand to the square mile.

(1964)

FROM

Dublin: A Portrait

VII

The official commemoration of the Easter Rising has just been held in Dublin as I write. The British have astonished Dubliners by regarding the men of the Rising as heroes; it would be easy to say about this admiration that it is one more example of the English habit of forgiving those you have injured. Certainly the English have short memories and the Irish have long ones: in fact the admiration has two more serious sources. First: in this year the British are remembering the loss of an equally patriotic and romantic generation, tens of thousands of them Irish, who lost their lives on the Somme. Secondly: the mass of British people in 1914 found it intolerable that an Irish settlement should have been delayed by a powerful section of their ruling class who were as oppressive to them as they were to the Irish. The Rising and the War disposed of those troubles.

Only one act of violence preceded this year's commemoration. Acts of violence are likely to last for ever in Ireland, for the Irish are privately vain of their taste for illegality and they enjoyed the gesture for its own sake. To commemorate the Rising, Kilmainham Jail, which had been in a state of ruin for years, was put into order and was opened as a sort of national shrine. In November 1965 I went to see how the work was getting on. Hundreds of tourists—mainly Irish-Americans—have visited the ruined jail every year. They scribble their names on the walls of the cells of this prison where so many Irish patriots were incarcerated, hanged or shot since the days of the United Irishmen. Here the leaders of the Rising were executed by the British. The jails of Ireland and especially of Dublin are old and brutal monuments. Kilmainham, in its rough granite, is the most horrible of them.

The driver who takes American tourists to visit the jail is eloquent about the brutality of British oppression; the British visitors are treated more guardedly. My driver, an old man who had fought against the British and who said his heart had been broken and his faith lost in the Civil War, was disgusted by my visit. The place, he said, was a monument to all the lies and betrayals of Irish history. He wanted the jail to be pulled down.

Inside, it was half-ruined. The roof had collapsed at one time, the grim little cells were rotted by damp, the floors had gone, one walked down freezing, dark, wrecked corridors, groping from plank to plank. One of the workmen, an old man who was doing some repairs, took me round the cells of the leaders of the Rising. We saw the broken gibbet on which (I believe he said) the Invincibles were hanged. He told the details of what each man had done. I saw the large cell which had two windows and which looked out on to a stone wall, where Parnell had been briefly imprisoned. His bust was there and there was an inscription cut into the sill. We went out into the exercise yard which is enclosed between the main block of the prison and the enormously high outer granite wall and then into the bleak yard where some of the men of the Rising were executed. In one corner was the spot where Connolly was shot. He had been badly wounded and carefully nursed in hospital—until he was well enough to sit up in a chair for execution! Nausea and hatred make the visitor wretched. The very fact that there are new granite chips in this death yard somehow appals. It is good for those of us who have escaped political imprisonment which, since 1916, has become a commonplace in our world, to consider the scene. Pearse longed to shed his blood: the British foolishly gratified his desire. From Tone and Emmet onwards the Irish patriot has always *wanted* to die. There is a most curious, obsessional desire in Ireland for "the last rites," life having only a doubtful meaning.

And then, at the most wretched moment of my visit, the absurd occurred, as it does again and again in Ireland. I was just about to leave when another visitor got into the prison. He had found the door open and he wandered towards us, a well-dressed, cheerful, vigorous-looking man in, I suppose, his early sixties; he looked like a prosperous business-man. He was English.

"I hope you don't mind," he said. "I was passing by. I thought I'd like to drop in on the old place. God, they've let it go. What a mess! What a shame! It wasn't like this in my time, the British kept it up, spick and span and proper. It's terrible. Oh yes, I was here. I was a naughty boy. They put me up there—in number three or four was it?—in the top gallery."

The old workman had been wary but at this he woke up.

"What was it?" he said.

"Well," said the man, "I've led a bit of a roving life, all over the world you might say, back and forth. I was a deserter. I was stationed in Galway. I was only a kid and I got into a spot of trouble down there—nothing really bad, well, we won't go into it now, it's a long time ago. Nowadays they'd let it pass but those were hard times. That's where they put me, up there."

"Is that a fact?" the old man began to grin.

"Yes, that's it, number three or four, top gallery. The man next door went mad and threw himself off and killed himself. There was no net in those days. What am I saying? I'm telling a lie. I was in here twice. That was when I was in Cork—more trouble, I deserted again. I deserted twice."

"Did you now?" said the old man who had his hands in his pockets and was scratching his legs with delight.

"Let's see the exercise yard," the Englishman said. "It's through there if I remember right."

The old man said: "That's right. Through this door."

"Do you see that? He remembers it!" the old man whispered to me laughing. "Come on now, I'll show you."

"It's a shame the way they've let it go," said the Englishman.

"No one seemed to care at all about it," apologised the old man.

"Oh, here it is," said the Englishman, aglow to be in the yard. "That's it. I reckon I know every stone in that wall. They made you run close to it. I have run round that wall hundreds of times."

"You're right there," said the elated old man.

"And the drummer—now where did he stand? Over there by the window in the corner, I think," said the Englishman.

"In the corner it was. You see he remembers everything," the old man said with admiration.

"Left, right, left, right, pick 'em up. The drum tap!" said the Englishman.

"Ah, the drum tap! The drum tap, it made you skip," cried the old man.

"The drum tap! They knew how to beat it out fast."

"Ah, they did that."

Reluctantly the Englishman left his playground.

"Was it in the Devons or the Foresters you said you were?" asked the old man.

"The Foresters."

"I was in the Fusiliers," said the old man. "We were in the Curragh."

They were charmed and they chattered. The Englishman gazed up at the cell.

"I think it was the third cell, perhaps I'm mixing it up with the second time. Or Arbour Hill Barracks—they had me there too. That was the third time."

"Three times. Powerful," said the old man whispering. And then, covering his mouth with his hand, he giggled: "I was in the bloody British Army too. I was a deserter myself. Ha! Ha!"

"Where were you then?" said the Englishman.

"I was in Solingen, never short of a razor blade there. And the girls cheering in the street when we got in," said the old man.

"You're bloody right. I was up there too!" said the Englishman. The two friends gazed at each other.

"It's a pity, it's a great pity it's been let go," the old man said.

"It's a shame. It looked decent once. To be candid I came here because I had a bit of trouble with my daughter. I'd forgotten all about it—well, the years go, you forget. But she found out and 'Oh dear, our dad in prison!'—you know? She was so upset I had to get the priest to calm her down. It's all right now. So, I thought, next time I'm over I'll have a look at the old place. I didn't expect this mess."

"Oh we're putting it right. We're getting in the show cases; there's been a delay in the cement," apologised the old man. "But we've got the toilets nearly finished. We're waiting for the pipes. It's in the Commandant's office. I'll show you. We've done a nice job here." We went into the toilets.

"That's it," said the Englishman. "They brought you in here. That's where he must have sat."

Toilets for tourists: is that how the history of a human agony ends?

(1967)

LONDON

No Londoner can be exact or reasonable about London. This place with the heavy-sounding name, like coal being delivered or an engine shunting, is the world's greatest unreasonable city, a monstrous agglomeration of well-painted property. The main part of the city, 120 square miles of low-lying and congested Portland stone, yellow brick and stucco, slate, glass and several million chimneys, lies a few minutes' flight from the North Sea. There are immense acreages of railway track, and the subsoil is a tangle of tunnels running into scores of miles. Such is the mere core of London; another 700 square miles of what was once pasture and woodland is now continuous red-faced suburb. People talk loosely about the number of London's inhabitants: there are certainly nine million. To the police it seems much more.

It is impossible to be exact about London because no one really has ever seen it. Once in, we are engulfed. It is a city without profile, without symmetry; it is amorphous, like life, and no one thing about it is definitive. A natural guess, for example, is that it is as gray and yellow as it looks; yet, from any small height it looks entirely green, like a forest, with occasional stone towers sticking out. The explanation is paradoxical: by preserving trees the Londoner, by far the most urban living creature, convinces himself he is living in the countryside.

Of the world's capitals London has been the most powerful and important for a good two hundred years, the capital of the largest empire since the Roman. It is now the capital of a Commonwealth. But to be a Londoner is still to be immediately, ineluctably, a citizen of the world. Half of the mind of every Londoner is overseas. If the French government falls, if there is dock trouble in New York, a riot in the Gold Coast, even the charwoman cleaning the office will mention the lugubrious fact. There is an old story that someone was once mad enough to ask a Cockney whether the London he came from was London, Ontario; the Cockney groaned "Nah! London the whole bloomin' world." Truculent, proud, even sentimental, yet the old hypocrite was piously complaining of the weight of the world upon the London mind.

Perhaps because of the weight and the worry, London is the least ostentatious of the world's capitals. It has little of the rhetorical architecture and the ambitious spacing of monuments and temples to be found in the capitals of the new democracies; none of the marble splash endowed by patriotic planners. Napoleon would turn in his grave in the Invalides if he could see Nelson's urn crowded among painters and bishops in the crypt of St. Paul's. The Houses of Parliament and Buckingham Palace are among the few great edifices to compose a view, and so—thanks to German bombers— was St. Paul's Cathedral for a few years during and after the war; but, for the rest, though London has its fine quarters, its monuments, palaces and even a triumphal arch or two, these have been eased into the city and are not ornately imposed upon it.

London excels in the things that segregate and preserve an air of privilege: the lovely terraces of the Regency, the sedate faces of the squares and of the moneyed or modest Georgian and Early Victorian streets. These are not collectors' pieces; they are the routine of central London. The Londoner is purse-proud and shows it in his domestic property rather than in imperial splash; and if in a moment of vainglory he builds a Pall Mall club that looks like the Foreign Office and a Foreign Office that looks like a cross between a Renaissance palace and a Turkish bath, he redresses the balance by putting the Prime Minister in a small private house called No. 10 down a side street and with only an iron railing—and a couple of policemen—to prevent us from putting our noses against the window.

But I am writing as if I had *seen* London, when the confusing fact is that I have only lived in it most of my life. I have just looked at the smear of gray sky through the window of my top-floor flat. It is in one of those blocks of pink structures which went up like so many vending machines in London between the wars, when architecture broke with the Victorian rotundity and the cheese-colored stucco of 150 years before. I closed the window to shut out the noise of the buses. Look at my hands. Already filthy.

I find myself siding with Henry James, who noticed the filth of London as soon as he arrived here, went on to say that it was not cheerful or agreeable, added that London was dull, stupid and brutally large and had a "horrible numerosity of society." Was anything left after that? Yes, he said; there was magnificence.

London is a prime grumbler. The weather, the traffic, the smoke, the dirty color get us down and we feel our life is being eaten up in those interminable bus and tube journeys through the marsh of brick—eaten up before we have even started to live. But gradually we begin to feel the magnificence that rises out of the gray, moody, Victorian splodge. We felt it in the sound of Big Ben growling like an old lion over the wet roofs in the silent, apprehensive nights of the war. Where Paris suggests pleasure, Rome the human passions of two thousand years, with assassination in every doorway, where New York suggests a ruthless alacrity, London suggests experience.

The manner of the city is familiar, casual, mild but incontrovertible.

London has this power not only of conserving the history of others but of making one feel personally historic. A young bus conductor, a youth with Korea in his face, said to me the other day: "That's all a thing of the past, like everything else nowadays." He was feeling historic already at twenty-five. Perhaps in all the very large cities of the world at the moment, people are beginning to feel they only have a past; the future seems short. But London has always turned the mind inward. Londoners vegetate.

The city also is something you get on your lungs, which quickens and dries your speech and puts a mask on the face. We breathe an acid effluence of city brick, the odors of cold soot, the dead rubbery breath of city doorways, or swallow a mouthful of mixed sulfuric that blows off those deserts of railway tracks which are still called Old Oak Common or Nine Elms without a blade of vegetation in sight for miles—we breathe these with advantage. They gave us headaches when we were young, but now the poison has worked and is almost beneficent to those born to it. So herrings must feel when they have been thoroughly kippered.

On top of this there is the climate. That is in itself aging. We are, for example, ten years older since eight o'clock this morning, for we woke up to fog, saw it melt into feeble sunshine, watched white clouds boil up and then stand still like marble. A thunderstorm? No, the temperature changes, shoots up, drops down, the sky blackens. At midday the lights come on in flats and shops. All those thousands of green desk lamps in the banks of the City are switched on. What does this mean? Snow this afternoon? Or rain? Probably rain but who can tell? We can't. In the next twenty-four hours we shall have lived a lifetime's weather. We shall have seen a dozen hopes and expectations annulled; we shall have been driven in on ourselves and on the defensive. We shall talk of what it was like yesterday, of the past.

Yet when Henry James used that word "magnificent" it was the London sky I at once thought of. London generates its own sky—a prolonged panorama of the battle between earth and heaven. For if the lower sky is glum over London and sometimes dark brown or soupy yellow, it is often a haze of violet and soft, sandy-saffron colors. If the basis is smoke and the next layer is smoke and fog banked up, the superstructure of cloud is frequently noble. White cumulus boils up over the city against a sky that is never blue as the Mediterranean knows blue, but which is fair and angelic. The sky space in our low city is wide.

And this sky has had another magnificence: it has been a battlefield. I never see a large white cloud now, against the blue, without going back to that afternoon when the Spitfires dived into it like silver fish, as the sirens went off over the British Museum. And many times in 1940 I saw the night sky go green instead of black, twitching like mad electricity, hammered all over by tens of thousands of sharp golden sparks as the barrage beat against it like steel against a steel door. The curling ribbons of fire that came down from heaven were almost a relief to see, with that unremitting noise. One was glad of silence, even if the silence was alight. One cloudless August afternoon green snow fell in dry, unmelting flakes in Holborn. We picked this new venture of the English climate off our coats: a V-2 had just fallen nearly two miles away in Hyde Park and had blown the leaves of the trees into these mysterious smithereens.

London is an agglomeration of villages which have been gummed together in the course of centuries. It is a small nation rather than a city, and its regions have never quite lost their original identity or even their dialects. The City of London, the administrative heart of the city, which begins at Aldgate suddenly, like a row of cliffs, is a province in itself. Yet a large part of central London is not muddle at all, for here it was planned in the late eighteenth and early nineteenth centuries, when the squares were laid out between Bloomsbury and Bayswater. The habit of making tree-shaded oases, in squares and private terraces, gave a respite from the vulgar uproar and ugly building of the general commercial scramble. The railed-in lawns and the green enclosures of the Inns of Court betray our love of privacy and privilege, and for delectable cliques, clubs and coteries, just as those acres and acres of little two-story houses show how much we like a little property to ourselves. This has been the despair of urban planners.

There are immense cheese-colored areas in Bayswater and elsewhere where Bernard Shaw's tall Heartbreak Houses have pillars like footmen's legs. Chelsea is one kind of place. Westminster another. Inner London is gray or yellow, outer London is red; that is about as much as can be said of the Victorian jungle, unless we name the slates shining like mirrors in the wet.

In that tired air, always heavy and often damp and lethargic, the grass grows green in the black soil of the gardens, the shrubs grow dusty and the dappled plane trees grow black. In the summer evenings we listen to their leaves turning over like the pages of endless office ledgers. We hear the ducks fly over from some pool of filthy water left on a bomb site to the wooded lakes in the parks. We hear the starlings at St. Martin's crying down the traffic. We hear owls. We even hear sheep in Regent's Park in the summer. A city so countrified cannot be megapolis.

We are tree lovers. In the winter the London trees are as black as processions of mourners and, like the weeds of some sooty gathering of widows, their higher branches are laced against the mist or the long, sad sunsets. The thing that reconciled us to those ruined miles in Holborn, Cheapside and round St. Paul's were the trees that grew rapidly out of burned-out basements where the safes had been kept; and the willow herb that grew in purple acres out of commercial brick.

The London tree grows out of poisoned soil, its roots are enclosed by stone and asphalt, and it breathes smoke. There is one heroic creature, raising its arms between two overtowering blocks of office buildings and the church of St. Magnus the Martyr in Billingsgate. Typewriters clatter among its branches instead of birds; and a boy who climbed it would come down black. Its survival shows how firmly Londoners cling to nature and, in life, to some corner of what has been.

Except in the curve of the river between Westminster and St. Paul's, there are no large vistas in London, and our small ones have come to us by luck and accident. I have a typical view of the London muddle from my flat. There is one of those Victorian streets of carefully painted small houses, with their classical doorways and their iron railings. (The Victorians did not know what to do with all the iron they produced and simply caged up everything in it.) I have counted 270 chimneys in a couple of hundred yards—cheap coal, cheap servants to carry it up from those basements. Now only about ten of those chimneys are smoking; we run on electricity and gas; but this population of London chimneys remains like millions of sets of old, unwanted teeth.

The street runs into a decaying square where the first publisher I knew used to live and poke his small Victorian fire in the late twenties; he wore button boots and believed in Animal Magnetism. A furniture depository has wrecked one end of the square. At the back of it are the mews: one smart mews flat, several garages with the chauffeurs cleaning and polishing and one of those doubtful "caffs" where the police are always asking questions. Until the espresso bars started there was a certain affinity between London coffee and crime.

Turn back, across the main street, and you are walking through Thackeray's *Vanity Fair* and *The Newcomes* into the country of the Victorian new rich and the pretty houses of their mistresses. Dickens lived near here in state. But close to their back doors was and is the toughest street in the neighborhood, a place for those fantastic fights between women who have had a pint or two. I once saw a lady pulled off her prey by three or four men.

"I can't take the 'ole ruddy lot of you on," she said, misunderstanding their intention. "I'm not an elephant."

The quarter has its gin palaces, its television shops, its cinemas, its plastic bars, a reputation for smash-and-grab, and the ripest old London music hall. There are only a few left. The idea is to go there, full of beer and with the family, and to laugh from the belly at mothers-in-law, double beds, perambulators and love from the point of view of the sexual treadmill. No Puritans here; on the other hand, not much art either. London has always liked its jokes to be common, full-fleshed, dirty and sanguine and its chorus girls to be pink, broad and breezy. It likes Britannia on the loose, with her helmet over one eye and her trident unspeakably meaningful.

The eye tours the slate roofs of the horizon and, presently, it stops short: there is that new aspect of the London skyline, the sudden gap. Ten or twelve houses went down over there in a cloud of dust during the war. These gaps and gashes are everywhere in London; some of them startle us. We see our ghosts. Up there (we say), where the sky is now, I used to dine with the So-and-so's. Or, there in that space were my first lodgings: the landlady used to tipple. Or, there, about thirty-five feet in the air, I was in love with a girl who read my fortune in my hand and infuriated me in predicting that I was to be the least important of the three great loves of her life. The back room where I wrote my first book is a piece of sky. To have survived such total destruction by ten or fifteen years makes one feel irrelevant. It makes life seem very long. The gardens of these destroyed houses are now haunted and sinister wilderness.

These gaps bring back the strangest thing that has ever happened to London: the silence of the city at night during the war. Only one writer has described it: Elizabeth Bowen, who sat it out in her cracked and boarded-up Regency house in the Park. One walked in those days down empty streets that stared like sepulchers, hearing only the echo of one's own heels. Voices carried far, as if across water. I remember two painted old ladies sitting up late on a bench in Lincoln's Inn Fields, and I could hear their solitary chatter from across the square. They were, of course, talking about the distant connections of the Royal Family.

Ever since that night in December 1940, when the City was burned out, the black crowds marching over London Bridge to their offices have seen a lifetime's seriousness made nonsense of. It was dumfounding to lose one's working past, affronting to pride and good sense. There has always been pride in trade and in London it was commemorated in the plaques and urns and epitaphs of Wren's churches. Men working in the city—selling shirts in Cheapside or insurance in London Wall—knew they were working in the birthplace of modern capitalism. They were heirs of Defoe and Lloyd. A guidebook to this part of London is useless now. Streets vanished.

Neighborhoods vanished. North of Cheapside one wanders in an abstract wilderness of streets without reason, for no buildings stand in them. London Wall is brick frieze three feet high to prevent one from falling into the cellars. Tears come into my eyes when I see the blackened husk of Bow Church. I suppose because the place had been made human by the nursery rhyme so suited to the children of merchants:

> *"When will you pay me,"*
> *Said the bells of Old Bailey.*
> *"I do not know,"*
> *Said the big bell at Bow.*

One thinks of mere impedimenta: the desks, the telephones, the filing systems, the teacups of the sacred quarter-of-an-hour for office tea, the counters and tills, the lifts that some people spent their working lives in. All gone. That wilderness north of Cheapside is misery; in the winter, when the snow is on it, or under the moon, it is the Void itself.

The wastes gave space and perspective to a city which the greedy middle-class individualism of trade had always grudged. All the fine planning in London, and any nobility it has, is aristocratic and royal; the rest of us, from the small shopkeeper to the great bureaucratic corporations, are consumed by the tenacious passion for property. The true Londoner would sooner have property than money; he would certainly sooner have it, no matter how muddled, than air or space.

This muddle of property, however, has its own richness. I worked in pungent London when I was young. Pungent London lies eastward of London Bridge. In the Boro' High Street, where you can still eat at one of those galleried inns that you probably thought existed only in the drawings of Cruikshank, I mooned in the heady smell of hops; in Tooley Street it is the Scandinavian trade in butter and eggs; in Pickle Herring Street, dry salted hides, rank and camphorous. Australian leather is being pulled off the lighters at Thames wharf, where the cranes sigh in their strange, birdlike communities. There is a strong smell of pepper, too, and the sour-mutton odor of wool. We dodged the crane hooks and got startling earfuls of the language of carmen, who are noted for their command of blasphemy. The cranes, the anchor chains and winches are clattering across the water, and steam and smoke go up dancing in the river wind. There are one or two public houses with terraces on the river, sitting as neat as pigeons between the warehouse walls. London is not a very self-regarding city; these wharves are its innumerable windows looking on the faraway world—to Africa, the Indies, China or the Levant.

But, for myself, Bermondsey was the place. There on the south bank they refer to London as the place "over the water." We worked in the stink of leather, listening to the splitting machines and the clogs of the hide men. The slum kids used to climb up the bars on the office windows and make faces at us and tie the swing doors so that we could not get out. When we caught these children their mothers turned up: "You take your bleedin' hands off that bleedin' kid." The Hide Market has been knocked silly now; Bermondsey and Rotherhithe are burned out, and where there was once a jungle of little houses, there now is London's naked clay, filling up with thousands of prefabricated huts that look like sets of caterpillar eggs. There are new tenements. One notices a rise in tone. At the Caledonian Market, where they sell everything from old clothes and worn-out gramophone records to antiques at the top West End prices, a good many stall holders talk the new B.B.C. English. "No, madam," one hears the incredible accent, "the date of this salt-cellar is 1765, not '75. One can see by the scroll."

In Throgmorton Street, we used to see the stock jobbers thick in the street. Inside the Stock Exchange we looked down on the littered floor and saw again what a passion for the market London has. For the stalls marked Diamonds, Industrials, Mines, and so on, are really gentlemanly versions of the vegetable market at Covent Garden, the meat market at Smithfield or the fish market of Billingsgate. The only difference is that a boss at the Stock Exchange puts on a top hat when he visits his banker; at the others, he sticks to his white dust coat, his cap or his bowler. The population of bowlers in London has declined, but in the conservative city clubs they can still be seen rowed up by the hundred like sittings of black eggs.

In Carlyle's London Library or under the dome of the whispering Reading Room of the British Museum, one may forget that London has the habit of markets and auctions. But at Christie's, the world-famous auction rooms of pictures, silver and china, they will knock down a Picasso or a Matisse, a Gainsborough or a Raphael, at a nod no one can see. The crowd is well-dressed and silent. Knowingness irradiates from inscrutable faces. It is like a chapel service, and the auctioneer is up to all the tricks of the sinners in the congregation: "I must ask you, sir, to stop preventing people from bidding. You turned round. Three or four times you have made a face." Such is the sensibility of this secretive business that a mere raised eyebrow can cause doubt. Where all are mad, all are cunning. It is the same at Sotheby's. You realize in these markets that London is composed of cliques, coteries and specialists, little clubbable collections, causeries, exclusivities, snobberies, of people in innumerable "games" played on secret knowledge, protecting people "in," keeping others "out," with dilatory blandness. It is untrue that we are white sepulchers. Our sepulchers are rosy.

In London, whatever you do, you have to be a "member." I have no doubt there are cliques at Covent Garden or Smithfield. It is different only in those instantaneous, outspoken markets of the street, that mark more clearly than anything one district from another. Berwick market for the foreigners, junk in the Portobello Road, dogs at Bethnal Green, pictures on the Embankment, jewelry and diamonds being sold on the street at Hatton Garden.

Petticoat Lane, just past Aldgate off the Whitechapel Road, is still the richest; this narrow mile, gashed by bomb sites and hemmed in by the East End sweatshops, is London's screaming parody of an Oriental bazaar. It is a mile deafened by voices that have burst their throat strings years ago and are down to tonsils and catarrh. "Nah then, come on closer. I'll tell you what I'll do. What's that? You're not my bloody sister. My family's like me, ugly as hell. Nah then, will any lady or gentleman present this morning do me the favah of lending me a pound note?" Or: "I'm not taking money this morning, not two pound, one pound, not eighteen, seventeen, fifteen, twelve shilling but"—bang on the book—"five shilling and sixpence for these beautiful cut-glass vases, the last. I'm frowning them away."

The crowd is dense here. You move six deep, chest to back, an inch at a time, jammed in by Cockneys, Jews, Negroes, Lascars and Chinese off the ships. And, head and shoulders above all, there will be that pink-feathered Zulu prince who can be seen any day anywhere between Aldgate and Tottenham Court Road, selling his racing tips and making the girls scream with his devouring smile. There will be a turban or two and, moving through them against the crowd, will come that tall, glum specter of the London streets with his billboard high above his head, denouncing the Jews for their wickedness in trading on Sunday morning. "The Wages of Sin," the notice reads, and people make way for him, "is Death." He passes the stalls where they are serving stewed eels by the cup and black-currant cordial by the glass. He passes the hot dogs and the sugared apples, the stalls of china, socks, watches, handkerchiefs, blankets, toys. A yell comes up from your boot. You have almost trodden on a little fellow who has sat down there suddenly in the middle of the street and is crying out, as if he were on fire: "Ladies! Ladies! Nylons a penny a pair!" And just when we are crushed and cannot move even our chests, there is the tinny sound of kettledrums, the wheeze of clarinet and trumpet, the boom of a soft slack drum. The blind men's band, with its one-legged collectors fore and aft, moves sternly through us all, raking in the cash.

For a year or two the City and the London market used to tempt me. There is a torpid pleasure in custom and routine which give their absorbent power to great cities. You could spend your life in those acres of desks under the thousands of green-shaded lamps that hang over them. There was that little temple in the middle of Lloyd's great temple of insurance, where the Lutine Bell was and still is, and where the red-robed and black-collared attendant in his velvet sat calling out the names of the underwriters like psalms throughout the day. You never realized before what a passion for guarantees the human race has and that London was the steady guarantor. I have never heard that Bell ring, as it is supposed to do, once for Bad News and twice for Good, and I am told that they have given up ringing it for Bad News because nowadays it would never stop ringing. They did ring it twice lately because some coastal steamer in the eastern Mediterranean and given up for lost had just crawled into Tobruk. Nothing happens at sea in any part of the world, but London suffers a seismographic tremor.

And then the spell of working in London owes something to its lingering medieval habit of working in districts; the tailors in Savile Row and their cutters in the Whitechapel Road; the car dealers in Great Portland Street; there are streets sweet to international banking, others committed to insurance; a street for merchant shipping, the "rag" or mantle trades round St. Paul's, as near as possible to Defoe's Cheapside—what is left of both—newspapers in Fleet Street. Even the Law splits up among the lawns and chambers of the Inns of Court, into Law and Equity. This is pleasant and, by middle age, one has gathered that London lives by and enjoys its inner self, purveying the careful illusion of leisure and the pretense that its business is private. But for a young man this was all privilege, mystery and a bore. One gets restless.

One morning in the First World War, a carman called Ninety burst into the office and shouted "Air Raid!" across the counter to us boys, and to show he had a proper respect for white collars, added the inevitable "Please" (I have heard the reception clerk at Broadcasting House say the same thing in the Blitz twenty-five years later—"Air Raid, please"—to call the boys to close the iron shutters). It did please. What a relief from the monotonous London rumble to hear a sound like doors banging in the sky. We left our desks. A flight of German aircraft flew as steady as mosquitoes in a clear May sky that was pimpled with gunfire. Black smoke was going up from Billingsgate.

Our boss, a white-bearded old lion of eighty, with the telephone in his shaking hand, was saying breathlessly to the head clerk: "Have you heard the news? The *Dunnottar Castle* has just docked. Send a boy to me." There were no boys. We were on the roof. It was about this time I decided that if I wanted to see the world London had so much experience of, the sooner I stopped seeing it from weighing slips, delivery orders, the foreign mail and the secondhand bookshops of the Charing Cross Road, the better. London would make me less impatient once I had got back from Paris, Rome, Madrid or New York.

What does strike me when I come back from these places now is that London is a masculine city, a place for male content and consequence. The men, I notice, dress better here than anywhere else; none knows the curl of a hat or the set of a shoulder better or wears clothes of finer quality. It is just as well, for the absurd variety of English chins, teeth and noses needs some redemption, and people who run so easily to eccentricity need strong rituals and conventions. This is not the idiotic London of Bertie Wooster and the Drones, for the man-about-town is an extinct type. But, we have a dandy for Prime Minister, and there are tens of thousands of less eminent males doing what Henry James called "the thing" properly.

Coming out of the cloakroom of a hotel during the war with my hat in my hand, I saw Sir Max Beerbohm give me a historical look. "In my youth," he said, "it was not correct to uncover one's head in an hotel." How low we had sunk. Such men suffer for us all. They bear the cruelty of the mirror of Narcissus with fortitude.

That young undersecretary to the Cabinet Minister who stands, without overcoat, in the biting January wind, outside Brooks's Club talking to a friend, knows that if he dies of pneumonia tomorrow he will have caught it, properly costumed, at the right address. It will satisfy him and we, who are not impeccable, know that he is suffering fashion for us. Just as the Guards are when they stamp at the Palace.

Nor does this London vanity afflict only a small class. Detectives and barrow boys, bank messengers and the man in the shop have it as a matter of *amour-propre*. I used to know a London leech gatherer who went barefoot, with his trousers rolled up, into the ponds on his strange search, but he always wore a white lining to his waistcoat and a carnation in his buttonhole when about his duties. Old Mr. Cox at the London Library, who knew every famous writer and scholar of the last sixty years, used to say with deep London approval: "I knew Mr. Pater. Very particular about his clothes, Mr. Pater was." Sartorially, we like to burn like Mr. Pater's "still blue flame."

Foreigners say that Londoners are less honest than they were before the war, but find us startlingly kind and clever since we have put aside the imperial mask. It is true, I am sure, that we are less starchy; but I am far from noticing any disastrous decline in our complacency, our traditional habit of lazy and vocal self-congratulation. It is also true that once we went out to the Empire; now the Commonwealth comes to us and adds to the polyglot vivacity of our streets.

These strangers come, of course, in the summer when London is green and the smoked white clouds boil over the sultry brick. Then the center of London becomes a foreign city. There are summer mornings at Victoria or Waterloo when the platforms become African or South American. The African tribes appear in all their topknots and shaven blackness: the Moslem turbans gather in the underground railway. The universities and schools have always had a large number of Hindus, Moslems and Chinese and, indeed, it is from their lips mainly that one hears authentic Oxford English. There have always been maharajahs at Claridge's, Africans at the British Museum, Canadians, Australians and New Zealanders in the Strand; and we would be hurt if there were not.

What surprises us is that the real foreigners now come to visit us, not for trade, but for pleasure. There are posses of Argentines in the art galleries of Bond Street. There are days when Piccadilly is German. Crowds of Scandinavians sit on the steps of Eros in Piccadilly taking photographs. Most astonishing are the young French who pour over for the pleasure of eating the *cuisine anglaise* in the Corner Houses! Most familiar, for they have always come here, are the Americans. We do not know and they do not know whether they are foreign or not.

The change is remarkable. Once visited for the power we had, we are, as I say, now visited for our pleasures. The effect is most notable in the police. It has been said that every Englishman desires to be a policeman, a just, tolerant, self-commanding man, and the police may be considered martyrs to our desire for what we call "the sterling qualities"—the stoical, slow and resistant. But, inevitably, the policeman becomes a giddy tourist guide; he begins to rock on his pedestal into a state of informative frivolity. He has always been good-natured; now he becomes witty. And so with other groups. Conductors get off buses—in defiance of regulations—to show a stranger the way; taxi drivers throw away their misanthropy; all barmaids, waiters, doormen, porters, club servants and chambermaids appear to have sat up the night before reading their Dickens, in order to turn out next morning as authentic characters from *Pickwick* or *David Copperfield*. The foreign touch has always ignited the strong inner fantasy life of the Londoner.

The desire for a Dickensian London is strongest among Russians and Americans. This has its dark side. The Russians search for cotton mills in Piccadilly and expect to find children starving to death up every chimney. There are Americans who expect to find the roaring hungry chaos of the home of the Industrial Revolution. The American student, like the American soldier, gets to know something more like the real contemporary London. The American Dickensian visits the shrine in Doughty Street, follows the ghosts through the quadrangles and the alleys of Lincoln's Inn Fields and the Temple, drinks a glass of warm beer in piety at that old coaching inn in Southwark and looks hopefully from London Bridge towards Rotherhithe for the fog to be coming up the river. He returns to his hotel and, as I say, finds the perpetual Dickens there, if the staff are not all Poles, Czechs, Italians or Irish.

Americans, too, are strong Johnsonians and are familiar with Wine Office Court and the Old Cheshire Cheese. Do they look at the Doctor's statue under the trees by the burned-out church near the Law Courts? They know Westminster Abbey, St. Paul's, the museums and galleries better than ourselves. Do they know the exquisite Soane Museum in Lincoln's Inn Fields with its collection of Hogarth's paintings? London is still Hogarthian underneath.

When they come from seeing the Italian paintings in the National Gallery, do they risk their lives in the middle of the traffic south of Trafalgar Square and regard one of the few beautiful statues in a city notorious for its commemoration of nonentities—the equestrian figure of Charles I gaily prancing down the street of his downfall? Do any go into the church of St. Stephen in Wallbrook, the perfect small classical seventeenth-century building, or consider the blue octagon interior of St. Clement Danes?

I would send my American friends down St. Peter's Square into Chiswick Mall, to go out to Strand-on-the-Green, to walk for days in the London squares, to drink at Jack Straw's Castle or The Spaniards on the Hampstead Heights, where one can look down at the whole London mess and get a breath of air. At Gravesend, you can get even a touch of the sea from the Thames estuary, and from the window of an inn built for an earl's mistress in the Regency, you can watch that magical procession of the ships of the world proceeding seawards, two or three a minute, at the top of the tide.

What the right-minded American comes to see in London is what we enjoy most ourselves: the sideshows. The city of markets is also a circus. We never know when we are going to run into the Brigade of Guards up to some ceremonial antic—I heard the Horse Guards this morning trooping off from the stables to the palace, and yesterday there were the royal and golden coaches picking up an ambassador at St. James's as if he were a piece of wedding cake and not a commissar and one-time graduate of the London School of Economics. They bur- ied an ambassador this week too. The Guards came across Bryanston Square to the single tap of a muffled drum, their arms reversed and like votaries of death itself in their gloomy Russian busbies. The minute gun went off in Hyde Park, the pigeons flew high off the hotels. It was well done and with pride.

The State never gives up a sideshow, a privilege, a title or a yard of scarlet or gold. In the House of Commons, before the free-for-all of Question Times begins, the Speaker walks like a specter in his silken knee breeches, with the Mace borne before him. We half grin at the solemnity and then, unaccountably, we straighten our faces. Our religion? Clearly we are ancestor worshipers; at any rate we worship their clothes and emblems.

There is humbug in this, of course. There was a good deal of clever humbug in *Alice in Wonderland*, and that book is the best guide to the inner life of London because it catches that London mood which is half solemn and half comic. A man will make jokes about some medieval office of vastly symbolical but slender real meaning, but in some private sense he will think the farce serious. We catch the feeling that, to relieve London of its crushing importance, we must have dreams that are half absurd, half elegant; we could hardly live under this weight without some grotesque or fancy. It is perhaps shady of us to be like this. John Quincy Adams thought it was plain hypocrisy. When the English are behaving badly, he said, they always pretend to be mad. At the House of Lords I heard a packed and humdrum collection of peers debate the outrageous fact of their existence in a democratic state. When Lord Salisbury said he could not offhand think of a logical defense of the hereditary principle and, for this reason, was disinclined to give it up, he was properly adjourning to *Alice in Wonderland*, and asserting the necessity of the London dream.

The clash between scarlet dream and pin-stripe reality is frank in the courts. They are the best booths in the London circus, easier to walk into than a news cinema and the only toothy bit of Dickensian London left. Dickens had the feeling for the London Wonderland. You can begin at the bottom with the police courts, a place like Bow Street. And here, as so often in this city, you are distracted and have to break off, for you are in a characteristic London muddle. For they have put an Opera House as fine as Milan's and the toughest police court of the city into the middle of Covent Garden vegetable market, so that you have to dodge the Black Maria and step over squashed oranges and cabbage stalks before you can see Fonteyn dance or hear Schwarzkopf sing.

Behind the market lorries is a church famous as a burial place for actors. The best collection of theatrical prints outside the museums is on the walls of the saloon bar of The Nag's Head public house, and at five in the morning the bar will be packed with market porters. One of the minor pleasures for women in London is to walk through Covent Garden early in the morning to a serenade of wolf cries, whistles, blunt suggestions, and the crucial bars of love songs from men of powerful voice. And here, in a strong smell of disinfectant, the Law hauls in its morning catch of thieves, prostitutes and drunks. People put in an hour at Bow Street before the pubs begin to open at 11:30.

Bow Street is crude casualty and is not dressed up. London's *Alice in Wonderland* really begins at the law courts of the Old Bailey, under its golden sword and scales, and continues at the Queen's Bench. When I was a child I used to sit at my father's office window watching the crowds queue for the murder trials at this ugly temple, which they put up in place of disreputable Old Newgate. This is a region of ghosts, doubly so since the war. In Dickens's time the Law was housed in eighteenth-century buildings and behaved with Gothic oddity; now it is housed in nineteenth-century

Gothic and behaves with a disturbing decorum. Yet pale oak paneling, with its suggestions of parliament, public libraries, choir stalls and the halls of modern universities, has not killed the waggishness of the Law. Wigs and scarlet robes, ermine and starched bibs, look alarming against this color. The real thing here is ourselves, foolish in our ordinary clothes but also rather aggressive, vulgar and impudent. There is nothing like the sight of a truculent witness, in a navy blue suit and with a bad accent, stonewalling Learned Counsel. The air is motionless, dry and tepid. A small cough, the turning of the pages of briefs, the quiet voices of lawyers, conducting as it seems not a trial but an insinuating conversation among educated friends— these stiffen behavior. A very thoughtful game of chess is going on at dictation speed. The Pawn goes into the box, Queen's Bishop stands up, King's Bishop sits down, a Knight scratches under his wig with a pen. Wrapped in his scarlet, that untakable piece the Lord Chief Justice, an old man with a face as hard as a walnut, restlessly moves his waxen hands.

The Law is a patient, tedious occupation and in London it relieves the boredom by its own little comedies.

"And you may think, m'lord," says Learned Counsel, "that it is not without significance that when the prisoner signed these cheques he appended the name of Ernest Stoney, a reference possibly to the circumstance that he was at that time without funds."

"Not one of your best, Mr. So-and-So," says the judge.

"An inadvertence, m'lord, an inadvertence," murmurs Counsel. He is satisfied. The calamities of legal wit are to be borne like the loss of Bishop's Pawn: the prisoner gets eighteen months. We laugh, the Usher calls silence in Court and we turn to look at the confidence man who tricks the colonials in some Strand hotel, the boy murderer with the vain smile on the lips—the Lord Chief does not frighten him—the row of conspiring company directors, respectable corner-seat men of the suburban train, the women of a lifetime's convictions, empurpled now by the uncomprehended load of her enmity toward us. We look at the newcomers since the war: the Poles, the West Africans, the West Indians who bring the angry pathos of their uprooting before the soft voices of their alien judges.

London is prolific in its casualties, its human waste and its eccentrics. We see that blowsy red-haired woman with the gray beard who dances and skips about the pavement in the Haymarket. A well-known trial to bus conductors, the woman always carries a spare hat concealed in a brown-paper bag for traveling by bus. She changes her hat and then sings out:

> He called me his Popsy Wopsy
> But I don't care.

And drops into a few unprintable words. We are very fond of her. There is the pavement artist who conducts a war with other street entertainers, especially those who use an animal to beg from the thousands of dog lovers, cat strokers, pigeon and duck feeders, the chronic animal lovers who swarm in London. "Worship God not animals," he scrawls in angry chalk on the pavement. There is the Negro bird warbler, ecstatic in his compulsion, and the King of Poland in his long golden hair and his long crimson robe. There are those solitaries with imaginary military careers and the frightening dry monotonous gramophone record of their battles and wounds. They are compelled, they utter, they click their heels, salute and depart. A pretty addled neighbor of mine used to mix up the washing of the tenants in her house when it hung on the line in her garden. She was getting her own back on the Pope, who had broken up her marriage to the Duke of Windsor. One has to distinguish between the divine mad and the people pursuing a stern, individual course. The elderly lady who arrives in white shorts on a racing bicycle at the British Museum every morning, winter and summer, is simply a student whom we shall see working under the gilded dome of the Reading Room. The taxi driver who answers you in the Latin he has picked up from the bishops he has been taking to and fro from the Athenaeum Club all his life is not consciously doing a comic turn. He is simply living his private life in public. As Jung says, we are dreaming all the time; consciousness merely interrupts. It was what Dickens noticed in Londoners a hundred years before.

We live in localities where we sharpen our particular foibles. The "local" public house is one gathering point, although television is emptying the pubs in the working-class districts. The London pubs are all different and live by character. For the stage, I think of the Salisbury, where a stage-door keeper the other day suggested to me that gin and eels made the ideal nightcap; El Vino's for the journalists, the York Minster for the French. We live on strong beer and gin and drink them standing in moody or explanatory groups. At a pub we like to reveal ourselves suddenly and at length to a few new friends; but we respect privacy too. I have seen a man sitting in the midst of a packed and roaring pub reading *The Economist* from cover to cover, unaware of the quarrel between the sailor and the tart, the racing talk, the slow description of a hospital operation or the whispers to the girl having her neck stroked. He was simply insulated.

People began to say before the war that London was becoming continentalized. So it was, in a superficial way. You can buy pizza in the mass restaurants without going to Soho and espresso coffee in the bars. Popular London lives by its mass diversions. For generations the city has been the world's capital of ballroom dancing, and its "pallys" are packed most of the week to see the exhibitions. Africans and Indians color the popular crowd and the great dancers are watched with a critical devotion that I have seen equaled only by Spaniards at the bullfight. The thousands who go to the ballet at Sadler's Wells or Covent Garden are a race in themselves.

And there is gambling; London is almost silenced in some quarters on Thursday nights, when people are doing their football pools, and again at six on Saturday when they hear the worst. There are the greyhound tracks—London's night betting machine; under the white floodlight that chemically green oval suggests the roulette tables of Monte Carlo. The mob goes to these places, the toughs, the spivs, the workers from the factories; but in the hot, carpeted bars of the people who are in the money you see the full heat of gambling, its secretiveness and its fantasies, as the floor is littered with betting slips. Living in London all my life, I had not met these Londoners before: the swarthy, brash, gold-ringed men, the Oriental-looking women in their furs or these startling blondes on the bar stools. Once more I had found another race, as I did when I followed the crowd who go to hear *Tosca* at Sadler's Wells or Shakespeare at the Old Vic, who have heard all the plays and all the operas you can name a dozen times over and call out for their favorite actors and actresses by name in an orgy of local religion.

Another London race is the race of arguers. We can never resist an argument. There are the human cockerels at lunchtime in squares like Lincoln's Inn Fields, crowing about every conceivable kind of political new dawn. But Sunday is the day for this essentially Puritan pleasure. We revel vulgarly in free speech. There are not only the dozen main meetings under the trees in Hyde Park but there are those earliest known manifestations of dialectical life on earth: the conjunction of two men standing nose to nose, with two or three idle friends attending, each proving the other wrong, not in rage but in quiet and disparaging parliamentary calm and pith. ("You say the Buddha is living—how do you know the Buddha is living? Have you seen the Buddha?") From a distance the shouting of Marble Arch sounds like a dog show. The red buses go round the Arch and add the uproarious, band-playing suggestion of merry-go-rounds and racers, but nothing can drown the argument. "My friends," the speakers shout, "believe!" Half a dozen voices call back, "Get on with it. You said that before." And some wit yells out, "Where was Moses born?"

"Believe! Believe!" What are we asked to believe? Some well-informed man is telling us that there are millions of gallons of water up in the sky— "What? Up there, Dad?" comes a voice—and that there will be a repetition of the Great Flood. We are asked to believe that Ireland will be free, that Russia wants war, that America wants war—or that they don't—a hymn strikes up next door, all the Truth societies are at it like mongrels, a lonely figure disputes the Virgin Birth relentlessly, an elderly man, gnawing at a bone, tells us the Pyramids hold the key to human destiny. And then we hear the melting Oxford voice of a colored man from the Gold Coast five yards away: "If I become Minister of Commerce in the Gold Coast—" What is he going to do? Something unpleasant to London, just as the Irish are, the Egyptians, the Russians, the South Americans, the men of God.

Insult, doom, destruction are offered to us. The crowds stand round grinning. The Guardsmen stand pink with pleasure. Sailors are delighted. The police stand by like hospital nurses. For nurse is never far off, gossipy at the moment, but always with an eye open. There is a nurse in every Londoner and nurse says things have got to be fair. One would be relieved if, as in wicked countries like France or Italy, things could be unfair—just for once. It is our weakness that we cannot manage that. "No," someone shouts out to an interrupter. "Let him say what he thinks. Go on, mate, say what you was going to say."

The Park is Babel. But in Trafalgar Square, at the foot of Nelson's Column and under the patriotic bas-relief of the Death of Nelson—for the British god is a sea god—you hear the Voice of the People. (They have put amplifiers on the noses of the lions there, which gives these soapy figures a new professorial look.)

The Irish poet W. B. Yeats, who used to wander, tall, remote and lonely, about the London streets when he had woken up from the detective story he had been reading in the Savile Club, despised Trafalgar Square meetings and once told me that in Dublin he had led a procession up Sackville Street—since re-named O'Connell Street—and had smashed ten thousand pounds' worth of plate glass. Such exaltations haven't been heard of in London—not since the days of the Duke of Wellington.

You have been looking at the Piero della Francescas in the National Gallery, watching the crowds there resting their feet on the sofas. You want some air and so, stepping over the face of Greta Garbo and the other Muses which have been done in mosaic in the hall, you come out into the Square. It is all pigeons, peanuts, prams and children getting wet and dirty in the capricious fountains; but round the plinth are the packed, studious-looking crowd, and the lions relaying the indignations of the speaker. He is almost certainly insulting the House of Commons and all those government offices down Whitehall. He is sickened by Downing Street. He is sarcastic about some "noble lord," for if we love lords we also love being rude about them. He is appealing to us, the People, to lift up our Voice and say no to something or other.

We look up at the sky. The appalling London pigeons fly round from their dung heaps on the top of Nelson's Column, the Gallery, the Admiralty Arch or St. Martin's. We listen to the babies crying. We stare at the advertising signs on the ugly buildings to the south, which remind us that if things are as bad as the speakers say, we can emigrate to any corner of the world. Most Londoners who look at those signs have relatives who have done so, and minds wander to what Jack is doing in New Zealand now, and how many years it is since Sis was in Durban, Saskatchewan or Singapore.

Yet we do not emigrate. We accumulate. More of us are pumped day and night into the tubes, more of us lie under the heavy trees in the parks in the summer, more of us greedily parade past the Oxford Street shops, more of us queue for the cinemas, cram the hotels and burst the buses. It is notorious that the English, who founded colonies and peopled new places, now do not fill the emigration quotas and do not care to move. Crowd life is intense life, and what the Londoner misses elsewhere is intensity, for intensity keeps him solid and obliges him to be clever. We have become the great urban nation which is bored by the open spaces. London is our macrocosm. It is no longer the nightmare city of the early Industrial Revolution; it has moderated though it continues to be vulgar and exuberant. It adds to the London spell that the future of this monstrosity, which never has more than a few weeks' supply of food in its store, is a gamble.

In any case London is traditionally free of hysteria, stoical and disciplined, but not beyond the resources of nature. Publicly powerful and often hated for that, London has always valued private life most. It is a place where whims have their rights, where nerves are not exacerbated, where one is at ease, where standardization of behavior is disliked and where the tone of casual conversation is affectionate. There is regard for what can last; this can be called vegetative, sentimental, unrealistic, muddled. A Londoner himself would call this feeling: passion.

(1956, 1989)

AMAZONIA

In South America there are two major experiences which humble and dwarf the traveler, which could easily exhaust a lifetime, which make him feel like an irrelevant insect: I have written of one of them—the Andes. There remains the Amazon, not only the greatest river in the world but the immense, almost untouched tropical forest which extends for nearly three thousand miles from the Andes to the mouth. Amazonia is a country in itself, totally without roads—for you cannot count the few miles of road that run out of Belém at the mouth, or from towns like Santarém, Manaus in Brazil and Iquitos in Peru—knowable only by the numberless waterways that spread like veins from the gross red arteries of the main rivers. Not always red; at Manaus, the great Rio Negro comes in gray and silver, and for miles the two unmixing waters—the Amazon and the Negro—flow side by side. It is hard to know which of these seas of water—they will rise more than forty feet when the rains come—is the main one. You are looking down on a huge brown drainage system of innumerable lakes and tributaries and there is no feature in the unchanging landscape by which you can pick them out and name them with certainty. From the paddle steamers that go up to Manaus—those flat-bottomed, wood-burning houseboats, several stories high, with their scores of hammocks slung on the lower decks so that they look like floating laundries—the continuous jungle is a low wall standing back from a vivid green verge of reeds and grass and sand. I flew a thousand miles up the Amazon from Belém to Manaus; and, once there, up the Rio Negro by boat.

From the air, the jungle is a close-packed carpet of what might be kale, starred by the palm trees or by puffs of silver. It is unchanging for thousands of miles, without hills or mountains, at any rate in the first fifteen hundred miles or more, and it is apparently uninhabited. Yet in a day's travel you come across numerous small riverside towns. The palm-thatched houses are propped on thin tall poles on the shore, against the seasonal floods, and there the river boats of all sizes, thatched or boarded against the sun, come with their fruit, their mandioca flour, their beans, their snakeskins, their cloth, to tie up or go phutting off on their daylong journeys up the blinding road of light. The alligator gazes at them from the bank, the angelfish cloud round them at the quays, the bloody piranha wait to attack in the streams and the pools.

In the boat the Indian family lives. The babies crawl about, the woman cooks or hangs out her washing, or calls to her neighbors—for these boats string along in tows, with the family parrot riding at the stern. These journeys start in the cool of dawn; by nine o'clock it is dangerous to expose your skin to the sun: in an hour you are blistered and in a fever of sunburn, deceived by the river breeze or the black, electric cloud-mountains of the coming tropical storm. When the rain comes, sky, forest and river turn to dirt and the spirits sink low, for the heat of the day is close and animal.

At first the jungle wall looks innocent and familiar like any stretch of creepered woodland we know, and there are places, above Manaus, where you would not be greatly surprised to see some well-known church spire rising. Then you notice the sudden flaunting of the fleshier trees, the liana curtains and the metallic leaves of the giant ferns, the immense bamboos and the scores of packed-in growths you may never know the names of, spreading their spell. You breathe the hot rot of the primeval forest floor. And there is a spell. This region acts like a drug. Men settle at Belém and then, once curiosity gets them up the river, they cannot rest until they have gone "further." I know a Brazilian engineer who took his wife and newborn baby up the river for months. "She knows that I am married also to the jungle," he said. Traders do well in Manaus and then sell out in order to get away to the upper, more savage reaches of the river. The climate reduces them to skin and bones, the bad diet ruins them, their will is eaten up by the lethargy of the forest, but they are held entranced by it. It is, they say, like a congenial poison and though sickness or exhaustion may make them glad to get out, they are just as likely to go back, as sailors go back to the sea on a bad ship they claim to hate.

The Amazon matches central Africa, but it is an Indian, not a Negro, region. Its soil is leached by rain and flood and can grow little in the way of crops and, of course, there are no cattle. Fresh meat, milk and vegetables must be flown in for those who cannot dispense with these luxuries. Those who live off the land live on nuts, fruits, beans, mandioca flour spread over tasteless dried meat, a little game and, when they can be had, turtles. The people of the Amazon are thin. The figures of the women are as straight as thin-armed boys. The people are all bone and have the Indian sharpness; yet they seem strong. They split the huge bolas of rubber with a blow of the machete; they load the boats, drive the trucks; they can hold the jaws of the alligators shut as they lever them out of the mud; they can hunt the puma, the peccary; they work in the rubber and jute factories. Near Manaus, oil men have found petroleum and are building a refinery. Along the riverbanks you see the tall sticks of the prospectors and engineers. There is a strong river trade in snakeskins, indeed in all animals. A boy of fourteen caught a black puma on a fishing line last year. His father, an Austrian collector from Bolivia, had to play it as you play a salmon. A hunter's story? Down at pretty Belém, at the delta, you pass the little shops where the jaguar and the alligator skins are cured.

We stand high up in the Opera House at Manaus and look down on what for forty years has been a dying city. We see the Negro and the Amazon rivers divide, immense melancholy highways through forest that surrounds us for thousands of miles. We are in a kind of midocean. It looks innocent. Hard to believe all the tales of the poison trees, the stinking and the narcotic blossoms, the pools solid with giant toads and heaped with alligators, the terrible processions of ants, the hourly battles between mantis and beetle, the fantastic and disgusting lives of the parasites, the awful breeding and killing that goes on every minute. The hummingbirds rape the passion flowers and when the birds have gone, the huge butterflies—biding their time—follow in flocks to the scene the birds have betrayed to them. Yet, if nature is incredible here, man, too, has been astonishing. He found the secret of the rubber tree and when we see these half-naked men splitting the balls of rubber in some city warehouse, we see an industry that once made millions, now reduced almost to its primitive state once more. He built Manaus in the boom. He imported the city mainly from Portugal, all the cobblestones and black-and-white marble of the pavements, almost all the bricks and tiles. Some marble, especially in the Opera House, came from Italy and England. In a few years he created a spectacular capital; in a few years the boom ended, and now the city rots, the steel rusts, the walls crack.

Yet Manaus is not dead. The Indians trade on the river, the big ships sometimes come up in the nut season, or the jute season. If the town has decayed, it is nonetheless full of life. The airplanes land at the handsome airport. There is a luxury hotel. The modern world has not given up here, even if most of the food has to be flown in at heavy expense to sustain the impudence of modern man. And when we go back to Belém at the Amazon's mouth and see the shipping there, we once more have that sense of dramatic awakening we feel everywhere in Brazil.

We wait at night at the airport of Belém, listening to the deafening noise of the crickets, for the plane to take us back to New York. We have flown over ten thousand miles in South America. We are standing only a mile or two from the huge red maw of the greatest river in the world. It has been a journey through superlatives of size, through all that Nature is capable of in mountain heights, river, jungle, desert and plain. What can we compare with those thousands of miles over the Peruvian desert or the Andes, or over the jungle of Brazil? What was mere romance to us has now become real memory. We have seen the unparalleled lights of Rio like brooches pinned and pearls strung over the sea. We have seen Cotopaxi in its shirt of snow, the cobbles of the Inca highways, the Cyclopean stone of their temples; we have stood under the rain tree and the ombú and have gazed over harbors sailors have told us of: Valparaíso and Callao, Macao and Pernambuco. We have eaten the mango, drunk the Chilean wine, kicked avocado pears in the streets. We have seen the alligator in his river and seen butterflies the size of handkerchiefs. We have been frozen and breathless at Titicaca and have eaten its wonderful giant trout; we have had the night sit on us like a hot elephant in the tropics. We have talked with Indians, Negroes, mestizos and mulattoes, with all the Spanish and Portuguese mixtures, with great men, with ordinary men and the poor. We have seen the Indian woman trotting down the street shuttling her llama wool; we have seen the wives and daughters of the millionaires of Lima, Buenos Aires and Rio, in their diamonds and emeralds. In Colombia, Ecuador, Peru, Chile, in the Argentine, Uruguay and Brazil, we have seen seven versions of Iberian civilization transplanted, some feudal, some ultra-modern, all violently different and continuing that tradition of explosive individuality which they brought from Europe. We have been plunged into a life whose values are often basically distinct from our own, and which is awake and creative. What, we must ask, will this continent become when it is fully opened up and its huge natural resources used? All travelers in South America are staggered by its wealth and its prospects. They are overcome by its beauty. We have had the incredible luck to see a continent at the moment of its awakening.

(1956, 1989)

NOVELS

FROM

Dead Man Leading

CHAPTER X

There was a late moon and the raiment of water, dividing the trees, made a scene of metals. Animals cried out in the forest through the night. There had been laughter about hostile Indians during the day, but now Wright and Phillips watched the yellow flame of a fire, no more than a scratch of yellow, on the distant bend of the river.

They were, they calculated, only a day and a half's journey from him. They slept uneasily under the white arc of the moon, and, after the usual sullen grumbling from the men, drank their coffee and started soon after sunrise. They sat advancing into the dazzling sun.

There was a monotony in the brief but overwhelming youth of these tropical dawns, when the land lay without shape like a divine breath upon the air. Phillips leaned eagerly forward and Wright stood keen and grey. His beard seemed to stiffen and his eyes, half closed against the new light, glittered like slits of dew. There was the smell of the trees in the water and the smell of the sleep sweat of the crew. There is to an ageing man nothing more cruel than the everlasting youth of the world, and it was not only the need of travelling fast and overtaking Johnson that made Wright stand up in the morning and impatiently urge on the crew, finally getting to work himself with the paddles; the impulse came also from the exquisite pangs of an envy for Johnson's youth, a desire to reclaim his own. Wright's temper sharpened and the crew grew sullen.

"Can't he see that's not the way to get these fellows to work," thought Phillips.

Phillips was a man not used to obeying or being obeyed.

As for Phillips, he saw Johnson in his camps and he saw the courage of Johnson. Not in imaginary encounters—there were pictures made for himself by his own fears—but he saw Johnson, still, alone, ordinary, unthinking. The essence of the courageous man's life is that nothing happens to him. Phillips took the paddle and felt the boat shoot on to Johnson's courage.

Suddenly Wright stopped paddling and called out.

"There's someone there," he pointed to the far bank.

Two figures were moving against the trees.

"It's Harry."

They all stopped and stood up in the drifting boat. Phillips put his hands to his mouth and shouted. The shout fell on the water and the forest. The two figures stood still on the shore. They made no sign.

"The police launch then went ashore," Phillips began.

Wright said, "Shut up. You're not to say anything like that to him."

Nearer and nearer the two figures came.

Silva and Johnson were standing there.

They were standing some yards from the water's edge, when Wright landed and walked up to them, two scrubbily bearded men with their clothes dirty and torn, the skin on their faces and their arms reddened and spotted and swollen. Johnson murmured something to Silva and they both grinned. They were looking at Phillips and not at Wright. Johnson said:

"Hullo. You know Silva. He's been fishing."

"Of course, I remember him," said Wright genially stretching a hand to Silva.

The crew came ashore and the four pretended to study them. Then Silva came forward and broke the awkward greetings:

"I will make us all some coffee."

They sat down on the ground and Wright talked of his journey. "It was my fire you saw last night. There are no Indians," Johnson said.

"We thought it was Indians cooking you," said Wright.

"There was a nasty smell in the air," Phillips said.

"Mosquitoes were our only trouble," Johnson said. He showed his swollen hands.

They gazed at Johnson and felt a deep affection for him in his comical situation, wondering how he would brazen it out, longing for him to do so. They prepared to laugh loudly at him, to heal the strange breach with laughter. But Johnson, like themselves, gave no hint. There was a set expression on his face of an enclosed man who would not explain. Wright's diplomacy was a diplomacy of suggestion: "You've proved your theory about the boat," or "What do you think about this river? It strikes me as being useful. The wrong river is often the best."

But all Johnson revealed was that he had no opinion about the river yet, because he had been ill for two days and they would have been much further up but for this.

"Food was getting short," he said.

He seemed to suggest that but for food they would not have caught him.

But as time passed Wright was beginning to lose interest in the comedy of their situation. Johnson was no longer symbol of youth or courage. The sun was at midday. Wright was a man of forty-nine. He had planned his purpose on the meridian of his life. He said quietly:

"You know we shall have to go back to the big river according to the plan we all agreed upon."

As he began speaking Phillips got up and called Silva away with him. Wright continued as they went out of earshot.

"I think your effort was a magnificent one, but we must work as a team and a sideline like this would waste time and we've lost too much as it is. I knew of course you were trying the canoe. Calcott got melodramatic about it but Phillips and I didn't worry. You shifted too! But now we've got to get back. We're a team, Harry."

Wright waited for Johnson to speak. At last Johnson said:

"I think you'd better send me back."

"What do you mean?"

"I'm sick."

"What is it?"

Johnson mumbled and then said:

"I've lost my nerve."

"Not sleeping?" said Wright.

"I've slept all right," said Johnson. His heavy shaggy head turned away from Wright. "It's my nerve."

"You've done too much," said Wright. "You had a start on us but you got away. You must have paddled like hell. You're just done in and want a rest."

Johnson did not answer.

"We've got the time," lied Wright. It is, Wright knew, a common delusion of men who spend their lives in exciting action that their nerve is going. It is an involuntary indecency of the spirit which, Wright knew, cannot be helped. The two men glanced at each other. They had known each other for years. They had climbed together, sailed together. They had described their doings, they had argued into the night. They had laughed at each other. Wright had the faculty of putting the young at their ease, of being merely the man who had lived longer, pretending with a skill they did not notice that this was a disadvantage. He listened. Yet now Johnson and Wright looked at each other with incomprehension. Engrossed in action, they knew each other's idiosyncrasies only.

"I've been looking at the maps to see if we could cut across-country," said Wright, cunningly trading on Johnson's passion for action. "When you're fit we'll have a look."

Johnson did not answer. His face was heavy, stubborn and inert. Wright persisted and went into the pros and cons of the journey, knowing it to be impossible. He talked a long time slowly coming to the judgement that it would be better to return to the main river. Johnson lived every moment of the deep humiliation of the return. He felt only the humiliation of being trapped, but how trapped or why trapped he did not know. He watched Silva wandering along the river's edge and thought of the days of freedom and the chains which Wright's quiet, even voice put upon him. He struggled to remember why it was he had run away from the expedition and could not remember. He would only remain defiant and enclosed, with a growing barrier of resentment against Wright in his heart.

"He used to flirt with young women under his wife's nose and make her jealous"—this irrelevant thought came into his head.

"Silva!" called Johnson, "Silva!"

"Yes?"

"Are both paddles in the boat?"

"Yes." To show Silva was his man.

This interrupted Wright.

"Extra crew will be useful," Wright said.

Johnson's resentment grew at this appropriation. He got up and surprised Wright by walking away. He walked out of the camp and then out of sight of it, and at once his gloom lifted. His eyes were alert, his face ready and lifted, his body waking into its extraordinary agility. The mad idea of going on alone, just as he was without food or arms, hovered in his head. Suddenly he stood still and, amazed at himself, broke into tears. They came without feeling and without warning and without meaning and the present moment seemed to melt from him like wax under a flame. Wright's bearded head appeared and went. His father's face came. He was, for a powerless moment, a child again and shouting at his father angrily, "The next time you cross the level crossing I hope the train comes along and kills you." This was a clear memory dislodged from the time when he was six. He had not wept for years and this memory jumped forward with the suddenness of the tears.

The tears were few. It was as if they had confessed; when his lips had been unable to speak they had spoken for him.

An air of embarrassment was in the camp. The idle crew sat under the trees gambling and quarrelling mildly and watching the Englishmen. Wright slept and Phillips tried unavailingly to draw out Johnson. Silva, observing everything, imagined that there was a quarrel about the division of the sale of the gold. Or perhaps about its whereabouts. Silva reckoned that if the expedition split, he would have a half-share with Johnson if he stuck to him. This was in Silva's imagination. In reality he did not believe the expedition was really going in search of gold but his was a mind whose fantasies never rested. He missed—it was the real hardship of the journey—his cigars. Phillips said to himself, "If Johnson stays, I shall stay." There was no reason for the expedition if Johnson were out of it. Phillips was depressed by the boredom of the daily camps and of this camp in particular. He could feel the slow turning of the earth, the irretrievable passage of time in his life. He thought chiefly of traffic and hot streets and restaurants. He traced the services of buses across the stream. While the others slept he propped up a mirror and shaved off several days of beard, admiring himself as he did this and sighing at the sleepers. He went over to Silva and nodded to them all.

"Crisis," he said. "Is Johnson mad?"

Silva shrugged his shoulders.

"Oh no," Silva said.

—

For Wright now the incident of the chase was closed and Johnson's "nerves" were already written off. Brusquer in speech now he was inactive, Wright was also bluntly decisive. Phillips had noted the change from his English manner of quiet, gay courtesy. Wright had the fever of his adventure but he was not one of those who believe in leading and commanding. If he had had twenty men he would have gone on his own way, leaving the others to imitate his diligence and his persistence. His orders were no more than sly digs, fragments of mockery.

Before sundown he said to Johnson:

"Let's try your boat and have a shot at something."

They took their guns and got into the boat.

It was a late afternoon like all the rest, the heat of the sun lessening with every beat, the distant trees softening in tone and hardening in outline. The two paddled with little noise, keeping a look-out for floating trees as they went near the wreckage of the banks. Wright spoke little and Johnson not at all.

Wright discovered one thing: that Johnson had intended going on. With the silver path of light between the deep shadows of the evening trees tranquil before him, broken only by the rising birds, Wright understood Johnson's wish. He said:

"I don't blame you for wanting to leave us. And I'm sorry to have to claim you back."

He spoke frankly for the first time; he felt there was no fear of injuring Johnson by the words.

"It is a good river," said Johnson.

After a while Wright said:

"Why did you want to leave us?"

Johnson's heart seemed to ring like a bell at this. He was touched by the delicacy and nearness of Wright, though he resented the intrusion.

"I wanted," he said, "to try this alone because my father came this way. I wanted to see."

Johnson was too simple to notice how this new motive had displaced the old haunting one.

"I would like to know what happened to my father."

"He was a good way beyond this."

"Yes."

Wright saw the father in the thick-shouldered, shaggy-haired figure of the son. He respected Johnson's motive, but he was instinctively shy of investigating such a curiosity any more. To Wright the emotions must be protected by convention. The rippling shadows of the trees and the strips of light between them passed under the boat like a silent moving cloth.

The first shot was Wright's. It sounded like a dropped plank and its echoes went hard against the trees and leapt back. The birds rose black in thousands against the sky. Swiftly Johnson paddled to the fallen bird before it sank. Time passed and Johnson got his shot. An excitement possessed them both. The trees had given place to a scattered scrub which grew thicker in the distance. The rays of the sun lengthened in it. They chose a good landmark, tied up the boat and went ashore. The mosquitoes and flies clouded round their hats.

They had landed at the entrance of a densely overgrown creek and were walking along the thick bush of the bank above it. They saw the droppings of four-footed animals. They trod down a procession of great ants. The land smelled dry and pungent and clean to the nostrils. The grasses were browned by the sun.

A mile up the creek the banks were lower and the water had dried out of it leaving only a bed of caked mud pocked with holes of dirty water. This water was often alive with movement whirling round and bubbling like a simmering stew. Wright cut a stick and sharpened it, saying there would be fish in these potholes left behind by the drying water of the creek, and they went down into the mud. The movement of the water was made by the whirling of innumerable small electric eels but beneath them were fish. Johnson watched Wright stabbing the pool with his spear. "Mustn't," thought Wright. "Mustn't stir up trouble." There was no sun in the bed of the creek. Johnson still carried his gun but Wright's lay on the bank. They were too engrossed, concentrated on the luck of each dip into the black water, to speak or to notice any other sounds and the failing of the sun.

Presently a scattering of birds and scampering of feet in the bushes twenty yards away where the creek-bed gave a sharp bend and went out of sight, made Johnson turn. An extraordinary movement of alarm was in the creek. Johnson moved to the firmer high bank alert for what was happening there. He thought the noise might be caused by wild pigs. He whispered quietly to Wright and went four or five yards nearer to the bend and was standing waist-deep in the bush. And now the confusion and rustling alarm, the flying up of birds spread down the opposite bank of the creek towards them. Wright stood shin-deep in the mud, looked up when Johnson called. He turned round to step out of the mud instinctively going for his gun. As his back was turned, the tall grasses on the bank opposite to him were broken down and the paws and head and shoulders of a jaguar appeared. It pulled up noiselessly at the bank's edge. In the grass its head was soft and marked with the greyish golden dustiness of an enormous moth; as suddenly and softly as the whirr of a moth the animal had appeared. It stood still, amazed, one paw on the top of the bank and one raised cat-fashion in wonder, arrested in its intent of running down the bank to its drinking place. Its eyes were like pits of gleaming honey. They had not seen Johnson.

"Tiger!" shouted Johnson. "Keep still! Don't shoot!" "Get to hell out of this," he yelled at the creature. With light guns like theirs the only hope was to startle the beast away. The jaguar had been considering in these seconds the figure of Wright heaving himself by a bush-stump out of the creek-bed. The air popped out of the pits of his heel-marks. He looked like a scrambling animal, though he was unaware of his danger until Johnson called. The shout from Johnson startled the creature. It gave a swift turn of the head, crouching as if to leap upon the new voice, and then in panic swept round in the breaking grasses to rush swiftly away. Johnson's gun was raised by instinct though his shot was too light for such an animal. He knew it was fatal to fire and wound. But now he could hear the beast breaking the bushes in flight he jumped into the mud and scrambled up the opposite bank to get a sight of it. Wright now aware of his escape shouted, "Don't shoot!" in his turn. Excitedly he was picking up his gun and turning to warn Johnson as he did so. Johnson stopped. His gun was pushed over the bank and he himself was half-lying on it, struggling to get up. In his hurry the gun went off and Wright shouted. Johnson lay still for a second in consternation at his accidental shot and then he realised that it was not his gun that had fired. He turned round and slithered comically down the bank, the dust pouring on to his head and shoulders, the thorns cutting his hands. He leaned staring against the bank at the end of his slide. There he saw Wright lying face downwards over his gun. Johnson blinked his eyes, wondering why Wright was lying down. "Why is he lying down to sleep? Is he tired?" Then he saw the nails of Wright's right boot and the toe twisted under a loop of root. Then the blood from his chest spreading under the arm of his khaki tunic.

Johnson crossed over to him and knelt beside him.

"Wright, what's happened?"

There was no movement and no reply. Carefully he turned Wright over and as he turned a murmur came from Wright's open mouth and the eyes quivered. His face was bloodless, red only in the faint fine veins on the cheek bones.

Johnson had no knowledge of what ought to be done for a man in Wright's case. His mind was a chaos. He undid the coat and saw now the burned hole in it and the tear in the blood-soaked cotton shirt. The charge had evidently entered the lung and Wright's faint breath was stertorous. Flies, the brown motuca, came in dozens at the smell of blood. They settled thickly on Wright's still face if Johnson for a moment ceased to drive them off. There was no drinkable water in the creek, only a black ooze, and neither carried any brandy. Johnson took off his coat and his shirt and the biting flies blackened on his bare skin, humming and whining, blowing into his face like a stinging, humming grit, as he tore his shirt to get long strips for bandages. He sickened as he wiped the wound and contrived to bind the strips round Wright's chest, putting a pad on the wound to staunch the thick drip of the blood. Wright's eyes opened in the middle of this and his lips moved, twisting with pain. "What happened?" Johnson said.

Wright could not answer.

To carry Wright on to the bank and leave him lying there to be tormented by the flies and by thirst and in the darkness a prey to any animal, while he got help? It would take two hours and he might be dead. The pulse was not strong. To carry him down to the river? That was a mile, a rough mile. The camp was a good three miles away, yet perhaps it was nearer across the bush. Hoping that in the quietness of the evening the sounds of shooting might attract attention, he went up the bank and fired ten shots in quick succession. He had only three left. But when the quietness had settled down again after the shots, the futility of the signal left him in despair. He was frightened by the silence. He shouted, knowing too that that was futile. He remembered his father had died in this country.

Wright moaned below the bank.

All that anxiety to know how: to reconstruct what had happened in those already hazed seconds when the jaguar had appeared and then fled, fought in Johnson's mind with this picture of his father's death and the agony of not knowing what to do. He went down the bank. Wright's eyes were still open. His lips tried to speak. His breath when it came roared like gas in a burner.

"I'm going to get you up to the top. Can you move?" There was no answer but a closing of the eyes.

The evening sky was becoming green and darker, the bush soundless and black. It seemed to Johnson he must get Wright down to the river where there was water and the boat. But when he put his arms under Wright, he could not move him. Three times he tried and the sweat poured down his face and chest. He was maddened by the flies. Then a brutality came into him and, cursing, he put his arms round the drunk, will-less body and lugged it up. Stumbling, falling, sprawling on top of Wright, straining until he felt his heart and stomach would burst, he got him half-way up the bank. There was a clear way here and he wedged Wright's feet against a bush. Wright's arms moved in agony. Johnson sat there gasping, swallowing his sweat, looking down like a hunted animal upon the wounded man, with pity and ferocity. There enters with the handling of the sick a kind of hatred, a rising of life to repel the assault of evil.

"The poor bloody fellow. The poor bloody fellow," gasped Johnson.

Then once more he struggled till he got Wright over his shoulder and tottered with him to the top. The blood came on to Johnson's skin.

The stars had not yet appeared and this night the moon was late in rising. The one pleasure of running through the rough and broken mile to the river's edge was the freedom from the flies. Bats were flying out of the bushes and the moths were tossing over the thorns. Johnson ran. He was exhausted when he got to the shore and lay breathless for a moment. Then he pulled in the boat and sluiced his hot body and his head with water from the bailing can. He filled it with water and wedging his hat over it to stop the water from spilling, he went back. He could not run now because of the water. But now in the dark the country was so changed that it was hard to find his way. He began to think he had gone too far and wandered back. He shouted. He turned again and at last the moans of Wright brought him to the place.

"I must get you moved before it is dark. I'll move you soon. Can you hear me? We'll soon be moving."

The water had revived Wright. He looked into Johnson's face and nodded.

What shall I tell them if he dies? What shall I say to his wife and to Lucy? It is my fault, coming up this river. No, it might have happened anyway. It was an accident. What was he doing? I didn't see. I was halfway up when I heard a shot. On what river? That was not the river you were going by. Why were you on the wrong river? My father died in this country. He went by this place. He might have died in this very place. No one knows where he died. The Indians come here. There are fires of Indians tonight and no bloody moon. If it could have happened on a moonlight night. If I had been up further, this would not have happened, he wouldn't have found me today. This is Lucy. This is the ruin Lucy has brought on me. No, it was an accident. . . .

"Can you put an arm round my shoulder? I say, can you put an arm round?" He hasn't strength in his arm. Shall we stay here? Shall I light a fire and the others are bound to come if we do not go back. How is it? He can't say anything.

There's a stupidity in the pitiable helplessness of the wounded. Wright moaned.

It is better if he moans. The flies have done. I wonder where the tiger is.

He went down to the creek, into the strange place which was nearly dark now, empty and without sound, where less than an hour before they had been poking in the mud-holes. A fish Wright had speared lay by the guns. The scene was not to be believed. Johnson found himself picking up the dead fish and bringing it back with the guns. He and Wright had seen it flap under the stick but had not even glanced to see it die.

Johnson hated the sight of the two idle guns now and they encumbered him; but he grimly made up his mind that if it killed him and it killed Wright he must carry Wright down to the river. If they waited, Wright, for all he knew, might die. He remade the bandages. The bleeding, he thought, had slackened. As he was putting on his coat Wright spoke and Johnson dropped to his knees to hear.

"Come here . . ." the voice faded.

"I am here. It's Harry. You're all right. I'm here. I'm going to get you down to the river."

(The wrong river.)

"Lucy . . ." said Wright.

"It's me, Harry. Not Lucy," said Johnson.

God, he's dying. He's dying and he's talking about Lucy, telling me he knows about Lucy. Would you deceive a man who is dying? Johnson knelt, with his face close to Wright's. The eyes were closed as if he were asleep and he stopped speaking.

I must get him back, dead or alive. I must carry him. Somehow he propped up Wright's body and, kneeling, got it on his shoulder, grasping him by the legs. He was strong now. He staggered up and stumbled forward in the thickening darkness under the first stars. He stumbled over roots, he tore his clothes on bushes, fanatically he followed the familiar bush of the creek bank. His shoulders were aching, his tongue out of his open mouth sucked in his sweat. Twice he rested and groped in the bush for sight or sound of the creek.

The stars were brilliant and clear. They shone with miraculous clarity, mapped clearly in their constellations. They placed a definite order before the eyes and one walked in the most marked and munificent light. But this order was in contrast to the confusion of the bush. Each tree where it touched the sky was like a bunch of black spears—each bush, each mass of grasses had this marked black head, clear and dramatic. And a voice seemed to come out of it, saying, "This is the way. You remember this bush, and then the five trees together and the scrub you skirted. You counted the bends and the rises." Each one stood distinct and black and certain. Johnson hesitated. Crouching under the groaning man, he turned round. Behind him, as before him, was the same array of definite shapes, a multitude of motionless caped figures. He swung round, but it was the same on either side of him. The definite things near by, the stars like tears in the branches, cold and brilliant, the heavens immaculate and lucid in their complexity. He listened for the sound of the river. There was no sound. The sweat went cold in his body. He lowered Wright gently to the ground and, turning with superstition at every pace to keep him in sight, stepped into the gap in the scrub where the creek was. He put his hat down on the gap and walked through.

There was no creek. There were twenty yards of low grass and rock with stones shining in the starlight and then a bank of scrub. This must be the creek. Carefully observing every step, he went to the bank, which was a foot or two higher than the land around him. There was no creek. He saw nothing, no line of bushes which he and Wright had appeared to follow hours earlier. He felt he had been lifted up and taken into country he had never seen before. From where he stood he could see his hat in the gap and he returned to it rapidly, dreading that it would vanish or change before he reached it. He got there. His hand was trembling as he took it and now he made for Wright. The world had opened loneliness upon him. In every direction it seemed certain that the river lay. The dark bush did not lose the distinctness, the simplicity of its shapes. He looked down upon the pale face of Wright.

"God, I'm a bloody fool," Johnson said. "How have I done this?" He stood stiff, ripples of coldness passing through his body, unable to decide anything. Once he thought he heard the sound of the river but it was a movement of night breeze sloughing in the distant trees and passing over them like some lost human breathing. He fought with all his slow will the impulse to dash here or there following this certainty and the other.

"Wait. Wait," he said.

He knelt down beside Wright and talked to him.

"Don't worry," he said. "We'll soon be there. I'll get you down somehow. Just taking a breather."

Wright's breathing seemed easier. The pulse was unchanged. The ground, Harry felt, was sodden with dew.

But this trick of calming and distracting himself and then of looking up with an open mind, to see the scene afresh and find conviction in a flash, did not succeed. There was a momentary illusion of vision, then it disolved.

He thought, "Shall I pray?"

If there were someone outside or above, with simple ease this person could point out the path to the river. It would be very simple. He thought, "Our Father which art in Heaven"; no, what's the use of panicking! I'm not going to wander round in circles. Light a fire. They'll see that. It can't be very long before they start searching.

He said, "This is not admitting defeat," and "Wright will not die." There is always some other small thing and after that another small thing which can be done before a man dies.

Harry had no watch. He stood trying to calculate the time. He set about lighting a fire, gathering the dry sticks. He took out his matches and his pipe and put it in his mouth. Then he could not, for some reason, smoke while Wright was lying there helpless. He lit the fire and as its light made a glowing room from which the sparks danced, his spirits rose. He did not like the thought of the black, distinct caped figures of the trees behind that unnatural and fluid wall of light. He worked hard collecting and piling on the sticks. The flame went up in a waving spire. He worked ceaselessly, taking no notice of Wright. "It was an accident. It was an accident." Branch after branch he brought and made a stack within reach of the fire. His whole life went into making the pile. The fire blazed high, yellow and dancing. Like an animal leaping, some yellow cat, the flame licked up in the dark, sending out claws at the darkness. He looked up and he and Wright seemed to be in a huge glowing temple, higher than the highest trees, wide and palatial. A fire that could be seen for miles. He shouted and listened. There was no answer, yet there had seemed to be a thousand faint answers, the movements of leaves or the scuttlings of night animals. He sat down beside Wright, exhausted, his throat dry; he realised now how his head ached and that he was sick with hunger.

But Johnson could not sit by the fire and wait. "In a moment," he said, "I will go and look for the river. If I make the fire high it will guide me. I can't be lost. I can get water for him."

Wright was murmuring again for water.

"Poor devil. I'll bring it you. Just getting a breather." The heat of the fire was strong and flat against his skin. He stared, exhausted, thinking out his plans.

And suddenly it was curiously easy, as if in the darkness a hand behind him guided him through the scrub. And it was near. Nearer than he would have imagined. They were camped, he discovered, within fifty yards—no, it seemed only twenty—from the river. The creek bank and its long clump were just as he remembered. He went down the bank of the river and so great was his joy that he did not even look for signs of the rescuers, but himself put down his hat—now the only thing he had for water—beside him and drank deeply from the river. It was cold and glorious water, so cold that it made his hot lips and his dry mouth sparkle with delight and his body shuddered.

Shuddering, in amazement, he woke up. The fire had gone low. He had dreamed.

He could not tell how long he had slept; it seemed only a few seconds; yet the lowness of the fire showed that it must have been much longer.

"Wright!" he called. "Wright!"

"Thank God," he said when Wright murmured.

Johnson could not see his face. He jumped up and put more sticks on the fire. His head was throbbing violently. The flame started at once, but now the glow was weary and wretched. His body ached. He heaped on the sticks.

"Good God," he said. "Where are they?"

He shouted to no answer.

"I must go now," he said.

He turned to shout again and then he saw he could not go.

Seated like a large dog at the rim of the circle of light, pale and dabbled by it and unmoving, was the jaguar. The animal had, indeed, been many yards nearer when the fire was low, but had turned back when Johnson had awoken and made it up.

Days afterwards, when Johnson could speak to Phillips of the happenings on this night, he said:

"It was the most bloody awful luck that we hadn't taken the rifle. I damn and curse myself for being such a fool. We shan't see another and he certainly won't come to sit and watch us, like that one did, as if we were a pair of clowns in a circus ring."

Johnson stood still with the branch in his halted hand frowning at the jaguar. Like nearly all animals they are, he knew, afraid of man and avoid him, but there is a point at which fear becomes fascination. If he stepped out of the exorcising circle of firelight and walked out into the dark in search of the river, the animal might recover from his trance and follow him.

"What do you want?" called Johnson sharply.

The creature pricked its ears.

"Clear off," Johnson shouted.

The jaguar rose and moved nervously away, but fascinated by the fire, did no more than move further round the circle. Once more he sat down like a dog with heavy front paws. Johnson knew he was safe with the fire. His real concern, amounting to a shocked anger with himself, was that he had fallen asleep; his only fear that he had slept for hours and that the camp party had not seen the glow of his fire because it was low. They might have passed hours before.

The life of Wright was the important thing. Harry picked up his gun and fired another shot. The echoes fell in a hard rebounding shower over the bush. The jaguar started up and crashed away into the darkness. There was the old silence swirling into stillness like a dark pond after a stone has been thrown into it, and the rim of the circle of light had a more sinister loneliness now that its sentinel had gone. It was not a time when it is easy to be patient. One counts the minutes.

There was no answering shot.

Johnson turned to Wright. His lips were cracked and bloodless, his tongue protruding and dry, his eyes staring. He murmured sometimes words and names which Johnson could not catch.

"Why the hell don't they come!" said Johnson. "Has he got to lie here and die because those fools don't answer?"

He stood up and fired again.

"They're coming," he said to Wright as the echoes rained. But he had no evidence that they were coming.

He cursed them quietly; but he was still most appalled by his own guilt in losing his way and in falling asleep. He was eaten by shame and by horror at himself, his ignorance, his incompetence and his guilt. He walked up and down looking at Wright, maddened by his inability to do anything. In his mind he continually saw a brilliantly lighted room—the drawing-room of Wright's house in England—and there Mrs Wright was reading and Lucy was standing by the open window. They were talking. Suddenly he was there walking across the room and they got up and walked quickly, exclaiming, towards him. They came very close to him, Lucy was laughing and the laughter and some words passed near to his face and then over and beyond him, and once more the room reappeared as it had been at first, with Mrs Wright and her book and Lucy at the open windows. They got up and came to him as before. Over and over again, with the tireless mechanism of pictures, these two scenes were enacted. He could not shake them out of his mind, as he bent to collect sticks or piled them on the fire or turned round to speak, for his own relief, to Wright. Johnson had never seen a dying man before.

He stood looking up at the darkness and the words came to him, "My luck has gone." He saw in the darkness the lighted room, the two women, and then beyond them hundreds of small fragments, glittering, out of his own life and his father like a shadow thrown upon it all. He felt again what he had felt intermittently during the past six months, that he had no longer a self, that he was scattered, disintegrated—nothing.

Then the jaguar returned and sat down in the rim of light and its eyes were as brilliant as motionless lamps.

"God!" exclaimed Johnson and, without thought, advanced running towards the creature with a burning root in his hand, shouting, "Get out, you fool! I'll beat your brains out if you don't clear out." He raised the torch of shrub high as he ran, shouting. The animal turned tail and sprang before him into the scrub breaking down the branches, and Johnson went after it. For fifty yards he ran and roosting birds clapped up in the dark. The ground rose and he heard the tiger still springing far away. And then Johnson dropped his arm in amazement. There was the river streaming in the rising moon within a hundred and fifty yards of the camp. There was the creek bank. He looked back. The camp which had seemed to be on rising ground was in a wide hollow and its light was invisible. The river was exactly in the direction from which he thought he and Wright had come after the accident.

He ran back to the camp. He marked the direction by the brand; and with rough care for Wright he knelt down and got him on his back. His weight was dead. Staggering with the man he made in the direction of the river. Wright groaned as he jolted over the rough ground.

There was no sign of the jaguar, no answer to his shout as he stood on the shore.

He paddled out to midstream to be in the path of the rising moon. "Then it must be nearly midnight." No action or sensation of Johnson was nervously harassed or feverish. His struggle with the weight of Wright, his staggering blindly through the bush, his guilt, his visions of Wright's home and of his own life, culminating in the words, "My luck has gone," he experienced slowly and laboriously. He passed through this suffering like an ox.

The current was with him. On the blank surface of the air were scratched the thin night-piping and croaking of water birds, but as the moon came up the surface began to glimmer. Faintly at first his shadow and the shadow of the gunwale were placed like hands upon the form of Wright and his face took on a deeper waxen whiteness.

"You're all right now. We're there," Johnson said. The warm wash of moonlight unclosed into a radiance rich like the whiteness of a lily and the river became like a white path of voluptuous funereal marble between cypresses in some southern cemetery. The night was warm.

All Johnson's thoughts were fixed on the camp, estimating the distance, noting landmarks, his eyes constantly searching for the gleam of the fire. Not for one moment did he think, "This is the end of the expedition," but he thought of the journey back to Calcott's town and who would take Wright there. To him every one of his paddle-strokes was something that detained Wright from dying. He was confident of his judgement though his luck had gone. His anxiety was that the others, who had not apparently come out to look for him, should have let their fire go out.

Presently, far ahead of him, he heard a shot. It came from far down the river and, seemingly, from the opposite bank to the one where the camp was. He took his gun and fired in answer to it. An answer quickly came. He paddled rapidly.

"They're here," he said.

Wright began to gasp and rave and then fell quiet.

Where the hell are they? What are they doing down there?

A strong smell of burning wood hung over the river, dry and acrid. It blew over from the opposite bank. He passed—he remembered it—the opening of a wide creek—and suddenly voices were plain. They were coming from the creek. Loudly another shot sounded. It was from the creek. He paused and shouted. He shouted several times. The voices came confusedly over the water and then there was an answering shout. He turned the canoe towards the sound and as he approached the creek mouth he saw their boat come down. Again he shouted and now there was no doubt about it. They called, and from under the fantastic shadows of the branches, the men rowing in the bows, the black craft appeared with Phillips and Silva standing in it. Then there's no one in the camp. The fools. Any animal may have pinched the stores.

They came alongside.

"Don't run me down," Johnson said. "There's been an accident. It's Wright. He's got shot."

Phillips and Silva looked down into the canoe. "We've been searching for you. The trees were fired opposite and we thought you were up the creek, cut off."

"Don't move him. But let's get to the camp quickly. Where is it?"

The men in the boat were silent. The Brazilians gazed down at the figure of Wright. "He's dead," they said among themselves. Feverishly they rowed over and Johnson went ahead of them, the two parties shouting across the water.

They arrived as Johnson was pulling his canoe into the shore. They jumped into the water, ignoring their boat to crowd round the canoe.

"Look after the boat," Johnson said. Two went shouting after it into the current to tie it up.

"He's unconscious," said Johnson. "Lift him carefully. It's the chest. He's lost blood."

Easily they lifted him ashore and laid him on their coats on the ground. They switched on their torches. The men were called to make up the fire. Johnson and Phillips knelt beside him and Silva was opening the medicine-box.

"Harry," said Phillips in a startled voice. "He's not unconscious. He's dead."

They both stared at the white face, the staring eyes, the protruding neck. "He's alive. He was speaking in the canoe." But when they felt the pulse and listened for the heart and put a mirror to his lips, they knew he was dead.

They stood up and all gathered round. Their torches played in balls of light about their feet and they stood in the vivid whiteness of the moon, looking speechlessly into one another's faces.

(1937)

FROM

Mr. Beluncle

ONE

Twenty-five minutes from the centre of London the trees lose their towniness, the playing fields, tennis courts, and parks are as fresh as lettuce, and the train appears to be squirting through thousands of little gardens. Here was Boystone before its churches and its High Street were burned out and before its roofs were stripped off a quarter of a mile at a time. It had its little eighteenth century face—the parish church, the alms-houses, the hotel, the Hall—squeezed by the rolls and folds of pink suburban fat. People came out of the train and said the air was better—Mr. Beluncle always did; it was an old town with a dormitory encampment, and a fizz and fuss of small private vegetation.

The Beluncles were always on the lookout for better air. Mr. Beluncle moved them out to Boystone from the London fume of Perse Hill when Henry was fourteen and had a bad accent picked up at half a dozen elementary schools.

"Aim high," said Mr. Beluncle, "and you'll hit the mark."

He wrote to six of the most expensive Public Schools in England and read the prospectuses in the evening to his family, treating them as a kind of poetry; blew up when he saw what the fees were, said, "Every week I pick up the paper and see some boy from Eton or Harrow has been sent to prison, dreadful thing when you think what it cost their fathers," and sent his boys to Boystone Grammar School.

The Beluncle boys lifted their noses appreciatively. The air was notably better than at Perse Hill Road. They were shy, reserved, and modest boys who kept away from one another in school hours and who rarely came home together. When they saw one another, they exchanged deep signals out of a common code of seriousness and St. Vitus's dance. "We are singular," they twitched. "No one understands us. We have a trick up our sleeves, but it is not time to play it." They separated and carried on with their shyness which took the form of talking their heads off.

The Beluncles talked with the fever of a secret society.

O'Malley was the frightening master at Boystone School. There was always silence when he came scraping one sarcastic foot into the room, showing his small teeth with the grin of one about to feast off human vanity.

He was a man of fifty with a head like an otter's on which the hair was drying and dying. He had a dry, haylike moustache, flattened Irish nostrils. He walked with small, pedantic, waltzing steps, as though he had a hook pulling at the seat of his trousers and was being dandled along by a chain. Mr. O'Malley was a terrorist. He turned to face the boys, by his silence daring them to move, speak, or even breathe. When he had silenced them, he walked two more steps, and then turned suddenly to stare again. He was twisting the screw of silence tighter and tighter. After two minutes had passed and the silence was absolute, he gave a small sharp sniff of contempt, and put his hands under the remains of his rotting rusty gown and walked to his desk.

One afternoon in the spring term, after the French period, O'Malley went straight to his desk in a temper and said in an exact and mocking voice:

"I have been asked by the headmaster," he said, "to inquire into your private lives. This is deeply distasteful to me, as a matter of principle. I do not consider, as I have told the headmaster, it is desirable to encroach on anyone's private affairs; nevertheless I am obliged to do so. Eh?" he suddenly asked.

The silence, beginning to slacken, suddenly tightened again.

"I am not going to have my history period wrecked by a piece," Mr. O'Malley's voice gave a squeal of temper, "of bureaucratic frivolity. I intend to get through this quickly. And," Mr. O'Malley's voice now became musical, sadistic, and languid, "any de-lays will in-ev-it-ably lead to three hours detention on Sat-ur-day for the whole form."

A delighted smile came on Mr. O'Malley's face, an open grin that raised his moustache. The otter seemed to be rising through the ripples.

"In alphabetical order I shall ask each boy in turn to tell me what he intends to do when he leaves this school and what religious denomination he belongs to. The replies," said Mr. O'Malley with scorn, "as to all official inquiries will, of course, be either dishonest or meaningless."

Mr. O'Malley opened a large red book. He looked like a man with knife and fork ready to enjoy an only too human meal.

"I'll take it alphabetically," he said, talking with his pen in his mouth.

"Anderson—what will Anderson do when he leaves school?"

"Clerk, sir," said Anderson.

"Clerk, sir," mocked Mr. O'Malley. "And what does Anderson think his religion is?"

"Church of England, sir," said Anderson.

"Church of England," said Mr. O'Malley, taking his pen out of his mouth and making a note of it. "Agnew?"

"Clerk and Church of England, sir."

"Alton? Clerk and Church of England?"

"Yes, sir."

"Yes, sir. Liar, sir," said Mr. O'Malley.

"Yes, sir."

"Andrews? Clerk and Church of England?"

"Yes, sir."

"Liar, sir," said Mr. O'Malley savagely. "Next, sir? Come on, sir. Baker, sir?"

Henry Beluncle saw the question coming towards him. For the first time in his life, he saw coming to him a chance he had often dreamed of: a chance to play the Beluncle trick. On the subject of religion the Beluncles were experts. The word "God" was one of the commonest in use in their family. It was a painful word. Its meaning was entangled in family argument. The deity was like some elderly member of the family, shut in the next room, constantly discussed, never to be disturbed, except by Mr. Beluncle himself who alone seemed jolly enough to go in and speak to Him. God was a kind of manager and an interminable conversationalist; a huge draft of capricious garrulity always emerged.

For God, in the Beluncle family, was always changing His mind. Once God had been a Congregationalist; once a Methodist. He had been a Plymouth Brother, the several kinds of Baptist, a Unitarian, an Internationalist; later, as Mr. Beluncle's business became more affluent, he had been a Steiner, a Theosophist, a New Theologian, a Christian Scientist, a Tubbite, and then had changed sex after Mrs. Eddy to become a follower of Mrs. Crowther, Mrs. Beale, Mrs. Klaxon, and Mrs. Parkinson—ladies who had deviated in turn from one another and the Truth. He had never been a Roman Catholic or a Jew.

Only once—it was just before the deity's change of sex, Henry seemed to recall—had there been no God in the Beluncle family. It had been a period of warmth and happiness. They had all had a seaside holiday that year, the only holiday in the history of the family. Mr. Beluncle himself had gone winkling. On Saturday afternoons Mr. Beluncle went for walks with his arm round Mrs. Beluncle's waist. There was fried fish in the evenings, a glass of stout now and then, and hot rides in char-à-bancs to commons where strong-scented gorse grew and people came home singing. The air smelled of cigars. Mrs. Beluncle was amorous and played the piano. Mr. Beluncle read booklets on salmon fishing—there being a canal at the back of the house—and Mrs. Beluncle used scent and was always warm-eyed, hot in the face, and had frilly blouses on Sundays. Up a tree in the garden, Henry and his brother George smoked pipes made out of elderberry wood and left notes for little girls under stones in neighbouring gardens.

And then, as on a long summer afternoon, when the castle of delicate and crinkled white cloud that lies remote without moving over the thousand red roofs of a bosky suburb, swells and rises and turns into the immense and threatening marble mass of impending thunder, and there is the first grunt of a London storm, God came back. A book called Productive Prayer, in a red cover, three and sixpence post free, came into Mr. Beluncle's soft hands. It was followed by one bearing the photograph of a fearless young man in horn-rimmed spectacles, called Christ: Salesman, and then by a pearl grey volume called *The Key to Infinity*. God came back but He had been cleaned of impurities: He was called Mind.

The simple change from God to Mind was like the change from gas to electric light to the Beluncles. Mrs. Beluncle dropped out of the discussion at the first contact. She did not understand what "this here Mind" was; for the first time in her life she was prevented from confusing theological argument by diversions into autobiography. There was an assuaging notion that whereas even Mr. Beluncle could not presume to be on equal terms with God, who according to the Bible was violent, jealous, revengeful, and incalculable, he could (as the leading mind of the family) know Mind in the natural course of business and affairs.

Henry Beluncle sat in an exposed place in the front of Mr. O'Malley's class. As Mr. O'Malley's question came towards him, Henry vividly saw the incident in which his family's life had crystallized in a new form. The changes in Mr. Beluncle's religion had corresponded very closely to the changes in his occupation and they had not always, by economic standards, been for the better. Wesleyans, Baptists, Internationalists had let one down. The Unitarian phase had been sharp, supercilious, and fatal. But from Mind onwards, the Beluncles had been a little better off. And then Mind had taken Mr. Beluncle—as far as the family could judge—out of the house rather more. If he was home late, delayed on Saturdays, unexpectedly away on Sundays, it was known that Mind was the cause. Mind appeared to move in higher circles socially than those of the Beluncle family, who indeed moved in no circles at all. (They held, as Mr. Beluncle used to say, the fort.) Occasional news of the Hon. This, Lord That, Sir Somebody This or Lady Something Else, fell like a lucky bird-dropping upon the house. And if Mind led Mr. Beluncle to slip an American word or two into his speech and despise his family a little, his family admired this in him.

In the old days before Mind, whenever Mr. Beluncle lost his faith or, rather, found a new one "more in harmony with modern business" one thing always happened. The furniture van would be at the door at once. The taxi arrived. Mrs. Beluncle would be sobbing; Mr. Beluncle would be catching two trains—one to put his family into and one for some business errand of his own. In the taxi, if Mrs. Beluncle was still weeping, Mr. Beluncle would sing:

> "Tell me the old, old story"

and go on with warmth, putting his arm round Mrs. Beluncle, to the second verse:

> "Tell me the story simply,
> For I forget so soon."

("Yes, you forget, you forget. I remember," Mrs. Beluncle called out.)

Or, if the removal was especially disastrous, Mr. Beluncle would sing a song to remind her of their courtship, like

> "Oh, dry those tears, oh, calm those fears—
> Life will be better tomorrow."

And Mr. Beluncle himself would shed a tear in this song and turn his face shyly to the cab window, in case his family should see it.

It was in the period of one of these disastrous removals—an episode known in the family as "what happened at the High Street"—that Mind had appeared. The Beluncles had found themselves suddenly moved from a new villa in South London to a basement flat in a reeking street within sound of the howling Thames, a street that appeared to have been cut through an immovable stench of railway smoke and vinegar. Henry and George were ill in bed. Leslie, their youngest brother, was ailing. Mrs. Beluncle, who met disaster by outdoing it in the untidiness of her clothes— hiding her nice things so as to be ready to sell them—went about in an old coarse apron, her blouse undone, her hair down her back, her shoes broken. She had refused always the expense of doctors and dentists for herself and now had a long and bad attack of toothache. She sat in front of the kitchen range holding a piece of brown paper with pepper and vinegar on it, to the fire, and then pressing it to her cheek, and as she did so, she rocked. Rocking led to soliloquy, soliloquy to catlike moans, and her children sat at the corners of the dark kitchen, excited by the sudden squalor of their surroundings, watching her distantly. They did not dare to go near her, or she would grip an arm of one of them, with her strong working fingers, and with a terrifying expression of agony and drama, cry out, as if she did not know them:

"Oh! If Gran could see me now!"

It was into this room Mr. Beluncle came, after a month away, with the smile, the bounce, the aplomb of a very highly tipped head waiter; and on his innocent lips was the word Mind. Gently and firmly, he took the brown paper from his wife; gently calmed the children; gently and firmly he told Mrs. Beluncle about a man at the Northern Hotel, Doncaster, who had told him about Mind.

"Did Mind make toothache?" Mr. Beluncle asked. "Of course he didn't. And yet you've just admitted Mind made everything that was made."

"You'll have to get your meal yourself. There's what's left in the saucepan," groaned Mrs. Beluncle.

"So you just *think* you've got toothache," said Mr. Beluncle kindly.

"You think you've had your dinner, go on," said Mrs. Beluncle.

"It's an illusion of the physical senses," said Mr. Beluncle, exalted. "Henry, you're supposed to be clever. Can a piece of bone feel anything?"

"Its nerves could perhaps," said Henry doubtfully.

"And did Mind make nerves?" asked Mr. Beluncle scornfully.

"No," murmured Henry.

"Of course not. The boy understands, old dear. It's simple logic. Now put that paper away, the smell's awful. Let's have some supper. I've been travelling since seven o'clock this morning."

The children smiled, waiting for the light to dawn on the crouching figure of Mrs. Beluncle. Suddenly she jumped up and screamed at their father.

"You wicked man, you dirty devil you, don't touch me. Talk about your sister, what about you . . ."

The children were sent to bed in the next room. They listened but grew tired of the haggle of voices and dropped asleep. Henry woke up again, thinking it was morning, but the gaslight still shone through the fan light over the door. He heard roars and shouts of fury coming from the kitchen. Mrs. Beluncle was screaming out about someone called "that woman."

What had Mr. Beluncle brought home? Some sublime and noble thing which Mrs. Beluncle tore to pieces every evening like an enraged dog.

Night after night, month after month, Henry Beluncle listened. Was it the Open Seal? Was it the Key to Infinity—for the word Infinite came in with Mind. Was it Mrs. Crowther's conference, Mrs. Klaxon's call, the Science of the Last Purification, the Art of Salesmanship, Universal Brotherhood, or Mrs. Parkinson's Group?

Henry Beluncle sat at his desk. His heart was racing. Even now he was not sure which kind of Mind had conquered his family.

"Belcher," said Mr. O'Malley.

It was the name before Henry's on the list.

"Grocery," said Belcher. "And Church of England."

Henry swallowed. Vanity decided him. He plunged.

"Father's business, sir," said Henry Beluncle. "And Mrs. Parkinson, sir."

"What?" exclaimed Mr. O'Malley, putting down his pen.

"Mrs. Parkinson, sir," said Henry.

It was not often that a smile of lyrical pleasure appeared on the small and injured face of Mr. O'Malley, but now his bitterness went. The little bosses of his cheeks became rosy, his muddy eyes closed to long slits of delight, his short teeth showed along the length of his mouth, and a long, almost sound-less laugh was going on in his head. He looked round the class from boy to boy, grinning with affection at each one, and then he turned to Henry Beluncle.

"Good God Almighty," said Mr. O'Malley.

"Yes, sir," said Henry Beluncle, standing up at his desk.

"Your parents are followers of Mrs. Parkinson?" said Mr. O'Malley.

"My father, sir."

"Do you know what the teachings of Mrs. Parkinson are, Beluncle?"

"Yes, sir. The Truth, sir."

"The Truth, sir. Balderdash, sir. Tommy rot, sir. Cheap, muddle-headed trash, sir."

Now he was on his feet, Henry felt no terror at all. He felt very strong. He had little idea of what the teachings of Mrs. Parkinson were but, hearing Mr. O'Malley's attack, Henry was at once convinced of the Divine inspiration and absolute rightness of Mrs. Parkinson.

"It is not, sir," said Henry, astonished at his own voice.

"How dare you contradict me, Beluncle!" said Mr. O'Malley. "Do you stand there in your idiocy and tell me that if you fell out of that window, three floors into the street, and broke your neck, you would say it was a false belief and hadn't happened?"

A murmur of laughter came from the other boys.

"Yes, sir."

"Yes, sir, no, sir, yes, sir," mocked Mr. O'Malley. "Would you, yes or no?"

"I would, sir."

"Oh, no, you wouldn't, sir," said Mr. O'Malley. "Oh, no, you wouldn't. You couldn't, sir. You'd be dead, sir. Don't add impudence to stupidity. And tell your father from me that if he is stuffing you up with that nonsense he is a lunatic."

Mr. O'Malley leaned back and presently a soft long dovelike call came from him:

"Ooo. Ooo. Ooo," he said softly and leaned confidingly to the class. "Now I understand. Now we can begin to follow the mind of Beluncle. Beluncle is a superior person. Beluncle is a snob. Beluncle is a fake, isn't that so, Beluncle? A snob, Beluncle? A fake, Beluncle? Answer me, Beluncle?"

"No, sir."

"No, sir. Yes, sir. A fool, sir, a conceited ass, sir, a lunatic, sir."

"My father," Henry Beluncle shouted, "is not a lunatic."

The boys began to murmur. The captain of the form got up and said politely:

"Excuse me, sir, Beluncle has as much right to his religion as you have to yours."

"Sit down. He hasn't," said Mr. O'Malley very surprised. But Henkel, the hot-tempered Jew, got up with a loud bang of his desk lid and shouted:

"His religion is as good as being an Irish Roman Catholic."

Mr. O'Malley jumped to his feet, knocked his books off his desk and rushed up to within three paces of Henkel.

"How dare you speak to me like that," said Mr. O'Malley. "I'm not Irish."

Three or four boys called out, "You've got an Irish name."

O'Malley waved his fist and rushed to where he thought the voices had come from.

"How dare you say I'm Irish," shouted Mr. O'Malley. "How dare you associate me with that murderous lot of treacherous blackguards," he screamed at them.

The uproar in the class stopped at once. They were astounded by Mr. O'Malley's outburst. They were not frightened by his rage. They sat back and waited to see, as connoisseurs, what form it would take next. What would Mr. O'Malley do now? Which of his well-known antics would he now perform? The classical tirade against liars which all the boys could recite; the famous hair-pulling performance; the question torture of Anderson: Do your parents live in a house, Anderson? Is there running water there, Anderson? What is water, Anderson? Tell me some of the purposes of water, Anderson? Have you ever applied water to your person, Anderson? Answer me, Anderson. Answer me, Anderson. A small dance of exquisite pleasure follows and then a cooing voice, Are you going to answer me, Anderson? Don't you think you'd better answer me? And so on, the cooing voice rising and rising until at last Mr. O'Malley leaps a yard forward with his hands out like claws with a sudden scream of, Answer! Anderson begins to blubber, is made to sit down, stand up, sit down, stand up, and is left standing while Mr. O'Malley walks to the other end of the form room, opens his mouth into a huge grin and picks his teeth with a match stick.

Which of these acts was it to be? Everyone could imitate them, Anderson best of all.

Mr. O'Malley returned to his desk and sat down. His colour had become greenish but slowly it returned. He stared at the thirty boys, going over the desks one by one. Each boy noted the movement of the eyes as they checked him. Mr. O'Malley seemed to be about to spring, for his hands held the edge of the desk, but he was steadying himself, while his heart quietened and his breath came back. For several minutes he remained like this and there was no sound. A master passing down the corridor looked admiringly through the window of the door at the sight of thirty Boystone boys motionless. Mr. O'Malley's methods were famous. At last Mr. O'Malley picked up his wooden pen and dipped it into the glass inkwell.

"Cowley," he said. "Future occupation? Religion? Come on."

———

There was a short flight of iron stairs at one end of the school building. A small court of admirers, sympathizers, and critics, surrounded Henry after school. These boys were all experts too. A hot argument about things Henry Beluncle had hardly heard of—so brief had been his family's dips into the innumerable Christian sects—sprang up. The state of grace, the Real Presence, the Divine Mercy, Original Sin, the Thirty-nine Articles, were bandied about. Henry Beluncle said:

"Mrs. Parkinson has cut all that out."

TWO

At twelve o'clock Mr. Beluncle's brown eyes looked up moving together like a pair of love-birds—and who were they in love with but himself? He put his nail scissors away in their little chamois case and the case went into the waistcoat pocket on the happy navy blue hill of his stomach where fifty years of life lay entwined with one another. The machines had stopped working too. Presently the eighteen men could be heard leaving the factory. A week had ended and Mr. Beluncle slackened and softened as the silence came to stand in his office. He looked out of the well-cleaned window at the wall of the factory opposite to his own and felt Saturday afternoon like a change of blood, the time when his office could have become a home to him. He went back to his desk and read again the country house advertisements in the Times and was wandering among shooting boxes and residences, sporting acres and paddocks, golf courses and mansions, travelling from one to the other in his car, seeing himself hit golf balls, ride horses, keep chickens, fish salmon, walk round his estate and stand before mantelpieces of all sizes. He was a short, deep, wide man, with grey hair kinked as if there were Negro in him. His skin was kippered by a life of London smoke but it quickly flushed to an innocent country ruddiness at the taste of food: his face was bland, heavy in jowl, formless and kind, resting on a second chin like a bottom on an air cushion. It was the face of a man who was enjoying a wonderfully boyish meal, which got better with every mouthful; but in the lips and in the lines from the fleshy nose there was a refined, almost spiritual, arresting look of insult and contempt. Mr. Beluncle was a snob about present pleasures; he was eager to drop old ones and to know the new. In his imaginary travels among the newspaper advertisements he got richer and richer, he moved from "well-appointed" residences to mansions and an occasional castle, he slowly raised his chin and insulted people right and left. He did not notice that he was doing this and, in fact, as he read, he felt more and more amiable; he doubled the pay of his workers, bought a fur coat for his wife, sent messages of love and peace to the unhappy masses in India and China, set the Russians free, until, at the spendthrift summit, he remembered his son.

A son: a shy, desirous, passionate, protective, disgusted, and incredulous play of feeling made its various marks on his face.

At once Mr. Beluncle marched out of his office, down the short corridor, to the general offices where his son worked with Chilly who was learning the business, and the clerks. Mr. Beluncle was going to tell his son not to wait any more and to go home. "I am not an ordinary employer. I am your father," he was humming to himself. "Enjoy the sun, the fresh air, go home to your mother. You love her—or you ought to love her—think of her down there longing for you to get back." The generous impulse was the pleasanter for a sweet flavour of self-pity in it. "At that boy's age I worked till ten o'clock at night on Saturday," he said, and the sensation was that Progress had been created by him for others, out of his sufferings.

But in Mr. Beluncle's dreams there was always a flaw. He opened the door of the general office, where half a dozen people worked. The first person he saw was this son of his, Henry, sitting at a long, high, old-fashioned mahogany desk that had been left when the office had been refurnished in the slump three or four years before. The boy had turned round from his desk on his high stool and was cleaning his nails with the edge of his season ticket. He was gazing in a sulky, childish, dejected dream at the sunlight on the factory wall which could be seen from this window also. The boy was such a stubborn, unorganized, weak replica of Mr. Beluncle with cheeks so young that one could cry out for care at the thought of a razor going over them. The father stopped short in horror and tenderness. A powerful feeling of anxiety possessed him. He forgot his intention in a shocked attempt to save the boy's character and life.

"One o'clock is your time," said Mr. Beluncle. "I don't like people idling away, watching the clock. The idle steal other people's time."

Mr. Beluncle added the moral out of modesty, to escape the fault of random accusation.

The boy blushed and his jaw hardened with quick, young temper. The clerks held their cynical pens for a moment.

"I have nothing to do," Henry Beluncle said, rudely sticking up for himself.

"If you are working for me," Mr. Beluncle said, his voice smoothing with a temper that was inexplicable to himself—it seemed to come from the small of his fat back, "it is your business to find something to do." He was shouting but only as someone shouts for help.

And Mr. Beluncle went out fast banging the door, getting away quickly with the self-effacement of one who has saved a life and does not wish to get a medal for it. Too ashamed to meet the looks of the experienced clerks, the boy opened his stock books again. His neck, his ears, his cheeks had reddened and he sat in a storm of humiliation. With the ingratitude of the rescued he wished he had been left to drown.

Mr. Beluncle marched back to his own room in a startled frame of mind. He had come down to earth; he was a man tortured, enslaved, tied down and unjustly treated by his own family.

He was followed into his office by his partner, a woman of forty-five, who was taller than himself, whose dark hair was dry but not yet grey and whose powerful uncoloured lips were crinkled and moved like irritable and exposed muscles.

"That is not the way to talk to your son," she said and she was holding a pair of spectacles open in her hand. She had only lately taken to wearing glasses and was forming the habit of taking them off when she talked of private matters. Mr. Beluncle, who had once admired her eyes, now took these sudden removals of the glasses as an uncalled-for reminder of his admiration.

He swung round to this surprise attack.

"Where were you?" he said.

"I was in the office. You didn't notice me," said Mrs. Truslove, speaking as if being conveniently invisible were a role, an achievement which had been painfully and satisfactorily built out of years of complaint. And in her white blouse and her grey coat and skirt, she had the neutrality, the protective colouring of irony and conscience.

"He is my employé," said Mr. Beluncle.

"He is your son," said Mrs. Truslove.

"Don't you start sticking up for him as if you were his mother," said Mr. Beluncle, turning his head sharply over his shoulder as he shot this remark at her. And Mr. Beluncle unmistakably conveyed, and meant to convey, that had he wished it, Mrs. Truslove could have been the mother of his son; but that he had not so wished.

Mrs. Truslove gave a shrug to one of her shoulders. She had picked up this foreign gesture from an Italian she had once worked for—it was the single feminine affectation in a woman who liked to be thought mannish, and had for Beluncle the irritation of a well-known habit—and she said that it was lucky for Mr. Beluncle that she was not the boy's mother. She intended the ambiguity of this sentence.

And here Mr. Beluncle found himself colouring in the large soft ears that stood out rather far from his puddingy head. He had been made, once more, to feel a foolish guilt by this woman who, unlike his wife, always looked him in the eyes.

"By Jove, that's good, Mrs. T. Ha! Ha!" Mr. Beluncle guffawed with a coarsening cloud of laughter intended to cover retreat. He had built up his career, his business, his trade connections on humorousness. "My word, do you know what you jolly nearly suggested. I say ... I say."

Mrs. Truslove did not laugh. Once more Mr. Beluncle was familiar with Mrs. Truslove's inability to see a joke. He found reluctantly that he had to respect this curious trait in people.

"I am going to tell the boy to go," she said. "I won't have you speak to him like that in front of the staff, it is wounding to his pride," she said. "And it is bad for the firm."

Mr. Beluncle's mouth stuck open with true astonishment. What he wished to say was "But that is what I *intended* to do. That is what a father must do; break and harden the boy before the world does. What is wrong with that boy is he's afraid of me."

"*I'll* go and tell him," Mr. Beluncle said. So Mr. Beluncle, with the insulting look which he had gathered in his day-dreams gone from his face, went back to the office smiling. That is to say he believed he was smiling. He was, in fact, scowling. Mr. Beluncle opened the door.

"You here still? Why haven't you gone?" said Mr. Beluncle.

"You told me not to go," the boy said.

"Don't flinch when I speak to you," said Mr. Beluncle. "There is no need to do that. I mean flinching conveys a bad impression. In fact," said Mr. Beluncle, the idea just occurring to him, as ideas continually did, and feeling it would be rather unfriendly not to mention it, "it might convey to those who don't know you, that you were hiding something."

The boy, who was no taller than his father, stared directly at him as if he were hypnotized.

"That's all," said Mr. Beluncle. "Go now and you won't miss the train."

Mr. Beluncle returned to his own room strengthened.

"The damn fool was just sitting there!" he laughed to Mrs. Truslove and he went round to his side of their large desk and began one of his favourite defences against her stare. This defence was to lift a few papers from one side of his desk to the other. If she spoke he would stop; if she was silent he would begin a return game from the other pile.

"Leave your boy alone," she said. "He has done nothing wrong. It is only your bad conscience."

Mr. Beluncle lowered a passing handful of letters to his blotter.

"Conscience!" he said. "I haven't got nothing on my conscience."

"Anything, Father," said Mrs. Truslove, correcting his English with quiet unexpected pleasantness and Mr. Beluncle was too grateful for her change of mood to take up that word "Father." He could have said, it was on the tip of his tongue to say, "Why do you always say 'father' in a certain way, what is the idea?"

"I am not a father," he wanted to say. She was his partner's widow, but this did not give her the right to call him "Father" in her low, unmusical, ridiculing voice. It was not her business to remind him that Nature, in the form of woman, had taken the initiative from him, and had made him no better than thousands of other damn fools: the supremely ridiculous thing: the father of a family. The annoying thing about Mrs. Truslove, during all the years she had been with him in the business since her husband's death, was this habit of telling him what a fortunate man he was, what a valuable and devoted wife, what pleasant children he had.

"Which way, Father?" when she took his arm in the evening as they left the office—he could hear her saying it. When she knew what she did know about his life! When she could see with her own eyes how bad things were, why, for what purpose, did she correct and remind? But she did. She always ended by every day convincing him he had the happiest marriage on earth. He would go home in a dream of happiness—that is to say with the insulting expression on his face—and the first thing that happened when he got to the house was that he flew into a rage at the sight of them all, wished he had never met his wife or begotten his children, and would moan slowly round his lawn like a bee, taking the honey of self-pity from flower to flower, longing to get back to his business again.

(1951)

SHORT STORIES

SENSE OF HUMOUR

It started one Saturday. I was working new ground and I decided I'd stay at the hotel the weekend and put in an appearance at church.

"All alone?" asked the girl in the cash desk.

It had been raining since ten o'clock.

"Mr Good has gone," she said. "And Mr Straker. He usually stays with us. But he's gone."

"That's where they make their mistake," I said. "They think they know everything because they've been on the road all their lives."

"You're a stranger here, aren't you?" she said.

"I am," I said. "And so are you."

"How do you know that?"

"Obvious," I said. "Way you speak."

"Let's have a light," she said.

"So's I can see you," I said.

That was how it started. The rain was pouring down on to the glass roof of the office.

She'd a cup of tea steaming on the register. I said I'd have one, too. What's it going to be and I'll tell them, she said, but I said just a cup
of tea.

"I'm TT," I said. "Too many soakers on the road as it is."

I was staying there the weekend so as to be sharp on the job on Monday morning. What's more it pays in these small towns to turn up at church on Sundays, Presbyterians in the morning, Methodists in the evening. Say "Good morning" and "Good evening" to them. "Ah!" they say. "Church-goer! Pleased to see that! TT, too." Makes them have a second look at your lines in the morning. "Did you like our service, Mister—er—er?"

"Humphrey's my name." "Mr Humphrey." See? It pays.

"Come into the office, Mr Humphrey," she said, bringing me a cup. "Listen to that rain."

I went inside.

"Sugar?" she said.

"Three," I said. We settled to a very pleasant chat. She told me all about herself, and we got on next to families.

"My father was on the railway," she said.

" 'The engine gave a squeal,' " I said. " 'The driver took out his pocket-knife and scraped him off the wheel.'"

"That's it," she said. "And what is your father's business? You said he had a business."

"Undertaker," I said.

"Undertaker?" she said.

"Why not?" I said. "Good business. Seasonable like everything else. High class undertaker," I said.

She was looking at me all the time wondering what to say and suddenly she went into fits of laughter.

"Undertaker," she said, covering her face with her hands and went on laughing.

"Here," I said. "What's up?"

"Undertaker!" she laughed and laughed. Struck me as being a pretty thin joke.

"Don't mind me," she said. "I'm Irish."

"Oh, I see," I said. "That's it, is it? Got a sense of humour."

Then the bell rang and a woman called out "Muriel! Muriel!" and there was a motor bike making a row at the front door.

"All right," the girl called out. "Excuse me a moment, Mr Humphrey," she said. "Don't think me rude. That's my boy friend. He wants the bird turning up like this."

She went out but there was her boy friend looking over the window ledge into the office. He had come in. He had a cape on, soaked with rain and the rain was in beads in his hair. It was fair hair. It stood up on end. He'd been economising on the brilliantine. He didn't wear a hat. He gave me a look and I gave him a look. I didn't like the look of him. And he didn't like the look of me. A smell of oil and petrol and rain and mackintosh came off him. He had a big mouth with thick lips. They were very red. I recognised him at once as the son of the man who ran the Kounty Garage. I saw this chap when I put my car away. The firm's car. A lock-up, because of the samples. Took me ten minutes to ram the idea into his head. He looked as though he'd never heard of samples. Slow,—you know the way they are in the provinces. Slow on the job.

"Oh Colin," says she. "What do you want?"

"Nothing," the chap said. "I came in to see you."

"To see me?"

"Just to see you."

"You came in this morning."

"That's right," he said. He went red. "You was busy," he said.

"Well, I'm busy now," she said.

He bit his tongue, and licked his big lips over and took a look at me. Then he started grinning.

"I got the new bike, Muriel," he said. "I've got it outside."

"It's just come down from the works," he said.

"The laddie wants you to look at his bike," I said. So she went out and had a look at it.

When she came back she had got rid of him.

"Listen to that rain," she said.

"Lord, I'm fed up with this line," she said.

"What line?" I said. "The hotel line?"

"Yes," she said. "I'm fed right up to the back teeth with it."

"And you've got good teeth," I said.

"There's not the class of person there used to be in it," she said. "All our family have got good teeth."

"Not the class?"

"I've been in it five years and there's not the same class at all. You never meet any fellows."

"Well," said I. "If they're like that half-wit at the garage, they're nothing to be stuck on. And you've met me."

I said it to her like that.

"Oh," says she. "It isn't as bad as that yet."

It was cold in the office. She used to sit all day in her overcoat. She was a smart girl with a big friendly chin and a second one coming and her forehead and nose were covered with freckles. She had copper-coloured hair too. She got her shoes through the trade from Duke's traveller and her clothes, too, off the Hollenborough mantle man. I told her I could do her better stockings than the ones she'd got on. She got a good reduction on everything. Twenty-five or thirty-three and a third. She had her expenses cut right back. I took her to the pictures that night in the car. I made Colin get the car out for me.

"That boy wanted me to go on the back of his bike. On a night like this," she said.

"Oh," she said, when we got to the pictures. "Two shilling's too much. Let's go into the one-and-sixes at the side and we can nip across into the two-shillings when the lights go down."

"Fancy your father being an undertaker," she said in the middle of the show. And she started laughing as she had laughed before.

She had her head screwed on all right. She said:

"Some girls have no pride once the lights go down."

Every time I went to that town I took a box of something. Samples, mostly, they didn't cost me anything.

"Don't thank me," I said. "Thank the firm."

Every time I took her out I pulled the blinds in the back seat of the car to hide the samples. That chap Colin used to give us oil and petrol. He used to give me a funny look. Fishy sort of small eyes he'd got. Always looking miserable. Then we would go off. Sunday was her free day. Not that driving's any holiday for me. And, of course, the firm paid. She used to take me down to see her family for the day. Start in the morning, and taking it you had dinner and tea there, a day's outing cost us nothing. Her father was something on the railway, retired. He had a long stocking, somewhere, but her sister, the one that was married, had had her share already.

He had a tumour after his wife died and they just played upon the old man's feelings. It wasn't right. She wouldn't go near her sister and I don't blame her, taking the money like that. Just played upon the old man's feelings.

Every time I was up there Colin used to come in looking for her.

"Oh Colin," I used to say. "Done my car yet?" He knew where he got off with me.

"No, now, I can't Colin. I tell you I'm going out with Mr Humphrey," she used to say to him. I heard her.

"He keeps on badgering me," she said to me.

"You leave him to me," I said.

"No, he's all right," she said.

"You let me know if there's any trouble with Colin," I said. "Seems to be a harum-scarum sort of half-wit to me," I said.

"And he spends every penny he makes," she said.

Well, we know that sort of thing is all right while it lasts, I told her, but the trouble is that it doesn't last.

We were always meeting Colin on the road. I took no notice of it first of all and then I grew suspicious and awkward at always meeting him. He had a new motor bicycle. It was an Indian, a scarlet thing that he used to fly over the moor with, flat out. Muriel and I used to go out over the moor to Ingley Wood in the firm's Morris—I had a customer out that way.

"May as well do a bit of business while you're about it," I said.

"About what?" she said.

"Ah ha!" I said.

"That's what Colin wants to know," I said.

Sure enough, coming back we'd hear him popping and backfiring close behind us, and I put out my hand to stop him and keep him following us, biting our dirt.

"I see his little game," I said. "Following us."

So I saw to it that he did follow. We could hear him banging away behind us and the traffic is thick on the Ingley road in the afternoon.

"Oh let him pass," Muriel said. "I can't stand those dirty things banging in my ears."

I waved him on and past he flew with his scarf flying out, blazing red into the traffic. "We're doing 58 ourselves," she said, leaning across to look.

"Powerful buses those," I said. "Any fool can do it if he's got the power. Watch me step on it."

But we did not catch Colin. Half an hour later he passed us coming back. Cut right in between us and a lorry—I had to brake hard. I damn nearly killed him. His ears were red with the wind. He didn't wear a hat. I got after him as soon as I could but I couldn't touch him.

Nearly every weekend I was in that town seeing my girl, that fellow was hanging around. He came into the bar on Saturday nights, he poked his head into the office on Sunday mornings. It was a sure bet that if we went out in the car he would pass us on the road. Every time we would hear that scarlet thing roar by like a horse-stinger. It didn't matter where we were. He passed us on the main road, he met us down the side roads. There was a little cliff under oak trees at May Ponds, she said, where the view was pretty. And there, soon after we got there, was Colin on the other side of the water, watching us. Once we found him sitting on his bike, just as though he were waiting for us.

"You been here in a car?" I said.

"No, motor bike," she said and blushed. "Cars can't follow in these tracks."

She knew a lot of places in that country. Some of the roads weren't roads at all and were bad for tyres and I didn't want the firm's car scratched by bushes, but you would have thought Colin could read what was in her mind. For nine times out of ten he was there. It got on my nerves. It was a red, roaring, powerful thing and he opened it full out.

"I'm going to speak to Colin," I said. "I won't have him annoying you."

"He's not annoying me," she said. "I've got a sense of humour."

"Here Colin," I said one evening when I put the car away. "What's the idea?"

He was taking off his overalls. He pretended he did not know what I was talking about. He had a way of rolling his eyeballs, as if they had got wet and loose in his head, while he was speaking to me and you never knew if it was sweat or oil on his face. It was always pale with high colour on his cheeks and very red lips.

"Miss MacFarlane doesn't like being followed," I said.

He dropped his jaw and gaped at me. I could not tell whether he was being very surprised or very sly. I used to call him "Marbles" because when he spoke he seemed to have a lot of marbles in his mouth.

Then he said he never went to the places we went to, except by accident. He wasn't following us, he said, but we were following him. We never let him alone, he said. Everywhere he went, he said, we were there. Take last Saturday, he said, we were following him for miles down the by-pass, he said. But you passed us first and then sat down in front, I said. I went to Ingley Wood, he said. And you followed me there. No, we didn't, I said, Miss MacFarlane decided to go there.

He said he did not want to complain but fair was fair. I suppose you know, he said, that you have taken my girl off me. Well, you can leave me alone, can't you?

"Here," I said. "One minute! Not so fast! You said I've taken Miss MacFarlane from you. Well, she was never your girl. She only knew you in a friendly way."

"She was my girl," was all he said.

He was pouring oil into my engine. He had some cotton wool in one hand and the can in the other. He wiped up the green oil that had overflowed, screwed on the cap, pulled down the bonnet and whistled to himself.

I went back to Muriel and told her what Colin had said.

"I don't like trouble," I said.

"Don't you worry," she said. "I had to have someone to go to all these places with before you came. Couldn't stick in here all day Sunday."

"Ah," I said. "That's it, is it? You've been to all these places with him?"

"Yes," she said. "And he keeps on going to them. He's sloppy about me."

"Good God," I said. "Sentimental memories."

I felt sorry for that fellow. He knew it was hopeless, but he loved her. I suppose he couldn't help himself. Well, it takes all sorts to make a world, as my old mother used to say. If we were all alike it wouldn't do. Some men can't save money. It just runs through their fingers. He couldn't save money so he lost her. I suppose all he thought of was love.

I could have been friends with that fellow. As it was I put a lot of business his way. I didn't want him to get the wrong idea about me. We're all human after all.

We didn't have any more trouble with Colin after this until Bank Holiday. I was going to take her down to see my family. The old man's getting a bit past it now and has given up living over the shop. He's living out on the Barnum Road, beyond the tram stop. We were going down in the firm's car, as per usual, but something went wrong with the mag. and Colin had not got it right for the holiday. I was wild about this. What's the use of a garage who can't do a rush job for the holidays! What's the use of being an old customer if they're going to let you down! I went for Colin bald-headed.

"You knew I wanted it," I said. "It's no use trying to put me off with a tale about the stuff not coming down from the works. I've heard that one before."

I told him he'd got to let me have another car, because he'd let me down. I told him I wouldn't pay his account. I said I'd take my business away from him. But there wasn't a car to be had in the town because of the holiday. I could have knocked the fellow down. After the way I'd sent business to him.

Then I saw through his little game. He knew Muriel and I were going to my people and he had done this to stop it. The moment I saw this I let him know that it would take more than him to stop me doing what I wanted.

I said:

"Right. I shall take the amount of Miss MacFarlane's train fare and my own from the account at the end of the month."

I said:

"You may run a garage, but you don't run the railway service."

I was damned angry going by train. I felt quite lost on the railway after having a car. It was crowded with trippers too. It was slow—stopping at all the stations. The people come in, they tread all over your feet, they make you squeeze up till you're crammed against the window, and the women stick out their elbows and fidget. And then the expense! A return for two runs you into just over a couple of quid. I could have murdered Colin.

We got there at last. We walked up from the tram stop. Mother was at the window and let us in.

"This is Miss MacFarlane," I said.

And mother said:

"Oh, pleased to meet you. We've heard a lot about you."

"Oh," mother said to me, giving me a kiss, "Are you tired? You haven't had your tea, have you? Sit down. Have this chair, dear. It's more comfortable."

"Well, my boy," my father said.

"Want a wash?" my father said. "We've got a wash basin downstairs," he said. "I used not to mind about washing upstairs before. Now I couldn't do without it. Funny how your ideas change as you get older."

"How's business?" he said.

"Mustn't grumble," I said. "How's yours?"

"You knew," he said, "we took off the horses: except for one or two of the older families we have got motors now."

But he'd told me that the last time I was there. I'd been at him for years about motor hearses.

"You've forgotten I used to drive them," I said.

"Bless me, so you did," he said.

He took me up to my room. He showed me everything he had done to the house. "Your mother likes it," he said. "The traffic's company for her. You know what your mother is for company."

Then he gives me a funny look.

"Who's the girl?" he says.

My mother came in then and said:

"She's pretty, Arthur."

"Of course she's pretty," I said. "She's Irish."

"Oh," said the old man. "Irish! Got a sense of humour, eh?"

"She wouldn't be marrying me if she hadn't," I said. And then I gave them a look.

"Marrying her, did you say?" exclaimed my father.

"Any objection?" I said.

"Now Ernest dear," said my mother. "Leave the boy alone. Come down while I pop the kettle on."

She was terribly excited.

"Miss MacFarlane," the old man said.

"No sugar, thank you, Mrs Humphrey. I beg your pardon, Mr Humphrey?"

"The Glen Hotel at Swansea, I don't suppose you know that?" my father said.

"I wondered if you did being in the catering line," he said.

"It doesn't follow she knows every hotel," my mother said.

"Forty years ago," the old man said. "I was staying at the Glen in Swansea and the head waiter . . ."

"Oh no, not that one. I'm sure Miss MacFarlane doesn't want to hear that one," my mother said.

"How's business with you, Mr Humphrey?" said Muriel. "We passed a large cemetery near the station."

"Dad's Ledger," I said.

"The whole business has changed so that you wouldn't know it, in my lifetime," said my father. "Silver fittings have gone clean out. Everyone wants simplicity nowadays. Restraint. Dignity," my father said.

"Prices did it," my father said.

"The war," he said.

"You couldn't get the wood," he said.

"Take ordinary mahogany, just an ordinary piece of mahogany. Or teak," he said. "Take teak. Or walnut."

"You can certainly see the world go by in this room," I said to my mother.

"It never stops," she said.

Now it was all bicycles over the new concrete road from the gun factory. Then traction engines and cars. They came up over the hill where the AA man stands and choked up round the tram stop. It was mostly holiday traffic. Everything with a wheel on it was out.

"On this stretch," my father told me, "they get three accidents a week." There was an ambulance station at the crossroads.

We had hardly finished talking about this, in fact the old man was still saying that something ought to be done when the telephone rang.

"Name of MacFarlane?" the voice said on the wire.

"No. Humphrey," my father said. "There is a Miss MacFarlane here."

"There's a man named Colin Mitchell lying seriously injured in an accident at the Cottage Hospital, gave me the name of MacFarlane as his nearest relative."

That was the Police. On to it at once. That fellow Colin had followed us down by road.

Cry, I never heard a girl cry, as Muriel cried, when we came back from the hospital. He had died in the ambulance. Cutting in, the old game he used to play on me. Clean off the saddle and under the Birmingham bus. The blood was everywhere, they said. People were still looking at it when we went by. Head on. What a mess! Don't let's talk about it.

She wanted to see him but they said "No." There wasn't anything recognisable to see. She put her arms round my neck and cried, "Colin. Colin," as if I were Colin and clung to me. I was feeling sick myself. I held her tight and I kissed her and I thought "Holiday ruined."

"Damn fool man," I thought. "Poor devil," I thought.

"I knew he'd do something like this."

"There, there," I said to her. "Don't think about Colin."

Didn't she love me, I said, and not Colin. Hadn't she got me? She said, yes, she had. And she loved me. But, "Oh Colin! Oh Colin!" she cried. "And Colin's mother," she cried. "Oh it's terrible." She cried and cried.

We put her to bed and I sat with her and my mother kept coming in.

"Leave her to me," I said. "I understand her." Before they went to bed they both came in and looked at her. She lay sobbing with her head in the pillow.

I could quite understand her being upset. Colin was a decent fellow. He was always doing things for her. He mended her electric lamp and he riveted the stem of a wine glass so that you couldn't see the break. He used to make things for her. He was very good with his hands.

She lay on her side with her face burning and feverish with misery and crying, scalded by the salt, and her lips shrivelled up. I put my arm under her neck and I stroked her forehead. She groaned. Sometimes she shivered and sometimes she clung to me, crying, "Oh Colin! Colin!"

My arm ached with the cramp and I had a crick in my back, sitting in the awkward way I was on the bed. It was late. There was nothing to do but to ache and sit watching her and thinking. It is funny the way your mind drifts. When I was kissing her and watching her I was thinking out who I'd show our new Autumn range to first. Her hand held my wrist tight and when I kissed her I got her tears on my lips. They burned and stung. Her neck and shoulders were soft and I could feel her breath hot out of her nostrils on the back of my hand. Ever noticed how hot a woman's breath gets when she's crying? I drew out my hand and lay down beside her and "Oh, Colin, Colin," she sobbed, turning over and clinging to me. And so I lay there, listening to the traffic, staring at the ceiling and shivering whenever the picture of Colin shooting right off that damned red thing into the bus came into my mind— until I did not hear the traffic any more, or see the ceiling any more, or think any more, but a change happened—I don't know when. This Colin thing seemed to have knocked the bottom out of everything and I had a funny feeling we were going down and down and down in a lift. And the further we went the hotter and softer she got. Perhaps it was when I found with my hands that she had very big breasts. But it was like being on the mail steamer and feeling engines start under your feet, thumping louder and louder. You can feel it in every vein of your body. Her mouth opened and her tears dried. Her breath came through her open mouth and her voice was blind and husky. Colin, Colin, Colin, she said, and her fingers were hooked into me. I got out and turned the key in the door.

In the morning I left her sleeping. It did not matter to me what my father might have heard in the night, but still I wondered. She would hardly let me touch her before that. I told her I was sorry but she shut me up. I was afraid of her. I was afraid of mentioning Colin. I wanted to go out of the house there and then and tell someone everything. Did she love Colin all the time? Did she think I was Colin? And every time I thought of that poor devil covered over with a white sheet in the hospital mortuary, a kind of picture of her and me under the sheets with love came into my mind. I couldn't separate the two things. Just as though it had all come from Colin.

I'd rather not talk any more about that. I never talked to Muriel about it. I waited for her to say something but she didn't. She didn't say a word.

The next day was a bad day. It was grey and hot and the air smelled of oil fumes from the road. There's always a mess to clear up when things like this happen. I had to see to it. I had the job of ringing up the boy's mother. But I got round that, thank God, by ringing up the garage and getting them to go round and see the old lady. My father is useless when things are like this. I was the whole morning on the phone: to the hospital, the police, the coroner—and he stood fussing beside me, jerking up and down like a fat india-rubber ball. I found my mother washing up at the sink and she said:

"That poor boy's mother! I can't stop thinking of her." Then my father comes in and says,—just as though I was a customer—

"Of course if Mrs Mitchell desires it we can have the remains of the deceased conveyed to his house by one of our new specially sprung motor hearses and can, if necessary, make all the funeral arrangements."

I could have hit him because Muriel came into the room when he was saying this. But she stood there as if nothing had happened.

"It's the least we can do for poor Mrs Mitchell," she said. There were small creases of shadow under her eyes which shone with a soft strong light I had never seen before. She walked as if she were really still in that room with me, asleep. God, I loved that girl! God, I wanted to get all this over, this damned Colin business that had come right into the middle of everything like this, and I wanted to get married right away. I wanted to be alone with her. That's what Colin did for me.

"Yes," I said. "We must do the right thing by Colin."

"We are sometimes asked for long-distance estimates," my father said.

"It will be a little something," my mother said.

"Dad and I will talk it over," I said.

"Come into the office," my father said. "It occurred to me that it would be nice to do the right thing by this friend of yours."

We talked it over. We went into the cost of it. There was the return journey to reckon. We worked it out that it would come no dearer to old Mrs Mitchell than if she took the train and buried the boy here. That is to say, my father said, if I drove it.

"It would look nice," my father said.

"Saves money and it would look a bit friendly," my father said. "You've done it before."

"Well," I said. "I suppose I can get a refund on my return ticket from the railway."

But it was not as simple as it looked, because Muriel wanted to come. She wanted to drive back with me and the hearse. My mother was very worried about this. It might upset Muriel, she thought. Father thought it might not look nice to see a young girl sitting by the coffin of a grown man.

"It must be dignified," my father said. "You see if she was there it might look as though she were just doing it for the ride—like these young women on bakers' vans."

My father took me out into the hall to tell me this because he did not want her to hear. But she would not have it. She wanted to come back with Colin.

"Colin loved me. It is my duty to him," she said. "Besides," she said, suddenly, in her full open voice—it had seemed to be closed and carved and broken and small—"I've never been in a hearse before."

"And it will save her fare too," I said to my father.

That night I went again to her room. She was awake. I said I was sorry to disturb her but I would go at once only I wanted to see if she was all right. She said, in the closed voice again, that she was all right.

"Are you sure?" I said.

She did not answer. I was worried. I went over to the bed.

"What is the matter? Tell me what is the matter," I said.

For a long time she was silent. I held her hand, I stroked her head. She was lying stiff in the bed. She would not answer. I dropped my hand to her small white shoulder. She stirred and drew up her legs and half turned and said, "I was thinking of Colin."

"Where is he?" she asked.

"They've brought him round. He's lying downstairs."

"In the front room?"

"Yes, ready for the morning. Now be a sensible girl and go back by train."

"No, no," she said. "I want to go with Colin. Poor Colin. He loved me and I didn't love him." And she drew my hands down to her breasts.

"Colin loved me," she whispered.

"Not like this," I whispered.

It was a warm grey morning like all the others when we took Colin back. They had fixed the coffin in before Muriel came out. She came down wearing the bright blue hat she had got off Dormer's millinery man and she kissed my mother and father good-bye. They were very sorry for her. "Look after her, Arthur," my mother said. Muriel got in beside me without a glance behind her at the coffin. I started the engine. They smiled at us. My father raised his hat, but whether it was to Muriel and me or to Colin, or to the three of us, I do not know. He was not, you see, wearing his top hat. I'll say this for the old boy, thirty years in the trade have taught him tact.

After leaving my father's house you have to go down to the tram terminus before you get on to the by-pass. There was always one or two drivers, conductors or inspectors there, doing up their tickets, or changing over the trolley arms. When we passed I saw two of them drop their jaws, stick their pencils in their ears and raise their hats. I was so surprised by this that I nearly raised mine in acknowledgment, forgetting that we had the coffin behind. I had not driven one of my father's hearses for years.

Hearses are funny things to drive. They are well-sprung, smooth-running cars, with quiet engines and, if you are used to driving a smaller car, before you know where you are, you are speeding. You know you ought to go slow, say 25 to 30 maximum and it's hard to keep it down. You can return empty at 70 if you like. It's like driving a fire engine. Go fast out and come back slow—only the other way round. Open out in the country but slow down past houses. That's what it means. My father was very particular about this.

Muriel and I didn't speak very much at first. We sat listening to the engine and the occasional jerk of the coffin behind when we went over a pot hole. We passed the place where poor Colin—but I didn't say anything to Muriel, and she, if she noticed—which I doubt—did not say anything to me. We went through Cox Hill, Wammering and Yodley Mount, flat country, don't care for it myself. "There's a wonderful lot of building going on," Muriel said at last.

"You won't know these places in five years," I said.

But my mind kept drifting away from the road and the green fields and the dullness, and back to Colin,—five days before he had come down this way. I expected to see that Indian coming flying straight out of every corner. But it was all bent and bust up properly now. I saw the damned thing.

He had been up to his old game, following us and that had put the end to following. But not quite; he was following us now, behind us in the coffin. Then my mind drifted off that and I thought of those nights at my parents' house, and Muriel. You never know what a woman is going to be like. I thought, too, that it had put my calculations out. I mean, supposing she had a baby. You see I had reckoned on waiting eighteen months or so. I would have eight hundred then. But if we had to get married at once, we should have to cut right down. Then I kept thinking it was funny her saying "Colin!" like that in the night; it was funny it made her feel that way with me, and how it made me feel when she called me Colin. I'd never thought of her in that way, in what you might call the "Colin" way.

I looked at her and she looked at me and she smiled but still we did not say very much, but the smiles kept coming to both of us. The light-railway bridge at Dootheby took me by surprise and I thought the coffin gave a jump as we took it.

"Colin's still watching us," I nearly said.

There were tears in her eyes.

"What was the matter with Colin?" I said. "Nice chap, I thought. Why didn't you marry him?"

"Yes," she said. "He was a nice boy. But he'd no sense of humour."

"And I wanted to get out of that town," she said.

"I'm not going to stay there, at that hotel," she said.

"I want to get away," she said. "I've had enough."

She had a way of getting angry with the air, like that. "You've got to take me away," she said. We were passing slowly into Muster, there was a tram ahead and people thick on the narrow pavements, dodging out into the road. But when we got into the Market Square where they were standing around, they saw the coffin. They began to raise their hats. Suddenly she laughed. "It's like being the King and Queen," she said.

"They're raising their hats," she said.

"Not all of them," I said.

She squeezed my hand and I had to keep her from jumping about like a child on the seat as we went through.

"There they go."

"Boys always do," I said.

"And another."

"Let's see what the policeman does."

She started to laugh but I shut her up. "Keep your sense of humour to yourself," I said.

Through all those towns that run into one another as you might say, we caught it. We went through, as she said, like royalty. So many years since I drove a hearse, I'd forgotten what it was like.

I was proud of her, I was proud of Colin and I was proud of myself. And, after what had happened, I mean on the last two nights, it was like a wedding. And although we knew it was for Colin, it was for us too, because Colin was with both of us. It was like this all the way.

"Look at that man there. Why doesn't he raise his hat? People ought to show respect for the dead," she said.

(1938)

THE EVILS OF SPAIN

We took our seats at the table. There were seven of us.

It was at one of those taverns in Madrid. The moment we sat down Juliano, the little, hen-headed, red-lipped consumptive who was paying for the dinner and who laughed not with his mouth but by crinkling the skin round his eyes into scores of scratchy lines and showing his bony teeth—Juliano got up and said, "We are all badly placed." Fernando and Felix said, "No, we are not badly placed." And this started another argument shouting between the lot of us. We had been arguing all the way to the restaurant. The proprietor then offered a new table in a different way. Unanimously we said, "No," to settle the row; and when he brought the table and put it into place and laid a red and white check tablecloth on it, we sat down, stretched our legs and said, "Yes. This table is much better."

Before this we had called for Angel at his hotel. We shook his hand or slapped him on the back or embraced him and two hung on his arm as we walked down the street. "Ah, Angel, the rogue!" we said, giving him a squeeze. Our smooth Mediterranean Angel! "The uncle!" we said. "The old scoundrel." Angel smiled, lowering his black lashes in appreciation. Juliano gave him a prod in the ribs and asked him if he remembered, after all these years, that summer at Biarritz? When we had all been together? The only time we had all been together before? Juliano laughed by making his eyes wicked and expectant, like one Andalusian reminding another of the great joke they had had the day poor So-and-So fell down the stairs and broke his neck.

"The day you were nearly drowned," Juliano said.

Angel's complexion was the colour of white coffee; his hair, crinkled like a black fern, was parted in the middle, he was rich, soft-palmed and patient.

He was the only well-dressed man among us, the suavest shouter. Now he sat next door but one to Juliano. Fernando was between them, Juan next to me and, at the end, Felix. They had put Caesar at the head of the table, because he was the oldest and the largest. Indeed at his age he found his weight tiring to the feet.

Caesar did not speak much. He gave his silent weight to the dinner, letting his head drop like someone falling asleep, and listening. To the noise we made his silence was a balance and he nodded all the time slowly, making everything true. Sometimes someone told some story about him and he listened to that, nodding and not disputing it.

But we were talking chiefly of that summer, the one when Angel (the old uncle!) had nearly been drowned. Then Juan, the stout, swarthy one, banged the table with his hairy hands and put on his horn-rimmed glasses. He was the smallest and most vehement of us, the one with the thickest neck and the deepest voice, his words like barrels rumbling in a cellar.

"Come on! Come on! Let's make up our minds! What are we going to eat? Eat! Eat!" he roared.

"Yes," we cried. "Drink! What are we going to drink?"

The proprietor, who was in his shirt sleeves and braces, said it was for us to decide. We could have anything we wanted. This started another argument. He stepped back a pace and put himself in an attitude of self-defence.

"Soup! Soup? Make up your minds about soup! Who wants soup?" bawled Juan.

"Red wine," some of us answered. And others, "Not red, white."

"Soup I said," shouted Juan. "Yes," we all shouted. "Soup."

"Ah," said Juan, shaking his head, in his slow miserable disappointed voice. "Nobody have any soup. I want some soup. Nobody soup," he said sadly to the proprietor.

Juliano was bouncing in his chair and saying, God he would never forget that summer when Angel was nearly drowned! When we had all been together. But Juan said Felix had not been there and we had to straighten that matter out. Juliano said:

"They carried him on to the beach, our little Angel on to the beach. And the beach superintendent came through the crowd and said, 'What's happening?' 'Nothing,' we said. 'A man knocked out.' 'Knocked out?' said the beach superintendent. 'Nothing,' we said. 'Drowned!' A lot of people left the crowd and ran about over the beach saying, 'A man has been drowned.' 'Drowned,' said the beach superintendent. Angel was lying in the middle of them all, unconscious, with water pouring out of his mouth."

"No! No!" shouted Fernando. "No. It wasn't like that."

"How do you mean, it wasn't like that?" cried Juliano. "I was there." He appealed to us, "I was there."

"Yes, you were there," we said.

"I was there. I was there bringing him in. You say it wasn't like that, but it was like that. We were all there." Juliano jumped protesting to his feet, flung back his coat from his defying chest. His waistcoat was very loose over his stomach, draughty.

"What happened was better than that," Fernando said.

"Ah," said Juliano, suddenly sitting down and grinning with his eyes at everyone, very pleased at his show.

"It was better," he said. "How better?"

Fernando was a man who waited for silence and his hour. Once getting possession of the conversation he never let it go, but held it in the long, soothing ecstasy of a pliable embrace. All day long he lay in bed in his room in Fuencarral with the shutters closed, recovering from the bout of the day before. He was preparing himself to appear in the evening, spruce, grey-haired and meaty under the deep black crescents of his eyebrows, his cheeks ripening like plums as the evening advanced, his blue eyes which got bloodshot early, becoming mistier. He was a man who ripened and moistened. He talked his way through dinner into the night, his voice loosening, his eyes misting, his walk becoming slower and stealthier, acting every sentence, as if he were swaying through the exalted phase of inebriation. But it was an inebriation purely verbal; an exaltation of dramatic moments, refinements upon situations; and hour after hour passed until the dawn found him sodden in his own anecdotes, like a fruit in rum.

"What happened was," Fernando said, "that I was in the sea. And after a while I discovered Angel was in the sea. As you know there is nothing more perilous than the sea, but with Angel in it the peril is tripled; and when I saw him I was preparing to get as far away as possible. But he was making faces in the water and soon he made such a face, so inhuman, so unnatural, I saw he was drowning. This did not surprise me for Angel is one of those men who, when he is in the sea, he drowns. There is some psychological antipathy. Now when I see a man drowning my instinct is to get away quickly. A man drowning is not a man. He is a lunatic. But a lunatic like Angel! But unfortunately he got me before I could get away. There he was," Fernando stood up and raised his arm, confronting the proprietor of the restaurant, but staring right through that defensive man, "beating the water, diving, spluttering, choking, spitting, and, seeing he was drowning, for the man was drowning, caught hold of me, and we both went under. Angel was like a beast. He clung to me like seaweed. I, seeing this, awarded him a knock-out—zum—but as the tenacity of man increases with unconsciousness, Angel stuck to me like a limpet, and in saving myself there was no escape from saving him."

"That's true," said Angel, admiring his finger nails. And Caesar nodded his head up and down twice, which made it true.

Juan then swung round and called out, "Eat! Food! Let us order. Let us eat. We haven't ordered. We do nothing but talk, not eat. I want to eat."

"Yes, come on," said Felix. "Eat. What's the fish?"

"The fish," said the proprietor, "is bacalao."

"Yes," everyone cried. "Bacalao, a good bacalao, a very good one. No, it must be good. No. I can't eat it unless it's good, very good and very good."

"No," we said. "Not fish. We don't want it."

"Seven bacalaos then?" said the proprietor.

But Fernando was still on his feet.

"And the beach inspector said, 'What's his name and address and has he any identity papers?' 'Man,' I said, 'he's in his bathing dress. Where could he keep his papers?' And Juan said, 'Get a doctor. Don't stand there asking questions. Get a doctor.'"

"That's true," said Juan gloomily. "He wasn't dead."

"Get a doctor, that was it," Angel said.

"And they got a doctor and brought him round and got half the Bay of Biscay out of him, gallons of it. It astonished me that so much water could come out of a man."

"And then in the evening," Juliano leaped up and clipped the story out of Fernando's mouth. "Angel says to the proprietor of the hotel . . ."

Juan's head had sunk to his chest. His hands were over his ears.

"Eat," he bawled in a voice of despair so final that we all stopped talking and gazed at him with astonishment for a few moments. Then in sadness he turned to me appealing. "Can't we eat? I am empty."

". . . said to the proprietor of the hotel," Fernando grabbed the tale back from Juliano, "who was rushing down the corridor with a face like a fish. 'I am the man who was drowned this morning.' And the proprietor who looked at Angel like a prawn, the proprietor said, 'M'sieu, whether you were drowned or not drowned this morning you are about to be roast. The hotel is on fire.'"

"That's right," we said. "The hotel was on fire."

"I remember," said Felix. "It began in the kitchen."

"How in the kitchen?"

This then became the argument.

"The first time ever I heard it was in the kitchen."

"But no," said Angel, softly rising to claim his life story for himself. Juliano clapped his hands and bounced with joy. "It was not like that."

"But we were all there, Angel," Fernando said, but Angel who spoke very rapidly said:

"No and no! And the proof of it is. What was I wearing?" He challenged all of us. We paused.

"Tripe," said Juan to me hopelessly wagging his head. "You like tripe? They do it well. Here! Phist!" he called the proprietor through the din. "Have you tripe, a good Basque tripe? No? What a pity! Can you get me some? Here! Listen," he shouted to the rest of the table. "Tripe," he shouted, but they were engrossed in Angel.

"Pyjamas," Fernando said. "When you are in bed you wear your pyjamas."

"Exactly, and they were not my pyjamas."

"You say the fire was not in the kitchen," shouted Fernando, "because the pyjamas you were wearing were not yours!" And we shouted back at Angel.

"They belonged to the Italian ambassador," said Angel, "the one who was with that beautiful Mexican girl."

Then Caesar, who, as I have said, was the oldest of us and sat at the head of the table, Caesar leaned his old big pale face forward and said in a hushed voice, putting out his hands like a blind man remembering:

"My God—but what a very beautiful woman she was," he said. "I remember her. I have never in my life," he said speaking all his words slowly and with grave concern, "seen such a beautiful woman."

Fernando and Angel, who had been standing, sat down. We all looked in awe at the huge, old-shouldered Caesar with his big pale face and the pockets under his little grey eyes, who was speaking of the most beautiful woman he had ever seen.

"She was there all that summer," Caesar said. "She was no longer young." He leaned forward with his hands on the table. "What must she have been when she was young?"

A beach, the green sea dancing down white upon it, that Mexican woman walking over the floor of a restaurant, the warm white houses, the night glossy black like the toe of a patent shoe, her hair black. We tried to think how many years ago this was. Brought by his voice to silence us, she was already fading.

The proprietor took his opportunity in our silence. "The bacalao is done in the Basque fashion with peppers and potatoes. Bring a bacalao," he snapped to a youth in the kitchen.

Suddenly Juan brought his fists on the table, pushed back his chair and beat his chest with one fist and then the other. He swore in his enormous voice by his private parts.

"It's eleven o'clock. Eat! For God's sake. Fernando stands there talking and talking and no one listens to anybody. It is one of the evils of Spain. Someone stop him. Eat."

We all woke up and glared with the defiance of the bewildered, rejecting everything he said. Then what he said to us penetrated. A wave roared over us and we were with him. We agreed with what he said. We all stood up and, by our private parts, swore that he was right. It was one of the evils of Spain.

The soup arrived. White wine arrived.

"I didn't order soup," some shouted.

"I said 'Red wine,'" others said.

"It is a mistake," the proprietor said. "I'll take it away." An argument started about this.

"No," we said. "Leave it. We want it." And then we said the soup was bad, and the wine was bad and everything he brought was bad, but the proprietor said the soup was good and the wine was good and we said in the end it was good. We told the proprietor the restaurant was good, but he said not very good, indeed bad. And then we asked Angel to explain about the pyjamas.

(1938)

The Oedipus Complex

"Good morning, Mr P.," said Mr Pollfax, rinsing and drying his hands after the last patient. "How's Mr P.?" I was always Mr. P. until I sat in the chair and he switched the lamp on and had my mouth open. Then I got a peerage.

"That's fine, my lord," said Mr Pollfax, having a look inside.

Dogged, with its slight suggestion of doggish, was the word for Mr Pollfax. He was a short man, jaunty, hair going thin with jaunty buttocks and a sway to his walk. He had two lines, from habitual grinning, cut deep from the nostrils, and scores of lesser lines like the fine hair of a bird's nest round his egg-blue eyes. There was something innocent, heroic and determined about Mr Pollfax, something of the English Tommy in tin hat and full pack going up the line. He suggested in a quiet way—war.

He was the best dentist I ever had. He got you into the chair, turned on the light, tapped around a bit with a thing like a spoon and then, dropping his white-coated arm to his side, told you a story. Several more stories followed in his flat Somerset voice, when he had your mouth jacked up. And then removing the towel and with a final "Rinse that lot out," he finished with the strangest story of all and let you go. A month or so later the bill came in. Mr Pollfax presents his compliments and across the bottom of it, in his hand, "Be good." I have never known a dentist like Mr Pollfax.

"Open, my lord," said Mr Pollfax. "Let's see what sort of life his lordship has been leading. Still smoking that filthy pipe, I see. I shall have to do some cleaning up."

He tapped around and then dropped his arm. A look of anxiety came on his face. "Did I tell you that one about the girl who went to the Punch and Judy show? No? Nor the one about the engine-driver who was put on sentry duty in Syria? You're sure? When did I see you last? What was the last one

I told you? That sounds like last April? Lord, you *have* been letting things go. Well," said Mr Pollfax, tipping back my head and squirting something on to a tooth, "we'll have a go at that root at the back. It's not doing you any good. It was like this. There was a girl sitting on the beach at Barmouth with her young man watching a Punch and Judy show . . ." (Closer and closer came Mr Pollfax's head, lower and lower went his voice.)

He took an instrument and began chipping his way through the tooth and the tale.

"Not bad, eh?" he said, stepping back with a sudden shout of laughter.

"Ah," I mouthed.

"All right, my lord," said Mr Pollfax, withdrawing the instrument and relapsing into his dead professional manner. "Spit that lot out."

He began again.

There was just that root, Mr Pollfax was saying. It was no good there. There was nothing else wrong; he'd have it out in a couple of shakes.

"Though, my lord," he said, "you did grow it about as far back in your throat as you could, didn't you, trying to make it as difficult as you could for Mr Pollfax? What we'll do first of all is to give it a dose of something."

He swivelled the dish of instruments towards me and gave a tilt to the lamp. I remembered that lamp because once the bulb had exploded, sending glass all over the room. It was fortunate, Mr Pollfax said at the time, that it had blown the other way and none of it had hit me, for someone might have brought a case for damages against someone—which reminded him of the story of the honeymoon couple who went to a small hotel in Aberdeen . . .

"Now," said Mr Pollfax, dipping things in little pots and coming to me with an injection needle; "open wide, keep dead still. I was reading Freud the other day. There's a man. Oedipus complex? Ever read about that? Don't move, don't breathe, you'll feel a prick, but for God's sake don't jump. I don't want it to break in your gum. I've never had one break yet, touch wood, but they're thin, and if it broke off you'd be in a nursing home three weeks and Mr Pollfax would be down your throat looking for it. The trouble about these little bits of wire is they move a bit farther into the system every time you swallow."

"There now," said Mr Pollfax.

"Feel anything? Feel it prick?" he said. "Fine."

He went to a cupboard and picked out the instrument of extraction and then stood, working it up and down like a gardener's secateurs in his hand. He studied my face. He was a clean-shaven man and looked like a priest in his white coat.

"Some of the stories you hear!" exclaimed Mr Pollfax. "And some of the songs. I mean where I come from. 'The Lot that Lily Lost in the Lottery'— know that one? Is your skin beginning to tingle, do you feel it on the tip of your tongue yet? That's fine, my lord. I'll sing it to you."

Mr Pollfax began to sing. He'd give it another minute, he said, when he'd done with Lily; he'd just give me the chorus of "The Night Uncle's Waistcoat Caught Fire."

"Tra la la," sang Mr Pollfax.

"I bet," said Mr Pollfax sadistically, "one side of his lordship's face has gone dead and his tongue feels like a pin cushion."

"Blah," I said.

"I think," he said, "we'll begin."

So Mr Pollfax moved round to the side of me, got a grip on my shoulders and began to press on the instrument in my mouth. Pressing and drawing firmly he worked upon the root. Then he paused and increased the pressure. He seemed to be hanging from a crowbar fixed to my jaw. Nothing happened. He withdrew.

"The Great Flood begins," said Mr Pollfax putting a tube in my mouth and taking another weapon from the tray.

The operation began again. Mr Pollfax now seemed to hang and swing on the crowbar. It was not successful.

"Dug himself in, has he?" muttered Mr Pollfax. He had a look at his instruments. "You can spit, my lord," he said.

Mr Pollfax now seized me with great determination, hung, swung, pressed and tugged with increased energy.

"It's no good you thinking you're going to stay in," said Mr Pollfax in mid-air, muttering to the root. But the instrument slipped and a piece of tooth broke off as he spoke.

"So that's the game is it?" said Mr Pollfax withdrawing. "Good rinse, my lord, while Mr Pollfax considers the position."

He was breathing hard.

Oh well, he said, there were more ways than one of killing a cat. He'd get the drill on it. There were two Jews standing outside Buckingham Palace when a policeman came by, he said, coming at me with the drill which made a whistling noise like a fishing line as he drew it through. The tube gurgled in my mouth. I was looking, as I always did at Mr Pollfax's, at the cowls busily twirling on the chimneys opposite. Wind or no wind these cowls always seemed to be twirling round. Two metal cowls on two yellow chimneys. I always remember them.

"Spit, my lord," said Mr Pollfax, changing to a coarser drill. "Sorry old man, if it slipped, but Mr Pollfax is not to be beaten."

The drill whirred again, skidding and whining; the cowls twirled on the chimneys, Mr Pollfax's knuckles were on my nose. What he was trying to do, he said, was to get a purchase.

Mr Pollfax's movements got quicker. He hung up the drill, he tapped impatiently on the tray, looking for something. He came at me with something like a button-hook. He got it in. He levered like a signal man changing points.

"I'm just digging," he said. Another piece of tooth broke off.

Mr Pollfax started when he heard it go and drew back.

"Mr Pollfax in a dilemma," he said.

Well, he'd try the other side. Down came the drill again. There were beads of sweat on his brow. His breath was shorter.

"You see," exclaimed Mr Pollfax suddenly and loudly, looking angrily up at his clock. "I'm fighting against time. Keep that head this way, hold the mouth. That's right. Sorry, my lord, I've got to bash you about, but time's against me."

"Why, damn this root," said Mr Pollfax, hanging up again. "It's wearing out my drill. We'll have to saw. Mr Pollfax is up against it."

His face was red now, he was gasping and his eyes were glittering. A troubled and emotional look came over Mr Pollfax's face.

"I've been up against it in my time," exclaimed Mr Pollfax forcefully between his teeth. "You heard me mention the Oedipus complex to you?"

"Blah," I managed.

"I started well by ruining my father. I took every penny he had. That's a good start, isn't it?" he said, speaking very rapidly. "Then I got married. Perfectly happy marriage, but I went and bust it up. I went off with a French girl and her husband shot at us out in the car one day. I was with that girl eighteen months and she broke her back in a railway accident and I sat with her six months watching her die. Six ruddy months. I've been through it. Then my mother died and my father was going to marry again, a girl young enough to be his daughter. I went up and took that girl off him, ran off to Hungary with her, married her and we've got seven children. Perfect happiness at last. I've been through the mill," said Mr Pollfax, relaxing his chin and shining a torch down my mouth, "but I've come out in the end."

"A good rinse, my noble lord," said Mr Pollfax.

"The oldest's fourteen," he said, getting the saw. "Clever girl. Very clever with her hands."

He seized me again. Did I feel anything? Well, thank God for that, said Mr Pollfax. Here we'd been forty minutes with this damned root.

"And I bet you're thinking why didn't Lord Pollfax let sleeping dogs lie, like the telephone operator said. Did I tell you that one about the telephone operator? That gum of yours is going to be sore."

He was standing legs apart, chin trembling, eyes blinking, hacking with the button-hook, like a wrestler putting on a headlock.

"Mr Pollfax with his back against the wall," he said, between his teeth.

"Mr Pollfax making a last-minute stand," he hissed.

"On the burning deck!" he gasped.

"Whence," he added, "all but he had fled."

"Spit," he said. "And now let's have another look." He wiped his brow. "Don't say anything. Keep dead still. For God's sake don't let it hear you. My lords, ladies and gentlemen, pray silence for Mr Pollfax. It's coming, it isn't. No, it isn't. It is. It is. There," he cried, holding a fragment in his fingers.

He stood gravely to attention.

"And his chief beside,
Smiling the boy fell dead,"
said Mr Pollfax. "A good and final spit, my lord and prince."

(1945)

THINGS AS THEY ARE

Two middle-class women were talking at half past eleven in the morning in the empty bar of a suburban public house in a decaying district. It was a thundery and smoky morning in the summer and the traffic fumes did not rise from the street.

"Please, Frederick," said Mrs Forster, a rentier who spoke in a small, scented Edwardian voice. "Two more large gins. What were you saying, Margaret?"

"The heat last night, Jill. I tossed and I turned. I couldn't sleep—and when I can't sleep I scratch," said Margaret in her wronged voice. She was a barmaid and this was her day off.

Mrs Forster drank and nodded.

"I think," said Margaret, "I mean I don't mean anything rude, but I had a flea."

Mrs Forster put her grey head a little on one side and nodded again graciously under a flowered hat, like royalty.

"A flea, dear?" she said fondly.

Margaret's square mouth buckled after her next drink and her eyes seemed to be clambering frantically, like a pair of blatant prisoners behind her heavy glasses. Envy, wrong, accusation, were her life. Her black hair looked as though it had once belonged to an employer.

"I mean," she began to shout against her will, and Frederick, the elderly barman, moved away from her. "I mean I wouldn't have mentioned it if you hadn't mentioned it."

Mrs Forster raised her beautiful arms doubtfully and touched her grey hair at the back and she smiled again.

"I mean when you mentioned that you had one yesterday you said," said

Margaret.

"Oh," said Mrs Forster, too polite to differ.

"Yes, dear, don't you remember, we were in here—I mean, Frederick! Were we in here yesterday morning, Frederick, Mrs Forster and me ..."

Frederick stood upright, handsome, old, and stupid.

"He's deaf, the fool, that's why he left the stage," Margaret said, glaring at him, knowing that he heard. "Jill, yesterday? Try and remember. You came in for a Guinness. I was having a small port, I mean, or were you on gin?"

"Oh, gin," said Mrs Forster in her shocked, soft, distinguished way, recognising a word.

"That was it, then," said Margaret, shaking an iron chin up and down four times. "It might have hopped."

"Hopped," nodded Mrs Forster pleasantly.

"I mean, fleas hop, I don't mean anything vulgar." Margaret spread her hard, long bare arms and knocked her glass. "Distances," she said. "From one place to another place. A flea travels. From here, at this end of the bar, I don't say to the end, but along or across, I mean it could."

"Yes," said Mrs Forster with agreeable interest.

"Or from a person. I mean, a flea might jump on you—or on me, it might jump from someone else, and then off that person, it depends if they are with someone. It might come off a bus or a tram." Margaret's long arms described these movements and then she brought them back to her lap. "It was a large one," she said. "A brute."

"Oh, large?" said Mrs Forster sympathetically.

"Not large—I mean it must have been large, I could tell by the bites, I know a small flea, I mean we all do—don't mind my mentioning it—I had big bites all up my leg," said Margaret, stretching out a long, strong leg. Seeing no bites there, she pulled her tight

serge skirt up with annoyance over her knee and up her thigh until, halted by the sight of her suspender, she looked angrily at Frederick and furtively at Mrs Forster and pulled her skirt down and held it down.

"Big as pennies, horrible pink lumps, red, Jill," argued Margaret. "I couldn't sleep. Scratching doesn't make it any better. It wasn't a London flea, that I know, Jill. I know a London flea, I mean you know a London flea, an ordinary one, small beastly things, I hate them, but this must have been some great black foreign brute. Indian! Frederick! You've seen one of those things?"

Frederick went with a small business of finger-flicking to the curtains at the back of the bar, peeped through as if for his cue. All bars were empty.

"Never," he said contemptuously when he came back, and turning his back on the ladies, hummed at the shelves of bottles.

"It's easy," Margaret began to shout once more, swallowing her gin, shouting at her legs, which kept slipping off the rail of the stool and enraged her by jerking her body, "I mean, for them to travel. They get on ships. I mean those ships have been in the tropics, I don't say India necessarily, it might be in Egypt or Jamaica, a flea could hop off a native onto some sailor in the docks."

"You mean, dear, it came up from the docks by bus," said Mrs Forster. "You caught it on a bus?"

"No, Jill," said Margaret. "I mean some sailor brought it up."

"Sailor," murmured Mrs Forster, going pale.

"Ted," said Margaret, accusing. "From Calcutta. Ted could have brought it off his ship."

Mrs Forster's head became fixed and still. She gazed mistily at Margaret and swayed. She finished her drink and steadied herself by looking into the bottom of the glass and waited for two more drops to come. Then she raised her small chin and trembled. She held a cigarette at the end of her thumb and her finger as if it were a stick of crayon and she were writing a message in blue smoke on the air. Her eyes closed sleepily, her lips sucked, pouted, and two tears rolled down her cheeks. She opened her large handbag and from the mess of letters, bills, money, keys, purses, and powder inside she took a small handkerchief and dabbed her eyes.

"Ah!" said Margaret, trying to get her arm to Mrs Forster, but failing to reach her because her foot slipped on the rail again, so that she kicked herself. "Ah, Jill! I only mentioned it, I didn't mean anything, I mean when you said you had one, I said to myself: 'That's it, it's an Indian. Ted's brought it out of the ship's hold.' I didn't mean to bring up Ted, Jill. There's nothing funny about it, sailors do."

Mrs Forster's cheeks and neck fattened amorously as she mewed and quietly cried and held her handkerchief tight.

"Here," said Margaret, mastering her. "Chin-chin, Jill, drink up, it will do you good. Don't cry. Here, you've finished it. Frederick, two more," she said, sliding towards Mrs Forster and resting one breast on the bar.

Mrs Forster straightened herself with dignity and stopped crying.

"He broke my heart," said Mrs Forster, panting. "I always found one in the bed after his leave was over."

"He couldn't help it," said Margaret.

"Oh, no," said Mrs Forster.

"It's the life sailors live," said Margaret. "And don't you forget, are you listening, Jill? Listen to me. Look at me and listen. You're among friends, Jill. He's gone, Jill, like you might say, out of your life."

"Yes," said Mrs Forster, nodding again, repeating a lesson. "Out of my life."

"And good riddance, too, Jill."

"Riddance," murmured Mrs Forster.

"Jill," shouted Margaret. "You've got a warm heart, that's what it is, as warm as Venus. I could never marry again after what I've been through, not whatever you paid me, not however much money it was you gave me, but you're not like me, your heart is too warm. You're too trusting."

"Trusting," Mrs Forster repeated softly, squeezing her eyelids.

"I tell you what it was," Margaret said. "You were in love, Jill," said Margaret, greedy in the mouth. "Can you hear me?"

"Yes, dear."

"That's what I said. It was love. You loved him and you married him."

Margaret pulled herself up the bar and sat upright, looking with surprise at the breast that had rested there. She looked at her glass, she looked at Mrs Forster's; she picked up the glass and put it down. "It was a beautiful dream, Jill, you had your beautiful dream and I say this from the bottom of my heart, I hope you will have a beautiful memory."

"Two months," sighed Mrs Forster, and her eyes opened amorously in a grey glister and then sleepily half closed.

"But now, Jill, it's over. You've woke up, woken up. I mean, you're seeing things as they are."

The silence seemed to the two ladies to stand in a lump between them. Margaret looked into her empty glass again. Frederick lit a cigarette he had made, and his powdered face split up into twitches as he took the first draw and then put the cigarette economically on the counter. He went through his repertory of small coughs and then, raising his statesman-like head, he listened to the traffic passing and hummed.

Mrs Forster let her expensive fur slip back from her fine shoulders and looked at the rings on her small hands.

"I loved him, Margaret," she said. "I really did love him."

"We know you loved him. I mean, it was love," said Margaret. "It's nothing to do with the age you are. Life's never over. It was love. You're a terrible woman, Jill."

"Oh, Margaret," said Mrs Forster with a discreet glee, "I know I am."

"He was your fourth," said Margaret.

"Don't, Margaret," giggled Mrs Forster.

"No, no, I'm not criticising. I never criticise. Live and let live. It wasn't a fancy, Jill, you loved him with all your heart."

Jill raised her chin in a lady-like way.

"But I won't be hit," she whispered. "At my age I allow no one to strike me. I am fifty-seven, Margaret, I'm not a girl."

"That's what we all said," said Margaret. "You were headstrong."

"Oh, Margaret!" said Mrs Forster, delighted.

"Oh, yes, yes, you wouldn't listen, not you. You wouldn't listen to me. I brought him up to the Chequers, or was it the Westmoreland?—no, it was the George—and I thought to myself, I know your type, young man—you see, Jill, I've had experience—out for what he could get—well, honest, didn't I tell you?"

"His face was very brown."

"Brown! Would you believe me? No, you wouldn't. I can see him. He came up here the night of the dance. He took his coat off. Well, we all sweat."

"But," sighed Mrs Forster, "he had white arms."

"Couldn't keep his hands to himself. Put it away, pack it up, I said. He didn't care. He was after Mrs Klebs and she went potty on him till Mrs Sinclair came and then that Mr Baum interfered. That sort lives for trouble. All of them mad on him—I bet Frederick could tell a tale, but he won't. Trust Frederick," she said with a look of hate at the barman, "upstairs in the billiard room, I shan't forget it. Torpedoed twice, he said. I mean Ted said: he torpedoed one or two. What happened to him that night?"

"Someone made him comfortable, I am sure," said Mrs Forster, always anxious about lonely strangers.

"And you were quite rude with me, Jill, I don't mean rude, you couldn't be rude, it isn't in you, but we almost came to words . . ."

"What did you say, Margaret?" said Mrs Forster from a dream.

"I said at your age, fifty-seven, I said you can't marry a boy of twenty-six."

Mrs Forster sighed.

"Frederick. Freddy, dear. Two more," said Mrs Forster.

Margaret took her glass, and while she was finishing it Frederick held his hand out for it, insultingly rubbing his fingers.

"Hah!" said Margaret, blowing out her breath as the gin burned her. "You bowled over him, I mean you bowled him over, a boy of twenty-six. Sailors are scamps."

"Not," said Mrs Forster, reaching to trim the back of her hair again and tipping her flowered hat forward on her forehead and austerely letting it remain like that. "Not," she said, getting stuck at the word.

"Not what?" said Margaret. "Not a scamp? I say he was. I said at the time, I still say it, a rotten little scamp."

"Not," said Mrs Forster.

"A scamp," said Margaret.

"Not. Not with a belt," said Mrs Forster. "I will not be hit with a belt."

"My husband," began Margaret.

"I will not, Margaret," said Mrs Forster. "Never. Never. Never with a belt.

"Not hit, struck," Mrs Forster said, defying Margaret.

"It was a plot, you could see it a mile off, it would make you laugh, a lousy, rotten plot," Margaret let fly, swallowing her drink. "He was after your house and your money. If he wasn't, what did he want to get his mother in for, a big three-storey house like yours, in a fine residential position? Just what he'd like, a little rat like that . . ."

Mrs Forster began a long laugh to herself.

"My grandfather," she giggled.

"What?" said Margaret.

"Owns the house. Not owns. Owned, I say, the house," said Mrs Forster, tapping the bar.

"Frederick," said Mrs Forster. "Did my grandfather own the house?"

"Uh?" said Frederick, giving his cuff links a shake. "Which house?"

"My house over there," said Mrs Forster, pointing to the door.

"I know he owned the house, dear," Margaret said. "Frederick knows."

"Let me ask Frederick," said Mrs Forster. "Frederick, you knew my grandfather."

"Uh?" said Frederick, leaning to listen.

"He's as deaf as a wall," Margaret said.

Frederick walked away to the curtain at the back of the bar and peeped through it. Nervously he came back, glancing at his handsome face in the mirror; he chose an expression of stupidity and disdain, but he spoke with a quiet rage.

"I remember this street," he raged, "when you could hardly get across it for the carriages and the footmen and the maids in their lace caps and aprons. You never saw a lady in a place like this."

He turned his back on them and walked again secretively to the curtain, peeped again, and came back stiffly on feet skewed sideways by the gravity of the gout and put the tips of his old, well-manicured fingers on the bar for them to admire.

"Now," he said, giving a socially shocked glance over the windows that were still half boarded after the bombing, "all tenements, flats, rooms, walls falling down, balconies dropping off, bombed out, and rotting," he said. He sneered at Margaret. "Not the same people. Slums. Riff-raff now. Mrs Forster's father was the last of the old school."

"My grandfather," said Mrs Forster.

"He was a gentleman," said Frederick.

Frederick walked to the curtains.

"Horrible," he muttered loudly, timing his exit.

There was a silence until he came back. The two women looked at the enormous empty public house, with its high cracked and dirty ceilings, its dusty walls unpainted for twenty years. Its top floor had been on fire. Its windows had gone, three or four times.

Frederick mopped up scornfully between the glasses of gin on the counter.

"That's what I mean," said Margaret, her tongue swelling up, her mouth side-slipping. "If you'd given the key to his mother, where would you have been? They'd have shut you out of your own house and what's the good of the police? All the scum have come to the top since the war. You were too innocent and we saved you. Jill, well, I mean if we hadn't all got together, the whole crowd, where were you? He was going to get into the house and then one night when you'd been over at the George or the Chequers or over here and you'd had one or two . . ."

Jill looked proudly and fondly at her glass, crinkled her childish eyes.

"Oh," said Jill in a little naughty-faced protest.

"I mean, I don't mean plastered," said Margaret, bewildered by the sound of her own voice and moving out her hand to bring it back.

"Not stinking, Jill, excuse me. I mean we sometimes have two or three. Don't we?" Margaret appealed to the barman.

"Uh?" said Frederick coldly. "Where was this?"

"Oh, don't be stupid," said Margaret, turning round suddenly and knocking her glass over, which Frederick picked up and took away. "What was I saying, Jill?"

A beautiful still smile, like a butterfly opening on an old flower, came onto Mrs Forster's face.

"Margaret," she confided, "I don't know."

"I know," said Margaret, waving her heavy bare arm. "You'd have been signing papers. He'd have stripped you. He might have murdered you like that case last Sunday in the papers. A well-to-do woman like you. The common little rat. Bringing his fleas."

"He—was—not—common," said Mrs Forster, sitting upright suddenly, and her hat fell over her nose, giving her an appearance of dashing distinction.

"He was off a ship," said Margaret.

"He was an officer."

"He said he was an officer," said Margaret, struggling with her corsets.

Mrs Forster got down from her stool and held with one hand to the bar. She laughed quietly.

"He—" she began.

"What?" said Margaret.

"I shan't tell you," said Mrs Forster. "Come here."

Margaret leaned towards her.

"No, come here, stand here," said Mrs Forster.

Margaret stood up, also holding to the bar, and Mrs Forster put her hands to Margaret's neck and pulled her head down and began to laugh in Margaret's ear. She was whispering.

"What?" shouted Margaret. "I can't hear. What is it?"

Mrs Forster laughed with a roar in Margaret's ear.

"He—he—was a man, Margaret," she whispered. She pushed her away.

"You know what I mean, Margaret," she said in a stern clear voice. "You do, don't you? Come here again, I'll tell you."

"I heard you."

"No, come here again, closer. I'll tell you. Where are you?"

Mrs Forster whispered again and then drew back.

"A man," she said boldly.

"And you're a woman, Jill."

"A man!" said Mrs Forster. "Everything, Margaret. You know—everything. But not with a belt. I won't be struck." Mrs Forster reached for her glass.

"*Vive la France!*" she said, holding up her glass, drank, and banged it down. "Well, I threw him out."

A lament broke from Margaret. She had suddenly remembered one of *her* husbands. She had had two.

"He went off to his work and I was waiting for him at six. He didn't come back. I'd no money in the house, that was seventeen years ago, and Joyce was two, and he never even wrote. I went through his pockets and gave his coats a shake, wedding rings poured out of them. What do you get for it? Your own daughter won't speak to you, ashamed to bring her friends to the house. 'You're always drunk,' she says. To her own mother. Drunk!" said Margaret. "I might have one or perhaps two. What does a girl like that know?"

With a soft, quick crumpling, a soft thump and a long sigh, Mrs Forster went to the floor and full-length lay there with a beautiful smile on her face, and a fierce noise of pleasure came from her white face. Her hat rolled off, her bag fell down, open, and spilling with a loud noise.

"Eh," said Frederick, coming round from behind the counter.

"Passed out again. Get her up, get her up quick," said Margaret. "Her bag, her money.

"Lift her on the side," she said. "I will take her legs."

They carried Mrs Forster to the broken leather settee and laid her down there. "Here's her bag," Margaret wrangled. "It's all there."

"And the one in your hand," said Frederick, looking at the pound note in Margaret's hand.

And then the crowd came in: Mrs Klebs, Mrs Sinclair, Mr Baum, the one they called Pudding, who had fallen down the area at Christmas, and a lot more.

"What's this?" they said. "Not again? Frederick, what's this?"

"They came in here," Frederick said in a temper. "Ladies, talking about love."

(1982)

WHEN MY GIRL COMES HOME

She was kissing them all, hugging them, her arms bare in her summer dress, laughing and taking in a big draught of breath after every kiss, nearly knocking old Mrs Draper off her feet, almost wrestling with Mrs Fulmino, who was large and tall. Then Hilda broke off to give another foreign-sounding laugh and plunged at Jack Draper ("the baby") and his wife, at Mr Fulmino, who cried out "What again?" and at Constance who did not like emotion; and after every kiss, Hilda drew back, getting her breath and making this sound like "Hah!"

"Who is this?" she said, looking at me.

"Harry Fraser," Mr Fulmino said. "You remember Harry?"

"You worked at the grocer's," she said. "I remember you."

"No," I said, "that was my brother."

"This is the little one," said Mrs Fulmino.

"Who won the scholarship," said Constance.

"We couldn't have done anything without him," said Mr Fulmino, expanding with extravagance as he always did about everything. "He wrote to the War Office, the Red Cross, the Prisoners of War, the American Government, all the letters. He's going to be our Head Librarian."

Mr Fulmino loved whatever had not happened yet. His forecasts were always wrong. I left the library years ago and never fulfilled the future he had planned for me. Obviously Hilda did not remember me. Thirteen years before, when she married Mr Singh and left home, I was no more than a boy.

"Well, I'll kiss him too," she said. "And another for your brother."

That was the first thing to happen, the first of many signs of how her life had had no contact with ourselves.

"He was killed in the war, dear," said Mrs Fulmino.

"She couldn't know," said Constance.

"I'm sorry," said Hilda.

We all stood silent, and Hilda turned to hold on to her mother, little Mrs Johnson, whose face was coquettish with tears and who came only up to Hilda's shoulder. The old lady was bewildered. She was trembling as though she were going to shake to pieces like a tree in the autumn. Hilda stood still, touching her tinted brown hair which was done in a tight high style and still unloosened, despite all the hugs and kissings. Her arms looked as dry as sand, her breasts were full in her green, flowered dress and she was gazing over our heads now from large yellow eyes which had almost closed into two blind, blissful curving lines. Her eyebrows seemed to be lacquered. How Oriental she looked on that first day! She was looking above our heads at old Mrs Draper's shabby room and going over the odd things she remembered, and while she stood like that, the women were studying her clothes. A boy's memory is all wrong. Naturally, when I was a boy I had thought of her as tall. She was really short. But I did remember her bold nose—it was like her mother's and old Mrs Draper's; those two were sisters. Otherwise I wouldn't have known her. And that is what Mr Fulmino said when we were all silent and incredulous again. We had Hilda back. Not just "back" either, but "back from the dead," reborn.

"She was in the last coach of the train, wasn't she, Mother?" Mr Fulmino said to Mrs Johnson. He called her "mother" for the occasion, celebrating her joy.

"Yes," said Mrs Johnson. "Yes." Her voice scraped and trembled.

"In the last coach, next the van. We went right up the platform, we thought we'd missed her, didn't we? She was," he exclaimed with acquisitive pride, "in the First Class."

"Like you missed me coming from Penzance," said Mrs Fulmino swelling powerfully and going that thundery violet colour which old wrongs gave her.

"Posh!" said Hilda. And we all smiled in a sickly way.

"Don't you ever do it again, my girl! Don't you ever do it again," said her mother, old Mrs Johnson, clinging to her daughter's arm and shaking it as if it were a bellrope.

"I was keeping an eye on my luggage," Hilda laughed.

Ah! That was a point! There was not only Hilda, there was her luggage. Some of it was in the room, but the bigger things were outside on the landing, piled up, looking very new, with the fantastic labels of hotels in Tokyo, San Francisco, and New York on it, and a beautiful jewel box in white leather on top like a crown. Old Mrs Draper did not like the luggage being outside the room in case it was in the way of the people upstairs. Constance went out and fetched the jewel box in. We had all seen it. We were as astonished by all these cases as we were by Hilda herself. After thirteen years, six of them war, we recognised that the poor ruined woman we had prepared for had not arrived. She shone with money. Later on, one after the other of us, except old Mrs Draper who could not walk far, went out and looked at the luggage and came back to study Hilda in a new way.

We had all had a shock. She had been nearly two years coming home from Tokyo. Before that there was the occupation, before that the war itself. Before that there were the years in Bombay and Singapore, when she was married to an Indian they always called Mr Singh. All those years were lost to us. None of us had been to India. What happened there to Mr Singh? We knew he had died—but how? Even if we had known, we couldn't have imagined it. None of us had been to Singapore, none of us to Japan. People from streets like Hincham Street do go to such places—it is not past belief. Knock on the doors of half the houses in London and you will find people with relations all over the world—but none of us had. Mention these places to us, we look at our grey skies and see boiling sun. Our one certainty about Hilda was what, in fact, the newspaper said the next day, with her photograph and the headline: *A Mother's Faith. Four Years in Japanese Torture Camp. London Girl's Ordeal.* Hilda was a terrible item of news, a gash in our lives, and we looked for the signs of it on her body, in the way she stood, in the lines on her face, as if we were expecting a scream from her mouth like the screams we were told Bill Williams gave out at night in his sleep, after he had been flown back home when the war ended. We had had to wait and wait for Hilda. At one time—there was a postcard from Hawaii—she was pinned like a butterfly in the middle of the Pacific Ocean; soon after there was a letter from Tokyo saying she couldn't get a passage. Confusing. She was travelling backwards. Letters from Tokyo were still coming after her letters from San Francisco.

We were still standing, waiting for Constance to bring in the teapot for the tea was already laid. The trolley buses go down Hincham Street. It is a mere one hundred and fifty yards of a few little houses and a few little shops, which has a sudden charmed importance because the main road has petered out at our end by the Lord Nelson and an enormous public lavatory, and the trolley buses have to run down Hincham Street before picking up the main road again, after a sharp turn at the convent. Hincham Street is less a street than an interval, a disheartened connection. While we stood in one of those silences that follow excitement, a trolley bus came by and Hilda exclaimed:

"You've still got the old trams. Bump! Bump! Bump!" Hilda was ecstatic about the sound. "Do you remember I used to be frightened the spark from the pole would set the lace curtains on fire when I was little?"

For, as the buses turned, the trolley arms would come swooping with two or three loud bumps and a spit of blue electricity, almost hitting Mrs

Draper's sitting-room window which was on the first floor.

"It's trolleys now, my girl," said old Mrs Draper, whose voice was like the voice of time itself chewing away at life. "The trams went years ago, before the war."

Old Mrs Draper had sat down in her chair again by the fire which always burned winter and summer in this room; she could not stand for long. It was the first remark that had given us any sense of what was bewildering all of us, the passing of time, the growing of a soft girl into a grown, hard-hipped woman. For old Mrs Draper's mind was detached from events around her and moved only among the signal facts and conclusions of history.

Presently we were, as the saying is, "at our teas." Mr Fulmino, less puzzled than the rest of us, expanded in his chair with the contentment of one who had personally operated a deeply British miracle. It was he who had got Hilda home.

"We've got all the correspondence, haven't we, Harry?" he said. "We kept it—the War Office, Red Cross, Prisoner of War Commission, everything, Hilda. I'll show it to you."

His task had transformed him and his language. Identification, registration, accommodation, communication, rehabilitation, hospitalisation, administration, investigation, transportation—well we had all dreamed of Hilda in our different ways.

"They always said the same thing," Mrs Fulmino said reproachfully. "No one of the name of Mrs Singh on the lists."

"I wrote to Bombay," said Mr Fulmino.

"He wrote to Singapore," said Mrs Fulmino.

Mr Fulmino drank some tea, wiped his lips and became geography.

"All British subjects were rounded up, they said," Mrs Fulmino said.

We nodded. We had made our stand, of course, on the law. Mrs Fulmino was authority.

"But Hilda was married to an Indian," said Constance.

We glanced with a tolerance we did not usually feel for Constance. She was always trying to drag politics in.

"She's a British subject by birth," said Mrs Fulmino firmly.

"Mum," Hilda whispered, squeezing her mother's arm hard, and then looked up to listen, as if she were listening to talk about a faraway stranger.

"I was in Tokyo when the war started," she said. "Not Singapore."

"Oh Tokyo!" exclaimed Mr Fulmino, feeling in his waistcoat for a pencil to make a note of it and, suddenly, realising that his note-taking days were over.

"Whatever the girl has done she has been punished for it," came old Mrs Draper's mournful voice from the chair by the fire, but in the clatter no one heard her, except old Mrs Johnson, who squeezed her daughter's arm and said:

"My girl is a jewel."

Still, Hilda's words surprised us. We had worked it out that after she and Mr Singh were married and went to Bombay he had heard of a better job in the state railway medical service and had gone to Singapore where the war had caught her. Mrs Fulmino looked affronted. If Mr Fulmino expanded into geography and the language of state—he worked for the Borough Council—Mrs Fulmino liked a fact to be a fact.

"We got the postcards," said Mrs Fulmino sticking to chronology.

"Hawaii," Mr Fulmino said. "How'd you get there? Swim, I suppose." He added, "A sweet spot, it looks, suit us for a holiday—palms."

"Coconuts," said young Jack Draper, who worked in a pipe factory, speaking for the first time.

"Be quiet," said his wife.

"It's an American base now," said Constance with her politically sugared smile.

We hesitated but let her observation pass. It was simple to ignore her. We were happy.

"I suppose they paid your fare," said Jack Draper's wife, a north-country woman.

"Accommodation, transportation," said Mr Fulmino. "Food, clothing. Everything. Financed by the international commission."

This remark made old Mrs Johnson cry a little. In those years none of us had deeply believed that Hilda was alive. The silence was too long; too much time had gone by. Others had come home by the thousand with stories of thousands who had died. Only old Mrs Johnson had been convinced that Hilda was safe. The landlord at the Lord Nelson, the butcher, anyone who met old Mrs Johnson as she walked by like a poor, decent ghost with her sewing bundles, in those last two years, all said in war-staled voices:

"It's a mother's faith, that's what it is. A mother's faith's a funny thing."

She would walk along, with a cough like someone driving tacks. Her chest had sunk and under her brown coat her shoulder blades seemed to have sharpened into a single hump. Her faith gave her a bright, yet also a sly, dishonest look.

"I'm taking this sewing up to Mrs Tracy's. She wants it in a hurry," she might say.

"You ought to rest, Mrs Johnson, like the doctor said."

"I want a bit of money for when my girl comes home," she said. "She'll want feeding up."

And she would look around perhaps, for a clock, in case she ought, by this time, to have put a pot on the stove.

She had been too ill, in hospital, during the war, to speak about what might have happened to Hilda. Her own pain and fear of dying deafened her to what could be guessed. Mrs Johnson's faith had been born out of pain, out of the inability—within her prison of aching bones and crushed breathing—to identify herself with her daughter. Her faith grew out of her very self-centredness. And when she came out from the post office every week, where she put her savings, she looked demure, holy and secretive. If people were too kind and too sympathetic with her, she shuffled and looked mockingly. Seven hospitals, she said, had not killed *her*.

Now, when she heard Mr Fulmino's words about the fare, the clothes, the food, the expense of it all, she was troubled. What had she worked for—even at one time scrubbing in a canteen—but to save Hilda from a charity so vast in its humiliation, from so blank a herding mercy. Hilda was hers, not theirs. Hilda kept her arm on her mother's waist and while Mr Fulmino carried on with the marvels of international organisation (which moved Mrs Fulmino to say hungrily, "It takes a war to bring it out"), Hilda ignored them and whispered to comfort her mother. At last the old lady dried her eyes and smiled at her daughter. The smile grew to a small laugh, she gave a proud jerk to her head, conveying that she and her Hil were not going to kowtow in gratitude to anyone, and Hilda, at last, said out loud to her mother what, no doubt, she had been whispering:

"He wouldn't let me pay anything, Mum. Faulkner his name

was. Very highly educated. He came from California. We had a fancy dress dance on the ship and he made me go as a geisha ... He gave me these ..." And she raised her hand to show her mother the bracelets on it.

Mrs Johnson laughed wickedly.

"Did he ...? Was he ...?" said Mrs Johnson.

"No. Well, I don't know," said Hilda. "But I kept his address."

Mrs Johnson smiled round at all of us, to show that in spite of all, being the poorest in the family and the ones that had suffered most, she and Hilda knew how to look after themselves.

This was the moment when there was that knock on the door. Everyone was startled and looked at it.

"A knock!" said Mr Fulmino.

"A knock, Constance," said young Mrs Draper who had busy north-country ears.

"A knock," several said.

Old Mrs Draper made one of her fundamental utterances again, one of her growls from the belly of the history of human indignation.

"We are," she said, "in the middle of our teas. Constance, go and see and tell them."

But before Constance got to the door, two young men, one with a camera, came right into the room, without asking. Some of us lowered our heads and then, just as one young man said, "I'm from the News," the other clicked his camera.

Jack Draper said, nearly choking:

"He's taken a snap of us eating."

While we were all staring at them, old Mrs Draper chewed out grandly:

"Who may they be?"

But Hilda stood up and got her mother to her feet, too. "Stand up all of us," she said eagerly. "It's for the papers."

It was the Press. We were in confusion. Mrs Fulmino pushed Mr Fulmino forward towards the reporter and then pulled him back. The reporter stood asking questions and everyone answered at once. The photographer kept on taking photographs and, when he was not doing that, started picking up vases and putting them down and one moment was trying the drawer of a little table by the window. They pushed Hilda and her mother into a corner and took a picture of them, Hilda calling to us all to "come in" and Mr Fulmino explaining to the reporters. Then they went, leaving a cigarette burning on one of old Mrs Draper's lace doyleys under the fern and two more butts on the floor. "What did they say? What did they say?" we all asked one another, but no one could remember. We were all talking at once, arguing about who had heard the knock first. Young Mrs Draper said her tea was spoiled and Constance opened the window to let the cigarette smoke out and then got the kettle. Mr Fulmino put his hand on his wife's knee because she was upset and she shook it off. When we had calmed down Hilda said:

"The young one was a nice-looking boy, wasn't he, Mum?" and Mr Fulmino, who almost never voiced the common opinion about anything but who had perhaps noticed how the eyes of all the women went larger at this remark, laughed loudly and said:

"We've got the old Hilda back!"

I mention this because of the item in the papers next day: A Mother's Faith. Four Years in a Japanese Torture Camp. London Girl's Ordeal.

Wonderful, as Mr Fulmino said. To be truthful, I felt uncomfortable at old Mrs Draper's. They were not my family. I had been dragged there by Mr Fulmino, and by a look now and then from young Mrs Draper and from Constance I had the feeling that they thought it was indecent for me to be there when I had only been going with Iris, Mr Fulmino's daughter, for two or three months. I had to be tolerated as one more example of Mr Fulmino's uncontrollable gifts—the gift for colonising.

Mr Fulmino had shot up from nothing during the war. It had given him personality. He was a short, talkative, heavy man of forty-five with a wet gold tooth and glossy black hair that streamlined back across his head from an arrow point, getting thin in front. His eyes were anxious, overworked and puddled, indeed if you had not known him you would have thought he had had a couple of black eyes that had never got right. He bowled along as he walked like someone absorbed by fondness for his own body. He had been in many things before he got to work for the Council—the Army (but not a fighting soldier) in the war, in auctions and the bar of a club. He was very active, confiding and enquiring.

When I first met him I was working at the counter of the Public Library, during the war, and one day he came over from the Council Offices and said, importantly:

"Friend, we've got a bit of a headache. We've got an enquiry from the War Office. Have you got anything about Malaya—with maps?"

In the next breath he was deflating himself:

"It's a personal thing. They never tell you anything. I've got a niece out there."

Honesty made him sound underhand. His manner suggested that his niece was a secret fortification somewhere east of Suez. Soon he was showing me the questionnaire from the Red Cross. Then he was telling me that his wife, like the rest of the Drapers, was very handsome—"a lovely woman" in more ways, his manner suggested, than one—but that since Hilda had gone, she had become a different woman. The transition from handsome to different was, he suggested, a catastrophe which he was obliged to share with the public. He would come in from fire-watching, he said, and find her demented. In bed, he would add. He and I found ourselves fire-watching together, and from that time he started facetiously calling me "my secretary."

"I asked my secretary to get the sand and shovel out," he would say about our correspondence. "And he wrote the letter."

So I was half a stranger at Hilda's homecoming. I looked round the room or out at the shops opposite and, when I looked back at the family several times, I caught Hilda's eyes wandering too. She also was out of it. I studied her. I hadn't expected her to come back in rags, as old Mrs Draper had, but it was a surprise to see she was the best-dressed woman in the room and the only one who looked as if she had ever been to a hairdresser. And there was another way in which I could not match her with the person Mr Fulmino and I had conjured. When we thought of everything that must have happened to her it was strange to see that her strong face was smooth and blank. Except for the few minutes of arrival and the time the reporters came, her face was vacant and plain. It was as vacant as a stone that has been smoothed for centuries in the sand of some hot country. It was the face of someone to whom nothing had happened; or, perhaps, so much had happened to her that each event wiped out what had happened before. I was disturbed by something in her—the lack of history, I think. We were worm-eaten by it. And that suddenly brought her back to me as she had been when she was a schoolgirl and when my older brother got into trouble for chasing after her. She was now sharper in the shoulders and elbows, no longer the swollen schoolgirl but, even as a girl, her face had the same quality of having been fixed and unchangeable between its high cheek bones. It was disturbing, in a face so anonymous, to see the eyes move, especially since she blinked very little; and if she smiled it was less a smile than an alteration of the two lines at the corners of her lips.

The party did not settle down quite in the same way after the reporters had been and there was talk of not tiring Hilda after her long journey. The family would all be meeting tomorrow, the Sunday, as they always did, when young Mrs Jack Draper brought her children. Jack Draper was thinking of the pub which was open now and asking if anyone was going over. And then, something happened. Hilda walked over to the window to Mr Fulmino and said, just as if she had not been there at the time:

"Ted—what did that man from the News ask you—about the food?"

"No," said Mr Fulmino widening to a splendid chance of not giving the facts. "No—he said something about starving the prisoners. I was telling him that in my opinion the deterioration in conditions was inevitable after the disorganisation in the camps resulting from air operations . . ."

"Oh, I thought you said we starved. We had enough."

"What?" said Mr Fulmino.

"Bill Williams was a skeleton when he came back. Nothing but a bowl of rice a day. Rice!" said Mrs Fulmino. "And torture."

"Bill Williams must have been in one of those labour camps," said Hilda. "Being Japanese I was all right."

"Japanese!" said Mr Fulmino. "You?"

"Shinji was a Japanese," said Hilda. "He was in the army."

"You married a Japanese!" said Mrs Fulmino, marching forward.

"That's why I was put in the American camp, when they came. They questioned every one, not only me. That's what I said to the reporter. It wasn't the food, it was the questions. What was his regiment? When did you hear from him? What was his number? They kept on. Didn't they, Mum?"

She turned to her mother who had taken the chance to cut herself another piece of cake and was about to slip it into her handkerchief, I think, to carry to her own room. We were all flabbergasted. A trolley bus went by and took a swipe at the wall. Young Mrs Draper murmured something and her young husband Jack said loudly, hearing his wife:

"Hilda married a Nip!"

And he looked at Hilda with astonishment. He had very blue eyes.

"You weren't a prisoner!" said Mrs Fulmino.

"Not of the Japanese," said Hilda. "They couldn't touch me. My husband was Japanese."

"I'm not stupid. I can hear," said young Mrs Draper to her husband. She was a plain-spoken woman from the Yorkshire coalfields, one of a family of twelve.

"I've nowt to say about who you married, but where is he? Haven't you brought him?" she said.

"You were married to Mr Singh," said Mrs Fulmino.

"They're both dead," said Hilda, her vacant yellow eyes becoming suddenly brilliant like a cat's at night. An animal sound, like the noise of an old dog at a bone, came out of old Mrs Draper by the fire.

"Two," she moaned.

No more than that. Simply, again: "Two."

Hilda was holding her handbag and she lifted it in both hands and covered her bosom with it. Perhaps she thought we were going to hit her. Perhaps she was going to open the bag and get out something extraordinary—documents, letters, or a handkerchief to weep into. But no—she held it there very tight. It was an American handbag—we hadn't seen one like that before, cream-coloured, like the luggage. Old Mrs Johnson hesitated at the table, tipped the piece of cake back out of her handkerchief on to a plate, and stepped to Hilda's side and stood, very straight for once, beside her, the old blue lips very still.

"Ted," accused Hilda. "Didn't you get my letters? Mother," she stepped away from her mother, "didn't you tell them?"

"What, dear?" said old Mrs Johnson.

"About Shinji. I wrote you. Did Mum tell you?" Hilda appealed to us and now looked fiercely at her mother.

Mrs Johnson smiled and retired into her look of faith and modesty. She feigned deafness.

"I put it all in the post office," she said. "Every week," she said. "Until my girl comes home, I said. She'll need it."

"Mother!" said Hilda, giving the old lady a small shake. "I wrote to you. I told you. Didn't you tell them?"

"What did Hilda say?" said Mr Fulmino gently, bending down to the old lady.

"Sh! Don't worry her. She's had enough for today. What did you tell the papers, Ted?" said Mrs Fulmino, turning on her husband. "You can't ever keep your big mouth shut, can you? You never let me see the correspondence."

"I married Shinji when the war came up," Hilda said.

And then old Mrs Draper spoke from her armchair by the fire. She had her bad leg propped up on a hassock.

"Two," said Mrs Draper savagely again.

Mr Fulmino, in his defeat, lost his nerve and let slip a remark quite casually, as he thought, under his voice, but everyone heard it—a remark that Mrs Fulmino was to remind him of in months to come.

"She strikes like a clock," he said.

We were stupefied by Mr Fulmino's remark. Perhaps it was a relief.

"Mr Fraser!" Hilda said to me. And now her vacant face had become dramatic and she stepped towards me, appealing outside the family. "You knew, you and Ted knew. You've got all the letters . . ."

If ever a man looked like the Captain going down with his ship and suddenly conscious, at the last heroic moment, that he is not on a ship at all, but standing on nothing and had hopelessly blundered, it was Mr Fulmino. But we didn't go down, either of us. For suddenly old Mrs Johnson couldn't stand straight any longer, her head wagged and drooped forward and, but for a chair, she would have fallen to the ground.

"Quick! Constance! Open the window," Mrs Fulmino said. Hilda was on her knees by her mother.

"Are you there, Hilly?" said her mother.

"Yes, I'm here, Mum," said Hilda. "Get some water—some brandy." They took the old lady next door to the little room Hilda was sharing with her that night.

"What I can't fathom is your aunt not telling me, keeping it to herself," said Mr Fulmino to his wife as we walked home that evening from Mrs Draper's, and we had said "Good-bye" to Jack Draper and his wife.

He was not hurt by Mrs Johnson's secretiveness but by an extraordinary failure of co-operation.

It was unwise of him to criticise Mrs Fulmino's family.

"Don't be so smug," said Mrs Fulmino. "What's it got to do with you? She was keeping it from Gran, you know Gran's tongue. She's her sister." They called old Mrs Draper Gran or Grandma sometimes.

But when Mr Fulmino got home he asked me in so that we could search the correspondence together. Almost at once we discovered his blunder. There it was in the letter saying a Mrs Singh or Shinji Kobayashi had been identified.

"Shinji!" exclaimed Mrs Fulmino, putting her big index finger on the page. "There you are, plain as dirt."

"Singh," said Mr Fulmino. "Singh, Shinji, the same name. Some Indians write Singh, some Shinji."

"And what is Kobayashi? Indian too? Don't be a fool."

"It's the family name or Christian name of Singh," said Mr Fulmino, doing the best he could.

Singh, Shinji, Shinji, Singh, he murmured to himself and he walked about trying to convince himself by incantation and hypnosis. He lashed himself with Kobayashi. He remembered the names of other Indians, Indian cities, mentioned the Ganges and the Himalayas; had a brief, brilliant couple of minutes when he argued that Shinji was Hindu for Singh. Mrs Fulmino watched him with the detachment of one waiting for a bluebottle to settle so that she could swat it.

"*You* thought Kobayashi was Indian, didn't you, Harry?" he appealed to me. I did my best.

"I thought," I said weakly, "it was the address."

"Ah, the address!" Mr Fulmino clutched at this, but he knew he was done for. Mrs Fulmino struck.

"And what about the Sunday papers, the man from the News?" she said. "You open your big mouth too soon."

"Christ!" said Mr Fulmino. It was the sound of a man who has gone to the floor.

I will come to that matter of the papers later on. It is not very important.

When we went to bed that night we must all have known in our different ways that we had been disturbed in a very long dream. We had been living on inner visions for years. It was an effect of the long war. England had been a prison. Even the sky was closed and, like convicts, we had been driven to dwelling on fancies in our dreary minds. In the cinema the camera sucks some person forward into an enormous close-up and holds a face there yards wide, filling the whole screen, all holes and pores, like some sucking octopus that might eat up an audience many rows at a time. I don't say these pictures aren't beautiful sometimes, but afterwards I get the horrors. Hilda had been a close-up like this for us when she was lost and far away. For myself, I could hardly remember Hilda. She was a collection of fragments of my childhood and I suppose I had expected a girl to return.

My father and mother looked down on the Drapers and the Johnsons. Hincham Street was "dirty" and my mother once whispered that Mr Johnson had worked "on the line," as if that were a smell. I remember the old man's huge crinkled white beard when I was a child. It was horribly soft and like pubic hair. So I had always thought of Hilda as a railway girl, in and out of tunnels, signal boxes and main line stations, and when my older brother was "chasing" her as they said, I admired him. I listened to the quarrels that went on in our family—how she had gone to the convent school and the nuns had complained about her; and was it she or some other girl who went for car rides with a married man who waited round the corner of Hincham Street for her? The sinister phrase "The nuns have been to see her mother" stuck in my memory. It astonished me to see Hilda alive, calm, fat and walking after that, as composed as a railway engine. When I grew up and Mr Fulmino came to the library, I was drawn into his search because she brought back those days with my brother, those clouts on the head from some friend of his, saying, "Buzz off. Little pigs have big ears," when my brother and he were whispering about her.

To Mrs Fulmino, a woman whose feelings were in her rolling arms, flying out from one extreme to another as she talked, as if she were doing exercises, Hilda appeared in her wedding clothes and all the sexuality of an open flower, standing beside her young Indian husband who was about to become a doctor. There was trouble about the wedding, for Mr Singh spoke a glittering and palatial English—the beautiful English a snake might speak, it seemed to the family—that made a few pock marks on his face somehow more noticeable. Old Mrs Draper alone, against all evidence—Mr Singh had had a red racing car—stuck to it that he was "a common lascar off a ship." Mrs Fulmino had been terrified of Mr Singh—she often conveyed— and had "refused to be in a room alone with him." Or "How can she let him touch her?" she would murmur, thinking about that, above all. Then whatever vision was in her mind would jump forward to Hilda, captured, raped, tortured, murdered in front of her eyes. Mrs Fulmino's mind was voluptuous. When I first went to Mr Fulmino's house and met Iris and we talked about Hilda, Mrs Fulmino once or twice left the room and he lowered his voice. "The wife's upset," he said. "She's easily upset."

We had not all been under a spell. Not young Jack Draper nor his wife, for example. Jack Draper had fought in the war and where we thought of the war as something done to us and our side, Jack thought of it as something done to everybody. I remember what he said to his wife before the Fulminos and I said "Good night" to them on the Saturday Hilda came home.

"It's a shame," said Jack, "she couldn't bring the Nip with her."

"He was killed," said his wife.

"That's what I mean," said Jack. "It's a bleeding shame she couldn't."

We walked on and then young Mrs Draper said, in her flat, northern laconic voice:

"Well, Jack, for all the to-do, you might just as well have gone to your fishing."

For Jack had made a sacrifice in coming to welcome Hilda. He went fishing up the Thames on Saturdays. The war for him was something that spoiled fishing. In the Normandy landing he had thought mostly of that. He dreamed of the time when his two boys would be old enough to fish. It was what he had had children for.

"There's always Sunday," said his wife, tempting him. Jack nodded. She knew he would not fall. He was the youngest of old Mrs Draper's family, the baby, as they said. He never missed old Mrs Draper's Sundays.

It was a good thing he did not, a good thing for all of us that we didn't miss, for we would have missed Hilda's second announcement.

Young Mrs Draper provoked it. These Sunday visits to Hincham Street were a ritual in the family. It was a duty to old Mrs Draper. We went there for our tea. She provided, though Constance prepared for it as if we were a school, for she kept house there. We recognised our obligation by paying sixpence into the green pot on the chiffonier when we left. The custom had started in the bad times when money was short; but now the money was regarded as capital and Jack Draper used to joke and say, "Who are you going to leave the green pot to, Mum?" Some of Hilda's luggage had been moved by the afternoon into her mother's little room at the back and how those two could sleep in a bed so small was a question raised by Mrs Fulmino whose night with Mr Fulmino required room for struggle, as I know, for this colonising man often dropped hints about how she swung her legs over in the night.

"Have you unpacked yet, Hilda?" Mrs Fulmino was asking.

"Unpacked!" said Constance. "Where would she put all that?"

"I've been lazy," said Hilda. "I've just hung up a few things because of the creases."

"Things do crease," said Mrs Fulmino.

"Bill Williams said he would drop in later," said Constance.

"That man suffered," said Mrs Fulmino, with meaning.

"He heard you were back," said Constance.

Hilda had told us about Shinji. Jack Draper listened with wonder. Shinji had been in the jute business and when the war came he was called up to the army. He was in "Stores." Jack scratched with delight when he heard this. "Same as I tried to work it," Jack said. Shinji had been killed in an air raid. Jack's wife said, to change the subject, she liked that idea, the idea of Jack "working" anything, he always let everyone climb up on his shoulders. "First man to get wounded. I knew he would be," she said. "He never looks where he's going."

"Is that the Bill Williams who worked for Ryan, the builder?" said Hilda.

"He lives in the Culverwell Road," young Mrs Draper said.

Old Mrs Draper speaking from the bowels of history, said:

"He got that Sellers girl into trouble."

"Yes," exclaimed Hilda, "I remember."

"It was proved in court that he didn't," said Constance briskly to Hilda. "You weren't here."

We were all silent. One could hear only the sounds of our cups on the saucers and Mrs Fulmino's murmur, "More bread and butter?" Constance's face had its neat, pink, enamelled smile and one saw the truthful blue of her small eyes become purer in colour. Iris was next to me and she said afterwards something I hadn't noticed, that Constance hated Hilda. It is one of the difficulties I have in writing, that, all along, I was slow to see what was really happening, not having a woman's eye or ear. And being young. Old

Mrs Draper spoke again, her mind moving from the past to the present with that suddenness old people have.

"If Bill Williams is coming, he knows the way," she said.

Hilda understood that remark for she smiled and Constance flushed. (Of course, I see it now: two women in a house! Constance had ruled old Mrs Draper and Mrs Johnson for years and her money had made a big difference.) They knew that one could, as the saying is, "trust Gran to put her oar in."

Again young Mrs Draper changed the subject. She was a nimble, tarry-haired woman, impatient of fancies, excitements and disasters. She liked things flat and factual. While the family gaped at Hilda's clothes and luggage, young Mrs Draper had reckoned up the cost of them. She was not avaricious or mean, but she knew that money is money. You know that if you have done without. So she went straight into the important question being (as she would say), not like people in the South, double-faced Wesleyans, but honest, plain and straight out with it, what are they ashamed of? Jack, her husband, was frightened by her bluntness, and had the nervous habit of folding his arms across his chest and scratching fast under his armpits when his wife spoke out about money; some view of the river, with his bait and line and the evening flies came into his panicking mind. Mr Fulmino once said that Jack scratched because the happiest moments of his life, the moments of escape, had been passed in clouds of gnats.

"I suppose, Hilda, you'll be thinking of what you're going to do?" young Mrs Draper said. "Did they give you a pension?"

I was stroking Iris's knee but she stopped me, alerted like the rest of them. The word "pension" is a very powerful word. In this neighbourhood one could divide the world into those who had pensions and those who hadn't. The phrase "the old pensioner" was one of envy, abuse and admiration. My father, for example, spoke contemptuously of pensioners. Old Mrs Draper's husband had had a pension, but my father would never have one. As a librarian (Mr Fulmino pointed out), I would have a pension and thereby I had overcome the first obstacle in being allowed to go out with his daughter.

"No," said Hilda. "Nothing."

"But he was your husband, you said," said Constance.

"He was in the army, you say," said young Mrs Draper.

"Inflation," said Mr Fulmino grandly. "The financial situation."

He was stopped.

"Then," said young Mrs Draper, "you'll have to go to work."

"My girl won't want for money," said old Mrs Johnson, sitting beside her daughter as she had done the day before.

"No," said young Mrs Draper. "That she won't while you're alive, Mrs Johnson. We all know that, and the way you slaved for her. But Hilda wants to look after you, I'm sure."

It was, of course, the question in everyone's mind. Did all those clothes and cases mean money or was it all show? That is what we all wanted to know. We would not have raised it at that time and in that way. It wasn't our way—we would have drifted into finding out—Hilda was scarcely home. But young Mrs Draper had been brought up hard, as she said, twelve mouths to feed.

"*I'm* looking after *you*, Mum," said Hilda, smiling at her mother.

Mrs Johnson was like a wizened little girl gazing up at a taller sister.

"I'll take you to Monte Carlo, Mum," Hilda said.

The old lady tittered. We all laughed loudly. Hilda laughed with us.

"That gambling place!" the old lady giggled.

"That's it," laughed Hilda. "Break the bank."

"Is it across water?" said the old lady, playing up. "I couldn't go on a boat. I was so sick at Southend when I was a girl."

"Then we'll fly."

"Oh!" the old lady cried. "Don't, Hil—I'll have a fit."

" 'The Man Who Broke the Bank at Monte Carlo,'" Mr Fulmino sang. "You might find a boy friend, Mrs Johnson."

Young Mrs Draper did not laugh at this game; she still wanted to know; but she did smile. She was worried by laughter. Constance did not laugh but she showed her pretty white teeth.

"Oh, she's got one for me," said Mrs Johnson. "So she says."

"Of course I have. Haven't I, Harry?" said Hilda, talking across the table to me.

"Me? What?" I said completely startled.

"You can't take Harry," said Iris, half frightened.

"Did you post the letter?" said Hilda to me.

"What letter?" said Iris to me. "Did she give you a letter?"

Now there is a thing I ought to have mentioned! I had forgotten all about the letter. When we were leaving the evening before, Hilda had called me quietly to the door and said:

"Please post this for me. Tonight."

"Hilda gave me a letter to post," I said.

"You did post it?" Hilda said.

"Yes," I said.

She looked contentedly round at everyone.

"I wrote to Mr Gloster, the gentleman I told you about, on the boat. He's in Paris. He's coming over at the end of the week to get a car. He's taking mother and me to France. Mr Gloster, Mum, I told you. No, not Mr Faulkner. That was the other boat. He was in San Francisco."

"Oh," said Mrs Johnson, a very long "oh" and wriggling like a child listening to a story. She was beginning to look pale, as she had the evening before when she had the turn.

"France!" said Constance in a peremptory voice.

"Who is Mr Gloster—you never said anything," said Mrs Fulmino.

"What about the currency regulations?" said Mr Fulmino.

Young Mrs Draper said, "France! He must have money."

"Dollars," said Hilda to Mr Fulmino.

Dollars! There was a word!

"The almighty dollar," said Constance, in the cleansed and uncorrupted voice of one who has mentioned one of the commandments. Constance had principles; we had the confusion of our passions.

And from sixteen years or more back in time or perhaps it was from some point in history hundreds of years back and forgotten, old Mrs Draper said: "And is this Indian married?"

Hilda—to whom no events, I believe, had ever happened—replied: "Mr Gloster's an American, Gran."

"He wants to marry her," said old Mrs Johnson proudly.

"If I'll have him!" said Hilda.

"Well, he can't if you won't have him, can he, Hilda?" said Mrs Fulmino.

"Gloster. G-L-O-S-T-E-R?" asked Mr Fulmino.

"Is he in a good job?" asked young Mrs Draper.

Hilda pointed to a brooch on her blouse.

"He gave me this," she said.

She spoke in her harsh voice and with a movement of her face that in anyone else one would have called excited, but in her it had a disturbing lack of meaning. It was as if Hilda had been hooked into the air by invisible wires and was then swept out into the air and back to Japan, thousands of miles away again, and while she was on her way, she turned and knocked us flat with the next item.

"He's a writer," she said. "He's going to write a book about me. He's very interested in me . . ."

Mrs Johnson nodded.

"He's coming to fetch us, Mum and me, and take us to France to write this book. He's going to write my life."

Her life! Here was a woman who had, on top of everything else, a life.

"Coming *here*?" said Mrs Fulmino with a grinding look at old Mrs Draper and then at Constance, trying to catch their eyes and failing; in despair she looked at the shabby room, to see what must be put straight, or needed cleaning or painting. Nothing had been done to it for years for Constance, teaching at her school all day, and very clean in her person, let things go in the house and young Mrs Draper said old Mrs Draper smelled. All the command in Mrs Fulmino's face collapsed as rapidly, on her own, she looked at the carpets, the lino, the curtains.

"What's he putting in this book?" said young Mrs Draper cannily.

"Yes," said Jack Draper, backing up his wife.

"What I tell him," Hilda said.

"What she tells him," said old Mrs Johnson sparkling. Constance looked thoughtfully at Hilda.

"Is it a biography?" Constance asked coldly. There were times when we respected Constance and forgot to murmur "Go back to Russia" every time she spoke. I knew what a biography was and so did Mr Fulmino, but no one else did.

"It's going to be made into a film," Hilda replied.

"A film," cried Iris.

Constance gleamed.

"You watch for American propaganda," said Constance. There you are, you see: Constance was back on it!

"Oh, it's about me," said Hilda. "My experience."

"Very interesting," said Mr Fulmino, preparing to take over. "A Hollywood production, I expect. Publication first and then they go into production."

He spread his legs.

None of us had believed, or even understood what we heard, but we looked with gratitude to Mr Fulmino for making the world steady again.

Jack Draper's eyes filled with tears because a question was working in him but he could not get it out.

"Will you be in this film?" asked Iris.

"I'll wait till he's written it," said Hilda with that lack of interest we had often noticed in her, after she had made some dramatic statement.

Mrs Fulmino breathed out heavily with relief and after that her body seemed to become larger. She touched her hair at the back and straightened her dress, as if preparing to offer herself for the part. She said indeed:

"I used to act at school."

"She's still good at it," said Mr Fulmino with daring to Jack Draper who always appreciated Mr Fulmino, but seeing the danger of the moment hugged himself and scratched excitedly under both armpits, laughing.

"You shouldn't have let this Mr Gloster go," said Constance.

Hilda was startled by this remark and looked lost. Then she shrugged her shoulders and gave a low laugh, as if to herself.

Mr Fulmino's joke had eased our bewilderment. Hilda had been our dream but now she was home she changed as fast as dreams change. She was now, as we looked at her, far more remote to us than she had been all the years when she was away. The idea was so far beyond us. It was like some story of a bomb explosion or an elopement or a picture of bathing girls one sees in the newspapers—unreal and, in a way, insulting to being alive in the ordinary daily sense of the word. Or, she was like a picture that one sees in an art gallery, that makes you feel sad because it is painted.

After tea when Hilda took her mother to the lavatory, Constance beckoned to Iris and let her peep into the room Hilda was sharing, and young Mrs Draper, not to be kept out of things, followed. They were back in half a minute:

"Six evening dresses," Iris said to me.

"She said it was Mr Faulkner who gave her the luggage, not this one who was going to get her into pictures," said Mrs Fulmino.

"Mr Gloster, you mean," said Constance.

Young Mrs Draper was watching the door, listening for Hilda's return.

"Ssh," she said, at the sound of footsteps on the stairs and, to look at us, the men on one side of the room and the women on the other, silent, standing at attention, facing each other, we looked like soldiers.

"Oh," said Constance. The steps we had heard were not Hilda's. It was Bill Williams who came in.

"Good afternoon one and all," he said. The words came from the corner of a mouth that had slipped down at one side. Constance drew herself up, her eyes softened. She had exact, small, round breasts. Looking around, he said to Constance: "Where is she?"

Constance lowered her head when she spoke to him, though she held it up shining, admiring him, when he spoke to us, as if she were displaying him to us.

"She'll be here in a minute," she said. "She's going into films."

"I'll take a seat in the two and fourpennies," said Bill Williams and he sat down at his ease and lit a cigarette.

Bill Williams was a very tall, sick-faced man who stooped his shoulders as if he were used to ducking under doors. His dry black hair, not oiled like Mr Fulmino's, bushed over his forehead and he had the shoulders, arms and hands of a lorry driver. In fact, he drove a light van for a textile firm. His hazel eyes were always watching and wandering and we used to say he looked as though he was going to snaffle something but that may simply have been due to the restlessness of a man with a poor stomach. Laziness, cunning and aches and pains were suggested by him. He was a man taking his time. His eyebrows grew thick and the way one brow was raised, combined with the side-slip of his mouth, made him look like some shrewd man about to pick up a faulty rifle, hit the bull's eye five times running at a fair and moan afterwards. He glanced a good deal at Constance. He was afraid of his manners before her, we thought, because he was a rough type.

"Put it here," said Constance, bringing him an ashtray. That was what he was waiting for, for he did not look at her again.

Bill Williams brought discomfort with him whenever he came on Sundays and we were always happier when he failed to come. If there was anything private to say we tried to get it over before he came. How a woman like Constance, a true, clean, settled schoolteacher who even spoke in the clear, practical and superior manner of someone used to the voice of reason, who kept her nails so beautifully, could have taken up with him, baffled us. He was very often at Mrs Draper's in the week, eating with them and Constance, who was thirty-five, quarrelled like a girl when she was getting things ready for him. Mrs Fulmino could not bear the way he ate, with his elbows out and his face close to the plate. The only good thing about the affair was that, for once, Constance was overruled.

"Listen to her," Bill Williams would say with a nod of his head. "A rank red Communist. Tell us about Holy Russia, Connie."

"Constance is my correct name, not Connie," she said.

Their bickering made us die. But we respected Constance even when she was a trial. She had been twice to Russia before the war and though we argued violently with her, especially Mr Fulmino who tried to take over Russia, and populate it with explanations, we always boasted to other people that she'd been there.

"On delegations," Mr Fulmino would say.

But we could not boast that she had taken up with Bill Williams. He had been a hero when he came back from Japan, but he had never kept a job since, he was rough and his lazy zigzagging habits in his work made even Constance impatient. He had for her the fascination a teacher feels for a bad pupil. Lately their love affair had been going better because he was working outside London and sometimes he worked at week-ends; this added to the sense of something vague and secretive in his life that had attracted Constance. For there was much that was secret in her or so she liked to hint—it was political. Again, it was the secretiveness of those who like power; she was the schoolmistress who has the threat of inside knowledge locked up in the cupboard. Once Mrs Fulmino went purple and said to her husband—who told me, he always told me such things—that she believed Constance had lately started sleeping with Bill Williams. That was because Constance had once said to her:

"Bill and I are individuals."

Mrs Fulmino had a row with Iris after this and stopped me seeing her for a month.

Hilda came back into the room alone. Bill Williams let his mouth slip sideways and spoke a strange word to her, saying jauntily to us: "That's Japanese."

Hilda wasn't surprised. She replied with a whole sentence in Japanese.

"That means"—but Bill Williams was beaten, but he passed it off. "Well, I'd best not tell them what it means," he said.

"East meets East," Mr Fulmino said.

"It means," said Hilda, "you were on the other side of the fence but now the gate is open."

Bill Williams studied her inch by inch. He scratched his head.

"Straight?" he said.

"Yes," she said.

"Stone me, it was bloody closed when we were there," said Bill Williams offensively, but then said: "They fed her well, didn't they, Constance? Sit down." Hilda sat down beside him.

"Connie!" he called. "Seen these? Just the job, eh?" He was nodding at Hilda's stockings. Nylons. "Now," he said to Hilda, looking closely at her. "Where were you? It got a bit rough at the finish, didn't it?"

Jack Draper came close to them to hear, hoping that Hilda would say something about what moved him the most: the enemy. Bill Williams gave him a wink and Hilda saw it. She looked placidly at Bill Williams, considering his face, his neck, his shoulders and his hands that were resting on his knees.

"I was okey doke," she said.

Bill Williams dropped his mouth open and waggled the top of his tongue in a back tooth in his knowing manner. To our astonishment Hilda opened her mouth and gave a neat twist to her tongue in her cheek in the same way.

Bill Williams slapped his knee and to cover his defeat in this little duel, said to all of us:

"This little girl's got yellow eyes."

All the colour had gone from Connie's face as she watched the meeting.

"They say you're going to be in pictures," said Bill Williams.

And then we had Hilda's story over again. Constance asked what papers Mr Gloster wrote for.

"I don't know. A big paper," said Hilda.

"You ought to find out," Constance said. "I'll find out."

"Um," said Hilda with a nod of not being interested.

"I could give him some of my experience," said Bill Williams. "Couldn't I, Connie? Things I've told you—you could write a ruddy book."

He looked with challenge at Hilda. He was a rival.

"Gawd!" he exclaimed. "The things."

We heard it again, how he was captured, where his battery was, the long march, Sergeant Harris who was hanged, Corporal Rowley bayoneted and left to die in the sun, the starvation, the work on the road that killed half of them. But there was one difference between this story and the ones he had told before. The sight of Hilda altered it.

"You had to get round the guards," he said with a wink. "If you used your loaf a bit, eh? Scrounge around, do a bit of trade. One or two had Japanese girls. Corporal Jones went back afterwards trying to trace his, wanted to marry her."

Hilda listened and talked about places she had lived in, how she had worked in a factory.

"That's it," said Bill Williams, "you had to know your way around and talk a bit of the lingo."

Jack Draper looked with affection and wonder at the talk, lowering his eyes if her eyes caught his. Every word entered him. The heat! she said. The rain. The flowers. The telegraph poles! Jack nodded.

"They got telegraph poles," he nodded to us.

You sleep on the floor. Shinji's mother, she mentioned. She could have skinned her. Jack, brought up among so many women, lost interest, but it revived when she talked of Shinji. You could see him mouthing his early marvelling sentence: "She married a Nip," but not saying it. She was confirming something he had often thought of in Normandy; the men on the other side were married too. A bloody marvel. Why hadn't she brought him home? He would have had a friend.

"Who looked after the garden when Shinji was called up?" he asked. "Were they goldfish, ordinary goldfish, in the pond?"

Young Mrs Draper shook her head.

"Eh," she said. "If he'd a known he'd have come over to change the water. Next time we have a war you just let him know."

Mrs Fulmino who was throbbing like a volcano said:

"We better all go next time by the sound of it."

At the end, Bill Williams said:

"I suppose you're going to be staying here."

"No," said Constance quickly, "she isn't. She's going to France. When is it, Hilda? When is Mr Gloster coming?"

"Next week, I don't know," said Hilda.

"You shouldn't have let him go!" laughed Bill Williams. "Those French girls will get him in Paree."

"That is what I have been saying," said Constance. "He gave her that brooch."

"Oh ah! It's the stockings I'm looking at," said Bill Williams. "How did you get all that stuff through the customs? Twenty cases, Connie told me."

"Twelve," said Hilda.

Bill Williams did not move her at all. Presently she got up and started clearing away the tea things. I will say this for her, she didn't let herself be waited on.

Iris, Mr and Mrs Fulmino and the young Drapers and their children and myself left Hincham Street together.

"You walk in front with the children, Iris," said Mrs Fulmino. Then they turned on me. What was this letter, they wanted to know. Anyone would have thought by their questions that I ought to have opened it and read it.

"I just posted it at the corner." I pointed to the pillar box. Mrs Fulmino stopped to look at the pillar box and I believe was turning over in her mind the possibility of getting inside it. Then she turned on her husband and said with contemptuous suspicion: "Monte Carlo!" As if he had worked the whole thing in order to go there himself.

"Two dead," she added in her mother's voice, the voice of one who would have been more than satisfied with the death of one.

"Not having a pension hasn't hurt her," said Mrs Draper.

"Not a tear," said Mrs Fulmino.

Jack and Mr Fulmino glanced at each other. It was a glance of surreptitious gratitude: tears—they had escaped that.

Mr Fulmino said: "The Japanese don't cry."

Mrs Fulmino stepped out, a bad sign; her temper was rising.

"Who was the letter to?" she asked me. "Was the name Gloster?"

"I didn't look," I said.

Mrs Fulmino looked at her husband and me and rolled her eyes. Another of our blunders!

"I don't believe it," she said.

But Mrs Fulmino did believe it. We all believed and disbelieved everything at once.

I said I would come to the report in the *News*. It was in thick lettering like mourning, with Hilda's picture: A Mother's Faith. Four Years in Jap Torture Camp. London Girl's Ordeal. And then an account of how Hilda had starved and suffered and been brain-washed by questioners. Even Hilda was awed when she read it, feeling herself drain away, perhaps, and being replaced by this fantasy; and for the rest of us, we had become used to living in a period when events reduced us to beings so trivial that we had no strong feeling of our own existence in relation to the world around us. We had been bashed first one way, then the other, by propaganda, until we were indifferent. At one time people like my parents or old Mrs Draper could at least trust the sky and feel that it was certain and before it they could have at least the importance of being something in the eye of heaven.

Constance read the newspaper report and it fulfilled her.

"Propaganda," she said. "Press lies."

"All lies," Mr Fulmino agreed with wonder. The notion that the untrue was as effective as the true opened to him vast areas to his powers. It was like a temptation.

It did not occur to us that we might be in a difficult situation in the neighbourhood when the truth came out, until we heard Constance and Bill Williams had gone over to the Lord Nelson with the paper and Constance had said, "You can't believe a word you read in the capitalist press."

Alfred Levy, the proprietor and a strong Tory, agreed with her. But was Hilda criticised for marrying an enemy? The hatred of the Japanese was strong at this time. She was not. Constance may not have had the best motives for spreading the news, we said, but it did no harm at all. That habit of double vision affected every one publicly. We lived in the true and the untrue, comfortably and without trouble. People picked up the paper, looked at her picture and said, "That's a shocking thing. A British subject," and even when they knew, even from Hilda's own lips the true story, they said, congratulating themselves on their cunning, "The papers make it all up."

Of course, we were all in that stage where the forces of life, the desire to live, were coming back, and although it was not yet openly expressed, we felt that curiosity about the enemy that ex-soldiers like Jack Draper felt when he wondered if some Japanese or some Germans were as fed up as he was on Saturdays by missing a day's fishing. When people shook Hilda's hand they felt they gave her life. I do not say there were not one or two mutterings afterwards, for people always went off from the Lord Nelson when it closed in a state of moralisation: beer must talk; the louts singing and the couples saying this or that "wasn't right." But this gossip came to nothing because, sooner or later, it came to a closed door in everybody's conscience. There were the men who had shot off trigger fingers, who had got false medical certificates, deserters, ration frauds, black marketeers, the pilferers of army stores. And the women said a woman is right to stand by her husband and, looking at Hilda's fine clothes, pointed out to their husbands that that kind of loyalty was sometimes rewarded; indeed, Mrs Fulmino asserted, by law.

We had been waiting for Hilda; now, by a strange turn, we were waiting for Hilda's Mr Gloster. We waited for a fortnight and it ran on into three weeks. George Hartman Gloster. I looked up the name on our cards at the library, but we had no books of his. I looked up one or two catalogues. Still nothing. It was not surprising. He was an American who was not published in this country. Constance came in and looked too.

"It is one of those names the Americans don't list," she said. Constance smiled with the cool air of keeping a world of meaningful secrets on ice.

"They don't list everything," she said.

She brought Bill Williams with her. I don't think he had ever been in a public library before, because his knowing manner went and he was overawed. He said to me:

"Have you read all these books? Do you buy them secondhand? What's this lot worth?"

He was a man always on the look-out for a deal; it was typical of him that he had come with Constance in his firm's light-green van. It was not like Constance to travel in that way. "Come on," he said roughly.

The weather was hot; we had the sun blinds down in the Library. We were in the middle of one of those brassy fortnights of the London summer when English life, as we usually know it, is at a standstill, and everyone changes. A new grinning healthy race with long red necks sticking out of open shirts and blouses appears, and the sun brings out the variety of faces and bodies. Constance might have been some trim nurse marching at the head of an official procession. People looked calm, happy and open. There was hardly ever a cloud in the sky, the slate roofs looked like steel with the sun's rays hitting them, and the side streets were cool in sharp shadow. It was a pleasant time for walking, especially when the sky went whitish in the distances of the city in the evening and when the streets had a dry pleasant smell and the glass of millions of windows had a motionless but not excluding stare. Even a tailor working late above a closed shop looked pleased to be going on working, while everyone else was out, wearing out their clothes.

Iris and I used to go to the park on some evenings and there every blade of grass had been wire-brushed by sunlight; the trees were heavy with still leaves and when darkness came they gathered into soft black walls and their edges were cut out against the nail varnish of the city's night. During the day the park was crowded. All over the long sweeps of grass the couples were lying, their legs at careless angles, their bottoms restless as they turned to the horseplay of love in the open. Girls were leaning over the men rumpling their hair, men were tickling the girls' chins with stalks of grass. Occasionally they would knock the wind out of each other with plunging kisses; and every now and then a girl would sit up and straighten her skirt at the waist, narrowing her eyes in a pretence of looking at some refining sight in the distance, until she was pulled down again and, keeping her knees together, was caught again. Lying down you smelt the grass and listened to the pleasant rumble of the distant traffic going round like a wheel that never stopped.

I was glad to know the Fulminos and to go out with Iris. We had both been gayer before we met each other, but seriousness, glumness, a sadness came over us when we became friends—that eager sadness that begins with thoughts of love. We encouraged and discouraged these thoughts in each other yet were always hinting and the sight of so much love around us turned us naturally away from it to think about it privately the more. She was a beautifully formed girl as her mother must have once been, but slender. She had a wide laugh that shook the curls of her thick black hair. She was being trained at a typing school.

One day when I was sitting in the park and Iris was lying beside me, we had a quarrel. I asked her if there was any news of Mr Gloster—for she heard everything. She had said there was none and I said, sucking a piece of grass:

"That's what I would like to do. Go round the world. Anywhere. America, Africa, China."

"A chance is a fine thing," said Iris, day dreaming.

"I could get a job," I said.

Iris sat up.

"Leave the Library?" she said.

"Yes," I said. "If I stay there I won't see anything." I saw Iris's face change and become very like her mother's. Mrs Fulmino could make her face go larger and her mouth go very small. Iris did not answer. I went on talking. I asked her what she thought. She still did not answer.

"Anything the matter?" She was sulking. Then she said, flashing at me:

"You're potty on that woman too. You all are. Dad is, Jack is; and look at Bill Williams. Round at Hincham Street every day. He'll be having his breakfast there soon. Fascinated."

"He goes to see Constance."

"Have you seen Constance's face?" she jeered. "Constance could kill her."

"She came to the Library."

"Ah," she turned to me. "You didn't tell me that."

"She came in for a book, I told you. For Mr Gloster's books. Bill Williams came with her."

Iris's sulk changed into satisfaction at this piece of news.

"Mother says if Constance's going to marry a man like Mr Williams," she said, "she'll be a fool to let him out of her sight."

"I'll believe in Mr Gloster when I see him," Iris said. It was, of course, what we were all thinking. We made up our quarrel and I took Iris home. Mrs Fulmino was dressed up, just putting the key in the door of her house. Iris was astonished to see her mother had been out and asked where she had been.

"Out," said Mrs Fulmino. "Have I got to stay in and cook and clean for you all day?"

Mrs Fulmino was even wearing gloves, as if she had been to church. And she was wearing a new pair of shoes. Iris went pale at the sight of them. Mrs Fulmino put her gloves down on the sitting-room table and said:

"I've got a right to live, I suppose?"

We were silenced.

One thing we all agreed on while we waited for Mr Gloster was that Hilda had the money and knew how to spend it. The first time she asked the

Fulminos and young Drapers to the cinema, Mrs Fulmino said to her husband:

"You go. I've got one of my heads."

"Take Jack," young Mrs Draper said. "I've got the children."

They were daring their husbands to go with her. But the second time, there was a party. Hilda took some of them down to Kew. She took old Mrs Johnson down to Southend—and who should they meet there but Bill Williams who was delivering some goods there, spoiling their day because old Mrs Johnson did not like his ways. And Hilda had given them all presents. And two or three nights a week she was out at the Lord Nelson.

It was a good time. If anyone asked, "Have you heard from Mr Gloster yet?" Hilda answered that it was not time yet and, as a dig at Constance that we all admired, she said once: "He has business at the American Embassy." And old Mrs Johnson held her head high and nodded.

At the end of three weeks we became restless. We noticed old Mrs Johnson looked poorly. She said she was tired. Old Mrs Draper became morose. She had been taught to call Mr Gloster by his correct name, but now she relapsed.

"Where is this Indian?" she uttered.

And another day, she said, without explanation:

"Three."

"Three what, Gran?"

"There've been two, that's enough."

No one liked this, but Mrs Johnson understood.

"Mr Gloster's very well, isn't he, Hil? You heard from him yesterday?" she said.

"I wasn't shown the letter," said old Mrs Draper. "We don't want a third."

"We don't," said Mrs Fulmino. With her joining in "on Gran's side," the situation changed. Mrs Fulmino had a low voice and the sound of it often sank to the floor of any room she was in, travelling under chairs and tables, curling round your feet and filling the place from the bottom as if it were a cistern. Even when the trolley bus went by Mrs Fulmino's low voice prevailed. It was an undermining voice, breaking up one's uppermost thoughts and stirring up what was underneath them. It stirred us all now. Yes, we wanted to say, indeed, we wanted to shout, where is this Mr Gloster, why hasn't he come, did you invent him? He's alive, we hope? Or is he also—as Gran suggests—dead?

Even Mr Fulmino was worried.

"Have you got his address?" he asked.

"Yes, Uncle dear," said Hilda. "He'll be staying at the Savoy. He always does."

Mr Fulmino had not taken out his notebook for a long time but he did so now. He wrote down the name.

"Has he made a reservation?" said Mr Fulmino. "I'll find out if he's booked."

"He hasn't," said Bill Williams. "I had a job down there and I asked. Didn't I, Connie?"

Mrs Fulmino went a very dark colour. She wished she had thought of doing this. Hilda was not offended, but a small smile clipped her lips as she glanced at Connie:

"I asked Bill to do it," she said.

And then Hilda in that harsh lazy voice which she had always used for announcements: "If he doesn't come by Wednesday you'll have to speak for me at your factory, Mr Williams. I don't know why he hasn't come, but I can't wait any more."

"Bill can't get you a job. You have to register," said Constance.

"Yes, she'll have to do that," said Mr Fulmino.

"I'll fix it. Leave it to me," said Bill Williams.

"I expect," said young Mrs Draper, "his business has kept him." She was sorry for Hilda.

"Perhaps he's gone fishing," said Jack Draper, laughing loudly in a kind way. No one joined in.

"Fishing for orders," said Bill Williams.

Hilda shrugged her shoulders and then she made one of those remarks that Grandma Draper usually made—I suppose the gift really ran through the family.

"Perhaps it was a case," she said, "of ships that pass in the night."

"Oh no, dear," said Mrs Johnson trembling, "not ships." We went to the bus stop afterwards with the Fulminos and the young Drapers. Mrs Fulmino's calm had gone. She marched out first, her temper rising.

"Ships!" she said. "When you think of what we went through during the war. Did you hear her? Straight out?"

"My brother Herbert's wife was like that. She's a widow. Take away the pension and they'll work like the rest of us. I had to."

"Job! Work! I know what sort of work she's been doing. Frank, walk ahead with Iris."

"Well," said young Mrs Draper, "she won't be able to go to work in those clothes and that's a fact."

"All show," said Mrs Fulmino triumphantly. "And I'll tell you something else—she hasn't a penny. She's run through her poor mother's money."

"Ay, I don't doubt," said young Mrs Draper, who had often worked out how much the old lady had saved.

Mr Gloster did not come on Wednesday or on any other day, but Hilda did not get a job either, not at once. And old Mrs Johnson did not go to

Monte Carlo. She died. This was the third, we understood, that old Mrs Draper had foreseen.

—

Mrs Johnson died at half past eight in the morning just after Constance had gone off to school, the last day of the term, and before old Mrs Draper had got up. Hilda was in the kitchen wearing her blue Japanese wrap when she heard her mother's loud shout, like a man selling papers, she said, and when Hilda rushed in her mother was sitting up in bed. She gripped Hilda with the ferocity of the dying, as if all the strength of her whole life had come back and she was going to throw her daughter to the ground. Then she died. In an hour she looked like a white leaf that has been found after a lifetime pressed between the pages of a book and as delicate as a saint. The death was not only a shock: from the grief that spread from it staining all of us, I trace the ugly events that followed. Only the frail figure of old Mrs Johnson, with her faith and her sly smile, had protected us from them until then, and when she went, all defence went with her.

I need not describe her funeral—it was done by Bickersons: Mr Fulmino arranged it. But one thing astonished us: not only our families but the whole neighbourhood was affected by the death of this woman who, in our carelessness, we thought could hardly be known to anyone. She had lived there all her life, of course, but people come and go in London, only a sluggish residue stay still; and I believe it was just because a large number of passing people knew just a little about her, because she was a fragment in their minds, that her death affected them. They recognised that they themselves were not people but fragments. People remembered her going into shops now and then, or going down to the bus stop, passing down a street. They remembered the bag of American cloth she used to carry containing her sewing—they spoke for a long time afterwards about this bag, more about it, indeed, than about herself.

Bickersons is a few doors from the Lord Nelson, so that when the hearse stood there covered with flowers everyone noticed it, and although the old lady had not been in that public house for years since the death of her husband, all the customers came out to look. And they looked at Hilda sitting in her black in the car when the hearse moved slowly off and all who knew her story must have felt that the dream was burying the dreamer. Hilda's face was dirty with grief and she did not turn her head to right or left as they drove off. I remember a small thing that happened when we were all together at old Mrs Draper's, after we had got her back with difficulty up the stairs.

"Bickersons did it very well," said Mr Fulmino, seeking to distract the old lady who, swollen with sadness, was uncomfortable in her best clothes. "They organise everything so well. They gave me this."

He held up a small brass disc on a little chain. It was one of those identity discs people used to wear on their wrists in the war.

"She had never taken it off," he said. It swung feebly on its chain. Suddenly, with a sound like a shout Mr Fulmino broke into tears. His face caved in and he apologised: "It's the feeling," he said. "You have the feeling. You feel." And he looked at us with panic, astonished by this discovery of an unknown self, spongy with tears, that had burst out and against whom he was helpless.

Mrs Fulmino said gently:

"I expect Hilda would like to have it."

"Yes, yes. It's for her," he said, drying his eyes and Hilda took it from him and carried it to her room. While she was there (and perhaps she was weeping too), Mr Fulmino looked out from his handkerchief and said, still sobbing:

"I see that the luggage has gone."

None of us had noticed this and we looked at Constance who said in a whisper: "She is leaving us. She has found a room of her own." That knocked us back. "Leaving!" we exclaimed. It told against Hilda for, although we talked of death being a release for the dead person we did not like to think of it as a release for the living; grief ought to hold people together and it seemed too brisk to have started a new life so soon. Constance alone looked pleased by this. We were whispering but stopped when we heard Hilda coming back.

Black had changed her. It set off her figure and although crying had hardened her, the skin of her neck and her arms and the swell of her breasts seemed more living than they had before. She looked stronger in body perhaps because she was shaken in mind. She looked very real, very present, more alive than ourselves. She had not heard us whispering, but she said, to all of us, but particularly to Mr Fulmino:

"I have found a room for myself. Constance spoke to Bill Williams for me, he's good at getting things. He found me a place and he took the luggage round yesterday. I couldn't sleep in that bed alone any more."

Her voice was shaky.

"She didn't take up much room. She was tiny and we managed. It was like sleeping with a little child."

Hilda smiled and laughed a little.

"She even used to kick like a kid."

—

Ten minutes on the bus from Hincham Street and close to the centre of London is a dance hall called "The Temple Rooms." It has two bands, a low gallery where you can sit and a soft drink bar. Quite a few West Indians go there, mainly students. It is a respectable place; it closes at eleven and there is never any trouble. Iris and I went there once or twice. One evening we were surprised to see Constance and Bill Williams dancing there. Iris pointed to them. The rest of the people were jiving, but Bill Williams and Constance were dancing in the old-fashioned way.

"Look at his feet!" Iris laughed.

Bill Williams was paying no attention to Constance, but looking around the room over her head as he stumbled along. He was tall.

"Fancy Auntie Constance!" said Iris. "She's getting fed up because he won't listen."

Constance Draper dancing! At her age! Thirty-eight!

"It's since the funeral," said Mr Fulmino over our usual cup of tea. "She was fond of the old lady. It's upset her."

Even I knew Mr Fulmino was wrong about this. The madness of Constance dated from the time Bill Williams had taken Hilda's luggage round to her room and got her a job at the reception desk in the factory at Laxton. It dated from the time, a week later, when standing at old Mrs Draper's early one evening, Constance had seen Hilda get out of Bill Williams's van. He had given her a lift home. It dated from words that passed between Hilda and Constance soon afterwards. Hilda said Williams hung around for her at the factory and wanted her to go to a dance. She did not want to go, she said—and here came the fatal sentences—both of her husbands had been educated men. Constance kept her temper but said coldly:

"Bill Williams is politically educated."

Hilda had her vacant look.

"Not his hands aren't," she said.

The next thing, Constance—who hardly went into a pub in her life—was in the Lord Nelson night after night, playing bar billiards with Bill Williams. She never let him out of her sight. She came out of school and instead of going home, marking papers and getting a meal for herself and old Mrs Draper, she took the bus out to the factory and waited for him to come out. Sometimes he had left on some job by the time she got there and she came home, beside herself, questioning everybody. It had been her habit to come twice a week to change her library books. Now she did not come. She stopped reading. At The Temple Rooms, when Iris and I saw her, she sat out holding hands with Bill Williams and rubbing her head into his shoulder, her eyes watching him the whole time. We went to speak to them and Constance asked:

"Is Hilda here tonight?"

"I haven't seen her."

"She's a whore," said Constance in a loud voice. We thought she was drunk.

It was a funny thing, Mr Fulmino said to me, to call a woman a whore. He spoke as one opposed to funny things.

"If they'd listened to me," he said, "I could have stopped all this trouble. I offered to get her a job in the council office but," he rolled his eyes, "Mrs F. wouldn't have it and while we were arguing about it, Bill Williams acts double quick. It's all because this Mr Gloster didn't turn up."

Mr Fulmino spoke wistfully. He was, he conveyed, in the middle of a family battle; indeed, he had a genuine black eye the day we talked about this. Mrs Fulmino's emotions were in her arms.

This was a bad period for Mr Fulmino because he had committed a folly. He had chosen this moment to make a personal triumph. He had got himself promoted to a much better job at the Council Offices and one entitling him to a pension. He had become a genuine official. To have promoted a man who had the folly to bring home a rich whore with two names, so causing the robbery and death of her mother, and to have let her break Constance's heart, was, in Mrs Fulmino's words, a crime. Naturally, Mr Fulmino regarded his mistakes as mere errors of routine and even part of his training for his new position.

"Oh well," he said when we finished our tea and got up to pay the bill, "it's the British taxpayer that pays." He was heading for politics. I have heard it said, years later, that if he had had a better start in life he would have gone to the top of the administration. It is a tragic calling.

If Hilda was sinister to Constance and Mrs Fulmino, she made a different impression on young Mrs Draper. To call a woman a whore was neither here nor there to her. Up north where she came from people were saying that sort of thing all day long as they scrubbed floors or cleaned windows or did the washing. The word gave them energy and made things come up cleaner and whiter. Good money was earned hard; easy money went easy. To young Mrs Draper Hilda seemed "a bit simple," but she had gone to work, she earned her living. Cut off from the rest of the Draper family, Hilda made friends with this couple. Hilda went with them on Saturday to the Zoo with the children. They were looking at a pair of monkeys. One of them was dozing and its companion was awake, pestering and annoying it. The children laughed. But when they moved on to another cage, Hilda said, sulkily:

"That's one thing. Bill Williams won't be here. He pesters me all the time."

"He won't if you don't let him," said young Mrs Draper.

"I'm going to give my notice if he doesn't stop," said Hilda. She hunched a shoulder and looked around at the animals.

"I can't understand a girl like Constance taking up with him. He's not on her level. And he's mean. He doesn't give her anything. I asked if he gave her that clip, but she said it was Gran's. Well, if a man doesn't give you anything he doesn't value you. I mean she's a well-read girl."

"There's more ways than one of being stupid," said young Mrs Draper.

"I wonder she doesn't see," said Hilda. "He's not delivering for the firm. When he's got the van out, he's doing something on the side. When I came home with him there was stuff at the back. And he keeps on asking how much things cost. He offered to sell my bracelet."

"You'd get a better price in a shop if you're in need," said young Mrs Draper.

"She'd better not be with him if he gets stopped on the road," said Jack, joining in. "You wouldn't sell that. Your husband gave it you."

"No. Mr Faulkner," said Hilda, pulling out her arm and admiring it.

Jack was silent and disappointed; then he cheered up.

"You ought to have married that earl you were always talking about when you were a girl. Do you remember?" he said.

"Earls—they're a lazy lot," said young Mrs Draper.

"I did, Jack," said Hilda. "They were as good as earls, both of them."

And to young Mrs Draper she said: "They wouldn't let another man look at me. I felt like a woman with both of them."

"I've nowt against that if you've got the time," said young Mrs Draper. She saw that Hilda was glum.

"Let's go back and look at the giraffes. Perhaps Mr Faulkner will come for you now Mr Gloster hasn't," young Mrs Draper said.

"They were friends," said Hilda.

"Oh, they knew each other!" said young Mrs Draper. "I thought you just . . . met them . . ."

"No, I didn't meet them together, but they were friends."

"Yes. Jack had a friend, didn't you?" said Mrs Draper, remembering.

"That's right," said Jack. He winked at Hilda. "Neck and neck, it was." And then he laughed outright.

"I remember something about Bill Williams. He came out with us one Saturday and you should have seen his face when we threw the fish back in the water."

"We always throw them back," said young Mrs Draper taking her husband's arm, proudly.

"Wanted to sell them or something. Black market perch!"

"He thinks I've got dollars," said Hilda.

"No, fancy that, Jack—Mr Gloster and Mr Faulkner being friends. Well, that's nice." And she looked sentimentally at Hilda.

"She's brooding," young Mrs Draper said to Mrs Fulmino after this visit to the Zoo. "She won't say anything." Mrs Fulmino said she had better not or she might say something. "She knows what I think. I never thought much of Bill Williams, but he served his country. She didn't."

"She earns her living," said Mrs Draper.

"Like we all do," said Mrs Fulmino. "And it's not men, men, men all day long with you and me."

"One's enough," said young Mrs Draper, "with two children round your feet."

"She doesn't come near me," said Mrs Fulmino.

"No," Mr Fulmino said sadly, "after all we've done."

———

They used to laugh at me when I went dancing with Iris at The Temple Rooms. We had not been there for more than a month and Iris said: "He can't stop staring at the band."

She was right. The beams of the spotlights put red, green, violet and orange tents on the hundreds of dancers. It was like the Arabian Nights. When we got there, Ted Coster's band was already at it like cats on dustbins and tearing their guts out. The pianist had a very thin neck and kept wagging his head as if he were ga-ga; if his head had fallen off he would have caught it in one of his crazy hands and popped it on again without losing a note; the trumpet player had thick eyebrows that went higher and higher as he tried and failed to burst; the drummers looked doped; the saxophone went at it like a man in bed with a girl who had purposely left the door open. I remember them all, especially the thin-lipped man, very white-faced with the double bass drawing his bow at knee level, to and fro, slowly, sinful. They all whispered, nodded and rocked together, telling dirty stories until bang, bang, bang, the dancers went faster and faster, the row hit the ceiling or died out with the wheeze of a balloon. I was entranced.

"Don't look as though you're going to kill someone," Iris said.

That shows how wrong people are. I was full of love and wanted to cry.

After four dances I went off to the soft drink bar and there the first person I saw was Bill Williams. He was wearing a plum-coloured suit and a red and silver tie and he stood, with his dark hair dusty-looking and sprouting forward as if he had just got out of bed and was ducking his head on the way to the bathroom.

"All the family here?" he asked, looking all round.

"No," I said. "Just Iris and me."

He went on looking around him.

"I thought you only came Saturdays," he said suspiciously. He had a couple of friends with him, two men who became restless on their feet, as if they were dancing, when I came up.

"Oh," said Bill Williams. Then he said, "Nicky pokey doda—that's Japanese, pal, for keep your mouth shut. Anyone say anything, you never see me. I'm at Laxton, get me? Bill Williams? He's on night shift. You must be barmy. OK? Seeing you," he said. "No sign of Constance."

And he walked off. His new friends went a step or two after him, dancing on their pointed shoes and then stopped. They twizzled round, tapping their feet, looking all round the room until he had got to the carpeted stairs at the end of the hall. I got my squash and when I turned round, the two men had gone too.

But before Bill Williams had got to the top of the stairs he turned round to look at the dancers in one corner. There was Hilda. She was dancing with a young West Indian. When I got back to our table she was very near.

I have said that Hilda's face was eventless. It was now in a tranced state, looking from side to side, to the floor, in the quick turns of the dance, swinging round, stepping back, stepping forward. The West Indian had a long jacket on. His knees were often nearly bent double as though he were going to do some trick of crawling towards her, then he recovered himself and turned his back as if he had never met her and was dancing with someone else. If Hilda's face was eventless, it was the event itself, it was the dance.

She saw us when the dance was over and came to our table breathlessly. She was astonished to see us. To me she said, "And fancy you!" She did not laugh or even smile when she looked at me. I don't know how to describe her look. It was dead. It had no expression. It had nothing. Or rather, by the smallest twitch of a muscle, it became nothing. Her face had the nakedness of a body. She saw that I was deaf to what Iris was saying. Then she smiled and in doing that, she covered herself.

"I am with friends over there"—we could not tell who the friends were—then she leaned to us and whispered:

"Bill Williams is here too."

Iris exclaimed.

"He's watching me," Hilda said.

"I saw him," I said. "He's gone."

Hilda stood up frowning.

"Are you sure? Did you see him? How long ago?"

I said it was about five minutes before.

She stood as I remember her standing in Mrs Draper's room on the first day when she arrived and was kissing everyone. It was a peculiar stance because she usually stood so passively; a stance of action and, I now saw, a stance of plain fright. One leg was planted forward and bent at the knee like a runner at the start and one arm was raised and bent at the elbow, the elbow pushed out beyond her body. Her mouth was open and her deep-set yellow eyes seemed to darken and look tired.

"He was with some friends," I said and, looking back at the bar. "They've gone now."

"Hah!" It was the sound of a gasp of breath. Then suddenly the fright went and she shrugged her shoulders and talked and laughed to all of us. Soon she went over to her friends, the coloured man and a white couple; she must have got some money or the ticket for her handbag from one of them, for presently we saw her walking quickly to the cloakroom.

Iris went on dancing. We must have stayed another half an hour and when we were leaving we were surprised to see Hilda waiting in the foyer. She said to me:

"His car has gone."

"Whose?"

"Bill Williams's car."

"Has he got a car?" Iris said.

"Oh, it's not his," said Hilda. "It's gone. That's something. Will you take me home? I don't want to go alone. They followed me here."

She looked at all of us. She was frightened.

I said, "Iris and I will take you on our way."

"Don't make me late," said Iris crossly. "You know what Mum is." I promised. "Did you come with him?"

"No, with someone else," Hilda said, looking nervously at the glass swing door. "Are you sure his friends went too? What did they look like?"

I tried to describe them.

"I've seen the short one," she said, frowning, "somewhere."

It was only a quarter of an hour's ride at that hour of the night. We walked out of The Temple Rooms and across the main road to the bus stop and waited under the lights that made our faces corpse-like. I have always liked the hard and sequinned sheen of London streets at night, their empty dockyard look. The cars come down them like rats. The red trolley bus came up at last and when we got in Hilda sat between us. The bus-load of people stared at her and I am not surprised. I have said what she looked like—the hair built up high, her bright green wrap and red dress. I don't know how you would describe such clothes. But the people were not staring at her clothes. They were staring at her eyebrows. I said before that her face was an extension of her nudity and I say it again. Those eyebrows of hers were painted and looked like the only things she had on—they were like a pair of beetles with turned up tails that had settled on her forehead. People laughed under their hands and two or three youths at the front of the bus turned round and guffawed and jostled and whistled; but Hilda, remember, was not a girl of sixteen gone silly, but a woman, hard rather than soft in the face, and the effect was one of exposure, just as a mask has the effect of exposing.

We did not talk but when the trolley arm thumped two or three times at a street junction, Hilda said with a sigh, "Bump! Bump! Bump!" She was thinking of her childhood in old Mrs Draper's room at Hincham Street. We got off the bus a quarter of a mile further on and, as she was stepping off, Hilda said, speaking of what was in her mind, I suppose, during the ride:

"Shinji had a gold wrist-watch with a gold strap and a golden pen. They had gone when he was killed. They must have cost him a hundred pounds. Someone must have stolen them and sold them.

"I reported it," Hilda said. "I needed the money. That is what you had to do—sell something. I had to eat."

And the stare from her mask of a face stated something of her life that her strangeness had concealed from us. We walked up the street.

She went on talking about that watch and how particular Shinji was about his clothes, especially his shirts. All his collars had to be starched, she said. Those had gone too, she said. And his glasses. And his two gold rings. She walked very quickly between us. We got to the corner of her street. She stopped and looked down it.

"Bill Williams's van!" she said.

About thirty houses down the street we could indeed see a small van standing.

"He's waiting for me," she said.

It was hard to know whether she was frightened or whether she was reckoning, but my heart jumped. She made us stand still and watch. "My room's in the front," she said. I crossed over to the other side of the street and then came back.

"The light is on," I said.

"He's inside," she said.

"Shall I go and see?" I said.

"Go," said Iris to me.

Hilda held my wrist.

"No," she said.

"There are two people, I think, in the front garden," I said.

"I'm going home with you," Hilda said to Iris decisively. She rushed off and we had to race after her. We crossed two or three streets to the Fulminos' house. Mrs Fulmino let us in.

"Now, now, Hilda, keep your hair on. Kill you? Why should he? This is England, this isn't China . . ."

Mr Fulmino's face showed his agony. His mouth collapsed, his eyes went hard. He looked frantic with appeal. Then he turned his back on us, marched into the parlour and shouted as if he were calling across four lines of traffic:

"Turn the wireless off."

We followed him into the room. Mrs Fulmino, in the suddenly silent room, looked like a fortress waiting for a flag to fall.

We all started talking at once.

"Can I stay with you tonight?" she said. "Bill Williams has broken into my house. I can't go there. He'll kill me." The flag fell.

"Japan," said Mrs Fulmino disposing of her husband with her first shot. Then she turned to Hilda; her voice was coldly rich and rumbling. "You've always a home here, as you well know, Hilda," she went on, giving a very unhomely sound to the word. "And," she said, glancing at her neat curtains to anyone who might be in ambush outside the window, "if anyone tries to kill you, they will have to kill," she nodded to her husband, "Ted and me first. What have you been doing?"

"I was down at The Temple. Not with Bill Williams," said Hilda. "He was watching me. He's always watching me."

"Now look here, Hilda, why should Bill Williams want to kill you? Have you encouraged him?"

"Don't be a fool!" shouted Mrs Fulmino.

"She knows what I mean. Listen to me, Hilda. What's going on between you and Bill Williams? Constance is upset, we all know."

"Oh keep your big mouth shut," said Mrs Fulmino. "Of course she's encouraged him. Hilda's a woman, isn't she? I encouraged you, didn't I?"

"I know how to look after myself," said Hilda, "but I don't like that van outside the house at this hour of night, I didn't speak to him at the dance."

"Hilda's thinking of the police," ventured Mr Fulmino.

"Police!" said Mrs Fulmino. "Do you know what's in the van?"

"No," said Hilda. "And that's what I don't want to know. I don't want him on my doorstep. Or his friends. He had two with him. Harry saw them."

Mrs Fulmino considered.

"I'm glad you've come to us. I wish you'd come to us in the first place," she said. Then she commanded Mr Fulmino: "You go up there at once with Harry," she said to him, "and tell that man to leave Hilda alone. Go on, now. I can't understand you"—she indicated me—"running off like that, leaving a van there. If you don't go I'll go myself. I'm not afraid of a paltry ... a paltry ... what does he call himself? You go up."

Mrs Fulmino was as good a judge of the possibilities of an emotional situation as any woman on earth: this was her moment. She wanted us out of the house and Hilda to herself.

We obeyed.

Mr Fulmino and I left the house. He looked tired. He was too tired to put on his jacket. He went out in his shirt sleeves.

"Up and down we go, in and out, up and down," said Mr Fulmino. "First it's Constance, now it's Hilda. And the pubs are closed."

"There you are, what did I tell you?" said Mr Fulmino when we got to Hilda's street. "No van, no sign of it, is there? You're a witness. We'll go up and see all the same."

Mr Fulmino had been alarmed but now his confidence came back. He gave me a wink and a nod when we got to the house.

"Leave it to me," he said. "You wait here."

I heard him knock at the door and after a time knock again. Then I heard a woman's voice. He was talking a long time. He came away.

He was silent for a long time as we walked. At last he said:

"That beats all. I didn't say anything. I didn't say who I was. I didn't let on. I just asked to see Hilda. 'Oh,' says the landlady, 'she's out.' 'Oh,' I said, 'that's a surprise.' I didn't give a name—'Out you say? When will she be back?' 'I don't know,' said the landlady, and this is it, Harry—'she's paid her rent and given her notice. She's leaving first thing in the morning,' the landlady said. 'They came for the luggage this evening.' Harry," said Mr Fulmino, "did Hilda say anything about leaving?"

"No."

"Bill Williams came for her luggage."

We marched on. Or rather we went stealthily along like two men walking a steel wire of suspicion. We almost lost our balance when two cats ran across the street and set up howls in a garden, as if they were howling us down. Mr Fulmino stopped.

"Harry!" he said. "She's playing us up. She's going off with Bill Williams."

"But she's frightened of him. She said he was going to kill her."

"I'm not surprised," said Mr Fulmino. "She's been playing him up. Who was she with at the dance hall? She's played everyone up. Of course she's frightened of him. You bet. I'm sorry for anyone getting mixed up with Bill Williams—he'll knock some sense into her. He's rough. So was her father."

"Bill Williams might have just dropped by to have a word," I said.

"Funny word at half past eleven at night," said Mr Fulmino. "When I think of all that correspondence, all those forms—War Office, State Department, United Nations—we did, it's been a poor turn-out. You might say," he paused for an image sufficiently devastating, "a waste of paper, a ruddy wanton waste of precious paper."

We got back to his house. I have never mentioned, I believe, that it had an iron gate that howled, a noise that always brought Mrs Fulmino to her curtains, and a clipped privet hedge, like a moustache, to the tiny garden.

We opened the gate, the gate howled, Mrs Fulmino's nose appeared at the curtains.

"Don't say a word," said Mr Fulmino.

Tea—the room smelled of that, of course. Mrs Fulmino had made some while we were out. She looked as though she had eaten something too. A titbit. They all looked sorry for Mr Fulmino and me. And Mrs Fulmino had had a titbit! In fact I know from Iris that the only thing Mrs Fulmino had got out of Hilda was the news that she had had a postcard from Mr Faulkner from Chicago. He was on the move.

"Well?" said Mrs Fulmino.

"It's all right, Hilda," said Mr Fulmino coldly. "They've gone."

"There," said Mrs Fulmino, patting Hilda's hand.

"Hilda," said Mr Fulmino, "I've been straight with you. I want you to be straight with me. What's going on between you and Bill Williams . . . ?"

"Hilda's told me . . ." Mrs Fulmino said.

"I asked Hilda, not you," said Mr Fulmino to his wife, who was so surprised that she went very white instead of her usual purple.

"Hilda, come on. You come round here saying he's going to kill you. Then they tell me you've given your notice up there."

"She told me that. I think she's done the right thing."

"And did you tell her why you gave your notice?" asked Mr Fulmino.

"She's given her notice at the factory too," said Mrs Fulmino.

"Why?" said Mr Fulmino.

Hilda did not answer.

"You are going off with Bill Williams, aren't you?"

"Ted!" Hilda gave one of her rare laughs.

"What's this?" cried Mrs Fulmino. "Have you been deceiving me? Deceit I can't stand, Hilda."

"Of course she is," said Mr Fulmino. "She's paid her rent. He's collected her luggage this evening—where is it to be? Monte Carlo? Oh, it's all right, sit down," Mr Fulmino waved Mrs Fulmino back. "They had a row at the dance this evening."

But Hilda was on her feet.

"My luggage," she cried, holding her bag with both hands to her bosom as we had seen her do once before when she was cornered. "Who has touched my luggage?"

I thought she was going to strike Mr Fulmino.

"The dirty thief. Who let him in? Who let him take it? Where's he gone?" She was moving to the door. We were stupefied.

"Bill Williams!" she shouted. Her rage made those artificial eyebrows look comical and I expected her to pick them off and throw them at us. "Bill Williams I'm talking about. Who let that bloody war hero in? That bitch up there . . ."

"Hilda," said Mr Fulmino. "We don't want language."

"You fool," said Mrs Fulmino in her lowest, most floor-pervading voice to her husband. "What have you been and done? You've let Bill Williams get away with all those cases, all her clothes, everything. You let that spiv strip her."

"Go off with Bill Williams!" Hilda laughed. "My husband was an officer."

"I knew he was after something. I thought it was dollars," she said suddenly.

She came back from the door and sat down at the table and sobbed.

"Two hundred and fifty pounds, he's got," she sobbed. It was a sight to see Hilda weeping. We could not speak.

"It's all I had," she said.

We watched Hilda. The painted eyebrows made the grimace of her weeping horrible. There was not one of us who was not shocked. There was in all of us a sympathy we knew how to express but which was halted—as by a fascination—with the sight of her ruin. We could not help contrasting her triumphant arrival with her state at this moment. It was as if we had at last got her with us as we had, months before, expected her to be. Perhaps she read our thoughts. She looked up at us and she had the expression of a person seeing us for the first time. It was like an inspection.

"You're a mean lot, a mean respectable lot," she said. "I remember you. I remember when I was a girl. What was it Mr Singh said, I can't remember— he was clever—oh well, leave it, leave it. When I saw that little room they put my poor mother in, I could have cried. No sun. No warmth in it. You just wanted someone to pity. I remember it. And your faces. The only thing that was nice was," she sobbed and laughed for a moment, "was bump, bump, bump, the trolley." She said loudly: "There's only one human being in the whole crew—Jack Draper. I don't wonder he sees more in fish."

She looked at me scornfully. "Your brother—he was nice," she said. "Round the park at night! That was love."

"Hilda," said Mrs Fulmino without anger. "We've done our best for you. If we've made mistakes I hope you haven't. We haven't had your life. You talk about ships that pass in the night, I don't know what you mean, but I can tell you there are no ships in this house. Only Ted."

"That's right," said Mr Fulmino quietly too. "You're overwrought."

"Father," said Mrs Fulmino, "hadn't you better tell the police?"

"Yes, yes, dear," agreed Mr Fulmino. "We'd better get in touch with the authorities."

"Police," said Hilda, laughing in their faces. "Oh God! Don't worry about that. You've got one in every house in this country." She picked up her bag, still laughing, and went to the door.

"Police," she was saying, "that's ripe."

"Hilda, you're not to go out in the street looking like that," said Mrs Fulmino.

"I'd better go with her," said Mr Fulmino.

"I'll go," I said. They were glad to let me.

—

It is ten years since I walked with Hilda to her lodgings. I shall not forget it, and the warm, dead, rubbery city night. It is frightening to walk with a woman who has been robbed and wronged. Her eyes were half-closed as though she was reckoning as she walked. I had to pull her back on to the pavement or she would have gone flat into a passing car. The only thing she said to me was:

"They took Shinji's rings as well."

Her room was on the ground floor. It had a divan and a not very clean dark green cover on it. A pair of shoes were sticking out from under it. There was a plain deal cupboard and she went straight to it. Two dresses were left. The rest had gone. She went to a table and opened the drawer. It was empty except for some letters.

I stood not knowing what to say. She seemed surprised to see me there still.

"He's cleared the lot," she said vacantly. Then she seemed to realise that she was staring at me without seeing me for she lowered her angry shoulders.

"We'll get them back," I said.

"How?" she said, mocking me, but not unkindly.

"I will," I said. "Don't be upset."

"You!" she said.

"Yes, I will," I said.

I wanted to say more. I wanted to touch her. But I couldn't. The ruin had made her untouchable.

"What are you going to do?" I said.

"Don't worry about me," she said. "I'm okey doke. You're different from your brother. You don't remember those days. I told Mr Gloster about him. Come to that, Mr Faulkner too. They took it naturally. That was a fault of Mr Singh"—she never called him by his Christian name—"jealousy."

She kicked off her shoes and sat down on the cheap divan and frowned at the noise it made and she laughed.

"One day in Bombay I got homesick and he asked me what I was thinking about and I was green, I just said 'Sid Fraser's neck. It had a mole on it'— you should have seen his face. He wouldn't talk to me for a week. It's a funny thing about those countries. Some people might rave about them, I didn't see anything to them."

She got up.

"You go now," she said laughing. "I must have been in love."

I dreamed about Hilda's face all night and in the morning I wouldn't have been surprised to see London had been burned out to a cinder. But the next night her face did not come and I had to think about it. Further and further it went, a little less every day and night and I did not seem to notice when someone said Bill Williams had been picked up by the police, or when Constance had been found half dead with aspirins, and when, in both cases, Mr Fulmino told me he had to "give assistance in the identification," for Hilda had gone. She left the day after I took her to her room. Where she went no one knew. We guessed. We imagined. Across water, I thought, getting further and further away, in very fine clothes and very beautiful. France, Mr Fulmino thought, or possibly Italy. Africa, even. New York, San Francisco, Tokyo, Bombay, Singapore. Where? Even one day six months after she had left when he came to the library and showed me a postcard he had had from her, the first message, it did not say where she was and someone in the post office had pulled off the stamp. It was a picture of Hilda herself on a seat in a park, sitting with Mr Faulkner and Mr Gloster. You wouldn't recognise her.

But Mr Gloster's book came out. Oh yes. It wasn't about Japan or India or anything like that. It was about us.

(1961)

THE LIARS

"We're all dressed up today," said the landlady, going downstairs to her husband in the kitchen, from the old lady's room. "Diamond rings, emerald necklace—she's put the lot on. I said to her: 'You're all dressed up for company, I see.' 'Yes,' she said, 'Harry's coming.' I mean, it's childish. I don't trust that man. He'd stop at nothing and he tells lies. And do you know what she said?"

"What did she say?" said the landlady's husband.

"It's Thursday, Mrs Lax, she says. It's my day for telling lies."

It was a February afternoon. Under her black wig, the old lady upstairs was sitting up in bed reading her father's Baudelaire. She read greedily; her eyes enlarged by her glasses, were rampaging over the lines; with her long nose and her long lips sliding back into her cheeks, she looked like a wolf grinning at the smell of the first snow and was on the hunt restlessly among the words.

> *Vous que dans votre enfer mon âme a poursuivies*
> *Pauvres soeurs, je vous aime autant que je vous plains*

She was murmuring avidly as she read. All over the bed were books, French and English, papers, detective novels that she had picked up and pushed away. On and off, in the long day, she had looked to see what was going on in the street; sleet had emptied it. The only thing that still caught her eye was an old blackbird gripping the branch of the plane tree outside her window; its wings hanging down, alone.

"You're late," said the old lady, pulling her shawl violently round her arms, taking off her glasses and showing her strong, expectant teeth, when

Harry came up to her room at four o'clock. The bold nose was naked and accusing.

Harry put the library books he had brought for her on the table under the window by her bedside. He was a tall, red-faced man with the fixed look of moist astonishment at having somehow got a heavy body into his navy-blue suit and of continually hearing news.

"I had my hair cut," he said, moving a small cane-seated chair out of the muddle of furniture into the middle of the room. The old lady waited impatiently for him to sit down.

"No," he said. The old lady took a deep breath and gave a small hungry smile.

"No," he said. "A terrible thing happened when I came out of the barber's." The old lady let out her breath peacefully and let her head slip aside on her pillow in admiration.

"I saw my double," Harry said.

Two years ago she had been in hospital, but before that Harry had the job of pushing her along the sea front in a bath chair on fine mornings. When she had been taken ill, he had started working in the bar and dining-room of the Queens Hotel. Now that she was bedridden he brought her books. First of all, in the days when he used to wheel her out, it was "Yes, Miss Randall" or "Is that a fact, Miss Randall?" while she chattered about the town as it was when she was a child there, about her family—all dead now—and about her father, the famous journalist and what he had done at Versailles after the 1914 war and his time in the Irish troubles, and her London life with him. And Harry told her about himself. "I was born in Enniskillen, ma'am." "Now that's a border town, isn't it Harry?" "It's like living on a tightrope ma'am. My father fought against the British." "Very foolish of him," said the old lady. "Oh, it was," said Harry. "He had us blown up." "The British *bombed* you, Harry?" "Not at all, it was one of father's bombs, home-made thing, it went off in the house." "Were you hurt, Harry?" "I was at my Auntie's. So I went to sea." "So you did, you told me, and the ship blew up too." "No ma'am it was the boiler. It was a Liverpool ship, the *Grantham*." "Two explosions, I don't believe you, Harry." "It's God's truth ma'am. It was in New York harbour. But I'd left her in Buenos Aires—there was always trouble on her." "And then you went to that hacienda—no, you got a job in an hotel first of all—isn't that it?" "Yes, in two or three hotels, ma'am until this American lady took me up to her hacienda." "To look after the horses?" "That is correct." "This was the lady who rode her horse up the steps into the dining-room?" "No ma'am," said Harry, "she rode it right inside and up the marble staircase into her bedroom." "She couldn't Harry. A mule yes, but not a horse." "That part was easy for her, ma'am, it was getting the horse down that was the trouble. She called us, the

Indian boy and myself, and we had to do that. Down twenty-five marble steps. She stood at the top shouting at us 'Mind the pictures.'" "I suppose there was an explosion there, too, Harry?" "No ma'am, but there were butterflies as large as plates flying through the air, enough to knock you down ... "

"Harry," said the old lady one day, "You're as big a liar as my sister's husband used to be."

Harry looked at her warily, then around him to see if there was anyone he could call to for help if there was trouble.

"It's God's truth," said Harry rapidly and anxiously.

"There's truth and there's God's truth," said the old lady. It was after this that she had to be taken off to hospital.

——

"So you saw your double, Harry," the old lady said. "Stand up and let me look at you."

Harry stood up.

"They've cropped you at the back, you're nearly blue. I'll tell you whose double you are, Harry. My sister's husband. He was in the hotel business like you."

"Is that a fact?" said Harry. "Did your sister marry?"

"I've been thinking about it ever since you went to work at the Queens," said the old lady. "He was taller and broader than you and he had fair hair, not black like yours and a very white face, a London night face—but the feet were the same, like yours, sticking out sideways. Sit down, Harry."

"I suppose," said Harry, who had heard versions of this story before. "I suppose he'd be the manager?"

"Manager!" shouted the old lady. "He wouldn't have considered it! Ambassador, Archbishop, Prime Minister, more like it. That is what he sounded like and what he looked like—anyway what we *thought* he was. He was the head waiter at a night-club."

She stared herself into silence.

"No, it's God's truth," said Harry, taking his chance. "I was coming out of the barber's and I forgot your books and went back for them and when I came to cross the street, the lights changed. There was a crowd of us there on the kerb and that was when I saw this fellow. He was standing on the other side of the street waiting to cross. I stared at him. He stared at me. We were the double of each other. I thought I was looking in a mirror."

The old lady let her head slip back peacefully on the pillow, a happy smile came on her face and she took a biscuit from the tin.

"Same clothes?" said the old lady slyly.

"Except for the hat," said Harry. "Same height. He was staring at me. Same nose, eyes, everything. And then the lights changed and he stepped off the kerb and I stepped off and we were still staring at each other. But when we got to the middle I couldn't look at him any longer and I looked away. We passed each other and I felt cold as ice down one side of my body."

"Did he turn round? Did *he* recognise you?"

"He did not. But after we passed I looked back and he wasn't there. No sign of him at all. I got to the kerb and I had a second look. He'd gone."

"He was lost in the crowd."

"He was not. There wasn't a crowd. He was the only one crossing from that side of the street. Except for the hat, it was me."

The pupils of Harry's eyes were upright, brown ovals. He had been wronged, so wronged that he looked puffed out, full of wind.

"It was like passing an iceberg in the Atlantic. Or a ghost," Harry said.

"You could say Deb's husband was a ghost," said the old lady. "He was living upstairs in the flat above us for three years before we met him. We used to hear his taxi at four in the morning. He was out all night and we were out all day. Deb at her art school and I worked on the paper my father used to work on."

"You mightn't have met at all," Harry said. "I never saw the night porter at the Queens for a year."

"I wish we hadn't," said the old lady.

"It would be accidental if you did. Would there have been an accident?" Harry said, putting on an innocent look. "When I was working on that hacienda with the American lady, the one with the horse in her bedroom . . ."

"There was an accident!" said the old lady. "You know there was. I told you, Harry."

"He left the stopper in his basin," Harry said.

"With the tap dripping," the old lady said. "Deb got home one evening and heard the water dripping through the ceiling on to father's desk. She put a bowl underneath it and it splashed all over father's books—we had a very pleasant flat, not like this. Father left us some very beautiful things. When I got home I was angry with Deb. She was a very dreamy girl. 'Why didn't you get the housekeeper up instead of letting it ruin everything?' I said. I had to ring for him—stone deaf, like your cook. Didn't you say the explosion on that ship, the *Cairngorm*, made your cook stone deaf?"

"On the *Grantham*," Harry said.

"You told me the *Cairngorm* before," said the old lady. "But never mind. He got his keys and went upstairs to see what was going on. That flat, Harry. It was empty. When I say empty, just the lino on the floor . . ."

"I've got lino at the Queens," said Harry. "Brown with white flowers."

"Nothing—nothing but a table and a bed and a couple of chairs. It was like a cell. It was like a punishment hanging over us. Not a book. There was a parcel of shirts from the laundry on the bed—that would have told us something if we'd looked."

"It would," said Harry.

"Four o'clock in the morning," said the old lady, "he came home. The taxi ticking down below in the street! Like a ghost in the night. Of course he came next day to apologise about the water. Harry, the moment he stood in the room, I knew I'd seen him before! I said to my sister 'I've seen that man somewhere.' The way he stopped in the doorway, looking across the room at Deb and me and the chairs, nodding at them as if he were telling us where to sit, the way he held his hands together as he spoke with his head bent. He had one of those kissing mouths—like a German. He looked at the books that had been splashed and said, 'Balzac and Baudelaire, very great men,' and looked fatter in the face after he said it. More important. We said they were father's books and my sister said 'Father was a special correspondent. Perhaps you've heard of him.' He said he'd heard people mention him at his club and it sounded as if he'd eaten father." The old lady laughed out loud at this idea of hers and left her mouth open for a while after she had laughed. "I'll tell you who he was like," she said excitedly, "that statue of George II. Or do I mean the Duke of Bedford?

"I wanted to get rid of him: he was so large and serious and he sounded as if he was making a speech to Parliament about what some painter he knew had said about art and the public. He knew a lot of people—cabinet ministers, actors, judges. Well, I said, when he'd gone, I don't know who he is but he's a man 'in the know!' Deb did not like my saying this. 'He's a journalist, I expect.' Before he went Deb asked him to have a drink with us one day. 'Let me look at my diary. Thursday I'm free and Sundays, unless I go away to stay,' he said. 'Come on Sunday,' Deb said. He came. We had people there. The first thing he did was to start handing round the drinks. It was *his* party. He owned us. He'd eaten us too. I couldn't take my eyes off him. One or two people were as curious as I was. 'Who is he? The editor of *The Times*? What does he do?' He wasn't like any of our friends, we were all younger. You know what I think drew us to him—girls are such fools—his conceit! He was as conceited as a gravestone. I watched him moving about. There was his round white face, rather puffy, and his head bowing like the whole of the House of Hanover—the House of Hanover were very stiff, I know, Harry, but you know what I mean—and talking about the Prime Minister and politics in a pooh-poohing way; but down below were his feet sticking out sideways and scampering about beneath him—like messenger boys. 'Which paper do you work for?' I asked him. 'I'm not a journalist,' he said. 'Oh', I said, 'the housekeeper said you were a journalist on night work. We hear your taxi every night. And do you know what he said? 'I asked the housekeeper about you when I took my flat here. I wanted to be sure it was a quiet house. He said you were two ladies out all day.' Snubs to us, I said to my sister after he had gone, but she said 'Fancy him asking about us!' and she danced round the room singing up at the ceiling 'I'm a lady out all day.' We could hear him upstairs walking about."

"Yes, but that's what I can't make out about this man," said Harry. "I was thinking about it yesterday. Why wouldn't he tell you what his job was?"

"He thought we were a pair of snobs," said the old lady. "I expect we were."

"Out all night, he could have been a printer," said Harry.

"Or the post office! Or the police! Nightwatchman. Actor. We thought of that," the old lady raced along. "It was clever of him: you see what he did. He didn't tell a single lie but he started us imagining things and telling lies to ourselves. Deb couldn't leave it alone. Every time he dodged our questions, she made something up."

The old lady pulled her arms out of the shawl and spread her arms wide.

"Burglar came into *my* head," she shouted. "I came home from the office one evening and there they were, both of them, sitting on the sofa and he was saying he had heard on the 'highest authority'—the highest authority, he actually used those words, I always called him the highest authority after that to annoy Deb—that the Cabinet had decided to legalise street betting. When he left I said to Deb 'Deb, that man is not in politics: he is in crime.' 'I can tell you he is not in crime,' Deb said, 'I asked him straight out.'"

Harry leaned forward and began to rub his hands up and down his sleeves making a sound like breath.

" 'I asked him straight out what he did,' Deb said, and he said he was very sorry but it was secret work, something he couldn't talk about, but not crime. He made her promise not to ask or try to find out, but he said he would tell her when he was free to say."

"If you'd looked at those shirts on his bed you'd have known the answer," Harry said. "Dress shirts."

"The head waiter at a smart night-club," the old lady said.

"And earning good money, I suppose," said Harry. "That is where he picked up his talk."

"I've told you all this before, Harry," said the old lady.

"Things come back," said Harry.

"The chief steward on the Grantham," said Harry, "used to pass himself off as the Captain when he went ashore. That was to girls too."

"Oh he talked very well and took us in. You can call him a waiter if you like but you know what I call him? Bluebeard."

"Bluebeard?" said Harry, very startled. "Was he married?"

"No, but he had Bluebeard in him," said the old lady. "A girl will do anything to find out a secret."

"That's true," said Harry.

The old lady stared at Harry, weighing him up. Then she said, in a lower voice: "I can talk to you, Harry. You're a married man. I mean you've been a married man. Show me your wife's picture again."

Harry opened his wallet and took out an old snapshot of a young girl with smooth dark hair drawn in an old-fashioned style round an oval face.

"She was pretty, Harry. Deb was fair and a bit plump." She looked at the photograph a long time and then gave it back to Harry who put it in his wallet again.

"You miss her, Harry."

"I do that."

"You would have had a home," said the old lady. "I haven't got a home. You haven't got a home—and yet, years ago, before we moved to London, my family had a large house in this town."

The old lady suddenly changed her mood and her voice became sarcastically merry.

"Bluebeard! Oh, we were all mystery! Secret service, Russian spies. When Deb went to bed at night, she started drawing back the curtains, turning out the lights and undressing by the light of the street lamp down below. And she would open the window wide—in the winter! The fog blowing in! She would stand in her nightdress and say 'Can't you feel the mystery of London? I want to feel I am everywhere in London seeing what everyone is doing this minute. Listen to it.' 'You'll get pneumonia,' I said. But it was love. He came down to see us very often now. One day he was saying something about the French Ambassador and French foreign policy, it sounded boastful and I said (I remember this) 'Father was one of Clemenceau's very few English friends'—which wasn't true. I told you he made us tell lies. That impressed him because before he went he asked us both out to dinner—at the Ritz! The Ritz! And that was where something funny happened—only a small thing. A party at another table started staring at him and I was sure I heard someone mentioned his name. I'm sure I heard one of the men say 'There's Charles,' and I said to him: 'Someone knows you over there.' 'No,' he said. 'They were talking about you. They were saying it was unfair a man taking out two pretty sisters.' Deb was very pleased. 'He's very well known,' she said. 'In that case, he can't be secret, can he?' I said.

"He never took us out again."

The old lady scowled.

"After that it was champagne, caviar, lobster. Up in his flat and Deb took her gramophone—I never went. 'He must be a cook,' I said and she said 'No, he sends out for it' and wouldn't speak to me for a week afterwards. She was clean gone. She gave up her classes because she couldn't see him during the day except on Thursdays and Sundays. She was mad about him. And she got very secretive, hiding things, not like her at all. I told her she'd have a bigger secret than she bargained for."

The old lady sniggered.

"I was jealous," said the old lady in a moping voice.

"Ah you would be I expect," Harry agreed.

"Yes," moped the old lady.

"And then," said Harry giving a loud slap to his knee. "There was this ring at the bell . . ."

The old lady looked suspiciously at him.

"The same as the time I told you about, when we docked at Marseilles— with that Algerian. Short black socks he had on and . . ."

The old lady woke up out of her moping, offended.

"Algerian! He was not an Algerian. He was a Cypriot. I was very surprised to hear a ring at that time of the evening. I thought it must have been one of those Jehovah's Witnesses. I went to the door and there he was, this little dark Cypriot with a bottle sticking out of his pocket—I thought he was drunk. He asked for Mr Charles. 'There is no Mr Charles here,' I said. 'What number do you want?' 'Six', he said."

"And you were four!" said Harry.

"'This is four,' I said pointing to the number on the door. Well you'd think people could read. 'Number six is upstairs.' And I shut the door quickly, I was frightened."

"You can mark a man with a bottle," said Harry. "I've seen that too."

"I heard him ring the bell upstairs. I heard talking. And then it was all quiet. Then suddenly I heard a shout and I thought the ceiling was coming down, like furniture being thrown about."

"An argument?" said Harry.

"An argument," said the old lady. She tightened her shawl round her and leaned back as if she were warding off blows.

"Screams, Harry! Lobster, Harry! Glass! And Deb rushing out to the landing making a horrible squeal like a dog being run over. I rushed out of our flat and up the stairs and there was Deb in her petticoat shrieking and just as I got to her the Cypriot rushed out with ketchup or blood, I don't know which, on his boots and ran downstairs. I pulled Deb out of the way. Her scream had stopped in her wide open mouth and she was pointing into the lobby of the flat. There was Charles getting up from the floor, in his shirt sleeves with blood all over his face. You couldn't walk for glass."

The old lady stared at Harry and, picking up Baudelaire's poems, contemptuously threw them to the end of the bed. Then slowly she smiled and Harry smiled. They smiled at each other with admiration.

"Yes," said Harry with a nod. "It's feasible." The old lady nodded back.

"It's feasible all right," Harry said. "The same as I was saying happened in Marseilles when I was in the Grantham—Egyptian onions from Alexandria—you could smell us all over the port. I went ashore with the second mate and we were having a drink in one of those cafés with tables on the street—only there five minutes and this Algerian comes in, a young fellow. He walks straight between the tables to the head waiter who was flicking flies off the fruit and shoots him dead. Not a word spoken. Same idea. The head waiter had been fiddling chicken and brandy, selling it on the side and when the boss tumbled to it, the waiter said this Algerian kitchen boy—that is what he was—had done it and the boss fired him. Same story. They're very hot-blooded down there. It was all in the papers."

"The Cypriot was kitchen boy at the club. Champagne, lobster, caviar, it all came from there! Week after week," said the old lady.

"Yes," said Harry.

"We kept it out of the papers, of course," said the old lady loftily.

"You don't want a thing like that in the papers," Harry agreed. "Just sweep up and say nothing, like that time at the Queens when Mr Armitage . . ."

"We had a reason," said the old lady. "I'll tell you something I never told you before. When Deb came screaming to the door, I didn't tell you—she had a broken bottle in her hand."

"Is that so!" said Harry very startled.

"It's true. That is what happened. It was Deb that did the fighting not the Cypriot. It was Deb."

"God Almighty," said Harry. "And she married him after that!"

"She didn't marry him," said the old lady. "I know I said she did, but she didn't. 'I wouldn't marry a man who cheated like that,' she said. She wouldn't speak to him. Or look at him. She wouldn't get a doctor to look after him. He had a terrible cut on his forehead. I had to clean it and bandage it and get him to the hospital and nurse him. She wouldn't go near him. And it wasn't because he'd cheated. Now she knew about him, the secret, she didn't want him. She was a girl like that. It was a pity. He did well for himself. I showed you the postcard of his hotel—it must be one of the biggest in Cannes. When you sit like that with your feet turned out, you remind me of him. He could tell the tale too," she suddenly laughed. "You're the double."

And then the landlady came in with tea and put the tray across the old lady's lap.

"There," she said. "Tea for two as the saying is. And don't you tire her out, Mr O'Hara. Another quarter of an hour."

The old lady frowned at the closed door when the landlady went and listened for her steps going down the stairs.

"I could have married him," the old lady said.

"Now this woman, Harry," she said quickly. "With the horse. She was after you, wasn't she? Why did she make you come up and get that horse down? Why couldn't she ride it down, she rode it up. You're trying to throw dust in my eyes ..."

"No, it was a fine horse and Irish bred," said Harry. "She bought it off a man who had lost his leg ..."

The afternoon had darkened. The bird that had been sitting on the tree all day had gone. Harry said "Good-bye" to the old lady. "See you next Thursday," he said.

"And don't be late. Don't let that woman at the Queens keep you. It's your day off," she called as he stood by the open door at the top of the stairs.

He went back along the front, listening to the laughter of the sea in the dark and then into the bar of the Queens Hotel. But because it was his half day off, on the other side of it, as a customer, drinking a small whisky and listening to what people had to say.

(1969)

THE CAMBERWELL BEAUTY

August's? On the Bath Road? Twice-Five August—of course I knew August: ivory man. And the woman who lived with him—her name was Price. She's dead. He went out of business years ago. He's probably dead too. I was in the trade only three or four years but I soon knew every antique dealer in the South of England. I used to go to all the sales. Name another. Naseley of Close Place? Jades, Asiatics, never touched India; Alsop of Ramsey? Ephemera. Marbright, High Street, Boxley? Georgian silver. Fox? Are you referring to Fox of Denton or Fox of Camden—William Morris, art nouveau—or the Fox Brothers in the Portobello Road, the eldest stuttered? They had an uncle in Brighton who went mad looking for old Waterford. Hindmith? No, he was just a copier. Ah now, Pliny! He was a very different cup of tea: Caughley ware. (Coalport took it over in 1821.) I am speaking of specialities; furniture is the bread and butter of the trade. It keeps a man going while his mind is on his speciality and within that speciality there is one object he broods on from one year to the next, most of his life; the thing a man would commit murder to get his hands on if he had the nerve, but I have never heard of a dealer who had; theft perhaps. A stagnant lot. But if he does get hold of that thing he will never let it go or certainly not to a customer—dealers only really like dealing among themselves—but every other dealer in the trade knows he's got it. So they sit in their shops reading the catalogues and watching one another. Fox broods on something Alsop has. Alsop has his eye on Pliny and Pliny puts a hand to one of his big red ears when he hears the name of August. At the heart of the trade is lust but a lust that is a dream paralysed by itself. So paralysed that the only release, the only hope, as everyone knows, is disaster; a bankruptcy, a divorce, a court case, a burglary, trouble with the police, a death. Perhaps then the grip on some piece of treasure will weaken and fall into the watcher's hands and even if it goes elsewhere he will go on dreaming about it.

What was it that Pliny, Gentleman Pliny, wanted of a man like August who was not much better than a country junk dealer? When I opened up in London I thought it was a particular Staffordshire figure, but Pliny was far above that. These figures fetch very little though one or two are hard to find: The Burning of Cranmer, for example. Very few were made; it never sold and the firm dropped it. I was young and eager and one day when a collector, a scholarly man, as dry as a stick, came to my shop and told me he had a complete collection except for this piece, I said in my innocent way: "You've come to the right man. I'm fairly certain I can get it for you—at a price." This was a lie; but I was astonished to see the old man look at me with contempt, then light up like a fire and when he left, look back furtively at me; he had betrayed his lust.

You rarely see an antique shop standing on its own. There are usually three or four together watching one another: I asked the advice of the man next door who ran a small boatyard on the canal in his spare time and he said, "Try Pliny down the Green: he knows everyone." I went "over the water," to Pliny; he was closed but I did find him at last in a sale-room. Pliny was marking his catalogue and waiting for the next lot to come up and he said to me in a scornful way, slapping a young man down, "August's got it." I saw him wink at the man next to him as I left.

I had bought myself a fast red car that annoyed the older dealers and I drove down the other side of Newbury on the Bath Road. August's was one of four little shops opposite the Lion Hotel on the main road at the end of the town where the country begins and there I got my first lesson. The place was closed. I went across to the bar of the hotel and August was there, a fat man of sixty in wide trousers and a drip to his nose who was paying for drinks from a bunch of dirty notes in his jacket pocket and dropping them on the floor. He was drunk and very offended when I picked a couple up and gave them to him. He'd just come back from Newbury races. I humoured him but he kept rolling about and turning his back to me half the time and so I blurted out:

"I've just been over at the shop. You've got some Staffordshire I hear."

He stood still and looked me up and down and the beer swelled in him.

"Who may you be?" he said with all the pomposity of drink. I told him. I said right out, "Staffordshire. Cranmer's Burning." His face went dead and the colour of liver.

"So is London," he said and turned away to the bar.

"I'm told you might have it. I've got a collector," I said.

"Give this lad a glass of water," said August to the barmaid. "He's on fire."

There is nothing more to say about the evening or the many other visits I made to August except that it has a moral to it and that I had to help August over to his shop where an enormous woman much taller than he in a black dress and a little girl of fourteen or so were at the door waiting for him. The girl looked frightened and ran a few yards from the door as August and his woman collided belly to belly.

"Come back," called the woman.

The child crept back. And to me the woman said, "We're closed," and having got the two inside, shut the door in my face.

The moral is this: if The Burning of Cranmer was August's treasure, it was hopeless to try and get it before he had time to guess what mine was. It was clear to him I was too new to the trade to have one. And, in fact, I don't think he had the piece. Years later, I found my collector had left his collection complete to a private museum in Leicester when he died. He had obtained what he craved, a small immortality in being memorable for his relation to a minor work of art.

I know what happened at August's that night. In time his woman, Mrs Price, bellowed it to me, for her confidences could be heard down the street. August flopped on his bed and while he was sleeping off the drink she got the bundles of notes out of his pockets and counted them. She always did this after his racing days. If he had lost she woke him up and shouted at him; if he had made a profit she kept quiet and hid it under her clothes in a chest of drawers. I went down from London again and again but August was not there.

Most of the time these shops are closed. You rattle the door handle; no reply. Look through the window and each object inside stands gleaming with something like a smile of malice, especially on plates and glass; the furniture states placidly that it has been in better houses than you will ever have, the silver speaks of vanished servants. It speaks of the dead hands that have touched it; even the dust is the dust of families that have gone. In the shabby places—and August's was shabby—the dealer is like a toadstool that has grown out of the debris. There was only one attractive object in August's shop—as I say—he went in for ivories and on a table at the back was a set of white and red chessmen set out on a board partly concealed by a screen. I was tapping my feet impatiently looking through the window when I was astonished to see two of the chessmen had moved; then I saw a hand, a long thin work-reddened hand appear from behind the screen and move one of the pieces back. Life in the place! I rattled the door handle again and the child came from behind the screen. She had a head loaded with heavy black hair to her shoulders and a white heart-shaped face and wore a skimpy dress with small pink flowers on it. She was so thin that she looked as if she would blow away in fright out of the place, but instead, pausing on tiptoe, she swallowed with appetite; her sharp eyes had seen my red car outside the place. She looked back cautiously at the inner door of the shop and then ran to unlock the shop door. I went in.

"What are you up to?" I said. "Playing chess?"

"I'm teaching my children," she said, putting up her chin like a child of five. "Do you want to buy something?"

At once Mrs Price was there shouting:

"Isabel. I told you not to open the door. Go back into the room."

Mrs Price went to the chessboard and put the pieces back in their places.

"She's a child," said Mrs Price, accusing me.

And when she said this Mrs Price blew herself out to a larger size and then her sullen face went black and babyish as if she had travelled out of herself for a beautiful moment. Then her brows levelled and she became sullen again.

"Mr August's out," she said.

"It is about a piece of Staffordshire," I said. "He mentioned it to me. When will he be in?"

"He's in and out. No good asking. He doesn't know himself."

"I'll try again."

"If you like."

There was nothing to be got out of Mrs Price.

In my opinion, the antique trade is not one for a woman, unless she is on her own. Give a woman a shop and she wants to sell something; even that little girl at August's wanted to sell. It's instinct. It's an excitement. Mrs Price—August's woman—was living with a man exactly like the others in the trade: he hated customers and hated parting with anything. By middle age these women have dead blank faces, they look with resentment and indifference at what is choking their shops; their eyes go smaller and smaller as the chances of getting rid of it became rarer and rarer and they are defeated. Kept out of the deals their husbands have among themselves, they see even their natural love of intrigue frustrated. This was the case of Mrs Price who must have been handsome in a big-boned way when she was young, but who had swollen into a drudge. What allured the men did not allure her at all. It is a trade that feeds illusions. If you go after Georgian silver you catch the illusion, while you are bidding, that you are related to the rich families who owned it. You acquire imaginary ancestors. Or, like Pliny with a piece of Meissen he was said to keep hidden somewhere—you drift into German history and become a secret curator of the Victoria and Albert museum—a place he often visited. August's lust for "the ivories" gave to his horse-racing mind a private oriental side; he dreamed of rajahs, sultans, harems and lavish gamblers which, in a man as vulgar as he was, came out, in sad reality, as a taste for country girls and the company of bookies. Illusions lead to furtiveness in every-day life and to sudden temptations; the trade is close to larceny, to situations where you don't ask where something has come from, especially for a man like August whose dreams had landed him in low company. He had started at the bottom and very early he "received" and got twelve months for it. This frightened him. He took up with Mrs Price and though he resented it she had made a fairly honest man of him. August was to be *her* work of art.

But he did not make an honest woman of her. No one disapproved of this except herself. Her very size, growing year by year, was an assertion of virtue. Everyone took her side in her public quarrels with him. And as if to make herself more respectable, she had taken in her sister's little girl when the sister died; the mother had been in Music Hall. Mrs Price petted and prinked the little thing. When August became a failure as a work of art, Mrs Price turned to the child. Even August was charmed by her when she jumped on his knee and danced about showing him her new clothes. A little actress, as everyone said, exquisite.

It took me a long time to give up the belief that August had the Cranmer piece—and as I know now, he hadn't got it; but at last I did see I was wasting my time and settled in to the routine of the business. I sometimes saw August at country sales and at one outside Marlborough something ridiculous happened. It was a big sale and went on till late in the afternoon and he had been drinking. After lunch the auctioneer had put up a china cabinet and the bidding was strong. Some outsider was bidding against the dealers, a thing that made them close their faces with moral indignation; the instinctive hatred of customers united them. Drink always stirred August morally; he was a rather despised figure and he was, I suppose, determined to speak for all. He entered the bidding. Up went the price: 50,5,60,5,70,5, 80,5,90. The outsiders were a young couple with a dog.

"Ninety, ninety," called the auctioneer.

August could not stand it. "Twice-Five," he shouted.

There is not much full-throated laughter at sales; it is usually shoppish and dusty. But the crowd in this room looked round at August and shouted with a laughter that burst the gloom of trade. He was put out for a second and then saw his excitement had made him famous. The laughter went on; the wonder had for a whole minute stopped the sale. "Twice-five!" He was slapped on the back. At sixty-four the man who had never had a nick-name had been christened. He looked around him. I saw a smile cross his face and double the pomposity that beer had put into him and he redoubled it that evening at the nearest pub. I went off to my car and Alsop of Ramsey, the ephemera man who had picked up some Victorian programmes, followed me and said out of the side of his mouth:

"More trouble tonight at August's."

And then to change the subject and speaking for every dealer south of the Trent, he offered serious news.

"Pliny's mother's dead—Pliny of the Green."

The voice had all the shifty meaning of the trade. I was too simple to grasp the force of this confidence. It surprised me in the following weeks to hear people repeat the news: "Pliny's mother's dead" in so many voices, from the loving memory and deepest sympathy manner as much suited to old clothes, old furniture and human beings indiscriminately, to the flat statement that an event of business importance had occurred in my eventless trade. I was in it for the money and so, I suppose, were all the rest—how else could they live?—but I seemed to be surrounded by a dreamy freemasonry, who thought of it in a different secretive way.

On a wet morning the following spring I was passing through Salisbury on market day and stopped in the square to see if there was anything worth picking up at the stalls there. It was mostly junk but I did find a pretty Victorian teapot—no mark, I agree—with a chip in the spout for a few shillings because the fever of the trade never quite leaves one even on dull days. (I sold the pot five years later for £8 when the prices started to go mad.) I went into one of the pubs in the square, I forget its name, and I was surprised to see Marbright and Alsop there and, sitting near the window, Mrs Price. August was getting drinks at the bar.

Alsop said to me:

"Pliny's here. I passed him a minute ago."

Marbright said: "He was standing in Woolworth's doorway. I asked him to come and have one, but he wouldn't."

"It's hit him hard his mother going," Marbright said. "What's he doing here? Queen Mary's dead."

It was an old joke that Gentleman Pliny had never been the same since the old Queen had come to his shop some time back—everyone knew what she was for picking up things. He only opened on Sundays now and a wealthy crowd came there in their big cars—a new trend as Alsop said. August brought the drinks and stood near, for Mrs Price spread herself on the bench and never left much room for anyone else to sit down. He looked restless and glum.

"Where will Pliny be without his mother," Mrs Price moaned into her glass and, putting it down, glowered at August. She had been drinking a good deal.

August ignored her and said, sneering:

"He kept her locked up."

There is always a lot of talking about "locking up" in the trade; people's minds go to their keys.

"It was kindness," Mrs Price said, "after the burglars got in at Sampson's, three men in a van loading it up in broad daylight. Any woman of her age would be frightened."

"It was nothing to do with the burglary," said August, always sensitive when crime was mentioned. "She was getting soft in the head. He caught her giving his stuff away when she was left on her own. She was past it."

Mrs Price was a woman who didn't like to be contradicted.

"He's a gentleman," said Mrs Price, accusing August. "He was good to his mother. He took her out every Sunday night of his life. She liked a glass of stout on Sundays."

This was true, though Mrs Price had not been to London for years and had never seen this event; but all agreed. We live on myths.

"It was her kidneys," moaned Mrs Price. One outsize woman was mourning another, seeing a fate.

"I suppose that's why he didn't get married, looking after her," said Marbright.

"Pliny! Get married! Don't make me laugh," said August with a defiant recklessness that seemed to surprise even himself. "The last Saturday in every month like a clock striking he was round the pubs in Brixton with old Lal Drake."

And now, as if frightened by what he said, he swanked his way out of the side door of the pub on his way to the Gents.

We lowered our eyes. There are myths, but there are facts. They all knew—even I had heard—that what August said was true, but it was not a thing a sensible man would say in front of Mrs Price. And—mind you—Pliny standing a few doors down the street. But Mrs Price stayed calm among the thoughts in her mind.

"That's a lie," she said peacefully as we thought, though she was eyeing the door waiting for August to come back.

"I knew his father," said Alsop.

We were soon laughing about the ancient Pliny, the Bermondsey boy who began with a barrow shouting "Old Iron" in the streets, a man who never drank, never had a bank account—didn't trust banks—who belted his son while his mother "educated him up"—she was a tall woman and the boy grew up like her, tall with a long arching nose and those big red ears that looked as though his parents had pulled him now this way now that in their fight over him. She had been a housekeeper in a big house and she had made a son who looked like an old family butler, Cockney to the bone, but almost a gentleman. Except, as Alsop said, his way of blowing his nose like a foghorn on the Thames, but sharp as his father. Marbright said you could see the father's life in the store at the back of the shop; it was piled high with what had made the father's money, every kind of old-fashioned stuff.

"Enough to furnish two or three hotels," Alsop said. Mrs Price nodded.

"Wardrobes, tables . . ." she said.

"A museum," said Marbright. "Helmets, swords. Two four-posters the last time I was there."

"Ironwork. Brass," nodded Mrs Price mournfully.

"Must date back to the Crimean War," said Marbright.

"And it was all left to Pliny."

There was a general sigh.

"And he doesn't touch it. Rubbish he calls it. He turned his back on it. Only goes in for the best. Hepplewhite, marquetries, his consoles. Regency."

There was a pause.

"And," I said, "his Meissen."

They looked at me as if I were a criminal. They glanced at one another as if asking whether they should call the police. I was either a thief or I had publicly stripped them of all their clothes. I had publicly announced Pliny's lust.

Although Mrs Price had joined in the conversation, it was in the manner of someone talking in her sleep; for when this silence came, she woke up and said in a startled voice:

"Lal Drake."

And screwing up her fists she got up and, pausing to get ready for a rush, she heaved herself fast to the door by which August had left for the Gents, down the alley a quarter of an hour before.

"The other door, missis," someone shouted. But she was through it.

"Drink up," we said and went out by the front door. I was the last and had a look down the side alley and there I saw a sight. August with one hand doing up his fly buttons and the other arm protecting his face. Mrs Price was hitting out at him and shouting. The language!

"You dirty sod. I knew it. The girl told me." She was shouting. She saw me, stopped hitting and rushed at me in tears and shouted back at him.

"The filthy old man."

August saw his chance and got out of the alley and made for the cars in the square. She let me go and shouted after him. We were all there and in Woolworth's doorway was Pliny. Rain was still falling and he looked wet and all the more alone for being wet. I walked off and, I suppose, seeing me go and herself alone and giddy in her rage she looked all round and turned her temper on me.

"The girl has got to go," she shouted.

Then she came to her senses.

"Where is August?"

August had got to his car and was driving out of the square. She could do nothing. Then she saw Pliny. She ran from me to Pliny, from Pliny to me.

"He's going after the girl," she screamed.

We calmed her down and it was I who drove her home. (This was when she told me, as the wipers went up and down on the windscreen, that she and August were not married.) We splashed through hissing water that was like her tears on the road. "I'm worried for the child. I told her, 'Keep your door locked.' I see it's locked every night. I'm afraid I'll forget and I won't hear him if I've had a couple. She's a kid. She doesn't know anything." I understood that the face I had always thought was empty was really filled with the one person she loved: Isabel.

August was not there when we got to their shop. Mrs Price went in and big as she was, she did not knock anything over.

"Isabel?" she called.

The girl was in the scullery and came with a wet plate that dripped on the carpet. In two years she had changed. She was wearing an old dress and an apron, but also a pair of high-heeled silver evening shoes. She had become the slut of the house and her pale skin looked dirty.

"You're dripping that thing everywhere. What have you got those shoes on for? Where did you get them?"

"Uncle Harry, for Christmas," she said. She called August Uncle Harry. She tried to look jaunty as if she had put all her hope in life into those silly evening shoes.

"All right," said Mrs Price weakly looking at me to keep quiet and say nothing.

Isabel took off her apron when she saw me. I don't know whether she remembered me. She was still pale, but had the shapeliness of a small young woman. Her eyes looked restlessly and uncertainly at both of us, her chin was firmer but it trembled. She was smiling too and, because I was there and the girl might see an ally in me, Mrs Price looked with half-kindness at Isabel; but when I got up to go the girl looked at me as if she would follow me out of the door. Mrs Price got up fast to bar the way. She stood on the doorstep of the shop watching me get into the car, swollen with the inability to say "Thank you" or "Goodbye." If the girl was a child, Mrs Price was ten times a child and both of them standing on the doorstep were like children who don't want anyone to go away.

I drove off and for a few miles I thought about Mrs Price and the girl, but once settled into the long drive to London, the thought of Pliny supplanted them. I had been caught up by the fever of the trade. Pliny's mother was dead. What was going to happen to Pliny and all that part of the business Pliny had inherited from his father, the stuff he despised and had not troubled himself with very much in his mother's time. I ought to go "over the water"—as we say in London—to have a look at it some time. In a few days I went there; I found the idea had occurred to many others. The shop was on one of the main bus routes in South London, a speckled early

Victorian place with an ugly red brick store behind it. Pliny's father had had an eye for a cosy but useful bit of property. Its windows had square panes (1810) and to my surprise the place was open and I could see people inside. There was Pliny with his nose which looked servile rather than distinguished, wearing a long biscuit-coloured tweed jacket with leather pads at the elbows like a Cockney sportsman. There, too, was August with his wet eyes and drinker's shame, Mrs Price swelling over him in her best clothes, and the girl. They had come up from the country and August had had his boots cleaned. The girl was in her best too and was standing apart touching things in the shop, on the point of merriment, looking with wonder at Pliny's ears. He often seemed to be talking at her when he was talking to Mrs Price. I said:

"Hullo! Up from the country? What are you doing here?" Mrs Price was so large that she had to turn her whole body and place her belly in front of everyone who spoke to her.

"Seeing to his teeth," she said nodding at August and, from years of habit, August turned too when his wife turned, in case it was just as well not to miss one of her pronouncements, whatever else he might dodge. One side of August's jaw was swollen. Then Mrs Price slowly turned her whole body to face Pliny again. They were talking about his mother's death. Mrs Price was greedy, as one stout woman thinking of another, for a melancholy tour of the late mother's organs. The face of the girl looked prettily wise and holiday-fied because the heavy curls of her hair hung close to her face. She looked out of the window, restless and longing to get away while her elders went on talking, but she was too listless to do so. Then she would look again at Pliny's large ears with a childish pleasure in anything strange; they gave him a dog-like appearance and if the Augusts had not been there, I think she would have jumped at him mischievously to touch them, but remembered in time that she had lately grown into a young lady. When she saw him looking at her she turned her back and began writing in the dust on a little table which was standing next to a cabinet; it had a small jug on it. She was writing her name in the dust I S A B ... And then stopped. She turned round suddenly because she saw I had been watching.

"Is that old Meissen?" she called out, pointing to the jug.

They stopped talking. It was comic to see her pretending, for my benefit, that she knew all about porcelain.

"Cor! Old Meissen!" said August pulling his racing newspaper out of his jacket pocket with excitement, and Mrs Price fondly swung her big handbag; all laughed loudly, a laugh of lust and knowledge. They knew, or thought they knew, that Pliny had a genuine Meissen piece somewhere, probably upstairs where he lived. The girl was pleased to have made them laugh at her; she had been noticed.

Pliny said decently: "No, dear. That's Caughley. Would you like to see it?"

He walked to the cabinet and took the jug down and put it on a table.

"Got the leopard?" said August, knowingly. Pliny showed the mark of the leopard on the base of the jug and put it down again. It was a pretty shapely jug with a spray of branches and in the branches a pair of pheasants were perching, done in transfer. The girl scared us all by picking it up in both hands, but it was charming to see her holding it up and studying it.

"Careful," said Mrs Price.

"She's all right," said Pliny.

Then—it alarmed us—she wriggled with laughter.

"What a funny face," she said.

Under the lip of the jug was the small face of an old man with a long nose looking sly and wicked.

"They used to put a face under the lip," Pliny said.

"That's right," said August.

The girl held it out at arm's length and, looking from the jug to Pliny, she said: "It's like you, Mr Pliny."

"Isabel!" said Mrs Price. "That's rude."

"But it is," said Isabel. "Isn't it?" She was asking me. Pliny grinned. We were all relieved to see him take the jug from her and put it back in the cabinet.

"It belonged to my mother," he said. "I keep it there," Pliny said to me, despising me because I had said nothing and because I was a stranger.

"Go into the back and have a look round if you want to. The light's on."

I left the shop and went down the steps into the long white storeroom where the white-washed walls were grey with dust. There was an alligator hanging by a nail near the steps, a couple of cavalry helmets and a dirty drum that must have been there since the Crimean War. I went down into streets of stacked up furniture. I felt I was walking into an inhuman crypt or worse still one of those charnel houses or ossuaries I had seen pictures of in one of my father's books when I was a boy. Large as the store was, it was lit by a single electric light bulb hanging from a girder in the roof and the yellow light was deathly. The notion of "picking up" anything at Pliny's depressed me, so that I was left with a horror of the trade I had joined. Yet feelings of this kind are never simple. After half an hour I left the shop. I understood before that day was over and I was back in the room over my own place that what had made me more wretched was the wound of a sharp joy. First, the sight of the girl leaving her name unfinished in the dust had made my heart jump, then when she held the vase in her hands I had felt the thrill of a revelation; until then I had never settled what I should go in for but now I saw it. Why not collect Caughley? That was it. Caughley; it was one of those inspirations that excite one so that every sight in the world changes; even houses, buses and streets and people are transfigured and become unreal as desire carries one away—and then, cruelly, it passes and one is left exhausted. The total impossibility of an impatient young man like myself collecting Caughley which hadn't been made since 1821 became brutally clear. Too late for Staffordshire, too late for Dresden, too late for Caughley and all the beautiful things. I was savage for lack of money. The following day I went to the Victoria and Albert and then I saw other far more beautiful things enshrined and inaccessible. I gazed with wonder. My longing for possession held me and then I was elevated to a state of worship as if they were idols, holy and never to be touched. Then I remembered the girl's hands and a violent day dream passed through my head; it lasted only a second or two but in that time I smashed the glass case, grabbed the treasure and bolted with it. It frightened me that such an idea could have occurred to me. I left the museum and I turned sourly against my occupation, against Marbright, Alsop and above all Pliny and August, and it broke my heart to think of that pretty girl living among such people and drifting into the shabbiness of the trade. I S A B—half a name, written by a living finger in dust.

One has these brief sensations when one is young. They pass and one does nothing about them. There is nothing remarkable about Caughley— except that you can't get it. I did not collect Caughley for a simple reason; I had to collect my wits. The plain truth is that I was incompetent. I had only to look at my bank account. I had bought too much. At the end of the year I looked like getting into the bankruptcy court unless I had a stroke of luck. Talk of trouble making the trade move; I was Trouble myself, dealers could smell it coming and came sniffing into my shop and at the end of the year I sold up for what I could get. It would have been better if I could have waited for a year or two when the boom began. For some reason I kept the teapot I had bought in Salisbury to remind me of wasted time. In its humble way it was pretty.

In the next six months I changed. I had to. I pocketed my pride and I got a dull job in an auctioneer's; at least it took me out of the office when I got out keys and showed people round. The firm dealt in house property and developments. The word "develop" took hold of me. The firm was a large one and sometimes "developed" far outside London. I was told to go and inspect some of the least important bits of property that were coming into the market. One day a row of shops in Steepleton came up for sale. I said I knew them. They were on the London Road opposite the Lion Hotel at the end of the town. My boss was always impressed by topography and the names of hotels and sent me down there. The shops were in the row where August and one or two others had had their business, six of them.

What a change! The Lion had been re-painted; the little shops seemed to have got smaller. In my time the countryside had begun at the end of the row. Now builders' scaffolding was standing in the fields beyond. I looked for August's. A cheap café had taken over his place. He had gone. The mirror man who lived next door was still there but had gone into beads and fancy art jewellery. His window was full of hanging knick-knacks and mobiles.

"It's the tourist trade now," he said. He looked ill.

"What happened to August?"

He studied me for a moment and said, "Closed down," and I could get no more out of him. I crossed the street to The Lion. Little by little, a sentence at a time in a long slow suspicious evening I got news of August from the barmaid as she went back and forth serving customers, speaking in a low voice, her eye on the new proprietor in case the next sentence that came out of her might be bad for custom. The sentences were spoken like sentences from a judge summing up, bit by bit. August had got two years for receiving stolen goods; the woman—"She wasn't his wife"—had been knocked down by a car as she was coming out of the bar at night—"not that she drank, not really drank; her weight really"—and then came the final sentence that brought back to me the alerting heat and fever of its secrets: "There was always trouble over there. It started when the girl ran away."

"Isabel?" I said.

"I dunno—the girl."

I stood outside the hotel and looked to the east and then to the west. It was one of those quarters of an hour on a main road when, for some reason, there is no traffic coming either way. I looked at the now far-off fields where the February wind was scything over the grass, turning it into waves of silver as it passed over them. I thought of Isab . . . running with a case in her hand, three years ago. Which way? Where do girls run to? Sad.

I went back to London. There are girls in London too, you know. I grew a beard, reddish: it went with the red car which I had managed to keep. I could afford to take a girl down to the south coast now and then. Sometimes we came back by the Brixton road, sometimes through Camberwell and when we did this I often slowed down at Pliny's and told the girls, "That man's sitting on a gold mine." They never believed it or, at least, only one did. She said: "Does he sell rings? Let us have a look."

"They're closed," I said. "They're always closed."

"I want to look," she said, so we stopped and got out.

We looked into the dark window—it was Saturday night—and we could see nothing and as we stared we heard a loud noise coming, it seemed, from the place next door or from down the Drive-in at the side of Pliny's shop, a sound like someone beating boxes or bath tubs at first until I got what it was:

drums. Someone blew a bugle, a terrible squeaky sound. There was heavy traffic on the street, but the bugle seemed to split it in half.

"Boys' Brigade, practising for Sunday," I said. We stood laughing with our hands to our ears as we stared into the dark. All I could make out was something white on a table at the back of the shop. Slowly I saw it was a set of chessmen. Chess, ivories, August—perhaps Pliny had got August's chessmen.

"What a din!" said the girl. I said no more to her for in my mind there was the long forgotten picture of Isabel's finger on the pieces, at Steepleton.

When I've got time, I thought, I will run over to Pliny's; perhaps he will know what happened to the girl.

And I did go there again, one afternoon, on my own. Still closed. I rattled the door handle. There was no answer. I went to a baker's next door, then to a butcher's, then to a pub. The same story. "He only opens on Sundays," or, "He's at a sale." Then to a tobacconist's. I said it was funny to leave a shop empty like that, full of valuable stuff. The tobacconist became suspicious.

"There's someone there all right. His wife's there."

"No she's not," his wife said. "They've gone off to a sale. I saw them." She took the hint.

"No one in charge to serve customers," she said.

I said I'd seen a chessboard that interested me and the tobacconist said: "It's dying out. I used to play."

"I didn't know he got married," I said.

"He's got beautiful things," said his wife. "Come on Sunday."

Pliny married! That made me grin. The only women in his life I had ever heard of were his mother and the gossip about Lal Drake. Perhaps he had made an honest woman of her. I went back for one last look at the chessmen and, sure enough, as the tobacconist's wife had hinted someone had been left in charge, for I saw a figure pass through the inner door of the shop. The watcher was watched. Almost at once I heard the tap and roll of a kettle drum, I put my ear to the letter box and distinctly heard a boy's voice shouting orders. Children! All the drumming I had heard on Saturday had come from Pliny's—a whole family drumming. Think of Pliny married to a widow with kids; he had not had time to get his own. I took back what I had thought of him and Lal Drake. I went off for an hour to inspect a house that was being sold on Camberwell Green, and stopped once more at Pliny's on the way back. On the chance of catching him. I went to the window: standing in the middle of the shop was Isabel.

Her shining black hair went to her shoulders. She was wearing a red dress with a schoolgirlish white collar to it. If I had not known her by her heart-shaped face and her full childish lips, I would have known her by her tiptoe way of standing like an actress just about to sing a song or give a dance when she comes forward on the stage. She looked at me daringly. It was the way, I remembered, she had looked at everyone. She did not know me. I went to the door and tipped the handle. It did not open. I saw her watching the handle move. I went on rattling. She straightened and shook her head, pushing back her hair. She did not go away. She was amused by my efforts. I went back to the window of the shop and asked to come in. She could not hear, of course. My mouth was opening and shutting foolishly. That amused her even more. I pointed to something in the window, signalling that I was interested in it. She shook her head again. I tried pointing to other things: a cabinet, an embroidered firescreen, a jar three feet high. At each one she shook her head. It was like a guessing game. I was smiling, even laughing, to persuade her. I put my hands to my chest and pretended to beg like a dog. She laughed at this and looked behind, as if calling to someone. If Pliny wasn't there, his wife might be, or the children. I pointed upwards and made a movement of my hands, imitating someone turning a key in a lock. I was signalling, "Go and get the key from Mrs Pliny," and I stepped back and looked up at a window above the shop. When I did this Isabel was frightened; she went away shouting to someone. And that was the end of it; she did not come back.

I went away thinking, Well, that is a strange thing!

What ideas people put into your head and you build fancies yourself— that woman in the bar at Steepleton telling me Isabel had run away and I imagining her running in those poor evening shoes I'd once seen, in the rain down the Bath Road, when what was more natural in a trade where they all live with their hands in one another's pockets—Pliny had married, and they had taken the girl on at the shop. It was a comfort to think of. I hadn't realised how much I had worried about what would happen to a naïve girl like Isabel when the break up came. Alone in the world! How silly. I thought, one of these Sundays I'll go up there and hear the whole story. And I did.

There was no one there except Pliny and his rich Sunday customers. I even went into the store at the back, looked everywhere. No sign of Isabel. The only female was a woman in a shabby black dress and not wearing a hat who was talking to a man who was testing the door of a wardrobe, making it squeak, while the woman looked on without interest, in the manner of a dealer's wife; obviously the new Mrs Pliny. She turned to make way for another couple who were waiting to look at it. I nearly knocked over a stack of cane chairs as I got past.

If there was no sign of Isabel, the sight of Pliny shocked me. He had been a dead man, permanently dead as wood, even clumsy in his big servile bones, though shrewd. Now he had come to life in the strangest, excited way, much older to look at, thinner and frantic as he looked about him this way and that. He seemed to be possessed by a demon. He talked loudly to people in the shop and was suspicious when he was not talking. He was frightened, abrupt, rude. Pliny married! Marriage had wrecked him or he was making too much money; he looked like a man expecting to be robbed. He recognised me at once. I had felt him watching me from the steps going down to the store. As I came back to the steps to speak to him he spoke to me first, distinctly in a loud voice:

"I don't want any of August's men here, see?"

I went red in the face.

"What do you mean?" I said.

"You heard me," he said. "You know what he got."

Wells of Hungerford was standing near, pretending not to listen. Pliny was telling the trade that I was in with August—publicly accusing me of being a fence. I controlled my temper.

"August doesn't interest me," I said. "I'm in property. Marsh, Help and Hitchcock. I sold his place, the whole street."

And I walked past him looking at a few things as I left.

I was in a passion. The dirty swine—all right when his mother kept an eye on him, the poor old woman, but now—he'd gone mad. And that poor girl! I went to the tobacconist for the Sunday paper in a dream, put down my money and took it without a word and was almost out of the door when the wife called out:

"Did you find him? Did you get what you wanted?" A friendly London voice. I tapped the side of my head.

"You're telling me," the wife said.

"Well, he has to watch everything now. Marrying a young girl like that, it stands to reason," said the wife in a melancholy voice.

"Wears him out, at his age," suggested the tobacconist.

"Stop the dirty talk, Alfred," said the wife.

"You mean he married the *girl*?" I said. "Who's the big woman without a hat—in the store?"

"What big woman is that?" asked the tobacconist's wife. "He's married to the girl. Who else do you think—there's no one else."

The wife's face went as blank as a tombstone in the sly London way.

"She's done well for herself," said the tobacconist. "Keeps her locked up like his mother, wasn't I right?"

"He worships her," said the woman.

I went home to my flat. I was nauseated. The thought of Isabel in bed with that dressed up servant, with his wet eyes, his big raw ears and his breath smelling of onions! Innocent? No, as the woman said, "She has done well for herself." Happy with him too. I remembered her pretty face laughing in the shop. What else could you expect, after August and Mrs Price.

The anger I felt with Pliny grew to a rage but by the time I was in my own flat Pliny vanished from the picture in my mind. I was filled with passion for the girl. The fever of the trade had come alive in me; Pliny had got something I wanted. I could think of nothing but her, just as I remember the look August gave Pliny when the girl asked if the jug was Meissen. I could see her holding the jug at arm's length, laughing at the old man's face under the lip. And I could see that Pliny was not mad; what was making him frantic was possessing the girl.

I kept away from Pliny's. I tried to drive the vision out of my mind, but I could not forget it. I became cunning. Whenever my job allowed it—and even when it didn't—I started passing the time of day with any dealer I had known, picked up news of the sales, studied catalogues, tried to find out which ones Pliny would go to. She might be with him. I actually went to Newbury but he was not there. Bath he couldn't miss and, sure enough, he was there and she wasn't. It was ten in the morning and the sale had just started. I ran off and got into my car. I drove as fast as I could the hundred miles back to London and cursed the lunchtime traffic. I got to Pliny's shop and rang the bell. Once, then several long rings. At once the drum started beating and went on as if troops were marching. People passing in the street paused to listen too. I stood back from the window and I saw a movement at a curtain upstairs. The drumming was still going on and when I bent to listen at the letter box I could hear the sound become deafening and often very near and then there was a blast from the bugle. It was a misty day south of the river and for some reason or other I was fingering the grey window and started writing her name, I S A B . . . hopelessly, but hoping that perhaps she might come near enough to see. The drumming stopped. I waited and waited and then I saw an extraordinary sight; Isabel herself in the dull red dress, but with a lancer's helmet on her head and a side drum on its straps hanging from her shoulders and the drum sticks in her hand. She was standing upright like a boy playing soldiers, her chin up and puzzling at the sight of the letters B A S I on the window. When she saw me she was confused. She immediately gave two or three taps to the drum and then bent almost double with laughter. Then she put on a straight face and played the game of pointing to one thing after another in the shop. Every time I shook my head, until at last I pointed to her. This pleased her. Then I shouted through the letter box: "I want to come in."

"Come in," she said. "It's open."

The door had been open all the time; I had not thought of trying it. I went inside.

"I thought you were locked in."

She did not answer but wagged her head from side to side.

"Sometimes I lock myself in," she said. "There are bad people about, August's men."

She said this with great importance, but her face became ugly as she said it. She took off the helmet and put down the drum.

"So I beat the drum when Mr Pliny is away," she said. She called him Mr Pliny.

"What good does that do?"

"It is so quiet when Mr Pliny is away. I don't do it when he's here. It frightens August's men away."

"It's as good as telling them you are alone here," I said. "That's why I came. I heard the drum and the bugle."

"Did you?" she said eagerly. "Was it loud?"

"Very loud."

She gave a deep sigh of delight.

"You see!" she said, nodding her head complacently.

"Who taught you to blow the bugle?" I said.

"My mother did," she said. "She did it on the stage. Mr Pliny—you know when Mr Pliny fetched me in his motor-car—I forgot it. He had to go back and get it. I was too frightened."

"Isab . . ." I said.

She blushed. She remembered.

"I might be one of August's men," I said.

"No you're not. I know who you are," she said. "Mr Pliny's away for the day but that doesn't matter. I am in charge. Is there something you were looking for?"

The child was gone when she put the drum aside. She became serious and practical: Mrs Pliny! I was confused by my mistake in not knowing the door was open and she busied herself about the shop. She knew what she was doing and I felt very foolish.

"Is there something special?" she said. "Look around." She had become a confident woman. I no longer felt there was anything strange about her. I drifted to look at the chessmen and I could not pretend to myself that they interested me, but I did ask her the price. She said she would look it up and went to a desk where Pliny kept his papers and after going through some lists of figures which were all in code she named the sum. It was enormous—something like £275 and I said, "What!" in astonishment. She put the list back on the desk and said, firmly:

"My husband paid £260 for it last Sunday. It was carved by Dubois. There are only two more like it. It was the last thing he did in 1785."

(I found out afterwards this was nonsense.)

She said this in Pliny's voice; it was exactly the sort of casual sentence he would have used. She looked expressionlessly and not at all surprised when

I said, "Valuable," and moved away.

I meant, of course, that she was valuable and in fact her mystery having gone, she seemed conscious of being valuable and important herself, the queen and owner of everything in the shop, efficiently in charge of her husband's things. The cabinet in the corner, she said, in an offhand way, as I went to look at it, had been sold to an Australian. "We are waiting for the packers." We! Not to feel less knowing than she was, I looked around for some small thing to buy from her. There were several small things, like a cup and saucer, a little china tray, a christening mug. I picked things up and put them down listlessly and, from being indifferent, she became eager and watched me. The important, serious expression she had had vanished, she became childish suddenly and anxious: she was eager to sell something. I found a little china figure on a shelf.

"How much is this?" I said. It was Dresden; the real thing. She took it and looked at the label. I knew it was far beyond my purse and I asked her the price in the bored hopeless voice one puts on.

"I'll have to look it up," she said.

She went to the desk again and looked very calculating and thoughtful and then said, as if naming an enormous sum:

"Two pounds."

"It can't be," I said.

She looked sad as I put it back on the shelf and she went back to the desk. Then she said:

"I tell you what I'll do. It's got a defect. You can have it for thirty-five shillings."

I picked it up again. There was no defect in it. I could feel the huge wave of temptation that comes to one in the trade, the sense of the incredible chance, the lust that makes one shudder first and then breaks over one so that one is possessed, though even at that last moment, one plays at delay in a breathless pause, now one is certain of one's desire.

I said: "I'll give you thirty bob for it."

Young Mrs Pliny raised her head and her brown eyes became brilliant with naïve joy.

"All right," she said.

The sight of her wrapping the figure, packing it in a box and taking the money so entranced me, that I didn't realise what she was doing or what I had done. I wasn't thinking of the figure at all. I was thinking of her. We shook hands. Hers were cold and she waved from the shop door when I left. And when I got to the end of the street and found myself holding the box I wondered why I had bought it. I didn't want it. I had felt the thrill of the thief and I was so ashamed that I once or twice thought of dropping it into a litter box. I even thought of going back and returning it to her and saying to her:

"I didn't want it. It was a joke. I wanted you. Why did you marry an awful old man like Pliny?" And those stories of Pliny going off once a month in the old days, in his mother's time, to Lal Drake that old whore in Brixton, came back to me. I didn't even unpack the figure but put it on the mantelpiece in my room, then on the top shelf of a cupboard which I rarely used. I didn't want to see it. And when in the next months—or even years—I happened to see it, I remembered her talking about the bad people, August's men.

But, though I kept away from Pliny's on Sundays, I could not resist going back to the street and eventually to the shop—just for the sight of her.

And after several misses I did see her in the shop. It was locked. When I saw her she stared at me with fear and made no signals and quickly disappeared—I suppose into the room at the back. I crossed the main road and looked at the upper part of the house. She was upstairs, standing at a window. So I went back across the street and tried to signal, but of course she could only see my mouth moving. I was obsessed by the way I had cheated her. My visits were a siege for the door was never opened now. I did see her once through the window and this time I had taken the box and offered it to her in dumb show. That did have an effect. I saw she was looking very pale, her eyes ringed and tired and whether she saw I was remorseful or not I couldn't tell, but she made a rebuking yet defiant face. Another day I went and she looked terrified. She pointed and pointed to the door but as I eagerly stepped towards it she shook her head and raised a hand to forbid me. I did not understand until, soon, I saw Pliny walking about the shop. I moved off. People in the neighbourhood must often have seen me standing there and the tobacconist I went to gave me a look that suggested he knew what was going on.

Then, on one of my vigils, I saw a doctor go to the side door down the Goods Entrance and feared she was ill—but the butcher told me it was Pliny. His wife, they said, had been nursing him. He ought to convalesce somewhere. A nice place by the sea. But he won't. It would do his wife good. The young girl has worn herself out looking after him. Shut up all day with him. And the tobacconist said what his wife had said a long time back. "Like his poor mother. He kept *her* locked in too. Sunday evening's the only time she's out. It's all wrong."

I got sick of myself. I didn't notice the time I was wasting for one day passed like a smear of grey into another and I wished I could drag myself away from the district, especially now Pliny was always there. At last one Saturday I fought hard against a habit so useless and I had the courage to drive past the place for once and did not park my car up the street. I drove on, taking side streets (which I knew, nevertheless, would lead me back), but I made a mistake with the one-ways and got on the main Brixton road and was heading north to freedom from myself.

It was astonishing to be free. It was seven o'clock in the evening and to celebrate I went into a big pub where they had singers on Saturday nights; it was already filling up with people. How normal, how cheerful they were, a crowd of them, drinking, shouting and talking; the human race! I got a drink and chose a quiet place in a corner and I was taking my first mouthful of the beer, saying to myself: "Here's to yourself, my boy," as though I had just met myself as I used to be. And then, with the glass still at my lips, I saw in a crowd at the other end of the bar Pliny, with his back half-turned. I recognised him by his jug-handle ears, his white hair and the stoop of a tall man. He was not in his dressy clothes but in a shabby suit that made him seem disguised. He was listening to a woman who had a large handbag and had bright blonde hair and a big red mouth who was telling him a joke and she banged him in the stomach with her bag and laughed. Someone near me said: "Lal's on the job early this evening." Lal Drake. All the old stories about Pliny and his woman came back to me and how old Castle of Westbury said that Pliny's mother had told him, when she was saying what a good son he was to her, that the one and only time he had been with a woman he had come home and told her and put his head in her laps and cried "like a child" and promised on the Bible he'd never do such a thing again. Castle swore this was true.

I put down my glass and got out of the pub fast without finishing it. Not because I was afraid of Pliny. Oh no! I drove straight back to Pliny's shop. I rang the bell. The drum started beating a few taps and then a window upstairs opened.

"What do you want?" said Isabel in a whisper.

"I want to see you. Open the door."

"It's locked."

"Get the key."

She considered me for a long time.

"I haven't got one," she said, still in a low voice, so hard to hear that she had to say it twice.

"Where have you been?" she said.

We stared at each other's white faces in the dark. She had missed me!

"You've got a key. You must have," I said. "Somewhere. What about the back door?"

She leaned on the window, her arms on the sill. She was studying my clothes.

"I have something for you," I said. This changed her. She leaned forward trying to see more of me in the dark. She was curious. Today I understand what I did not understand then; she was looking me over minutely, inch by inch—what she could see of me in the sodium light of the street lamp—not because I was strange or unusual—but because I was not. She had been shut up either alone or with Pliny without seeing another soul for so long. He was treating her like one of his collector's pieces, like the Meissen August had said he kept hidden upstairs. She closed the window. I stood there wretched and impatient. I went down the Goods Entrance ready to kick the side door down, break a window, climb in somehow. The side door had no letter box or glass panes, no handle even. I stood in front of it and suddenly it was opened. She was standing there.

"You're *not* locked in," I said.

She was holding a key.

"I found it," she said.

I saw she was telling a lie.

"Just now?"

"No. I know where he hides it," she said lowering her frank eyes.

It was a heavy key with an old piece of frayed used-up string on it.

"Mr Pliny does not like me to show people things," she said. "He has gone to see his sister in Brixton. She is very ill. I can't show you anything."

She recited these words as if she had learned them by heart. It was wonderful to stand so near to her in the dark.

"Can I come in?" I said.

"What do you want?" she said cautiously.

"You," I said.

She raised her chin.

"Are you one of August's men?" she said.

"You know I'm not. I haven't seen August for years."

"Mr Pliny says you are. He said I was never to speak to you again. August was horrible."

"The last I heard he was in prison."

"Yes," she said. "He steals."

This seemed to please her; she forgave him that easily. Then she put her head out of the doorway as if to see if August were waiting behind me.

"He does something else, too," she said.

I remembered the violent quarrel between August and poor Mrs Price when she was drunk in Salisbury—the quarrel about Isabel.

"You ran away," I said.

She shook her head.

"I didn't run away. Mr Pliny fetched me," she said and nodded primly, "in his car. I told you."

Then she said: "Where is the present you were bringing me?"

"It isn't a present," I said. "It's the little figure I bought from you. You didn't charge me enough. Let me in. I want to explain."

I couldn't bring myself to tell her that I had taken advantage of her ignorance, so I said:

"I found out afterwards that it was worth much more than I paid you. I want to give it back to you."

She gave a small jump towards me. "Oh please, please," she said and took me by the hand. "Where is it?"

"Let me come in," I said, "and I will tell you. I haven't got it with me. I'll bring it tomorrow, no not tomorrow, Monday."

"Oh. Please," she pleaded. "Mr Pliny was so angry with me for selling it. He'd never been angry with me before. It was terrible. It was awful."

It had never occurred to me that Pliny would even know she had sold the piece; but now, I remembered the passions of the trade and the stored up lust that seems to pass between things and men like Pliny. He wouldn't forgive. He would be savage.

"Did he do something to you? He didn't hit you, did he?"

Isabel did not answer.

"What did he do?"

I remembered how frantic Pliny had been and how violent he had sounded, when he told me to get out of his shop.

"He cried," she said. "He cried and he cried. He went down on his knees and he would not stop crying. I was wicked to sell it. I am the most precious thing he has. Please bring it. It will make him better."

"Is he still angry?"

"It has made him ill," she said.

"Let me come in," I said.

"Will you promise?"

"I swear I'll bring it," I said.

"For a minute," she said, "but not in the shop."

I followed her down a dark passage into the store and was so close that I could smell her hair.

Pliny crying! At first I took this to be one of Isabel's fancies. Then I thought of tall, clumsy, servant-like Pliny, expert at sales with his long-nosed face pouring out water like a pump, repentant, remorseful, agonised like an animal, to a pretty girl. Why? Just because she had sold something? Isabel loved to sell things. He must have had some other reason. I remembered Castle of Westbury's story. What had he done to the girl? Only a cruel man could have gone in for such an orgy of self-love. He had the long face on which tears would be a blackmail. He would be like a horse crying because it had lost a race.

Yet those tears were memorable to Isabel and she so firmly called him "Mr Pliny." In bed, did she still call him "Mr Pliny"? I have often thought since that she did; it would have given her a power—perhaps cowed him.

At night the cold white-washed store-room was silent under the light of its single bulb and the place was mostly in shadow, only the tops of stacked furniture stood out in the yellow light, some of them like buildings. The foundations of the stacks were tables or chests, desks on which chairs or small cabinets were piled. We walked down alleys between the stacks. It was like walking through a dead, silent city, abandoned by everyone who once lived there. There was the sour smell of upholstery; in one part there was a sort of plaza where two large dining tables stood with their chairs set around and a pile of dessert plates on them. Isabel was walking confidently. She stopped by a dressing-table with a mirror on it next to a group of wardrobes and turning round to face it, she said proudly:

"Mr Pliny gave it all to me. And the shop."

"All of this?"

"When he stopped crying," she said.

And then she turned about and we faced the wardrobes. There were six or seven, one in rosewood and an ugly yellow one and they were so arranged here that they made a sort of alcove or room. The wardrobe at the corner of the alley was very heavy and leaned so that its doors were open in a manner of such empty hopelessness, showing its empty shelves, that it made me uneasy. Someone might have just taken his clothes from it in a hurry, perhaps that very minute, and gone off. He might be watching us. It was the wardrobe with the squeaking door which I had seen the customer open while the woman whom I had thought to be Mrs Pliny stood by. Each piece of furniture seemed to watch—even the small things, like an umbrella stand or a tray left on a table. Isabel walked into the alcove and there was a greeny-grey sofa with a screwed up paper bag of toffees on it and on the floor beside it I saw, of all things, the lancer's helmet and the side drum and the bugle. The yellow light scarcely lit this corner.

"There's your drum," I said.

"This is my house," she said, gaily now. "Do you like it? When Mr Pliny is away I come here in case August's men come . . ."

She looked at me doubtfully when she mentioned that name again.

"And you beat the drum to drive them away?" I said.

"Yes," she said stoutly.

I could not make out whether she was playing the artless chld or not, yet she was a woman of twenty-five at least. I was bewildered.

"You are frightened here on your own, aren't you?"

"No I am not. It's nice."

Then she said very firmly:

"You will come here on Monday and give me the box back?"

I said: "I will if you'll let me kiss you. I love you, Isabel."

"Mr Pliny loves me too," she said.

"Isab . . ." I said. That did move her.

I put my arm round her waist and she let me draw her to me. It was strange to hold her because I could feel her ribs, but her body was so limp and feeble that, loving her as I did, I was shocked and pulled her tightly against me. She turned her head weakly so that I could only kiss her cheek and see only one of her eyes and I could not make out whether she was enticing me, simply curious about my embrace or drooping in it without heart.

"You *are* one of August's men," she said getting away from me. "He used to try and get into my bed. After that I locked my door."

"Isabel," I said. "I am in love with you. I think you love me. Why did you marry a horrible old man like Pliny?"

"Mr Pliny is not horrible," she said. "I love him. He never comes to my room."

"Then he doesn't love you," I said. "Leaving you locked up here. And you don't love him."

She listened in the manner of someone wanting to please, waiting for me to stop.

"He is not a real husband, a real lover," I said.

"Yes, he is," she said proudly. "He takes my clothes off before I go to bed. He likes to look at me. I am the most precious thing he has."

"That isn't love, Isabel," I said.

"It is," she said with warmth. "You don't love me. You cheated me. Mr Pliny said so. And you don't want to look at me. You don't think I'm precious."

I went to take her in my arms again and held her.

"I love you. I want you. You are beautiful. I didn't cheat you. Pliny is cheating you, not me," I said. "He is not with his sister. He's in bed with a woman in Brixton. I saw them in a pub. Everyone knows it."

"No he is not. I *know* he is not. He doesn't like it. He promised his mother," she said.

The voice in which she said this was not her playful voice; the girl vanished and a woman had taken her place and not a distressed woman, not a contemptuous or a disappointed one.

"He worships me," she said and in the squalid store of dead junk she seemed to be illumined by the simple knowledge of her own value and looked at my love as if it were nothing at all.

I looked at the sofa and was so mad that I thought of grabbing her and pulling her down there. What made me hesitate was the crumpled bag of toffees on it. I was as nonplussed and, perhaps, as impotent as Pliny must have been. In that moment of hesitation she picked up her bugle and standing in the aisle, she blew it hard, her cheeks going out full and the noise and echoes seemed to make the shadows jump. I have never heard a bugle call that scared me so much. It killed my desire.

"I told you not to come in," she said. "Go away."

And she walked into the aisle between the furniture, swinging her key to the door.

"Come back," I said as I followed her.

I saw her face in the dressing-table mirror we had passed before, then I saw my own face, red and sweating on the upper lip and my mouth helplessly open. And then in the mirror I saw another face following mine—Pliny's. Pliny must have seen me in the pub.

In that oblong frame of mahogany with its line of yellow inlay, Pliny's head looked winged by his ears and he was coming at me, his head down, his mouth with its yellowing teeth open under the moustache and his eyes stained in the bad light. He looked like an animal. The mirror concentrated him and before I could do more than half turn he had jumped in a clumsy way at me and jammed one of my shoulders against a tall-boy.

"What are you doing here?" he shouted.

The shouts echoed over the store.

"I warned you. I'll get the police on you. You leave my wife alone. Get out. You thought you'd get her on her own and swindle her again."

I hated to touch a white-haired man but, in pain, I shoved him back hard. We were, as I have said, close to the wardrobe and he staggered back so far that he hit the shelves and the door swung towards him so that he was half out of my sight for a second. I kicked the door hard with my left foot and it swung to and hit him in the face. He jumped out with blood on his nose. But I had had time to topple the pile of little cane chairs into the alleyway between us. Isabel saw this and ran round the block of furniture and reached him and when I saw her she was standing with the bugle raised like a weapon in her hand to defend the old man from me. He was wiping his face. She looked triumphant.

"Don't you touch Mr Pliny," she shouted at me. "He's ill."

He *was* ill. He staggered. I pushed my way through the fallen chairs and I picked up one and said: "Pliny, sit down on this." Pliny with the bleeding face glared and she forced him to sit down. He was panting. And then a new voice joined us; the tobacconist came down the alley.

"I heard the bugle," he said. "Anything wrong? Oh Gawd, look at his face. What happened, Pliny? Mrs Pliny, you all right?" And then he saw me. All the native shadiness of the London streets, all the gossip of the neighbourhood came into his face.

"I said to my wife," he said, "something's wrong at Pliny's."

"I came to offer Mr Pliny a piece of Dresden," I said, "but he was out at Brixton seeing his sister, his wife said. He came back and thought I'd broken in and hit himself on the wardrobe."

"You oughtn't to leave Mrs Pliny alone with all this valuable stock, Mr Pliny. Saturday night too," the tobacconist said.

Tears had started rolling down Pliny's cheeks very suddenly when I mentioned Brixton and he looked at me and the tobacconist in panic.

"I'm not interested in Dresden," he managed to say.

Isabel dabbed his face and sent the tobacconist for a glass of water.

"No, dear, you're not," said Isabel.

And to me she said: "We're not interested."

That was the end. I found myself walking in the street. How unreal people looked in the sodium light.

(1974)

DID YOU INVITE ME?

Rachel first met Gilbert at David and Sarah's, or it may have been at Richard and Phoebe's—she could not remember—but she did remember that he stood like a touchy exclamation mark and talked in a shot-gun manner about his dog. His talk jumped so that she got confused; the dog was his wife's dog but was he talking about his dog or his wife? He blinked very fast when he talked of either. Then she remembered what David (or maybe Richard) had told her. His wife was dead. Rachel had a dog, too, but Gilbert was not interested.

The bond between all of them was that they owned small, white stuccoed houses, not quite alike—hers alone, for example, had Gothic churchy windows which, she felt, gave her point—on different sides of the park. Another bond was that they had reached middle life and said nothing about it, except that Gilbert sharply pretended to be younger than the rest of them in order to remind them they had arrived at that time when one year passes into the next unnoticed, leaving among the dregs an insinuation that they had not done what they intended. When this thought struck them they would all—if they had the time—look out of their sedate windows at the park, the tame and once princely oasis where the trees looked womanish on the island in the lake or marched in grave married processions along the avenues in the late summer, or in the winter were starkly widowed. They could watch the weekend crowds or the solitary walkers on the public grass, see the duck flying over in the evenings, hear the keeper's whistle and his shout, "All Out" when the gates of the park closed an hour after sunset; and at night, hearing the animals at the zoo, they could send out silent cries of their own upon the place and evoke their ghosts.

But not Gilbert. His cry would be a howl and audible, a joint howl of himself and this dog he talked about. Rachel had never seen a man so howling naked. "Something must be done about him," she thought every time she met him. Two years ago, Sonia, his famous and chancy wife had died—"on the stage," the headlines in the London newspapers said, which was nearly true—and his eyes were red-rimmed as if she had died yesterday, his angry face was raw with drink or the unjust marks of guilt and grief. He was a tall man, all bones, and even his wrists coming out of a jacket that was too short in the sleeve, seemed to be crying. He had also the look of a man who had decided not to buy another suit in his life, to let cloth go on gleaming with its private malice. It was well known—for he boasted of it himself—that his wife had been much older than he, that they quarrelled continually and that he still adored her.

Rachel had been naked too, in her time when, six or seven years before, she had divorced her husband. Gilbert is "in the middle of it," she thought. She had been "through it" and had "come out of it," and was not hurt or lonely any more and had crowded her life with public troubles. She was married to a newspaper column.

"Something really *must* be done about him," she said at last out loud to David and Sarah, as she tried to follow Gilbert's conversation that was full of traps and false exit lines. For his part, he sniffed when he spoke to them of Rachel.

"Very attractive woman. Very boring. All women are boring. Sonia was a terrible bore sometimes, carrying on, silly cow. What of it? You may have remarked it: I'm a bore. I must go. Thank you Sarah and David, for inviting me and offering me your friendship. You did invite me, didn't you? You did? I'm glad. I have no friends. The friends Sonia and I invited to the house were hers not mine. Old codgers. I must go home and feed her dog."

They watched him go off stiffly, a forty-year-old.

An outsider he was, of course, because of loss. One feels the east wind— she knew that. But it was clear—as she decided to add him to her worries— that he must always have been that. He behaved mechanically, click, click, click, like a puppet or an orphan, homelessness being his vanity. This came out when David had asked Gilbert about his father and mother in her presence. From David's glances at his wife Rachel knew they had heard what he said many times before. Out came his shot, the long lashes of his childish eyes blinking fast.

"Never met the people." He was showing contempt for a wound. He was born in Singapore, he said. One gathered the birth had no connection with either father or mother. She tried to be intelligent about the city.

"Never saw the place," he said. The father became a prisoner of the Japanese; the mother took him to India. Rachel tried to be intelligent about India.

"Don't remember it," he said. "The old girl"—his mother sent him home to schools and holiday schools. He spent his boyhood in camps and dormitories, his army-life in Nissen huts. He was twenty when he really "met" his parents. At the sight of him they separated for good.

No further answers. Life had been doled out to him like spoonfuls of medicine, one at a time; he returned the compliment by doing the same and then erected silences like packs of cards, watching people wait for them to fall down.

How, Rachel asked, did the raw young man come to be married to Sonia, an actress at the top of the tree, fifteen years older than he? "The old girl knew her," he said; she was his mother's friend. Rachel worried away at it. She saw, correctly, a dramatic woman with a clever mouth, a surrogate mother—but a mother astute in acting the part among her scores of grand and famous friends. Rachel had one or two famous friends too, but he snubbed her with his automatic phrase:

"Never met him."

Or

"Never met her."

And then Rachel, again correctly, saw him standing in the doorway of Sonia's drawing-room or bringing drinks perhaps to the crowd, like an uncouth son; those wrists were the wrists of a growing boy who silently jeered at the guests. She heard Sonia dressing him down for his Nissen hut language and his bad manners—which, however, she encouraged. This was her third marriage and it had to be original. That was the heart of the Gilbert problem; Sonia had invented him; he had no innate right to be what he appeared to be.

So Rachel, who happened to be writing an article on broken homes, asked him to come round and have a drink. He walked across the park from his house to hers. At the door he spoke his usual phrase:

"Thank you for inviting me. You did invite me, didn't you? Well, I thank you. We live on opposite sides of the park. Very convenient. Not too near."

He came in.

"Your house is white and your dog is white," he said.

Rachel owned a dog. A very white fox terrier came barking at him on a high, glassy note, showing a ratter's teeth. Rachel was wearing a long pale blue dress from her throat to the tips of her shoes and led him into the sitting-room. He sank into a soft silky sofa with his knees together and politely inspected her as an interesting collection of bones.

"Shall I ever get up from this?" he said patting the sofa. "Silly question. Yes I shall, of course. I have come, shortly I shall go." He was mocking someone's manners. Perhaps hers. The fox terrier which had followed him into the small and sunny room sniffed long at Gilbert's shoes and his trouser legs and stiffened when he stroked its head. The dog growled.

"Pretty head," he said. "I like dogs' heads." He was staring at Rachel's head. Her hair was smooth, neat and fair.

"I remarked his feet on the hall floor, tick, tick, tick. Your hall must be tiled. Mine is carpeted."

"Don't be so aggressive, Sam," said Rachel gravely to the dog.

"Leave him alone," said Gilbert. "He can smell Tom, Sonia's bull terrier. That's who you can smell isn't it? He can smell an enemy."

"Sam is a problem," she said. "Everyone in the street hates you, Sam, don't they? When you get out in the garden you bark and bark, people open their windows and shout at you. You chase cats, you killed the Gregory boy's rabbit and bit the Jackson child. You drive the doctor mad. He throws flower pots at you."

"Stop nagging the poor animal," said Gilbert. And to the dog he said: "Good for you. Be a nuisance. Be yourself. Everyone needs an enemy. Absolutely."

And he said to himself: "She hasn't forgiven her husband." In her long dress she had the composure of the completely smoothed over person who might well have nothing on underneath. Gilbert appreciated this, but she became prudish and argumentative.

"Why do you say 'absolutely,'" she said, seeing a distracting point for discussion here. "Isn't that relative?"

"No," said Gilbert with enjoyment. He loved a row. "I've got an enemy at my office. Nasty little creepy fellow. He wants my job. He watches me. There's a new job going—promotion—and he thinks I want it. So he watches. He sits on the other side of the room and is peeing himself with anxiety every time I move. Peeing himself, yes. If I leave the room he goes to the door to see if I'm going to the director's office. If I do he sweats. He makes an excuse to go to the director to see if he can find out what we've been talking about. When I am working on a scheme he comes over to look at it. If I'm working out costs he stares with agony at the lay-out and the figures. 'Is that Jameson's?' He can't contain himself. 'No, I'm doing my income tax,' I tell him. He's very shocked at my doing that in office hours and goes away relieved. He'll report that to the director. Then a suspicion strikes him when he is half-way back to his desk and he turns round and comes over again panting. He doesn't believe me. 'I'm turning inches into centimetres,' I say. He still doesn't believe me. Poor silly bugger."

He laughed.

"Wasn't that rather cruel?" she said. "Why centimetres?"

"Why not? He wants the French job. Boring little man. Boring office. Yes."

Gilbert constructed one of his long silences. Rachel saw skyscrapers, pagodas, the Eiffel Tower and little men creeping up them like ants. After a while Gilbert went on and the vision collapsed:

"He was the only one who came from the office to Sonia's funeral. He brought his wife—never met her before—and she cried. The only person who did. Yes. He'd never missed a show Sonia was in."

"So he isn't an enemy. Doesn't that prove my point," she said solemnly. Gilbert ignored this.

"They'd never met poor Sonia," he said. And he blinked very fast.

"I never met your wife either, you know," said Rachel earnestly. She hoped he would describe her; but he described her doctors, the lawyers that assemble after death.

"What a farce," he said.

He said: "She had a stroke in the theatre. Her words came out backwards. I wrote to her two husbands. Only one replied. The theatre sent her to hospital in an ambulance—the damn fools. If you go to hospital you die of pneumonia, bloody hospital won't give you enough pillows, you lie flat and you can't get your breath. What a farce. Her brother came and talked, one of those fat men. Never liked the fellow."

She said how terrible it must have been.

"Did she recover her speech? They sometimes do."

"Asked," he said, "for the dog. Called it god."

He got up suddenly from the sofa.

"There! I have got up. I am standing on my feet. I am a bore," he said. "I shall go."

As he left the room the terrier came sniffing at his heels.

"Country dogs. Good ratters. Ought to be on a farm."

She plunged into a confidence to make him stay longer.

"He used to be a country dog. My husband bought him for me when we lived in the country. I know" (she luxuriated in a worry) "how important environment is to animals and I was going to let him stay—but when you are living alone in a city like London—well there are a lot of burglaries here."

"Why did you divorce your husband?" he asked as he opened the front door. "I shouldn't have asked. Bad manners. I apologise. I was rude. Sonia was always on to me about that."

"He went off with a girl at his office," she said staunchly.

"Silly man," said Gilbert looking at the dog. "Thank you. Goodbye. Do we shake hands? You invited me, now it is my turn to invite you. That is the right thing, of course it is. We must do the right thing. I shall."

Weeks passed before Gilbert invited Rachel. There were difficulties. Whatever he decided by day was destroyed by night. At night Sonia would seem to come flying out of the park saying the house had belonged to her.

She had paid for it. She enumerated the furniture item by item. She had the slow, languid walk of her stage appearances as she went suspiciously from room to room, asking what he had done with her fur coats and where her shoes were. "You've given them to some woman." She said he had a woman in the house. He said he asked only David and Sarah; she said she didn't trust Sarah. He pleaded he had kept the dog. When he said that, her ghost vanished saying he starved the poor thing. One night he said to her, "I'm going to ask Rachel, but you'll be there."

"I damn well will," she said. And this became such a dogma that when, at last, he asked Rachel to come, he disliked her.

His house was not so sedate as hers which had been repainted that year—his not. His windows seemed to him—and to her—to sob. There was grit on the frames. When he opened the door to her she noted the brass knocker had not been polished and inside there was the immediate cold odour of old food. The hall and walls echoed their voices and the air was very still. In the sitting-room the seats of the chairs, one could see, had not been sat on for a long time, there was dust on the theatrical wallpaper. Hearing her, Sonia's dog, Tom, came scrabbling the stair carpet and rushed into the room hysterically at both of them, skidding on rugs, snuffling, snorting, whimpering and made at once for her skirts, got under her legs and was driven off on to a sofa of green silk, rather like hers, but now frayed where the dog's claws had caught.

"Off the sofa, Tom," said Gilbert. The dog ignored this and snuffled from its squat nose and gazed from wet eyes that were like enormous marbles. Gilbert picked up a rubber bone and threw it to the dog. Down it came and the racing round the room began again. Rachel held her glass in the air for safety's sake and the dog jumped at it and made her spill whisky on her dress. In this confusion they tried to talk.

"Sonia liked being photographed with Tom," he said.

"I only saw her on the stage once. She was very beautiful," she said. "It must have been twelve years ago. Gielgud and another actor called Slade were in it. Was it Slade? Oh dear! My memory!"

"Her second husband," he said.

He picked up the dog's rubber bone. The dog rushed to him and seized it. Man and dog pulled at the bone.

"You want it. You won't get it," said Gilbert while she seemed to hear her husband say: "Why can't you keep your mouth shut if you can't remember things?" And Gilbert, grinning in his struggle with the dog said:

"Sonia always had Tom to sleep on our bed. He still does. Won't leave it. He's on it even when I come back from the office."

"He sleeps with you?" she said with a shudder.

"I come home. I want someone to talk to."

"What d'you do with him when you go to your office?" The dog pulled and snorted. "The woman who comes in and cleans looks after the dog," he said. And went on: "Your house has three storeys, mine has two, otherwise the same. I've got a basement full of rubbish. I was going to turn it into a flat but Sonia got worse. Futile. Yes, life is futile. Why not sell the damn place. No point. No point in anything. I go to the office, come back, feed the dog and get drunk. Why not? Why go on? Why do you go on? Just habit. No sense in it."

"You do go on," she said.

"The dog," he said.

I must find some people for him to meet. He can't live like this, she thought. It is ghastly.

When she left, he stood on the doorstep and said:

"My house. Your house. They're worth four times what we gave for them. There it is."

She decided to invite him to dinner to meet some people—but who could she ask? He was prickly. She knew dozens of people but, as she thought of them, there seemed, for the first time, to be something wrong with all of them. In the end she invited no one to meet him.

"On a diet, silly cow," he thought when she came to the door but he fell back on his usual phrase as he looked about the empty room.

"Did you invite me? Or shall I go away? You did invite me. Thank you. Thank you."

"I've been in Vienna with the Fladgates. She is a singer. Friends of David and Sarah."

"Fladgates? Never heard of the people," he said. "Sonia insulted someone in Vienna. I was drunk. Sonia never drank anything—that made her insults worse. Did your husband drink?"

"Indeed not."

He sat down on the sofa. The evening—Sonia's time. He expected Sonia to fly in and sit there watching this woman with all her "problems" hidden chastely except for one foot which tipped up and down in her shoes under her long dress. But—to his surprise—Sonia did not come. The terrier sat at Rachel's feet.

"How is your enemy?" she said as they drank. "The man in the office."

"He and his wife asked me to dinner," he said.

"That's kind," she said.

"People are kind," he said. "I've remarked that."

"Does he still watch you?"

"Yes. You know what it was? He thinks I drink too much. He thinks I've got a bottle in my desk. It wasn't the job that was worrying him. We are wrong about people. I am. You are. Everyone is."

When they went in dinner candles were on the table.

"Bloody silly having candles," he said to himself. And when she came in with the soup, he said:

"We had candles. Poor Sonia threw them out of the window once. She had to do it in a play."

The soup was iced and white and there was something in it that he could not make out. But no salt. That's it, he thought, no salt in this woman. Writing about politics and things all day and forgets the salt. The next course was white too, something chopped or minced with something peculiar, goodness knew what. It got into his teeth. Minced newsprint, he thought.

"Poor Sonia couldn't cook at all," he said, pushing his food about, proud of Sonia. "She put dishes on the floor near the stove, terrible muddle and rushed back to hear what people were saying and then an awful bloody stink came from the kitchen. I used to go down and the potatoes had burned dry and Tom had cleared the plates. Bloody starvation. No dinner."

"Oh no!" she said.

"I live on chops now. Yes," he said. "One, sometimes two, every day, say ten a week. Am I being a bore? Shall I go?"

Rachel had a face that had been set for years in the same concerned expression. That expression now fell to pieces from her forehead to her throat. Against her will she laughed. The laugh shook her and was loud; she felt herself being whirled into a helpless state from the toes upwards. Her blood whirled too.

"You laughed!" he shouted. "You did not protest. You did not write an article. You laughed. I could see your teeth. Very good. I've never seen you laugh before."

And the dog barked at them.

"She laughed," he shouted at the dog.

She went out to make coffee, very annoyed at being trapped into laughing. While he waited, the dog sat undecided, ears pricked, listening for her and watching him like a sentry.

"Rats," whispered Gilbert to the dog. It stood up sharply.

"Poor bastard. What a life," he said.

The dog barked angrily at him and when she came in, he said: "I told your dog he ought to be on a farm."

"You said that before," she said. "Let us have coffee next door." They moved into the next room and she sat on the sofa while she poured the coffee.

"Now *you* are sitting on the sofa. I'm in this armchair," he said, thinking of life tactically. "Sonia moved about too. I used to watch her going into a room. Where will she sit next? Damned if I ever got it right. The same in restaurants. Let us sit here, she'd say, and then when the waiter came to her chair, she'd say, 'No, not here. Over there.' Never knew where she was going to settle. Like a fly. She wanted attention. Of course. That was it. Quite right."

"Well," she said coldly, "she was an actress."

"Nothing to do with it," he said. "Woman."

"Nonsense," she said, hating to be called a woman and thought, "It's my turn now."

"My husband," she said, "travelled the whole time. Moscow, Germany, Copenhagen, South Africa, but when he got home he was never still, posing to the animals on the farm, showing off to barns, fences, talking French and German to birds, pretending to be a country gentleman."

"Let the poor man alone," he said. "Is he still alive?"

"I told you," she said. "I won't bore you with it all."

She was astonished to find herself using his word and that the full story of her husband and herself she had planned to tell and which she had told so many people, suddenly lost interest for her. And yet, anyway, she thought, why shouldn't I tell this man about it? So she started, but she made a muddle of it. She got lost in the details. The evening, she saw, was a failure. He yawned.

If there was one thing Rachel could honestly say it was that she had not thought of her husband for years. She had not forgotten but he had become a generality in the busyness of her life. But now, after the evening when Gilbert came to dinner, her husband came to life and plagued her. If an aeroplane came down whistling across the wide London sky, she saw him sitting in it—back from Moscow, Capetown, Copenhagen, descending not upon her, but on another woman. If she took the dog for a run in the park, the cuddling couples on the grass became him and that young girl; if babies screamed in their prams they were his children; if a man threw a ball it was he; if men in white flannels were playing cricket, she wondered if he was among them. She imagined sudden, cold meetings and ran through tirades of hot dialogue. One day she saw a procession of dogs tails up and panting, following a bitch, with a foolish grin of wet teeth in their jaws and Sam rushed after them; she went red in the face shouting at him. And yet she had gone to the park in order to calm herself and to be alone. The worst thing that could happen would be to meet Gilbert, the cause of this, but, like all malevolent causes, he never showed his face. She had wished to do her duty and be sorry for him, but not for him to become a man. She feared she might be on the point of talking about this to a woman, not a woman she knew well—that would be disastrous—but, say, to some woman or girl sitting alone on a park seat or some woman in a shop; also a confidence she would regret all her life. She was touchy in these days and had a row with the doctor who threw flower pots at her dog. She petted the animal. "Your head is handsome," she said, stroking its head, "but why did you go after that silly bitch?" The dog adored her when she said this. "You're vain," she said to it.

Gilbert *did* go to the park but only on Saturdays when the crowds came. He liked seeing the picnics, the litter on the grass; he stood still with pleasure when babies screamed or ice-cream dripped. He grinned at boys throwing water from drinking fountains and families trudging, drunks lying asleep, and fat girls lying half on top of their young men and tickling their faces with grass. "The place is a damn bedroom. Why not? Where else can they go? Lucky, boring people. I've got a bedroom and no one in it."

One Saturday, after three days of rain, he took his dog there and—would you believe it?—there the whole crowd was again, still at it, on the wet grass. The trouble with Sonia was that she thought the park was vulgar and would never go there—went once and never again, hadn't brought the right shoes.

He remarked this to his dog as he let it off its leash. The animal scampered round him in wide circles; came back to him and then raced off again in circles getting wider and wider, until it saw a man with string in his hand trying to fly a kite. The kite was flopping on the ground, rose twenty or thirty feet in the air and then dived again. The dog rushed at the kite, but the man got it up again, higher this time. Gilbert walked towards the man. "Poor devil, can't get it up," he said as he walked. He got near the man and watched his struggles.

Then the kite shot up high and Gilbert watched it raving there until suddenly it swept away higher still. Gilbert said: "Good for him." The boredom of the grey afternoon was sweet. He lit a cigarette and threw the empty packet on the grass and then he found he had lost sight of the dog. When he saw it again it was racing in a straight line towards a group of trees by the lake. It was racing towards another dog. A few yards away from the dog it stopped and pranced. The dog was a terrier and stopped dead, then came forward. They stood sniffing at each other's tails and then jumped round muzzle to muzzle. They were growling, the terrier barked and then the two dogs flew at each other's necks. Their play had turned to a war, their jaws were at each other's necks and ears. Gilbert saw at once it was Rachel's dog, indeed Rachel was running up shouting, "Sam. Sam." The fight was savage and Tom had his teeth in.

"Stop them," Rachel was shouting. "Stop them. They'll kill each other. He's got him by the throat."

And then she saw Gilbert: "You!"

Gilbert was enjoying the fight. He looked around and picked up a stick that had fallen from a tree.

"Stop them," she shouted.

"Get yours by the collar, I'll get mine," he shouted to her.

"I can't. Sam! Sam! They're bleeding."

She was dancing about in terror, trying to catch Sam by the legs.

"Not by the legs. By the collar, like this, woman," he shouted. "Don't put your arms round him, you idiot. Like this. Stop dancing about."

He caught Tom by the collar and lifted him as both dogs hung on to each other.

"You're strangling him. I can't, I can't," she said. Gilbert brought his stick down hard on the muzzles of the dogs, just as she was trying to grasp Sam again.

"You'll kill them."

He brought the stick down hard again. The dogs yelped with pain and separated.

"Get the leash on," he said, "you fool."

Somehow she managed it and the two dogs now strained to get at each other. The terrier's white neck and body were spotted with blood and smears of it were on her hands.

Gilbert wiped their spit off his sleeve.

They pulled their dogs yards apart and she stared at him. It infuriated her that he was laughing at her with pure pleasure. In their stares they saw each other clearly and as they had never seen each other before. To him, in her short skirt and her shoes muddied by the wet grass, her hair disordered and the blood risen to her pale face, she was a woman. The grass had changed her. To her he was not a pitiable arrangement of widower's tricks, but a man on his own. And the park itself changed him in her eyes; in the park he, like everyone else there, seemed to be human. The dogs gave one more heave to get at each other.

"Lie down, Sam," Gilbert shouted.

She lifted her chin and was free to hate him for shouting at her animal.

"Look after yours. He's dangerous," she called back, angered by the friendliness of his face.

"Damn silly dogs enjoyed it. Good for them. Are you all right? Go up to the kiosk and get a drink—if I may I'll follow you up—see you're all right."

"No, no," she put out a loud moan—far too loud. "He's bleeding. I'll take him home," and she turned to look at the park. "What a mess people make." And now walking away shouted a final accusation: "I didn't know you brought your dog here."

He watched her go. She turned away and dragged the struggling terrier over the grass uphill from the lake. He watched her walking unsteadily.

"Very attractive figure," he thought. "Silly cow. Better go home and ring her up."

He turned and on the way back to his house he could still see her dancing about on the grass and shouting. He went over the scene again and repeated his conclusion. "She's got legs. Never seen them before. A woman. Must be. Full of life." She was still dancing about as he put a bowl of water down for the dog. It drank noisily and he gave it another bowl and then he washed the dog's neck and looked at its ear. "Nothing much wrong with you," he said. He fed the animal and soon it jumped on the sofa and was instantly snorting, and whimpering and shaking into sleep.

"I must ring her up, yes, that is what I must do."

But a neighbour answered and said Rachel had gone to the vet and she had come back in a terrible state and had gone to bed with one of her migraines.

"Don't bother her," he said. "I just rang to ask how the dog was."

Rachel was not in bed. She was standing beside the neighbour and when the call was over, she said:

"What did he say?"

"He asked about the dog."

"Is that all?"

"Yes."

This flabbergasted her.

In the middle of the night she woke up and when her stupefaction passed she damn well wished he was there so that she could say, "It didn't occur to you to apologise. I don't like being called a fool. You assume too much. Don't think I care a damn about *your* dog." She was annoyed to feel a shudder pass through her. She got out of bed and looking out of her window at the black trees, saw herself racing across the park to his house and pulling that dog of his off his bed. The things she said! The language she used! She kicked the dog out of the room and it went howling downstairs. She went back to bed weak and surprised at herself because, before she realised it, Sam became Tom in her hand. She lay there stiff, awake, alone. Which dog had she kicked? Sam or Tom?

In his house Gilbert locked up, poured himself a strong whisky, then a second, then a third. Uncertain of whom he was addressing, Rachel or Sonia, he said, "Silly cow," and blundered drunkish to bed. He woke up at five very cold. No dog. The bed was empty. He got out of bed and went downstairs. For the first time since Sonia had died the dog was asleep on the sofa. He had forgotten to leave his door open.

In the morning he was startled to hear Sonia's voice saying to him in her stage voice: "Send her some flowers. Ask her to dinner."

So he sent the flowers and when Rachel rang to thank him he asked her to dinner—at a restaurant.

"Your house. My house," he said. "Two dogs."

There was a long silence and he could hear her breath bristling.

"Yes, I think it has to be somewhere else," she said. And added: "As you say, we have a problem."

And after this dinner and the next, she said:

"There are so many problems. I don't really know you."

They talked all summer and people who came regularly to the restaurant made up stories about them and were quite put out when in October they stopped coming. All the proprietor had heard was that they had sold their houses—in fact he knew what they'd got for them. The proprietor had bought Sonia's dog. There was a terrier, too, he said, but he didn't know what had happened to that.

(1974)

THE MARVELLOUS GIRL

The official ceremony was coming to an end. Under the sugary chandeliers of what had once been the ballroom of the mansion to which the Institute had moved, the faces of the large audience yellowed and aged as they listened to the last speeches and made one more effort of chin and shoulder to live up to the gilt, the brocaded panels of the walls and the ceiling where cherubs, clouds and naked goddesses romped. Oh, to be up there among them, thought the young man sitting at the back, but on the platform the director was passing from the eternal values of art to the "gratifying presence of the Minister," to "Lady Brigson's untiring energies," the "labours of Professor Exeter and his panel" in the Exhibition on the floor below. When he was named the Professor looked with delight at the audience and played with a thin gold chain he had taken from his pocket. The three chandeliers gave a small united flicker as if covering the yawns of the crowd. The young man sitting at the back stared at the platform once more and then, with his hands on his knees, his elbows out and his eye turned to the nearest door got ready to push past the people sitting next to him and to be the first out—to get out before his wife who was on the platform with the speakers. By ill-luck he had run into her before the meeting and had been trapped into sitting for nearly two hours, a spectator of his marriage that had come to an end. His very presence there seemed to him an unsought return to one of those patient suicides he used to commit, day after day, out of drift and habit.

To live alone is to expose oneself to accident. He had been drawing on and off all day in his studio and not until the evening had he realised that he had forgotten to eat. Hunger excited him. He took a bus down to an Italian restaurant. It was one of those places where the proprietor came out from time to time to perform a private ballet. He tossed pancakes almost up to the ceiling and then dropped them into a blaze of brandy in the pan—a diversion that often helped the young man with the girls he now sometimes took there. The proprietor was just at the blazing point when two women came into the restaurant in their winter coats and stood still, looking as if they were on fire. The young man quickly gulped down the last of a few coils of spaghetti and stood up and wiped his mouth. The older, smaller of the two women was his wife and she was wearing a wide hat of black fur that made her look shorter than he remembered her. Free of him, she had become bizarre and smaller. Even her eyes had become smaller and, like mice, saw him at once and gave him an alert and busy smile. With her was the tall, calm girl with dark blue eyes from their office at the Institute, the one she excitedly called "the marvellous girl," the "only one I have ever been able to get on with."

More than two years had gone by since he and his wife had lived together. The marriage was one of those prickly friendships that never succeeded—to *his* astonishment, at any rate—in turning into love, but are kept going by curiosity. It had become at once something called "our situation;" a duet by a pair of annoyed hands. What kept them going was an exasperated interest in each other's love affairs, but even unhappiness loses its tenderness and fascination. They broke. At first they saw each other occasionally, but now rarely; except at the Institute where his drawings were shown. They were connected only by the telephone wire which ran under the London pavements and worried its way under the window ledge of his studio. She would ring up, usually late at night.

"I hope it's all right," she'd say wistfully. "Are you alone?"

But getting nothing out of him on that score, she would become brisk and ask for something out of the debris of their marriage, for if marriages come to an end, paraphernalia hangs on. There were two or three divans, a painted cupboard, some rugs rolled up, boxes of saucepans and frying pans, lamps—useful things stored in the garage under his studio. But, as if to revive an intimacy, she always asked for some damaged object; she had a child's fidelity to what was broken: a lampshade that was scorched, an antique coal bucket with one loose leg, or a rug that had been stained by her dog Leopold whose paws were always in trouble. Leopold's limp had come to seem to the young man, the animal's response to their hopeless marriage. The only sound object she had ever wanted—and got into a temper about it—was a screwdriver that had belonged to her father whom she detested.

Now, in the restaurant, she put up a friendly fight from under the wide-brimmed hat.

"I didn't know you still came here," she said.

"I come now and again."

"You must be going to the opening at the Institute."

"No," he said. "I haven't heard of it."

"But I sent you a card," she said. "You must go. Your drawings are in the Exhibition. It's important."

"Three drawings," said the girl warmly.

"Come with us," his wife said.

"No. I can't. I'm just going to pay my bill."

A lie, of course. She peered at his plate as if hoping to read his fortune, to guess at what he was up to. He turned to the girl and said with feeling:

"Are you better now?"

"I haven't been ill," said the girl.

"You said she'd been in hospital," he said to his wife.

"No I didn't," she said. "She went to Scotland for a wedding."

A quite dramatic look of disappointment on the young man's face made the girl laugh and look curiously at him. He had seen her only two or three times and knew nothing much about her, but she was indeed "marvellous." She was not in hospital, she was beautiful and alive. Astounding. Even, in a bewildering way, disappointing.

The waiter saved him and moved them away.

"Enjoy yourselves," said the young man. "I'm going home."

"Goodbye," the girl turned to wave to him as she followed his wife to the table.

It was that "goodbye" that did for him. It was a radiant "goodbye," half laughing, he had seen her tongue and her even teeth as she laughed. Simply seeing him go had brought life to her face. He went out of the restaurant and in the leathery damp of the street he could see the face following him from lamp to lamp. "Goodbye, goodbye," it was still saying. And that was when he changed his mind. An extraordinary force pulled his scattered mind together; he determined to go to the meeting and to send to her, if he could see her in the crowd, a blinding, laughing, absolute Goodbye for ever, as radiant as hers.

Now, as he sat there in the crowded hall there was no sign of her. He had worn his eyes out looking for her. She was not on the platform with his wife and the speakers of course. The director, whose voice suggested chocolate, was still thanking away when, suddenly, the young man did see her. For the light of the chandeliers quivered again, dimmed to a red cindery glow and then went out, and as people gasped "Oh," came on strongly again and one or two giggled. In that flash when everyone looked up and around, there was a gap between the ranks of heads and shoulders and he saw her brown hair and her broad pale face with its white rose look, its good-humoured chin and the laugh beginning on it. She turned round and she saw him as he saw her. There are glances that are collisions, scattering the air between like glass. Her expression was headlong in open conniving joy at the sight of things going wrong. She was sitting about ten rows in front of him but he was not quick enough to wave for now, "plonk," the lights went out for good. The audience dropped *en masse* into the blackness, the hall sank gurgling to the bottom of the sea and was swamped. Then outside a door banged, a telephone rang, feet shuffled and a slow animal grunting and chattering started everywhere and broke into irreverent squeals of laughter.

Men clicked on their lighters or struck matches and long anarchic shadows shot over the walls. There was the sudden heat of breath, wool, fur and flesh as if the audience had become one body.

"Keep your seats for a moment," the director said from the darkness, like God.

Now was the time to go. Darkness had wiped out the people on the platform. For the young man they had become too intimate. It had seemed to him that his wife who sat next to her old lover, Duncan, was offering too lavish a sight of the new life she was proposing to live nowadays. Duncan was white-faced and bitter and they were at their old game of quarrelling publicly under their breath while she was tormenting him openly by making eyes at the Professor who was responding by making his gold chain spin round faster and faster. The wife of the director was studying all this and preparing to defend her husband in case the longing in those female eyes went beyond the Professor and settled on *him*.

How wrong I was about my wife's character, the young man thought. Who would have thought such wistful virginity could become so rampant. The young man said: "Pull yourself together, Duncan. Tell her you won't stand any more of it. Threaten her with Irmgard . . ."

Darkness had abolished it all.

It was not the darkness of the night outside. This darkness had no flabby wet sky in it. It was dry. It extinguished everything. It stripped the eyes of sight; even the solid human rows were lumped together invisibly. One was suddenly naked in the dark from the boots upwards. One could feel the hair on one's body growing and in the chatter one could hear men's voices grunting, women's voices fast, breath going in and out, muscles changing, hearts beating. Many people stood up. Surrounded by animals like himself he too stood up, to hunt with the pack, to get out. Where was the girl? Inaccessible, known, near but invisible. Someone had brought a single candle to the desk at which the director stood like a spectre. He said:

"It would seem, ladies and gentlemen, that there has been a failure of the . . . I fear the . . . hope to procure the . . ."

There was a rough animal laugh from the audience and, all standing up now, they began to shuffle slowly for the doors.

"Get out of my way. Please let me pass," the young man shouted in a stentorian voice which no one heard for he was shouting inside himself. "I have got to get to a girl over there. I haven't seen her for nearly a year. I've got to say 'Goodbye' to her for the last time."

And the crowd stuck out their bottoms and their elbows, broadened their backs and grew taller all around him, saying:

"Don't push."

A man, addressing the darkness in an educated voice, said: "It is remarkable how calm an English crowd is. One saw it in the Blitz."

The young man knocked over a chair in the next row and in the next, shoving his way into any gap he could find in the clotted mass of fur and wool, and muttering:

"I've only spoken to her three times in my life. She is wearing blue and has a broad nose. She lives somewhere in London—I don't know where—all I know is that I thought she was ill but it turns out that she went to a wedding in Scotland. I heard she is going to marry a young man in Canada. Think of a girl like that with a face as composed as a white rose, but a rose that can laugh—taking her low voice to Canada and lying at night among thousands of fir trees and a continent of flies and snow. I have got to get to the door and catch her there and say 'Goodbye.'"

He broke through four rows of chairs, trod on feet and pushed, but the crowd was slow and stacked up solid. Hundreds of feet scraped. Useless to say to them:

"A fox is among you. I knew when I first saw this girl that she was to be dreaded. I said just now in a poetic way that her skin is the colour of a white rose, but it isn't. Her hair has the gloss of a young creature's, her forehead is wide and her eyebrows are soft and arching, her eyes are dark blue and her lips warm and helpless. The skin is really like bread. A marvellous girl—everyone says so—but the sure sign of it is that when I first saw her I was terrified of her. She was standing by an office window watching people in the street below and talking on the telephone and laughing and the laughter seemed to swim all over her dress and her breasts seemed to join in and her waist, even her long young legs that were continuing the dance she had been at—she was saying—the night before. It was when she turned and saw me that my sadness began.

"My wife was there—it was her office—and she said to me in a whisper: " 'She is marvellous, isn't she? The child enjoys herself and she's right. But what fools girls are. Sleep with all the boys you like, don't get married yet, it's a trap, I keep telling her.'

"I decided never to go to that office again."

———

The crowd shuffled on in the dark. He was choking in the smell of fur coats, clamouring to get past, to get to the door, angrily begging someone to light one more match—"What? Has the world run out of matches and lighters?"—so that he could see her, but they had stopped lighting matches now. He wanted to get his teeth into the coat of a large broad woman in front of him. He trod on her heels.

"I'm sorry," he wanted to say. "I'm just trying to say 'Goodbye' to someone. I couldn't do it before—think of my situation. I didn't care—it didn't matter to me—but there was trouble at the office. My wife had broken with that wretched man Duncan who had gone off with a girl called Irmgard and when my wife heard of it she made him throw Irmgard over and took him back and once she'd got him she took up with the Professor—you saw him twiddling his gold chain. In my opinion it's a surprise that the Exhibition ever got going, what with the Professor and Duncan playing Cox and Box in the office. But I had to deliver my drawings. And so I saw this girl a second time. I also took a rug with me, a rug my wife had asked for from the debris. Oh yes, I've got debris.

"The girl got up quickly from her desk when she saw me. I say *quickly*. She was alone and my sadness went. She pointed to the glass door at the end of the room.

" 'There's a Committee meeting. She's in there with her husband and the others.'

"I said—and this will make you laugh Mrs Whatever-your-name-is, but please move on—I said:

" 'But I am her husband,' I said.

"With what went on in that office how could the girl have known? I laughed when I said this, laughing at myself. The girl did not blush; she studied me and then she laughed too. Then she took three steps towards me, almost as if she was running—I counted those steps—for she came near enough to touch me on the sleeve of my raincoat. Soft as her face was she had a broad strong nose. In those three steps she became a woman in my eyes, not a vision, not a sight to fear, a friendly creature, well-shaped.

" 'I ought to have known by your voice—when you telephone,' she said.

"Her mistake made her face shine.

" 'Is the parcel for the Exhbition?' she said.

"I had put it on a chair.

" 'No, it's a rug. It weighs a ton. It's Leopold's rug.'

" 'I've got to go,' I said. 'Just say it's Leopold's. Leopold is a dog.'

" 'Oh,' she said. 'I thought you meant a friend.'

" 'No. Leopold wants it, apparently. I've got a lot of rugs. I keep them in the garage at my studio. You don't want a rug, do you? As fast as I get rid of them some girl comes along and says, "How bare your floor is. It needs a rug," and brings me one. I bet when I get back I'll find a new one. Or, I could let you have a box of saucepans, a Hoover, a handsaw, a chest of drawers, firetongs, a towel rail . . .'

"I said this to see her laugh, to see her teeth and her tongue again and to see her body move under its blue dress which was light blue on that day. And to show her what a distance lay between her life and mine.

" 'I've got to go,' I said again but at the door I said,

" 'Beds too. When you get married. All in the garage.'

"She followed me to the door and I waved back to her."

To the back of the fur-coated woman he said, "I can be fascinating. It's a way of wiping oneself out. I wish you'd wipe yourself out and let me pass. I shall never see her again."

And until this night he had not seen her again. He started on a large design which he called *The Cornucopia*. It was, first of all, a small comic sketch of a dustbin which contained chunks of the rubbish in his garage—very clever and silly. He scrapped it and now he made a large design and the vessel was rather like the girl's head but when he came to drawing the fruits of the earth they were fruits of geometry—hexagons, octagons, cubes, with something like a hedgehog on top, so he made the vessel less like a girl's head; the thing drove him mad the more he worked on it.

September passed into October in the parks and once or twice cats on the glass roof of the studio lost their balance and came sliding down in a screech of claws in the hurly-burly of love.

One night his wife telephoned him.

"Oh God. Trouble," he said when he heard her plaintive voice. He had kept out of her way for months.

"Is it all right? Are you alone?" she said. "Something awful has happened. Duncan's going to get married again. Irmgard has got her claws into him. I rang Alex—he always said I could ring—but he won't come. Why am I rejected? And you remember that girl—she's gone. The work piles up."

"To Canada?" he said.

"What on earth makes you say that?" she said in her fighting voice.

"You said she was."

"You're always putting words into my mouth. She's in hospital."

"Ill," he said. "How awful. Where is she?"

"How do I know?" she said. "Leopold," and now she was giggling. "Leopold's making a mess again. I must ring off."

"I'm sorry," he said.

Ill! In hospital! The picture of the girl running towards him in the office came back to him and his eyes were smeared with tears. He felt on his arms and legs a lick of ice and a lick of fire. His body filled with a fever that passed and then came back so violently that he lost his breath. His knees had gone as weak as string. He was in love with the girl. The love seemed to come up from events thousands of years old. The girl herself he thought was not young but ancient. Perhaps Egyptian. The skin of her face was not rose-like, nor like bread, but like stone roughened by centuries. "I am feeling love," he said, "for the whole of a woman for the first time. No other woman exists. I feel love not only for her face, her body, her voice, her hands and feet but for the street she lives in, the place she was born, her dresses and stockings, her bus journeys, her handbags, her parties, her dances. I don't know where she is. How can I find out? Why didn't I realise this before?"

Squeezed like a rag between the crowd he got to the doorway and there the crowd bulged and carried him through it backwards because he was turning to look for her. Outside the door was an ambitious landing. The crowd was cautiously taking the first steps down the long sweep of this staircase. There was a glimmer of light here from the marble of the walls and that educated man gripped his arm and said, "Mind the steps down," and barred the young man's way. He fought free of the grip and stood against the wall. "Don't be a damn fool," said the educated man, waving his arms about. "If anyone slips down there, the rest of you will pile on top of them." The man now sounded mad. "I saw it in the war. A few at a time. A few at a time," he screamed. And the young man felt the man's spit on his face. The crowd passed him like mourners, indecipherable, but a huge woman turned on him and held him by the sleeves with both hands. "Thornee! Thornee! Where are you? You're leaving me," she whimpered. "Dear girl," said a man behind her. "I am here." She let go, swung round and collided with her husband and grabbed him. "You had your arm round that woman," she said. They faded past. The young man looked for a face. Up the stairs, pushing against the procession going down, a man came up sidling against the wall. Every two or three steps he shouted, "Mr Zagacheck?" Zagacheck, Zagacheck, Zagacheck came nearer and suddenly a mouth bawled into the young man's face with a blast of heavily spiced breath.

"Mr Zagacheck?"

"I am not Mr Zagacheck," said the young man in a cold clear voice and as he said it the man was knocked sideways. A woman took the young man's hand and said:

"Francis!" and she laughed. She had named him. It was the girl, of course. "Isn't this wild? Isn't it marvellous? I saw you. I've been looking for you," she said.

"I have been looking for you."

He interlaced his fingers with her warm fingers and held her arm against his body.

"Are you with your wife?" she said.

"No," he said.

She squeezed his hand, she lifted it and held it under her arm.

"Are you alone?" he said.

"Yes."

"Good," he said. "I thought you'd gone." Under her arm he could feel her breast. "I mean for good, left the country. I came to say 'Goodbye.'"

"Oh yes!" she said with enthusiasm and rubbed herself against him. "Why didn't you come to the office?"

He let go of her hand and put his arm round her waist.

"I'll tell you later. We'll go somewhere."

"Yes!" she said again.

"There's another way out. We'll wait here and then slip out by the back way."

The crowd pressed against them. And then, he heard his wife's voice, only a foot away from him. She was saying: "I'm not making a scene. It's you. I wonder what has happened to the girl."

"I don't know and I don't care," the man said. "Stop trying to change the subject. Yes or no? Are you?"

The young man stiffened: "This is the test. If the girl speaks the miracle crashes."

She took his arm from her waist and gripped his hand fiercely. They clenched, sticking their nails into each other, as if trying to wound. He heard one of the large buttons on his wife's coat click against a button of his coat. She was there for a few seconds; it seemed to him as long as their marriage. He had not been so close to his wife for years. Then the crowd moved on, the buttons clicked again and he heard her say:

"There's only Leopold there."

In a puff of smoke from her cigarette she vanished. The hands of the girl and Francis softened and he pressed hard against her.

"Now," he whispered. "I know the way."

They sidled round the long wall of the landing, passing a glimmering bust—"Mr Zagacheck," he said—and came to the corner of a corridor, long and empty, faintly lit by a tall window at the end. They almost ran down it, hand in hand. Twice he stopped to try the door of a room. A third door opened.

"In here," he said.

He pulled her into a large dark room where the curtains had not been drawn, a room that smelled of new carpet, new paint and new furniture. There was the gleam of a desk. They groped to the window. Below was a square with its winter trees and the headlights of cars playing upon them and the crowd scattering across the roads. He put his arms round her and kissed her on the mouth and she kissed him. Her hands were as wild as his.

"You're mad," she said. "This is the director's room," as he pushed her on to the sofa but when his hands were on the skin of her leg, she said, "Let's go."

"When did you start to love me?" he said.

"I don't know. Just now. When you didn't come. I don't know. Don't ask me. Just now, when you said you loved me."

"But before?"

"I don't know," she said.

And then the lights in the building came on and the lights on the desk and they got up, scared, hot-faced, hot-eyed, hating the light.

"Come on. We must get out," he said.

And they hurried from the lighted room to get into the darkness of the city.

(1974)

THE VICE-CONSUL

Under the blades of the wide fan turning slowly in its Yes-No tropical way, the vice-consul sloped in his office, a soft and fat man, pink as a ham, the only pink man in the town, and pimpled by sweat. He was waiting for the sun to go down into the clouds over the far bank of the estuary, ten miles wide here, and to put an end to a bad week. He had been plagued by the officers and crew of a Liverpool ship, the *Ivanhoe*, smoking below in the harbour. There was trouble about shipping a puma.

His Indian clerk put his head in at the door and said in the whisper of the tropics, "Mr McDowell's here."

Years at this post on the river had reduced the vice-consul's voice also to the same sort of whisper, but he had a hoarseness that gave it rank. He believed in flying off the handle and showing authority by using allusions which his clerk could not understand.

"Not the bloody Twenty-third Psalm from that blasted tramp again," he said and was glad McDowell heard it as he pushed in earnestly after the clerk. McDowell was a long-legged man with an unreasonable chin and emotional knees.

"I've brought Felden's licence," he said.

"I ought to have had it a week ago," said the vice-consul. "Have you got the animal aboard yet? It was on the dock moaning away all day. You could hear it up here."

"We've got it on deck," said McDowell.

"Typical hunter," said the vice-consul, "thinking he could ship it without a licence. They've no feeling for animals and they're liars too."

"No hearts," said McDowell.

At this low hour at the end of the day, the vice-consul did not care to have a ship's officer trump his own feelings.

It was part of the vice-consul's martyrdom during his eight years at the port that he was, so to say, the human terminus on whom hunters, traders, oilmen, television crews, sailors whose minds had been inflated by dealing with too much geography, dumped their boasts. Nature in the shape of thousands of miles of jungle, flat as kale, thousands of miles of river, tributaries, drifting islands of forest rubbish, not to mention millions of animals, snakes, bloodsucking fish, swarms of migrating birds, butterflies and biting insects, had scared them and brought them down to the river to unload their fantasies.

"Take your boa constrictor..." they began. "Take your alligator... Take your marching ant..."

Now he had to "take" a man called Felden who had tried to stuff him up with the tale that his fourteen-year-old son had caught the beast on his fishing line in a backwater above Manaos.

The vice-consul was a sedentary man and longed to hear a fact. "When do you sail?" he said when McDowell sat down on an upright chair which was too small for him.

"The day after tomorrow," said McDowell.

"I can't say I'll be sorry to see you lot go," said the vice-consul, making his usual speech to departing sailors. "I'd like to know where the hell your company gets its crews."

"I'm from Belfast," said McDowell, placing his hands on those knees.

"Oh, nothing personal," said the vice-consul. He stamped the licence, pushed it across his desk and stood up, but McDowell did not move. He leaned forward and said, "Would you do me a favour?"

"What favour?" said the vice-consul, offended.

McDowell started to caress his knees as if to get their help. "Would you be able to recommend a dentist in the town?" he said.

The vice-consul sat down, made a space on his desk and said, "Well, that's a change. I thought you were going to tell me you had got yourself clapped like the rest of your crew and wanted a doctor. Dentist? Afraid not. There isn't a dentist in the place, not one I'd recommend, anyway. You've been here three weeks and can see for yourself. Half the population have no teeth at all. None of the women, anyway. Go down the street, and if you're not careful, you can walk straight down their throats."

McDowell nodded. The vice-consul wanted more than a nod.

"It stands to reason," he said, expanding. "What do they get to eat? Dried meat and manioc covered in bird droppings, fish that tastes of newspaper from the bloody river. No fresh milk, no fresh meat, no fresh vegetables—everything has to be flown in and they can't afford it. It would kill them if they could."

McDowell shook his head and kept his knees still. "Catholic country," he said.

"No topsoil," said the vice-consul, putting on a swagger. "If you've got a pain in the jaw, I'm sorry. Take my advice and do what I do. Get on the next plane to Miami. Or Puerto Rico if you like. It'll cost you a penny or two but it's the only way. Sorry for you. Painful."

"Oh," said McDowell, sitting back like an idol. "My teeth are all right," he said.

"Then what do you want a dentist for?"

"It's my dentures," McDowell said, gleaming as he made the distinction.

"All right—dentures," said the vice-consul.

"They've gone. Stolen."

The vice-consul looked at McDowell for a long time. The jaws did not move, so he turned sideways and now studied McDowell, screwing up one annoyed eye. The man swallowed.

"Mr McDowell," he said, taking the syllables one by one. "Are you feeling the heat? Just give your mouth a tap. If I'm not mistaken, you're wearing them."

McDowell let his arms fall to his sides and parted his lips: a set of teeth gleamed as white and righteous as a conjuring trick. "I never sail without me spares," he said.

The vice-consul wasn't going to stand funny business from British subjects. He had an air for this.

"Very wise," he said. "You fellows are always getting your teeth knocked out by your pals. Makes you careful, I suppose. What do you want me to do? You've got a captain, haven't you?" He became suspicious. "I suppose you're not thinking of Filing an Official Complaint," he said, pulling a form out of his drawer, waving it at McDowell and putting it back, "because I can tell you, officially, that who pinches what from whom on the bloody Ivanhoe is no concern of mine, unless it's connected with mutiny, wounding, murder or running guns."

The vice-consul knew this kind of speech by heart.

The sun had floundered down into the clouds; he shouted to his clerk to put on the light but switched it on himself. He decided to match McDowell on the meaning of words.

"You said 'stole,' McDowell. You must have some prize thieves in your crew. But will you tell me how you get a set of dentures out of a man's head against his will, even when he's asleep, unless he's drugged or tied up. Were you drunk?"

"I've never touched a drop in my life," said McDowell.

"I suppose not," said the vice-consul coldly.

"I took them out myself. I always put my dentures in a glass."

"So I should hope," said the vice-consul. "Filthy leaving them in. Dangerous too. What else did they take? Watch? Wallet? Glasses?"

McDowell spoke carefully, picking over the peculiarity of an austere and personal case. "Only my dentures," he said. "It wasn't the crew. I don't mix with them. They read magazines. They never think. I wasn't aboard," he said softly, adding to his mystery. "It wasn't at night. I was ashore. In the afternoon. Off duty."

The Indian clerk put his head in at the door and looked anxiously from McDowell to the vice-consul.

"What do you want now? Can't you see I'm busy?" said the vice-consul. The man's head disappeared and he shut the door.

McDowell stretched his long arms and placed his hands on his knees and his fingers began to drag at his trousers. "I saw it with my own eyes," he said. "I saw this girl with them. When the rain started."

"What girl?" the vice-consul said, lighting a cigar and putting a haze of smoke between himself and his torment. "The rainy season started six weeks ago," he swaggered. "You get your thunderstorm every afternoon. They come in from the west and build up over the river at two o'clock to the minute and last till ten past three. You can set your watch by them."

The vice-consul owned the climate.

"Tropical rain," he said grandly, "not the drizzle you get in Belfast. The rain comes down hot, straight out of the kettle, floods the streets and dries up in ten minutes, not a sign of it except the damn trees grow a foot higher. The trouble is that it doesn't clear the air: the heat is worse afterwards. You feel you're breathing—I don't know—boiled stair carpet my wife says, but that's by the way." He waved at the smoke. "You'll tear the knees of those trousers of yours if you don't leave them alone."

A dressy man, he pointed his cigar at them. McDowell's knees stuck out so far that the vice-consul, who was a suspicious man, felt that they were making a displeasing personal claim on him. They indeed gave a jump when McDowell shouted in a voice that had the excitement of sudden fever, "I can stand thunder. But I can't stand lightning, sheet or forked. It brings my dinner up. It gets under your armpits. A gasometer went up in Liverpool when I was a boy and was blown blazing across the Mersey—"

"I thought you said you came from Belfast," said the vice-consul. "Lightning never bothers me."

"There was this thunderbolt," said McDowell, ignoring him, and his voice went to a whisper. "I'm in the entrance of this hotel, looking at the alligator handbags to take one home for my wife and I've just picked one up and down comes this bolt, screaming behind my back, with a horrible violet flame, and sends me flying headfirst up the passage. There's a girl there, polishing the floor, and all the lights go out. The next thing, I'm in an open doorway, I'm pitching headfirst on to a bed in the room and I get my head under the clothes. It's like the end of the world and I'm praying into the pillow. I think I am dead, don't I?"

"I don't know," said the vice-consul coldly. "But what do you do at sea? And where was this place?"

"It's natural at sea," said McDowell, calming down. "The Columbus. Yes, it would be the Columbus."

"Never heard of it," said the vice-consul.

"I don't know how long I am there, but when it gets quieter I look up, the lightning is going on and off in the window and that's when I see this girl standing by the mirror—"

"The one who was polishing the floor, I suppose," said the vice-consul with contentment.

"No," said McDowell, "this one was in the bed when I fell on it, on top of her, I told you."

"You didn't. You pulled her in," said the vice-consul.

McDowell stopped, astonished, but went on, "Standing by the mirror, without a stitch of clothing on her. Terrible. She takes my dentures out of the glass, and the next thing, she opens her mouth wide and she's trying to fit them, this way and that, to her poor empty gums."

"You couldn't see all that in a flash of lightning. You must have switched the light on," said the vice-consul.

McDowell slapped his knee and sat back in a trance of relief. "You're right," he said gratefully. "Thank God you reminded me. I wouldn't want to tell a lie. The sight of her with her poor empty mouth destroyed me. I'll never forget it. It'd break a man's heart."

"Not mine," said the vice-consul. "It's disgusting. Shows ignorance too. No two human jawbones are alike."

"The pitiful ignorance, you're right!" said McDowell. "I called out to her, 'Careful what you're doing! You might swallow them. Put them back in the glass and come back to bed.'"

The tropical hoarseness left the vice-consul's voice. "Ah," he shouted and put his cigar down. "I thought we'd come to it. In plain English, you had come ashore to commit fornication."

"I did not," said McDowell, shocked. "Her sister works for the airline."

"Oh, it's no business of mine. I don't care what you do, but you were in bed with that girl. You said so yourself. But why in God's name did you take your dentures out? In the middle of the afternoon?"

McDowell was even more shocked. He sat back sternly in his chair. "It would have looked hardly decent," he said, "I mean on an occasion like that, for any man to keep his teeth in when a poor girl had none of her own. It was politeness. You'd want to show respect. I've got my principles."

He became confident and said, "My dentures have gold clips. Metal attracts lightning—I mean, if you had your mouth open, you might be struck dead. That's another reason why I took them out. You never know who the Lord will strike."

"Both of you, I expect," said the vice-consul.

"Yes," said McDowell, "but you've got to think of others."

The vice-consul got out his handkerchief and wiped his face and his head.

"You'd never get away with this twaddle in a court of law," said the vice-consul. "None of this proves she stole your dentures."

"She had gone when I woke up, and they had gone. The rain was pouring down outside or I would have gone after her," said McDowell.

"And you wouldn't have caught her if you had," said the vice-consul with deep pleasure. "She sold them before she got to the end of the street. You can say goodbye to that lot. You're wasting my time. I've got two other British ships docking in an hour. I've told you what to do. Keep clear of the police. They'll probably arrest you. And if you want a new set of dentures, go to Miami as I said."

"But they're not for me," exclaimed McDowell. "I want them for this girl. I've got the money. It's wrong to steal. Her sister knows it and so does she. If you see a soul in danger, you've got to try and save them."

"God help me," said the vice-consul. "I've got enough trouble in this port as it is, but as a matter of interest, who told you to go to this place—the Columbus—to buy handbags? You can get them at every shop in the town. The river's crawling with alligators."

McDowell nodded to the outer office where the Indian clerk sat. "That gentleman."

"He did, did he?" said the vice-consul, laughing for the first time and achieving a louder shout to his clerk.

The Indian clerk came in. He loved to be called in when the vice-consul was talking business. He gleamed with the prestige of an only assistant. The vice-consul spoke to him in Portuguese with the intimacy of one who sketches his way through a language not his own. The clerk nodded and nodded and talked eagerly.

"My clerk says," said the vice-consul, in his large way, "that you came in at midday the day before yesterday and asked where you could get a girl. He says he knows the airline girl and her sister. He knows the whole family. The father has the barbershop opposite the church and he is a dentist too. He buys up teeth, mostly after funerals."

The clerk nodded and added a few words.

"He says he fixed him up. He says this man's got the biggest collection of teeth in the town."

The clerk's neck was thin; he was like wood. He opened his mouth wide with pride for McDowell to see. There were five sharp steel teeth and two with gold in them.

The vice-consul went on, "He says he often sells them to missionaries. The Dominicans have a mission here. The poor devils come back from far up in the Indian settlements looking like skeletons after three years and with their teeth dropping out. I told you: no calcium. No fresh vegetables. No milk. The climate . . ."

The Indian said no more.

McDowell got up and moved towards the clerk suspiciously, setting his chin. "What's he say about the Dominicans?" said McDowell in a threatening way.

The vice-consul said, "He says you could go down to this man, this barber chap, and you might find your teeth."

The Indian nodded.

"If you don't—well, they've been snapped up and are being flown up the river. Sorry, McDowell, that's all we can do. Take my advice and get back double-quick to your ship. Good day."

The vice-consul picked up some papers and called to McDowell as he left the room, "They'll be up there, preaching The Word."

The following day the vice-consul went out to the Ivanhoe to have a last drink with the captain and to have a look at the puma, and grinned when it opened its mouth and snarled at him. The captain said McDowell would be all right once he got to sea, and went on to some tale about a man who claimed to have a cat that backed horses.

It's the bloody great river that does it, the vice-consul thought as he was put ashore afterwards and as he walked home in the dark and saw all the people whispering in their white cotton clothes, looking like ghosts. He was thinking it was only another year before his leave and that he was the only human being in the town.

(1980)

THE FIG TREE

I checked the greenhouses, saw the hose taps were turned off, fed the Alsatian, and then put the bar on the main gate to the Nursery and left by the side door for my flat. As I changed out of my working clothes I looked down on the rows of labelled fresh green plants. What a pleasure to see such an orderly population of growing things gambling for life—how surprising that twenty years ago the sight of so much husbandry would have bored me.

When I was drying myself in the bathroom I noticed Sally's bathcap hanging there and I took the thing to the closet in the bedroom, and then in half an hour I picked up Mother at her hotel and drove her to Duggie and Sally's house, where we were to have dinner. I supposed Mother must have seen Sally's bathcap, for as we passed the Zoo she said, "I do wish you would get married again and settle down."

"Dutch elm disease," I replied, pointing to the crosses on one or two trees in the Park.

The Zoo is my halfway mark when I go to Duggie and Sally's—what vestiges of embarrassment I feel become irrelevant when I have passed it.

"It worries your father," Mother said.

Mother is not "failing." She is in her late seventies and Father was killed in the war thirty years ago, but he comes to life in a random way, as if time were circular for her. Father seems to be wafted by, and sows the only important guilt I have—I have so little memory of him. Duggie has said once or twice to Sally that though I am in my early forties, there are still signs that I lacked a father's discipline. Duggie, a speculative man, puts the early whiteness of my hair down to this. Obviously, he says, I was a late child, probably low in vitality.

Several times during this week's visit I have taken Mother round the shops she likes in London. She moves fast on her thin legs, and if age has shortened her by giving her a small hump on her shoulders, this adds to her sharp-eyed, foraging appearance. She was rude, as usual, to the shop assistants, who seemed to admire this—perhaps because it reminded them of what they had heard of "the good old days." And she dressed with taste, her makeup was delicate, and if her skin had aged, it was fine as silk; her nose was young, her eyes as neat as violets. The week had been hot, but she was cool and slightly scented.

"Not as hot as we had it in Cairo when your father was alive," she said in her mannish voice.

Time was restored: Father had returned to his grave.

After being gashed by bombs during the war, the corner of early-Victorian London where Duggie and Sally live has "gone up." Once a neighbourhood of bed-sitters, now the small houses are expensive and trim; enormous plane trees, fast-growing sycamores, old apple and pear trees bearing uneatable fruit, crowd the large gardens. It was to see the garden and to meet Duggie, who was over from Brussels on one of his monthly trips, that Mother had really come: in the country she is an indefatigable gardener. So is Sally, who opened the door to us. One of the unspoken rules of Sally and myself is that we do not kiss when I go to her house; her eyes were as polite as glass (and without the quiver to the pupils they usually have in them) as she gave her hand to my mother. She had drawn her fair hair severely back.

"Duggie is down in the garden," Sally said to Mother and made a fuss about the steps that lead down from her sitting-room balcony. "These steps my husband put in are shaky—let me help you."

"I got used to companionways going to Egypt," said Mother in her experienced voice. "We always went by sea, of course. What a lovely garden."

"Very wild," said Sally. "There used to be a lawn here. It was no good, so we dug it up."

"No one can afford lawns nowadays," said my mother. "We have three. Much better to let nature take its course."

It is a clever garden of the romantic kind, half of it a green cavern under the large trees where the sun can still flicker in the higher branches. You duck your way under untidy climbing roses; there is a foreground, according to season, of overgrown marguerites, tobacco plants, dahlias, irises, lilies, ferns—a garden of wild, contrived masses. Our progress was slow as Mother paused to botanise until we got to a wide, flagged circle which is shaded by a muscular fig tree. Duggie was standing by the chairs with a drink in his hand, waiting for us. He moved a chair for Mother.

"No, I must see it all first," Mother said. "Nice little magnolia."

I was glad she noticed that.

There was a further tour of plants that "do well in the shade"—"Dear Solomon's-seal," she said politely, as if the plant were a person. A bird or two darted off into other gardens with the news—and then we returned to the chairs set out on the paved circle. Duggie handed drinks to us, with the small bow of a tall man. He is lazily well-made, a bufferish fellow in his late fifties, his drooping grey moustache is affable—"honourable" is how I would describe the broad road of sunburned baldness going over his head. His nose is just a touch bottled, which gives him the gentlemanly air of an old club servant, or rather of being not one man but a whole club, uttering impressions of this and that. Out of this club his private face will appear, a face that puts on a sudden, fishy-eyed stare, in the middle of one of his long sentences. It is the stare of a man in a brief state of shock who has found himself suspended over a hole that has opened at his feet. His job takes him abroad a good deal and his stare is also that of an Englishman abroad who has sighted another Englishman he cannot quite place. Not being able to get a word in while the two women were talking, he turned this stare on me. "I missed you the last time I was home," he said.

Again, it is my rule that I don't go to the house unless he is there.

"How is that chest of yours?"

I gave a small cough and he gave me a dominating look. He likes to worry about my health.

"The best thing your uncle ever did for you was to get you out of the city. You needed an open-air life."

Duggie, who has had to make his own way, rather admires me for having had a rich uncle.

Was he shooting a barb into me? I don't think so. We always have this conversation: he was born to repeat himself—one more sign of his honourableness.

Duggie takes pride in a possessive knowledge of my career. He often says to Sally, "He ought to put on weight—white hair at his age—but what do you expect? Jazz bands in Paris and London, hanging round Chelsea bars, playing at all that literary stuff, going into that bank—all that sort of nonsense." Then he goes on, "Mother's boy—marrying a woman twelve years older than himself. Sad that she died," he adds. "Must have done something to him—that breakdown, a year in the sanatorium, he probably gambled. Still, the Nursery has pulled him together. Characteristic, of course, that most of the staff are girls."

"It's doing well," he said in a loud confidential voice, nodding at the fig tree by the south wall, close to us.

"What a lovely tree," Mother said. "Does it bear? My husband will only eat figs fresh from the tree."

"One or two little ones. But they turn yellow and drop off in June," said Sally.

"What it needs," Duggie said, "is the Mediterranean sun. It ought to be in Turkey, that is where you get the best figs."

"The sun isn't enough. The fig needs good drainage and has to be fertilised," Mother said.

"All fruit needs that," said Duggie.

"The fig needs two flies—the Blastophaga and, let me see, is it the Sycophaga? I think so—anyway, they are Hymenoptera," Mother said.

Duggie gazed with admiration at my mother. He loves experts. He had been begging me for years to bring her over to his house.

"Well, we saved its life, didn't we, Teddy?" he said to me and boasted on his behalf and mine. "We flagged the area. There was nothing but a lake of muddy water here. How many years ago was that?"

"Four or five," I said.

"No!" said Duggie. "Only three."

Was he coming into the open at last and telling me that he knew that this was the time when Sally and I became lovers? I think not. The stare dropped out of his face. His honourable look returned.

—

Sally and Duggie were what I call "Monday people" at the Nursery. There is a rush of customers on the weekend. They are the instant gardeners who drive in, especially in the spring and autumn, to buy everything, from plants already in bud and flowers, the potted plants, for balconies of flats. The crowd swarms and our girls are busy at the counter we had to install to save costs as the business grew. (The counter was Duggie's idea: he could not resist seeing the Nursery as one of his colonies.) But on Monday the few fanatic gardeners come, and I first became aware of Sally because she was very early, usually alone, a slight woman in her late thirties with her straw-blond hair drawn back from a high forehead in those days, a severe look of polite, silent impatience which would turn into a wide, fastidious grimace like the yawn of a cat if anyone spoke to her. She would take a short step back and consider one's voice. She looked almost reckless and younger when she put on glasses to read what was on the sacks and packets of soil, compost, and fertiliser in the store next to the office, happiest in our warm greenhouses, a woman best seen under glass. Her eyebrows were softer, more downily intimate than anything else about her. They reminded me when I first saw her of the disturbing eyebrows of an aunt of mine which used to make me blush when I was a boy. Hair disturbs me.

One day she brought Duggie to the Nursery when I was unloading boxes of plants that came from the growers and I heard her snap at him, "Wait here. If you see the manager, ask about grass seed and stop following me round. You fuss me."

For the next half-hour she looked round the seedlings or went into the greenhouses while Duggie stood where he was told to stand. I was near him when the lorry drove off.

"Are you being attended to?" I said. "I'll call a girl."

He was in his suspended state. "No, I was thinking," he said in the lazy voice of a man who, home from abroad and with nothing to do, was hoping to find out if there were any fellow thinkers about. "I was thinking, vegetation is a curious thing," he said with the predatory look of a man who had an interesting empire of subjects to offer. "I mean, one notices when one gets back to London there is more vegetation than brick. Trees," he said. "Plants and shrubs, creeper, moss, ivy," he went on, "grass, of course. Why this and not that? Climate, I suppose. You have laurels here, but no oleander, yet it's all over the Mediterranean and Mexico. You get your fig or your castor-oil plant, but no banana, no ginkgo, no datura. The vine used to swarm in Elizabethan times, but rare now, but I hear they're making wine again. It must be thin. The climate changed when the Romans cut down the forests." For a moment he became a Roman and then drifted on, "Or the Normans. We all come down to grass in the end."

He looked at our greenhouses.

"My job takes me away a lot. I spend half the year abroad," he said. "Oil. Kuwait."

He nodded to the distant figure of his wife. She was bending over a bed of tobacco plants.

"We spent our honeymoon in Yucatán," he said with some modest pomp. He was one of those colonising talkers, talking over new territory.

"But that is not the point," he said. "We can't get the right grass seed. She sows every year, but half of it dies by the time summer comes. Yet look at the Argentina pampas." He was imposing another geography, some personal flora of his own, on my Nursery. Clearly not a gardener: a thinker at large.

I gave him the usual advice. I took him to a shed to show him sacks of chemicals. His wife came back from the flower beds and found us. "I've been looking for you everywhere," she said to him. "I told you to wait where you were." She sounded to be an irritable woman.

He said to me, in an aloof, conspiring way, ignoring her, "I suppose you wouldn't have time to drop round and have a look at our lawn? I mean, in the next week or two—"

"It will be too late by then," she interrupted. "The grass will be dead. Come along," and she made that grimace—a grimace that now struck me as a confidence, an off-hand intimation.

He made an apologetic gesture to me and followed her obediently out of the Nursery.

—

I often had a word or two with Sally when she came alone: grass seed seemed to be the couple's obsession. She said it was his; he said it was hers. I was a kind of umpire to whom they appealed when we met.

So one afternoon in November when I was delivering laurels to a neighbour of theirs down the street, I dropped in at their house.

A fat young man was sitting sedately on a motorbike outside it, slowly taking off a fine pair of gauntlets. Sitting behind the screen of the machine, he might have been admiring himself at a dressing-table mirror. In his white crash helmet he looked like a doll, but one with a small black moustache.

"Those lads get themselves up, don't they?" I said to Duggie, who came to the door.

"Our tenant," Duggie said. "He has the flat in the basement. He uses the side entrance. Under our agreement he does not use the garden. That is reserved for ourselves. Come through—I had these iron steps put in so that my wife has strictly private access to the garden without our interfering with him or he with us. My wife would have preferred a young married couple, but as I pointed out, there would be children. One has to weigh one thing against another in this life—don't you find?"

We went down to the garden. Their trouble was plain. The trees were bare. Half of the place was lifeless soil, London-black and empty. The damp yellow leaves of the fig tree hung down like wretched rags, and the rest had fallen flat as plates into a very large pool of muddy water that stretched from one side of the garden to the other. Overnight, in November, a fig collapses like some Victorian heroine. Here—as if she were about to drown herself. I said this to Duggie, who said, "Heroine? I don't follow."

"You'll never grow a lawn here. Too much shade. You could cut the trees down . . ."

At this moment Sally came down and said, "I won't have my trees cut down. It's the water that's killing everything."

I said that whole districts of London were floating on water. Springs everywhere, and the clay held it.

"And also, the old Fleet River runs underground in this district," I said. "The only thing you can do is to put paving down."

"The Fleet River? News to me," said Duggie, and he looked about us at other gardens and houses as if eager to call out all his neighbours and tell them. "Pave it, you say? You mean with stones?"

"What else?" said Sally curtly and walked away. The garden was hers.

"But, my dear," he called after her, "the point is—what stones? Portland? Limestone?"

The coloniser of vegetation was also a collector of rock. A load of geology poured out of him. He ran through sandstone, millstone grit, until we moved on to the whinstone the Romans used on Hadrian's Wall, went on to the marble quarries of Italy and came back to the low brick wall of their garden, which had been damaged during the war.

Presently there was the howling and thumping of jazz music from the basement flat.

"I told you that man has girls down there," Sally said angrily to her husband. "He's just come in. He's turning the place into a discothèque. Tell him to stop—it's intolerable."

And she looked coldly at me as if I too were a trespasser, the sort of man who would kick up a shindy with girls in a quiet house. I left. Not a happy pair.

———

I sent him an estimate for paving part of the garden. Several months passed; there was no reply and his wife stopped coming to the Nursery. I thought they were abroad. Then in the spring Duggie came to the Nursery with his daughter, a schoolgirl, who went off to make up confidently to a van driver.

Duggie watched her and then said to me, "About those paving stones. My wife has been ill. I had a cable and flew home."

"I hope it was not serious?"

He studied me, considering whether to tell me the details, but evidently—and with that kind of reluctance which suggests all—changed his mind. "The iniquitous Rent Act," he said disparagingly, "was at the bottom of it."

He gave an outline of the Act, with comments on rents in general. "Our tenant—that boy was impossible, every kind of impertinence. We tried to get rid of him but we couldn't. The fellow took us to court."

"Did you get an order against him?" I asked.

Duggie's voice hurried. "No. Poor fellow was killed. Drove his motorbike head-on into a lorry, a girl with him too. Both killed. Horrible. Naturally, it upset my wife: she blames herself. Imagination," he apologised. Duggie spoke of the imagination accusingly.

"The man with the little black moustache?" I asked.

"She wouldn't have a married couple there," he said.

"I remember," I said. "You mentioned it."

"Did I?" he said. He was cheered by my remembering that.

"You see," he said. "It was clearly laid down in the agreement that he was not to go into the garden under any pretext, but he did. However, that is not what I came about. We're going to pave that place, as you suggested. It will take her mind off it all." He nodded to the house. "By the way, you won't say anything to her, will you? I'm away so much the garden is everything to her."

Shortly after this I took one of our men over to the house. Duggie was stirred at the end of the first day when he came home from his London office to see we had dug up a lot of brick rubble—chunks of the garden wall which had been knocked down by blast during the war. On the second day he came back early in the afternoon and stood watching. He was longing to get hold of my man's pickaxe. The man put it down and I had turned around when I heard the dead sound of steel on stone and a shout of "Christ!" from Duggie. He had taken the pickaxe and brought it down hard on a large slab of concrete and was doubled up, gripping his wrists between his legs, in agony. Sally came to the balcony and then hurried down the steps. Her appearance had changed. She was plumper than she had been, there was no sign of illness, and she had done her hair in a new way: it was loosened and she often pushed it back from her cheeks.

"You are a fool, Duggie," she said.

The man was shovelling earth clear of the slab of concrete, which tilted down deep into the earth.

"It's all right. It's all right. Go away. I'm all right," said Duggie.

"What is it?" he said.

"Bleeding air-raid shelter," my gardener said. "There's one or two left in the gardens round here. A gentleman down the road turned his into a lily pond."

He went on shovelling and dug a hole. The concrete ended in a tangle of wire and stone. It had been smashed. He kneeled down on the ground and said, "The end wall has caved in, full of wet muck." He got up and said, disappointed, "No one in it. Saved some poor bloke's life. If he copped it, he wouldn't have known, anyway."

Sally made a face of horror at the gardener. "Those poor people," she said. "Come indoors. What a fool you are, Duggie."

Duggie refused to go. Pain had put him in a trance: one could almost see bits of his mind travelling out of him as he called triumphantly to her, "Don't you see what we've got, my dearest?" he cried, excitement driving out his pain. He was a man whose mind was stored with a number of exotic words: "We've got a *cenote*."

How often we were to hear that word in the next few days! For months after this he must have continued startling people with it in his office, on buses, men in clubs, whoever was sitting next to him in aircraft on his way to Kuwait.

"What is a cenote?" I said, no doubt as they did.

"It's an underground cistern," he said. "You remember Yucatán, Sally— all those forests, yet no water. No big rivers. You said, 'How did the Mayas survive?' The answer was that the Maya civilisation floated on underground cisterns."

Duggie turned to me, calling me Teddy for the first time. "I remember what you said about London floating on underground rivers—it's been on my mind ever since you said it. Something was there at the back of my mind, some memory, I couldn't get it. There it is: a cenote. That's where your fig tree has been drinking, Sally. You plant your fig tree on a tank of water and the rubble drains it.

"Sally and I saw dozens of cenotes, all sizes, some hundred feet deep on our honeymoon," he confided to me.

Sally's eyes went hard.

"The Mayans worshipped them: you can see why. Once a year the priests used to cut out the heart of a virgin and throw it into the water. Propitiation," he said.

"It's an act for tourists at the nightclubs there," said Sally drearily.

"Yes," Duggie explained to us and added to me, "Fake, of course."

Sally said, "Those poor people. I shall never go into this garden again."

In the next few days she did not come down while we turned the ruin into a foundation, and the following week Duggie superintended the laying of the stones. His right arm was in a sling.

When the job was finished Duggie was proud of the wide circle of stones we had laid down.

"You've turned my garden into a cemetery. I've seen it from the window," Sally said.

Duggie and I looked at each other: two men agreeing to share the unfair blame. She had been ill; we had done this job for her and it had made things worse.

Imagination, as Duggie had said. Difficult for him. And I had thought of her as a calm, sensible woman.

—

It happened at this time I had to go to the Town Hall about a contract for replanting one of the neglected squares in the borough, and while I was there and thinking of Duggie and Sally I tried to find out who had lived in their house and whether there was any record of air-raid casualties. I went from office to office and discovered nothing. Probably the wrong place to go to. Old cities are piled on layer after layer of unrecorded human lives and things. Then Duggie sent a cheque for our work, more promptly too than most of our customers do. I thought of my buried wife and the rot of the grave as I made out a receipt. It occurred to me that it would be decent to do something for Duggie. I was walking around the Nursery one morning when I saw a small strong magnolia, a plant three feet high and already in bud. It was risky to replant it at this time, but I bound it, packed it, and put it in a large tub and drove to their house one Saturday with it, to surprise them. Sally came to the door with a pen in her hand and looked put-out by my sudden call. I told her I had the plant in the van.

"We didn't order anything. My husband is in Kuwait—he would have told me. There must be a mistake."

The pen in her raised hand was like a funny hostile weapon, and seeing me smile at it, she lowered her hand.

"It's not an order. It's a present. In the van," I said. She looked unbelieving at the van and then back at me. In the awkward pause my mind gave an unintended leap. I forgot about Duggie.

"For you," I said. I seemed to sail away, off my feet.

"For me?" she said. "Why for me?"

I was astonished. Her face went as white as paper and I thought she was going to faint. She stood there, trembling. The pen dropped out of her hand to the floor and she turned round and bent to pick it up and stood up again with a flustered blush as if she had been caught doing something wrong.

"You're the gardener," I said. "Come and look."

She did not move, so I started off down the few steps to the gate. She followed me and I saw her glance, as if calling for protection to the houses on either side of her own.

"Why should you do this?" she said in an unnatural voice. I opened the gate, but she made me go through first.

The swollen rusty-pink and skin-white buds of the plant were as bright as candles in the darkness of the van.

"Advertising," I said with a salesman's laugh. She frowned, reproaching me doubtfully. But when she saw the plant she said, "How lovely!"

My tongue raced. I said I had been thinking of the paved circle in the middle of the garden; the magnolia would stand there and flower before the trees shaded the place, and that it could be moved out of the tub wherever she wanted it in the garden later in the year.

"You mean that?" she said.

So I got out a trolley, put up a board, and wheeled the plant down from the van carefully. It was very heavy.

"Be careful," she said. She opened the side entrance to the garden and followed me there.

"No muddy puddle now. It's gone," I boasted. It was a struggle getting the heavy tub in place and she helped me.

"You've got a gardener's strong hands," I said.

I looked around and then up at the trees. Her wide mouth opened with delight at the plant.

"How kind you are," she said. "Duggie will love it."

I had never been alone with her in this garden and, I remember, this was privileged ground. She walked around and around the plant as if she were dancing.

"It will be in full bloom in ten days," I said. "It will cheer up the fig tree. It's trying to bud."

"This time of the year," she said, despising it, "that tree looks like a chunk of machinery."

A half-hour passed. We went back to the house and she thanked me again as I pushed the trolley.

"Leave it there," she said. "I must give you some tea or a drink. How lucky I was in. You should have telephoned."

In the sitting-room she laughed as she looked back at the plant from the window. It was, I realised, the first time I had heard her laugh. It was surprising not to hear Duggie's voice. She went off to make tea and I sat in an armchair and remembered not to put my dirty hands on the arms. Then I saw my footmarks coming across the carpet to me. I felt I had started on a journey.

I noticed she frowned at them and the cups skidded on the tray when she came back with the tea.

I said apologetically, "My boots!"

Strange words, now that I think of it, for the beginning of a love affair; even she gaped at them as if they had given me away.

When she had only half filled my cup she banged the teapot down, got up and came across to squeeze my hand.

"Oh, you are so *kind, kind,*" she said and then stepped back to her chair quickly.

"You *are* a friend," she said.

And then I saw tears were dropping down her cheeks. Her happy face had collapsed and was ugly. "I'm sorry to be so silly, Mr Ormerod," she said, trying to laugh.

Ten shelves of Duggie's books looked down, their titles dumb, but listening with all ears as I sat not knowing what to do, for, trying to laugh, she sobbed even more and she had to get up and turn her back to me and look out of the window.

"It's all right," she said with her back to me. "Don't let your tea get cold. My husband wanted to put an urn there," she said. "I suppose he told you."

Duggie had not been able to control his drifting mind.

"This is the first time I've been in the garden since you were here last," she said, turning round.

"By the way," I said, "if you're worrying about the shelter, I can tell you—I've looked up the records at the Town Hall. There were no casualties here. There was no one in the shelter."

I did not tell her no records could be traced. Her tears had made my mind leap again.

"Why on earth did you do that?" she said, and she sat down again.

"I had the idea it was worrying you," I said.

"No, not at all," she said, shaking after her cry, and she put on an off-hand manner and did not look at me.

"The shelter? Oh, that didn't worry me," she said. "The war was thirty years ago, wasn't it? One doesn't have to wait for bombs to kill people. They die in hospital, don't they? Things prey on my husband's mind. He's a very emotional man; you mightn't think it. I don't know whether he told you, we had trouble with a young man, a tenant. It made Duggie quite ill. They flew him home from Kuwait."

I was baffled. She had exactly reversed the story Duggie had told me.

She said with the firm complacency of a married woman, "He talks himself into things, you know."

After she said this there was a question in her eyes, a movement like a small signal, daring me for a moment. I was silent and she began talking about everyday things, in a nervous way, and intimacy vanished.

She stood at the door and gave a half wave as I left, a scarcely visible wave, like a beckon. It destroyed me. Damn that stupid man, I thought when I got home and stood at the stove getting a meal together. The telephone rang and I turned the stove off. I thought the call was from my mother—it was her hour—but the voice was Sally's, firm but apologetic. "You've left your trolley. I thought you might need it."

O blessed trolley! I said I'd come at once. She said curtly she was going out. That, and the hope that she was not interrupting my dinner, were the only coherent, complete sentences she spoke in one of the longest calls I have ever had. On her side it was a collection of unfinished phrases with long silences between them, so that once or twice she seemed to have gone away—silences in which she appeared to be wrestling with nouns, pronouns, and verbs that circled round an apology and explanation that was no explanation, about making "that silly scene." No sooner was she at the point of explanation than she drifted off it. It struck me that listening to her husband so much, she had lost the power of talking.

There was something which, "sometime in the future," she would like to ask me, but it had gone from her mind. "If there is a future," she added too brightly. Her silences dangled and stirred me. The manner was so like Duggie's: it half exasperated me and I asked her if she would have dinner with me one day. "Dinner?" This puzzled her. She asked if I had had my dinner. The idea died and so did the conversation. What affectation, I thought afterwards. Not on my side: desire had been born.

But on the following day I saw her waiting in one of our greenhouses. She was warmer under glass. I had collected my trolley. That, for some reason, pleased her. She agreed to have dinner with me. "Where on earth are we going?" she said when we drove off.

"Away from the Nursery," I said. I was determined to amuse her. "To get away from the thieves."

"What thieves?" she said.

"The old ladies," I said.

It is well known, if you run a nursery, that very nice old ladies sometimes nip off a stem for a cutting or slip small plants into their bags. Stealing a little gives them the thrill of flirtation. I said that only this week one of them had come to me when I was alone in a greenhouse and said, "Can I whisper something to you? I have a dreadful confession to make. I have been very naughty. I stole a snippet of geranium from you in the summer and it has struck!"

Sally said, "And what about old men? Don't they steal?"

My fancy took a leap. "Yes, we've got one," I said, "but he goes in for big stuff."

There was a myth at our Nursery that when a box of plants was missing or some rare expensive shrub had been dug up and was gone, this was the work of a not altogether imaginary person called Thompson who lived in a big house where the garden abutted on our wall. Three camellias went one day, and because of the price he was somehow promoted by the girls and became known as "Colonel" Thompson. He had been seen standing on a stepladder and looking over our wall. I invented a face for the colonel when I told Sally about this. I gave him a ripe nose, a bald head, a drooping moustache; unconsciously I was describing Duggie. I went further: I had caught the colonel with one leg over the wall, and when I challenged him he said, "Looking for my dog. Have you seen my dog?"

Sally said, "I don't believe you."

This was promising. A deep seriousness settled on us when we got to the restaurant. It was a small place. People were talking loudly, so that bits of their lives seemed to be flying around us, and we soon noticed we were the quietest talkers there, talking about ourselves, but to our plates or the tablecloth, crumbling bread and then looking up with sudden questions. She ate very fast; a hungry woman, I thought. How long, she asked suddenly, raising a fork to her mouth, how long had I known my wife before we were married? Four months, I said. She put her fork down.

"That was a rush," she said. "It took Duggie and me seven years."

"Why was that?"

"I didn't want to get married, of course," she said.

"You mean you lived together?" I said.

"Indeed not. We might not even have married *then*," she said, "but his firm was sending him to Mexico for three years. We knew each other very well, you know. Actually," she mumbled now, "I was in love with someone else." She now spoke up boldly, "Gratitude is more important than love, isn't it?"

"Is that the question you wanted to ask me," I said, "when you telephoned?"

"I don't think I said that," she said.

I was falling in love with her. I listened but hardly heard what she said. I was listening only to my desire.

"Gratitude? No, I don't," I said. "Not when one is young. Why don't you go with him on his jobs?"

"He likes travel, I don't," she said. "We like each other. I don't mind being alone. I prefer it. You're alone, aren't you?"

Our conversation stopped. A leaden boredom settled on us like a stifling thundercloud. I whispered, looking around first to be sure no one heard me, and in a voice I scarcely recognized as my own, "I want you."

"I know," she said. "It's no good," she said, fidgeting in her chair and looking down at the cloth. Her movement encouraged me.

"I've loved you ever since—"

She looked up.

"—since you started coming to the Nursery," I said.

"Thank you, but I can't," she said. "I don't go to bed with people. I gave that up when my daughter was born."

"It's Duggie?" I said.

She was startled and I saw the grimace I knew.

She thought a long time.

"Can't you guess?" she said. And then she leaned across and touched my hand. "Don't look so gloomy. It's no good with me."

I was not gloomy. That half wave of the hand, the boredom, the monotony of our voices, even the fact that the people at the next table had found us so interesting that they too had started whispering, made me certain of how our evening would end.

"Let us go," I said.

I called a waiter and she watched me pay the bill and said, "What an enormous tip." In our heavy state, this practical remark lightened us. And for me it had possessive overtones that were encouraging; she stood outside, waiting for me to bring the car with that air women have of pretending not to be there. We drove off and when I turned into a shopping street almost empty at this hour I saw our heads and shoulders reflected in the windows of a big shop, mocking us as we glided by: two other people. I turned into a street of villas; we were alone again and I leaned to kiss her on the neck. She did not move, but presently she glanced at me and said, "Are you a friend?"

"No," I said. "I'm not."

"I think I ought to like that," she said. And she gripped my arm violently and did not let it go.

"Not at my house," she said.

We got to my flat and there she walked across the sitting-room straight to the window and looked down at the long greenhouses gleaming in the dark.

"Which is Colonel Thompson's house?" she said.

I came up behind her and put my arms round her and she watched my daring hands play on her breasts with that curiosity and love of themselves that women have, but there was a look of horror on her face when I kissed her on the mouth, a hate that came (I know now) from the years of her marriage. In the next hours it ebbed away, her face emptied, and her wide lips parted with greed.

"I don't do things like this," she said.

—

The next day she came to me; on the third day she pulled me back as I was getting out of bed and said, "Duggie's coming home. I have something bad to tell you, something shameful." She spoke into my shoulder. "Something I tried to tell you when I telephoned, the day you came with the plant, but I couldn't. Do you remember I telephoned to you?

"I told a lie to Duggie about that young man, I told Duggie he attacked me." She said, "It wasn't true. I saw him and his girl at night from my bedroom window going into the garden with their arms round each other, to the end of it, under the trees. They were there a long time. I imagined what they were doing. I could have killed that girl. I was mad with jealousy—I think I was really mad. I went out into the garden many nights to stop them, and in the afternoons I worked there to provoke him and even peeped into their window. It was terrible. So I told Duggie. I told him the boy had come up behind me and pulled at my clothes and tried to rape me. I tore my blouse to prove it. I sent a cable to Duggie. Poor Duggie, he believed me. He came back. I made Duggie throw the boy out. You know what happened. When the boy was killed I thought I would go out of my mind."

"I thought you said Duggie was ill," I said.

"That is what I'm ashamed of," she said. "But I was mad. You know, I hated you too when Duggie brought you in to do those stones. I really hated anyone being in the garden. That is why I made that scene when you brought the magnolia. When you came to the door I thought for an awful moment it was the boy's father coming for his things; he did come once."

I was less shocked than unnerved. I said, "The real trouble was that you were lying to yourself." I saw myself as the rescuer for a moment.

"Do you think he believed you?" I said.

She put on the distant look she used to have when I first met her, almost a look of polite annoyance at being distracted from her story. Then she said something that was true. "Duggie doesn't allow himself to believe what he doesn't want to believe. He never believes what he sees. One day I found him in the sitting-room, and he started to pull a book out of the bookcase and closed it with a bang and wiped his eyes. 'Dust,' he said. 'Bad as Mexico.' Afterwards I thought, He's been crying."

"That was because he knew he was to blame," I said.

I went to my window and looked at the sky. In the night he would be coming across it.

"What are we going to do?" I said. "When shall I see you? Are you going to tell him?"

She was very surprised. "Of course not," she said, getting out of bed.

"But we must. If you don't, I shall."

She picked up her dress and half covered herself with it. "If you do," she said, "I'll never see you again, Colonel Thompson."

"He'll find out. I want to marry you."

"I've got a daughter. You forget that. He's my husband."

"He's probably got some girl," I said lightly.

The gentleness went out of our conversation.

"You're not to say that," she said vehemently. We were on the edge of a quarrel.

"I have got to go," she said. "Judy's coming home. I've got to get his suits from the cleaners and there are some of yours."

My suits and Duggie's hanging up on nasty little wire hangers at the cleaners!

—

We had a crowd of customers at the Nursery and that took my mind off our parting, but when I got back to my flat the air was still and soundless. I walked round my three rooms expecting to see her, but the one or two pictures stared out of my past life. I washed up our empty glasses. Well, there it is, I thought cynically. All over. What do you expect? And I remembered someone saying, "Have an affair with a married woman if you like, but for God's sake don't start wanting to marry her."

It was a help that my secretary was on holiday and I had to do all the paperwork at night. I also had my contract for re-planting the square the council had neglected and did a lot of the digging myself. As I dug I doubted Sally and went over what I knew about her life. How did she and Duggie meet? What did they say? Was Sally flaunting herself before her husband, surprising and enticing him? I was burned by jealousy. Then, at the end of the week, before I left for the square at half past eight, I heard her steps on the stairs to my office. She had a busy smile on her face.

"I've brought your suits," she said. "I'm in a rush." And she went to hang them in their plastic covers on the door, but I had her in my arms and the suits fell to the floor.

"Is it all right?" I said.

"How do you mean?" she said.

"Duggie," I said.

"Of course," she said complacently.

I locked the door. In a few minutes her doubts and mine were gone. Our quarrel was over. She looked at me with surprise as she straightened her skirt.

Happiness! I took one of our girls with me to the square and stood by lazily watching her get on with her work.

After lunch I was back at the Nursery and I was alarmed to see Duggie's bald head among the climbing greenery of our hothouse.

He was stooping there, striped by sunlight, like some affable tiger. I hoped to slip by unseen, but he heard me and the tiger skin dropped off as he came out, all normality, calling, "Just the man! I've been away."

I gave what must have been the first of the small coughs, the first of a long series with which I would always greet him and which made him put concern into his voice. I came to call it my "perennial hybrid"—a phrase that struck him and which he added to his vocabulary of phrases and even to his reflections on coughs in general, on Arab spitting and Mexican hawking.

"I came over to thank you for that wonderful magnolia. That was very kind. I missed it in flower but Sally says it was wonderful. You don't know what it did for her. I don't know whether you have noticed, she's completely changed. She looks years younger. All her energy has come back." Then in a louder voice: "She has forgotten all that trouble. You must have seen it. She tells me she has been giving you a hand, your girl's away."

"She was very kind. She took my suits to the cleaners."

He ignored this. We walked together across the Nursery and he waved his hand to the flower beds. Did I say that his daughter was with him? She was then a fat girl of thirteen or fourteen with fair hair like her mother's.

"Fetched them," said the pedantic child, and from that time her gaze was like a judgement. I picked a flower for her as they followed me to the door of my office.

"By the way," he said, "what did you do about that fellow who gets over the wall? Sally told me. Which wall was it?"

Sally seemed to tell him everything.

"He's stopped. That one over there."

He stood still and considered it. "What you need is a wire fence, with a three-inch mesh to it; if it was wider, the fellow could get his toe in. It would be worth the outlay—no need to go in for one of those spiked steel fences we put up round our refineries." He went on to the general question of fences: he had always been against people who put broken glass on walls.

"Unfair," he said. He looked lofty—"Cruel, too. Chap who did that ought to be sent off the field.

"Come and have a drink with us this evening," Duggie said.

I could think of no excuse; in fact I felt confident and bold now, but the first person I saw at the house was Duggie wearing a jacket far too small for him. It was my jacket. She had left his suits at my office and taken mine to her own house.

Duggie laughed loudly. "Very fishy, I thought, when I saw this on my bed. Ha-ha! What's going on? It would be funnier still if you'd worn mine."

Sally said demurely she saw nothing funny in that. She had only been trying to help.

"Be careful when Sally tries to help." He was still laughing. The comedy was a bond. And we kept going back to it. Judy, her daughter, enjoyed this so much that she called out, "Why doesn't Mr Ormerod take our flat?"

Our laughter stopped. Children recklessly bring up past incidents in their parents' lives. Duggie was about to pour wine into Sally's glass and he stopped, holding the bottle in the air. Sally gave that passing grimace of hers and Duggie shrank into instant protective concern and to me he seemed to beg us all for silence. But he recovered quickly and laughed again, noisily— too noisily, I thought.

"He has to live near the Nursery, don't you, Teddy? Colonel Thompson and all that."

"Of course," said Sally easily. "Duggie, don't pour the wine on the carpet, please."

It was a pleasant evening. We moved to the sitting-room and Sally sat on the sofa with the child, who gazed and gazed at me. Sally put her arm round her.

—

Three years have passed since that evening when Judy spoke out. When I look back, those years seem to be veiled or to sparkle with the mists of an October day. How can one describe happiness? In due time Duggie would leave and once more for months on end Sally and I would be free, and despite our bickerings and jealousies, our arguments about whether Duggie knew or did not know, we fell into a routine and made our rules. The stamp of passion was on us, yet there was always in my mind the picture of her sitting on the sofa with her daughter. I came to swear I would do nothing that would trouble her. And she and I seemed able to forget our bodies when we were all together. Perhaps that first comedy had saved us. My notion was that Duggie invented me, as he had invented her. I spend my time, she says, inventing Duggie. She invented neither of us.

Now I have changed my mind. After that evening when the child Judy said, "Why doesn't Mr Ormerod take our flat?" I am convinced that Duggie knew—because of his care for Sally, even because he knew more than either of us about Sally and that tenant of theirs who was so horribly killed on his motorbike. When he turned us into fictions he perhaps thought the fiction would soon end. It did not. He became like a weary, indulgent, and distant emperor when he was home.

But those words of Judy's were another matter. For Duggie, Judy was not a fiction. She was his daughter, absolutely his, he made her. She was the contradiction of his failure. About her he would not pretend or compromise. I am now sure of this after one or two trivial events that occurred that year. One afternoon the day before he was due home—one of those enamelled misleading October days, indeed—Sally was tidying the bedroom at my flat. I was in the sitting-room putting the drinks away and I happened to glance down at the Nursery. I saw a young woman there, with fair hair, just like Sally's, shading her eyes from the sun, and waving. For a moment I thought it was Sally who had secretly slipped away to avoid the sad awkwardness of those business-like partings of ours. Then I saw the woman was a young girl—Judy. I stepped back out of sight. I called Sally and she came with a broom in her hand.

"Don't go near the window like that"—she was not even wearing a bra—"look!"

"It's Judy! What is she up to? How long has she been there?" she said.

"She's watching us," I said. "She knows!"

Sally made that old grimace I now so rarely see.

"The little bitch," she said. "I left her at home with two of her school friends. She can't know I'm here."

"She must do," I said. "She's spying."

Sally said crisply, "Your paranoia is a rotten cover. Do you think I didn't know that girl's got a crush on you, my sweetheart? Try not to be such a cute old man."

"Me? Try?" I said jauntily.

And then, in the practical manner of one secure in the higher air of unruffled love, she said, "Anyway, she can't see my car from there. She can't see through walls. Don't stand there looking at her."

She went back to tidying the flat and my mind drifted into remembering a time when I was a boy throwing pebbles at the window of the girl next door. What a row there was with her mother!

I forgot Judy's waving arm. Duggie came home and I was not surprised to see him wandering about the Nursery two days later like a dog on one of his favourite rounds, circling round me from a distance, for I was busy with a customer, waiting for his chance. He had brought Judy with him. She was solemnly studying the girls, who with their order books and pencils were following undecided customers or directing the lost to our self-service counter inside the building. Judy was murmuring to herself as if imagining the words they said. She was admiring the way one of the girls ordered a youth to wheel a trolley-load of chrysanthemums to the main gate.

When I was free Duggie came quickly to me. "That counter works well," he said. He was congratulating himself, for the counter had been his idea, one item in his dreamy possession of the place. "It has cut down the labour costs. I've been counting. You've got rid of three girls, haven't you?"

"Four," I said. "My secretary left last week to get married."

Judy had stopped watching and came up with him. Yes, she had grown. The child whose face had looked as lumpish as a coffee mug, colourless too, had suddenly got a figure, and her face was rounded. Her eyes were moist with the new light of youth, mingling charmingly with an attempt at the look of important experience. She gazed at me until Duggie stopped talking, and then she said, "I saw you the day before yesterday"—to show she had started to become an old hand—"at your window. I waved to you."

"Did you?" I said.

"You weren't in your office," she said.

Cautiously I said, "I didn't see you."

"You were ironing your shirts."

A relief.

"Not me. I never iron my shirts," I said. "You must have seen the man who lives in the flat below. He's always ironing his shirts, poor fellow. He usually does it at night."

"On the third floor," the girl said.

"I live on the fourth, dear," I said.

"How awful of me," the girl said.

To save her face Duggie said, "I like to see women scrubbing clothes on stone—on a riverbank."

"That's not ironing, Daddy," she said.

There was the usual invitation to come to his house for a drink now that he was back. I did my cough and said I might drop in, though as he could see, we were in a rush. When I got to his house I found a chance to tell Sally. "Clever of her," I said. "It was a scheme to find out which floor I live on."

"It was not what you think," Sally said.

The evening was dull and Sally looked unwell and went to bed early. Duggie and I were left to ourselves and he listened to me in an absent-minded way when I told him again about my secretary leaving. He said grumpily, "You ought to leave the girls alone and go in for older women," and went on to say that his sister-in-law was coming to stay, suggesting that married life also had its troubles. Suddenly he woke up, and as if opportunity had been revealed to him in a massive way he said, "Come and have dinner with me at my club tomorrow."

The invitation was half plea, half threat. *He* was being punished. Why not myself also?

Duggie's club! Was this to be a showdown? The club was not a bolt-hole for Duggie. It was an imperial institution in his life and almost sacred. One had to understand that, although rarely mentioned, it was headquarters, the only place in England where he was irrefutably himself and at home with his mysteries. He did not despise me for not having a club myself, but it did explain why I had something of the homeless dog about me. That clubs bored me suggested a moral weakness. I rose slightly in his esteem once when I told him that years ago my uncle used to take me to *his* club. (He used to give me a lot to drink and lecture me on my feckless habits and even introduced me to one or two members—I suppose to put stamina in me.) These invitations came after my wife's death, so that clubs came to seem to me places where marriages were casketed and hidden by the heavy curtains on the high windows.

There was something formidable in Duggie's invitation, and when I got to his club my impression was that he had put on weight or had received a quiet authority from being only among men, among husbands, in mufti. It was a place where the shabby armchairs seemed made of assumptions in leather and questions long ago disposed of.

In this natural home Duggie was no longer inventive or garrulous. Nods and grunts to the members showed that he was on his true ground.

We dined at a private table. Duggie sat with his back to an old brocade curtain in which I saw some vegetable design that perhaps had allayed or taken over the fantasies of the members.

A couple of drinks in the bar downstairs and a decanter of wine on the table eased Duggie, who said the old chef had had a stroke and that he thought the new chef had not got his hand in yet. The sweetbreads had been runny the last time; maybe it would be better to risk the beef.

Then he became confessional to put me at my ease: he always came here when his sister-in-law came to stay. A difficult woman—he always said to Sally, "Can't you put her off? You'll only get one of your migraines after she has been."

"I thought Sally didn't look too well," I said.

"She's having a worrying time with Judy," he said. "Young girls grow up. She's going through a phase."

"She is very lovely."

He ignored this. "Freedom, you know! Wants to leave school. Doesn't work. Messed up her exams."

"Sex, I suppose," I said.

"Why does everyone talk about sex?" said Duggie, looking stormy. "She wants to get away, get a flat of her own, get a job, earn her living, sick of the old folks. But a flat of her own—at sixteen! I ask you."

"Girls have changed."

Duggie studied me and made a decision. I now understood why I had been asked.

"I wondered," said Duggie, "has she ever said anything to you—parents are the last to hear anything."

"To me?"

"Friend of the family—I just wondered."

"I hardly ever see her. Only when Sally or you bring her to the Nursery. I can't see the young confiding in me. Not a word."

Duggie was disappointed. He found it hard to lose one of his favourite fancies: that among all those girls at the Nursery I had sublimated the spent desires of my youth. He said, taking an injured pride in a fate, "That's it. I married into a family of gardeners."

And then he came out with it—the purpose of this dinner: "The girl's mad to get a job in your nursery. I thought she might have been sounding you out—I mean, waving to that fellow ironing his shirt."

"No. Nothing," I said.

"Mad idea. You're turning people away! I told her. By the way, I don't want to embarrass you. I'm not suggesting you should take her on. Girls get these ideas. Actually, we're going to take her away from that school and send her to school in Switzerland. Alps, skiing. Her French and German are a mess. Abroad! That is what she needs."

Abroad! The most responsive string in Duggie's nature had been struck. He meant what he said.

"That will be hard on Sally," I said. "She'd miss her terribly."

"We've got to do the best for the girl. She knows that," said Duggie.

And without warning the old stare, but now it was the stare of the interrogator's lamp, turned on my face, and his manner changed from the brisk and business-like to the commandingly off-hand.

"Ironical," he said. "Now, if Sally had wanted a job at your nursery, that would be understandable. After all, you deal with all those Dutch and French, and so on. Her German's perfect. But poor Judy, she can't utter."

"Sally!" I laughed. "She'd hate it."

Duggie filled my glass and then his own very slowly, but as he raised the decanter he kept his eye on me: quite a small feat, indeed like a minor conjuring trick, for a man who more than once had knocked a glass over at home and made Sally rush to the kitchen for a cloth.

"You're quite wrong," he said. "I happen to know."

Know what? "You mean *she's* mentioned it," I said.

"No, no, of course not," he said. "But if you said the word, I'm certain of it. Not last year, perhaps. But if Judy goes to Switzerland, she'll be alone.

She'd jump at it."

Now the wine began to work on him—and on me, too—and Duggie's conversation lost its crisp manner. He moved on to one of his trailing geographical trances; we moved through time and space. The club became subtropical, giant ferns burst out of the club curtains, liana hung from the white pillars of the dining-room, the other members seemed to be in native dress, and threading through it all was the figure of Sally, notebook in hand. She followed us downstairs to the bar, which became a greenhouse, as we drank our port. No longer wretched because her daughter had gone, no longer fretting about the disastrous mess she had made of her life when she was young, without a mother's experience to guide her. I heard Duggie say, "I know they're moving me to Brussels in a few months and of course I'll be over every weekend—but a woman wants her own life. Frankly," he said with awe in his voice, "we *bore* them."

The club resumed its usual appearance, though with an air of exhaustion. The leather chairs yawned. The carpets died. A lost member rose from the grave and stopped by Duggie and said, "We need a fourth at bridge."

"Sorry, old boy," said Duggie.

The man went off to die elsewhere.

"And no danger," said Duggie, "of her leaving to get married."

And now, drunkish as we were, we brought our momentous peace conference to an end. The interrogator's lamp was switched on again just before we got to our feet and he seemed to be boring his way into my head and to say, "You've taken my wife, but you're bloody well not going to get my daughter into your pokey little fourth-floor flat ironing your shirts."

I saw the passion in his mottled face and the powerful gleam of his honourable head.

—

After Sally had put up a fight and I had said that sending Judy away was his revenge, Sally came to work for me. Duggie had married us and I became as nervous and obsequious as a groom. There was the awkwardness of a honeymoon. She dressed differently. She became sedate—no strokings and squeezes of love were allowed: she frowned and twisted away like a woman who had been a secretary all her life. She looked as young and cross as a virgin. She went back to her straight-back hair style; I was back in the period when I was disturbed by the soft hair of her eyebrows. Her voice was all telephone calls, invoices, orders, and snapping at things I had forgotten to do. She walked in a stately way to the filing cabinet. Only to that object did she bend: she said what a mess her predecessor or I had left it in. If she went downstairs to the yard when the lorries arrived, she had papers in her hand. The drivers were cocky at first and then were scared of her. And in time she destroyed our legend—the only unpopular thing she did—the legend of

Colonel Thompson. Dog or no dog, he had never come over the wall. The thief, she discovered, had been one of our gardeners. So Colonel Thompson retired to our private life.

Before this, our life had been one of beginnings, sudden partings, unexpected renewals. Now it hummed plainly along from day to day. The roles of Duggie and myself were reversed: when Duggie came home once a week now from Brussels, it was he who seemed to be the lover and I the husband. Sally grew very sharp with both of us and Duggie and I stood apart, on our dignity.

—

I have done one thing for him. I took my mother to dine with him, as I have said.

"What a saintly man," she said as we drove away. "Just like your father. He's coming to see me next time they're at their cottage."

(1980)

Cocky Olly

At the end of term I often give a lift to two or three of my students who are going back to London. They talk; I listen. Halfway, about forty miles from the city, where the motorway rises and slices through the Downs, cutting one off from the towns that are merely names on the road signs, I interrupt their chatter to point out one or two prehistoric barrows. The youngsters listen politely. When we pass the sign, "NEXT EXIT FORDHAMPTON," where a winding side road drops itself into the wooded country, I have the impulse to say that down there is a turning to Clapton St Luke, Fogham, and the Marshes—one of the paradises of my childhood—but I check it. And farther on we pass Newford, where I was at school when I was a girl, forty years ago. One of these days, when there is no one with me, I plan to go and look at these places, but I never do. The main road whips it all away.

I hear Newford is larger now; people commute from there to London. Only a few used to take a train from Fordhampton, with its main street running down the hill to the small river, where we would lean from the bridge hoping to see the private trout in the pool where rich Londoners, one of them a Cabinet Minister, used to fish at weekends. On Monday mornings, when I was waiting at our station for the train to take me to school, the Cabinet Minister would be dressed in bowler hat, black coat, and striped trousers, and carrying his official case. Unlike the rest of the passengers, he would be trotting up to the end of the platform and back, often fifteen times: I counted. If my father drove me to the station he would give his big laugh and say loudly for anyone to hear, "Bloody politician. Up to no good." I was a weekly boarder at the school in Newford, and at first my mother drove me all the way and then would pick me up on Saturday mornings and drive me home to Upper Marsh, a different country, almost an island between the

Downs, where the village people had a more drawling way of talking than the people in the towns. I had picked up the habit before my school days, from the children I played with on the farm near our house.

Marsh Hole really was like a deep hole, where four lanes met at a big farm. Our house was a mile up the road to Upper Marsh, a red mock-Tudor villa that I used to boast was Elizabethan. It was built between the wars. I also thought it was immense, but it was small. It looked out onto a large field of kale. At the back of our house (which my school friend Augusta called "the eyesore") lay a two-mile stretch of water meadow that went to the foot of the bald Downs themselves. Rarely did one see anyone walking across it and not often any cattle grazing, either. The endless pampas (as I used to call it—one of my favourite words) was alive with insects in the spring and summer, and, from my bedroom, I used to feel I had only to stretch my finger to touch the prehistoric barrow at the top of the far-off hill and the curious chalk track that went in a zigzag scratch almost to the top. The water meadow began at a hedge at the bottom of our steep garden. I remember when I was thirteen gazing at it and feeling it all belonged to our family. This was because the people at Lower Marsh, half a mile farther down our lane, had exactly the same view, although we could not see their house even in the winter. A mound or tongue of coppice kept us from the sight of our nearest neighbours. Lower Marsh had a short avenue of elms leading to a farm where I used to play with the village boys. Lower Marsh House itself was large and grey, with big windows. The village boys said it was haunted. A strange tall man with a long black beard sometimes came out of it, and once I saw him in the road piddling into the hedge near our house. Another time, a funeral hearse went by and after that the black-bearded man did not appear again. But my mother told me I could not have seen all this, because I wasn't even born. Yet it is very vivid to me, and now I think I must have heard my parents talking of some such event much later.

But I know for a fact that years later Lower Marsh House was occupied by Major Short and his wife and a young boy, because I saw them hitting a shuttlecock in the air once or twice as we drove past. Often at weekends if we were walking by we could see two or three cars parked in the avenue of elms.

"Guests!" my mother would say.

"Weekend riffraff," my father said. "Gang of traitors. Pacifists, longhaired pansies, atheists, bathing stark naked in that swimming-pool. Friends of Hitler and Stalin. Calls himself a major."

"Well, he was," my mother would say.

"First World War," said my father, who was a brigadier.

"But, Buzzer," my mother said—Buzzer was my father's army nickname: they used to say he buzzed like a wasp—"didn't Major Short do rather well in that war, got a medal and was badly wounded?"

"Got himself blown up, some fool dug him out."

I always thought of the Major as a kind of fair-haired elephant, with a huge chest, lying under tons of French mud. My father had also been wounded. His left arm creaked and he wore a black glove on his artificial hand. He was a slight man with red hair and scalded patches on his face and a high, sandy kind of voice with grit in it, and when he talked of the Major he would get into a temper. Then he'd laugh in the middle of it, and more than once he added, "Sends his boy to a god-awful boarding school in Dorset run by pansies and refugees wearing sandals, where the boys live in trees. Girls, too. No wonder the little bastard runs away."

"Surely not in trees, Buzzer," my mother would say in her high, thrilled, happy voice. I think that my mother and father were thrilled by each other.

"Ruined by that nanny they had, too," Father went on. "Not a lad I'd care to have in my command."

These outbursts cheered my father. He was often up and down to the War Office in London or away fishing. At home he would either be ordering Mother's plants about in the garden or sitting for hours playing patience with his one hand. "Crash, crash, tinkle, tinkle, tinkle," he would call out as he put a winning deal down. He was thinking of glass flying about in French villages when shells burst during that war.

Another thing that annoyed my father was that the Shorts did not go to church. We were forbidden to know them. Mother said it was nothing to do with that old war. The real trouble was that our land almost joined theirs and that the Major had cut down several fir trees at the edge of it. My father, Mother said in her heavenly voice, liked cover.

As for myself, I often thought about "the little bastard" Benedict, who not only lived in trees but was a "run-away" as well: that worried Mother, too. In spite of the quarrel between the two men, I believed Mother and Mrs Short sometimes met in Newford. They belonged to a musical group, a quartet. More than once I saw the boy shopping with his father and mother in Fordhampton, jumping up and down with excitement as he called to them to look at the posters of a gangster film at the cinema and talking with a spluttering lisp. He had black hair like his mother's and her same sunburned toasted skin—because he lived in trees, perhaps—and he was handsome in his mother's way. I used to wonder if he had run away that very day. He was two years younger than I.

At fourteen, I was a studious girl. I longed to be a monitor at my school and I thought, as my father did, that Benedict was spoiled and that he ought to be "taken in hand." Often when I was out in our garden and looking at the Downs rising straight out of the marsh I was fascinated by the chalky track rising to the top and I would think of Benedict "running" forty miles, at least, across country, and coming down that track as he came at last in sight of his home. I soon found out that in fact he did not run far. He had the nerve to telephone his father once he had escaped from that school of his and his father drove out at night, to pick him up outside some pub on the road. I was awed by this crime.

This and the thought of all those guests "bathing naked" in the "traitors'" house at Lower Marsh gripped me. In the holidays I would sometimes get through the hedge at the bottom of our garden and follow the rough ground until their house came into view and I would see the lawn of the Shorts' garden and keep an eye open for a sight of the runaway. Once, I thought I saw him with his mother walking across the water meadow picking wild flowers. Another time, he was coming in our direction and then drifted away. I used to think if he came near our garden I would shout out to him, "What are you doing here? This is private property!" At last I decided to be illegal myself one weekend and to climb through our hedge and then walk cautiously all along the meadow till I could get a full view of the Shorts and their friends. Getting through the hedge always excited me. The air seemed freer on the other side, the smells different. I did this many times just for something to do, and at first went no nearer. I always took an apple with me, throwing it up and down as I walked, for I thought this would make the Shorts think I was passing by accident. Sometimes there was no one there, sometimes only Mrs Short digging in her garden. If it was a weekend there would be several men and women sitting in basket chairs on the long veranda or on the lawn. The lawn looked rough, but sometimes they played a mixture of bowls and croquet. In time I got bolder, passing within twenty yards of their garden. No sign of naked atheists or a swimming pool and only once a sight of Benedict, running from player to player. I heard the Major booming at him.

I gave up bothering about the Shorts. One hot and heavy afternoon at the end of that summer when the clouds hardly moved and the water meadow was as still as a photograph I got through our hedge again and walked across the water meadow, soon eating my apple, because I was thirsty. I looked at the St John's-wort, a yellow flower that swarms with disgusting caterpillars. The insects were biting and I kept brushing off the flies that were swirling round my head. I remember the swallows and crows were flying low. I was making for the wood at the bottom of the Downs and when I got there the wood pigeons had stopped cooing. Even the flies had gone. The wood had that cankered, damp smell—the smell of toadstools. It came into my head to see if there were any Red Blushers, which excited me, because there might be also what my fungus book called Poisonous or False Red Blushers—not that I would touch them but I liked to give myself a fright by staring at poisonous things and congratulating myself on knowing the difference. I didn't go too deeply into the wood but just shuffled through the dead leaves. The wood was darker, and presently I felt a big warm spit of rain on my face. Suddenly a shot went off, and I nearly jumped out of my skin and the silent wood pigeons came clattering out of the trees and went circling over the marsh. Then there was a long silence. I hurried out of the wood, and crackling sticks seemed to be coming after me. Suddenly the runaway came running out, carrying a gun. There were tears on his white face as he rushed at me.

"Quick! Quick!" he screeched. "I've shot a bird. It's streaming with blood. It's frightful. It's still alive. It's flapping about." And he grabbed hold of my arm.

I brushed back my hair. I heard myself saying in my father's voice, "Stop waving that gun about. You can't leave a wounded bird." I shook off his arm. "Show me where it is," I said.

"Up here! Up here!" he shouted out.

The bird was lying on the ground flapping one wing. There was blood on it and its white lids were closing upward. Benedict was afraid to touch it.

"It's got diphtheria," he said. "That's why I shot it."

I knelt to pick it up.

"Birds don't get diphtheria," I said.

"They do," he screeched.

In a moment it was dead and horribly warm.

"We must bury it," I said.

"No," he said and stepped away. He was white and frantic.

"Come back," I said. "We can't leave it here. It's cruel." When I was small we always buried a bird if we found one dead.

"You must bury it," I ordered. "Dig a hole." He had no knife. Nor had I. I told him to get a stick. He obeyed and we started digging a hole in the soft ground.

"Make it deep," he said. He was excited now. At last the hole was deep enough and I put the poor bird in and raked the earth back. "More leaves, more leaves," he said. "In case a stoat digs it up."

"Did you get permission to have that gun?" I said. We were very hot about "getting permission" for things at school.

"It's Glan's," he said. Glanville was his father. "Is this your half-term?"

"No," I said. "I'm a weekly boarder."

"The Devil lives here," he said. He had decided to frighten me.

"That's stupid," I said. "He doesn't exist."

"It's a she-devil," he said and he started jumping about in a jeering way.

"You're dotty," I said.

I now felt several drops of rain, then it was pattering down. This stopped us talking and we looked up. There was a strange change of light and then a rumbling noise. The air was hot and heavy. Thunder! We hurried out of the wood, which was filled with a new sour smell, and just as we got out of the trees there was a long yellow flash of lightning. The peal of thunder came at once.

Benedict gave one of his shrill laughs. "We'll be struck dead," he screeched.

"We must get away from the trees," I said. And then the rain came drenching down so that we could hardly see his distant house through it.

We started to run. My blue-and-white cotton dress was soaked at once, and we were nearly blinded by the rain. There was another flash as we stumbled through the humps of the meadow and then mud splashed our legs. We were running towards the Shorts' house; thank goodness my father was away fishing. We got across the ditch onto Benedict's forbidden lawn and ran up to the veranda of the house. I looked around as we ran: no swimming-pool in sight. The Major's wife was standing there calmly, and then the Major came out.

"Ah," he said in a calm, insinuating, conspiratorial voice. "The frightful Benedict and who has he brought with him? Is it the apple girl? I wonder. Yes, it is the apple girl."

I realised I had been watched from the house every time I walked past. I was afraid of him.

"Oh, Benedict, you're drowned," his mother said. "What a bore you are. What on earth got into your head, when you know the Crowthers and the others are coming any minute. And look at poor dear Sarah. Get inside." How did she know my name?

"Shall I take the firearm?" said Glanville Short to Benedict. "I wonder how it came into your possession?"

All houses have their smell. The Shorts' house was larger than ours and smelled of thyme and oil paint and old wood fires.

We were taken up the plain polished stairs of the house—the stairs of *our* house were carpeted—passing paintings of geometric faces which looked new. I remember two fat pink naked nymphs dancing on a big seashell and two naked young men standing looking at them. We passed a large room upstairs with bookcases going up to the ceiling and a picture of that tall man with the long black beard sitting in a basket chair and stroking a cat. I was pushed into a bathroom.

"Get it all off, I think, don't you, Sarah, my dear?" said Mrs Short, who had a book in her hand. "While I see to Benedict."

What a bathroom! There was a blown-up painting or photograph of an ancient ruin, which continued on three walls of the room from floor to ceiling. I rubbed myself with a towel. When Mrs Short came back I was staring at the painting.

"Is that the Roman Forum?" I said, showing off.

"No, that is Persepolis, my dear. In Persia." She pointed to a figure on a grand but broken stairway. "They say it is Darius—you remember?—but it doesn't seem possible. Now, I don't know what we're going to fit you out with." She had brought a bundle of shorts and jerseys with her.

"We were burying a dead bird," I said.

"We could turn the legs up. Do you mind shorts?"

People coming, I thought, as I dried my hair. How awful.

"Please don't bother," I said as I pulled on the shorts. "May I ring my mother?"

"Now you're a boy—what do you make of that? Rather fun? How is your mother? I missed her at the chamber music last week."

So that rumour was true! I had always suspected that although we were ordered by my father not to know the Shorts, she and my mother still met at Newford.

"Rather chic, I think," she said, looking at me. "You must come down and get warm."

We went along the corridor and round corners to a second flight of stairs, down to a kitchen and through a cloakroom with a telephone in it, and then across the hall into a large morning room, where there was a music stand with a sheet of music on it near a large window, and a violin propped against one wall. A radio was on a big table with books and newspapers and also on the same table there was a large, unfinished jigsaw puzzle spread out.

And that is how I remember Emma Short always: a small woman with small, brown brilliant eyes, as dark as Benedict was, wearing a plain but pretty dress, chattering and eagerly questioning herself as she stands before the large puzzle of some famous picture—a cathedral or a castle perhaps, with a river in the foreground. This one also had the figure of a man with a boat on the river. She is standing there picking up a piece and saying, "How beastly they are to put so much water in these things. It's cheating. What a bore. Ah, now—here, do you think? No. No. Ah, perhaps here? You must look at the little wiggles." And she put a curly piece of the puzzle into its place.

"You must know Mrs Figg," she said.

"She teaches us French," I said, surprised.

"I *know*!" said Mrs Short with a laugh. "Too extraordinary. What do you make of her? Odd, do you find? Her hats! Is Augusta a friend of yours? She's coming."

Augusta Chambers, head girl of my school! Augusta—to see me dressed up like this!

I said again I must telephone to my mother to fetch me.

"Glan will do that," she said. "You must have some tea to warm you up."

Through the window I saw two or three cars arrive. People and their children were soon jabbering in the hall. I heard Benedict screeching at them. As they came into the room Benedict was pulling Augusta's father by the wrist and saying, "Foxey, Foxey, you're a murderer, a murderer. I'm going to report it to the police."

"The number is 3052," said Augusta's father. "Shall I get it for you?"

There was a crowd of people taking off their coats in the hall. Benedict let Foxey's hand go, and Augusta came to me and said, "What fun." She whispered, "Benedict is mad, as usual."

I was muttering that I must go and getting nearer to the door to escape when Glanville Short stopped me. "I have told your mother," he said. "You're staying to tea."

Suddenly we were in a dining-room, sitting round a very large painted table, which seemed to be an astrological map.

"Your marvellous table," said Augusta. And to me, "Emma designed it. Isn't it wonderful?"

I was still embarrassed by my ridiculous clothes. I had never seen so many people in my life, all talking their heads off. At home we lived to ourselves, as my father said. Doors were always shut in our house. Here all the doors were open and names were flying about. Everyone was asking questions about other people. Benedict was screeching. The walls of the room were painted pale violet. A number of people I had never heard of were declared "mad." A Mary somebody was "too extraordinary about her dogs." There was news that someone called Stephanie had lost the manuscript of a novel she was writing, on a bus, for the second time.

"What do you make of Chester?" someone said.

The city or some person? I could not guess. I was out of my depth in this new language, but Benedict was listening eagerly, as if enchanted by mockery when his father spoke.

Augusta's handsome brother sat between me and Emma Short. He asked where I lived and went to school. When I told him about school, he said, "Bad marks—it's on the Right Bank," which amused him. It was a long time, almost a year, before I found out what he meant, and by then I was mad about him. People like the Shorts were sometimes called the Left Bank of an imaginary river like the Seine. Newford was very Right Bank, Fordhampton was very Left.

Suddenly tea was over. Emma Short groaned. "It's still raining," she said. "What a bore. No croquet."

"But Emma," said Augusta's brother, "we could take umbrellas."

"Yes!" shouted Benedict, getting up. "Umbrellas, umbrellas—we'll get umbrellas!"

"I think it will have to be Cocky Olly," said Glan Short.

And they all shouted, "Yes, Cocky Olly!"

"I don't know it," I said.

"You do know it," Benedict insisted. "You must do. This is Cocky Olly Lane—everyone plays it. It's Prisoner's Base."

"Cocky Olly" is the name that jumps into my mind even now when I drive past the signpost to Fordhampton. And when I look back on it who could have been more of a Cocky Olly than myself, chasing the runaway boy across the fields.

"Cocky Olly!" we all shouted.

"No one to go into the bedrooms," said Emma Short. "Library and bathrooms are free."

"Including, I hope," said Foxey, "the pig's bathroom." He meant that Glanville had kept half a pig in brine in one of the bathrooms during the war. I had heard of this at home, and I had been told that it was illegal to cure a pig without registering the fact with the agricultural inspector. My father always said Major Short ought to be reported to the inspector and sent to jail.

And so with Foxey as Cocky Olly to start us off, the grown-ups and we children raced up the stairs and hid all over the house. Soon we were shouting warning cries of "Cocky Olly on the back stairs!" as everyone raced away. "Cocky Olly in the library!" "Cocky Olly in the passage!" "Cocky Olly in Annie's room!" and we raced up another flight, and Augusta, who had been caught, was shouting, "Rescue, rescue!" and Benedict was crying for rescue, too. I got to him and touched him. He was free. He was the most excited of us all. Round the house, up and down, we went. On a desk in the library, where Glanville worked, I came upon a huge book called *The Building of the Pyramids.* It was written, Augusta told me, by that old man with the long black beard—the one I had seen peeing into the hedge, whose portrait was on the wall, not easy to see because the afternoon was dark. The rain was still coming down. Then the hue and cry came again, the sound of scattering people. I ran along the passage and made for a door where the passage turned a corner. Benedict had scooted there. We collided and stepped back into a small room where the curtains were drawn. Suddenly Benedict locked the door. "That's not fair," I said. I can hear myself, even now, saying it.

Benedict said in his shrill voice, "There's a dead body in here."

I was not going to be scared by him. I remembered what Foxey had done when Benedict called him a murderer.

"Yes," I said. "I know. I've reported it. It's on the floor. Give me the key or I'll put the light on."

He gave me the key at once.

"This is your room," I said.

"It isn't," he said. "It used to be Nanny's, but we threw her out." I told him he couldn't scare me, and, in fact, after that I couldn't get rid of him. He followed me everywhere as we chased round in the game.

The grown-ups had gone down to the drawing room and eventually, hot and puffed, we went in to join them. It was a greenish silky room. Glanville was handing out orange juice to cool us down, and small glasses of gin, I suppose, to the grown-ups and to Augusta's brother, too. Glanville moved slowly, politely, with a sly conspiring look in his eyes as he gave us our drinks. He had been in the middle of telling a story when we rushed in, and now he continued. He had been on a jury at Winchester, he said, and there was evidence from a policeman who said he had seen the prisoner signalling to a confederate on a racecourse, and then the judge had said, "A signal, officer? Would you be kind enough to do the signal for us?" and the officer made strange movements with his hand. The judge said, "Officer, would you mind doing that again?"

Glanville had a gift for acting. He could make you feel guilty by rolling his eyes and looking mysterious. In a fish shop in Fordhampton when I was with my mother we once heard him saying in his quiet accusing voice to the fishmonger, "Have you fish?"

I looked round at the pictures on the walls of the drawing room. There were two clowns and there was a painting of a sculptured head of a girl in profile, mounted on a short marble stand, a girl with large eyes, very beautiful.

"It's a Stolz," Augusta whispered to me.

"No, it isn't," said her brother. "It's a Webb in her Stolz period." And to me he said, in Mrs Short's manner, "What do you make of it?"

"It looks chopped off," I said. I saw Augusta's brother was disappointed in me.

I looked at the heads of all the people in the room. They seemed to be like people from another planet. I was in love with them all and did not want to leave. And then Foxey said, "We must go," and Augusta said to me, "We'll drop you."

"No, I'll walk. It's only up the lane."

"You must come again," said Mrs Short.

"I wonder whether we shall see more of the apple girl," said Glan in his conspiring mocking tone. "I think we shall."

I remember sitting next to Augusta's brother in the back of the car and Benedict waving frantically to us.

"Where are your clothes?" my mother asked when I was dropped at our house.

I had forgotten them.

"What a sight you look."

I could not stop talking about everything and everyone I had seen—the house, the huge tea table, the puzzle on Mrs Short's table, the Persepolis in the bathroom. I explained that it was not my fault I had gone there, but I was worried about what my father would say. Mother made light of it. All she wanted to know was whether Benedict had played his violin.

This startled me.

"He is going to be good," my mother said in her thrilled voice. She was astonished that I did not know.

I could not go to sleep for thinking about it all: the rooms, the stairs, the girl's head, Benedict locking me in the room, and Augusta's brother. I looked at my room and hated our furniture and the smell of polish, and wanted to run away.

It was only in the morning that I remembered I had not seen the swimming-pool.

—

I admit that I left my wet clothes behind so that I would be able to return. The following morning, I went back to Lower Marsh openly by the road and down the avenue of elms, with a bundle of the Shorts' clothes under my arm, but kept back the shirt until it could be washed. The air was fresher after the storm. The front door of the house was open. There was no bell or knocker. I could hear Glanville talking on the telephone, which perhaps for some secret reason was in the cloakroom. At our house we had a proper telephone fitted in our hall.

I heard Glanville say on the telephone, "So you think well of Gentle Annie do you? I had rather fancied—" and I think he said "Monte Cristo." And then, "Rather dangerous, do you think? The going will be heavy after all the rain. Well, we must hope." Then he must have changed the subject, for in a conspiring, private voice he was saying, "I am inclined to agree with you, Foxey. I fancy that Oedipus is coming into the open. He is digging a grave in the garden—indeed, two graves. But we don't despair, Foxey. There is a filly, and we're pinning our hopes there. We shall have to see how it goes. Goodbye, Foxey."

Now what was that about?

Then he came out of the cloakroom and saw me.

"Ah, what have we here? The apple girl without her apple. She has brought a parcel. What can that be?"

He took the parcel and then, in his plotting way, said, "We must discover where the frightful Benedict is. Do you think he may be in the garden? Shall we go and see?"

I had decided that when he was buried under tons of earth by a land mine, or whatever it was, in the First World War, Glanville must have saved his life by asking himself innumerable questions. Perhaps that is silly, but he always looked at me or anyone else so steadily as he spoke that he was outside time and his blue eyes cast a spell. This made me shy, because he was not an old man. Now he led me through the house onto the long veranda and we looked down across the lawn. No sign of Benedict, so we went round the side of the house and there, in the paddock, we saw him. He was digging with difficulty in the tufty grass, and when we got to him we saw he had taped out two long rectangles side by side and had dug a few spadefuls of earth out of the end of one. As we watched, Benedict stuck the garden fork into the ground and danced around it.

"Can he be looking for buried treasure?" the Major asked.

Benedict jumped about crying, "Guess, guess, guess. Don't tell her, Glan."

I said he was making a flowerbed.

"No, no, no," he called out. "Guess."

Mrs Short came up from the garden and the Major explained why I was there. Benedict was annoyed because we were not talking to him.

"He says it is a swimming-pool—one for men, one for ladies," said Mrs Short.

We all laughed.

Benedict looked from one to the other of us. "I have changed it," he said. "It's an Egyptian tomb for Pharaoh."

"And this one, perhaps, for his wife?" said the Major, pointing to the second rectangle.

"Where is the pyramid?" I said.

"It's going to be a barrow," said Benedict. "An ancient mound."

The Major and his wife strolled away, and Benedict and I were left alone. I picked up the garden fork and tried to dig. "Don't do that," he said, and pulled the fork from me, rather frightened. "It's boring," he said.

It was a lazy morning, one of those long mornings—how long they are when one is young—when you wander about and every minute is as long as an hour.

"I'm going to see the dead bird," he said at last.

I did not want to go home. I thought, This is where I want to stay, so I followed him. We crossed the hedge into the water meadow, where the air was cool, and listened to the swish of our shoes against the wiry grass and watched the insects jump away and stopped to listen to the larks singing like electric bells high up in the sky and tried to see them, and we seemed to walk from one electric bell to another. Like Benedict I was playing at running away. First he went ahead fast, but I soon caught up and passed him.

"Beat you," I said, and rumpled his head as I passed. He began to chase me. We passed the end of the wood where the dead bird was and got across the stream, where we messed about with sticks in the water and startled birds. Then we began to climb. I wanted to get to the top of the barrow, but it was longer and higher than I had imagined it would be. The view grew wider and wider and went on for miles, and there was no sound now. We were high above the singing larks. I could see our house and Benedict's standing quiet with the sun on them. We stopped and sat down. We were sitting on the bones of people who had died *millions* of years ago. There was no sound here except the wind, but then we heard the baaing of a ram. It sounded to me like the voice of a buried man, but I did not say this. We got up from where we were sitting and looked for it but could see nothing. The sound must have come from the ram far below. I nearly said, "The heights! How I love them!" but I didn't. Benedict, I thought, is too young; I was centuries older than he was. I wanted to stay there for ever—not with Benedict but, say, with Augusta's brother, and when we stood for a last look on the miles of flat fields and clumps of trees where there would be a church tower and little houses on the far side, with a road wriggling round a wood, I wanted to go there, too. Suddenly—I don't know why—thinking of Augusta's brother, I marched up to Benedict and kissed him and ran off. He didn't like this and picked up a thorny stick and chased after me.

I stopped. "Why do you run away from school?" I asked severely.

"I hate it," he said at once. "It's boring. I'm not going back."

The Devil was there, he went on. Benedict and the Devil! The Devil was dressed in red, he said. This time the Devil was the man who taught music there at his school. He was ignorant, stupid.

It was getting late. We went stumbling down the steep path, and as we got lower I could hear the skylarks again, no higher than my shoulder but far out over the fields below. I could almost have caught one of them.

When we got down to the meadow Benedict was angry when I said I had to get back home. "Stay, stay," he said, "I'll let you dig." But I said no, I didn't want to dig. He followed me across the meadow to our hedge, still saying "Stay." I said I had to pack up and go back to school in the afternoon. When I got through the hedge and called out "Goodbye," he shouted "I hate you!" I saw him walking away and then suddenly he ran and then he was out of sight. I don't know why I kissed him when we were on the barrow.

Everything changed at my school in Newford after that party at Lower Marsh. Augusta, who was a good deal older than I and taller, had never taken much notice of me, but now she came floating round me like a swan. She had long golden hair and large grey dreaming eyes that narrowed and dwelled on you in an inspecting way. She said, "I didn't know you knew the Shorts," in a way that suggested I had hidden a secret from her. Her voice seemed to float on romantic secrets. She was also our chief mimic and gossip. She'd do Mrs Figg's sarcastic voice, and she knew which teacher was in love with an old don at Oxford who was married. She called two girls who doted on the art master "Picasso's Doves," and the headmistress "the blessed St Agnes." To be with her was like reading a novel in serial parts; she paused and we knew there were chapters to come.

I told her that we did not really know the Shorts, though my mother, I thought, often met Mrs Short at a musical quartet at Newford.

She narrowed her questioning eyes. "I adore Glan and Emma, don't you?"

And before I knew what I was saying I said there was some trouble about fir trees.

"Fir trees!" said Augusta with a laugh that egged me to go on, but I had come to a lame end.

We were going into supper and Mrs Figg passed us. "Don't dawdle, Sarah," she said.

I was not a dawdling girl, and I saw that I must have been copying Augusta's dawdling walk. It was new to me, and I felt I had grown up several months. As we separated and went to our different tables Augusta said, off-hand, "Of course, Benedict's quite mad. My father says it goes back to that awful pious nurse he had. She used to tell him that the Devil would get him and that he would go to hell. And then there was that awful Webb business." And, with that, she glided away.

But the phrase "that awful Webb business" and Augusta walking away with her I-know-more-than-you-do look made me dog Augusta whenever I could. And I could see by her face that she noticed this. We went off the next day to play tennis on the school court. She was a slapdash tennis player, and even the few balls that came over the net seemed to know something. When we left the court and went to our dormitory to change I said, "My father didn't cut down those fir trees. It was old Webby who used to work for the Shorts as well as for us."

Augusta stood there with her blouse off. Her grown-up breasts, larger than mine, seemed to be staring at me. The bell rang and we hadn't washed.

"Run along," she said. "Actually," she said—we all said "actually" in a cutting way in those days—"I was talking about Glanville's first wife. She died years ago. She drowned."

I felt I was like some silly fish dangling on a hook in hot air. I could not breathe.

"Come along, girls," Mrs Figg called from the door of the dormitory. I choked my way into my clothes. I sluiced my face and through the water I saw the astonishing stone face of the drowning Webb in the drawing room at Lower Marsh.

Poor Benedict, I thought, and I ran down the clattering stairs to the dining room. I mumbled my way through grace and saw Augusta across the room saying grace beautifully, her lovely chin raised. Later she ate slowly, while I was racing through my food and spilled my milk. I was still wriggling on Augusta's hook. I was in her power.

But Augusta was merciful to me, or else, I suppose, she saw the kind of opportunity she loved. If she was dreamy, she was also crisp.

In our free time it was easy for girls to be in twos, lying in the grass, and at last I was able to say, "Poor Benedict, his mother drowned." This explained the strange things he did, and his talk of the body in the room.

"I did not say that," said Augusta scornfully. "Emma is his mother. Glan was married to Webb. Then he married Emma. What a thing to say! Did your father say that? If he did, it's very wicked," she said sharply.

I said no, he'd never said anything like that, nor my mother, I swore. Augusta was still suspicious of this, but at last she saw how confused I was, and she forgave me. She said that Glanville had married a Miss Webb when he came home after the First World War; everyone was mad about her. It was not until much later that I began to wonder how Augusta knew the story. It must have happened before the war and she wasn't born then. But she said that Webb had gone off to Egypt with a painter called Stolz and that he had left her, and so she had come home and drowned herself in the river at Fordhampton.

The one where father can't afford to fish, I thought. And then I thought of Benedict digging a grave for Pharaoh and his wife in his garden.

I had already told Augusta about this the day after Cocky Olly, but when I mentioned it again now, Augusta cut the story short. "That boy is always digging," she said. "He wants to be an archaeologist, like that man in Glanville's library." And she said dreamily, "I would never be a second wife, unless he was like Glanville."

We got up from the grass laughing. I mean, I laughed; Augusta didn't. Anyway, she said, Emma and Glan were sending Benedict to the grammar school in Newford. That would stop him running away because he'd come home every day by train. And she gave me one of her narrow-eyed looks. The Shorts were her possession.

—

The long holidays began. My father took us to Devonshire to stay in a hotel near a place where he went fishing. Mother and I went on long walks, and the only event of the day was to come back by the bridge over the river to catch sight of him. We were not allowed to go near him when he was fishing. Once or twice we drove ten miles to a high red-faced cliff—they were not chalky cliffs as they are in our part of the country. The waves were forever staining the sand red near the shore. We used to park on the cliff with other cars and walk not too near the edge and look at the sea glittering some days and on others tumbling fast down the Channel. I loved the Channel because it was wider here. This was the only time I thought of the Shorts and

Benedict, for they were in Brittany. *La mer*: what a beautiful word! We had a set book by Pierre Loti to read in the holidays. My mother said she, too, had had to read it at school when she was a girl, yet she was no help with the words I didn't know.

So, back home again. It seemed dull. I rushed to my post at the end of our garden and looked across the water meadow, but there was no sight of Benedict on the first day. In the middle of the week I did see him in the distance with a girl taller than he and making for his house. I waved. They did not see me, and I tried to make myself look larger when they came into closer view. I waved again. They still did not see me. I felt something like a red-hot electric wire run through me—a wire that seemed to turn into a flame, as if I were alight. Then I went icy cold. Benedict was with Augusta! I was flaming with jealousy. I watched till they went out of sight.

My father was in the garden talking to my mother, who was pulling up weeds. I got carried away and went out to the road and walked along to the Shorts' drive. There were cars outside the house, one of them Foxey's red car. A party. And I wasn't invited. I was stiff with misery. I went back to my room and tried to read, but I was listening, for hours it seemed to me, to hear the cars drive away. When I went to bed my jealousy went. I remembered that the next week I would see Benedict on the train to and from school.

But at first this was not so. On the first day of term Augusta told me that Benedict's mother was going to drive him to his grammar school and bring him back each day. So I became a parcel again on my weekly journey. On Monday mornings I saw the politician doing his morning trot up and down the platform, and weekend people going to London with their papers, and a few grammar-school boys who got in at King's Mill and played cards all the way. Their school caps had a yellow ring round them. On Saturday afternoons there was always a large crowd of them going back to their homes in King's Mill or Fordhampton. About a dozen of them would stand on the platform bashing one another with their cases, and cheeking the woman who ran the buffet. Sometimes she turned them out. They crowded round the slot machines and tried to force them to yield up coins. I used to sit on a seat watching them. The porters grinned at the boys, but the ticket inspector hated the way they pushed past him. Sometimes a boy would be pushed onto my seat and I would walk away higher up the platform. There was a fat boy who was always eating chocolate.

The first Saturday I saw Benedict on the platform, he was keeping clear of the other boys. "Hullo," he said eagerly in his high voice, and the fat boy mocked, "Squeaky's got a little t-tart."

They stared at us and then went on pushing one another around. Benedict was carrying his violin case. I had never seen that before. I asked him why he wasn't wearing the school cap.

"Because I hate it," he said.

I can't remember what we talked about except that I told him that I had seen him with an old lady walking across the water meadow and had waved to him. He was startled.

"A witch," he said.

"No, it wasn't," I said. "It was Augusta. Don't tell her I said that."

"I'll tell," he said.

I knew he would, because every now and then after our train came in and we took our seats he said, "I'll tell, I'll tell."

At Fordhampton, Glan was waiting for him, and my mother was there as well.

"Aha!" said Glanville in his insinuating way. "The apple girl."

"It seems damn silly," said my father to my mother when I got home. "Why couldn't he have given Sarah a lift and saved you the trouble? Save petrol, too. Typical socialist."

"You don't give the boy a lift," Mother said.

"Don't be an owl," Father said. "That man's got nothing to do."

So every Monday and Saturday I travelled on the train with Benedict. He had become quieter and it seemed that he had settled into the school. It was "beastly" there, of course, but chiefly, he said, because the music master was angry when he told him the school piano was out of tune. He also hated Prayers, and the fat boy who got into the train at King's Mill was the Devil. This came out one morning when a man across from us was reading a newspaper with a headline in big print: "CLIFF MURDER: HUNT FOR BRIGHTON YOUTH." Benedict began jumping up and down in his seat and said the fat boy had done it. "It's Fatty! It's Fatty!" he said in a furious whisper. I told him not to be silly. At school I told Augusta this was now the only sign of Benedict's being mad, but she had changed this term. She said it was Glanville who put these ideas into his son's head. Foxey said so, too. But after this Benedict was calm. One day he brought his stamp collection and he showed it to me, and once I ruffled his black hair when he said I was as fat as Augusta. I knew what he meant: I was growing up. I told him Augusta would marry him if he was not careful, and I laughed because he looked scared. He was very polite after that.

—

I enjoyed those train rides and I missed him for two weeks when he had flu. I was glad to see him when he reappeared on the platform at Newford Station. I had got there late because I had gone into one of the shops in the town to buy a lipstick like Augusta's. I had run all the way from the shop, frightened that I had missed the train. At first I didn't see Benedict. Some boys were crowded round the fat boy as usual, begging him to give them a bit of his chocolate. The fat boy was backing away from them and Benedict was watching. The fat boy was sly and stood back against the wall, looking around for some way of escape. One boy was pulling at his arm. Suddenly the fat boy broke from them and went up to Benedict, snatched his cap from his pocket, and cried, "Put your cap on, Squeaky, or I'll report you."

Benedict stood holding his violin case and did not put his cap on, and the fat boy suddenly stepped forward and pulled the cap down over Benedict's eyes and face. I called out, "Leave him alone."

And then I saw Benedict do a stupid thing. He pulled his cap off and sent it flying off the platform and onto the railway track, and then, white with fright, he dashed at the fat boy and struck him on the shoulder with his violin case, screeching out, "I'll kill you!"

The fat boy moved away, frightened. Two women were watching us, and one of them said, "I will report you to your headmaster," and she said to her friend, "It's Major Short's boy." I got Benedict by the sleeve and we walked away from the crowd. I was giddy with temper and walked him far up the platform, and when I looked back I saw the boys gaping at the cap lying on the railway line. Two boys were beginning to follow us, but the others were still crowding round Fatty. And then the train came in. I got Benedict into a first-class carriage in front. Three of Fatty's crowd raced up looking for us, but I pulled down the blind. I could hear the porters bawling, and the boys ran back. We sat still; the compartment had a notice saying "Ladies Only." There was a long wait and a strange silence at our end of the train. I let down the window and saw some of the boys getting off the train, all laughing. I heard a porter shout, "Not this train!" A whistle blew. The train, I saw, was much longer than the train we usually took.

"We're on the wrong train," I said. "It's the express. Quick. It doesn't stop at Fordhampton," and I tried to open the door. Then the train—one of the new diesels—moved out fast. I turned round. Benedict was lounging back on the seat.

"I knew!" he said, laughing at me.

"You beast," I said.

I was scared. I saw the last of the pink houses of Newford and heard the chime of the signal box, as final and frightening as if it were killing itself with laughter. My father and mother would be waiting for me at Fordhampton and the train would whiz through. And that woman from Lower Marsh who had heard me shout in the mixup with the boys—she would report it all to my father. I lost my head.

"Why didn't you tell me it was the wrong train?" I said. "I hate you."

"I'm running away," he said, delighted by my terror. "I hate that school. I hate Glanville. I'm not going back."

There is a long wooded stretch outside Newford and all the leaves on the trees seemed to be talking about us. Had he planned it?

"Where are you going?" I said.

He was sitting there gloating and grinning. "To London," he said.

"But that's in the opposite direction. This train goes to Bath."

"I'll get a London train there," he said.

"You're mad. It's hundreds of miles away."

What frightened me was that I had only two shillings on me.

"How much money have you got?" I said.

"My aunt lives in Bath. She'll give me the money," he said.

The train was speeding. Two little stations went by like a shout.

"The Devil is on this train," he said with glee. "I saw him on the platform."

I was standing up still, and the train swerved at King's Mill when it crossed the river. A man was fishing there. I fell onto my seat. I was tired of Benedict and his Devil.

"I'll rape you," he said.

"You won't," I said. "Silly little Squeaky." And I got up and rumpled his hair. "You'd better look at your violin. You smashed it when you hit that boy."

This stopped him. He opened his case and took out his violin and looked at it very carefully and then he took up his bow and played one or two notes. They sounded very sad. All this time I had been trying not to cry, and it was the sound of those notes, like someone speaking, that stopped me. In that moment I recovered my wits. I looked about the compartment and noticed the communication cord. A notice said "Emergency. To Stop Train Pull the Cord. Penalty for Improper Use £5." I was scared. When the train got near Fordhampton I knew I was going to pull the cord and make it stop there. I sat down and got out one of my school books and pretended to read, but I was looking at the fields. When the train got to Flour Mill I would get ready to pull the cord. This calmed me. I got up and said, "I am going to the lavatory." I was dying to go. "There's one for you at the other end of the corridor," he said.

There was the door marked "Toilet Vacant." I went in. The window was of frosted glass so that I couldn't see out, but I could tell by the sound of the train crossing the river where we were. We'd crossed one bridge. There were two more to come. I knew how long that took. I wasn't long in the lavatory before someone tried the door. I waited. Then I pulled the catch. It had stuck. It wouldn't open at first; when it did there was the ticket inspector on the other side. The inspector always tested the door in order to catch any one hiding from him. He was a big man with a red face and a black moustache like a wet paintbrush.

"Sorry, Miss. Ticket, please."

"It's in my bag in the compartment," I said. He looked at my hat—we wore straw hats with a red band at my school—and slowly followed me to the compartment. Benedict was not there, and as I opened my bag I heard a deep rumbling noise, louder than the noise of river bridges. We were rushing over the High Street at Fordhampton. The station platform screeched at us, people flew away in a stream of dots, the green top of the town hall danced away, and the brick orphanage on the outskirts of the town looked down on us from fifty narrow windows. I had forgotten this was an express train. With a final clap Fordhampton vanished, the points clattered, and the oak woods closed in on us. Benedict came into the compartment.

"Ticket," the ticket inspector said to Benedict, who got out his train pass.

"We're going to Bath," Benedict said coolly.

"You're in first class!" said the inspector. "Fordhampton, it says here. That your violin? We've passed Fordhampton."

He took my train pass and looked at it and said the same thing. Then he sat down with us and got out a printed pad. "Both going to Bath? Plenty of room in third class in the next coach."

He slowly turned the pages of his pad. "You'll be owing me some money," he said. "Ten pounds each. You got in at Newford, I see. It comes expensive." He looked very sly when he said this and then sighed and said sharply, "First class—let me see. Fifteen pounds each, I make it. Holidays begun early, eh? Playing in a concert?" He was looking around in the compartment, and I knew he was trying to see if we had smashed the lightbulbs or slashed the seat.

"We got into the wrong train and some boys locked us in. We thought it was the Fordhampton train," I said. "My father is waiting for us. He's a brigadier. It's terrible. No one told us at Newford. I'm not going to Bath, and we missed our lunch."

"Well, it will be a long wait," said the inspector. "But your friend's going to Bath. With his violin?"

"No, I'm going to London. I'm in the school orchestra," Benedict said calmly.

I was so amazed I could only say, "Benedict!"

"I am," said Benedict.

"It's a funny way to go to London. Down to Bath, up to London, wrong way round. Cost you more. Twenty-five pounds, I make it."

"Where is the buffet car?" said Benedict, putting on an important voice.

The inspector said it was two coaches back. "Stay where you are," he said. He got up slowly. He put his pad in his pocket and said he'd be back later on. We waited and waited.

"Why did you tell such lies? We'll be arrested."

"Let's go to the buffet car," Benedict said. "I'm hungry."

If only I hadn't bought that lipstick. With only my two shillings, we couldn't pay for lunch.

The train broke out of the Downs, where there was a white horse carved on the hill, and into unknown country, herds of cows in the fields, farms, chickens, horses galloping away. This flat country went on, mile after mile. Farther and farther. I worried where we would go in Bath, where we would sleep the night. Terrible tales came into my mind of girls attacked on trains. I was thinking about what my father had said about the Shorts.

"You're not giving a concert," I said. "You can't even play."

"I can," he said. He opened his case and got his violin out, but I asked if he had got any money. He pulled out a few coppers from his pocket. "Come on," he said. "Let's go to the buffet car. I'll tell them to send the bill."

But before we could move the inspector came back with a young man who stood in the doorway studying us and murmured something I couldn't catch.

"Stand up, Ben," this man said.

"My name is Benedict," said Benedict. He could be as cool and ironical as Glanville.

The young man said, annoyed, "Where's your school cap?"

I burst out, "A boy threw it on the line at Newford when the train was coming in."

"What was his name?" asked the man.

"Fatty," said Benedict.

"Better check at Castle Wadney," said the young man to the inspector. They went off down the corridor.

The train was gliding past wide fields of mustard, a few big clouds were hanging still in the sky. Presently the train slowed down almost to a standstill, and when I looked out I saw a gang of men standing back: they were working on the line. I can still remember every one of their faces looking up at me. Then we crawled past watercress beds to Castle Wadney, a town on a hill but with no castle that I could see. The train had stopped.

"Police," whispered Benedict excitedly.

The inspector came back and said, "Soon get you back, Miss. You're getting out here."

At that busy station porters were rolling milk cans down the platform. We were taken to the stationmaster's office, a dark room smelling of ink and tea. The stationmaster was drinking a cup in between talking on the telephone, and there was a machine somewhere that clicked dot, dot, dash. A man at another table called "Brighton on the line for you" to a very clean young man with hair short at the neck, who went to the telephone.

One of these new men looked at our train passes and asked our names again. I showed him mine on my exercise book. Someone was having a row with the stationmaster, who held the phone away from his ear.

"Sure it's not Knowles?" the smooth young man asked Benedict.

"Short. Short. Short," Benedict jeered.

"Short," I joined in. "I mean he's Short, I'm—"

"I'm asking him," said the smooth young man. "How do I know your name's Short, son?" he asked.

And then Benedict did a thing I'll never forget. He turned his back to the man and pulled the neck of his jacket clear of his neck until the name tape was showing.

The detective held the jacket and called to the two new men. "Take a dekko at this."

" 'Short,' " they both said. "OK, Sonny."

"Hold on, they're on the line," said the stationmaster into the telephone. Then he beckoned to us.

Glanville was on the line. Emma, too. And my father. When we had stopped talking to them the two inspectors had gone and so had our train. We were going to be sent back on the 3.44.

One of the detectives said, "Sorry, Miss." And the other said, "On the lookout for a lad from Brighton. You won't miss your concert," he said to Benedict and went off.

"Watch out," whispered Benedict. "They'll follow us." He was delighted.

The stationmaster took us to the buffet and told the woman there to give us what we asked for and to give the bill to him. He told Benedict his daughter was taking piano lessons. We were put on the 3.44 to Fordhampton, and I felt sad going back.

"It was the Brighton Cliff Murder," said Benedict. "They thought we were in on it."

And indeed a youth had taken the hand brake off his parents' car, jumped out, and left them to go over the cliff. There was a picture of a boy very like Benedict with curly hair. We saw it all when a man got in at one of the stops with the picture on the inside page and a headline saying "HUNT MOVES TO WEST COUNTRY." I muttered to Benedict, "Keep quiet or I'll strangle you."

Benedict started bouncing with delight on his seat. He said that Glan had told him all about the murder. And he started to tell me. The Devil would be in it, I knew.

"Stop it," I said. "Not now. You promised me."

The train was a slow one. The man got out at Stockney. And then I said, "Why did you say you were going to Bath?"

"To see the Roman ruins," he said.

"But you said London, too, to give a concert," I said. I couldn't keep up with him.

"I am going to the College of Music next term," he said.

I began to tease him. "There was a devil on *this* train—it was you," I said and gave him a push.

There is nothing to say about our arrival at Fordhampton, except that my mother was talking to Mrs Short, and Benedict was talking all the time to Glan, telling him how he had shown his name tape to the detective. Father was talking to the stationmaster, who was shaking his head.

"I gave the stationmaster at Newford a blowing up," Father said. "I mean, suppose they'd been troops?"

"It's the staff, you know what I mean," said the stationmaster. "Your daughter's here."

"Oh," said my father, astonished to see me. And then he saw Glanville and stiffened. "All present and correct," he said sarcastically.

In the car driving home I began telling my father and mother what had happened, but Father said, "Wait till we get home."

Mother said, "You should have pulled the alarm cord."

Father said, "Costs five pounds. I haven't got five pounds."

I didn't say anything about Benedict's saying he was running away. Father was already revelling in the war he was now beginning with the railway company. He was going to write to the chairman at once. He was going to get someone at the War Office to blow them up. Mother's eyes shone.

When I went to school on Monday Benedict was not on the train, but Mrs Figg had heard the story, because Mother had rung the school. Augusta knew, too. Then she told me that once a man had exposed himself in a train when she was there, in a full compartment!

What did she do? "Nothing," she said grandly. "I turned my head away and looked out of the window."

That weekend my mother picked me up at my school and Benedict at his and drove us back to the Shorts, and I was invited for tea. Father said it was the least they could do.

Mrs Short was standing by her puzzle when I got there, a new one of a castle.

"It's a beast," she said. There were a dozen people at that beautiful table and Benedict was crowing and interrupting his father. Then it was Cocky Olly again and all of us racing around.

(1989)

THE IMAGE TRADE

What do you make of the famous Zut—I mean his stuff in this exhibition?
Is he just a newsy collector of human instances jellied in his darkroom, or is
he an artist—a Zurbarán, say, a priest searching another priest's soul?
Pearson, one of a crowd of persons, was silently putting these questions to
them on a London bus going north.

Last July, Pearson went on, he was at home. The front-door bell rang.
"He's here! On time!" his beautiful wife said. She was scraping the remains
of his hair across his scalp. "Wait," she said, and turning him round, she gave
a last sharp brush to his shoulders and sent him dibble-dabbing fast down
three flights of stairs to the door. There stood Zut, the photographer, with
his back to Pearson and on impatient feet, tall and thin in a suit creased by
years of air travel. He was shouting to Mrs Zut, who was lugging two heavy
bags of apparatus up the street to the house. She got there and they turned
round.

As a writer, in the news too and in another branch of the human-image
trade, Pearson depended on seeing people and things as strictly they are not.
The notion that Zut and his wife could be a doorstep couple offering to buy
old spectacles or discarded false teeth, a London trade, occurred to him, but
he recovered and, switching on an eager smile, bowed them into the house.
They marched past him down the hall, briskly, like a pair of surgeons, to the
foot of the stairs and looked back at him.

"I hope you had no difficulty in finding this—er—place," Pearson said,
vain of difficulty as a sort of fame.

"None," said Zut. "She drives. I read the street map." Mrs Zut had not put
down her load. Zut seemed to ask, Are you the body?

Well, said Pearson spaciously, where did they want to "do," or "take"—

he hesitated between saying "it" or "me." He said this to all photographers, waving a hand, offering the house. Zut looked up at the stairs and the high ceiling.

Pearson said, Ground-floor dining room, tall windows, books? Upstairs by half-landing, a balcony, or would you say patio, flowers, shrubs, greenery, a pair of Chinese dogs in stone, view of neighbouring gardens? Down below, garden seat under tree, could sit there taking the air. And talking of air, have often been done—if that is the word—outside in the street, in overcoat and fur hat by interesting railings, coat buttoned or unbuttoned. No? Or first-floor sitting room. High windows again, fourteen feet in fact, expensive when curtaining, but chairs easy or uneasy, large mirror, peacock feathers on wife's desk, quite a lot of gilt, *chaise-longue* indeed. Have often been done there, upright or lying full length. *Death of Chatterton* style.

Zut said, "Furniture tells me nothing. Where do you work?"

"Work?" said Pearson.

"Where you write," said Zut.

"Oh, that," said Pearson. "You mean the alphabet, sentences? At the top. Three flights up, I'm afraid," apologising to Mrs Zut. (Writer, writing at desk, rather a cliché for a man like Zut—no?)

Already Zut was taking long steps up the stairs, followed by Mrs Zut, who refused to give up her two rattling bags, Pearson looking at Mrs Zut's grey hair and peaceful back as he came after them. From flight to flight they went and did not speak until they were under a fanlight at the top. In a pause for breath Pearson said, "Burglar's entry."

Zut ignored this and, pointing to a door, "In here?" he said.

"No, used to be children's bathroom. Other door." The door was white on the outside, yellowing on the inside. They marched in.

"It smells of—what would you say?—decaying rhubarb, I'm afraid. I smoke a pipe."

There was the glitter of permafrost in Zut's hunting eyes as he studied the room. There were two attic windows; the other three walls were blood red but stacked and stuffed with books to the ceiling. They were terraced like a football crowd, in varieties of anoraks, a crowd unstirred by a slow game going on among four tables where more books and manuscripts were in scrimmage.

"That your desk?" said Zut, pointing to the largest table.

"I'm a table man," said Pearson, apologising, bending to pick up one or two matches and a paper clip from the floor. "I migrate from table to table." And drew attention to a large capsized photograph of the Albert Memorial propped on a chest of drawers. Accidentally, Zut kicked a metal wastepaper basket as he looked round. It gave a knell.

Yes, Pearson was inclined to say (but did not), this room has a knell. Authors die. Dozens of funerals of unfinished sentences here every day. It is less a study than a—what shall I say?—perhaps a dockyard for damaged syntax? Or, better still, an immigration hall. Papers arrive at a table, migrate to other tables or chairs, and, when they are rubber-stamped, get stuffed into drawers. By the way, outgoing mail on the floor. Observe the corner bookcase, the final catacomb—my file boxes. I like to forget.

Mrs Zut dropped to her knees near a window and was opening the bags.

Now (Pearson was offering his body to Zut), what would you like me to be or do? Stand here? Or there? Sit? Left leg crossed over right leg, right over left? Put on a look? Get a book at random? Open a drawer? Light a pipe? Talk? Think? Put hand on chin? Great Zut, make your wish known.

Talk, Zut. All photographers talk, put client at ease. Ask me questions. Dozens of pictures of me have been taken. I could show you my early slim-subaltern-on-the-Somme-waiting-to-go-over-the-top period. There was my Popular Front look in the Thirties and Forties, the jersey-wearing, all-the-world's-a-coal-mine period, with close-ups of the pores and scars of the skin and the gleam of sweat. There was the editorial look, when the tailor had to let out the waist of my trousers, followed by the successful smirk. In the Sixties the plunging neckline, no tie. Then back to collar and tie in my failed-bronze-Olympic period. Today I fascinate archaeologists—you know, the broken pillar of a lost civilisation. Come on, Zut. What do you want?

Zut looked at the largest table. It had a clear space among pots of pencils, ashtrays, paper clips, two piles of folders for the execution block—a large blotter embroidered by pen wipings, and on it was a board with beautiful clean white paper clipped to it.

"There," said Zut, pointing to the chair in front of it. Zut had swollen veins on his long hands. "Sit," he said.

Pearson sat. There was a hiss from Mrs Zut's place on the floor, close to Zut. She had pulled out the steel rods of a whistling tripod. Zut gave a push to her shoulder. Up came a camera. She screwed it on and Zut fiddled with it, calling for more and more little things. What fun you have in your branch of the trade, said Pearson. You have little things to twizzle. Well, I have paper clips, pipe cleaners, scissors, paste. I try out pens, that's all—to save me from entering the wilderness, the wilderness of vocabulary.

But now Zut was pulling his creased jacket over his head and squinting through the camera at Pearson, who felt a small flake of his face fall off. And at that moment Zut gave Mrs Zut a knock on her arm. "Meter," he said. Then he let his coat slip back to his shoulders and stepped from the end of the table to where Pearson was sitting and held the meter, with shocking intimacy, close to Pearson's head. He looked back at the window, muttering a word. Was the word "unclean"? And he turned to squint through the camera and looked up to say, "Take your glasses off."

My glasses. My only defence. Can't see a thing. He took them off.

Ah, Zut, I see you don't talk, because you are after the naked truth, you are a dabbler in the puddles of the mind. As you like, but I warn you I'm wise to that.

"Don't smile."

I see, you're not a smile-please man, muttered Pearson. Oh, Zut, you've such a shriven look. If you take me naked, you will miss all the *et cetera* of my life. I am all *et cetera*. But Zut was back under his jacket, spying again, and then he did something presumptuous. He came out of his jacket, reached across the table, and moved a pot of pencils out of the way. The blue pot, that rather pretty et cetera that Pearson's wife had found in a junk shop next to the butcher's—now a pizza café—twenty-four years ago on a street not in this district. Zut, you have moved a part of my life to another table, it will hate being there, screamed Pearson's soul. How dare you move my wife?

Anything else?

"Not necessary," said Zut and, reaching out, gave Mrs Zut a knock on the arm. "Lamp," he said between his teeth.

Mrs Zut scrabbled in the bag and pulled out a rubbery cord; at the end was a clouded yellow lamp, a small sickly moon. She stood up and held it high.

Zut gave another knock on her arm as he spied into the camera.

"Higher," he said.

Up went the lamp. Another knock.

"Keep still. You're letting it droop," said Zut. Oh, Florence Nightingale, can't you, after all these years, hold it steady?

"Look straight into the camera," called Zut from under his jacket.

"Now write," said Zut.

"Write? Where?"

"On that paper."

"Pen or pencil?" said Pearson. "Write what?"

"Anything."

"Like at school."

Pearson tipped the board on the edge of the table.

"Don't tip the board. Keep it flat."

"I can't write flat. I never write flat," Pearson said. And I never write in public, if anyone is in the room. I grunt. I make a noise.

I bet you can't photograph a noise.

Pearson glanced at Zut. Then, sulking, he slid the board back flat on the table and felt the room tip up.

Zut, Pearson murmured. I shall write: Zut keeps on hitting his wife. Zut keeps on hitting his wife. Can't write that. He might see. Zut, I am going to diddle you. I shall write my address, 56 Hill Road Terrace, with the wrong post code—N6 4DN. Here goes: 56 Hill Road Terrace, 56 Hill Road Terrace . . .

"Keep on writing," said Zut.

Pearson continued 56 Hill Road Terrace and then misspelled "terrace." Out of the corner of his eye he saw the little yellow lamp.

"Now look up at me," said Zut.

The room tipped higher.

"Like that. Like that. Like that," hissed Zut. "Go on. Now go on writing."

Click, click, click, went the shutter of the camera. A little toad in the lens has shot out a long tongue and caught a fly.

"You're dropping it again," said Zut, giving Mrs Zut a punch.

"Good," the passionate Zut called to Pearson, then came out of his jacket.

"My face has gone," Pearson said.

But how do you know you've got *me*? My soul spreads all over my body, even in my feet. My face is nothing. At my age I don't need it. It is no more than a servant I push around before me. Or a football I kick ahead of me, taking all the blows, in shops, in the streets. It knows nothing. It just collects. I send it to smirk at parties, to give lectures. It has a mouth. I've no idea what it says. It calls people by the wrong names. It is an indiscriminate little grinner. It kisses people I've never met. The only time my face and I exchange a word is when I shave. Then it sulks.

Click, went the camera.

Pearson sat back and put down his pen and dropped his arm to his side.

"Will you do that again," said Zut. "The way you just dropped your arm," Zut said.

Pearson did it.

"No," said Zut. "We've missed it."

Pearson was hurt, and apologised to Mrs Zut, the dumb goddess. Not for worlds would he upset her husband. She simply gazed at Zut.

Zut himself straightened up. The room tipped back to its normal state. Pearson noticed the long lines down the sides of Zut's mouth, wondered why the jacket did not rumple his grey hair. Cropped, of course. How old was he? Where had he flown from? Hovering vulture. Unfortunate Satan walking up and down the world looking for souls. Satan on his treadmill. I bet your father was in, say, the clock trade, was it?—and when you were a boy you took his watch to pieces looking for Time. Why don't you *talk*? You're not like that man who came here last year and told me that he waited until he felt there was a magnetic flow uniting himself and me. A technological flirt. Nor are you like that other happy fellow with the waving fair hair who said he unselfed himself, forgot money, wife, children, all, for a few seconds to become me!

Zut slid a new plate into the camera and glanced up at the ceiling. It was smudged by the faint shadows of the beams behind it. A prison or cage effect. Why was he looking at the ceiling? Did he want it to be removed?

Pearson said, "Painted only five years ago. And look at it! More expense." Zut dismissed this.

"Look towards the window," said Zut.

"Which one?" said Pearson.

"On the right," said Zut. "Yes. Yes." Another blow on that poor woman's arm.

"Lamp—higher. Still higher."

Click, click from the toad in the lens.

"Again," said Zut.

Click. Click. Another click.

"Ah!" said Zut, as if about to faint.

He's found something at last, Pearson thought. But, Zut, I bet you don't know where my mind was. No, I was not looking at the tree-tops. I was looking at a particular branch. On a still day like this, there is always one leaf skipping about at the end of a branch on its own while the rest of the tree is still. It has been doing that for years. Why? An *et cetera*, a distinguished leaf. Could be me. What am I but a leaf?

One more half-hearted click from the camera, and then Zut stood tall. He had achieved boredom.

"I've got all I want," he muttered sharply to his wife.

All? said Pearson, appealing. There are tons of me left. I know I have a face like a cup of soup with handles sticking out—you know?—after it has been given a couple of stirs with a wooden spoon. A speciality in a way. What wouldn't I give for bone structure, a nose with bone in it!

Zut gave a last dismissive look around the room.

"That's it," he said to his wife.

She started to dismantle the tripod. Zut walked to the photograph of the Albert Memorial on the chest near the door, done by another photographer, and studied it. There was an enormous elephant's head in the foreground. Zut pointed. "Only one eye," he said censoriously.

"The other's in shadow," said Pearson.

"Elephants have two eyes," said Zut. And then, "Is there a . . ."

"Of course, of course, the door on the left."

Pearson was putting the muscles of his face back in place. He was alone with Mrs Zut, who was packing up the debris of the hour.

"I have always admired your husband's work," he said politely.

"Thank you," she said from the floor, buckling the bags.

"Remarkable pictures of men—and, of course, women. I think I saw one of you, didn't I, in his last collection?"

"No," she said from the floor, looking proud. "I don't allow him to take my picture."

"Oh surely—"

"No," she said, the whole of herself standing up, full-faced, solid and human.

"His first wife, yes. Not me," she said resolutely, killing the other in the ordinary course of life.

Then Zut came back, and in procession they all began thanking their way downstairs to the door.

—

At the exhibition Pearson sneaked in to see himself, stayed ten minutes to look at his portrait, and came out screaming, thinking of Mrs Zut.

An artist, he said. Herod! he was shouting. When the head of John the Baptist was handed to you on that platter, the eyes of that beautiful severed head were peacefully closed. But what do I see at the bottom of your picture. A high haunted room whose books topple. Not a room indeed, but a dank cistern or aquarium of stale water. No sparkling anemone there but the bald head of a melancholy frog, its feet clinging to a log, floating in literature. O Fame, cried Pearson, O Maupassant, *O Tales of Hoffmann*, O Edgar Allan Poe, O Grub Street.

Pearson rushed out and rejoined the human race on that bus going north and sat silently addressing the passengers, the women particularly, who all looked like Mrs Zut. The sight of them changed his mind. He was used, he said, to his face gallivanting with other ladies and gentlemen, in newspapers, books, and occasionally on the walls of galleries like that one down the street. Back down the street, he said, a man called Zut, a photographer, an artist, not one of your click-click men, had exhibited his picture, but by a mysterious accident of art had portrayed his soul instead of mine. What faces, Pearson said, that poor fellow must see just before he drops off to sleep at night beside the wise woman who won't let him take a picture of her, fearing perhaps the Evil Eye. A man in the image trade, like myself. Pearson called back as he got off the bus. Not a Zurbarán, more a Hieronymus Bosch perhaps. No one noticed Pearson getting off.

(1989)

BIOGRAPHY

FROM

The Gentle Barbarian:
The Life and Work of Turgenev

CHAPTER 3

What Turgenev needed in order to outgrow the dilettante self was not only a change of mind but, above all, a deepening of his power to feel. He had not yet known the force of passion.

In November of 1843 Pauline Viardot-Garcia, the Spanish singer, came from Paris to Petersburg to sing the part of Rosina in *Il Barbiere di Seviglia* at the magnificent opera house which had been remodelled and which could hold an audience of three thousand people. Italian opera had not been heard there for a generation and the season aroused wild enthusiasm. It was a triumph for the young singer and for her middle-aged husband who was her impresario. She had succeeded in London but had been edged out of the Paris opèra by the established prima donnas.

The event was not one that a poet and young man of fashion could miss but Turgenev was in a bad way for money because his mother now refused to pay off his heavy debts and kept him to a very small allowance. She had been amused by *Parasha* as a personal present but she was not going to do anything for a common scribbler who dragged the family name into the papers. He could earn very little by his occasional writing, but he somehow got a cheap seat at the opera and saw on the stage a slight young married woman of twenty-two, three years younger than himself, with no figure and almost ugly to look at. She had black hair, a wide mouth, a heavy underlip that seemed continuous with her chin and a very long neck. The effect was of sullenness in a strong, gypsyish way, the hooded eyes were large and black, the pupils lifting in one of those asserting Spanish stares of mockery and pride; yet the stare would break into sudden vivacity, warmth and enticing smiles. And then the voice!

Musset, who had known Pauline Garcia and had been in love with her when she was seventeen, said the voice had "the velvetness of the peach and youth," and had written a poem in which the first verse runs:

> *Oui femme, tel est votre empire;*
> *Vous avez ce fatal pouvoir*
> *De nous jeter par un sourire*
> *Dans l'ivresse ou le désespoir.*

But the last verse contains the lines:

> *Mais toute puissance sur terre*
> *Meurt quand l'abus en est trop grand,*
> *Et qui sait souffrir et se taire*
> *S'éloigne de vous en pleurant.*

The extravagant words of Heine about her voice are well-known:

> Her ugliness is of a kind that is noble and, if I might almost say beautiful, such as sometimes enchanted and inspired the great lion-painter Delacroix . . . The Garcia recalls to your mind not so much the civilised beauty and tame grace of our European homeland, as the terrible splendour of an exotic wilderness and during some moments of her impassionated performance, especially when she opens wide her large mouth with its dazzling white teeth and smiles with such savage sweetness and delightful ferocity, you feel as though the monstrous plants and animals of India and Africa were about to appear before your eyes as though giant palms festooned with thousands of blossoming lianas were shooting up— and you would not be surprised to see a leopard or a giraffe or even a herd of young elephants stampede across the stage.

Musset was more precise. Recalling the resemblance of her voice to the voice of her famous sister, La Malibran, he said there was "the same timbre, clear, resonant, audacious; that Spanish *coup de gosier*" which has something, at the same time, so harsh and so sweet in it that it reminded him of the taste of wild fruit.

Heine's grotesque images magnify the reality. Pauline Viardot was an exotic: her inheritance came from the Triana. The strictly dedicated young artist, who had been brought up in cultivated circles in Paris, had race in her. She had the fine carriage of Spanish women; she sparkled in repose. Many other writers speak of something noble in her plain masculine face; in her portraits which are, of course, idealised, there is something else:

authority. Such a strange figure must instantly have brought back to Turgenev the half-barbarous spell of his plain mother. Love at first sight, Jane Austen said, was a sign of giddiness: Turgenev certainly had the reputation of giddiness in Petersburg. But with him, love at first sight seems to have been a recognition of an earlier image printed in the heart.

If the voice of Pauline Viardot was part primitive and a gift of nature, it was exquisitely schooled beyond the rough spontaneity of popular Andalusian singing. An exacting musical culture had produced it: Pauline was born into a family who had been musicians for three generations. Her father, Manuel del Popolo Garcia, had been born in Seville in 1775; her grandfather had been a gypsy and as a child had been one of the harsh, shrill choristers of Seville cathedral and had become very quickly a professional singer and composer. Manuel Garcia's wife is said to have been an actress with all the hard-headedness of the theatre in her. There had been nothing for a poor ambitious man like Manuel in Spain and, being enormously energetic, subject to strong impulses, and having the gifts of a showman, he had moved the family in a business-like way to Paris. There he soon made a reputation as a tenor and pushed on to Italy, where he sought out Rossini who wrote for him the part of Almaviva in *Il Barbiere di Seviglia*: the opera in which Turgenev first heard Pauline was almost the Garcia family's property. Her father and her famous sister, La Malibran, had made their names in it.

In considering the character of Pauline one has to look more closely at the influence of this elder sister's life and fame. She was much older than Pauline, who was a child when her sister was already celebrated in Europe and America. In her scholarly life of Pauline Viardot and her indispensable account of her relationship with Turgenev, *The Price of Genius*, published in 1964, to which all writers on Turgenev owe a debt, April Fitzlyon tells us that La Malibran became the incarnation, the goddess of the Romantic movement. Every poet worshipped her. Beautiful and of great independence of spirit she had caused an upheaval in the Garcia family by quarrelling with her father and marrying Malibran, an American banker, when they were in New York. Manuel had been unrelenting and even cruel in the training he had given his daughter and she had married Malibran to get away from him. She was not cast down by the failure of her marriage— her husband went bankrupt at once and became unimportant in her life— she eventually divorced him and after many love affairs married a gifted Belgian violinist. The extraordinary girl was not only a singer but a talented painter and a daring horsewoman.

One early adventure of the Garcia family—of which Pauline and all of them were proud—occurred when Manuel, having done well in New York, dragged his family to Mexico, where again they made a small fortune and decided to go back to France. On the rough and dangerous journey from Mexico City to Vera Cruz they were attacked by brigands who soon disposed of the frightened escort of soldiers and robbed the party of everything. Although Pauline was frightened—she was only seven—she used to say in old age "all this was terribly beautiful, I liked it." And apparently, the excited and cheerful Garcias laughed all the way to Vera Cruz afterwards.

—

Pauline had scarcely known her marvellous and tragic sister. La Malibran was killed at the age of twenty-eight in a riding accident when she went to sing in Manchester. The father was more tender with Pauline. She would have preferred to have been a pianist and was very accomplished, but singing was the family tradition and she was persuaded by her sister's fame to emulate her. To La Malibran singing had come by nature, she had an unmatched ease and range of voice and could move from tragedy to comedy without effort. She was indeed lazy. Not so Pauline: she worked at whatever she was doing (the family said), "like an ant." By temperament she was an intellectual; she applied her will and very good mind to her task of acquiring range by will and this quality was to have a special appeal to Turgenev's deep regard for critical intellect. Throughout her life, music critics were amazed by a singer who studied the literary texts of the operas she sang in. There are two more aspects of her character as an artist: the story of her sister's life warned her against a reckless marriage and the Bohemian love affairs that had followed. Pauline was no rebel. And there was the influence of her shrewd mother who embodied the cautious business sense of a family of geniuses who put their art first.

When Turgenev was carried away by Pauline's voice in Petersburg he was listening to an achieved artist who had worked hard as he had not and, who although three years younger than himself, was already an idol. She was well-educated. She was a quick linguist. She was married and a mother. Her French husband, Louis Viardot, was in his forties. He was the capable and honourable son of a respectable judge and, in addition to being her impresario, had a modest reputation as a translator, a writer of travel books and studies of European painting.

There was nothing reckless in this marriage, even though Pauline's husband was in his forties, twenty-one years older than herself; she respected him, she relied on him absolutely but was not in love. The curious and sensible marriage had been arranged by George Sand, who had known the Garcias and Louis Viardot for years: and it can be said, at any rate, to have satisfied George Sand's ruling maternal passion. More than once, after her own unhappy marriage, she had been attracted to young women and in the young Pauline she saw a girl whose independence as an artist of growing powers would need protection from the dangerous temptations and illusions from which she herself had suffered in her own early scandalous days. In middle age, however, George Sand's motives were never quite simple: her jealousy was aroused when she heard Musset, one of her own disastrous and discarded lovers, was courting the girl, who, luckily, was disgusted by his drinking and his libertine life; but that would still leave her open to folly. George Sand worshipped the artist in Pauline and indeed was using her as a model for the ideal artist-heroine of her longest and most famous novel, *Consuelo*. Pauline always said that the portrait perfectly described what she herself was like and wished morally to be, although the wild adventures of the book were romantic invention.

Louis Viardot might be thought a comic middle-aged figure: he was short, he had a large nose which was a gift to caricaturists, he looked as if he were going to tip over; people found him dull, inclined to fuss and a pedant. (In one of his *Prose Poems*, "The Egoist," Turgenev is thought to have portrayed him as the imperturbable right-thinking man.) He was a decent man of principle. If public opinion in France or, indeed abroad, was to be considered—he shared the Republican and anti-clerical opinions of George Sand and particularly of Lerroux the Radical politician who had been her lover; but Pauline's mind was in her art. She knew he lacked the engaging, child-like qualities; if she did not love him she respected him and, with the utmost dignity and consideration, he loved her deeply. She had never loved anyone except her father and, perhaps, in Louis she saw a father reborn. It was noticed that she often called him "Papa."

Turgenev went night after night to hear the singer. He pushed into his friends' boxes—he couldn't afford one of his own—and he shouted his admiration. His gentleness and shyness vanished as his shrill voice screamed applause, his mad behaviour was the joke of the season. There is nothing like the sight of a giant who is out of his mind. There was no performance without it. People told Pauline that the noisy ass with the long chestnut hair was a young landowner, a good shot and a feeble poet. The young singer had the pretty tactics of fame at her finger tips: an admirer who was far richer than Turgenev had given her a huge bearskin which was spread on the floor of her dressing-room and there she sat like an idol and four of her admirers were allowed the privilege of sitting at a proper distance on the paws. It was a long time before Turgenev was allowed to join her privileged admirers in her dressing-room and win his right to a paw. Once there, the quick, serious charm, the wit and his power of telling and acting amusing untrue stories came back to him. His French and German were perfect. But surrounded as she was by more important admirers, Pauline took little notice of him.

Turgenev had to be content to concentrate on Louis Viardot, who, like himself, was often pushed into the background and, in the classic fashion of such triangular beginnings, it was the men who became friends first. Writing his books of travel and art, managing the opera company and Pauline's career, seeing to it that she would indeed be another Malibran, developing her distinct personality and style—these were the lasting preoccupations of Louis Viardot's busy life. But once business was over, Louis Viardot saw a flattering and aspiring young writer with whom he had a quite unexpected taste in common. It was decisive. Louis was fanatical to the point of comedy as a sportsman: he loved slaughter, as Pauline once said. He loved shooting birds in season and out. The sportsmen of Spasskoye and of Courtavenel in France, where Louis had bought a converted medieval chateau and estate, had a subject less strenuous than a love of music.

And there was more than that. The man of forty and the young man of twenty-five had other things in common. Pauline's Spanish spell had also caught Louis. He had written a book on Spain and had translated *Don Quixote*—not very well, they say. There was also the bond of politics: the two men were rationalists and democrats. Viardot was even thought to be politically dubious by the Russian secret police. The pair were at one in their hatred of serfdom. Louis was much taken by the clever young man and saw he could be congenial and useful. He saw that Pauline could clinch her popular success by singing a few Russian songs and that Turgenev was the man to teach her something of the language. Certainly they all met for this useful purpose, in the Viardots' apartment in Petersburg.

Pauline herself was captivated by the mixture of Oriental barbarity and polish in Court Society in Petersburg where everyone spoke French. She was persuaded to sing some Spanish gypsy songs to Russian gypsies: both parties were convinced that Russia and Spain had far more in common than they had with Western Europeans and in this their instinct was right. It is an irony that Turgenev, the Westerner who believed the future of Russia lay in learning from Europe, should have been brought to his one great and lasting passion by what looks like an atavism: her Spanishness had its Islamic roots; his own, remote though they might be, had something of this too. The Andalusian wit and feeling that underlay her French upbringing responded to his lazy, open Russianness. There was more than the buried image of his mother in Pauline, more than the attraction of a common love of music and the belief in the supremacy of art, more even than the conventional attractions of a handsome man for a plain woman, or of a young Quixote for a young woman who was set on the practical matters of her career.

The Viardots left Russia. The following year they came back to Petersburg and then went on to Moscow, where Turgenev took his mother to hear Pauline sing. His mother had heard the gossip about his absurd behaviour. She was annoyed. She did not mind him going to bed with serf girls or having an older mistress of his own class—he had been having an affair with a miller's wife when he was out shooting near Petersburg just before meeting Pauline—but to dangle so seriously after a foreign actress killed any chance of the marriage his mother had hoped he would make. After hearing the singer she sulked, but came away saying "It must be admitted the damn gypsy sings well."

—

The embittered, ill and ageing sovereign of Spasskoye was at this period of her life, showing her own ever-increasing powers as an actress. She had, as we know, broken with her son Nikolai because of his disgraceful marriage; cutting Ivan's allowance to next to nothing had not prevented him from stooping to literature and accepting an invitation from the Viardots to visit them in France. (He went, on the pretext that he had to see a doctor about his eyes.) She could not stand the company of her brother-in-law who had come to live in the house and got rid of him. Worse: the old gentleman had married and very happily. In spite of everything, she longed for the sons who would not obey her and she put on fantastic and malevolent scenes. One year she announced that there would be no Easter Festival—an appalling sacrilege in the eyes of her peasants and her neighbours. She ordered the priest to stop the ringing of the church bells and though the servants laid the great table in the hall with the Sèvres porcelain and had set out the bright red eggs, the lamb made of butter and the Easter cake, she made them clear it all away untouched.

In another scene she sent for the priest to hear her confession, but when he got there she called for her house serfs to be assembled and told the priest she wanted to be confessed publicly. The priest protested that this was against the laws of the church but she shouted and threatened till the terrified man gave in.

The most powerful scene occurred on the date of Ivan's birthday, a sacred day for her. She ordered him to come home. Budding orange trees were placed in tubs on the verandahs, the cherry trees were brought out of the forcing sheds. A great feast with the foods Ivan loved was laid out on the tables in the stone gallery, the flags of the Lutovinovs and Turgenevs were hoisted over the house and she had a signpost erected on the road on which the words *Ils reviendront* were painted. Neither son came, and retiring to her room she announced that she was dying. She called for Ivan's portrait and called out, "*Adieu*, Jean. *Adieu*, Nikolai. *Adieu, mes enfants.*" As the household wept she ordered them to bring in the icon of the Holy Virgin of Vladimir. She lay on her bed imitating the death rattle with her favourites kneeling at her bedside—they knew it was all a farce—and obliged the forty servants from the highest to the lowest to come in and kiss her hand in farewell. When this was done she suddenly called out in a stentorian voice to

Polyakov, her chief servant: "Bring some paper." Her box of loose sheets for making strange notes was at her bedside and when it was given to her, she wrote down:

> Tomorrow the following culprits must appear in front of my window and sweep the yard. You were overjoyed that I was dying. You were drinking and celebrating a name day and your mistress dying!

The next day the drinkers, from the principal servants downwards, were made to put on smocks with circles and crosses on their backs and clean out the yards and gardens with brooms and shovels in sight of her terrifying window.

—

In the following year—in 1846, according to Mme. Zhitova—Ivan did come home to ask her to recognise his brother's marriage and to give him money. She stormed and refused. They got on to the subject of serfdom. Mme. Zhitova says she heard a conversation. It could have been matched, in this period, in landowners' houses in Ireland or in the American South.

"So my people are badly treated! What more do they need? They are very well fed, shod and clothed, they are even paid wages. Just tell me how many serfs do receive wages?"

"I did not say that they starve and are not well-clothed," began Ivan Sergevitch cautiously, stammering a little, "but they tremble before you."

"What of it?"

"Listen mama, couldn't you now, this minute, if you wanted, exile any one of them?"

"Of course I could."

"Even from a mere whim?"

"Of course."

"Then that proves what I have always told you. They are not people—they are things."

"Then according to you they ought to be freed?"

"No, why? I don't say that, the time hasn't come yet."

"And won't come."

"Yes it will come, it will come soon," cried Ivan Sergevich passionately in the rather shrill voice he used when excited and he walked quickly round the room.

"Sit down, your walking about worries me," his mother said.

"I see you are quite mad."

The Viardots' third season in Petersburg lasted until the spring of 1845 and they returned to France. Turgenev resigned from his post in the Civil

Service on the excuse that he was having serious trouble with his eyes and accepted an invitation to stay with the Viardots at Courtavenel. There are signs that Pauline had lost her indifference and was falling in love against her will, and Turgenev spoke of this time as "the happiest time of my life." From any other man these words would indicate that he had conquered, that the love was returned and fulfilled; but one notices that when he became the master of the love story, he is far more sensitive to the beginnings of love than to its fulfilment, to the sensation of being—to use one of his titles—"on the eve" of love, of standing elated as he waits for the wave to curl and fall. The spring—and also the autumn—mean more to him than high summer.

He went back to Petersburg and had some small successes writing for *The Contemporary*, a new review which was making an impression, and was distraught at being unable to see her. At last, in 1847, he borrowed money and went to Paris again and the Viardots let the penniless writer stay on at Courtavenel whether they were away or not. They were often away for months on end, as Pauline travelled from success to success all over Europe. If, as some believe, they ever became lovers, it was in the next three years and if they did not, it was the time when what has been called "a loving friendship" sparkled and crystallised.

Courtavenel was a strange and spacious house. It was close to Rozay-en-Brie and lay in dull but good shooting country, convenient for Paris. Louis Viardot had bought it from a Baron. It had two faces. The older face dated from the sixteenth century and had towers, a moat and a drawbridge; the modern one suggested bourgeois wealth and respectability, just the place for a prosperous family who entertained largely and would soon acquire a town house in the rue de Douai in Montmartre where they would go in the winter. When the Viardots went off they left behind them Pauline's mother and her in-laws, her little girl and her governess, and a crowd of servants and gardeners, guests and visitors continued to come and go. When Dickens stayed there with the Viardots he complained that there was a general air of transience about the place; it was like a railway junction where people were changing trains, but to Turgenev such a life had all the easy-going openness of life in a Russian country house, without the provincial stagnation. The lonely young man who had not been able to stand life with his mother at Spasskoye had found a home and a cheerful family. He became a great friend of Mme. Garcia, Pauline's mother, who was affectionate and full of salty Spanish proverbs. Pauline wrote letters to her mother and occasionally to him and they were read and re-read aloud; and he wrote amusing letters on his own and the family's behalf and showed them to her mother before he sent them so that she could add postscripts of her own.

It is on the letters that Turgenev wrote to Pauline at this period—and indeed all his life—that we have chiefly to rely for our conjectures about their mysterious relationship and especially for our sight of his character. He wrote to her constantly about what he was doing, the people he met and especially about his reading and about her music and her performances, for he followed every report of them. Our trouble is that although she made time to write to him in her distracted life, only a handful of her letters have survived. He longed for them; occasionally some—to judge by his replies— were delightful for a lover to receive; but there is not a sensual or even an extravagant word of feeling in the few we have. She chattered away but is reticent and no more than affectionate.

The question of Turgenev's relationship with Pauline and the changes in it are important. It was the opinion of a large number of his Russian contemporaries that his love for her was fatal to his talent, for it was an obsession that took him away from Russia and damaged his understanding of his own country. It was also their opinion that she enslaved him and reduced him to the state of her *cavalier servant* and that he became the humiliated figure in a *ménage à trois*, and that his love was not a strength but a sign of his chronic weakness of will, at the root of his pessimism and his melancholy.

Turgenev called Courtavenel "the cradle of his fame." There at the age of twenty-eight he felt that *épanouissement de l'être* which gave him his first important subjects. His letters of this time are the happy letters of a mind finding itself and growing. It is a cultivated mind. It is endlessly curious. It is spirited and critical: the letters are brilliant, changeable, discursive talk, all personality. One can see that Pauline Viardot was drawn to him by not only his gaiety and his serious interest in her art, but his ease as a natural teacher. He was flattering, but the flattery was instructed. For example, he told her she had not quite mastered tragic parts where her talent would eventually lie—Iphigenia would suit her, but Goethe was "a shade calm" because "Thank God you come from the Midi—still there is something composed in your character."

Turgenev read everything rapidly and with excitement. He tells her that he has picked up a book by a fool called Daumer who holds the theory that Primitive Judaic Christianity was simply the cult of Moloch revived. A silly theory, but there is a terrible side to Christianity: the bloody, disheartening, anti-human side of a religion which set out to be a religion of love and charity. It is painful to read of the flagellation, the processions, worship of relics, the autos-da-fé, the hatred of life, the horror of women, all those wounds and all that talk of blood.

Under her husband's influence Turgenev's conversation was peppered with bits of Spanish. Pauline, of course, knew the language well. Turgenev took Spanish lessons at Courtavenel and was soon reading Calderón. Of

Calderón's *Devoción de la Cruz* he says he is the greatest Catholic dramatic poet since Shakespeare—like him, the most humane and the most anti-Christian: He has

cette foi immuable, triomphante, sans l'ombre d'un doute ou même d'une réflexion. Il vous écrase à force de grandeur et de majesté, malgré tout ce que cette doctrine a de répulsif et d'atroce. Ce néant de tout ce qui constitue la dignité de l'homme devant la volonté divine, l'indifférence profonde pour tout ce que nous appelons vertu ou vice avec laquelle la Grâce se répand sur son élu—est encore un triomphe pour l'esprit humain, car l'être qui proclame ainsi avec tant d'audace son propre néant, s'élève par cela même à l'égal de cette Divinité fantasque, dont il se reconnaît être le jouet.

He has moved on to Calderón's *La Vida Es Sueño* with its wild energy, its profound and sombre disdain for life, its astonishing boldness of thought, set side by side with Catholic fanaticism at its most inflexible. Calderón's Segismund is the Spanish Hamlet. That life is a dream will be both context and impulse when Turgenev found his genius in poetic realism and already we see him forming his theory of the contrasting characters of Hamlet and Don Quixote. But a Hamlet who marks the difference between the South and the North. Hamlet is the more reflective, subtle and philosophic; the character of Segismund is simple, naked and as penetrating as a dagger: one fails to act through irresolution, doubt and brooding: the other acts—for his southern blood drives him to do so—but even as he acts he knows that life is only a dream. (The lover is subtly trying to stir her southern blood and draw out her Spanishness.)

Contemporary literature, he reflects, is in a state of transition. It is eclectic and reflects no more than the scattered sentiments of their author. There is no great dominant movement—perhaps industrialism will take the place of literature; perhaps that will liberate and regenerate mankind. So perhaps the real poets are the Americans who will cut a path through Panama and invent a transatlantic electric telegraph. (Once the social revolution has been achieved a new literature will be born!) He doesn't suppose that a spirit as discriminating, simple, straight-forward and serious as hers is has much patience with the stories of Diderot: he is too full of paradox and fireworks, though sometimes he has new and bold ideas. It is by his *Encyclopaedia* he will live and by his devotion to freedom. (There will be more than a touch of Diderot in the construction of Turgenev's stories.)

Louis Viardot has asked him to arrange his library. There is a list of books read: M. Ott's *History* is the work of a Catholic Democrat—something against nature: that idea merely produces monsters. There are other nauseating books on history in the library: Rolteck, for example, with his flat, emphatic style but there are the spirited letters of Lady Mary Wortley

Montagu; an absurd Spanish novel; Bausset's *Napoleon*, the book of a born lackey; a dull translation of Virgil's *Eclogues*, not exactly a marvel in the original. He has started on the *Koran* but despite its good sense he knows it will all lead sooner or later to the usual Oriental flatulence.

But he knows that what she will most want is news of the theatre, what he is doing and the small events of life in Paris where he goes to buy the papers for critiques of her performances and to stroll in the Tuileries and to watch the pretty children and their staid nurses and enjoy the crisp autumn air. Autumn on a fine day is rather like Louis XIV in old age. He expects she'll laugh at that idea. "Well, go on laughing to show your teeth."

Another day he goes to the woods at Ville d'Avray:

> *L'impression que la nature fait sur l'homme est étrange. Il y a dans cette impression un fonds d'amertume fraîche comme tous les odeurs des champs, un peu de mélancholie sereine comme dans les chants d'oiseaux*

and adds that he adores the reality, the changes, the dangers, the habits, the passing beauty of life. While he is rearranging Louis Viardot's library the servant is polishing, washing, tidying, sweeping, waxing from morning to night. One night as he goes up to bed he hears two deep sighs that passed in a puff of air close to him. It froze him. Suppose the next moment a hand had touched him: he would have screamed like an eagle. (Question: Are the blind afraid of ghosts?) He lists the sounds he heard one night as he stood by the drawbridge: the throb of the blood in his ears, the rustle of leaves, the four crickets in the courtyard, fish rising in the moat, a dull sound from the road, the ping of a mosquito. He goes out to look at the stars and writes what will become one of the certainties of his life:

> *Cette chose indifférente, impérieuse, vorace, égoiste, envahissante, c'est la vie, la nature . . .*

Still, tell Louis there are a lot of quail about and shooting begins on the 25th. There is a plague of orange tawneys (*rougets*). In an hour her aunt has caught "*cinquante, cincuenta, fünfzig,* fifty," on her face and neck. He's scratching himself with both hands. They're all waiting for Mlle. Berthe's arrival, *para dar a comer a los bichos* ("to give the bugs a meal"), as Don Pablo says, as a useful diversion. M. Fougeux arrives, the king of bores. Turgenev goes rowing and puffing around the moat with him. The moat needs dredging. Fougeux is a man who speaks only in clichés and quotations. Over and over again he says "Nature is only a vast garden." God!

One night he has a long fantastic flying dream. He is walking along a road lined with poplars and is obliged to sing the line "*À la voix de la mère*" a hundred times before he will be allowed to get home. He meets a white figure who calls himself his brother and who turns him into a bird. He finds he has a long beak like a pelican and off they fly:

> I can remember it still, not simply in the head, *but* if I can so express myself, with my whole body.

They fly over the sea and below he sees enormous fish with black heads and he knows he has to dive for them because they are his food. A secret horror stops him. The sun suddenly rises and burns like a furnace. And so on. (Perhaps he was dreaming about his mother, his brother and the carp lying deep in the fish pond at Spasskoye. Many times in his later writings he evokes gross sinister fishes rising out of the deep water to threaten him. A great many years later, in a gloomy period of his life, he put this dream into a rhapsodic fantasy called *Phantoms:* it has little merit but suggests an erotic excitement or the frustration and fear of it.)

———

From her exhausting tours and the applause of audiences in London, Germany and Austria, the singer and her husband returned at intervals to Courtavenel to rest. They had taken in the young Gounod and Turgenev was for a time a little jealous of Pauline's interest in his work: there was some local gossip—George Sand indeed wrote to Pauline asking if he were "a good man"—but the friendship seems to have been strictly musical in its interests, though when Gounod suddenly married, his wife made trouble when Louis and Pauline sent her a bracelet.

On Sundays Turgenev would go off shooting with Louis or would go for charming walks with Pauline. They lay under the trees talking or reading books aloud or in the house he would go through the works she was studying. If there were parties Turgenev danced with her; he was an excellent dancer. On ordinary evenings, the family of aunts sat about reading, knitting and sewing, and an uncle taught Pauline's rather spoiled little daughter Spanish, Gounod worked on a musical score, and Turgenev told stories.

Then Louis and Pauline were off again and every few days he was writing to her. The letters begin, Bonjour or Dear Madame Viardot, and there were friendly messages to Viardot. To hers, Viardot often added a postscript. Nothing could have been more correct; but by 1848, his letters often end in ardent phrases in German. She is his "dearest Angel." Again "Thank you a thousand, thousand times for . . . you know why . . . you the best and dearest of women . . . what happiness you gave me then . . ." And "Give me your kind and delicate hands so that I can press and kiss them a long time . . . Whatever a man can think, feel and say, I say it and feel it now."

Her hands were beautiful and he worshipped them all his life. In a letter sent to her in 1849 he said in German:

> All day I have been lost in a magical dream. Everything, everything, all the past, all that has been poured irresistibly and spontaneously into my soul . . . I am whole . . . I belong body and soul to my dear Queen. God bless you a thousand times.

In July '49 at Courtavenel he went off to a village fête, studied the faces and watched the sweating dancers. He passed the next day alone and wrote to her in German:

> I cannot tell you how much I have thought of you every day, when I got back to the house I cried out your name in ecstasy and opened my arms with longing for you. You must have heard and seen me!

There is a line in one letter in which, once only, he addresses her as "*du*." From this and from the paragraphs in German some biographers have thought that Pauline and he had become physically lovers and that German was used to hide the fact from her husband who is said not to have known the language. This is most unlikely: Louis had been many times to Germany; as a capable translator in a bilingual family, he must at least have picked up some German in the course of his business and indeed from Pauline's singing. German is more likely to be "a tender little language" between intimate friends and Turgenev, the polyglot, liked to spice his letters with foreign words for he could not use more than a word or two of Russian to her. Perhaps in using German he was simply using the romantic language of the sublime he had learned in Berlin when he was nineteen. Expressions of love are at once more extravagant and frequent in a foreign tongue and, for that reason, have the harmless sense of theatrical fantasy or flattery: platonic love affairs live by words and not deeds. George Sand wrote with the same exaltation in her novels; and young women of the period would expect no less from a correspondent, especially from the Russian "openness." There is no sign that Pauline ever replied to Turgenev in such terms.

It is impossible to say more about the nature of this love for the moment; but there is strong reason to suspect that Pauline, duty or no duty, "hot southern blood" (as she once or twice said) or not, was one of those gifted young women who do not feel physical passion until later in life and have something mannish in their nature. And what about the guilt Turgenev may have felt in being in love with the wife of a generous friend? This is also a mystery: there is only a slight sign of this embarrassment in his stories.

In their biographies, Yarmolinsky, Magarshack and April Fitzlyon differ considerably in their interpretation. Yarmolinsky is vivid, engaging and ironical in the disabused manner of the nineteen-twenties and regards the love affair as purely platonic on both sides, a deep *amitié amoureuse*, which would go a long way to explaining why Turgenev never gave it up and why Louis Viardot tolerated it. (Louis was to become the father of four children.) Magarshack asserts that Pauline did become Turgenev's mistress and that the affair came quickly to an end because she gave him up for Ary Scheffer, the painter, who often came to Courtavenel and that when she and Turgenev were reconciled she was unfaithful to him and her husband again. He also accepts the common gossip that her second daughter, Didie, and her son Paul were probably Turgenev's children. Neither of these writers has closely considered the character of Pauline and all the evidence as searchingly as April Fitzlyon has done. She believes that Pauline did fall seriously in love with Turgenev and indeed felt passion for the first time; that it is just possible they were briefly lovers, though to neither of them was physical love important—indeed Pauline may have been put off by a dislike of "conjugal duty"—and that, in any case, she put her art before personal relationships always and is well-known to have disapproved of the Bohemian morals of her profession. Far from having been her lover, Ary Scheffer—a man as old as her husband and a stern moralist—would be the counsellor who prevented her from leaving her husband for Turgenev and made her control her heart by her will which was certainly very strong. She says it is indeed just possible in the case of the son that Turgenev was the father, but it is unlikely and there is no evidence. And that although Turgenev made bitter remarks in the vicissitudes of his attachment to her and in his masochistic way said that he lived under her heel as many of his incredulous friends thought, he endured what he did endure because he was in love with his own chivalrous love.

In this situation Louis Viardot behaved with dignity and concealed the pain he must have felt. He was passionately in love with his wife and was no cynic: he remained friends with Turgenev all his life, although some thought their attitude to each other formal.

The situation indeed changed, as we shall see.

—

Whatever went on at Courtavenel in those early years there is no doubt that Louis and his wife must have regarded Turgenev affectionately as an extraordinary and exotic case. Viardot himself, as a traveller and one who had felt the Spanish spell of his wife, must have felt the Russian spell of Turgenev. They must have been astounded by the story of his barbarous experience at Spasskoye, and have been amazed that the giant had grown to be grave and gentle, as well as gifted. And Louis must have recognised a wit and a mind far richer than his own. The Viardots felt concern for his talent and both pointed to the dangers of idleness to a man who was rich enough to do nothing. Pauline was no amateur: she was an artist and a professional and it can never have entered her head that Turgenev, who was incapable of managing money or any practical matter, could replace her husband. One can see by their kindness, and especially Louis Viardot's, that although they saw his distinction and originality, their feeling must have been protective. Viardot had no small vanity in his own taste and exercised an almost fatherly right to give sound advice to the feckless aristocrat and was aware of having two artists on his hands whom he could keep in order. He was a rational man but quietly firm in requiring moral behaviour and decorum. There is a line in *A Month in the Country*, the play that Turgenev began to write before he left Courtavenel and which in many respects is drawn on his situation as a lover. Rakitin, the lover, is made to say at the crisis of the play:

"It is time to put an end to these morbid, consumptive relations."

Consumptive? Or self-consuming? It strikes one that those words must have been actually spoken at Courtavenel not by Turgenev but by Viardot. They have his manner.

There comes a moment, in one of the last letters Turgenev was to write from Courtavenel, when he adds a sentence in German:

What is the matter with Viardot? Is he upset because I am living here?

(1977)

Chekhov: A Spirit Set Free

SAKHALIN

Although friends of Chekhov had heard him say that he saw no difficulty in chasing two or even more hares at the same time, they were alarmed when, in 1890, the news leaked out that he was planning to travel across Russia and Asia to the Russian penal colony on the island of Sakhalin, Russia's notorious Botany Bay in the Far East. The nomad had been reborn. When he asked Suvorin to back him, Suvorin refused. That hare, Suvorin said, had died more than a generation ago. Even the story of *Manon Lescaut* was dead. Chekhov's duty was to literature, not to documentary investigation. And in any case, there was no trans-Siberian railway; the appalling land journey through barbarous country would kill him. Stirred by opposition and anxious to refute both his liberal and radical critics, who accused him of lacking "a general political idea," Chekhov fought back.

> Sakhalin can be useless and uninteresting only to a society which does not exile thousands of people to it. . . . We have sent *millions* of men to rot in prison, have destroyed them—casually without thinking, barbarously . . . have depraved them, have multiplied criminals, and the blame for all this we have thrown upon the gaolers and red-nosed superintendents. Now all educated Europe knows that it is not the superintendents that are to blame, but all of us. . . . The vaunted [political idealists of the] sixties did nothing for the sick and for prisoners, so breaking the chief commandment of Christian civilization.

When Mikhail Chekhov was asked what had put the idea into his brother's head, he said it was an accident: Anton had happened to read a penal document lying about in an office. In Petersburg the gossip was that he wanted to go in order to recover from an unhappy love affair with a married woman, Lydia Avilova, a sentimental novelist. This is certainly untrue. After his death she wrote *Chekhov in My Life*, which has been shown to be a wishful illusion. More interestingly, when he had graduated as a doctor he had not written his dissertation, and the desire to make amends by writing a serious medical document that would qualify him was strong. Indeed on his return from Sakhalin he did submit a manuscript to the university, where it was at once rejected as unacademic.

There is no doubt that Chekhov felt he had the "duty of repaying my debt to medicine." But it is very important also that ever since his boyhood he had been a passionate reader of the journeys of Przhevalsky, the greatest of Russian explorers, and had read Humboldt's journey across the steppe and George Kennan's famous expedition to Siberia. More intimately human are his words to a friend, the writer Ivan Shcheglov, who supposed, naturally, that Chekhov was going simply to observe and "get impressions." Chekhov replied that he was going "simply to be able to live for half a year as I have not lived up to this time. Don't expect anything from me."

Suvorin gave in. Chekhov got his sister, his brother Alexander and friends to do exhaustive research for him in Petersburg. Among other responsibilities he had to see that his family had enough money to live on while he was away. He described his own state of excitement medically: "It's a form of lunacy: Mania Sakhalinosa."

He set off at last late in April 1890 on a four-thousand-mile journey that would last over three months. He had been spitting blood that winter. His sister and a few friends saw him off on the river steamer at Yaroslavl. He was equipped with a heavy leather coat and a short one, top boots, a bottle of cognac, a knife "useful for cutting sausages and killing tigers" and a revolver for protection against brigands—he never had to use it.

His account of his land and river journey is told in vivid letters to his sister and his mother.

The rain poured down during the river trip to the ravines of Kineshma. After leaving the steamer he took to the road, jolted in an open public coach from one posting house to the next, though he hired private carriages when he could, and sat there freezing "like a goldfinch in a cage."

He writes to his sister:

> I have my fur coat on. My body is all right, but my feet are freezing. I wrap them in the leather overcoat, but it is no use. I have two pairs of breeches on. . . . Telegraph poles, pools, birch copses flash by. Here we overtake some emigrants. . . . We meet tramps with pots on their back; these gentry promenade all over . . . . Siberia without hindrance. One time they will murder some poor old woman to

take her petticoat for their leg-wrappers; at another they will strip from the verst post the metal plate with the number on it—it might be useful; at another will smash the head of some beggar or knock out the eyes of some brother exile; but they never touch travellers. . . .

He is by now well past the Urals. If the small towns are gray and miserable, the country people are "good and kindly," and

have excellent traditions. Their rooms are simply furnished but clean, with claims to luxury; the beds are soft, all feather mattresses and big pillows. The floors are painted or covered with homemade linen rugs.

No bugs, no "Russian smell." The explanation: these people have forty-eight acres of black earth, which they farm themselves.

But it cannot all be put down to prosperity. . . . One must give some of the credit to their manner of life. . . . they don't search in each other's heads in your presence. . . . There is a cleanliness of which our Little Russians can only dream, yet the Little Russians are far and away cleaner than the Great Russians.

Food! Pies and pancakes are good, but all the rest is not for what Chekhov calls his "European" stomach. Duck broth is disgusting and muddy; there is the terrible "brick tea" tasting like a "decoction of sage and beetles."

The last of the bad Moscow air was out of his lungs and he had stopped coughing. But in Siberia there were freezing gales, food was scarce; the bad roads, the floods and the days and nights of jolting along brought on his cough again and he spat blood. He had bought a cart of his own by now because it was cheaper, but he was continually repairing it. His cheap boots cramped his feet and for the rest of the journey he suffered agonies from piles. His whole body was aching.

He changes to a public coach. It is like traveling on roads flooded to the size of lakes and he has to be rowed across them. As for fellow passengers—they seem chiefly to have been drunkards and boasters. There was a police officer who had written a play and insisted on reading it. He also exhibited a nugget of gold. There was constant talk about gold in Siberia.

Tomsk turns out to be a dull and drunken town—"a pig in a skullcap" and the acme of "mauvais ton." It is regarded as a distinction that all its governors die in it.

After the freezing gales the heat of summer comes suddenly. He had his first bath at Irkutsk, "a very European town," and threw away his filthy clothes and bought new ones. Then on by river steamer to the famous Lake Baikal, a little sea in itself, and at last he reached a paradise on the Amur

River. On the left, the Russian shore; on the right, wild and deserted China. What a region for a summer villa, among duck, grebes, herons and all sorts of creatures with long beaks, young girls smoking cigarettes, old ladies smoking pipes. Marvelous crags and forests, everyone talking about gold, gold, gold.

> And what liberalism! Oh what liberalism. . . . People are not afraid to talk aloud here. There's no one to arrest them and nowhere to exile them to, so you can be as liberal as you like. The people for the most part are independent, self-reliant and logical. If there is any misunderstanding at Ustkara, where the convicts work (among them many politicals who don't work), all the Amur region is in revolt. . . . . An escaped convict can travel freely on the steamer to the ocean, without any fear of the captain's giving him up. This is partly due to the absolute indifference to everything that is done in Russia.

At last, after two and a half months, on July 5, 1890, he is at Nikolayevsk, a town of respectable smugglers on the Tatar Strait and the port of embarkation for the island of Sakhalin on the other side of the strait. On the crossing he found himself with three hundred soldiers and several prisoners, one he notices "accompanied by his five-year-old daughter, who clung to his shackles as he came up the gangway."

The first sight of the town itself alarmed him. Smoke was drifting across the strait from huge fires. He eventually wrote in *The Island: A Journey to Sakhalin:*

> The horrifying scene, compounded of darkness, the silhouettes of mountains, smoke, flames and fiery sparks, was fantastic. On my left monstrous fires were burning, above them the mountains, and beyond the mountains a red glow rose to the sky from remote conflagrations. It seemed that all of Sakhalin was on fire.

Chekhov had had no difficulty in getting permission to talk to the convicts or the settlers, but his official permit forbade him to talk with political prisoners. He had given practical forethought to his inquiry and he had shrewdly decided to begin by making his personal census of the population. He devised a card of twelve questions, which requested simple particulars of each settler's status, age, religion, education and year of arrival, and included the very cogent question: Married in Russia or in Sakhalin? He claimed to have filled out ten thousand of those cards. There was no Impressionist in Chekhov, the doctor. Most of the settlers were of peasant origin and illiterate. Some didn't know where they came from. There were twice as many men as women in the penal colony, and in addition there were the "bachelor soldiers," who were as dangerous, he noted, as "roughnecks building a railroad" near a Russian village.

If he is writing a flat documentary prose and rather overloads his book with the statistics, he has the storyteller's eye for the grim and the bizarre. When word of a new delivery of woman convicts gets around, we shall see, the road is crowded with men going south to the port of arrival. These are known to everyone, not without irony, as the "suitors," or prospective bridegrooms.

They actually look like bridegrooms. One has donned a red bunting shirt, another wears a curious planter's hat, a third sports shining new high-heeled boots, though nobody knows where he bought them or under what circumstances. When they arrive at the post they are permitted to enter the women's barracks and they are left there with the women. The suitors wander around the plank beds, silently and seriously eyeing the women; the latter sit with downcast eyes. Each man makes his choice. Without any grimaces, without any sneers, very seriously, they act with humanity toward the ugly, the old and those with criminal features. . . . If some younger or older woman "reveals herself" to a man, he sits down beside her and begins a sincere conversation. She asks if he owns a samovar and whether his hut is covered with planks or straw. . . . Only after the housekeeping examination has been completed, when both feel that a deal has been made, does she venture to say: "You won't hurt me in any way, will you?"

The conversation is over. The civil marriage is completed and he takes his "cohabitant" home.

With the exception of women from the privileged classes or those who arrived with their husbands, all female convicts became "cohabitants." Most of the women convicts were neurotics who had been "sentenced for crimes of passion or crimes connected with their families." They say, "I came because of my husband," or "I came because of my mother-in-law."

Most are murderers, the victims of love and family despotism. Even those who are sent out here for arson and for counterfeiting are being punished for their love affairs, since they were enticed into crime by their lovers.

Now they were "settled." Twenty years before Chekhov's time such women were sent to brothels.

Chekhov made a study of the grim mining settlements all over the island. Due was a place of violent brawls and robberies. On another journey there is a place called Upper Armudan, famous for its cardplayers. They gambled here with their rations and clothing. Once he was obliged to stay in a garret in the jail because the only other room was fully occupied by bugs and cockroaches. The jailer said these creatures "win all the time."

It seemed as though the walls and ceiling were covered with black crepe, which stirred as if blown by a wind. From the rapid and disorderly movements of portions of the crepe you could guess the composition of this boiling, seething mass.

During his journeys Chekhov came across dozens of criminal life stories. He got used to the apathy of the women, but the lot of the children born there horrified him.

What is terrifying in the cities and villages of Russia is commonplace here.... When children see chained convicts dragging a wheelbarrow full of sand, they hang onto the back of the barrow and laugh uproariously.

They played Soldiers-and-Convicts and Vagrants among themselves and knew the exact meaning of "executioner," "prisoners in chains," and "cohabitant." He records a talk with a boy of ten.

"What is your father's name?" I asked him.
"I don't know," he answered....
"You are living with your father and don't know his name? That is disgraceful."
"He's not my real father."
"What do you mean, he's not your real father?"
"He's my mother's cohabitant."
"Is your mother married or a widow?"
"A widow. She came because of her husband."
"What do you mean, she came because of her husband?"
"She killed him."

In spite of this Chekhov was convinced that the children were "the most useful, the most necessary and the most pleasant" creatures on the island and that the convicts themselves felt this too. The children loved their "impure mothers and criminal fathers more than anything else in the world. ... often children are the only tie that binds men and women to life, saving them from despair and a final disintegration." Yet the parents seemed indifferent to child prostitution.

The most horrifying pages of the book are those describing a flogging. Chekhov steeled himself to watch it and to record almost every stroke and all the screams of the criminal and the cold professional attitude of the flogger, counting out the strokes. Chekhov was impelled to identify himself with all the pain on the island. The one relief from the sight of human degradation came to him from the sights of nature: the crops, the forests, the animals, birds and shoals of fish. He studied the agriculture of the island very seriously. Writing the book when he was back home was a trying labor for one who was not by nature a documentary journalist. He added very enlightening footnotes. The book did not appear until 1895.

By October he was glad to leave Sakhalin, glad to stop being a doctor, examining human degradation, and to be a free globe-trotter. He left on a steamer by way of Hong Kong and Singapore. He reveled above all in Ceylon, where, he claimed in a letter to Alexander, he had made love to a dark girl under the palm trees; he also acquired three mongooses, and then went on to Odessa. At Tula his mother and sister met him, and then home to Moscow. He had been away eight months. He was thirty. He told his friends and family:

> I can say I have lived! I've had everything I want. I have been in Hell which is Sakhalin and in Paradise which is Ceylon.

He was restless. This labor of writing a "book of statistics" hung over him like a punishment for a long time, for once more he was frantic about money. He had spent more than he could afford. His mind was full of stories begging to be written.

The man so conscientious in his duties inevitably craved once more for escape and evasion. The "cure" was more travel and, although protesting, he jumped recklessly at the chance of a trip to Europe with Suvorin. The distraction was indeed a cure. On Sakhalin he had simply worked too hard; now with Suvorin and Suvorin's son he moved from barbarism to civilization. Vienna amazed him. He had never seen anything like this in his life.

> I have for the first time realized. . . . that architecture is an art. And here the art is not seen in little bits, as with us, but stretches over several miles. And then on every side street there is sure to be a bookshop. . . . It is strange that here one is free to read anything and to say what one likes.

They went on to Venice: "For us poor and oppressed Russians it is easy to go out of our minds here in a world of beauty, wealth, and freedom," he writes. And in another letter: "And the house where Desdemona lived is to let!"

On they went to Bologna and Florence. What works of art! What singing! What neckties in the shops! In Naples he was enchanted by the famous aquarium and studied the grace and viciousness of the exotic fish. He climbed Vesuvius and looked down on the crater and heard "Satan snoring under cover of the smoke." In Monte Carlo he could not resist a gamble and lost more than he could afford. "If I had money to spare I would spend the whole year gambling"—and, in one sense, his own life had become a gamble. In Nice he thought the luxury of the resort vulgarized the scenery. In Paris there were riots, but he thought the French "magnificent." He was impressed at the Chamber of Deputies, where he heard a free and stormy debate on the behavior of the police in the riots. Imagine the freedom to criticize the police! For once in his life he was staying in luxury hotels. He loved the Moulin Rouge but he eventually tired of "men who tie boa constrictors round their bodies, ladies who kick up to the ceiling, flying people, lions, *cafés chantants*, dinners and lunches." He wanted to get back to work. His depression had gone.

On Mondays, Tuesdays and Wednesdays I write my Sakhalin book, on the other days, except Sunday, my novel, and on Sundays, short stories.

He had paid his debt to medicine.

(1988)

LITERARY CRITICISM

MARK TWAIN

THE AMERICAN PURITAN

After reading Hemingway and Faulkner and speculating upon the breach of the American novel with its English tradition, we go back to the two decisive, indigenous Americans who opened the new vein—Mark Twain and Edgar Allan Poe. Everything really American, really non-English comes out of that pair of spiritual derelicts, those two scarecrow figures with their half-lynched minds. Both of them, but particularly Twain, represent the obverse side of Puritanism. We have never had this obverse in England, for the political power of Puritanism lasted for only a generation and has since always bowed if it has not succumbed to civilised orthodoxy. If an Englishman hated Puritanism, there was the rest of the elaborate English tradition to support him; but American Puritanism was totalitarian and if an American opposed it, he found himself alone in a wilderness with nothing but bottomless cynicism and humorous bitterness for his consolation. There has never been in English literature a cynicism to compare with the American; at any rate we have never had that, in some ways vital, but always sardonic or wretched, cynicism with its broken chopper edge and its ugly wound. We have also never had its by-product: the humorous philosophers; Franklin's Poor Richard, the Josh Billingses, the Artemus Wards, the Pudd'nhead Wilsons and Will Rogerses with their close-fisted proverbs:

"Training is everything. The peach was once a bitter almond: cauliflower is nothing but a cabbage with a college education."

Or

"Consider well the proportion of things. It is better to be a young June bug than an old bird of Paradise."

I say we have never had this kind of thing, but there is one exception to prove the rule and to prove it very well, for he also is an uprooted and, so to speak, colonial writer. Kipling with his "A woman is always a woman, but a good cigar is a smoke" is our first American writer with a cynicism, a cigar-stained humour and a jungle book of beliefs which, I think, would be a characteristic of our literature if we become seriously totalitarian in the future. For English totalitarianism would create the boredom and bitterness of the spiritual wilderness, as surely as Puritanism did in America.

When Mark Twain turned upon the religion of his childhood because it was intolerable, he was unaware that it would destroy him by turning him into a money-grubber of the most disastrously Puritan kind. Fortunately the resources of the imagination are endless even when a fanatical philosophy wrecks human life, genius and happiness. Out of the mess which Twain made of his life, amid the awful pile of tripe which he wrote, there does rise one book which has the serenity of a thing of genius. *Huckleberry Finn* takes the breath away. Knowing his life, knowing the hell from which the book has ascended, one dreads as one turns from page to page the seemingly inevitable flop. How can so tortured and so angry a comedian refrain from blackguarding God, Man and Nature for the narrow boredom of his early life, and thus ruin the gurgling comedy and grinning horror of the story? But an imaginative writer appears to get one lucky break in his career; for a moment the conflicts are assimilated, the engine ceases to work against itself. The gears do not crash and *Huckleberry Finn* hums on without a jar. America gets its first and indisputable masterpiece. The boyhood of Huck Finn is the boyhood of a new culture and a new world.

The curious thing about *Huckleberry Finn* is that, although it is one of the funniest books in all literature and really astonishing in the variety of its farce and character, we are even more moved than we are amused by it. Why are we moved? Do we feel the sentiment of sympathy only? Are we sighing with some envy and self-pity? "Alas, Huck Finn is just what I would have been in my boyhood if I had had half a chance." Are we sorry for the vagrant, or are we moved by his rebellion? These minor feelings may play their part; but they are only sighs on the surface of the main stream of our emotion. Twain has brought to his subject far more than this personal longing; he has become the channel of the generic American emotion which floods all really American literature—nostalgia. In that brilliant, hit-or-miss book, *Studies in Classical American Literature*, which is either dead right or dead wrong, D. H. Lawrence called this feeling the longing of the rebel for a master. It may be simply the longing for a spiritual home, but it is as strong in Mark Twain as it is implicit in Hemingway. One finds this nostalgia in Anglo-Irish literature which is also colonial and, in a less lasting way, once again in the work of Kipling. The peculiar power of American nostalgia is that it is not only harking back to something lost in the past, but suggests also the tragedy of a lost future. As Huck Finn and old Jim drift down the Mississippi from one horrifying little town to the next and hear the voices of men quietly swearing at one another across the water about "a chaw of tobacco"; as they pass the time of day with the scroungers, rogues, murderers, the lonely women, the frothing revivalists, the maundering boatmen and fantastic drunks, we see the human wastage that is left behind in the wake of a great effort of the human will, the hopes frustrated, the idealism which has been whittled down to eccentricity and mere animal cunning. These people are the price paid for building a new country. The human spectacle is there. It is not, once you have faced it—which Dickens did not do in *Martin Chuzzlewit*, obsessed as he was by the negative pathos of the immigrant—it is not a disheartening spectacle; for the value of a native humour like Twain's is that it records a profound reality in human nature: the ability of man to adjust himself to any circumstance and somehow to survive and make a life.

Movement is one of the great consolers of human woe; movement, a process of continual migration is the history of America. It is this factor which gives Twain's wonderful descriptions of the journey down the Mississippi its haunting overtone and which, naturally enough, awakens a sensibility in him which is shown nowhere else in his writings and which is indeed vulgarly repressed in them:

> ... then we set down on the sandy bottom where the water was about knee-deep and watched the daylight come. Not a sound anywhere—perfectly still—just like the whole world was asleep, only sometimes the bull-frogs a-clattering may be. The first thing to see, looking away over the water, was a kind of dull line—that was on the woods on t'other side—you couldn't make nothing else out; then a pale place in the sky; then more paleness, spreading around; then the river softened up, away off, and wasn't black any more but grey; you could see little dark spots drifting along, ever so far away—trading scows ... and such things; and long black streaks—rafts; sometimes you could hear a sweep screaking; or jumbled-up voices, it was so still, and sounds come so far; and by-and-by you could see a streak on the water which you know by the look of the streak that there's a snag in the swift current which breaks on it and that streak looks that way; and you see the mist curl up off the water, and the east reddens up, and the river, and you make out a log cabin in the edge of the woods, away on the bank t'other side of the river, being a woodyard likely, and piled by them cheats so you can throw a dog through it anywheres ...

And afterwards we would watch the lonesomeness of the river, and kind of lazy along and by-and-by, lazy off to sleep. Wake up, by-and-by, and look to see what done it, and may be see a steamboat, coughing along upstream, so far off towards the other side you couldn't tell nothing about her only whether she was sternwheel or side wheel; then for about an hour there wouldn't be nothing to hear nor nothing to see—just solid lonesomeness. Once there was a thick fog, and the rafts and things that went by was beating tin pans so the steam boats wouldn't run over them. A scow or a raft went by so close we could hear them talking and cussing and laughing—heard them plain; but we couldn't see no sign of them; it made you feel crawly, it was like spirits carrying on that way in the air. Jim said he believed it was spirits; but I says, "No, spirits wouldn't say 'dern this dem fog.' "

(Note the word "way" in this passage; it is a key nostalgic word in the American vocabulary, vaguely vernacular and burdened with the associations of the half-articulate. It is a favourite Hemingway word, of course: "I feel *that way*"—not the how or what he feels of the educated man.)

The theme of *Huckleberry Finn* is the rebellion against civilisation and especially against its traditions:

I reckon I got to light out for the Territory ahead of the rest, because Aunt Sally she's going to adopt me and sivilize me and I can't stand it. I been there before.

Huck isn't interested in "Moses and the Bulrushers" because Huck "don't take no stock of dead people." He garbles European history when he is discussing Kings with Jim, the Negro. Whether Huck is the kind of boy who will grow up to build a new civilisation is doubtful; Tom Sawyer obviously will because he is imaginative. Huck never imagines anything except fears. Huck is "low down plain ornery," always in trouble because of the way he was brought up with "Pap." He is a natural anarchist and bum. He can live without civilisation, depending on shrewd affections and loyalty to friends. He is the first of those typical American portraits of the underdog, which have culminated in the poor white literature and in Charlie Chaplin—an underdog who gets along on horse sense, so to speak. Romanticism, ideas, ideals are repugnant to Huck; he "reckons" he "guesses," but he doesn't think. In this he is the opposite of his hero, Tom Sawyer. Tom had been telling "stretchers" about Arabs, elephants and Aladdin's lamp. Huck goes at once "into a brood."

I thought all this over for two or three days, and then I reckoned I would see if there was anything in it. I got an old tin lamp and an irony ring and went out into the woods and rubbed it till I sweat like an Injun, calculating to build a palace and sell it; but it wasn't no use, none of the genies came. So then I judged that all that stuff was only just one of Tom Sawyer's lies. I reckoned he believed in the A-rabs and elephants, but as for me I think different. It has all the marks of a Sunday school.

That is, of American Puritan civilisation, the only civilisation he knew.

"Ornery," broody, superstitious, with a taste for horrors, ingenious, courageous without knowing it, natural, sound-hearted, philosophical in a homely way—those are the attributes of the gorgeous, garrulous Huck and they give a cruelly extravagant narrative its humanity. He obliges you to accept the boy as the devastating norm. Without him the violence of the book would be stark reporting of low life. For if *Huckleberry Finn* is a great comic book it is also a book of terror and brutality. Think of the scenes: Pap and d.t.'s chasing Huck round the cabin with a knife; Huck sitting up all night with a gun preparing to shoot the old man; Huck's early familiarity with corpses; the pig-killing scene; the sight of the frame house (evidently some sort of brothel) floating down the Mississippi with a murdered man in it; the fantastic events at the Southern house where two families shoot each other down in vendetta; the drunken Boggs who comes into town to pick a quarrel and is eventually coolly shot dead before the eyes of his screaming young daughter by the man he has insulted. The "Duke" and the "King," those cynical rascals whose adventures liven up the second half of the story, are sharpers, twisters and crooks of the lowest kind. Yet a child is relating all this with a child's detachment and with a touch of morbidity. Marvellous as the tale is, as a collection of picaresque episodes and as a description of the mess of frontier life, it is strong meat. Sometimes we wonder how Twain's public stomached such illusionless reporting. The farce and the important fact that in this one book Mark Twain never forced a point nor overwrote—in the Dickens way for example—are of course the transfiguring and beguiling qualities. His corpse and coffin humour is a dry wine which raises the animal spirits. Old Jim not only looked like a dead man after the "King" had painted him blue, but like one "who had been dead a considerable time."

Judiciousness is carried to the comic limit. And then, Mark Twain is always getting the atmosphere, whether he picks up the exact words of loafers trying to borrow tobacco off one another or tells a tall story of an hysterical revival meeting.

Atmosphere is the decisive word. *Huckleberry Finn* reeks of its world. From a sensitive passage like:

> When I got there it was all still and Sunday-like, and hot and the hands was gone to the fields; and there was them kind faint dronings of bugs and flies that makes it seem so lonesome and like everybody's dead . . .

to descriptions of the silly, dying girl's ridiculous poetry, the sensibility draws a clear outline and is never blurred and turned into sentimentality. One is enormously moved by Huck's view of the world he sees. It is the world not of Eden, but of the "old Adam," not the golden age of the past, but the earthly world of a reality which (we feel with regret) we have let slip through our fingers too carelessly. Huck is only a crude boy, but luckily he was drawn by a man whose own mind was arrested, with disastrous results in his other books, at the schoolboy stage; here it is perfect. And a thousand times better than the self-conscious adventures of Stevenson's *Treasure Island* and *Kidnapped*.

Is *Huckleberry Finn* one of the great works of picaresque literature? It is, granting the limits of a boy's mind in the hero and the author, a comic masterpiece; but this limitation is important. It is not a book which grows spiritually, if we compare it to *Quixote, Dead Souls* or even *Pickwick*; and it is lacking in that civilised quality which you are bound to lose when you throw over civilisation—the quality of pity. One is left with the cruelty of American humour, a cruelty which is softened by the shrewd moralisings of the humorous philosophers—the Josh Billingses, the Artemus Wards, and the Will Rogerses. And once Mark Twain passed this exquisite moment of his maturity, he went to bits in that morass of sentimentality, cynicism, melodrama and vulgarity which have damned him for the adult reader.

(1942)

SAMUEL RICHARDSON

CLARISSA

The modern reader of Richardson's *Clarissa* emerges from his experience exhausted, exalted and bewildered. The book is, I fancy, the longest novel in the English language; it is the one most crowded with circumstantial detail; it is written in the most dilatory of narrative manners, i.e., in the form of letters. It is a tale perceived through a microscope; it is a monstrosity, a minute and inordinate act of prolonged procrastination. And the author himself is a monster. That a man like Samuel Richardson should write one of the great European novels is one of those humiliating frolics in the incidence of genius. The smug, juicy, pedestrian little printer from Derbyshire, more or less unlettered, sits down at the age of 50 and instructs young girls in the art of managing their virtue to the best advantage. Yet, ridiculous as Pamela is, her creator disarms criticism by a totally new ingredient in the novel: he knows how to make the reader weep. And, stung by the taunts of the educated writers of his time, Richardson calmly rises far above *Pamela* when he comes to the story of Clarissa Harlowe; he sets the whole continent weeping. Rousseau and even Goethe bow to him and take out their handkerchiefs; the vogue of sensibility, the first shoots of the Romantic movement, spring from the pool of Richardson's pious tears like the grateful and delicate trees of an oasis. Yet there he is, plump, prosaic, the most middling of middling men, and so domestically fussy that even his gift of weeping hardly guarantees that he will be a major figure. Is there not some other strain in this dull and prodigiously painstaking little man? There is. Samuel Richardson was mad.

I do not mean that Richardson was a lunatic. I do not mean he was mad as Swift was mad. At first sight, an immeasurable smugness, an endlessly pettifogging normality seem to be the outer skin of Richardson's character. We know, as I have already said, that from his youth he was an industrious and timid young man who was, for some reason or other, used by young women who wanted their love letters written. Profoundly sentimental, he sat like some pious old cook in her kitchen, giving advice to the kitchen maids, and when he came to write novels he was merely continuing this practical office. He lived vicariously like some sedentary lawyer who has to argue the disasters of other people's lives letter by letter, but who himself never partakes. Genteel, he is, nevertheless, knowing; prim and cosy, he is, nevertheless, the victim of that powerful cult of the will, duty and conscience by which Puritanism turned life and its human relations into an incessant war. There is no love in Puritanism; there is a struggle for power. Who will win the daily battle of scruple and conscience—Pamela or the young squire; Clarissa or Lovelace? And yet what is urging Richardson to this battle of wills? What is it that the Puritan cannot get out of his mind, so that it is a mania and obsession? It is sex. Richardson is mad about sex.

His is the madness of Paul Pry and Peeping Tom. I said just now that *Clarissa* is a novel written under the microscope; really it is a novel written about the world as one sees it through the keyhole. Prurient and obsessed by sex, the prim Richardson creeps on tip-toe nearer and nearer, inch by inch, to that vantage point; he beckons us on, pausing to make every kind of pious protestation, and then nearer and nearer he creeps again, delaying, arguing with us in whispers, working us up until we catch the obsession too. What are we going to see when we get there? The abdication, the seduction, the lawful deflowering of a virgin in marriage are not enough for him. Nothing short of the rape of Clarissa Harlowe by a man determined on destroying her can satisfy Richardson's phenomenal day-dream with its infinite delays.

The principle of procrastinated rape is said to be the ruling one in all the great best-sellers. It was in Richardson's genius that he was able to elevate the inner conflict of the passions and the will to an abstract level, so that the struggle of Clarissa and Lovelace becomes a universal battle-piece; and, in doing this, Richardson was able to paint it with the highly finished realism of the Dutch painters. At the beginning one might simply be reading yet another novel of intrigue, which just goes on and on; and but for the incredible suspense in the narrative I think many readers must have given up *Clarissa* by the end of the first volume. It is not until the third and fourth volumes are reached, when Richardson transposes his intrigue into the sustained and weeping music, the romantic tragedy of Clarissa's rape and long preparation for death, that we get his measure. She dies piously, yet like a Shakespearean conferring greatness upon all around her by the starkness of her defeat. At the beginning we are not prepared for this greatness in Clarissa; even in that last volume we are often uncertain of her real stature. It is not easy for virginity to become Virtue. Would she be anything without Lovelace? And yet, we know, she is the crown upon Lovelace's head. He too becomes tragic under her judgment as she becomes tragic by his act. These two reflect glory upon each other, like saint and devil. But in the first volume there is no difficulty about deciding who is the greater as a character or as an abstract conception. Lovelace has her beaten hands down. A practical and languid correspondence wakes up when he takes pen in hand. Anna Howe, the "pert" friend, makes circles round her. Arabella, with her nose out of joint, is livelier comedy. The scheming brother, the gouty father with his paroxysms, the supplicating and fluttering mother, and the endearing uncles with their unendearing family solidarity, make a greater mark on our minds than the all-too-articulate Clarissa does. Our one hope is that witty Miss Howe is right when she teases Clarissa with maidenly self-deception. "The frost piece," as Lovelace called her, looks exactly like one of those fascinating prudes whose minds are an alphabet that must be read backwards. But no; though she will enchant us when she is rattled, with cries like "Oh, my Nancy, what shall I do with this Lovelace?" her course and her motives are clear to her; and we begin the slow and painful discovery of a virtue which finds no exhilaration except in scruple. We face an inexhaustible determination, and this is exhausting to contemplate, for Clarissa is as interested in the organisation of human motives as Richardson himself; and he insinuates himself in her character so thoroughly, niggling away with his "ifs" and his "buts," that he overwhelms her, as Flaubert overwhelmed Madame Bovary.

Still this does not take from the drama of Clarissa's situation, and does, in fact, increase the suspense of it. If we skip—and of course we do, looking up the letters in the obliging synopsis—we do not, as in other novels, find ourselves caught out by an overlooked sub-plot; we are back in the main situation. Will the family relent? Will Lovelace abduct, marry, rape or reform? There's hardly a sub-plot worth mentioning in this huge novel. It follows the labyrinth of a single theme. And though we turn to Anna Howe for glimpses of common sense, and for a wit to enliven the glum belligerents of what Lovelace—always a psychologist and nearly a Freudian—called "the Harlowe dunghill" with its wills and deeds of settlement, we see in Clarissa's stand something more than a virtuous daughter bullied by her parents. She is a lawyer in family morals, and in Lovelace's too; but she is the first heroine in English fiction to stand against the family. Richardson called them "the embattled phalanx," and in *Clarissa* he goes to the heart of the middle-class situation: money, accretion of estate, the rise in the world, the desire to found a family, in conflict with the individual soul. She and Lovelace complement each other here. She thinks her family ought not to do evil to her, yet takes their evil upon herself; she is not a rebel but is tricked and driven into becoming an outcast and at last a saint. Like Lovelace, she has asked too much, "for people who allow nothing will be granted nothing; in other words, those who aim at carrying too many points will not be able to carry any." Yes, and those who put up their price by the device of reluctance invite the violence of the robber. By setting such a price upon herself, Clarissa represents that extreme of puritanism which desires to be raped. Like Lovelace's, her sexuality is really violent, insatiable in its wish for destruction.

Lovelace is Richardson's extravagant triumph. How did such a burning and tormented human being come out of that tedious little printer's mind? In the English novel Lovelace is one of the few men of intellect who display an intellect which is their own and not patently an abstract of their author's intellectual interests. He is half-villain, half-god, a male drawn to the full, and he dominates English fiction. He is all the more male for the feminine strains in his character: his hatred of women, his love of intrigue, his personal vanity, his captiousness and lack of real humility. A very masculine novelist like Fielding is too much a moralist, and too confidently a man, to catch a strain like that. And how Lovelace can write! When Clarissa's letters drag, like sighing Sunday hymns, or nag at us in their blameless prose, like the Collect for the day, the letters of Lovelace crackle and blaze with both the fire and the inconsequence of life. His words fly back and forth, throwing out anecdotes and the characters of his friends, with wonderful transitions of mood. In one paragraph he is writing a set apostrophe to Clarissa, full of longing and half-way to repentance. He shakes the mood off like a man who is drunk with grief and throws off this description of his gouty old kinsman:

And here (pox of his fondness for me; it happens at a very bad time) he makes me sit hours together entertaining him with my rogueries (a pretty amusement for a sick man!) and yet, whenever he has the gout, he prays night and morning with his chaplain. But what must *his* notions of religion be, who, after he has nosed and mumbled over his responses, can give a sigh or groan of satisfaction, as if he thought he had made up with Heaven; and return with a new appetite to my stories?—encouraging them, by shaking his sides with laughing at them, and calling me a sad fellow, in such an accent as shows he takes no small delight in his kinsman.

The old peer has been a sinner in his day, and suffers for it now; a sneaking sinner, *sliding*, rather than *rushing* into vices, for fear of his reputation; or rather, for fear of detection, and positive proof; for this sort of fellow, Jack, has no real regard for reputation. Paying for what he never had, and never daring to rise to the joy of an enterprise at first hand, which bring him within view of a tilting or the honour of being considered as the principal man in a court of justice.

To see such a Trojan as this just dropping into the grave which I hoped ere this would have been dug, and filled up with him; crying out with pain and grunting with weakness; yet in the same moment crack his leathern face into a horrible laugh, and call a young sinner charming varlet, encoring him as formerly he used to do the Italian eunuchs; what a preposterous, what an unnatural adherence to old habits.

Or there is the awful description of that old procuress, Mrs Sinclair, a horror out of Rowlandson, who advances upon Clarissa on the night of the rape, when all Richardson's fascination with carnal horror breaks out. There is a double terror in it, because Lovelace himself is writing as if trying to drive evil out of his mind by a picture of evils still greater:

The old dragon straddled up to her, with her arms kemboed again, her eyebrows erect like the bristles upon a hog's back, and, scowling over her shortened nose, more than half hid her ferret eyes. Her mouth was distorted. She pouted out her blubber-lips, as if to bellow up wind and sputter into her horse-nostrils, and her chin was curdled, and more than usually prominent with passion.

The temperate, lawyer-like mind of Richardson does not prepare one for passages like this. When there is matter-of-factness in the eighteenth century, one expects it to be as regular as Pope's couplets were. But Richardson is not consistent. In the sheer variety of their styles the letters in this novel are astonishing. The bovine uncles, the teasing parenthetical Miss Howe, the admonitory Belford, the curt Colonel Morden, heading for his duel, the climbing neurotic brother whose descendants were no doubt in the British Union of Fascists, all have their styles, and they are as distinctive as Lovelace's or Clarissa's. Richardson is the least flat, the most stereoscopic novelist of an age which ran the plain or formal statement to death in the end. Another point: he is a writer of indirect narrative. We are shown scenes at second hand, for the epistolary method requires it so; and we become used to a sort of memoranda of talk and action which will tire our inward eye because our judgment is called upon at the same time. So there are many reported scenes which are relative failures, for example, the early and rather confusing ones between Clarissa and her mother. One has a muddled impression of two hens flying up in the air at each other and scattering their feathers. Yet even in this kind of scene Richardson can, at times, write talk which is direct and put action wonderfully under our eye. The scene of the rape is tremendous in this respect; and so is the awful picture of the brothel when Mrs Sinclair breaks her leg and the harridans come out in their night attire; and there is the comic, savage picture of Lovelace defeating the attempt of his family to try him. But where Richardson shook off the slavery of his own method is shown at its best, I think, in Belford's letter describing the prison scene where the two prostitutes offer to bail Clarissa out:

> "We are surprised at your indifference, Miss Harlowe. Will you not write to any of your friends?"
>
> "No."
>
> "Why, you don't think of tarrying here always."
>
> "I shall not live always."

Even in those few lines one sees Richardson advancing his inner narrative and, if one continues this conversation, one also sees him patiently and unerringly preserving character. One might almost say that prolix as it was, his method was economical, given his chosen end. The slowness comes from an excess of examination, not an excess of words. No prose has fewer redundancies.

We come to the death scene. The torment of Lovelace pacing his horse past the gate of the house he dare not enter, though Clarissa lies dying within, is not rhetorical. It is defiant as fits a being so saturnine, it is in the mind as becomes a man of intellect, it is the changeable, imploring, ranging madness of a clever mind that has met its conqueror. Lovelace is a villain no man hates, because he is a man. He is candid, if he is vain. He can argue like Iago or debate like Hamlet, and in between send a purse of a few guineas to a rogue who has helped him to his present catastrophe. It is strange to think of him—the only Don Juan in English fiction and done to the last Freudian detail. Clarissa dies like a swan amid the formal melody of a prose into which Richardson fell without affectation.

> Her breath being very short, she desired another pillow. Having two before, this made her, in a manner, sit up in her bed; and she spoke then with more distinctness; and seeing us greatly concerned, forgot her own stutterings to comfort us; and a charming lecture she gave us, though a brief one, upon the happiness of a timely preparation, and upon the hazards of a late repentance, when the mind, as she observed, was so much weakened, as well as the body, as to render a poor soul hardly able to contend with its natural infirmities.

It is a strong test of the illusion that Richardson has cast upon us that we think of Lovelace like a shadow cast upon Clarissa as she dies; and of Clarissa rather than of Lovelace when *he* appears. These lives are known by their absences; they are inextricable, tangled in the thousands of words they have spoken about each other, and are swept away at last into other people's words.

(1946)

SCOTT

"No one reads Scott now": how often one has heard these words! I have no doubt they are true, at any rate true of English readers. At some time in the last 30 years feeling against dialect and especially the Scottish dialect has hardened into a final dislike. It is troublesome to the eye, it is a language which nags and clatters; one would as soon read phonetics. And then dialect suggests the overweening conceit of local virtue, and if anything has died in the last 30 years, it is regionalism. Our society—why pretend?—has made war on regionalism and has destroyed it. We may question whether, under any disguise, it can be reborn in the modern world. That is the first difficulty when we look at the long brown row of the Waverley novels that have stood high out of reach on our shelves, unopened since our childhood. And here the second difficulty arises. We read Scott in our childhood and he is not suitable reading for children; few of the great novelists are. Why should a man, writing in his maturity, scarred by life, marked by the evils of the world, its passions and its experience in his blood, be consigned to the young who know nothing of themselves or the world? The fault is partly Scott's: this great man, the single Shakespearean talent of the English novel, drew far too often the heroes and heroines which have always appealed to the adolescent and gently reared reader—wooden idealisations, projections of our more refined, sixteen-year-old wishes. At sixteen we are in love with those sexless heroines with their awful school-mistressy speeches. We are in love with those stick-in-the-mud heroes whose disinterestedness and honour pervert the minds of boys with a tedious and delusive idealism. One grows up in the daydream that Scott has generated to discover it is a swindle; and one never forgives him.

Yet, if we except this serious criticism for the moment, and measure Scott in the light of the full noon of life, we see that he belongs to that very small group of our novelists—Fielding and Jane Austen are the chief of them—who face life squarely. They are grown up. They do not cry for the moon. I do not mean that to be grown up is the first requirement of genius. To be grown up may be fatal to it. But short of the great illuminating madness, there is a power to sustain, assure and enlarge us in those novelists who are not driven back by life, who are not shattered by the discovery that it is a thing bounded by unsought limits, by interests as well as by hopes, and that it ripens under restriction. Such writers accept. They think that acceptance is the duty of a man.

An error of our boyhood reading of Scott is, I fancy, the easy assumption that Scott is primarily an historical novelist. There is more reason to think of him as a comic writer. We would make a similar kind of error about Defoe, Fielding or Richardson if we took them at their word and believed that their only aim was to reform morals. The historical passion of Scott or the moral passion of these other novelists was the engine of their impulse. Where that engine took them is another matter. Hazlitt saw this when, in his too drastic way, he said that Scott was interested in half of life only: in the past of man and not in what he might become; and Hazlitt went to the length of thinking Godwin's *Falkland* fit to be compared with *Waverley*. But Scott's history meant simply his preoccupation with what is settled—and, after all, a great deal is settled for better or worse, in human life and character. One might even see in Scott's history the lame man's determination to impose and ennoble normality. The feuds of the clans are done with, the bloody wars of the Border are over, Jacobitism is a mere sentiment notable for its ironical inconsistencies as well as its heroic gestures. A period has ended and, for a novelist, there is no more favourable moment. Now he can survey. Scott gazes upon it all like a citizen who has dressed up. Now, vicariously, he can be physically heroic; but the real result of the historical impulse is not history but an immense collection of small *genre* pieces, a huge gallery of town and country faces in their inns, their kitchens, their hovels, their farms and their rambling houses. And the painting of them is as circumstantial, as middle-class—in the anti-romantic sense—and as non-aristocratic as anything of Hogarth's. Scott does not revive the past or escape into it; he assimilates it for his own time and for his own prejudices. He writes like a citizen. He asserts the normal man, the man who has learned to live with his evil; what his evil might have done with him if he had not learned to live with it can be guessed from the grotesque declamations of *The Black Dwarf*, the creature who cuts himself off from mankind.

The Black Dwarf is not a good novel. There are awkward lumps of unreality in it. The bad thing is the central drama, and this points to Scott's obvious fault as a novelist. He has an immense memory and the necessary taste for improving on memory. He has the power to present the outside of a character and to work from the outside to the inside. But once inside, he discovers only what is generic. That is the fault. He has, I would say, no power to work from the inside to the outer man. There is nothing feminine in him. So the black dwarf is excellent when he is seen as local recollection, a piece of Border hearsay, and no one could surpass Scott in portraying that tortured head, with its deep-sunken pin-point eyes, the almost legless and hairy little body with its huge feet and the enormous voice that issues from the abortion. But when we come to the mind of this tortured creature, when he speaks, what we get is not horror but a dreary, savage Calvinist lecture. The black dwarf's misanthropy is a mere exercise, a sermon turned inside out. There is a complete breakdown of the imagination: compare this story with Turgenev's *Lear of the Steppes*. I suspect that as we continue our rediscovery of Scott we shall often find that the chief drama of the novels breaks down in this way, for the great protagonists of fiction begin from the inside of a writer. One is inclined to divide the Scott characters into two classes: the secondary and minor ones who are real and are truly recollected, the children of his wonderful memory; and the major ones who are the awkward, stage figures of an imagination that is cut off from the sap of life. To go back to Hazlitt: Scott lacked a vital sense, the sense of what people may become. His history was not real history. It was the settled, the collectible, the antique.

I turn to *The Chronicles of the Canongate*, the tales of the second series, to see whether my last sentence is too sweeping. There is *The Highland Widow*. Here is real history—but you notice at once—history without costume. History in the rags of the people. The widow's husband has been a bandit, the Robin Hood of a clan that has almost died out. Her son perceives that times have changed; he enlists in the army which was once his father's enemy. The mother is appalled by the disgrace and plots to restore her son to a life of crime. The tragedy which is enacted springs from the clash of two orders of virtue, and the virtue of one age has become the vice of the age that succeeds it. There is no dialect in this story. It is heroic and not Hogarthian. It is the kind of thing that Mérimée and Pushkin took from Scott. And here, better than in his more elaborate compositions, we see the mark of Scott's genius as a story-teller. I say nothing of the suspense of which he is always a master; I am thinking of his power of suggesting the ominous, the footsteps of fate coming to meet one on the road. Frequently Scott used the supernatural and the hints of second sight to get this effect, and they are all the more effective for being explained as the domestic beliefs of his characters which the author himself hesitates to accept. But in *The Highland Widow* we come upon one of those real omens, one of those chance remarks made by a stranger which have another meaning to the one who hears. It is a device much used by Hardy. In Scott's story the young soldier has been drugged by his fanatical mother so that he shall not return to his regiment. The boy wakes up and rushes out to find what day of the week it is, for he fears more than anything else the degradation of his honour. The first person he meets is a minister, who replies: "Had you been where you should have been yesterday, young man, you would have known that it was God's Sabbath." The two meanings of those words mark the crisis of the tale, and after looking back upon it one realises how ingenious and masterly has been the construction of a simple story. The end we could foresee; the means we could not, and it is in the means that Scott always shows the power of a master.

It is less the business of the novelist to tell us what happened than to show how it happened. The best things in Scott arise out of the characters. He especially understands, as I said before, the generic differences between people. He understands the difference between the fisherman and the farmer, the shepherd and the drover, and so on. He understands, in other words, what all ordinary, simple, observant men know about one another: the marks of their trade, their town, their family. (His view of women is that of the simple man: he knows them by their habits in the house. In love he does not know them at all.) The tale called *The Two Drovers* is a fine example of Scott's watchfulness of male character. The honour of Robin, the Highland drover, seems to be quaint silliness to Wakefield, the stolid Yorkshireman; the sense and fair play of Wakefield, who cannot believe that enmity will survive a little amateur boxing, are meaningless to the Highlander. Each is reasonable—but in a different way. The clash when it comes is tragic; again two kinds of virtue are irreconcilable. The scene in the inn is wonderfully true to the men there, and the talk slips naturally off their clumsy tongues. Wakefield has challenged Robin to fight with his fists. Robin can't see how this will mend a quarrel.

Harry Wakefield dropped the hand of his friend or rather threw it from him.

"I did not think I had been keeping company for three years with a coward."

"Coward pelongs to none of my name," said Robin, whose eyes began to kindle, but keeping the command of his temper. "It was no coward's legs or hands, Harry Waakfelt, that drew you out of the fords of Frew, when you was drifting ower the plack rock, and every eel in the river expected his share of you."

"And that is true enough, too," said the Englishman, struck by the appeal.

"Adzooks!" exclaimed the bailiff—"sure Harry Wakefield, the nattiest lad at Whitson Tryste, Wooler Fair, Carlisle Sands, or Stagshaw Bank, is not going to show the white feather? Ah, this comes of living so long with kilts and bonnets—

men forget the use of their daddles."

"I may teach you, Master Fleecebumpkin, that I have not lost the use of mine," said Wakefield, and then went on. "This will never do, Robin. We must have a turn-up or we shall be the talk of the countryside. I'll be d____d if I hurt thee—I'll put on the gloves gin thou like. Come, stand forward like a man!"

"To be peaten like a dog," said Robin, "is there any reason in that? If you think I have done you wrong, I'll go before your shudge, though I neither know his law nor his language."

A general cry of "No, no—no law, no lawyer, a bellyful and be friends" was echoed by the bystanders.

"But," continued Robin, "if I am to fight, I have no skill to fight like a jackanapes, with hands and nails."

And here once more the agent of tragedy is moving slowly down the road towards the two friends—the drover who is carrying Robin's dirk for him, to keep him out of trouble and to circumvent the fate that was foretold at the beginning of the story.

Except in the outbursts of *The Black Dwarf,* Scott appears to see evil as a fatality that ensues from the nature of the times. The civil wars have made men narrow and ruthless, and he writes at the end of an era, surveying the broken scene and pleading for tolerance. The crimes in *The Chronicles of the Canongate* are "errors of the understanding," not examples of absolute wickedness. When we turn to *The Antiquary* we meet another side of his talent; his humour. I wonder how many of those who, like myself, had not read Scott since their schooldays will recall that Scott is one of the great comic writers? It is not purely Scottish humour, depending on the canniness of the speaker or on a continuous sly, nervous snigger, or on the grotesque and pawky asides of dialect. Scott's humour, like his best prose, is cross-bred with the English eighteenth century. Sterne and Fielding have put red blood into it. A character like Jonathan Oldbuck does not make thin jokes down his nose, but stands solidly and aglow beside all the well-found comics of our literature. The secret is that Scott's animal spirits are high, as Fielding's were. I have always enjoyed that strange scene in the early pages of *The Antiquary* in which Oldbuck supervises the rescue of the foolish, snobbish, bankrupt, treasure-hunting Sir Arthur, and his stick of a daughter, from the rising tide. Jonathan Oldbuck, who has only an hour before been snubbed by the angry baronet, now watches the men heave the scarcely conscious gentleman up the rock:

"Right, right, that's right, too—I should like to see the son of Sir Gamelyn de Guardover on dry land myself—I have a notion he would sign the abjuration oath, and the Ragman-roll to boot, and acknowledge Queen Mary to be nothing better than she should be, to get alongside my bottle of old port that he ran away from, and left scarce begun. But he's safe now, and here a' comes—(for the chair was again lowered, and Sir Arthur made fast in it, without much consciousness on his own part)—Here a' comes—bowse away, my boys!—canny wi' a tenpenny tow—the whole barony of Knockwinnock depends on three plies of hemp—respice finem, respice funem—look to your end—look to the rope's end."

I can read about half of *The Antiquary* and enjoy the flavours of what I read. After that I skip through the preposterous plot and willingly leave the wooden Lovel and the disdainful Miss Wardour to the pleasure of talking like public statues to each other. In one respect it must be admitted they do surpass modern lovers. Severely regulated by their families and by circumstance, these antique couples are obliged to know their subject. The obstacles to love ensure that the lovers shall concentrate.

The criticism that Scott cannot draw a heroine has to be modified after we have read *The Heart of Midlothian*. To judge by this book Scott could not draw a hero. For neither the pious, pettifogging Butler nor the wicked George Staunton can be called human beings of anything but conventional interest. Effie and Jeanie Deans are quite another matter. They are peasants and Scott condescends to them with the gentlemanliness of his time, but they are alive as his peasants always are. Scott's inability to draw women life-size seems to be due to the fact that he can think of them only as creatures high above him, or safely below him; and the ones below are drawn better than the ones above. The maid is more interesting than the mistress. We owe this romantic and pedestalled conception of women partly to the lame man's feeling of inferiority. He idealised what he could not approach. But these idealisations also arise from that curious split in the puritan middle-class mind which had begun to unsex itself so that it might devote all its will to the adventure of getting on in the world of money or honour, leaving the warmer passions to the lower orders. But unlike the early Victorian novelists, Scott is not a prude. Miss Bellendon's maid, in *Old Mortality*, nudges, winks and uses all her enticements on the soldiery; speech is very free in the farms and the inns; only Miss Bellendon in her castle stands like a statue and talks like an epitaph. Once Scott is free of these inhibitions—and in the main they are fixed by considerations of class—Scott describes women as well as they can be described from the point of view of a man in the house; that is as scolding, fussing, gossiping, pestering, weeping, wilful and mercenary adjuncts of domestic life. They can always answer back. They never forgive a slight, they can always be persuaded to condone a crime. Expressed without satire but with sense and geniality this view has inspired many robust minor portraits of womanhood in Scott. The loveliness and attraction of Di Vernon in *Rob Roy* is due, I fancy, to the fact that she has a good deal of male in her. What is missing from all these portraits is the vitalising element: the sense a woman has of herself, the sense of what she may become—that sense of our fate which alone gives meaning to our character. And as I have said before, Scott's direct intuitive sense of that fate seems to have been weak; he grasps the importance of it only through the labours of the historian and the documentary artists. His researches, not his instinct, gave us his remarkable portrait of the passionate mother in *The Highland Widow,* and his researches also revealed to him, in the same way, the larger meaning of Jeanie Deans's character in *The Heart of Midlothian.*

A modern novelist who rewrote The Heart of Midlothian would cer-tainly stress the unconscious jealousy which Jeanie must have felt towards her younger sister by her father's second marriage. We would say that Jeanie's refusal to tell the lie that would save Effie from the scaffold was not a stern moral act, but an animal retaliation; for psychology has altered for us the nature of many ethical dilemmas. Scott ignores the evident jealousy. And though Effie, in a remarkable prison scene, flies out at her sister, we are left with the impression that Jeanie is either too stupid or too conceited in her conscience to be endured. But Scott's strength in the handling of the situation between the two women comes from his knowledge of the effect of history upon them. They are children of history. And the one part of history Scott knew inside out was its effect upon the conscience. Jeanie's refusal to tell a lie had generations of Calvinistic quarrelling behind it, the vituperations of the sectaries who had changed the sword of the clan wars and the civil wars for the logic-chopping of theology. Instead of splitting skulls, they had taken to splitting hairs. The comedies, the tragedies, the fantastic eloquence and tedious reiteration of these scruples of conscience are always brilliantly described by Scott, who has them in his blood. And so Jeanie's refusal to lie and her journey to London on foot to seek her sister's pardon are not the result of conceit, heartlessness or even literalness of mind: they are the fruit of history.

And a history which produces not only plump, dumb, resolute figures like hers, but men of roystering violence like the bloody Porteous, tortured believers in predestination like Staunton, fanatics like old Deans, cranks like Saddlebright, lunatic harlots like Madge Wildfire, adventuresses like Effie, wonderful sea-lawyers of the criminal world of old Edinburgh, like Ratcliffe, the thief, and wonderful fools like the gaping old laird of Dumbiedikes. There is none of the sentimentality which Dickens spread like a bad fog over the suffocated bastards, baby-farmers, harlots and criminals of his novels; none of the melodrama. Scott's realism belongs to the time when gentlemen knew the mob because they were not yet afraid of the mob. There is only one false episode in *The Heart of Midlothian*, and that is the wildly improbable meeting between Jeanie and George Staunton at his father's vicarage in England, and we owe that to the influence of the theatre on the English novel. For that matter, none of the English scenes is really good and the final third of the novel is a failure. Here Jeanie is diminished as a character by the condescension of the author. But when she is in Scotland, we feel the force of her country and her fate in her, and these make her into a woman. One sees her even more clearly and fully late in the book when it is she, the rescuer, who has to pay tribute to Effie, the adventuress, who has, after all, got away with it. Scott was too much the man of the world to prevent Effie getting away with a good deal more than Dickens or even Thackeray were later on to allow their giddy-pated or wicked women. Scott recorded wilfulness in women with an appreciative eye; and an ear cocked for the back answer.

It has often been said that the decay of our interest in problems of conscience is a major cause of the feebleness of the modern novel; but there have been many poor novels stuffed tight with conscience. Might we not say more justly that the problems of conscience have changed? Our habit is to weigh man against society, civilisation against man or nature; individuals against groups. The greatness of *The Heart of Midlothian* arises, first of all, in the scope that the problem of conscience gave to Scott's imagination. He was not arguing in a void. His argument was creating real people and attracting real people to it. He made the story of Effie's murdered baby a national story. And then how wide his range is! The scenes in the Tolbooth are remarkable, and especially those that are built about the figure of Ratcliffe when the governor is working to turn him into an informer. Scott had the eighteenth-century taste for rogues, and their talk is straight from nature.

"Why, I suppose you know you are under sentence of death, Mr. Ratcliffe?" replied Mr. Sharpitlaw.

"Ay, so are a', as that worthy minister said in the Tolbooth Kirk the day Robertson wan off; but naebody kens when it will be executed. Gude faith, he had better reason to say than he dreamed of, before the play was played out that morning!"

"This Robertson," said Sharpitlaw, in a lower and something like a confidential tone, "d'ye ken, Rat—that is, can ye gie us ony onkling where he is to be heard tell o'?"

"Troth, Mr. Sharpitlaw, I'll be frank wi' ye: Robertson is rather a cut abune me—a wild deevil he was, and mony a daft prank he played; but except the Collector's job that Wilson led him into, and some tuilzies about run goods wi' the guagers and the waiters, he never did ony thing that came near our line o' business."

"Umph! that's singular, considering the company he kept."

"Fact, upon my honour and credit," said Ratcliffe, gravely. "He keepit out o' our little bits of affairs, and that's mair than Wilson did; I hae dune business wi' Wilson afore now. But the lad will come on in time; there's nae fear o' him; naebody will live the life he has led, but what he'll come to sooner or later."

"Who or what is he, Ratcliffe? You know, I suppose?" said Sharpitlaw.

"He's better born, I judge, than he cares to let on; he's been a soldier, and he has been a playactor, and I watna what he has been or hasna been, for as young as he is, sae that it had daffing and nonsense about it."

"Pretty pranks he has played in his time, I suppose?"

"Ye may say that," said Ratcliffe, with a sardonic smile, "and" (touching his nose) "a deevil amang the lasses."

"Like enough," said Sharpitlaw. "Weel, Ratcliffe, I'll no stand niffering wi' ye; ye ken the way that favour's gotten in my office; ye maun be usefu'."

"Certainly, sir, to the best of my power—naething for naething—I ken the rule of the office," said the exdepredator.

Then there is Scott's power of describing a crowded scene. I am thinking of the long narrative about the crowd's storming of the Tolbooth and the killing of Porteous. Scott has looked it all up, but his own version is so alive, so effortless, so fast moving. Every detail tells; the very pedantry of it is pedantry washed down by the rough wine of life. Everything is carried off with the authority of a robust and educated style, the style of a man fit to understand, master and govern, a man endlessly fair and excitingly patient in his taste for human nature. He understands popular clamour. He understands the mysteries of loyalty—all the diverse loyalties of a man's life and trade.

And after that Scott has the story-teller's ability to build a great scene and to make a natural use of it. I'm thinking of the search in the dark on Salisbury Crag when the police have persuaded Ratcliffe to help them catch Robertson, and Ratcliffe has brought Madge Wildfire with him to show them all the way. Madge is semi-lunatic, and Ratcliffe has to use all his guile to keep her to the job. He knows her mind is stuffed full of old wives' tales, and he reminds her of a notorious murder that was done on the Crag years before—a story the reader has already been prepared for: Scott's antiquarian asides ought never to be skipped—but Ratcliffe's cunning is turned against him at the moment of its success by the madness of the woman. She accuses him of being as bad as the murderer.

"I never shed blood," he protested.

"But ye hae sauld it, Ratton—ye hae sauld blood mony a time."

That chance shaft hits Ratcliffe's conscience and wrecks the expedition. In a short chapter Scott has ingeniously extracted every kind of surprise and apprehension; and without any frivolity or artifice. This adventure could have happened; indeed, we say, if we had had eyes at the back of our heads, we would have known that it must have happened so, fabulous as it is. Scott's knowledge gives a sense of necessity to his picture of life, and his freedom in mixing the comic with the serious, even at the most dramatic moments, adds to this pleasant sense. He is not overdriven by his imagination, whereas a writer like Dickens was. Scott, like Fielding, has both feet firmly on the ground.

Rob Roy is admired—but for one or two scenes only when we examine the matter, and it is really a poor novel. At first sight the claims of *Old Mortality* are less emphatic upon the reader's attention, and since Scott repeated himself so often one is tempted to neglect this novel. It should not be neglected. Into this book Scott put all his tolerance and civilisation, his hatred of fanaticism, and illuminated the subject of the religious wars in Scotland with all his irony, humour, all his wiriness of intellect and all his human sympathy. In Burley he drew the rise and the corruption of the fanatical character, and I do not know any other in Scott whose character grows and changes so convincingly. There is real movement here; elsewhere the sense of movement in his characters is more the result of Scott's habit of dissertation than a real enacting of change. The portrait of Claverhouse is debonair, and the battle scene when the insurgents rout him is almost Tolstoyan; how much Scott owes to a sincere pleasure, even a joy, in the accoutrement of life. One can see how the Russians, like Tolstoy, Gogol and Pushkin first of all, must have been caught by Scott's wonderful pictures of the eccentric lairds. The miser in *Old Mortality*, or the ridiculous, gaping laird in *The Heart of Midlothian*, must have fathered many a landlord in *Dead Souls* and other Russian stories. Where the Russians were to succeed and where Scott failed was in conveying the sense of an abiding destiny going on beyond the characters described. For Scott life is a book that one closes; to the Russians it is a book that one opens. And although one feels his animal zest for life, one feels it as a delightful recollection of hours that are ended, not as the perturbation or languor of the hour which has still to go by on the clock as we read.

One looks up the critics. What did Scott add to the English novel? Is he just another Fielding, but planted in Scottish history? Has he simply added a change of scene and material? It looks like that at first glance: he is a writer from the outside looking in. But I think there is something else. I would like to argue that Scott is a complement to Richardson—an analytical and psychological novelist who describes to us the part of our motives formed by public events. He is certainly the first novelist to describe the political influence of religion and the peculiar significance of superstitions and legend in the mind; and he uses them to illustrate the promptings of unconscious guilt and fear. One sees this in the character of Ratcliffe in *The Heart of Midlothian* and in innumerable instances elsewhere; Scott does not use his apparitions and legends merely for the purpose of putting a shiver or a laugh in his story. They are there to convey hidden processes of mind. No English novelist has added to that sense of a general or public mind, and certainly no great novelist—Hardy is the atheistical exception—has used religion as Scott used it.

(1946)

CHARLES DICKENS

EDWIN DROOD

When lately I was reading *The Mystery of Edwin Drood* I felt extremely the want of some sort of guidance on the Victorian fascination with violent crime. What explains the exorbitant preoccupation with murder, above all? In earlier periods, when life was cheaper, rape, seduction, incest were the crimes favoured by literature. If we look to literature rather than to life, it is certain the Victorian writers took over murder from the popular taste of the eighteenth century, and succeeded—against the outcry of the older critics—in making it respectable. But in the nineteenth century one detects, also, the rise of a feeling (so curiously expressed by a popular writer on the melodrama a few years ago, I have forgotten his name) that "murder is cleaner than sex." There is a clue there, I think. There is a clue, too, in the fact that organised police forces and systems of detection were not established until the Napoleonic wars—we are bound to become fascinated by the thing we punish—and another more sinister clue lies in the relative freedom from war after 1815. A peaceful age was horrified and fascinated, for example, by the ritual murders of the Indian thugs. Where else can we look? To the megalomania that was a natural field for the Romantic movement? To the guilt that is deposited in the mind after a ruthless exertion of the will, such as the Victorians made at the time of the Industrial Revolution? To the social chaos before the Fifties, when tens of thousands were uprooted, and if they did not rise with the rising tide were left to sink into the slums or to stand out alone in violent rebellion? The more one reads of the unrest and catastrophes of the nineteenth century, in social or in private life, the more one is appalled by the pressure which its revolution applied to human beings. And when we read again the rant of the melodramas, when we listen to the theatre organ of Bulwer-Lytton in *Eugene Aram*, and read the theatrical pages of Dickens, we feel, after the first shock of distaste, that these people are responding to a pressure which is not exerted upon us in the same degree. The violence of the scene suggests a hidden violence in the mind, and we begin to understand how assuaging it must have been, in novels like *Oliver Twist* or *The Mystery of Edwin Drood*, to see the murderer's conscience displayed in terms of nightmare and hysteria.

Assuaging to the Victorians, but not to us. We are not driven by the same dynamo. *Edwin Drood* stands at the parting of the ways between the early Victorian and the modern attitude to murder in literature, and also, I suspect, at the beginnings of a change in Dickens himself. The earlier murders of Dickens belong to the more turbulent decades of the nineteenth century. By the late Fifties a calm had been reached; the lid had been levered back on to the pot of society and its seething had become a prosperous simmer. When Wilkie Collins wrote *The Moonstone* and Dickens, not to be outdone, followed it with *Edwin Drood*, we begin the long career of murder for murder's sake, murder which illustrates nothing and is there only to stimulate our skill in detection and to distract us with mystery. The sense of guilt is so transformed that we do not seek to expiate it vicariously on the stage; we turn upon the murderer and hunt him down. Presently, in our time, the hunt degenerates into the conundrums of the detective novel which, by a supreme irony, distracts us from our part in the mass murders of two wars. One or two critics have suggested that the struggle with the unfamiliar technique of the hunt was too much for Dickens and that it killed him and his novel. We cannot know whether this is so; but both those who dismiss the book as the last leaden effort of a worn-out man, and those who observe that it is the most careful and private of Dickens's novels, are agreed that it is pitched in a key he has never struck before.

What is that key? Before I add my answer to the dozens that have been made, it seems important to define one's own attitude to Dickens. I am totally out of sympathy with the hostile criticism of Dickens which has been made during the last twenty years, which has ignored his huge vitality and imaginative range and has done no more than to say he lacked taste and that he sacrificed a profound view of human nature to the sentimentalities and falsities of self-dramatisation. To me it is a perversion of criticism to suggest that you can have the virtues of a writer without his vices, and the discovery of Dickens's failures does not make his achievement less. I swallow Dickens whole and put up with the indigestion. I confess I am not greatly interested in the literary criticism which tells me where he is good and where he is bad. I am glad to be instructed; but for us, at the present time, I think there is far more value in trying to appreciate the nature of his creative vitality and the experience that fed it—a vitality notably lacking in our own fiction. Now when we turn to *Edwin Drood* we do find some of the old Dickens. There is Mr Sapsea, for example, with his own account of his courtship, that beautiful shot plum in the middle of romantic love and Victorian marriage:

> "Miss Brobity's Being, young man, was deeply imbued with homage to Mind. She revered Mind, when launched or, as I say, precipitated, on an extensive knowledge of the world. When I made my proposal, she did me the honour of being so over-shadowed with a species of Awe, as to be able to articulate only the two words 'Oh Thou!' meaning myself. Her limpid blue eyes were fixed upon me, her semi-transparent hands were clasped together, pallor overspread her aquiline features, and, though encouraged to proceed, she never did proceed a word further . . . She never did and never could find a phrase satisfactory to her perhaps—too—favourable estimate of my intellect. To the very last (feeble action of the liver) she addressed me in the same unfinished terms."

That is the old Dickens, but a shadow is upon Mr Sapsea. The tomb of Mrs Sapsea is, we are told, to be used by Jasper, the murderer, for his own purpose. Durdles, the drunken verger, tapping the walls of the cathedral for evidence of the "old uns," is to be roped in. The muscular Christian, Mr Crisparkle, sparring before his mirror in the morning, is marked down by the plot; and that terrifying small boy, the Imp or Deputy, who is employed by Durdles to stone him homewards when he is drunk, will evidently be frog-marched into the witness box. Dickens is submitting to discipline, and how fantastically severe it was may be seen in Edmund Wilson's *The Wound and the Bow*. The background loses some of its fantasy, but the best things in *Edwin Drood* are the descriptions of the cathedral, the town and countryside of Rochester which are recorded with the attentive love one feels for things that are gracious and real. Chesterton thought that something of the mad, original Dickens was lost in this realism; other critics explain it as the influence of mid-Victorian settling down. Mr Edmund Wilson seems to suggest that in *Edwin Drood* one finds the mellowness and the bitterness of the man who sets out with some confidence equipped to master his devil and to dominate his wound. I do not find a loss in this picture of Cloisterham:

> Cloisterham is so bright and sunny in these summer days, that the cathedral and the monastery-ruin show as if their strong walls were transparent. A soft glow seems to shine from within them, rather than upon them from without, such is their mellowness as they look forth on the hot cornfields and the smoking roads that distantly wind among them. The Cloisterham gardens blush with ripening

fruit. Time was when travel-stained pilgrims rode in clattering parties through the city's welcome shades; time is when wayfarers, leading a gypsy life between hay-making time and harvest, and looking as if they were just made of the dust of the earth, so very dusty are they, lounge about on cool doorsteps, trying to mend their unmendable shoes, or giving them to the city kennels as a hopeless job, and seeking others in the bundles that they carry, along with their yet unused sickles swathed in bands of straw. At all the more public pumps there is much cooling of the bare feet, together with much bubbling and gurgling of drinking with hand to spout on the part of these Bedouins; the Cloisterham police meanwhile looking askant from their beats with suspicion, and manifest impatience that the intruders should depart from within the civic bounds, and once more fry themselves on the simmering high roads.

The shocks in *Edwin Drood* come not from the sudden levelling of his fantasy and the appearance of realism. They occur when Dickens acts his realism—see the showdown between Jasper and Rosa—and we realise that it is really alien to Dickens's gift that his people should be made to talk to each other. When he attempts this he merely succeeds in making them talk at each other, like actors. His natural genius is for human soliloquy not human intercourse.

In criticism of the English novel and in appeals to what is called "the English tradition," there has been a misunderstanding, I think, about this intrinsic quality of Dickens. One hears the word Dickensian on all sides. One hears of Dickens's influence on the English novel on the one hand, and of the failure of the English novel to produce a comparable genius. While the word Dickensian lasts, the English novel will be suffocated. For the convivial and gregarious extravagance and the picaresque disorder which are supposedly Dickensian are not Dickens's especial contribution to the English novel. They are his inheritance from Sterne, Smollett and, on the sentimental side, from Richardson, an inheritance which may be traced back to the comedy of Jonson. What Dickens really contributed may be seen by a glance at the only novelists who have seriously developed his contribution—in Dostoevsky above all and, to a lesser degree, in Gogol. (There is more of Dickens, to my mind, in James Joyce's *Ulysses* than in books like *Kipps* or *Tono Bungay*.) For the distinguishing quality of Dickens's people is that they are solitaries. They are people caught living in a world of their own. They soliloquise in it. They do not talk to one another; they talk to themselves. The pressure of society has created fits of twitching in mind and speech, and fantasies in the soul. It has been said that Dickens creates merely external caricatures, but Mr Sapsea's musings on his "somewhat extensive knowledge" and Mr Crisparkle's sparrings in front of his mirror are fragments of inner life. In how many of that famous congress of "characters"—Micawber, Barkis, Moddles, Jingle, Mrs Gamp or Miss Twitteron: take them at random—and in how many of the straight personages, like Jasper and Neville Landless in *Edwin Drood*, are we chiefly made aware of the individual's obliviousness of any existence but his own? The whole of Dickens's emotional radicalism, his hatred of the utilitarians and philanthropists and all his attacks on institutions, are based on his strongest and fiercest sense: isolation. In every kind of way Dickens was isolated. Isolation was the foundation not only of his fantasy and his hysteria, but also—I am sure Mr Edmund Wilson is correct here—of the twin strains of rebel and criminal in his nature. The solitariness of people is paralleled by the solitariness of things. Fog operates as a separate presence, houses quietly rot or boisterously prosper on their own. The veneer of the Veneerings becomes almost tangible, whipped up by the repetitions. Cloisterham believes itself more important than the world at large, the Law sports like some stale and dilapidated circus across human lives. Philanthropy attacks people like a humour or an observable germ. The people and the things of Dickens are all out of touch and out of hearing of each other, each conducting its own inner monologue, grandiloquent or dismaying. By this dissociation Dickens brings to us something of the fright of childhood, and the kind of realism employed in *Edwin Drood* reads like an attempt to reconstruct and co-ordinate his world, like a preparation for a final confession of guilt.

(1946)

GEORGE ELIOT

She looked unusually charming today from the very fact that she was not vividly conscious of anything but of having a mind near her that asked her to be something better than she actually was.

It is easy to guess which of the mid-Victorian novelists wrote these lines. The use of the word "mind" for young man, the yearning for self-improvement in the heroine, and, lastly, the painful, reiterating English, all betray George Eliot. This description of Esther Lyon in *Felix Holt* might have been chipped out in stone for George Eliot's epitaph and, as we take down a novel of hers from the shelf, we feel we are about to lever off the heavy lid of some solid family tomb. Yet the epitaph is not hers alone. The unremitting ethic of self-improvement has been the sepulchre of all mid-Victorian fiction except *Wuthering Heights*. Today that ethic no longer claims the Esther Lyons of the English novel. The whole influence of psychology has turned our interest to what George Eliot would have called the downward path, to the failures of the will, the fulfilment of the heart, the vacillations of the sensibility, the perception of self-interest. We do not wish to be better than we are, but more fully what we are; and the wish is crossed by the vivid conflicts set up in our lives by the revolution that is going on in our society. The bottom has fallen out of our world and our Esthers are looking for a basis not for a ceiling to their lives.

But this does not mean that Esther Lyon is falsely drawn or that she is not a human being. Using our own jargon, all we have a right to say is that the objects of the super-ego have changed; and, in saying this, we should recall a minor point of importance. It is this. Not only English tradition from Fielding onwards, but no less a person than the author of the *Liaisons Dangereuses* delight in the delectable evasions of the prig and the reserve of the prude; and it would indeed be absurd to cut the aspirations to virtue out of characters and to leave only the virtue that is attained or is already there. The critic needs only to be clear about the kind of aspiration that is presented to him; and here we perceive that what separates us from Esther Lyon and her creator is a matter of history. She is impelled by the competitive reforming ethic of an expanding society. One might generalise without great danger and say that in all the mid-Victorian novels the characters are either going up in the world, in which case they are good; or they are going down in the world, in which case they are bad. Whereas Goldsmith and Fielding revelled in the misadventures of the virtuous and in the vagaries of Fortune—that tutelary goddess of a society dominated by merchant-speculators—a novelist like George Eliot writes at a time when Fortune has been torn down, when the earned increment of industry (and not the accidental coup of the gambler) has taken Fortune's place; and when character is tested not by hazard but, like the funds, by a measurable tendency to rise and fall.

Once her ethic is seen as the driving force of George Eliot we cease to be intimidated by it, and she emerges, for all her lectures, as the most formidable of the Victorian novelists. We dismiss the late-Victorian reaction from her work; our fathers were bored by her because they were importuned by her mind; she was an idol with feet of clay and, what was worse, appeared to write with them. But it is precisely because she was a mind and because she was a good deal of the schoolmistress that she interests us now. Where the other Victorian novelists seem shapeless, confused and without direction, because of their melodramatic plots and subplots and the careless and rich diversity of their characters, George Eliot marks out an ordered world, and enunciates a constructed judgment. If we read a novel in order to clarify our minds about human character, in order to pass judgment on the effect of character on the world outside itself, and to estimate the ideas people have lived by, then George Eliot is one of the first to give such an intellectual direction to the English novel. She is the first of the rulers, one of the first to cut moral paths through the picturesque maze of human motive. It is the intimidating rôle of the schoolmistress. And yet when we read a few pages of any of her books now, we notice less the oppression of her lectures and more the spaciousness of her method, the undeterred illumination which her habit of mind brings to human nature. We pass from the romantic shadows into an explicit, a prosaic but a relieving light.

Two of George Eliot's novels, it seems to me, will have a permanent place in English literature. As time goes by *Adam Bede* looks like our supreme novel of pastoral life; and I cannot see any novel of the nineteenth century that surpasses *Middlemarch* in range or construction. With *Adam Bede*, it is true, the modern reader experiences certain unconquerable irritations. We are faced by a sexual theme, and the Victorians were constitutionally unable to write about sexual love. In saying this we must agree that no English writer since the eighteenth century has been happy in this theme, for since that time we have lost our regard for the natural man and the equanimity required for writing about him. The most we have a right to say about the Victorians is that, like the ingenious people who bricked up the windows of their houses and painted false ones on the wall, in order to escape the window tax, the Victorian novelists always chose to brick up the bedroom first.

Now in *Adam Bede* we are shocked by two things: the treatment of Hetty Sorel and by the marriage of Dinah and Adam at the end. It is clear that George Eliot's attitude to Hetty is a false one. The drawing of Hetty is neither observation from life nor a true recasting of experience by the imagination; it is a personal fantasy of George Eliot's. George Eliot was punishing herself and Hetty has to suffer for the "sins" George Eliot had committed, and for which, to her perhaps unconscious dismay, she herself was never punished. We rebel against the black-and-white view of life and when we compare *Adam Bede* with Scott's *Heart of Midlothian*, to which the former confessedly owes something of its plot, we are depressed by the decline of humanity that has set in since the eighteenth century. Humanity has become humanitarianism, uplift and, in the end, downright cruelty. The second quarrel we have with this book arises, as I have said, from the marriage of Adam and Dinah. There is no reason why a man who has suffered at the hands of a bad woman should not be rewarded and win the consolations of a good woman. If Adam Bede likes sermons, we say, better than infidelity let him have them: we all choose our own form of suffering. But George Eliot told lies about this marriage; or rather, she omitted a vital element from it. She left out the element of sexual jealousy or if she did not leave it out, she did not recognise it, because she could not admit natural passions in a virtuous character. In that scene where Hetty pushes Dinah away from her in her bedroom, where Hetty is dressing up and dreaming her Bovary-like dreams, the reader sees something that George Eliot appears not to see. He is supposed to see that Hetty is self-willed; and this may be true, but he sees as well that Hetty's instincts have warned her of her ultimate rival. The failure to record jealousy, and the attempt to transmute it so that it becomes the ambiguous if lofty repugnance to sin, spring from the deeper failure to face the nature of sexual passion.

This failure not only mars George Eliot's moral judgment but also represses her power as a story-teller. When Adam comes to Arthur Donnithorne's room at the Hermitage, Arthur stuffs Hetty's neckerchief into the wastepaper basket out of Adam's sight. The piece of silk is a powerful symbol. The reader's eye does not leave it. He waits for it to be found. But no, it simply lies there; its function is, as it were, to preach the risks of sin to the reader. Whereas in fact it ought to be made to disclose the inflammatory fact that the physical seduction took place in this very room. George Eliot refuses to make such a blatant disclosure not for æsthetic reasons, but for reasons of Victorian convention; and the result is that we have no real reason for believing Hetty has been seduced.Her baby appears inexplicably. The account of Hetty's flight is remarkable—it is far, far better than the corresponding episode in *The Heart of Midlothian*—but the whole business of the seduction and crime, from Adam's fight with Arthur Donnithorne in the woods to Hetty's journey to the scaffold, seems scarcely more than hearsay to the reader. And the reprieve of Hetty at the gallows adds a final unreality to the plot. It must also be said—a final cruelty.

Yet, such is George Eliot's quality as a novelist, none of these criticisms has any great importance. Like the tragedies of Hardy, *Adam Bede* is animated by the majestic sense of destiny which is fitting to novels of work and the soil. Majestic is perhaps the wrong word. George Eliot's sense of destiny was prosaic, not majestic; prosaic in the sense of unpoetical. One must judge a novel on its own terms; and from the beginning, in the lovely account of Dinah's preaching on the village green, George Eliot sets out the pieties which will enclose the drama that is to follow. Her handling of the Methodists and their faith is one of the memorable religious performances of English literature, for she neither adjures us nor satirises them, but leaves a faithful and limpid picture of commonplace religion as a part of life. When she wrote of the peasants, the craftsmen, the yeomen, the clergy and squires of Warwickshire, George Eliot was writing out of childhood, from that part of her life which never betrayed her or any of the Victorians. The untutored sermons of Dinah have the same pastoral quality as the poutings of Hetty at the butter churn, the harangues of Mrs Poyser at her cooking, or the remonstrates of Adam Bede at his carpenter's bench. In the mid-Victorian England of the railway and the drift to the towns, George Eliot was harking back to the last of the yeomen, among whom she was born and who brought out the warmth, the humour, the strength of her nature. We seem to be looking at one of Morland's pictures, at any of those domestic or rustic paintings of the Dutch school, where every leaf on the elm trees or the limes is painted, every gnarl of the bark inscribed, every rut followed with fidelity. We follow the people out of the hedgerows and the lanes into the kitchen. We see the endless meals, the eternal cup of tea; and the dog rests his head on our boot or flies barking to the yard, while young children toddle in and out of the drama at the least convenient moments. Some critics have gibed at the dialect, and dialect is an obstacle; but when the great moments come, when Mrs Poyser has her "say out" to the Squire who is going to evict her; or, better still, when Mrs Bede laments the drowning of her drunken husband, these people speak out of life:

"Let a-be, let a-be. There's no comfort for 'e no more," she went on, the tears coming when she began to speak, "now they poor feyther's gone, and I'n washed for and mended, an' got's victual for him for thirty 'ear, an' him allays so pleased wi' iverything I done for him, an' used to be so handy an' do the jobs for me when I war ill an' cambered wi' th' babby, an' made me the posset an' brought it upstairs as proud as could be, an' carried the lad as war as heavy as two children for five mile an' ne'er grumbled, all the way to Warson Wake, 'cause I wanted to go an' see my sister, as war dead an' gone the very next Christmas as e'er come. An' him to be drownded in the brook as we passed o'er the day we war married an' come home together, an' he'd made them lots o' shelves for me to put my plates an' things on, an' showed 'em me as proud as could be, 'case he know'd I should be pleased. An' he war to die an' me not to know, but to be a-sleepin' i' my bed, as if I caredna nought about it. Eh! an' me to live to see that! An' us as war young folks once, an' thought we should do rarely when we war married. Let a-be, lad, let a-be! I wonna ha' no tay; I carena if I ne'er ate nor drink no more. When one end o' th' bridge tumbles down, where's th' use o' th' other stannin'? I may's well die, an' foller my old man. There's no knowin' but he'll want me."

Among these people Dinah's religion and their quarrels with her about it are perfectly at home; and George Eliot's rendering is faultless. English piety places a stress on conduct and the guidance of conscience; and George Eliot, with her peasant sense of the laws and repetitions of nature, easily converted this working theology into a universal statement about the life of man. Where others see the consequences of sin visited upon the soul, she, the Protestant, saw them appear in the event of a man's or woman's life and the lives of others. Sin is primarily a weakness of character leading to the act. To Arthur Donnithorne she would say, "Your sin is that your will is weak. You are unstable. You depend on what others say. You are swayed by the latest opinion. You are greedy for approbation. Not lust, but a weak character is your malady. You even think that once you have confessed, your evil will turn out good. But it cannot, unless your character changes." And to Hetty she says, "Your real sin was vanity." It is a bleak and unanswerable doctrine, if one is certain that some kinds of character are desirable and others undesirable; psychologically useful to the novelist because it cuts one kind of path deeply into human nature, and George Eliot knows each moral character like a map. If her moral judgment is narrow, it enlarges character by showing us not merely the idiosyncrasy of people but propounds their type. Hetty is all pretty kittenish girls; Arthur is all careless young men. And here George Eliot makes a large advance on the novelists who preceded her. People do not appear haphazard in her books. They are not eccentrics. They are all planned and placed. She is orderly in her ethics; she is orderly in her social observation. She knows the country hierarchy and how a squire is this kind of man, a yeoman another, a teacher, a publican, a doctor, a clergyman another. They are more than themselves; they are their group as well. In this they recall the characters of Balzac. You fit Dinah among the Methodists, you fit Methodism into the scheme of things, you fit Adam among the peasants. Behind the Poysers are all the yeomen. George Eliot's sense of law is a sense of kind. It's a sense of life which has been learned from the English village where every man and woman has his definition and role.

I doubt if any Victorian novelist has as much to teach the modern novelists as George Eliot; for although the English novel was established and became a constructed judgment on situations and people after she had written, it did not emulate her peasant sense of law. Hardy alone is her nearest parallel, but he differed from her in conceiving a fate outside the will of man and indifferent to him. And her picture of country life is really closer to the country we know than Hardy's is, because he leaves us little notion of what the components of country society are. The English peasant lived and still lives in a milder, flatter world than Hardy's; a world where conscience and self-interest keep down the passions, like a pair of gamekeepers. It is true that George Eliot is cut off from the Rabelaisian malice and merriment of the country; she hears the men talk as they talk in their homes, not as they talk in the public-houses and the barns. But behind the salty paganism of country life stands the daily haggle of what people "ought" and "didn't ought" to do; the ancient nagging of church and chapel. All this is a minor matter beside her main lesson. What the great schoolmistress teaches is the interest of massive writing, of placing people, of showing how even the minds of characters must be placed among other minds.

When we turn from *Adam Bede* to *Middlemarch* we find a novel in which her virtues as a novelist are established and assured; and where there is no sexual question to bedevil her judgment. No Victorian novel approaches *Middlemarch* in its width of reference, its intellectual power, or the imperturbable spaciousness of its narrative. It is sometimes argued by critics of contemporary literature that a return to Christianity is indispensable if we are to produce novels of the Victorian scale and authority, or indeed novels of any quality at all; but there are the novels of unbelievers like George Eliot and Hardy to discountenance them. The fact is that a wide and single purpose in the mind is the chief requirement outside of talent; a strong belief, a strong unbelief, even a strong egoism will produce works of the first order. If she had any religious leanings, George Eliot moved towards Judaism because of its stress on law; and if we think this preference purely intellectual and regard worry, that profoundly English habit of mind, as her philosophy, the point is that it was congenital, comprehensive worry. A forerunner of the psychologists, she promises no heaven and threatens no hell; the best and the worst we shall get is Warwickshire. Her world is the world of will, the smithy of character, a place of knowledge and judgments. So, in the sense of worldly wisdom, is Miss Austen's. But what a difference there is. To repeat our earlier definition, if Miss Austen is the novelist of the ego and its platitudes, George Eliot is the novelist of the idolatries of the super-ego. We find in a book like *Middlemarch*, not character modified by circumstance only, but character first impelled and then modified by the beliefs, the ambitions, the spiritual objects which it assimilates. Lydgate's schemes for medical reform and his place in medical science are as much part of his character as is his way with the ladies. And George Eliot read up her medical history in order to get his position exactly right. Dorothea's yearning for a higher life of greater usefulness to mankind will stay with her all her days and will make her a remarkable but exasperating woman; a fool for all her cleverness. George Eliot gives equal weight to these important qualifications. Many Victorian novelists have lectured us on the careers and aspirations of their people; none, before George Eliot, showed us the unity of intellect, aspiration and nature in action. Her judgment on Lydgate as a doctor is a judgment on his fate as a man:

> He carried to his studies in London, Edinburgh and Paris the conviction that the medical profession as it might be was the finest in the world; presenting the most perfect interchange between science and art; offering the most direct alliance between intellectual conquest and the social good. Lydgate's nature demanded this combination: he was an emotional creature, with a flesh and blood sense of fellowship, which withstood all the abstractions of special study. He cared not only for "Cases," but for John and Elizabeth, especially Elizabeth.

The Elizabeth who was not indeed to wreck Lydgate's life, but (with far more probability) to corrupt his ideas and turn him into the smart practitioner, was Rosamond, his wife. Yet, in its own way, Rosamond's super-ego had the most distinguished ideals. A provincial manufacturer's daughter, she too longed idealistically to rise; the desire was not vulgar until she supposed that freedom from crude middle-class notions of taste and bearing could only be obtained by marriage to the cousin of a baronet; and was not immoral until she made her husband's conscience pay for her ambitions. The fountain, George Eliot is always telling us, cannot rise higher than its source.

Such analyses of character have become commonplace to us. When one compares the respectable Rosamond Lydgate with, say, Becky Sharp, one sees that Rosamond is not unique. Where *Middlemarch* is unique in its time is in George Eliot's power of generalisation. The last thing one accuses her of is *unthinking* acceptance of convention. She seeks, in her morality, the positive foundation of natural law, a kind of Fate whose measures are as fundamental as the changes of the seasons in nature. Her intellect is sculptural. The clumsiness of style does not denote muddle, but an attempt to carve decisively. We feel the clarifying force of a powerful mind. Perhaps it is not naturally powerful. The power may have been acquired. There are two George Eliots: the mature, experienced, quiet-humoured Midlander who wrote the childhood pages of *The Mill on the Floss*; and the naïve, earnest and masterly intellectual with her half-dozen languages and her scholarship. But unlike the irony of our time, hers is at the expense not of belief, but of people. Behind them, awful but inescapable to the eye of conscience, loom the statues of what they ought to have been. Hers is a mind that has grown by making judgments—as Mr Gladstone's head was said to have grown by making speeches.

Middlemarch resumes the observation and experience of a lifetime. Until this book George Eliot often strains after things beyond her capacity, as Dorothea Casaubon strained after a spiritual power beyond her nature. But now in *Middlemarch* the novelist is reconciled to her experience. In Dr Casaubon George Eliot sees that tragedy may paralyse the very intellect which was to be Dorothea's emancipation. Much of herself (George Eliot said, when she was accused of portraying Mark Pattison) went into Casaubon, and I can think of no other English novel before or since which has so truthfully, so sympathetically and so intimately described the befogged and grandiose humiliations of the scholar, as he turns at bay before the vengeance of life. Casaubon's jealousy is unforgettable, because, poisonous though it is, it is not the screech of an elderly cuckold, but the voice of strangled nature calling for justice. And notice, here, something very characteristic; George Eliot's pity flows from her moral sense, from the very seat of justice, and not from a sentimental heart.

Middlemarch is the first of many novels about groups of people in provincial towns. They are differentiated from each other not by class or fortune only, but by their moral history, and this moral differentiation is not casual, it is planned and has its own inner hierarchy. Look at the groups. Dorothea, Casaubon and Ladislaw seek to enter the highest spiritual fields—not perhaps the highest, for us, because, as we have seen, the world of George Eliot's imagination was prosaic and not poetic—still, they desire, in their several ways, to influence the standards of mankind. There is Lydgate, who is devoted to science and expects to be rewarded by a career. He and his wife are practical people, who seek power. The pharisaical Bulstrode, the banker, expects to rise both spiritually and financially at once, until he sits on the right hand of God, the Father; a businessman with a bad conscience, he is the father of the Buchmanites and of all success-religions. The Garths, being country people and outside this urban world, believe simply in the virtue of work as a natural law and they are brought up against Fred Vincy, Rosamond's brother. He, as a horsey young man educated beyond his means, has a cheerful belief in irresponsible Style and in himself as a thing of pure male beauty with a riding crop. We may not accept George Eliot's standards, but we can see that they are not conventional, and that they do not make her one-sided. She is most intimately sympathetic to human beings and is never sloppy about them. When Vincy quarrels with Bulstrode about Fred's debts, when Casaubon's jealousy of Ladislaw secretes its first venom, when Lydgate tries vainly to talk about money to his wife or Fred goes to his erratic old uncle for a loan, vital human issues are raised. The great scenes of *Middlemarch* are exquisite, living transpositions of real moral dilemmas. Questions of principle are questions of battle; they point the weapons of the human comedy, and battle is not dull. In consequence, George Eliot's beliefs are rarely boring, because they are energies. They correspond to psychological and social realities, though more especially (on the large scale) to the functions of the will; they are boring only when, in the Victorian habit, she harangues the reader and pads out the book with brainy essays.

I see I have been writing about *Middlemarch* as though it was a piece of engineering. What about the life, the humour, the pleasure? There are failures: Dorothea and Ladislaw do not escape the fate of so many Victorian heroes and heroines who are frozen by their creator's high-mindedness. Has George Eliot forgotten how much these two difficult, sensitive and proud people will annoy each other by the stupidity which so frequently afflicts the intellectual? Such scruples, such play-acting! But Lydgate and Rosamond quarrelling about money; Rosamond quietly thwarting her husband's decisions, passing without conscience to love affairs with his friends and ending as a case-hardened widow who efficiently finds a second father for her family—these things are perfect. Mary Garth defying the old miser is admirable. But the most moving thing in the book—and I always think this is the real test of a novelist—is given to the least likeable people. Bulstrode's moral ruin and his inability to confess to his dull wife are portrayed in a picture of dumb human despondency which recalls a painting by Sickert. One hears the clock tick in the silence that attends the wearing down of two lives that can cling together but dare not speak.

The humour of George Eliot gains rather than loses by its mingling with her intellect. Here we feel the sound influence of her girlish reading of the eighteenth-century novelists who were above all men of education. This humour is seen at its best in scenes like the one where the relations of the miser come to his house, waiting to hear news of his will; and again in the sardonic description of the spreading of the scandal about Bulstrode and Lydgate. George Eliot followed causes down to their most scurrilous effects. She is good in scandal and public rumour. Her slow tempo is an advantage, and it becomes exciting to know that she will make her point in the minor scenes as surely as she will make it in the great ones. Mrs Dollop of The Tankard has her short paragraph of immortality:

> [She had] "often to resist the shallow pragmatism of customers disposed to think their reports from the outer world were of equal force with what had 'come up' in her mind."

Mr Trumbull, the auctioneer, is another portrait, a longer one, smelling of the bar and the saleroom. Dickens would have caricatured this gift from heaven. George Eliot observes and savours. Characteristically she catches his intellectual pretensions and his offensive superiority. We see him scent the coming sale and walk over to Mary Garth's desk to read her copy of Scott's *Anne of Geierstein*, just to show that he knows a book when he sees one:

> "The course of four centuries," he reads out unexpectedly, "has well enough elapsed since the series of events which are related in the following chapters took place on the continent."

That moment is one of the funniest in the English novel, one of those mad touches like the insertion of a dog stealing a bone, which Hogarth put into his pictures.

There is no real madness in George Eliot. Both heavy feet are on the ground. Outside of *Wuthering Heights* there is no madness in Victorian fiction. The Victorians were a histrionic people who measured themselves by the Elizabethans; and George Eliot, like Browning and Tennyson, was compared to Shakespeare by her contemporaries. The comparison failed, if only because madness is lacking. Hysteria, the effect of the exorbitant straining of their wills, the Victorians did, alas, too often achieve. George Eliot somehow escapes it. She is too level-headed. One pictures her, in life, moralising instead of making a scene. There is no hysteria in *Middlemarch*; perhaps there is no abyss because there is so much determination. But there is a humane breadth and resolution in this novel which offers neither hope nor despair to mankind but simply the necessity of fashioning the moral life. George Eliot's last words on her deathbed might, one irreverently feels, be placed on the title-page of her collected works: "Tell them," she is reported to have said, "the pain is on the left side." Informative to the last and knowing better than the doctor, the self-made positivist dies.

(1946)

HONORÉ DE BALZAC

POOR RELATIONS

The small house on the cliff of Passy, hanging like a cage between an upper and lower street, so that by a trick of relativity, the top floor of the Rue Berton is the ground floor of the Rue Raynouard, has often been taken as a symbol of the life of Balzac. The custodian of the house—now a Balzac museum with the novelist's eternal coffee-pot, his dictionary of universal knowledge and with his appalling proof sheets framed on the wall—shows one the trap-door by which Balzac escaped to the lower floor in the Rue Berton. Down it the fat breathless novelist of forty-one went stumbling and blurting, like his own prose, to the Seine. Two houses in one, a life with two front doors, dream and reality; the novelist, naïve and yet shrewd, not troubling to distinguish between one and the other. Symbol of Balzac's life, the house is a symbol of the frontier life, the trap-door life of the great artists, who have always lived between two worlds. There Balzac wrote his letters to Madame Hanska in Poland, the almost too comprehensive, explanatory and eloquent letters of a famous and experienced writer who has the art, indeed the habit, of self-projection at his finger-tips; there, when the letters were posted, he went to bed with the docile housekeeper who was finally to turn round and blackmail him, and so provide him with the horrifying last chapters of Le Cousin Pons. At this house in the worst year of his life, the least blessed with that calm which is—quite erroneously— supposed to be essential to the novelist, Balzac wrote this book and La Cousine Bette, respectively the best constructed and the most fluent and subtle of his novels.

A new Life of Balzac was published in Paris in 1944. It is called simply

Vie de Balzac and is by André Billy. This biography contains nothing new, but it gathers all the immense biographical material in a couple of volumes. Its detail is as lively and exhaustive as a Balzac novel; the manner is warm but sceptical, thorough but not dry. Very rightly, M. Billy looks twice and three times at everything Balzac said about his life, for he is dealing with the hallucinations of the most extraordinary egotist in the history of literature. One can imagine a less diffuse biography; one in which the picture of his time played a greater part and where every detail of a chaotic Bohemian career was not played up to the same pitch. But given the gluttony of Balzac's egotism and the fertility of his comedy, one is not inclined to complain.

Like the tons of bronze and antiques—Balzac estimated the weight and value of himself with the care of an auctioneer's valuer—with which he darkened the house he finally took for Madame Hanska when he had got his hands on some of her fortune, the novels of Balzac weigh upon the memory. The reader is as exhausted as the novelist by the sheer weight of collection. One is tempted to see him as the stolid bulldozer of documentation, the quarrying and expatiating realist, sharpening his tools on some hard view of his own time. He seems to be stuck in his task. Yet this impression is a false one, as we find whenever we open a novel of his again. Balzac is certainly the novelist who most completely exemplifies the "our time" novelist, but not by his judgments on his society. He simply *is* his time. He is identified with it, by all the greedy innocence of genius. The society of rich peasants brought to power by revolution and dictatorship, pushing into business and speculation, buying up houses and antiques, founding families, grabbing at money and pleasure, haunted by their tradition of parsimony and hard work, and with the peasant's black and white ideas about everything, and above all their weakness for fixed ideas, is Balzac himself. He shares their illusions. Like them he was humble when he was poor, arrogant when he was rich. As with them, his extravagance was one side of the coin; on the other was the face of the peasant miser. The cynic lived in a world of romantic optimism. We see the dramatic phase of a century's illusions, before they have been assimilated and trodden down into the familiar hypocrisies. To us Balzac's preoccupation with money appears first to be the searching, scientific and prosaic interest of the documentary artist. On the contrary, for him money was romantic; it was hope and ideal. It was despair and evil. It was not the dreary background, but the animating and theatrical spirit.

Balzac learned about money, as M. Billy says, at his printing works in the Rue du Marais. He expected to find that fallen aristocrat, the goddess Fortune of the eighteenth century; instead he found that in the nineteenth century the goddess had become a bourgeois book-keeper. His laundry bills, his tailor's bill, his jeweller's bills were mixed with the printing accounts. The imagination of the businessman is always governable; Balzac's was not. Financially speaking, Balzac was out of date. Like his father, who also was willing to work hard enough, he sought for Fortune not for Profit; far from being an example of Balzac's realism, his attitude to money is really the earliest example of his Romantic spirit. Balzac's attitude to money was that of a man who did not understand money, who could not keep it in his hands, the plagued spendthrift and natural bankrupt. His promissory notes were a kind of poetry in his early years; later on they became articles of moral indignation; in the end—to quote M. Billy's delightful euphemism, he lost all "pudeur morale." The creation of debts began as exuberance; it became an appetite, one of those dominant passions which he thought occurred in all natures, but which really occur only among the most monstrous egotists. Madame Hanska's fortune did not calm him. He went on buying here and there, incurring more debts, scheming without check. And the last people he thought of paying were his wretched relations and especially his mother. To her, he behaved with the hypocrisy and meanness of a miser and the worse he treated her the more he attacked her.

At this point it is interesting to compare Balzac with Scott whom he admired and consciously imitated. Madame Hanska's estate in Poland was for many years his visionary Abbotsford; the passion for antiques, the debts, and the crushing labour, the days and nights of writing without sleep, were Abbotsford too. Balzac saw himself as an aristocrat; Scott saw himself as a laird: they are by no means the first or last writers to provide themselves with distinguished ancestors. He went to the length of travelling to Vienna as a Marquis, with coronets on his luggage; it was ruinous, he discovered, in tips. But the honourable Scott was broken by debts; they drove him to work as a duty; they wore out his imagination. Balzac, on the contrary, was certainly not ruined as a writer by his debts. His debts were a natural expression of a voracious imagination. One may doubt whether any of his mistresses moved his inspiration—though clearly their maternal sympathy was necessary—but one can be certain that Balzac's imagination was ignited by the romance of purchase, by the mere sensual possession of things. The moving impulse in his life was, as he said, the discovery of the "material of civilisation," the literal materials; and although he considered this a scientific discovery, it was really a mysticism of things. Every object he bought, from the famous walking-stick to the museum pieces, represented an act of self-intoxication that released the capacity—so vital to the creative artist—to become unreal.

It is easy, as M. Billy says, a hundred years after, to blame Madame Hanska for delaying her marriage with Balzac and for adding the afflictions of reluctance and jealousy to his life of appalling labour, but obviously he was possessed by a kind of madness, and he would have stripped her of all her property. One understands her hesitation after reading his later and maniacal letters about money and things.

> Je suis sûr qu'au poids il y aura, dans notre maison, trois mille kilogrammes de cuivres et bronzes dorés. C'est effrayant, le bronze! Cette maison est, comme je te le disais, une mine de cuivre doré, car mon ébéniste me disait qu'il y en a mille kilogrammes. À huit francs le kilo, à vendre aux chaudronniers, c'est trente-deux mille francs de valeur réelle. Juge de la valeur, en y ajoutant le valeur d'art.

Ruinous. There was no "valeur d'art". His brain gave way under the strain of his schemes and combinations. Yet, *Le Cousin Pons* and *La Cousine Bette* were written in that year; and when Pons makes the fortune of his persecutors with his collection of antiques which they had despised, one sees Balzac avenging himself for the complaints of his mistress. No; he was not weighed down by debts, in the sense of having his talent ruined by them. His extravagances floated him on the vital stream of unreality. He was the Micawber for whom things were only too continuously "turning up," a Micawber who worked. Balzac and Micawber are, it is interesting to note, contemporary financiers of the period.

The ox-like groans, the animal straining and lamentation of Balzac, his boasting, his bosom-beating letters to women like Madame Carraud, before whom he parades in the rôle of the indomitable martyr of circumstance, have created an imaginary Balzac. One sees—his own phrase—"the galley slave of fame." A rather different impression was formed by his contemporaries. Once he had put his pen down he was childishly gay:

> Naïveté, puérilité, bonté, ces trois mots reviennent sous la plume de tous les contemporains. Le portrait de Balzac que nous a laissé le poète des Meditations se trouve confirmé en tous points par celui qu'a tracé George Sand: puéril et puissant, toujours envieux d'un bibelot et jamais jaloux d'une gloire, sincère jusqu'à la modestie, vantard jusqu'à la hâblerie, confiant en lui-même et dans les autres, très expansif, très bon et très fou, avec un sanctuaire de raison intérieure où il rentrait pour tout dominer dans son œuvre, cynique dans la chasteté, ivre en buvant de l'eau, intempérant de travail et sobre d'autres passions, positif et romanesque avec un égal excès, crédule et sceptique, plein de contrastes et de mystères...

Some indeed found him grubby, ill-kempt and uncouth. Hans Andersen hardly recognised the dandy of the evening party in the tousselled Bohemian of the following day. There was a Rue Raynouard and a Rue Berton in his appearance and in his nature.

Instant in his admirations and schemes, Balzac was like a child for whom everything happens *now* and in a *now* that is connected with no future. Certainly with no future of incurred obligations. The burden of Balzac's life is not apparent until one sees him at work; and then we see that not debt but his method of writing was the fatal aggravation.

In a sense Balzac is a made, or rather re-made writer. There were times when he rushed down to the printers at eleven o'clock at night and they took the chapter of his novel page by page as he wrote it. But such moments of inspired exhibitionism were rare. In general Balzac strikes one as being the gifted talker whose mind congests when he sits down to write what he has just spoken. No doubt he could have turned out the cheap thrillers of his early period as easily as he spoke; but with his other books the process was agonising. There would be several versions of the text, each one smothered with erasures and additions; chapters were put into different places, more chapters were sandwiched in between. Pages and pages scrapped, more pages added. The historian of the contemporary scene had only to go out of his door to see a new thing to squeeze somewhere into the text. And this was not the end of the confusion and the struggle. Once the printers had sorted out the manuscript and had produced their galleys, the ungovernable author began a hardly less drastic process of destruction and reconstruction. Night after night, from midnight until seven—and these were merely regular hours. There were days and nights of almost continuous labour without sleep. Il ne savait pas sa langue, said Gautier. The time spent and the printers' costs would have eaten seriously into earnings not already mortgaged by extravagance.

Let us return to the double house in the Rue Raynouard and look once more at the two great novels Balzac wrote in that small room above the trap-door, when his brain was already breaking under the appetites he imposed upon it. Open *Le Cousin Pons*. There is the expected chapter, that roughly and in a domineering way generalises and clears a space for the characters in the Parisian scene. And then, like a blow in the face, comes the brutal sentence: "On n'a jamais peint les exigences de la gueule." One stops dead. What on earth has poor Pons done that his fastidious habit of dining at the expense of his better-off relations should become a treatise on the trough? Comically treated, of course; Balzac examined the dossier of human nature with the quizzical detachment of some nail-biting, cigar-strained Chief of Police who is going rapidly up in the world; who has seen so many cases; who thanks heaven that he does not make the moral law and that a worldly Church stands between himself and the Almighty. Passion, even when it is a passion for the best food, always becomes—in the experience of the Chief of Police—a transaction; Pons trades the little errands he runs on behalf of the family for the indispensable surprises of the gourmet. In the pursuit of that appetite he is prepared to ruin himself where other men, more voluptuously equipped by nature, will wreck themselves in the capture and establishment of courtesans. Sex or food, money or penury, envy or ambition—Balzac knows all the roads to ruin. If only men and women were content with their habits instead of craving the sublimity of their appetites.

But Pons is a type. He is a poor relation. In that isolation of a type, one detects the main difference between the French and English novels. The English novel has never lived down its early association with the theatre, and has always had to wrestle with a picaresque or artificial plot. But even if this had not been so, we could never have been a nation of moralists. Our instinct is to act; our interest in morals is a practical interest in results. The French novel—and how obvious this is in Balzac—is dominated on the contrary by a sense of law. Behind the individual lies the type, behind the act lies a law governing the act. The French novelists are the lawyers of the passions; they proceed from the prototype to the particular and then carry it back for comparison. Subtle and litigious in tactic, they conclude that human experience, however bizarre, however affecting, can never escape the deep inscription of its category or evade the ordinance of some general idea.

To an English taste there must always be something arbitrary in such a structure. Natural Protestants, we resist a determinism so Roman and so Catholic. But we must be abashed by the double reference in which French fiction is so rich. Look at the delightful Pons. His character has so many departments. He is an old man, an ugly man, an outmoded but respected musician, a dandy survived from an earlier period, a collector of antiques, a poor man, a careful man, a simple man who is not quite so simple—see his valuable collection of pictures and bric-à-brac cunningly picked up for next to nothing—a sexless man, a gourmet, a hanger-on, shrewd in his own world, lost in the society into which he has grown up. Pons is the kind of character who, inevitably, becomes fantastic in the English novel simply because no general laws pin him down. He would become a static "character." Instead Balzac takes all these aspects of Pons and mounts each one, so that Pons is constructed before our eyes. We have a double interest: the story or plot, which is excellent in suspense, drama and form—this is one of Balzac's well-constructed novels, as it is also one of the most moving—and the exact completion, brick by brick, of Pons and his circle. There are the historical Pons—he is an *incroyable* left-over from the Directoire—the artistic Pons, the financial Pons, the sociable Pons, the moral Pons, and in the end Pons dying, plundered, defiant, a man awakened from his simplicity and fighting back, the exquisitely humble artist turned proud, sovereign and dangerous in his debacle. Pons is a faceted stone, and part of the drama is the relation of each facet with the others. Thus his fantastic dress is related, via dandyism, to his small, esteemed, but out-of-date position in the world of art. That adjoins his love of good living—picked up in smarter days—which links up with the solitariness and social spryness of the bachelor, his timidity and his sexual innocence. We have the portrait of a man who in every trait suggests some aspect of the society in which he lives. The history of his time is explicit in him. Yet he is not a period piece. A period piece is incapable of moral development and the development of a moral theme is everything in the novels of Balzac, who facilitates it by giving every character not merely a time and place, but also an obsession. Among English novelists only Henry James, George Eliot and, on occasions, Meredith, move their drama not from incident to incident, but from one moral situation or statement to the next. (In Meredith's *The Egoist* one recalls the tension, tightening page by page, that precedes the accusation: "You are an egoist.") So it is with the story of Pons. He is snubbed by his ignorant relations who do not realise even the financial value of his collection of antiques and pictures. In consequence, rather than be dropped or ridiculed, he gives up his beautiful dinners and retires to taste the blessings of the concierge's motherly cooking and pure friendship with the delightful Schmucke, a man even more simple than himself. At that point an English novelist might have given up. The lesson was clear. But Balzac, like Henry James, saw that drama lies in the fact that there is no end to moral issues. For him—recomplication, further research. And so, just as Pons is getting a little tired of his landlady's cooking, society tempts him again. His relations apologise, and Pons is one of those good men who cannot bear other people to say they are in the wrong. He conceives a grandiose scheme for returning good for evil. He will find a husband for the unmarriageable daughter. He will announce the enormous value of his collection and leave it to her in his will. Result, gratitude? Not a bit of it. The family is longing to wipe out the memory of their humiliating apology by vengeance, and when the marriage scheme collapses, they finish with Pons. Once more we have come to a natural end of the novel. But once more Balzac recomplicates. Pons falls into the grip of his concierge, who has suddenly become covetous now that she has two harmless, childless, womanless old men in her power; and his downfall is ensured by the very innocence of Schmucke, who cannot believe evil of anyone.

Balzac is the novelist of our appetites, obsessions and our *idées fixes*, but his great gift—it seems to me—is his sense of the complexity of the human situation. He had both perceptions, one supposes, from his peasant origins, for among peasants, as he was fond of saying, the *idée fixe* is easily started; and their sense of circumstance overpowers all other consideration in their lives. A character in Balzac is so variously situated in history, in money, in family, class and in his type to begin with; but on top of this Balzac's genius was richly inventive in the field least exploited by the mass of novelists: the field of probability. It is very hard to invent probabilities. This simply means that Balzac knew his people as few novelists ever know their characters. The marriage scene in *Le Cousin Pons* for example: there we have the rich German all set to marry the daughter of the family. The awful facts of the "régime dotal"—a phrase repeated in pious chorus by the family with the unction usually reserved for statesmen like "God is Love"—have been accepted by him. He has merely to say the word. At this tense moment the German electrifies everyone by asking the unexpected question: Is the girl an only child? Yes, she is. Then he must withdraw. A man of forty is an idiot who marries a girl who has been spoiled in her childhood. She will use the fact that he is so much older than herself to prove she is always right. That way lies hell. The respectability of the institution of marriage is in itself no satisfaction.

But *Le Cousin Pons* moves from one surprising probability to the next, backed by the massed ranks of human circumstance. The change in the character of the charming, motherly landlady of Pons who suddenly takes on the general professional character of the concierges of her district creates another powerful situation—powerful because so isolated are we, so obsessed with possibility and hope, that the probable is unperceived by us. The last thing we care to believe is that we are governed by type and environment. Balzac believed nothing else.

I do not know that I would put anything in *Le Cousin Pons* above the first part of *La Cousine Bette*, though I like Pons better as a whole. Pons is the old bachelor. Bette is the old maid. The growth of her malevolence is less subtly presented than the course of Pons's disillusion, because Balzac had the genius to show Pons living with a man even simpler than himself. One sees two degrees of simplicity, one lighting the other, whereas Bette stands alone; indeed, it may be complained that she is gradually swamped by the other characters. She is best in her obscurity, the despised poor relation, the sullen peasant, masculine, counting her humiliations and her economies like a miser, startling people with her bizarre reflections. They laugh at her and do not conceive the monstrous fantasies of her painful virginity. And we are moved by her in these early pages when she is hiding her Polish artist, shutting him in his room like a son, driving him to work; or, later, when Madame Marneffe gives Bette the shabby furniture. Bette is a wronged soul; and when her passion does break it is, as Balzac says, sublime and terrifying. Her advance to sheer wickedness and ven- geance is less convincing, or, rather, less engrossing. It is a good point that she is the eager handmaid and not the igniting cause of ruin; but one draws back, incredulously, before some of her plots and lies. Acceptable when they are naïve, they are unacceptable when they fit too efficiently the melodramatic intrigue of the second part of the book. But the genius for character and situation is here again. La Marneffe, rooted in love's new middle-class hypocrisy and growing into a sanctimonious courtesan, is nicely contrasted with the besotted Baron who had grown up in an earlier period—"between the wars" in fact—when the fashion of love was brisker and more candid. That situation alone is a comic one. The diplomatic farce of La Marneffe's supposed pregnancy is brilliant. The lies and short repentances of the sexagenarian Baron are perfect. Only Adeline does not, to my mind, come off in this novel; and here we come upon Balzac's rather dubious advocacy of marital fidelity. He sounds as little convinced as a public speaker haranguing his way to conviction. Adeline's pathetic attempt to sell herself, in order to save her husband's fortunes, is embarrassing to read; are we to admire virtue because it is stupid? Balzac protests too much.

No one has surpassed Balzac in revealing the great part played by money in middle-class life; nor has anyone excelled him in the portraits of the parvenu. Henry James alone, coming at the zenith of middle-class power, perceived the moral corruption caused by money; but money had ripened. It glowed like a peach that is just about to fall. Balzac arrived when the new money, the new finance of the post-Napoleonic world, was starting on its violent course; when money was an obsession and was putting down a foundation for middle-class morals. In these two novels about the poor relation, he made his most palatable, his least acrid and most human statements about this grotesque period of middle-class history.

(1946)

IVAN TURGENEV

THE RUSSIAN DAY

What is it that attracts us to the Russian novelists of the nineteenth century? The aristocratic culture made more vivid by its twilight? The feeling, so readily understood by English readers, for *ennui*? No. The real attraction of that censored literature is its freedom—the freedom from our kind of didacticism and our plots. The characters of our novels, from Fielding to Forster, get up in the morning, wash, dress and are then drilled for their rôles. They are propelled to some practical issue in morality, psychology or Fortune before the book is done. In nineteenth-century Russia, under the simpler feudal division of society, there is more room to breathe, to let the will drift, and the disparate impulses have their ancient solitary reign. In all those Russian novels we seem to hear a voice saying: "The meaning of life? One day that will be revealed to us—probably on a Thursday." And the day, not the insistence of the plot or purpose, is the melodic bar. We see life again, as we indeed know it, as something written in days; its dramas not directed by the superior foreknowledge of the writer, but seeming to ebb and flow among the climaxes, the anticlimaxes, the yawnings of the hours. Turgenev, who knew English literature well, used to say that he envied the English novelists their power to make plots; but, of course, he really disdained it. The surprises of life, the sudden shudders of its skin, are fresher and more astonishing than the imposed surprises of literary convention or the teacher's lesson. And in seeing people in terms of their anonymous days, the Russians achieved, by a paradox, a sense of timelessness in their books. Gogol, for example, seems to date far less than Dickens. In the Russians there is a humility before the important fact of human inertia, the half-heartedness of its wish to move and grow, its habit of returning into itself. This is true of Turgenev; obviously true of Chekhov, and I think also of Dostoevsky. His dynamism and complex narratives are the threshings and confusions of a writer who—if we consult his notebooks and letters—could never bind his mind to a settled subject or a fixed plot.

Yet the use of the eventless day could not alone give the Russian novel its curious power; indeed, it can be its weakness. No novelists are easier to parody than the Russians. Those people picking their noses at the windows or trying on their boots while they go through passion and remorse! The day is a convention like any other. What gives those novels their power, and these persons their gift of moving us, is something which comes from a profound sense of a presence haunting the day. There lies on those persons, even on the most trivial, the shadow of a fate more richly definitive than the fate of any individual human being. Their feet stand in time and in history. Their fate is corporate. It is the fate of Russia itself, a fate so often adjured with eloquence and nostalgia, oftener still with that medieval humility which has been unknown to us since the Renaissance, and which the Russians sometimes mystically identify with the fate of humanity itself.

I have been reading Turgenev again and dipping occasionally into Avraham Yarmolinsky's thorough and discerning evaluation of him. It was a great advantage to the Russian novelists that they were obliged to react to the Russian question; a great advantage, too, that the Rus—sian question was to become a universal one: the question of the rise of the masses. The consequence is that Turgenev's political novels—especially *Rudin* and even *Fathers and Sons*—are less dated outside of Russia than they are inside it, for we can afford to ignore the detail of their historical context. I first read *Rudin* during the Spanish Civil War and, when he died on his foreign barricade, Rudin seemed to me (and still does seem) one of "the heroes of our own time." At the end of all Turgenev's political stories one may detect the invisible words "And yet . . ." left there by his hesitant and tentative genius. He is so close to the ripple of life's process of becoming that at the very moments of decision, departure, farewell, he seems to revise and rejuvenate. The leaf falls, but the new bud is disclosed beneath the broken stalk.

Turgenev solved the Russian problem for himself, as he solved his personal question by an ingenious psychological trick. It is rather irritating, it is a little comic when we see it in the light of his personal character, but it was serious and successful. It was the trick of assuming a premature old age. Now this device was a legacy of Byronism. One can see how it must have infuriated his younger contemporaries to hear him declare that at thirty-five his life was finished; and then to have him live another thirty years in full possession of his gracious and pertinent faculties. The trick was a kind of alibi. For behind the mist of regret, that autumnal resignation, the tenderness and the wave of the scented handkerchief in a good-bye that was never quite good-bye, there was a marksman's eye. Yarmolinsky speaks of him stalking his characters as he stalked his grouse on the steppe of Orel or Kaluga. Every time he picks off his man and notes, as he does so, his place in the Russian fauna. Look at this from *A Nest of Gentlefolk:*

> I want above all to know what you are like, what are your views and convictions, what you have become, what life has taught. (Mihalevitch still preserved the phraseology of 1830.)

The comic side of this adroit sense of time—so precise, so poetic and moving in his writing—comes out in Turgenev's private life. His autumnal disguise enabled him to give his large number of love affairs a protective fragility. The autumn is the hunting season.

A Sportsman's Sketches, A Nest of Gentlefolk, Fathers and Sons—those are the perfect books. Turgenev is the poet of spring who eludes the exhausting decisions and fulfilments of summer and finds in the autumn a second and safer spring. He is the novelist of the moments after meetings and of the moments before partings. He watches the young heart rise the first time. He watches it fall, winged, to the common distorted lot. The young and the old are his fullest characters: the homecoming and death of Bazarov and the mourning of his parents are among the truest and most moving things in literature. To this tenderness, this capacity to observe the growth of characters and the changes of the heart, as the slow days of the steppe change into the years that rattle by in Petersburg or Baden, there is, as I have said, a shrewd, hard-headed counterpart, the experienced shot:

> In the general the good-nature innate in all Russians was intensified by that special kind of geniality which is peculiar to all people who have done something disgraceful.

Or:

> Of his wife there is scarcely anything to be said. Her name was Kalliopa Karlovna. There was always a tear in her left eye, on the strength of which Kalliopa Karlovna (she was, one must add, of German extraction) considered herself a woman of great sensibility.

Or:

> Panshin's father, a retired cavalry officer and a notorious gambler, was a man of

insinuating eyes, a battered countenance, and a nervous twitch about the mouth.

Looking back over the novels, one cannot remember any falsified character. One is taken from the dusty carriage to the great house, one meets the landowners and the servants, and then one watches life produce its surprises as the day goes by. Turgenev has the perfect discretion. He refrains from knowing in advance. In *Rudin* we are impressed by the bellows of the local Dr Johnson; enter Rudin, and the brilliant young man demolishes the doctor, like a young Shelley; only himself to suffer exposure as the next day shows us more of his character.

His people expose themselves, as in life people expose themselves, fitfully and with contradiction. The art is directed by a sense which the English novel has never had—unless Jane Austen had something of it—the sense of a man's character and life being divisible into subjects. Career, love, religion, money, politics, illness and the phases of the years are in turn isolated in a spirit which is both poetic and scientific. There is no muddle in Turgenev. Romantic as he may be, there is always clarity, order and economy. He writes novels as if he were not a story-teller, but a biographer.

It was Edward Garnett who, in defending the disputed portrait of Bazarov, pointed out that Bazarov ought to have been judged as the portrait not of a political type, but of the scientific temperament. (There is nothing wrong with Bazarov really, except that Turgenev showed him in the country, where he was a fish out of water, instead of in the city.) This temperament was Turgenev's, and because of it one easily discounts the inevitable sad diminuendo of his tales, the languid dying away which is the shadow of his own wish in his work. The rest stands clearly and without date. But the method has one serious weakness. It almost certainly involved drawing directly from life, and especially it meant that Turgenev was (or thought he was) stimulated to write by an interest in living persons for their own sakes. Turgenev knew his own lack of invention, his reliance on personal experience, and he studied character with the zeal of a botanist watching a flower; but, in fact, the study of character, for a novelist, means the selection or abstraction of character. What is selected is inevitably less than what is there, and since Turgenev was (as he said) governed by the actual life story which he saw, he does not add to or transform his people. They have the clarity of something a little less than life. What is missing from them is that from which he personally recoiled—fulfilment. There are spring and autumn—there is no summer. If success is described, it is by hearsay. Marriage, for Turgenev, is either scandal or rather embarrassing domesticity, something for a fond, indulgent smile, but a quick get-away. Strangely enough, it is his objectivity which leads to his limpness.

There are two qualifications to add to this criticism. One is suggested by

A Sportsman's Sketches. His people derive a certain fullness from their part in the scene of the steppe, which none described better than he. In this book, his scrupulous habit or necessity of stopping short at what he saw and heard gave his portraits a laconic power and a terrible beauty. There the Russian day brings people to life in their random moments. The shapelessness of these pieces is the powerful shapelessness of time itself. The other qualification is the one I have indicated at the beginning of this essay. If his people lack the power to realise themselves because Turgenev himself lacked it in his own life, they have their roots in the fate of Russia. You localise them in a destiny which is beyond their own—tragic, comic, whatever they are—in the destiny of their society. They may fail, Russia goes on. One remembers that startling chapter at the end of *A Nest of Gentlefolk*, where, after the bitter end of Liza's love, the novelist returns to the house. One expects the last obligatory chords of romantic sorrow, but instead, there is the cruel perennial shock of spring:

> Marfa Dmitrievna's house seemed to have grown younger; its freshly painted walls gave a bright welcome; and the panes of its open windows were crimson, shining in the setting sun; from these windows the light merry sound of ringing young voices and continual laughter floated into the street.

The new generation had grown up. It is the most tragic moment of his writing, the one most burdened with the mystery of time as it flows through the empty light of our daily life.

(1946)

HENRY JAMES

THE NOTEBOOKS OF HENRY JAMES

The notebooks of the great authors are the idlest kind of reading as, for their writers, they have so often been the idlest kind of writing: in the forest of life they mark the trees to be felled. It is always a moment this, delicate and touch-and-go, when a piece of life is chipped off and is still neither life nor art, a fragment with the sap, the tang, the freshness still on it, to be picked up and considered. We are at a beginning, and there is a kind of pathos in knowing that presently this bright bit will be lost to life and become an anonymous, altered and perhaps undecipherable piece in the forbidding structure of a work of art. To some minds, and especially the critical, there will be a pleasure in tracing the history of that chip from the time when it flew off the axe until it found its present home in what Henry James called "the real thing"; to lazier minds there is the pleasure of being there as the first stroke rings, even when it rings flat and untrue. "A good deal might be done with Henry Pratt," wrote Henry James, recalling an evening with this friend of his in Venice. How one responds to that suddenly decisive and injudicious cry. Hurrah, the woodman has not spared the tree! Bring Henry Pratt in here. Let us *all* look him over. Let us keep him here, with the soil on his roots, while we make up our ingenious minds. That is one pleasure of notebooks: they are dramatic. A character, a scene, a smudge of scenery, half a dozen lines of talk, a few epigrams with no visible means of support, are caught in all their innocence. The other attraction is the strangeness of the workshop. Here are not only the acceptable ideas but the unacceptable, the discarded, the litter of a profession, the failures.

The Notebooks of Henry James belong to the working kind. Even the opening judgment on his first twelve years as a writer is done to clear the mind and not to indulge his memory. The great are monsters of efficiency, the mills work day and night. What strikes us is how much James's notes were used. Hawthorne's long notes, for example, seem to have been a studied alternative to his real subjects. Dostoevsky's—as far as we know them by quotation—generate fog rather than precision, though we may regard Dostoevsky as a note-writer whose object is to work up a fog of the right density. With James the matter is all literal: the American genius is technical and for production. The *Prefaces*, the anecdotes that have come down to us, show that nothing was lost: James was presentable and publishable in his very socks. His life was an arrangement in words, born to circulate.

These *Notebooks* of his were begun in Boston when he was thirty-eight and when he feared that he had let too many impressions slip by, and they cover thirty years. They confirm that the word was totally his form of life, as if sentences rather than blood ran in his veins. Outside of words lay the unspeakable:

> Meanwhile the soothing, the healing, the sacred and salutary refuge from all these vulgarities and pains is simply to lose myself in this quiet, this blessed and uninvaded workroom, in the inestimable effort and refreshment of art, in resolute and beneficent production. I come back to it with a treasure of experience, of wisdom, of acquired material, of (it seems to me) seasoned fortitude and augmented capacity. Purchased by disgust enough, it is at any rate, a boon that now I hold it, I feel I wouldn't, I oughtn't to have missed. Ah, the terrible law of the artist—the law of fructification, of fertilisation, the law by which everything is grist to his mill—the law in short of the acceptance of all experience, of all suffering, of all life, of all suggestion, sensation and illumination.

And again:

> To live in the world of creation—to get into it and stay in it...

This is a language, with its "inestimables," its "alls," its "boons" and "beneficences," which oddly recalls the otherworldly language (so blandly assuming solid rewards on earth) of his contemporaries, the American Transcendentalists: like them Henry James was turning in to a private Infinite which would give the painful American gregariousness a sense of privacy. His words to Logan Pearsall Smith who had described a desire to excel in literature (I quote from Simon Nowell Smith's *The Legend of the Master*) are the proper conclusion:

There is one word—let me impress upon you—which you must inscribe on your banner, and that word is Loneliness.

Loneliness, like a pair of empty eyes, stares between the lines of this volume. We see the empty silent room, the desk, the lost, blank face of the well-dressed writer. Already as he takes his pen, he is far away from the dinner party he has just left. He is caught by "the terrible law." As fast as Emerson he is turning matter into spirit. Nearly every note is made after a meeting with people whose words, or what he knows of their lives, have provided him with one of his "germs," and at first sight, these pages might pass as the record of a vast sociability, a discreet mass of anonymous gossip. James himself, once attacked by Alphonse Daudet for frequenting people below his own intellectual level, might appear like another Thackeray ruined by dining out, or like the Major in *The Real Thing* with "the blankness, the deep intellectual repose of twenty years of country-house visiting." (The American editors of the *Notebook*, F. O. Mathiessen and Kenneth B. Murdock, point out that the French critic exaggerated: Henry James had a great many distinguished friends and some of the notes clearly are prompted by them. It is an illusion that a novelist needs high company continually, unless that happens to be his material; the conditions of the intellectual life are dangerously inclined to cut the novelist off from ordinary people who expose themselves less guardedly than the intellectuals do.) But examine a typical note carefully: the memoranda of Henry James are not jottings and reminders. They are written out, hundreds of them, at length. They are not snatched out of time, but time is in them; already the creative process has begun. A glance shows how much of James's life must have passed in the immense labour of almost continuous writing, and writing out in full detail, as if to fill the emptiness of the day with the succulence of its lost verbatim. The earliest reference to *What Maisie Knew*—a story which may be followed from behind James's shoulder in many entries in this volume—is not a hurried shorthand. It might be a minute passed from one civil servant to another:

Two days ago, at dinner at James Bryce's, Mrs. Ashton, Mrs. Bryce's sister, mentioned to me a situation that she had known of, of which it struck me immediately that something might be made in a tale. A child (boy or girl would do, but I see a girl, which would make it different from *The Pupil*) was *divided* by its parents in consequence of their being divorced. The court, for some reason, didn't, as it might have done, give the child exclusively to either parent but decreed that it was to spend its time equally with each—that is alternately. Each parent married again and the child went to them a month, or three months about—finding with the one a new mother and the other a new father. Might not something be done with the idea of an odd and particular relation springing up . . .

James's method is uncommon among writers and explains why his *Notebooks* are more fertile than most others we have been allowed to see. A full, superfluous, self-communing phrase like, "Might not something be done . . ." slows down the too bright idea, roots it in the mind, gives it soil. The slower the process of note-making the more likely it is to have sap and growth. James passing minutes to himself, James in colloquy, writing himself long and intimate letters: the note becomes one of those preliminary private outpourings, a "voluminous effusion . . . so extremely familiar, confidential and intimate—in the form of an interminable garrulous letter addressed to my own fond fancy." Not only is his material the subject: he himself is in it, adjured, egged on and cozened. Strange cries, like the whimper of hounds on the scent, comically, not without mockery—and yet touchingly and even alarmingly: "I have only to let myself go"—break out. In life he is an outsider, but not in letters:

I have brought this little matter of Maisie to a point at which a really detailed scenario of the rest is indispensable for a straight and sure advance to the end. Let me not, just Heaven—not, God knows, that I *incline* to!—slacken in my deep observance of this strong and beneficent method—this intensely structural, intensely hinged and jointed preliminary frame . . .

The coverts are drawn:

What is this IX, then, the moment, the stage *of*? Well, of a more presented, a more visible cynisme, on the part of everybody. What *step* does the action take in it? *That of Sir C's* detachment from Ida—

Then comes the view:

Ah this *divine* conception of one's little masses and periods in the scenic light— as rounded Acts; this patient, pious, nobly "vindictive" (vindicating) application of the same philosophy and method—I feel as if it still (above all, Yet) had a great deal to give me, and might carry me as far as I dream! God knows how far—into the flushed, dying day—that is! *De part et d'autre Maisie* has become a bore to her parents—with Mrs. Wix to help to prove it.

And so from field to field he runs, down to that kill, so protracted, so lovingly delayed lest one thrill of the chase be lost—"Do I get anything out of Folkestone?"—where Mrs Wix at last "*dit son fait* to—or about."

We could not ask for a more explicit statement of the compulsive quality of the creative process; in fact, one could say that any other quality is excluded from these notes. There is little that is casual or speculative. "Writing maketh an exact man." The conception is musical or mathematical. Method has become a divinity. There are few descriptions of places though there is a warm evocation of what London meant to him in the early and almost pathetically impersonal summing up of his life at the beginning of the book. Our picture is continually of crowds of people, in clubs or drawing rooms; but not of people seen—for they are not usually described—but of people being useful to Henry James, in some way working for him, wired in unknown to themselves and all unworthily to his extraordinary system of secretive illumination. The lonely man lends them his foreign mind. Abstract notions occasionally are flashed to him: "What is there in the idea of Too Late?"—the idea of a passion or friendship long desired? But, generally, the information is trite. Even where the neatest plot is boxed, we see how the deliberate endeavour to heighten consciousness, which contains the whole of Henry James's art, has transformed it at once (after, we can ask how much this very deliberateness lost for him as a novelist). Situation, dilemma rather than character, except in a very general way, mark the *Notebooks*; there is little portraiture and one would not gather much of James's richness in this respect, a richness which displaces for many heretical readers the metaphysical interest of the double and triple turning of the screw upon them. How many readers, like hungry, but well-provided spiders, run carelessly over that elaborate and mathematical web, shimmering with knots and subtleties from one beautifully trussed fly to the next.

For other novelists the value of Henry James's *Notebooks* is immense and to brood over them a major experience. The glow of the great impresario is on the pages. They are unwearyingly readable and endlessly stimulating, often moving and are occasionally relieved by a drop of gossip. (It is amusing to see him playing with the plot of *Trilby* which was offered to him by Du Maurier.) Of no other stories and novels in the language have we been shown that crucial point where experience or hearsay has suddenly become workable and why it has. We see ideas taken too briskly; we see bad ideas and good ones, we see the solid mature and the greatest ventures, like *The Ambassadors*, spring from a casual sentence. The ability to think of plots and to see characters is common; the difficulty is that one plot kills the next, that character sticks in the mud, and the novelist is motionless from sheer ability to see and to invent too much. What made James a fertile writer was his brilliant use of what, as I have said before, can only be called a slowing-down process. His material begins to move when the right difficulty, the proper technical obstruction or moral load is placed on it. The habit of imposing himself, rather than the gift of a great impressionability, appears to have been his starting point; there was a conscious search by a consciousness that had been trained. For the kind of writer who stands outside life as James did, who indeed has no *life* in life, has to create himself before he can create others.

(1953)

JAMES BOSWELL

BOSWELL'S LONDON

The discovery of cache after cache of Boswell's manuscripts, journals and letters at Malahide and Fettercairn between 1925 and 1948 is one of the truly extraordinary events in the history of English letters. It gave us the original journal of the *Tour to the Hebrides*, published in 1785, and now we have a totally new manuscript, appearing 180-odd years after it was written. This is the London journal which Boswell wrote in 1762 and 1763 when, twenty-three years old, he came to London to get a commission in the Guards, and, failing in that, met the man who was to be his god, his subject and his insurance of fame. What, we wonder, will be the state of our old editions of the *Life* of Johnson when the manuscripts yet to be seen are published? The *Life* has been a kind of lay scripture to the English, for it contains thought in our favourite, pragmatic form, that is to say, masticated by character. The book has been less a biography than a sort of parliamentary dialogue containing a thundering government and an adoring and obliging opposition. It will be strange if the proverbial and traditional characters are altered, though in the last generation the clownish Boswell has risen in esteem, and beyond Macaulay's derision. He has changed from the burr on the Doctor's coat-tails into an original blossom of the psychological hothouse.

Here we get on the dangerous ground of Plutarchian contrast. If Boswell created himself, we must never forget that Johnson made that possible. We lean to Boswell now because we have been bred on psychologists rather than philosophers, and love to see a man drowning in his own contradictions and self-exposures. The Doctor, who believed in Virtue, believed inevitably in repression, where we have been taught that it is immoral to hide anything. Boswell's very lack of foundation, his lack of judgment, are seen merely as the price he pays for the marvellous fluidity, transparency and curiosity of his nature. Dilapidation is his genius. Yet if Boswell is a genius we cannot forget that the Doctor is a saint, a man of richer and more sombre texture than his parasite. He is a father-figure, but not in the mechanical fashion of psychological definition; he is a father-figure enlarged by the religious attribute of tragedy. It was the tragic apprehension that was above all necessary for the steadying of Boswell's fluctuating spirit and for the sustaining of his sympathetic fancy.

The marvel is that at the age of twenty-three Boswell was already turning his gifts upon himself in the *Journal*. Professor Pottle, his lively American editor, thinks that his detachment is more complete than that of Pepys or Rousseau. Boswell's picture of himself has indeed the accidental and unforeseeable quality of life which better organised, more sapient or more eloquent natures lose the moment they put pen to paper. Boswell's detachment comes from naïveté and humility. He was emotionally surprised by himself. To one who had been knocked off his balance by a severe Presbyterian upbringing the world is bound to be a surprising place. To those who have lived under intense pressure, what happens afterwards is a miracle and release is an historical event. If the will has been destroyed by a parent like Lord Auchinleck, it may be replaced by a shiftless melancholy, an abeyance of spirits, and, from that bewilderment, all life afterwards will seem an hallucination, when a high-blooded young man engages ingenuously with it.

There is an obscure period in Boswell's youth when he joined the Roman Catholic Church. We do not know whether passion, giddiness, his irrational fears, or his tendency to melancholy, moved him to this step. But native canniness got him out of the scrape which socially and materially would have been a disaster in that age, and we can be grateful that the confessional did not assuage what Puritan diarising has preserved. For that confession contains more than an account of his sins; it contains his sillinesses, his vanities, moods, snobberies, the varying temperatures of his aspirations. "I have a genius for Physick," he says. For what did he not think he had genius? If only he could find out how to develop it! No symptom was too small when he studied the extraordinary illness, the remarkable fever, the very illusion of being a Self, James Boswell.

Exhibitionism? Vanity? The *Journal* was not private. It was posted every week to a friend, one of the inevitable devotions of the hero-worshipper. It is amazing that a young man should be an ass with such art, that judgment should not sprout anywhere. How rare to see a fool persisting in folly to the point of wisdom. One of the earliest comedies in the book is his lamentable affair with the actress Louisa. Calculation is at the bottom of it. Meanness runs through it, yet it is an exquisitely defenceless tale. In time he hoped to have a mistress who was a woman of fashion, but social inexperience and poverty—he is wonderfully stingy, a real hungry Scot of the period—held him back. As an actress Louisa could *cheaply* create the illusion of the woman of fashion. All this is innocently revealed later by introspection; at the beginning he is all fine feeling. To emphasise the fineness of feeling, he astutely points out, in his first timid advances to Louisa, that love is above monetary considerations. Presently he begins to believe his own propaganda; he is in love and to the extent of lending the woman £2. In the seduction, his sexual powers at first disappoint and then suddenly surpass anything he (or Louisa) has ever heard of. The next time he has a shock. Love has vanished. He is an unstable character. Presently he discovers she has introduced him to the "Signor Gonorrhœa." Despair, rage, moral indignation—can he have left the path of Virtue?—hard bargainings with the surgeon, melancholy, the ridicule of friends, nothing to do but to stay at home and read Hume's *History*. Philosophy calms him until the surgeon sends his bill. (In the matter of cash, the dissolving selves of Boswell always come together with certainty.) He writes to Louisa, points out what she has cost him, and asks for his £2 back, and says he is being generous. The doctor's bill was £5:

> Thus ended my intrigue with the fair Louisa which I flattered myself so much with and from which I expected at least a winter's safe copulation.

To be so transparent, thinking neither of the impression he makes upon himself nor of the figure he will cut before his friend, is possibly to be fatuous. But Boswell's fatuousness, which seems to arise from a lack of will or centre in his life, is inspired. Instead of will, Boswell had that mysterious ingredient of the soul, so admired in the age of sensibility: "my genius," or, as we would say, his "id." On that point only is his *amour propre* unyielding. Drowning in midstream, unable to reach the shore of Virtue and swept back into Vice and Folly, he clings to the straw of his "genius" and spins round and round until, what is he but a frantic work of art?

"How well I write!" he exclaims, after flattering a peer in six lines of doggerel. How wonderfully "facetious" he is with the Earl, how wonderful are "the sallies of my luxuriant imagination."

> How easily and cleverly do I write just now! I am really pleased with myself, words come skipping to me like lambs upon Moffat Hill; and I turn my periods smoothly and imperceptibly like a skilful wheelwright turning tops in a turning loom. There's a fancy! There's a smile.

Sheridan punctures him brutally, but Garrick comes along:

> "Sir," said he, "you will be a great man. And when you are so, remember the year 1763. I want to contribute my part towards saving you. And pray, will you fix a day when I shall have the pleasure of treating you with tea." I fixed the next day. "Then Sir," said he, "the cups shall dance and the saucers skip."

Like Moffat lambs, no doubt; fancy has been at work on Garrick's talk. Boswell continues innocently:

> What he meant by my being a great man I can understand. For really, to speak seriously, I think there is a blossom about me of something more distinguished than the generality of mankind.

If only it can be left to grow, instead of being chilled by "my melancholy temper" and dishevelled by "my imbecility of mind." The extraordinary thing is that a man so asinine should be so right.

The words of a man fuddled by middle-age? No, we have to re-mind ourselves, they are the words of a coxcomb of twenty-three. Hypochondria, as well as the prose manner of the time, has doubled his age. "Taking care of oneself is amusing," he says, filling his spoon with medicine. Life is an illness we must enjoy. In goes the thermometer at every instance. How is the genius for greatness? How is the fever for getting into the Guards, for chasing after English peers and avoiding the Scottish—if their accents are still bad—the fever for the theatre, for planning one's life, for wrecking the plan by the pursuit of "monstrous" whores or by fanciful fornication on Westminster Bridge; the fever for wit; for being like Mr Addison; for a trip down the river; for lashings of beef; for cutting down his expenses and for freedom from error and infidelity in the eyes of Providence? Boswell goes round London with his biography hanging out of his mouth like the tongue of a panting dog, until the great climax comes. "I am glad we have met," says the Doctor, and the dog with the genius beneath the skin has found its master.

Boswell's picture of life in London drawing-rooms, coffee-houses, taverns and streets is wonderful. It is done by a man much alone—and such make the best observers—to whom every word heard is precious. Listening to the plays, listening to the ordinary talk at Child's, he makes his first experiment in that dramatic dialogue which later was to give the *Life* its crowning quality. His ear is humble as Child's:

> 1ST CITIZEN: Pray, doctor, what became of that patient of yours? Was not her skull fractured?

PHYSICIAN: Yes, To pieces. However, I got her cured.

2ND CITIZEN: Good Lord!

Transparency is his gift of nature; affectability turns it into art; his industry, above all, fashions it. For Boswell stumbled soon upon the vital discovery that experience is three parts hallucination, when he made up his diary, not drily on the spot but three or four days late. He had, as his present American editor shrewdly points out, a little foreknowledge. His "genius" taught him to prepare the way for surprises which the reader could not know. It is one of his cunning strokes—he was not a regular theatre-goer for nothing—to repeat to Louisa, at the calamitous end of the affair, the words she had primly used at the beginning of it: "Where there is no confidence, there is no bond." And he is plotting, too, for that moment—surely handed to him by his Genius and not by Life—when she will send his £2 back in a plain envelope without a word. To illustrate, no doubt, his genius for stinginess. By the end, when the Doctor comes, the Journal overlaps the Life, but until then this is new Boswell, disordered and unbosomed.

(1953)

TOBIAS SMOLLETT

THE UNHAPPY TRAVELLER

There is one in every boat train that leaves Victoria, in every liner that leaves New York, in every bar of every hotel all over the world: the unhappy traveller. He is travelling not for pleasure but for pain, not to broaden the mind but, if possible, to narrow it; to release the buried terrors and hatreds of a lifetime; or, if these have already had a good airing at home, to open up colonies of rage abroad. We listen to these martyrs, quarrelling with hotel keepers, insulting cooks, torturing waiters and porters, the scourges of the reserved seat and viragos of the sleeping car. And when they return from their mortifications it is to insult the people and the places they have visited, to fight the battle over the bill or the central heating, again and again, with a zest so sore that we conclude that travel for them is a continuation of domestic misery by other means.

Character that provokes fuss or incident is valuable to the writer of travel books, and it is surprising that this liverish nature, so continuously provocative, has rarely been presented. I do not forget the hostile travellers who, after being cosseted by the best hotels, turn round and pull their hosts to pieces, but to those who travel because they hate travelling itself. Of these Smollett is the only good example I can think of, and after 180 years his rage still rings out. Why is he still readable? Literature is made out of the misfortunes of others. A large number of travel books fail simply because of the intolerable, monotonous good luck of their authors. Then, it is a pleasure to be the spectator and not the victim of bad temper. Again, Smollett satisfies a traditional and secret rancour of the English reader: our native dislike of the French even when we are Francophile; and recalls to us the old blisters of travel, the times *we* have been cheated, the times we threatened to call the police, the times when *we* could not face the food or the bedroom. But these are minor reasons for Smollett's readableness. We could, if we wanted to do so, let out a louder scream ourselves. Smollett is readable because he is a lucid author—as the maddened often are—writing, as Sir Osbert Sitwell says in his well-packed preface to a new edition, "in a beautifully clear, easy, ordered, but subtle English, a style partly the result of nature, and partly of many years of effort." It is the sane, impartial style which makes his pot-boiling *History of England* still worth dipping into and *Humphry Clinker* nutritious to the end.

There is one more explanation of his instant readability. There is an ambiguity, always irresistible, in books of travel if in some way the unguarded character of the author travels with him like a shadow on the road. Smollett draws his own dour, stoical, irascible character perfectly. It is vital, too, that the author should have an interesting mind. Smollett has. He is not a gentleman on tour, but a doctor, and he carries the rash habit of diagnosis with him. His observations, like his quarrels, are built up with light but patient documentation. His passions are not gouty explosions, but come because his sense of fact, order and agreement has been in some minor particular outraged. It is laughable, but before the end we feel a touch of pity. If (it had slowly been borne in on him by the time his journey was done) he had been content to be cheated a little, to pay a trifle extra, to forget the letter of his bargains, if he had not bothered about the odd sous, he would have travelled faster in comfort and happiness. Alas, it was impossible. The one-time ship's surgeon who had made his own way in the world on little education, whose sense of inferiority had not been reduced either by a rich marriage nor by great monetary success in his profession, who had been thrown into prison (and very rightly) for libel after an outrageous attack on his admiral, and had sought out gratuitous quarrels with every English writer of his time, was not the man to allow others any latitude. The quarrel was what he wanted. Since the author of Tom Jones was not on the Continent Smollett took it out of the innkeepers.

It began on the Dover Road where

> the chambers are in general cold and comfortless, the bed paltry, the cooking execrable, the wine poison, the attendance bad, the publicans insolent; there is not a tolerable drop of malt liquor to be had from London to Dover.

It continues in Boulogne where the people are filthy, lazy, "incompetent in the mechanical arts," priest-ridden, immoral, their wine bad—he drank no good wine in France—and their cooking worse. Smollett, who was travelling with his wife and servants, five persons in all, preferred to buy and prepare his own food, such were his British, albeit Scottish, suspicions of the French *ragoût*. As for the French character, vanity is "the great and universal mover of all varieties and degrees." A Frenchman will think he owes it to his self-esteem to seduce your wife, daughter, niece and even your grandmother; if he fails he deplores their poor taste; if you reproach him, he will reply that he could not give higher proof of his regard for your family:

> You know Madam [Smollett writes to an imaginary correspondent], we are naturally taciturn, soon tired of impertinence, and much subject to fits of disgust. Your French friend intrudes upon you at all hours: he stuns you with his loquacity: he teases you with impertinent questions about your domestic and private affairs; he attempts to meddle in your concerns; and forces his advice upon you with unwearied importunity; he asks the price of everything you wear and, so sure as you tell him, undervalues it, without hesitation: he affirms it is bad taste, ill-contrived, ill-made; that you have been imposed upon both with respect to fashion and the price ...

Has this race of egotists and *petits-maîtres* any virtues? They have "natural capacities" (it appears) but ruined by giddiness and levity and the education of the Jesuits. It is, however, unfair to describe them as insincere and mean:

> High flown professions of friendship and attachment constitute the language of common compliment in this country, and are never supposed to be understood in the literal acceptation of the words; and if their acts of generosity are rare, we ought to ascribe that rarity not so much to a deficiency of generous sentiments, as to their vanity and ostentation, which, engrossing all their funds, utterly disable them from exerting the virtues of beneficence.

No, there is nothing to be said for the French. Their towns are often better than their inhabitants and in the descriptions of places we see Smollett's virtue as a writer. Clearly, like some architectural draughtsman, ingeniously contriving his perspectives, he has the power to place a town, its streets, its industries, its revenues and even its water supply, before us like a marvellous scale model. We get a far clearer notion of what a French town was like in the 1760s than we can form for ourselves of an English town today. Smollett was a sick man on this journey, he was travelling in search of health, and he brings to what he sees the same diagnostic care that he brought to the illnesses of others or his own; but he had grown up under the matter-of-fact and orderly direction of his time. Even when one of his inevitable rows begins—he swears he has been given bad horses, bad servants, bad meals, made to wait beyond his turn at the coaching stations and so on—they are conducted with all the sense of orderly manœuvre which he must have observed in his life at sea. We know exactly where he sat and where the innkeeper stood when the row began, and how often the doctor banged up the window of the coach and—one can see his ugly, peevish, stone-yellow face, for in a fit of repentance he describes it—refused to budge until the bargain was fulfilled to the letter. The astonishing thing is that he is always defeated; but petulance has no authority. Here is a typical upset at Brignolles—it was followed by worse at Luc: there the whole town turned out to see the defeat of the Doctor:

> At Brignolles, where we dined, I was obliged to quarrel with the landlady, and threatened to leave her house, before she would indulge us with any sort of fresh meat. It was meagre day, and she had made her provision accordingly. She even hinted some dissatisfaction at having heretics in the house; but I was not disposed to eat stinking fish, with ragouts of eggs in onions ... Next day when we set out in the morning from Luc, it blew a north-westerly wind so extremely cold and biting that even a flannel wrapper could not keep me warm in the coach. Whether the cold had put our coachman in a bad humour, or he had some other cause of resentment against himself, I know not; but when we had gone about a quarter of a mile, he drove the carriage full against the corner of a garden wall and broke the axle tree.

"Resentment against himself!" Smollett would understand that. It is the antidote to Sterne.

A useful and detailed *Life* of Smollett has just been written by a conscientious American scholar, Mr Lewis Mansfield Knapp. One sees that Smollett, caught between Grub Street and the gentleman writers, a commercially popular professional who made enough money to employ ghosts and hacks, was a man of hyper-sensitive, jealous yet remorseful temper, ardent and generous, yet easily stung and quick to sting. His sensibility has led to the suggestion that the passages of grossness and brutality, his chamber-pot humour, are not the broad comedy of a man who liked a dirty joke and the writing on the lavatory wall, but disclose a horror of the flesh, the wincing of the man with a skin too few. Like many doctors, he jokes brutally about the body because it shocks him. Up to a point this seems to me certainly true: to deny it is to deny the double mind of many eighteenth-century writers who were not less moved to reform manners because it happened to pay them to be gross and licentious in presenting the case. Smollett in his *Travels* is a fastidious man; he has the doctor's dislike of filth and the eighteenth century (as we see again in the case of Swift) saw the beginning of a hatred of filth in the person and the home. The bad temper of Smollett, though it was aggravated by ill-health, became, to some extent, a protest against the squalor, incompetence and cruelty which impeded the sensible desires of the civilised man. He liked decorum. He hated the raffish, the Bohemian and the wild. He was, in short, one of the earliest respectable men, when respectability was a weapon of reform; when it meant that you were jeered at for objecting to capital punishment, flogging, the public exposure of bodies broken on the wheel by the roadside, and the maddening disorderliness of a system of travel which belonged to the Middle Ages and not to 1763. Smollett's temper was, in some respects, a new, frost-bitten bud of civilisation, of which sick, divided and impossible men are frequently the growing point.

(1953)

SAKI

THE PERFORMING LYNX

"I'm living so far beyond my income," says one of the characters in Saki's *The Unbearable Bassington*, "that we may almost be said to be living apart." That is a pointer to Saki's case: it is the fate of wits to live beyond the means of their feeling. They live by dislocation and extravagance. They talk and tire in the hard light of brilliance and are left frightened and alone among the empty wine-glasses and tumbled napkins of the wrecked dinner-table. Saki was more than a wit. There was silence in him as well. In that silence one sees a freak of the travelling show of story-tellers, perhaps a gifted performing animal, and it is wild. God knows what terrors and cajoleries have gone on behind the scenes to produce this gifted lynx so contemptuously consenting to be half-human. But one sees the hankering after one last ferocious act in the cause of a nature abused. The peculiar character called Keriway who crops up unexplained in the middle of the Bassington novel tells the story of a "tame, crippled crane." "It was lame," Keriway says, "that is why it was tame."

What lamed and what tamed Saki? The hate, passion, loneliness that closed the hearts of the children of the Empire-builders? Like Thackeray, Kipling and Orwell, Saki was one of the children sent "home" from India and Burma to what seemed to them loveless care. Saki did not suffer as Kipling suffered, but we hear of an aunt whom his sister described as a woman of "ungovernable temper, of fierce likes and dislikes, imperious, a moral coward, possessing no brains worth speaking of and a primitive disposition." A Baroness Turgenev, in short. She is thought to be the detested woman in *Sredni Vashtar*, one of Saki's handful of masterpieces, the tale of the boy who plotted and prayed that she should be killed by a ferret. Boy and ferret were satisfied. But something less pat and fashionably morbid than a cruel aunt at Barnstaple must lie behind Saki's peculiarity, though she may go some way to explain his understanding of children. We are made by forces much older than ourselves. Saki was a Highland Scot and of a race that was wild and gay in its tribal angers. Laughter sharpens the steel. He belonged—and this is more important—to an order more spirited, melancholy, debonair and wanton than the pudding Anglo-Saxon world south of the Border, with its middle-class wealth, its worry and its conventions. He could not resist joining it, but he joined to annoy. *The Unbearable Bassington* is a neat piece of taxidermy, a cheerful exposure of the glass case and contents of Edwardian society, a footnote to *The Spoils of Poynton*. In a way, Saki has been tamed by this society, too. Clovis likes the cork-pop of an easy epigram, the schoolboy hilarity of the practical joke and the fizz of instant success—"The art of public life consists to a great extent of knowing exactly where to stop and going a bit further" and so on—he is the slave of the teacup and dates with every new word. His is the pathos of the bubble. But Saki has strong resources: he is moved by the inescapable nature of the weariness and emptiness of the socialite life, though unable to catch, like Firbank, the minor poetry of fashion. Francesca is too shallow to know tragedy, but she will know the misery of not being able to forget what she did to her son, all her life. She is going to be quietly more humiliated every year. And then, Saki's other resource is to let the animals in with imprudent cruelty. The leopard eats the goat in the Bishop's bathroom, the cat rips a house-party to pieces, the hounds find not a fox but a hyena and it comfortably eats a child; the two trapped enemies in the Carpathian forest make up their feud and prepare to astonish their rescuers with the godly news but the rescuers are wolves. Irony and polish are meant to lull us into amused, false comfort. Saki writes like an enemy. Society has bored him to the point of murder. Our laughter is only a note or two short of a scream of fear.

Saki belongs to the early period of the sadistic revival in English comic and satirical writing—the movement suggested by Stevenson, Wilde, Beerbohm, Firbank and Evelyn Waugh—the early period when the chief target was the cult of convention. Among these he is the teaser of hostesses, the shocker of dowagers, the mocker of female crises, the man in the incredible waistcoat who throws a spanner into the teacup; but irreverence and impudence ought not to be cultivated. They should occur. Otherwise writers are on the slippery slope of the light article. Saki is on it too often. There is the puzzling half-redeeming touch of the amateur about him, that recalls Maurice Baring's remark that he made the mistake of thinking life more important than art. But the awkwardness, the jumpiness in some of these sketches, the disproportion between discursion and incident or clever idea has something to do with the journalism of the period—Mr Evelyn Waugh's suggestion—and, I would add, some connection with the decadence of club culture. The great period of that culture was in the mid-nineteenth century: by the early 1900s it had run into the taste for the thin, the urbane and the facetious; and to sententious clichés: Lady Bastable is "wont to retire in state to the morning-room," Clovis makes a "belated appearance at the breakfast-table;" people "fare no better" and are "singularly" this or that. The cinema, if nothing else, has burned this educated shrubbery out of our comic prose. But Saki's club prose changes when he is writing descriptions of nature (in which he is a minor master), when he describes animals and children or draws his sharp new portraits. His people are chiefly the stupid from the country, the natterers of the drawing-room and the classical English bores, and though they are done in cyanide, the deed is touched by a child's sympathy for the vulnerable areas of the large mammals. He collected especially the petty foibles and practical vanities of women (unperturbed by sexual disturbance on his part), and so presented them as persons, just as he presented cats as cats and dogs as dogs.

> Eleanor hated boys and she would have liked to have whipped this one long and often. It was perhaps the yearning of a woman who had no children of her own.

Or there is the scene between the pleasant Elaine who, having just become engaged to be married, decides to increase her pleasure by scoring off her aunt and her country cousin who has also just got engaged. Saki is clear that Elaine is a thoroughly nice girl:

> "There is as much difference between a horseman and a horsy man as there is between a well-dressed man and a dressy one," said Elaine judicially, "and you have noticed how seldom a dressy woman really knows how to dress. An old lady of my acquaintance observed the other day, some people are born with a sense of how to clothe themselves, others acquire it, others look as if their clothes had been thrust upon them."

A stale joke? Beware of Saki's claws; he goes on in the next sentence:

> She gave Lady Caroline her due quotation marks, but the sudden tactfulness with which she looked away from her cousin's frock was entirely her own idea.

Saki's male bores and male gossips are remarkable in our comic literature, for he does not take the usual English escape of presenting them as eccentrics. Bores are bores, classifiable, enjoyable like anacondas or the lung-fish. There is Henry Creech with "the prominent, penetrating eyes of a man who can do no listening in the ordinary way and whose eyes have to perform the functions of listening for him." And bores have lives. When Stringham made a witty remark for the first time in his life in the House of Commons one evening, remarking indeed that "the people of Crete unfortunately make more history than they can consume locally," his wife grasped that some clever woman had got hold of him and took poison.

E. V. Knox's edition of Saki's tales (published by Collins) is a pleasant one, but it inexplicably omits all the stories from *Beasts and Superbeasts* in which Saki was at his best. I do not much care for Saki's supernatural stories, though I like the supernatural touch: the dog, for example, in *The Unbearable Bassington*, at the ghastly last dinner-party. His best things are always ingenious: the drama of incurring another's fate in *The Hounds of Fate*, the shattering absurdity of *Louis*, the artificial dog; and the hilarious tale of the tattooed Dutch commercial traveller who is confined to Italy because he is officially an unexportable work of art. The joke, for Saki, is in the kill. On the whole, it is the heart that is aimed at. He is always richly informed in the vanities of political life and does it in a manner that recalls Disraeli. Except for novels by Belloc, there has been none of this political writing since. Artificial writers of his kind depend, of course, on the dangerous trick-logic of contrivance. Success here is a gamble. For morality he substitutes the child's logic of instinct and idea.

The Unbearable Bassington is one of the lasting trifles. Its very surprising quality is the delicate apprehension of pleasure and misery. Saki was short of pity. He was an egoist and had no soothing word for pain. He knew that certain kinds of pain cannot be forgotten. Self-dramatisation, self-pity, none of the usual drugs, can take that stone from the heart. He is thoughtful but will offer nothing. In this frivolous novel Saki begins to mature. His next novel, *The Coming of William*, written in 1912 and warning lazy and corrupt Society of the German menace, was good propaganda. He imagined an England annexed to Germany and it makes uncomfortable reading; for silly Society turns instantly to collaboration. There is a more serious discomfort here; a disagreeable anti-Semitism shows more plainly in this book and one detects, in this soldierly sado-masochist, a desire for the "discipline" of authoritarian punishment. He is festive and enjoyable as the wild scourge; but the danger obviously was that this performing lynx, in the demi-monde between journalism and a minor art, might have turned serious and started lecturing and reforming his trainer. In earlier and more spontaneous days, he would have eaten him.

(1965)

GEORGE MEREDITH

MEREDITH'S BRAINSTUFF

Does anyone know what to think of Meredith's novels now? I think not. The lack of sympathy is complete. Difficult to read in his own time, he is almost impenetrable to ourselves. "Full of good brainstuff," Gissing said of *Diana of the Crossways*, and added joyfully that the true flavour of this book came out only after three readings! It was Meredith's brain that annoyed his early critics; today we suspect his heart. Insincerity and freakishness are held against him. Yet, we ought to feel some contact, for he is the first modern highbrow novelist in the sense of being the first to write for the minority and to be affected, even if unconsciously, by the split in our culture. George Eliot, his rival intellectual, was not so affected.

Those who visited the chalet at Box Hill in the period of Meredith's old age and fame were astonished by the mass of French novels there. He set out, as the French do, to facet life so that it became as hard as a diamond, to shape it by Idea. (At the time of the death of his second wife, he wrote: "I see all round me how much Idea governs," and Idea was "the parent of life as opposed to that of perishable blood.") The notion sometimes gave an intellectual dignity to his creations, but just as often dignity was merely stance. For Meredith's imagination housed the most ill-assorted ideas: there was dandyism, there was the oracular Romance of his claim to be a Celt, there was the taste for German fantasy, the feeling for supermen and women and the heroic role of the fittest. If we follow his own habit of metaphorical association, we find ourselves saying that the descendant of two generations of naval and military tailors in Portsmouth was born to the art of dressing-up. In fact, his grandfather, and his father before him, had been as fantastic in their lives as he was in his novels; the son was able to survive his own self-deceptions by the aid of wit. The difficulty of Meredith does not lie in his thought, but in its conceits, in the flowered waistcoats of his intellectual wardrobe. Gosse used to object to this passage from the description of a scene at the gaming table:

> He compared the creatures dabbling over the board to summer flies on butcher's meat, periodically scared by a cloth. More in the abstract, they were snatching at a snapdragon bowl. It struck him that the gamblers had thronged on an invitation to drink the round of seed-time and harvest in a gulp. Again they were desperate gleaners, hopping, skipping, bleeding, amid a whizz of scythe blades, for small wisps of booty. Nor was it long before the presidency of an ancient hoary Goat-Satan might be perceived with skew-eyes and pucker-mouth, nursing a hoof on a tree. Our medieval Enemy sat symbolical in his deformities, as in old Italian and Dutch thick-line engravings of him. He rolled a ball for souls, excited like kittens, to catch it tumbling into the dozens of vacant pits.

Brainstuff, indeed. For our welfare (Meredith warned us) Life was always trying to pull us away from consciousness and brainstuff. On the other hand, "Matter that is not nourishing to brains can help to constitute nothing but the bodies that are pitched on rubbish heaps." Human felicity is always trying (he said in a letter) to kill consciousness. There is often an extraordinary violence in Meredith's neo-pagan metaphors.

Meredith, like Browning, had too many ideas. And, as in his novels, so in his life, the brilliant egoist appeared to be an artificial construction. An American biographer, Professor Lionel Stevenson, notes in *The Ordeal of George Meredith* that by the time he was fifty, Meredith "had completely molded himself in a dramatic personality." He had become the Comic Spirit in person and if there was overstrain, it was for clear personal reasons: "The components had been collected with a kind of genius. Impenetrably screened behind it lurked the Portsmouth tailor shop, the bankrupt father, and the dreadful decade of his first marriage." The price was that he did not inspire intimacy:

> It was not that he seemed either aloof or insincere; but he created the effect of a perpetual and consummate theatrical performance and the pilgrims to Box Hill were not so much consorting with a friend as they were appreciating a unique work of art.

It would be misleading to continue to press a comparison between Meredith's life and his work as a novelist. Professor Stevenson is concerned with the writing life and very little with literary criticism. He comments on the novels, as they come along, but does not examine them in much detail. He notes (what Henry James deplored) Meredith's evasion of the *scène à faire*, for example, it is the point of all Meredith's novels, as Professor Stevenson admirably says, that the chief characters shall be tried by ordeal. They are burned in the fire of their own tragic or comic illusions and emerge from self-deception into self-knowledge. Yet, in *Diana of the Crossways*, the scene where Diana commits the folly of letting a political secret out of the bag is skipped. Is she an hysterical egoist? Is she as immoral as she appears? Has she merely lost her head? Only a direct account of the scene at the newspaper office, where she hands over the secret, can tell us. Meredith was no story-teller—a fatal defect, above all in the days of the three-volume novel. He is a novelist who gesticulates about a story that is implicitly already told. The cage of character is his interest. The rest of Professor Stevenson's criticism is appreciative but not considerable. I find only one point of disagreement. He says that Meredith was the first to introduce something close to natural dialogue in the English novel. Certainly Meredith breaks the convention in which dialogue had been written up to this time; the result is not natural speech. Meredith simply applied his own allusiveness to dialogue, and allusiveness happens to be a characteristic of ordinary speech anyway; he was too full of himself to see the characters or speech of other people, except in so far as they could be elaborated as "idea" and in stylised form. Meredith's dialogue is simply Meredith cutting a figure in his own society.

As a biography Professor Stevenson's *Life* tells a well-known story competently. A writer has not much time for living and Meredith's life is one more variant on the theme of the calamities of authorship. There is the aloof, handsome, snobbish youth making that first break with his environment by sheer pride of obsession. There is the unhappy marriage to Peacock's daughter and the hardening of the heart—yet Meredith's heart must have hardened in childhood. And then the literary grind follows. *The Ordeal of Richard Feverel* is a failure, so is *Evan Harrington. Harry Richmond* gets a few admirers. His integrity was untouched by neglect; he worked without a public until he was fifty, and by that time, his health went to pieces. The tall, eagle-faced man, the non-stop wit, talker and laugher, with his bouts of "manly" boisterousness and back-slapping, had always been a dyspeptic. Now he suddenly became deaf. He presently had the symptoms of locomotor ataxia. To keep his family he had ground away for years as a publisher's reader and wrote three articles a week for a provincial newspaper. For years also he made a small annual sum by reading to an old lady once a week. His letters are full of the groans of laborious authorship. At fifty he had had enough, but he was fated to live into his eighties, unable to hear speech or music; unable to walk, which had been his chief pleasure in life. He was drawn about in a donkey chair. He was sixty before he became famous; the relative comfort of his old age was only in part due to his success—he inherited a little money from an aunt. In his personal life, he had seen the death of his two wives and the son whom he had once adored, but who had become estranged from him after his second marriage. A psychologist might say that Meredith's life is an ironical illustration of the theory that we get what we are conditioned to desire. The death of his mother in very early childhood, and the pride and fecklessness of his father, had formed Meredith for self-sufficiency and loneliness: the brain rapidly filled in the hollows left by affections which had been denied. His own affections certainly became intellectual; his love letters are clearly of the kind that exhaust the feeling in an excessive flow of lyrical expression. He grieved over the death of his wife, but he *had* compared her to a mud fort! Friends found an annoying disconnection between brain and heart. There was one reward. It seems frequently to come to the egoistic temperament: the exciting, if heartless, power of living in the present. He tore up old letters and, in old age, is said to have scorned the common consolation of that time: living in the past. The torrential talker, the magician, was in short a picturesque monster, relishing his scars. One whimsical young American admirer—mentioned by Professor Stevenson—made the shrewd, even Meredithean remark, that he would probably have been happier and better organised if he had been a woman.

To return to the unreadableness of Meredith. He is not unreadable; he exists a page at a time; he is quotable, to be skipped through. The large characters like Sir Willoughby Patterne or Richmond Roy are myths. Meredith is tedious only in his detail; when he intends to be preposterous he is wonderful, as he is in that scene in *Harry Richmond*, where Richmond Roy poses publicly as an equestrian statue. Meredithean irony is excessive, as all the brainstuff is, but it is excellent when the character or the scene is fantastic enough for him. He is impossible until one submits to his conception of Romance; after that he is only hard work. He is a rhapsodist who writes about people who are really souls moving impatiently out of their present into their future, towards destruction or self-knowledge. They are pagan souls in the poetic sense, not characters in the moralistic sense; giants of the Celtic tradition, grotesques in the German; all their geese are swans. Their lives are portrayed as heightened exercises in their integrity and their sense of honour. Professor Stevenson remarks that Meredith was attacked with ridicule until he was fifty, not only because he was a pagan who could not tell a story and at odds with popular realism, but because Romance was out. His fame began when Romance came in. Stevenson and Conrad contain strange echoes. Chesterton's suburban romance owes a lot to him. D. H. Lawrence was the last to be influenced by him. Another element in making his fame was the rise of feminism. It is very hard for ourselves to imagine another revival in Romance. What a future generation of novelists may find stimulating in him is that preoccupation of his with what he called "the idea." He enlarged the novel with a brilliant power of generalisation. It was spoiled, as so much English fiction has been, by the obsession with romantic class-consciousness, but in *Beauchamp's Career*, or even in a clumsy novel like One of Our Conquerors, he has an ability to generalise about society as living history. And his presentation of character—Diana Merion, for example, in *Diana of the Crossways*—as idea and person at once, is a fertile addition to the old English tradition of character types, removed from our moralising habit. The pile of French novels at the chalet, the attempt to turn Molière into English, had their point.

Harry Richmond contains fewer difficulties of style than most of his work, chiefly because it is written in the first person. Meredith was a poetic or rhapsodic novelist, and *Harry Richmond* is a romance about the serious deceits and comedies of romance. Several of the characters are more than life-size, or speak and live in the heightened language of an imagination which is sometimes fine, at other times wooden or uncertain of its level; but there is no doubt that Meredith creates a complete world. Critics have often said that Meredith's taste for the chivalrous and high-sounding takes him clean out of the nineteenth century and sends his novels floating away in clouds of non-existent history. They have said that we can never pin him down to time and place, and that he is intellectually Ruritanian. This is only superficially true. We must take into consideration a novelist's temperament before we judge like that. Because Meredith's mind was microscopic, because his subject again and again is people's imaginative, ideal, future-consuming view of themselves and of their environment, this does not mean that they have no known place in a recognisable world. Nothing could be more thoroughly Victorian in imagination than *Harry Richmond*; if the neo-medieval colouring is precisely that, this novel reads as if it were an attempt to glamorise Victorian life out of recognition. This is a well-known habit among the poets of the nineteenth century. The cult of the picturesque history can be described as an escape from the grim squalor of the industrial revolution; but we can also think of it as a confident and imperial enterprise of colonisation. The Victorians were high-feeders on what is felt to be foreign in time or place. *Harry Richmond* is cast in the imperial frame of mind, and if Meredith can be justly accused of being merely Ruritanian, he did not fall into the ludicrous which so often imperils (shall we say?) Tennyson's historical or legendary poems. The very pretences of Harry Richmond's fantastic father to the throne of England and to royal blood expresses the rising, exuberant side of the situation in England at that time when people were very liable to be plethoric about the greatness of their history. The plot and many details of narration are also true to the period. It was a time of violent changes of fortune in private life, of tremendous claims to estates and titles. Meredith is known to have got the idea for Richmond Roy's wild claim from the fact that William the Fourth had many children by an Irish actress, and also from the marriage of George IV to Mrs Fitzherbert. Meredith's remoteness has been greatly exaggerated by critics brought up on realism.

The spell of *Harry Richmond*—for to read it is to pass into trance—exists because of the brilliant handling of an impossible subject. If Meredith had confronted Richmond Roy's claim squarely and realistically he would have been lost. His art lies in building up the character of the father as the romantic and charming figure seen by his child, and then in gradually disclosing that he is first an adventurer, living in state one minute and in a debtor's prison the next; at last, by evasive insinuation, comes the royal claim. Richmond Roy grows larger and larger, richer in resource and effrontery, more and more triumphant for every setback, but skating on thinner and thinner ice the farther he goes. Meredith learned from French novelists the method of working up to the key phrase. The moment the farmers on whom Harry Richmond is boarded when he is a child start deferring to him, and are heard at last to whisper superstitiously "Blood rile," the thrill is aesthetic. It has exactly the effect of the words "You are an egoist" when they are spoken to Sir Willoughby Patterne and when they transform the tension and tighten the focus of that book. Richmond Roy has been too obviously compared with Micawber; he is far more complex than that; his follies and dreams have genius. He is not a windbag; he is a fine actor. He is nearer to Falstaff. Richmond Roy alarms. He alarms when he brazenly orders scarlet liveries, permitted only to the Royal Family, for his postilions. He alarms by his knowledge of our weaknesses. He can bounce his way into buying a château or a yacht. He can spellbind a foreign court and rout the hostess of Bath. Notoriety he thrives on. His impudence when he poses as an equestrian statue at the German court is splendid. These imaginative episodes set off the scurvy ones; the father's nasty relationships with the press, his unscrupulous robbery of his adoring son, his caddish exploitation of the young man's love for the German princess, his cold-hearted swindling of his sister-in-law. He pretends that the money came from personages who are anxious to keep him quiet. He is a mountebank, and if we are glad in the end that Squire Beltham exposes him in good Squire Western style, it is not really because we like to see vice punished, but because the rogue has got too maddening and has reached an hysterical and pathetic stage where he will become a figure too farcical to bear his real weight as a symbol; hence his tragedy. Meredith works up to that proper conclusion but, like a great artist, explores all the other possibilities first. He has the piling-on instinct of the story-teller. We are delighted towards the end when Richmond Roy is confronted with another false claimant, a so-called Dauphin who claims to have marks on his body which prove his heredity. Meredith is clever enough to give this episode twice; in two different kinds of gossip, one showing Richmond Roy the master of an insulting situation, the other through Squire Beltham's hilarious British scorn. Meredith's mastery of comedy does not exclude the low and, indeed, in the low he is not tempted to his vice of over-polishing. When the ladies retire from the dinner table—a nice touch that—the squire lets go:

> They got the two together, William. Who are you? I'm a Dauphin; who are you? I'm Ik Dine, bar sinister. Oh, says the other; then I take precedence of you! Devil a bit, says the other; I've got more spots than you. Proof, says one. You first, t'other. Count, one cries. T'other sings out. Measles. Better than a dying Dauphin, roars t'other; and swore both of 'em 'twas nothing but port wine stains and pimples. Ha! Ha! And, William, will you believe it?—the couple went round begging the company to count spots to prove their big birth. Oh Lord, I'd ha' paid a penny to be there! A Jack of Bedlam Ik Dine damned idiot!—makes the name o' Richmond stink.

It has been said that Meredith is not a story-teller—but a story need not depend very much on plot; it can and does in Meredith depend on pattern and the disclosure of character through events. The weakness is that the fantastic father engrosses the great part of the interesting incident; when he is off-stage our interest flags. Meredith's narrative is not a straight line; it is a meandering back and forth in time, a blending of events and commentary and this Meredith must have gone for instinctively, because he is wooden in straightforward narration. We follow an imagination that cannot bear precision. He depends on funking scenes, on an increasing uncertainty about how exactly events did occur. There is a refusal to credit reality with importance until it has been parcelled out between two or three minds and his own reflections on it. Even in the duel scene in Germany, the excellence is due to the ironical telescoping of the event; we are hearing Meredith on the duel, telling us what to look at and what not to bother about. The effect is of jumping from one standstill scene to another. Life is not life, for him, until it is over; until it is history. (One sees this method in the novels of William Faulkner.) The movement is not from event to event, but from situation to situation, and in each situation there is a kernel of surprising incident. In realism he is tedious. One can almost hear him labouring at what he does not believe in and depending on purely descriptive skill.

The love scenes in *Harry Richmond* present a double difficulty to ourselves. The mixture of realism and high romance is awkward; we are made to feel the sensuality of lovers in a way remarkable to mid-Victorian novels; their words appear to be a highfalutin way of taking the reader's mind off it and, in this respect, Meredith's pagan idealism is no more satisfactory than the conventional Christian idealism of other novelists. Like Scott, Meredith is always better at the minor lovers than the major ones. His common sense, touched by a half-sympathetic scorn, is truer than his desire, which is too radiantly egocentric. In Meredith's personal life, his strongest and spontaneous feelings of love were those of a son and a father, and this is, of course, the theme of *Harry Richmond*. That is why, more than any of his other works, this one appears to be rooted in a truth about the human heart. In erotic love, Meredith never outgrew his early youth and the fact over-exhilarates and vulgarises him by turns.

Harry Richmond is thought to be less encumbered than Meredith's other novels because it is written in the first person. Unfortunately, as Mr Percy Lubbock pointed out some years ago in *The Craft of Fiction*, the first person has to be both narrator and actor in his own story, and in consequence stands in his own light. I do not believe that this is a serious fault in *Harry Richmond* as a story, for what carries us forward is Meredith's remarkable feeling for the generosity, impulsiveness and courage of youth and its splendid blindness to the meaning of its troubles. Harry is blinded by romantic love for his father and the German princess; he is weak in not facing the defects of the former and in not being "great" enough for the latter; but both these sets of behaviour are honourable and have our sympathy. With his father he shares a propensity for illusion and romance and is cured of them. Since he is the narrator we have only his word for it, and one is far from convinced that Harry Richmond has been cured or even examined. Put the story in Henry James's hands and one sees at once that the whole question of illusion or romance would have been gone into far more deeply. It is the old Meredithean trouble; he is an egoistical writer, fitted out with the egoistical accomplishments, and one who can never be sufficiently unselfed to go far into the natures of others. His portraits start from him, not from them, and the result is that he is only picturesque, a master of ear and eye, a witty judge of the world, a man a good deal cutting a figure in his own society; we are given brilliant views of the human heart, but we do not penetrate it. He has no sense of the calamitous, no sense of the broken or naked soul, and— fatally—no sense of evil. More than any other novelist of his age, he has the Victorian confidence and in a manner so dazzling and profuse that it is natural they called him Shakespearean. In the effusive Victorian sense, he was; but Shakespearean merely linguistically, glamorously, at second hand, without any notion of human life as passion or of suffering as more than disappointment. He is a very literary novelist indeed.

(1965)

MIGUEL DE CERVANTES

QUIXOTE'S TRANSLATORS

Don Quixote has been called the novel that killed a country by knocking the heart out of it and extinguishing its belief in itself for ever. The argument might really be the other way on. *Don Quixote* was written by the poor soldier and broken tax-collector with the hand maimed in his country's battles because the Spanish dream of Christian chivalry and total power had passed the crisis of success. The price of an illusion was already being paid and Cervantes marked it down. When Don Quixote recovered his sanity, his soul lost its forces, and he died. What must strike the foreign reader is the difference between the book as it appears to Spaniards and as it appears to the world outside of Spain. The difference is that in Spain *Don Quixote* had a basis in contemporary fact; outside Spain it is morality, metaphysics, fable. The romances of chivalry were read during the Counter-Reformation and specifically moved two of the Spanish saints to action—St Teresa and St Ignatius de Loyola. Longing for the freedom of a man as her brothers went off to the New World, St Teresa read these books with excitement, and Loyola's famous vigil at Manresa was made consciously in imitation of Amadis, and might be a chapter of *Don Quixote*.

Outside Spain, the novel began a new life in countries where the idea of chivalry had no tradition of national awakening and power, where the tragic core was missing. To the English and French translators who got to work a few years after the book was published, *Don Quixote* was simply the greatest of the picaresque novels, indeed the only great one in a genre which elsewhere kept strictly to exaggeration, meaninglessness and popular anarchy. The book became farce—though the contemporary Shelton sins far less than Motteux who translated the book at the beginning of the eighteenth century—a string of adventures and scenes of horseplay tied up with ironical conversations about the noble disadvantages of idealism and its conflict with proverbial self-interest. If we turn to the English novelists who, in the early eighteenth century, were deeply influenced by the tale, we can see how they altered the characters of Don Quixote and Sancho to suit the new middle-class morality. Don Quixote, especially, the violent and subtle madman with his visions of the lost Golden Age, becomes in England a mere eccentric, an unaccountable squire, a hilarious Scot in Smollett, an unworldly but rough-and-tumble clergyman in Fielding. Figures like Parson Adams are misfits, cranks, clowns, often enlightened but always simple and without authority; whereas Don Quixote's mind is darkened and dignified by the counsels of his madness. He has the endless resource of the neurotic; he has pride and the habits of pride and command. In England, the ingenious gentleman is opposed by the worthy forces of self-interest, so much admired in Cheapside. The question is practical: idealism or realism? The answer always sentimental: failure is lovable and what is lovable is commercial. These imitators in the sensible eighteenth century delight in freaks because they love individuality; but they do not enter, as Cervantes in his great mercy did, into that universal region of the human spirit where the imagination reigns like an ungovernable and fretful exile in a court of shadows.

The late Samuel Putnam translated *Don Quixote* and three of the *Exemplary Novels*. They were published in handsome volumes printed on a fine large page—a great advantage—and contain a critical account of many earlier translations and a very large collection of valuable notes; altogether a scholarly piece of work by an American amateur. He had translated a good deal of Brazilian literature. Mr Putnam believed *Don Quixote* to be one of the dying classics and thought an accurate and contemporary translation might revive it. Compared with Shelton, the abominated Motteux—the one guessed and the other added colour—with Ormsby, Jervas and even the Penguin done efficaciously (especially in the dialogue) by J. M. Cohen, Putnam's translation is toned down. This means that the fine shading of the irony of Cervantes becomes clear and Mr Putnam has taken great trouble with the difficult proverbs. A few contemporary colloquialisms, mainly American, surprise but do not seem out of place; there is often a mildness in Mr Putnam which leads him to choose a weak word or phrase where the Castilian is strong, terse and concrete; and in straining after accuracy he has missed sometimes the note of repartee or satirical echo in the conversations of Don Quixote and Sancho. In the scene at the inn with Maritornes and the muleteer, and in the chapter following, Motteux, Jervas and Cohen—to take only three—are superior in vigour to Mr Putnam, whose colloquial phrases have a citified smoothness from easy over-use. To give an example: Don Quixote is about to reveal that the daughter of the supposed Castilian had come to him in the night, but stops to make Sancho swear that he will tell no one about this until after the Knight is dead, for he will not allow anyone's honour to be damaged. Sancho replies, without tact, that he swears, but hopes that he will be free to reveal the secret tomorrow, on the grounds that: "It's just that I am opposed to keeping things too long—I don't like them to spoil on my hands."

Both Motteux and Cohen stick closer to the more vigorous original image. The Spanish word is "go mouldy" or even "rot," and not "spoil." Literally "go mouldy on me." In the earlier chapter one can catch Motteux adding direct, eighteenth-century animal coarseness where Cervantes is not coarse at all; in fact, *Don Quixote* is unique in picaresque literature in its virtual freedom from obscenity, except in some of the oaths. When Maritornes rushes to Sancho's bed to hide there from her angry master, Motteux writes:

> The wench ... fled for shelter to Sancho's sty, where he lay snoring to some tune; there she pigged in and lay snug as an egg.

This is picturesque, but it has arisen from the mistranslation of two words in the text. Possibly it is an improvement on Cervantes who wrote merely that "she went to Sancho's bed and curled up in a ball." Mr Putnam's pedantry spoils his accuracy here for, instead of "ball," he writes, "ball of yarn." The objection to Motteux is that in making Cervantes picturesque and giving him Saxon robustness, he endangers the elegance and the finely drawn out subtleties of the original. Motteux was half-way to Smollett, which is a long way from Cervantes. The picturesque and pungent in Cervantes lie wholly in Sancho's proverbs, where Mr Putnam excels. When Doña Rodriguez says that she can see "the advantage which a maiden duenna has over a widow, but he who clipped us kept the scissors," Sancho comes out strong and to the life:

> "For all of that," Sancho said, "when it comes to duennas there's so much to be clipped, according to what my barber tells me, that it would be better not to stir the rice even though it sticks."

Don Quixote begins as the description of a shy, timid, simple, eccentric provincial gentleman who, after the first clash with reality, develops an always growing complexity of mind that is the satisfying and diverting substance of the book. For as he goes deeper into delusion, so he is dogged by a dreadful doubt and self-knowledge. At the end, when Sancho returns home leading his master, with their roles reversed—for it is he, the realist, who has triumphed, having governed an island and having even rescued maidens in distress—Don Quixote is said to have failed in all, but to have known glory and to have won the supreme victory: victory over himself. The novel is a powerful example of the process of the growth of a work of art in a writer's mind, and of the luck of writing. For at the end of the first part, which Cervantes at one time regarded as the end of the book, one can see the idea in crisis and at the point of breaking down. Some critics have thought that the irrelevant stories stuffed into the end of the First Part show a fear that the reader will be bored by the colloquies of two characters only: and that he also wished to show that he was not a mere popular writer, but could write a polished, psychological short story in the best manner of the time. (He, indeed, succeeded in the story of Don Fernando and Dorothea and, in the latter, drew a delightful analytical portrait of cleverness in women.) But in the long interval between the two parts, the idea matured and became richer in fantasy, invention and intellectual body; the range of character became wider and success—so bitterly delayed in Cervantes's life—released confident powers that delight us because they delight in themselves. Not only does Don Quixote's own case branch into its full intricacy; not only are we now taken into all the casuistries of the imaginative life; by a master-stroke, Sancho is infected. The peasant gets his dream of material power, like some homely Trade Unionist, to put against the gentleman's dream of glory. Realism turns out to be as contagious to fantasy as idealism is. *Don Quixote* begins as a province, turns into Spain and ends as a universe, and far from becoming vaguer as it becomes more suggestive, it becomes earthier, more concrete, more certain in real speech and physical action. *Don Quixote* does not collapse, as the Second Part of Gogol's *Dead Souls* does, because Cervantes is not mad. He remains pragmatic, sceptical and merciful; whereas Gogol got the Russian Messianic bit between his teeth and went off his head. Spanish fantasy goes step by step with Spanish sanity. Nor, if we read *Don Quixote* truly, can it be described as a work of disillusion, if we mean by that the spiritual exhaustion which follows a great expense of spirit. The Spanish crack-up had begun, but it had only just begun. The force of that national passion was still felt. Though Cervantes was the broken soldier, though he was imprisoned, hauled before the Inquisition, and knew all the misery and confusion that the Spanish expansion abroad had left behind at home, he was not the enemy of the Spanish idea. He valued arms more than literature, as he explicitly said— incidentally in the character of Cardenio he drew an excellent portrait of a coward. What *Don Quixote* does is to enact the tragedy of experience as something still passionate though commingled with reflection: experience now more deeply felt. The comic spirit of the book is not satirical or tired, but is vital, fully engaged and positive. The wisdom runs with the events, not after them. It is stoical, not epicurean; sunlit, not eupeptic; civilised, not merely robust. *Don Quixote* bridges the gulf between two cultures, not by an inhuman cult of the people, but by excellence of intellect; by the passion a writer has for his means; by irony and love.

(1965)

LEO TOLSTOY

THE DESPOT

The life of Tolstoy is a novel that might have been written by Aksakov in its beginning, by Gogol in the middle and by Dostoevsky in the years following the conversion. He was not so much a man as a collection of double-men, each driven by enormous energy and, instinctively, to extremes. A difficulty for the biographer is that while we grin at the sardonic comedy of Tolstoy's contradictions and are stunned by his blind egotism, we are also likely to be infected by his exaltation: how is this exclamatory life to be brought to earth and to be distributed into its hours and days? And besides this there is the crucial Russian difficulty which the Russian novel revels in and which mystifies ourselves: there seems to be no such person as a Russian alone. Each one appears in a crowd of relations and friends, an extravagantly miscellaneous and declaiming tribal court. At Yasnaya Polyana the house was like an inn or caravanserai. There is the question of avoiding Tolstoy as a case or a collection of arguments. And the final affront to biography is the fact that Tolstoy exhaustively presented his life nakedly in his works.

One's first impression of Henri Troyat's remarkable Life is that we have read all this before and again and again, either in the novels or the family's inveterate diaries. So we have, but never with M. Troyat's management of all the intimacies in the wide range of Tolstoy's life. He was a man always physically on the move, even if it was only from room to room; even if it was simply gymnastic exercise, riding, hunting at Yasnaya Polyana. He is in Petersburg or Moscow, in the Caucasus, in Georgia, in Germany, England, France and Italy; and when he moves, his eyes are ceaselessly watching, his impulses are instantly acted on. His military career, his wild life, are packed with action and mind-searching. In sheer animality he outpaces everyone; in spirit and contradictions too. The amount of energetic complexity he could put into the normal search for a girl to marry outdoes anything that the most affectable sentimental novelist could conceive. Marriage, when it did come, was abnormal in its very domesticity. M. Troyat writes:

> Sonya was not sharing the destiny of one man but of ten or twenty, all sworn enemies of each other; aristocrat jealous of his prerogatives and people's friend in peasant garb; ardent Slavophil and Westernising pacifist; denouncer of private property and lord aggrandising his domains; hunter and protector of animals; hearty trencherman and vegetarian; peasant-style Orthodox believer and enraged demolisher of the church; artist and contemptuous scorner of art; sensualist and ascetic...

M. Troyat has managed to make this live with the glitter of the days on it. His book is a triumph of saturation. He has wisely absorbed many of Tolstoy's small descriptions of scene and incident and many of his phrases into the text. So when Tolstoy rushes off to one of his outrageous bullyings of his aunts in Moscow, we are at once back in a drawing room scene in *Resurrection*, and one can see M. Troyat going adroitly to the novels for exact moments of the life. He has learned the master's use of casual detail. He has learned his sense of mood and also of "shading" the characters. He does not lose an instance of the ironic and even the ridiculous in Tolstoy's behaviour, but—and this is of the utmost importance—he keeps in mind the tortured necessity of Tolstoy's pursuit of suffering, and his knowledge of his situation. The conscience of the prophet often performs farcical moral antics, but fundamentally its compulsions are tragic. One can be angered by Tolstoy's hypocrisies, but also know that they agonised Tolstoy himself.

A test for the biographer is the exposition of Tolstoy's great quarrels. They are so absurdly jealous that the temptation must be to leave them in their absurdity. M. Troyat does better than this. The row with Turgenev, the breach and the reconciliation years later when Turgenev had become a garrulous old man, has never been so well-placed and made to live, as in this book. The comedy of the reconciliation brings laughter and tears to the eyes. There Tolstoy sits at the family table making enormous Christian efforts to repress his undying jealousy of the elegant and clever man who enraptures the family. Tolstoy grunts while Turgenev shows the girls how one dances the cancan in Paris. It is a farce that contains the sadness of the parting of irreconcilables; even more than that, for Turgenev is a dying man and does not fear death. He is interested in his disease and is sure that death is the end of all. The still vigorous Tolstoy is terrified of death; his flesh demands immortality. The search for God was really a return to childhood, an attempt at rejuvenation, but in Tugenev, Tolstoy was faced by a man who lived by an opposite principle. At thirty-five Turgenev had hit upon the infuriating device of attaining serenity by declaring his life was over, and then living on as a scandal until his sixties. One is present at a country house scene in a heart-rending play by Chekhov, where the elders are tortured and the young people laugh.

The story of Tolstoy's marriage is one of the most painful stories in the world; it is made excruciating by the insane diary-keeping of the parties. They exchanged hatreds, crossed them out, added more; from the very beginning the habit of confession was disastrous and brutal. Like the Lawrences and the Carlyles, the Tolstoys were the professionals of marriage; they knew they were not in it for their good or happiness, that the relationship was an appointed ordeal, an obsession undertaken by dedicated heavyweights. Now one, now the other, is in the ascendant. There is almost only one genial moment, one in which the Countess conquered with a disarming shrewdness that put her husband at a loss. It occurs when the compromise about the copyrights is reached. The Countess decides she will publish her share of his works herself and consults Dostoevsky's widow, who has been very business-like in a similar undertaking. The two ladies meet enjoyably and profitably; the Countess is soon making a lot of money, she is happy—to Tolstoy's annoyance. The art he had denounced was, as if by a trick, avenging itself on his conscience. He was made to look foolish and hypocritical. And yet, after all, they were short of money and his wife had proved she was right.

If there had been no struggle for power between the couple—and on both sides the feeling for power was violent—if there had been no struggle between the woman who put her children and property first and the man who put his visions before either; if there had been no jealousy or cruelty, there was enough in the sexual abnormality of both parties to wreck their happiness. Even though mere happiness was their interest for only a short period of their lives. She hated sexual intercourse and was consoled by the thought that by yielding to his "maulings," she gained power; and he, whose notions of sexual love approached those of primitive rape, hated the act he could not resist. His sexuality tortured him. He hated any woman after he had slept with her. Conscious of being short and ugly, he was appalled that women were magnetised by him. Into this question—so alluring to psychologists—M. Troyat does not go very far; he simply puts down what is known and, of course, a great deal is known. It is an advantage, and in conformity with his method, that M. Troyat has not gone on the usual psychological search. He would far sooner follow Tolstoy in his daily life, tortured by lust or remorse, than dig into the unconscious. The fact is that

Tolstoy seems to have known something nearer to love in his devotion to his aunts and to one or two elusive and distinguished older women.

About the Works M. Troyat has many interesting things to say. Because he was many men Tolstoy was able to get into the skins of many men, and the Countess understood that he was most fulfilled and made whole by the diversion of his protean energies into imaginative writing. On that she is unassailable; even his messianic passion produced religious fables of great purity and beauty; and in *Resurrection*, the recognition of the moral integrity of the prostitute is a triumph of Tolstoy's psychological perspicuity in a novel that does not promise it. Tolstoy's fear of death had a superb imaginative expression in *The Death of Ivan Ilich*—but, it is to be noted, this was not written in one of the passionate phases of his life, but in a period of coldness that was almost cynical. M. Troyat has a sentence which describes Tolstoy's love of quarrelling and his promise to reform, but only for the pleasure of going back on his promise, a sort of moral slyness, which contains a comment on his nature as an artist:

> Impenitent old Narcissus, eternally preoccupied with himself, he blew on his image in the water, for the sheer pleasure of seeing it come back when the ripples died away.

It is at the rippling stage, when he has dissolved himself, that he is an artist. And, of course, very conscious of what he is doing. He is watchful as an animal that sees every surface movement, he builds his people from innumerable small details of things seen. A misplaced button may tell all. He "shades"—that is to say, he builds out of contradictory things: a cold dry character will be shown in a state of surprising emotion partly because this is true to nature, but also because that gives him an extra dimension that will surprise the reader. Tolstoy rewrites a scene again and again in order that the reader shall not know in the course of a conversation whose side he is on. He makes a great point of impartiality. Although *Anna Karenina* strikes the reader as a novel with a clear idea, set out in orderly manner and of miraculous transparency, the fact is that Tolstoy did not know what he was going to do when he started, and many times, in altered versions, changed the characters and the plot. He groped very much as Dostoevsky did, though not in a fog of suggestion, but rather among an immense collection of facts. The Countess and her daughters had to copy out many versions and the printers found on his pages a mass of rewriting which even Balzac cannot have equalled. One can see—and this is true of many artists—that the trivial idea from real life takes its final form only as the subject is finally assimilated to the self or experience of the author. He is edging towards a vicarious self-analysis.

It is fitting that this Life should have been done in Tolstoyan fashion with constant attention to the vivid and betraying surface. Not a single incident among the thousands of incidents fails in this respect. Yet the whole is not novelised. There is no imagined dialogue: it finds its place out of the immense documentation. The commentary is ironical, but a just sense of the passions involved is there: perhaps M. Troyat leans more to the side of the Countess but she is drawn as a woman, not as a cause, and we see her change, just as we see Tolstoy as an incalculable man. The complexity of the long final quarrel and the flight is made clear, and the narrative, at this dreadful point, is without hysteria. One can't forget such things as the old man sitting on a tree stump in the wood, secretly altering his will; or the Countess rushing out half-naked to pretend to drown herself in the pond. Then comes that awful train journey in the Third Class: the dim, inadequate figure of the worshipping doctor who went with Tolstoy; the whispers of the passengers who knew they had the great man with them; the bizarre scene at the station when the press arrived and were not allowed to take pictures of the station because it was illegal to photograph railway stations: the face of the demented Countess at the window as she looks at her dying husband to whom she is not allowed to speak—the whole scene is like the death of a modern Lear. As Isaiah Berlin wrote in *The Hedgehog and the Fox*, Tolstoy

died in agony, oppressed by the burden of his intellectual infallibility and his sense of perpetual moral error: the greatest of those who can neither reconcile, nor leave unreconciled, the conflict of what there is with what there ought to be.

(1979)

GABRIEL GARCÍA MÁRQUEZ

THE MYTH MAKERS

It has often been said of the Spanish nature and—by extension—of those who have inherited Iberian influences in South America, that the ego is apt to leap across middle ground and see itself as a universe. The leap is to an All. The generalisation itself skips a great deal too, but it is a help towards beginning to understand the astonishing richness of the South American novelists of recent years. Their "All"—and I think of Vargas Llosa and García Márquez among others—is fundamentally "the people," not in the clichés of political rhetoric, but in the sense of millions of separate lives, no longer anonymous but physically visible, awash in historical memory and with identities.

After reading *Leaf Storm*, the novella written by Gabriel García Márquez when he was only nineteen, but not published until 1955, one sees what a distance lies between this effort and his masterpiece *One Hundred Years of Solitude*. The young author sows the seed of a concern with memory, myth and the nature of time which bursts into lovely shameless blossom in his later book. We get our first glimpse of the forgotten town of Macondo (obviously near Cartagena), a primitive place, once a naïve colonial Eden; then blasted by the "leaf storm" of the invading foreign banana-companies, and finally a ghost town, its founders forgotten. Shut up in a room in one of its remaining family houses is an unpleasant doctor who "lives on grass"— a vegetarian?—whom the town hates because he once refused to treat some men wounded after a civil rising. Now, secluded for goodness knows how many years, he has hanged himself, and the question is whether the town will riot and refuse to have him buried. The thing to notice is that, like so many South American novelists, García Márquez was even then drawn to the inordinate character—not necessarily a giant or saga-like hero, but someone who has exercised a right to extreme conduct or aberration. Such people fulfil a new country's need for legends. A human being is required to be a myth, his spiritual value lies in the inflating of his tale.

Far better than *Leaf Storm* are some of the short stories in the new collection, and one above all: "The Handsomest Drowned Man in the World." The story is an exemplary guide to the art of García Márquez, for it is a celebration of the myth-making process. Somewhere on the seashore children are found playing with the body of a drowned man, burying it, digging it up again, burying it. Fishermen take the corpse to the village, and while the men go off to inquire about missing people, the women are left to prepare the body for burial. They scrape off the crust of little shells and stones and weed and mess and coral in which the body is wrapped and then they see the man within:

> They noticed that he bore his death with pride for he did not have the lonely look of other drowned men who came out of the sea or that haggard needy look of men who drowned in rivers . . . he was the tallest, strongest, most virile and best built man they had ever seen . . . They thought if that magnificent man had lived in the village, his house would have had the widest doors, the highest ceiling, and the strongest floor, his bedstead would have been made from a midship frame held together by iron bolts and his wife would have been the happiest woman. They thought he would have had so much authority he could have drawn fish out of the sea simply by calling their names.

The women imagine him in their houses; they see that because he is tall, the doors and ceilings of their houses would have to be higher and they tell him affectionately to "mind his head" and so on. The dead god has liberated so much fondness and wishing that when the body is at last formally buried at sea it is not weighed down by an anchor, for the women and the men too hope that the dead man will realise that he is welcome to come back at any time.

There is nothing arch or whimsical in the writing of this fable. The prose of García Márquez is plain, exact, subtle and springy and easily leaps into the comical and the exuberant, as we find in *One Hundred Years of Solitude*. In that book the history of the Buendía families and their women in three or four generations is written as a hearsay report on the growth of the little Colombian town; it comes to life because it is continuously leaping out of fact into the mythical and the myth is comic. One obvious analogy is with Rabelais. It is suggested, for example, that Aureliano Segundo's sexual orgies with his concubine are so enjoyable that his own livestock catch the fever. Animals and birds are unable to stand by and do nothing. The rancher's life is a grandiose scandal; the "bonecrusher" in bed is a heroic glutton who attracts "fabulous eaters" from all over the country. There is an eating duel with a lady known as "The Elephant." The duel lasted from a Saturday to a Tuesday, but it had its elegance:

> While Aureliano ate with great bites, overcome by the anxiety of victory, The Elephant was slicing her meat with the art of a surgeon and eating it unhurriedly and even with a certain pleasure. She was gigantic and sturdy, but over her colossal form a tenderness of femininity prevailed . . . later on when he saw her consume a side of veal without breaking a single rule of good table manners, he commented that this most delicate, fascinating and insatiable proboscidian was in a certain way the ideal woman.

The duel is beautifully described and with a dozen inventive touches, for once García Márquez gets going there is no controlling his fancy. But note the sign of the master: the story is always brought back to ordinary experience in the end. Aureliano was ready to eat to the death and indeed passes out. The scene has taken place at his concubine's house. He gasps out a request to be taken to his wife's house because he had promised not to die in his concubine's bed; and she, who knows how to behave, goes and shines up his patent leather boots that he had always planned to wear in his coffin. Fortunately he survives. It is very important to this often ruthless, licentious and primitive epic that there is a deep concern for propriety and manners.

As a fable or phantasmagoria *One Hundred Years of Solitude* succeeds because of its comic animality and its huge exaggerations which somehow are never gross and indeed add a certain delicacy. García Márquez seems to be sailing down the bloodstream of his people as they innocently build their town in the swamp, lose it in civil wars, go mad in the wild days of the American banana company and finally end up abandoned. The story is a social history but not as it is found in books but as it muddles its way forward or backward among the sins of family life and the accidents of trade. For example, one of the many Aurelianos has had the luck and intelligence to introduce ice to Macondo. To extend the ice business was impossible without getting the railroad in. This is how García Márquez introduces the railroad:

> Aureliano Centeno, overwhelmed by the abundance of the factory, had already begun to experiment in the production of ice with a base of fruit juices instead of water, and without knowing it or thinking about it, he conceived the essential fundamentals for the invention of sherbet. In that way he planned to diversify the production of an enterprise he considered his own, because his brother showed no signs of returning after the rains had passed and the whole summer had gone by with no news of him. At the start of another winter a woman who was washing

clothes in the river during the hottest time of the day ran screaming down the main street in an alarming state of commotion.

"It's coming," she finally explained. "Something frightful like a kitchen dragging a village behind it."

There are scores of rippling pages that catch the slippery comedies and tragedies of daily life, at the speed of life itself: the more entangled the subject the faster the pace. García Márquez is always ready to jump to extremes; it is not enough for a girl to invite two school friends to her family's house, she invites seventy horrible girls and the town has to be ransacked for seventy chamber pots. Crude or delicate an incident may be, but it is singular in the way ordinary things are. Almost every sentence is a surprise and the surprise is, in general, really an extension of our knowledge or feeling about life, and not simply a trick. Ursula, the grandmother of the Buendía tribe, the one stable character, is a repository of superstitious wisdom, i.e., superstition is a disguised psychological insight. In her old age, we see her revising her opinions, especially one about babies who "weep in the womb." She discusses this with her husband and he treats the idea as a joke. He says such children will become ventriloquists; she thinks that they will be prophets. But now, surveying the harsh career of her son who has grown up to be a proud and heartless fighter of civil wars, she says that "only the unloving" weep in the womb. And those who cannot love are in need of more compassion than others. An insight? Yes, but also it brings back dozens of those talks one has had in Spain (and indeed in South America) where people kill the night by pursuing the bizarre or the extreme by-ways of human motive.

In no derogatory sense, one can regard this rapid manner of talk—nonstop, dry and yet fantastical—as characteristic of café culture: lives pouring away in long bouts of chatter. In North America its characteristic form is the droll monologue; in South America the fantasy is—in my limited reading—more agile and imaginative, richer in laughter and, of course, especially happy in its love of the outrageous antics of sexual life.

One Hundred Years of Solitude denies interpretation. One could say that a little Arcady was created but was ruined by the "Promethean ideas" that came into the head of its daring founder. Or that little lost towns have their moment—as civilisations do—and are then obliterated. Perhaps the moral is, as García Márquez says, that "races condemned to one hundred years of solitude do not get a second chance on earth." The notion of "the wind passeth over it and it is gone" is rubbed in; so also is the notion Borges has used, of a hundred years or even infinite time being totally discernible in a single minute. But what García Márquez retrieves from the history he has surveyed is a Homeric laughter.

Life is ephemeral but dignified by fatality: the word "ephemeral" often crops up in *The Autumn of the Patriarch*, which has been well translated by Gregory Rabassa—the original would be beyond even those foreigners who read Spanish.

The Patriarch who gives the novel its moral theme is the elusive despot of a South American republic and we hear him in the scattered voices of his people and his own. As a young wild bull he is the traditional barefoot peasant leader; later he is the confident monster ruthlessly collecting the spoils of power, indifferent to murder and massacre, sustained by his simple peasant mother, surviving by cunning. Still later, in old age, he is a puppet manipulated by the succeeding juntas, who are selling off the country to exploiters, a Caliban cornered but tragic, with a terrifying primitive will to survive. His unnamed republic looks out on the Caribbean from a barren coast from which the sea has receded, so that he believes, as superstitiously as his people do, that foreigners have even stolen the sea.

By the time the novel opens he is a myth to his people. Those who think they have seen him have probably seen only his double, though they may have glimpsed his hand waving from a limousine. He himself lives among the remnants of his concubines and the lepers and beggars that infest the Presidential fort. His mother is dead. He stamps round on his huge feet and is mainly concerned with milking his cows in the dairy attached to his mansion. Power is in the hands of an untrusted Minister. The President no longer leaves the place but drowses as he reads of speeches he has never made, celebrations he has never attended, applause he has never heard, in the newspaper of which only one copy is printed and solely for himself. He is, in short, an untruth; a myth in the public mind, a dangerous animal decaying in "the solitary vice" of despotic power, fearing one more attempt at assassination and, above all, the ultimate solitude of death.

At first sight the book is a capricious mosaic of multiple narrators. We slide from voice to voice in the narrative without warning, in the course of the long streaming sentences of consciousness. But the visual, animal realism is violent and forever changing: we are swept from still moments of domestic fact to vivid fantasy, back and forth in time from, say, the arrival of the first Dutch discoverers to the old man looking at television, in the drift of hearsay and memory.

The few settled characters are like unforgettable news flashes that disturb and disappear: the richness of the novel will not be grasped in a single reading. We can complain that it does not progress but returns upon itself in widening circles. The complaint is pointless: the spell lies in the immediate force of its language and the density of narrative. We can be lost in those interminable sentences and yet once one has got the hang of the transitions from one person to the next it is all as sharp as the passing moment because García Márquez is the master weaver of the real and the conjectured. His descriptive power astounds at once, in the first forty pages where the narrator is a naïve undefined "we," i.e., the people. They break into the fortress of the tragic monster and find their Caliban dead among the cows that have long ago broken out of the dairy and graze off the carpets in the salons of the ruined Presidencia and even have appeared, lowing like speakers, on the balconies. This is from the opening scene:

> When the first vultures began to arrive, rising up from where they had dozed on the cornices of the charity hospital, they came from farther inland, they came in successive waves, out of the horizon of the sea of dust where the sea had been, for a whole day they flew in slow circles of the house of power until a king with bridal feathers and a crimson ruff gave a silent order and that breaking of glass began, that breeze of a great man dead, that in and out of vultures through the windows imaginable only in a house which lacked authority, so we dared go in too and in the deserted sanctuary we found the rubble of grandeur, the body that had been pecked at, the smooth maiden hands with the ring of power on the bone of the third finger, and his whole body was sprouting tiny lichens and parasitic animals from the depths of the sea, especially in the armpits and the groin, and he had the canvas truss of his herniated testicle which was the only thing that had escaped the vultures in spite of its being the size of an ox kidney; but even then we did not dare believe in his death because it was the second time he had been found in that office, alone and dressed and dead seemingly of natural causes during his sleep, as had been announced a long time ago in the prophetic waters of soothsayers' basins.

Only his double had been able to show him his "untruth": that useful ignoramus died of poison intended for his master. There had been a period when the President really was of the people, the easy joker who might easily get an upland bridegroom murdered so that he himself could possess the bride. The dictator's peasant mother who carried on in his mansion, sitting at her sewing machine as if she were still in her hut, was the only one aware of his tragedy. (Once when he was driving to a ceremonial parade she rushed after him with a basket of empties telling him to drop them at the shop when he passed. The violent book has many homely touches.) His brutal sexual assaults are not resented—he fucks with his boots and uniform on—but when very late he comes to feel love, he is at a loss. On a Beauty Queen of the slum called the Dog District, he pours gadgets and imported rubbish, even turns the neighbourhood into a smart suburb: she is immovable and he is almost mad.

He kidnaps a Jamaican novice nun and marries her, but two years pass before he dares go to bed with her. She spends her time bargaining for cheap toys in the market. She surrenders to him not out of love but out of pity and teaches him to read and sign his name. The market people hate her trading habits and her fox furs and set dogs on her and her children: they are torn to pieces and eaten. There is a frightful scene where his supposedly loyal Minister organises an insurrection. The old man's animal instinct detects a plot in the conspiracy. The Minister warns him: "So things are in no shape for licking your fingers, general Sir, now we really are fucked up." The wily President won't budge but sends down a cartload of milk for the rebels and when the orderly uncorks the first barrel there is a roar and they see the man

> floating on the ephemeral backwash of a dazzling explosion and they saw nothing else until the end of time in the volcanic heat of the mournful yellow mortar building in which no flower ever grew, whose ruins remained suspended in the air from the tremendous explosion of six barrels of dynamite. That's that, he sighed in the Presidential palace, shaken by the seismic wind that blew down four more houses around the barracks and broke the wedding crystal in cupboards all the way to the outskirts of the city.

The President turns to his dominoes and when he sees the double five turn up, he guesses that the traitor behind the rebellion is his old friend of a lifetime, the Minister. He is invited to a banquet and, at the stroke of twelve, "the distinguished Mayor General Roderigo de Aguilar entered on a silver tray, stretched out, garnished with cauliflower and laurel, steeped with spices and oven brown—and, in all his medals, is served up roast." The guests are forced to eat him.

García Márquez is the master of a spoken prose that passes unmoved from scenes of animal disgust and horror to the lyrical evocation, opening up vistas of imagined or real sights which may be gentle or barbarous. The portrait of the mother who eventually dies of a terrible cancer is extraordinary. He has tried to get the Papal Nuncio to canonise her and, when Rome refuses, the President makes her a civil saint and has her embalmed body carried round the country. Avidly the people make up miracles for her. Once more, in his extreme old age and feeble, there is another insurrection, plotted by a smooth aristocratic adviser. The President survives. In his last night alive he wanders round the ruined house, counting his cows, searching for lost ones in rooms and closets; and he has learned that because of his incapacity for love he has tried to "compensate for that infamous fate with the burning cultivation of the solitary vice of power" which is a fiction. "We (the multiple narrator concludes less tritely) knew who we were while he was left never knowing it for ever..." The "All" is not an extent, it is a depth.

(1979)

S. J. PERELMAN

THE CON-MAN'S SHADOW

Humorists have a hard life. As a matter of habit the reader comes round to saying, "I don't think he's funny any more," the point being that life is so unfunny that the pace gets hotter with every joke. There is the inborn feeling that the humorist is a temporary fellow. A jester must not be allowed to approach the norm. He has to divert you from the intolerable or make you digest it. The difficulty is that while stomach-ache becomes funnier the worse it gets, the stomach-ache genre becomes standardised. In her introduction to The *Most of S. J. Perelman* Dorothy Parker says of humorists in general that they find a little formula and "milk it till it moos with pain." Her list is rather more American than European: "the tyrannical offspring, the illiterate business associate (American), the whooping devil-may-care spinster, the man trying to do a bit of carpentry and the virtuous criticisms of the little wife, mainly European." The virtuous wife in America is outsize: she arrives home grandiose, in mink, to take hell out of the husband who has burned the dinner. As S. J. Perelman, or rather his stand-in Prebbleman, remarks of his Xanthippe, she has the classical, martyred look of someone who would be "a wow as St Joan at a Little Theatre."

The one or two English humorists I have met have been sad men, anxious of eye, hag-ridden by efficiency of mind, mechanically ulcerated and teetering on the edge of religious conversion or the hospital. Their writings have usually contradicted this impression. The English thin man has a fat man inside him, a creature dilatory, sedentary and nourishing his joke, often over-nourishing it. Our humorists have mostly been juicy men dwelling in the belly of society; or, if this was not possible for them, have become mad cherubs like Carroll or Lear. The one general characteristic of the English humorists, good or bad, is that they are at home, dreaming private follies or shut up under lock and key in the attic, but still in the family. There is a profound satisfaction in the perils of the public face. Even if the family rejects, the pubs and clubs accept. The clubs, alas, in the older generation, have been a disaster for English humour; there it falls into persiflage. The best Americans escape this. Homelessness and the nomadic—as Miss Constance Rourke instructed us in her classic work on *American Humour*— are basic to the American tradition. So is overstatement, that Elizabethan gift which we carelessly exported lock, stock and barrel to America. So is the monologue which has been left, by us, to the Irish—see Beckett and Joyce. Our humorists—even Saki and Anstey—have had good digestions, the joke with them being that they knew that they bloody well *had* to digest what was given to them and put a peculiar face on it. Less subjected to the pressures of a dense society, Americans have had the freedom to send up howls of enjoyable pain at the raw muck set before them and instead of being digressive they have put a poker face on their duodenums. The elongated joke has been important to both traditions, but this has worked to the advantage of the American humorist who relies so much on monologue; the European cult of conversation may inspire refinement in comedy but is likely to comb all the nits out of the hair. The American monologue leaves the nits in. It can also dip into myth and, to be endurable, this has to be enlivened by image and pungency of language. In England, since the decline of the joke of middle-class periphrasis, we are only just beginning to explore exaggeration again; and at the very moment when American humour shows some signs of becoming middle-class, the sick joke being fundamentally suburban.

The huge advantage of American humour, as one sees it in S. J. Perelman, is in the punishment of character and the use of language. Unlike Thurber who has been much admired by us, Perelman is not an understater who suddenly throws out an almost spiritual blossom. He drops ash into the dessert. Perelman either grew up with burlesque or soon got caught up in it. Immediate action is his need. An idea has to seize him. His very best things have come out of grotesque experiences in Hollywood; or when, not having enough time to read Palgrave's *Golden Treasury*, he has had to feed on the advertising columns of glossy papers. One gets the impression that English humorists snub the commercials, whereas an American like Perelman regards them as part of the general awful meal that makes us what we don't want other people to be. Having acquired a stomach of zinc, he knows it's his duty to swallow the poison, like someone who feels it a duty to see what cyanide does to the system. As a character, he is a harassed detective, stuck in some lobby, chain-smoking, pedantic, always in disguise, with the air of one about to follow footprints and tracking something down. He is Groucho

Marx's more sensitive alter ego, the con-man's shadow. What one owes to the other, apart from cigars, may be conjectured from Groucho's letters—especially those to Kurnitz—which are very funny about Hollywood. The T. S. Eliot letters suffer, on both sides, from the paralysis which occurs when a highest common factor meets a lowest common denominator and both are awed. On the evidence, Perelman's life has been passed in film studios, dressing rooms, cigar stores, hotels, tailor's, barber's, steak grottoes and in bad journeys on inferior shipping lines to the phoney Orient. He will be caught —trying to hide behind *Time* or *Harper's Bazaar*—by acquaintances with names like Spontoon, Henbane, Follansbee and Crump who, spotting his lonely but springy figure, have treated him like flypaper and have buzzed in an ear made for higher things. He has been the sort of man who having, for the moment, to identify himself with a No. 1 Stripteaseuse who has married a young Maharajah, can say that "although she had little need of paper work in her line of business," she is obliged to be "the only ecdysiast on record with a Zoroastrian amanuensis." The phrase is her agent's. She breaks it down into the following:

> A skinny little man with a big bugle on which one flange has a diamond the size of your pinkie welded into it. He has a shift embroidered with rubies and around his neck five strands of pearls like Mary Garden or Schumann-Heink in the Victor Book of Opera.

Flustered by the pass he makes at her after this aesthetic impression, she asks what about his family in Cawnpore. "Don't you," she asks, "have any wives?" It is at the centre of this tradition of American humour to build up a rococo fantasy and then slap its face with a wet towel. Mr Perelman has that art. Many a gorgeous balloon goes "pop" at the touch of his cigar tip. Occasionally, under the name of Prebbleman, he is at home, usually minding something in the oven and waiting for his Joan of Arc to come back, rather late, in something new and blinding, and full of complaint. He defends himself: "I haven't the faintest clue to what you're foompheting about." Wherever else he may fail it is not in adding a valuable word to the gag book. And he is soon off to a sentimental reunion of the old alumni of Dropsical High. There the old folk are "acquiring a skinful" wearing paper hats, clutching phials of adrenalin, nitroglycerin and other restoratives.

Again the puncturing anticlimax: "I give them a wide berth because they may topple on to me during a seizure and wrinkle my suit." The noise is deafening. In it one hears "the clash of bridge work and the drum fire crackle of arteries snapping like pipe stems"; the chief speaker, recovering from his third stroke, has a voice that "ripples from his tongue as if strained across an entire creek of gravel."

Perelman's speciality, like O. Henry's and Mark Twain's, is Fraud. He looks at the landscape and it is gashed and bill-boarded with the poetic news that here someone made a killing and cleared out quickly. The inner life of a grey Puritan culture is dramatic, gaudy and violent; fraud, in the sense of the double-think, double appearance or fact and the image that palms them off, is basic. The tall story, wearisome in Europe, so that a Münchausen is a bore and a meaningless liar who wastes your time, has a more nourishing role in the American tradition. Fantasy—in English comics—has a different part to play. The distinction is suggested by comparing the extravagances of, say, Dickens with those of the O. Henry, Twain and Perelman school. The speeches of Mrs Gamp or Mr Pecksniff are, in essence, soliloquies that fountain out of their inner lives. They tell us less about the scene in which they live than about the privacies of their minds and of their history. The flights of a Carroll, a Lear, a Beerbohm, an Anstey or a Wodehouse reject the oppressive scene around them and assert the rights of private vision in a culture which has generally been obsessed—as John Stuart Mill said— with the necessity of a social discipline. The exaggerations of the American humorists have a different impulse. If you look at their greedy use of the grotesque, you see that they are guzzling impedimenta and nameable products. You hardly see the people there but you see American paraphernalia; their metaphors take you on to the joints or to what is happening semi-legally on the sidewalk. Chicken Inspector No. 23 Perelman of the Fraud Squad surveys the field of conspicuous waste, the biggest fraud of the lot, with a buyer's hypnotised eye. He is the un-innocent abroad; at his best in the subjects of showbiz, he is a tangy raconteur, though I find him less speedy when he turns his idea into a script with dialogue. This is odd since he has been one of the finest script writers in the funny business; indeed, remembering the Marx Brothers, a genius. He is above all a voice, a brisk and cigary voice, that keeps up with his feet as he scampers, head-down, upon the trail; in his own words "button-cute, rapier-keen and pauper poor" and having "one of those rare mouths in which butter has never melted." He has a nose for non-news. For a long time the English humorists have suffered from having achieved the funny man's dream; they have either gone straight for the information or have succumbed to the prosaic beauty of their own utterance. They are "facetious" without being Boswell. Mr Perelman is not entirely free of the English vice. I have caught him adding an unnecessary "I said with hauteur" or "I said with dignity." This weakness he may have picked up on his annual visits to those fake cathedral closes of ours in Savile Row. (The metaphor is his.) But he does not wear thin. There are four or five narky things in the present book which are as good as anything in *Crazy Like a Fox.*

(1985)

SAUL BELLOW

JUMBOS

Saul Bellow has the most effusive intelligence of living American novelists. Even when he is only clever he has a kind of spirited intellectual vanity that enables him to take on all the facts and theories about the pathetic and comically exposed condition of civilised man and distribute them like high-class corn so that the chickens come running to them. That is the art of the novelist who can't resist an idea: to evoke, attract that "pleasing, anxious being," the squawking, dusty, feverish human chicken. Aldous Huxley could always throw the corn but nothing alive came fluttering to it.

But immensely clever novelists have to beware of self-dispersal when they run to great length. I enjoy Saul Bellow in his spreading carnivals and wonder at his energy, but I still think he is finer in his shorter works. *The Victim* was the best novel to come out of America—or England—for a decade. *The Dangling Man* is good, but subdued; *Seize the Day* is a small grey masterpiece. If one cuts out the end, *Henderson the Rain King* is at once profound and richly diverting in its fantasy. These novels had form; their economy drove their point home.

By brevity Bellow enhanced our experience. And, to a European reader—though this may be irrelevant—he seems the only American of this generation to convey the feel and detail of urban America, preserving especially what is going on at the times when nothing is going on: the distinctive native ennui, which is the basic nutrient of any national life.

It is when he turns to longer books, chasing the mirage of "the great American novel," that Bellow weakens as he becomes a traveller, spreading the news and depending on the presence of a character who is something like a human hold-all, less a recognisable individual than a fantastic piece of bursting luggage. His labels, where he has been, whom he has met in his collision with America are more suggestive than his banal personal story. In *Herzog,* the hero or rather the grandiose victim, is a gifted Jewish professor and polymath with a rather solemn pretension to sexual prowess. He seems a promising exemplar of the human being exposed to everything without the support of a settled society or fixed points of belief or value. This theme has offered the American novelist a chance to show his vitality for a long time now and the Jewish novelists have done strikingly well with it, for as a group they have acutely felt the sense of a missing law or covenant.

What has happened to Moses Herzog, this restless dabbler in the ideas of four centuries? He is having a breakdown because his second wife has destroyed his sexual confidence. He sees himself—and Mr Bellow sees him—prancing through one marriage and several liaisons with success and then marrying the all-time bitch; exhibitionist, hysteric, looter of his brain, spender of his money, far-seeing in matters of law and property, adulterous, glamorously second-rate but adroit with the castrating scissors. To add insult, not to mention symbolism, to injury, the man she goes off with is a one-legged radio phoney. The ruthless and learned Moses, a walking university, begins to look like a Jumboburger who has been told he has lost his mustard. His earlier women may say "Serve him right," but neither they nor the reader are likely to think his sufferings of much importance when, in a ham ending, he solemnly shacks up with a tremendously international woman called Ramona—of all names—who is apt to come swaggering out of the bathroom with her hand on her hip like a dagger-carrying flamenco dancer, and wearing black frilly panties with saucy ribbons. Twice during the novel she clinches the entire deal by serving the gourmet the only dish, apparently, she knows how to cook: Shrimp Arnaud, washed down with a bottle of Pouilly Fuissé. His earlier ladies must have thought they had paid a high price. Why didn't they think of applying this particular nostrum to the exposed soul of modern man? One knows that the fantasy life of university professors is often surprisingly gaudy, that the minds of experts on seventeenth-century thought or the *condition humaine* often drift off to Hollywood in the evenings. If this is Mr Bellow's ironical realism it certainly describes the feeble state of contemporary erotic fancy: but I detect no irony. Yet irony and self-irony are usually Mr Bellow's strength. What is more, the one or two love affairs in the book suggest that Moses is looking for easily punishable women without his or Mr Bellow's knowing it. In a moment of insight Moses wonders if his obsession with sex and love isn't really feminine. The reader is likely to go further and ask whether Moses is not hermaphrodite.

Structurally and in content, the story of *Herzog* is unsustaining. But what

Herzog sees, the accidental detail of his experience, is very impressive. Here he grows. He really has got a mind and it is hurt. It is a tribute to Mr Bellow's reserves of talent that the novel survives and over-grows its own weaknesses. The muddle Moses is in, his sense of victimisation, are valuable. His paranoia is put, by Mr Bellow, to excellent use. If the theme is lost, we have the American scene. Moses is not really exposed, but his New York and Chicago are. Mr Bellow has something like a genius for place. There is not a descriptive insinuator of what, say, a city like New York is like from minute to minute who comes anywhere near him. Some novelists stage it, others document it; he is breathing in it. He knows how to show us not only Moses but other people, moving from street to street, from room to room in their own circle of uncomprehending solitude. Grasping this essential of life in a big city he sees the place not as a confronted whole, but continually askance. His senses are especially alive to *things* and he catches the sensation that the *things* have created the people or permeated them. This was the achievement of *The Victim*, and it is repeated in *Herzog*. A wanderer, he succeeds with minor characters, the many small figures in the crowd who suggest millions more. The dialogue of a Puerto Rican taxi driver, a Chicago cop, a low lawyer, a Jewish family, people brash, shady or saddened by the need of survival and whose ripeness comes out of the dirty brick that has trapped them, is really wonderful. It is far superior to Hemingway's stylised naturalism: Bellow's talk carries the speakers' life along with it. Their talk makes them move. They involve Moses with themselves and show him living, as all human beings do, in a web spun by others as well as by himself.

The habit of seeing things askance or out of the corner of his eye has given Mr Bellow an even more important quality: it keeps alive a perpetual sense of comedy and feeds his originality. There is sometimes talk of a taste for elegance in his book; spoken of like that, as a sort of craving or innate possession, it sounds very nearly vulgar. But there is an implicit elegance of mind in his writing: it sharpens the comic edge and dares him to spirited invention. As far as the comedy is concerned it has all the fatality of Jewish comedy, that special comedy of human undress and nakedness of which the Jewish writers are the world's masters. The other gift of Mr Bellow is his power of fantastic invention. He has hit upon a wonderful device for conveying Herzog's nervous breakdown. How to deal with his paranoia—if that is what it is—how to make it contribute not only to the character of Herzog but also to the purpose of the book? Mr Bellow decides that Herzog's dottiness shall consist in writing unfinished letters to all kinds of people living and dead, known and unknown—to his women friends, to editors, tutors, professors, philosophers, to his dead mother, to the President. It is the habit of the mad and Moses is not mad; but he at once is comically and seriously disturbed by every kind of question. Is romanticism "split religion"? "Do the visions of genius become the canned goods of intellectuals?" He writes to Eisenhower asking him "to make it all clear in a few words." He begins addressing M. de Jouvenal about the aims of political philosophy. The letters are really the scribbles of an exhausted mind. Travelling in the subway Moses evokes the dream figure of a Dr Shrödinger at Times Square:

> It has been suggested (and why not) that reluctance to cause pain is actually an extreme form, a delicious form of sensuality, and that we increase the luxuries of pain by the injection of a moral pathos. Thus working both sides of the street. Nevertheless, there are moral realities, Herzog assured the entire world as he held his strap in the speeding car.

Since Moses is a man of intellect these addresses are often interesting in themselves; but chiefly they convey the dejected larking of a mind that has been tried by two contradictory forces: the breakdown of the public world we live in and the mess of private life. In which world does he live? He is absurd yet he is fine; he is conceited yet he is raw. He is a great man yet he is torpedoed by a woman who "wants to live in the delirious professions"— trades in which the main instrument is your opinion of yourself and the raw material is your reputation or standing. At times he lives like a sort of high-class Leopold Bloom, the eternal Jewish clown; at others he is a Teufelsdröckh; again he is the pushing son of the bewildered Polish-Jewish immigrant and failed boot-legger, guilty about his break with the past, nagged by his relations, his ambitions punctured.

As a character Moses is physically exact—we know his domestic habits—but mentally and emotionally amorphous. Any objection to this is cancelled by his range as an observer-victim. It is a triumph that he is not a bore and does not ask our sympathy.

The outsize heroes of Bellow's long novels are essentially moral types who have been forced by the American scene to behave like clowns. They are the classic American monologue in person, elephantine chunks of ego. In *Humboldt's Gift* we meet the clown as performing poet:

> A wonderful talker, a hectic non-stop monologist and improvisator, a champion detractor: to be loused up by Humboldt was really a kind of privilege. It was like being the subject of a two-nosed portrait by Picasso or an eviscerated chicken by Soutine ...

One recognises the voice at once: it has the dash, the dandyism, the easy control of side-slipping metaphor and culture-freaking which gives pace to

Saul Bellow's comedies. He is above all a performer, and in *Humboldt's Gift* he tells the story of performance in the person of Citrine, Humboldt's worshipper, disciple and betrayer.

As a youth Citrine had kneeled before the great manic depressive who had passed the peak of his reputation and was left, gin bottle in hand, cursing American materialism for what it does to genius and the life of the imagination. Humboldt was shrewd enough to see that the young Citrine was on the make, but was glad to have an ally among the young: everything went well, in a general alcoholic way, until Citrine did a frightful thing: he wrote a Broadway success which made him a sudden fortune. He had gone straight to the top of the tree. This was more than the crumbling, middle-aged poet could bear: he did not mind that Citrine had portrayed him as a knockabout Bohemian character; what he resented was the money going into Citrine's pocket. By this time Humboldt has become the classic American drunken genius and hospital case who shows up American philistinism. Getting out of Bellevue, Humboldt has a delightful time with the psychiatrists:

> Even the shrewd Humboldt knew what he was worth in professional New York. Endless conveyor belts of sickness or litigation poured clients and patients into these midtown offices like dreary Long Island potatoes. These dull spuds crushed psychoanalysts' hearts with boring character problems. Then suddenly Humboldt arrived. Oh Humboldt! He was no potato! He was papaya, a citron, a passion fruit ... And what a repertory he had, what changes of style and tempo. He was meek at first—shy. Then he became child-like, trusting, then he confided ... He said he knew what husbands and wives said when they quarrelled ... People said ho-hum and looked at the ceiling when you started this. Americans! With their stupid ideas about love and their domestic tragedies. How could you bear to listen to them after the worst of wars and the most sweeping of revolutions, the destruction, the death camps, the earth soaked in blood ... The world looked into American faces and said: "Don't tell me these cheerful, well-to-do people are suffering ... Anyway I'm not here to discuss adolescent American love-myths"—this was how Humboldt talked. Still, I'd like you to listen to this.

And, suddenly blazing up, he howled out all the melodramas of American scandal and lust. The lawyers had heard it a thousand times—but they wanted to hear it again from a man of genius. He had become what the respectable professionals long for—their pornographer.

As admirers of Saul Bellow's work know, he is a master of elaborately patterned narrative that slips back or forward in time, circulating like Sterne, like Proust even. Sterne did this because he loved human inertia:

Bellow is out for every tremor of the over-electrified American ego: he is expert in making characters disappear and then reappear swollen and with palms itching for more and more instant life. Humboldt will die in an elevator, but he will haunt the novel to the end like Moby Dick: even contemporary ghosts are jumbo size. The story moves to Chicago and there, on native ground, Citrine fills out. He is Cleverness and Success in person:

> It was my turn to be famous and to make money, to get heavy mail, to be recognised by influential people, to be dined at Sardi's and propositioned in padded booths by women who sprayed themselves with musk, to buy Sea Island cotton underpants and leather luggage.

His troubles with the tax man, with his ex-wife's lawyers who are stripping him of everything they can get hold of, seem to excite rather than depress him. His sexual life is avid and panicky: he hopes to outsmart middle age. He has bouts of hypochondria. These are enjoyable because he is very frank about his vanity: his touchiness, as middle age comes on, is the making of him as a comic figure. Gleam as he may with success, he cherishes what his wife calls his "cemetery bit"; he has a bent for being a victim: ironical and sentimental, he also knows he is as hardheaded as that other famous twelve-year-old charmer, David Copperfield.

Once Humboldt is dead, Citrine is without a necessary enemy, and here Mr Bellow makes a very interesting find: Rinaldo Cantabile, a small crook with the naïve notion that he can "make" the top Mafia. Unlike Humboldt, there is nothing myth-attracting in Cantabile. He is a loud, smart, nasty smell; he understands the first lesson of gangsterdom: to humiliate your victim; but he is an ass. We remember that Citrine is out to explore the American love-hate of Culture and Genius and indeed takes us round colleges and foundations: Cantabile is introduced to suggest that the Mafia might get a foot in here. Cantabile even thinks he can terrorise Citrine into seeing that Cantabile's wife gets a Ph.D. by fraud. My own view is that he does not make the grade as a compelling menace: he is without the extra dimension given to Bellow's strongly felt characters.

However, good comes of Cantabile, for he gets Mr Bellow back to Chicago. That city is the hero of *Humboldt's Gift*. No American novelist surpasses Bellow in the urban scene. He knows Chicago intimately from the smell of old blood in the hot nights to the rust on its fire escapes and the aluminium glint of the Lake. He knows the saunas:

> the wooden posts were slowly consumed by a wonderful decay that made them soft brown. They looked like beavers' fur in the golden vapour ... The Division Street steam-bathers don't look like the trim proud people downtown ... They

are vast in antique form. They stand on thick pillow legs affected with a sort of creeping verdigris or blue-cheese mottling of the ankles ... you feel these people are almost conscious of obsolescence, of a time of civilisation abandoned by nature and culture. So down in the super-heated sub cellars all these Slavonic cavemen and wood demons with hanging laps of fat and legs of stone and lichen boil themselves and splash ice-water on their heads by the bucket. Upstairs, on the television screen in the locker room, dudes and grinning broads make smart talk or leap up and down ... Below, Franush, the attendant, makes steam by sloshing water on the white-hot boulders.

The secret of Mr Bellow's success is that he talks people into life and never stops pouring them in and out of his scenes. In this book the women are particularly well-drawn. Citrine's sexual vanity is a help here: once satisfied, he is taken aback by the discovery that women have other interests—the delightful delinquent Demmie is reformed, but in sleep at night her buried life comes out in groans and howls as she wrestles with the devil, and she wakes up next day fresh as a daisy to get down on her knees for redemption by scrubbing floors. Denise is the climbing wife of the climbing man. Vassar girl, seductive and respectable—what more does she want? The ear of top people at the White House; she wants to tell them what she has just read in *Newsweek!* And then Renata—a fate for more than one Bellow hero—Spanishy, flamenco-ish, vulgar, genial, sexually voracious, knows her Ritzes, and while willing to listen to high-class intellectual talk for a while, makes it clear that her price is very high and her fidelity at perpetual risk. These women are real, even likeable. Why? I think because in some clever way Mr Bellow shows them moving through their own peculiar American day, which is unlike the day of Citrine. One might press the point further and say that Bellow's characters are real to us because they are physical objects— Things. What other tenderness can a materialist society contain?

It says a great deal for Bellow's gift that although he can raise very boring subjects and drop names like an encyclopaedia or a digest, he has tact and irony. He is crisp. But two-thirds of the way through this novel he lands himself with a tangle of dramatic situations as complex as, say, the last act of a Restoration comedy. Here he lost me. Humboldt—it turns out—had repented of calling Citrine a Judas and traitor; had even left him a money-making film script—put into the hands of the right phoney director it should make a fortune. It does. Citrine does not take the money, indeed he behaves so well that it looks as though in saving his soul from corruption he may lose Renata. One curious act he does perform: he has Humboldt and his mother disinterred and re-buried in a decent cemetery. That's one thing you can do for artists.

(1980)

GERALD BRENAN

THE SAYINGS OF DON GERALDO

There is a moment in the old age of a writer when he finds the prospect of one more long haul in prose intimidating and when he claims the right to make utterances. We grow tired of seeing our experience choked by the vegetation in our sentences. We opt for the pithy, the personal, and the unapologetic. For years we have had a crowd of random thoughts waiting on our doorstep, orphans or foundlings of the mind that we have not adopted; the moment of the aphorism, the epigram, the clinching quotation has come. So, in his eighties, Gerald Brenan has sat in his Spanish house, ignoring the fame that has gathered around him as the unique interpreter of Spanish history, politics, and literature, his energetic past as a sort of scholar-gypsy in Europe, Morocco, his previous hopes as a poet and novelist, and his interest as a confessional biographer, and has set about polishing his *pensées* in this miscellany which he has called dismissively *Thoughts in a Dry Season*. ("Dry" is the wrong word: the juices are very active in him.)

Brenan has always been a man of vast reading in many languages, interested in everything from religion, politics, literature, men, women, animals, down to flowers, trees, birds, and insects: he has lived for inquiry and discovery. Although he left school young and is innocent of the university, he cannot be called an autodidact. Greek and Latin came easily to him, he is not a dogmatic "knower" but, as he says, a "learner," and he has had the advantage of rarely having reviewed a book or given a lecture. A Chair has not allured him. None of his sayings is therefore a regurgitation. He confesses to having kept a commonplace book earlier in his life, but he did not keep it up. His only regret is that the exigencies of modern publishing have made him cut out his longer reflections on history, philosophy, politics, and the phases of the revolution we are now passing through and which have been his passionate preoccupation since, I suppose, the Spanish Civil War.

Since Brenan, or Don Geraldo as the Spaniards call him, has been my closest friend for the last forty years, I cannot look at the present volume with detachment. I have sat by his blazing wood fire in his Spanish house listening to him talk this book into existence. I see and hear him rather than read it. The tall man whose glasses flash as if he were sending out signals, as he slippers about the room talking fast and softly while he looks above my head into a vast distance, or looks down suddenly as if puzzled by my existence, pops up between the lines of the printed page.

He is an egoist, a performer, who invites one into the upper air of his fantasies and insights. He is one of those excited conversationalists who at once define and transform the people, places, and ideas that have set them off. If he is an encyclopaedia, it is an encyclopaedia that has wings. He will punctuate his talk with the most elegant of smoker's coughs and the most enticing of suggestions or gossipy innuendo. I have often wished I could transcribe his manner of conversation, his sudden darts into some preposterous item of sexual news, his pleasant malice, the jokes that enliven the quirks of learning and his powers of generalisation, but the thing escapes me. But now, in the epigrams and discursive entries in this book, I hear his voice.

How does Brenan talk, what is his manner? Here it all is. This is Brenan, any day, on his terrace or by the fire or talking his way up Spanish paths, passing from village to village, switching, for example, from the idea that no village loves the next village, but only the next village but one, and that this may have its roots in Arab habit, to expounding on the cultivation of plants, the habits of birds, the moral and social influences of architecture, the problems of abstract art, T. S. Eliot's deficiency in historical sense, the nature of pretty girls, the ups and downs of sexual life, the phases of marriage, the patterns of theology, the difference between the nature of the poet and the prose writer, the differing formalities of the Mediterranean, the northern European, the Muslim, and the American cultures and their historical causes. Things are things and events are events, and he knows all about them, but they suddenly take off and become ideas and then become part of the flow of historic instances before they drop into some comical anecdote.

He has arranged his utterances in groups about life, love, marriage, death, religion, art and architecture, literature, writing, people, nature, places, introspection, and dreams. He has invented a terse Chinese sage, Ying Chü.

In his talking life these matters will run from one to another and we shall have scarcely time to agree or disagree. Here I shall note varieties in his manner, remembering that what may sound dogmatic and like a sharp military order—for there is something of the curt soldier in him—is really put forward as a question he invites us to dispute.

Poverty is a great educator. Those who have never known it lack something.

Most of our personal opinions lie on the board like iron filings. But pass the magnet of a strong emotion over them and they will change overnight and point in the opposite direction.

On love:

Some girls only fall in love with ugly men. These are the girls who when they were children preferred golliwogs to dolls.

Love and admiration often precede sexual attraction and may even exclude it. Think of Stendhal and the fiasco. The following is a real Geraldo-ism:

But women also have their problems. Thus making love to a girl for the first time can be like going into a dark room and fumbling for the electric switch. Only when a man has found it will the light come full on.

Marriage:

In a happy marriage it is the wife who provides the climate, the husband the landscape.

On religion he is a moderate sceptic. He does not care for utilitarianism. He is not a humanist because he does not feel "Man is a sufficiently noble animal to be given absolute power over his destiny." He needs authority:

What authority I do not know, but my need has made me a fellow traveller of the religious, though I shall get out of their bus several stations before the end.

(He is close to Montaigne. Above all he admires Montaigne's prose, but "not in translation.")

The paintings that move him most are those that express a moment in time when things seem to be arrested and made to stand still.

I am not drawn to Rubens because in his paintings every little detail is on the move. Nothing has weight, there is no rest for the mind, one thinks chiefly of the skill and mastery.

On painting, he passes from the pensée to the essay, but the pensée punctuates the essay. On the abstract painters:

there is no struggle in their canvases, no tension—only choices and hesitations.

Yet the works of the American abstract expressionists

surge up from some deep layer on the borders of the unconscious and make a strong emotional impression.

The essay goes on to architecture—

Modern States [being strictly utilitarian] are the natural enemies of good architecture.

—and an analysis of the Romanesque, the Gothic, and the Byzantine, and praise for the Muslims for their "abnormal sensitivity to small variations." These are intended to "lull the senses," and he has a eulogy of the mosque of Adrianople. All this ends with an odd kind of aside that gives a sparkle to the learned phrases of his talk. The bishop who completed Salisbury Cathedral had been Queen Philippa's chaplain, a dwarf who was notoriously impotent. He built the finest spire in England.

The entries become longer when he moves to literature. He looks at Stendhal ("an amateur in a nation of professionals"), Balzac, Flaubert, Henry James, Quevedo, Italo Svevo—a talking author very close to him, indeed I often confuse my friend with him—Jane Austen and even P. G. Wodehouse, Góngora and many other poets, and each paragraph contains a startling apercu,. These pages are too long to quote but I have heard many of them thrown off in high moments of his talk where they were as precise as they are in print; his conversation has the glancing quality of something rapt and yet prolonged. His afterthoughts are sudden:

Who, for example, among English writers of talent could have written a serious poem on dentifrice, as Apuleius did, except Nabokov? And in their use of erotic subjects for unerotic ends they are also similar.

Or:

The cliché is dead poetry. English, being the language of an imaginative race, abounds in clichés, so that English literature is always in danger of being poisoned by its own secretions.

Whereas French writing—until "Sartre eroded the language"—relied on the precision of its syntax. All the same, clichés,

> if well chosen, provide a rest for the mind and give a more leisurely movement to the sentence . . . A good deal can be done by words that are vague and plastic: consider the use that Vergil makes of the word *res*.

So one listens to Brenan's talk for its vivacity and for the extraordinary breadth of its interests. In one section he amuses himself by bringing in his imaginary Chinese sage to whom modern rulers, from Hitler onward, come to ask advice. The troubled Nixon asks whether there is any chance of being born again in another life in which he could fulfil his potentialities. The sage reminds him that if he is reborn he will find that billions of others will be reborn—"including all your compatriots"—and suggests he will cease to be tormented by this craving for immortality if he reflects on this, before breakfast.

As for himself, there are discreet revelations: he has the writer's shame before his own writing. Out of dullness he wakes up when he gets to his desk, but cannot believe that he is the "I" who has written and is praised. Modesty? No, he says, conceit. Fog surrounds him: only intuition can give access to the vague shapes he discerns in the fog. All his remarks on nature—on the toad, the snail, insects, and birds—are delightful to hear. He is a connoisseur of the distribution of the olive. To walk with him is to see creatures, trees, rocks, and soils come to life, not only because he knows so much, but because what he knows comes lightly to his tongue. A bore would have stunned us with more information. He does not inform: he incites. There is no melancholy in this Jacques:

> Rain, rain, rain. It brings out all the scents—roses, heliotrope, lemon leaves, loquat flowers, freesias, but subduing them a little and mixing them with the smell of the wet earth. This garden is where I should like to live if I were blind, because in its soft air the sounds as well as the scents have a soothing and memory-provoking quality. Ordinarily the senses take in too much. One would better enjoy using one's eyes if they recorded fewer things, because the less clearly objects are defined, the greater is the charge of emotional associations they carry.

Brenan ends by cursing the critics of poetry who insist on "explicating."

He is no sentimentalist. He is always exacting. Be careful: if he is drawing his portrait he may be drawing yours. It will be sharp and yet you will be enlarged by his fantasy. Thousands of Malagueños came to his funeral when lately he died.

(1990)

MOLLY KEANE

IRISH BEHAVIOUR

After the Treaty in the Twenties the Anglo-Irish gentry—the "Ascendancy" as they were called—rapidly became a remnant. Some stormed out shouting insults at the receding Wicklow Hills. Those who stayed on resorted to irony; for centuries they had been a caste in decline on a poor island-within-an-island in Britain's oldest colony. They stuck to their wild passions for huntin', shootin', fishin', the turf, drink, and, above all, genealogy, as the damp rose in their fine but decaying houses. Debts and mortgages gathered around them, but they had long settled for not knowing history socially except when it presented itself in the form of family trees (sometimes done in tapestry) going back to the Normans, the Elizabethans, even to Charlemagne.

The snobbery approached, as Stendhal would have said, the Sublime. In their time this race had produced great generals, clever colonial servants, excellent playwrights, writers in prose and poetry. In these last, their particular gift lay in clear swift writing, in the unrelenting, almost militant comedy of manners or in uproarious farce. How often, in the expectant stare of their eyes, one noticed a childlike or raging innocence and the delight in mischief. Their condition was the nearest thing in Western Europe to, say, Gogol's or Turgenev's Russian landowners, and this in the ever-changing light of an often graceful landscape, and in a climate that either excited the visionary in them or drove them in on themselves.

As one who knew something of the period of Molly Keane's *Good Behaviour* I was astonished to find there no hint of the Irish "Troubles," the Rising of 1916, the later civil war, or the toll of burned-down houses. Was this an instance of the Anglo-Irish, indeed of the general Irish habit of euphemism and evasion? What, of course, is not unreal to Molly Keane is the game of manners, the instinctive desire to keep boring reality at bay, yet to be stoical about the cost.

The Victorian and Edwardian codes stayed on far longer in southern Ireland than in England. *Good Behaviour* was less a novel than a novelised autobiography which exposes the case of Anglo-Irish women, especially in the person of the narrator, a shy, large, ungainly, horsey girl. The males, young or old, are always away, either fighting in the 1914 war or shooting and fishing or dangling after less innocent girls abroad. For the women at home sex is taboo, yet marriage is the only hope—so long as you remember that by their nature "It's a thing men do, it's all they want to do, and you won't like it." Love, like sex, is really a state of cease-fire. One of the rules of good behaviour is that you say nothing about it unless it is done by animals. The native Catholic servants, untroubled by the use of euphemism or "place," burst with gaudy oaths to your face. They are chiefly excited by illness and death and are passionate adepts at wakes and the "last rites." The young girl has to rise above it all. Her duty is to know the voice of command that "puts people in their places."

So the amiable war hero and landowner, the girl's father, reckless in the saddle, will have a heart attack in mysterious circumstances; he is a charming drinker and accepted pursuer of young girls when he goes to London. When he is dying his freezing wife is indifferent; her role is to conserve the "things" of the family—pictures, silver, fine inherited furniture, and the remains of the status and money. The role of the young girl is to control the war between wife, nurse, and the head-tossing servant who sneaks into the sickroom with fatal draughts of whiskey. She is the peasant with the pacifying art of giving sexual relief under the sheets: she pretends she is warming the old man's feet. What does the daughter crave? All the excitements of the freedom she has heard of in the Twenties: to be loved by the young man who has merely flirted in a gentlemanly way at a dance or two, and has vanished. She is red-faced, gauche, and clumsy in society, and has scarcely been educated by an ignorant governess hired mainly to teach her a few phrases of French as an item of gentility. What she craves is the assurance that her father is convinced of her virginity and that he loves her: he certainly hates his selfish wife. In the end he *does* show that he loves his daughter. He punishes his wife by leaving the girl the property. And the book ends with that great national festival, the classic Irish funeral at which the girl gets majestically drunk.

This book is an entertainment which in part recalls the one outstanding Irish novel of the nineteenth century, *The Real Charlotte* by E. O. Somerville and Martin Ross—the latter was the more sensitive and serious partner in the collaboration of Somerville and Ross in, for example, *Further Experiences of an Irish R.M.* Somerville was the mistress of country house farce and its metaphors ("Birds burst out of holly bushes like corks out of soda water bottles." We remember old Flurry Knox whose "grandmother's curry" was so powerful that "you'd take a splint off a horse with it.") Ross was the subtler social moralist who could almost match Mrs Gaskell's *Wives and Daughters* or, on native grounds, Maria Edgeworth.

Molly Keane's real novel, substantial and ingeniously organised, is the more recent *Time After Time.* It is more Ross than Somerville in temper than the earlier book. Now good behaviour is in abeyance, although its shadow is there. We are now in a period closer to the present day. Still no politics, though there is a horrified glance at a political crime abroad, the Holocaust.

For the rest, the Irish imbroglio tells its own tale. Elderly Jasper Swift and his three sisters look back on past glories as they quarrel in the Big House while its remaining acres have become a wilderness. The family are all old, the youngest in her sixties, the others in their late seventies. There are no comic servants, there is little money. Jasper, once at Eton, paces about in the patched clothes of his dressy youth: he has been left the terrible legacy of looking after his bickering and pitiless sisters. His realm is in the kitchen. He does the cooking, specialising in dubious menus with strange sauces which he recalls from his gourmet past; some of the stuff has been rescued from the dogs and cats and is made anonymous by a last-minute scattering of herbs. He is a quiet, nervy fellow and doesn't bother now to conceal his faintly homosexual past; a sort of half-fey cunning saint whose main relief—apart from cooking—is ruling his sisters by getting his own back. They are tough, high-spirited, unsexed ladies but bottled in illusions about their youth. In a confusing narrative which ingeniously brings back glimpses of the family past—and without any clumsy use of flashback so that the past secretes itself in fragments—we are grateful that the ladies are conveniently called April, May, and June.

Fiercely they lock their bedrooms against one another. They have all, including Jasper, been emotionally maimed by the monstrous, possessive will of their "darling Mummie," long ago dead. We are back in a forgotten Anglo-Irish, perhaps totally Irish, puzzle: how do the women survive? The answer is by secretiveness, rancour; liberated by isolation, they go "underground" and "make do," all expert in the "home truth."

Shut up in her room, seventy-five-year-old April, the ex-beauty, lives among the beautiful dresses of her past. She is a childless widow—she knows what the others don't, that "thing men do." (Her husband, a pornographer, liked "doing it" on trains.) She lives in the past, and is deaf and carries a pad on which the others have to write down what they have to say. Her chief occupations are weight-watching and push-ups. Her deafness seems to enhance what was once beauty: she is "armoured for loneliness." She sips vodka and is bemused by tranquillisers.

May's room is as bleak as a room in a nursing-home. She looks and lives like a robot, has never been desired, but is frantically busy as a bad artist. She makes pictures out of tweed, grasses, dead flowers, and leather. She loves to collect china rabbits—her obsession. She is also light-fingered where bright little objects are concerned: tinsel, marbles, anything that shines—a jackdaw. Her dexterity with her hands is astonishing for she was born with a "cropped right hand with only two fingers." She knows how to conceal this wound at local talks on flower arrangement. She is in conspiracy also with the local antique dealer—a new type in modern Ireland—and is not above some skilful stealing.

Baby June, the youngest, aged sixty-four, has reverted to the peasant condition and is indeed a by-blow. Fit to do the work of two men, illiterate, she is a powerful girl in the stables and has been, in her time, a rider who was the terror of every point-to-point in the country and was "the shape and weight of a retired flat race jockey." She is an expert at delivering calves, killing lambs, knows how to deal with farrowing pigs. She clumps into the house, satisfied by the blood on her hands and clothes. Her closest friend and pupil is a pious Catholic stable-lad she is training to become a jockey. Around the sisters crowd their lascivious dogs and cats in Jasper's filthy kitchen. (*His* cat sits on the bread board.)

And then, a pitiless figure descends on them—old indeed, fat but in gorgeous clothes, reeking of Paris and insinuation. She is Leda, half-Jewish, the daughter of a famous restaurateur in Vienna who had married into the family before the 1940 war. To her cousins she brings back the childhood memories of past wealth and pleasure. Miraculously they feel rejuvenated. They had never liked to talk about her because of her Jewish blood, for they were sure she had been trapped by the Nazis and had died in Belsen. They half-remember that, when staying with them as a girl, she had been suddenly, without explanation, and in one of the high moments of "good behaviour"—"so sorry you cannot stay"—firmly sent off at a moment's notice by "darling Mummie," a genius of the final goodbye. Perhaps it was something to do with Daddy or Jasper? It doesn't matter now: they are ravished by her miraculous chatter. They are overcome by pity for her state: she is blind. Only Baby June, illiterate, dirty, has no time for her. Jasper himself, the man who had always longed to be "more of a Human Being," is excited. He returns to compete with Vienna in his kitchen. Leda, in short, brings the family to life. They put her in Mummie's sacred room and thenceforth she worms their secrets out of them. It is a seduction with a special compensation: her blindness. She cannot see how aged they all are, any more than she can know her own ugliness.

But when we see Leda installed alone in Mummie's sacred room we watch her do a strange thing. She gropes towards the wardrobe where Mummie's beautiful dresses still hang and, fingering the material, pulls the finest one out and spits all over it. Leda, we see, is here for vengeance. (Here is the real echo of the appalling jealousy Martin Ross evoked in *The Real Charlotte*.) One by one she worms out the eager secrets: April, full of erotic notions, picked up from her dead husband the pornographer; May the artist and nimble shoplifter; guilty Baby June who once shot Jasper in the eye when she was a child of seven; and Jasper, with his peculiar meetings with a local monk. At a terrible breakfast scene she comes out with all of it. Jasper in his lazy, evasive, semi-saintly way gladly makes himself out to be worse than the sisters who drive him mad, in order not to look nicer than they are.

There is more to this thoroughly well-organised traditional study of intrigue, malice, and roguery. It is rich and remarkable for the intertwining of portraits and events. It is spirited, without tears. The ingenious narrative is always on the move and has that extraordinary sinuous, athletic animation that one finds in Anglo-Irish prose. Mrs Keane has a delicate sense of landscape; she is robust about sinful human nature and the intrigues of the heart, a moralist well weathered in the realism and the evasions of Irish life. No Celtic twilight here! Detached as her comedy is, it is also deeply sympathetic and admiring of the stoicism, the *incurable* quality of her people. When Leda herself is exposed and is taken off and put back with her nuns again, a helpless, cynical, evil creature, April relentlessly goes with her, almost like a wardress, to make her do her slimming exercises. Jasper, who has never quite been able to become a "human being," has one less sister to torment and turns once more to his cooking and gardening. So Irish realism, with the solace of its intrigues, dominates this very imaginative and laughing study of the anger that lies at the heart of the isolated and the old, and their will to live.

(1990)

John Osborne

A BETTER CLASS OF PERSON

John Osborne has always been a master of spoken diatribe, whether it is of the "bloody but unbowed" kind or the picturesque confessional of wounds given and received. In his vigorous autobiography *A Better Class of Person* he has the wound-licking grin of the only child who has been through the class mill and is getting his own back—very much a comic Mr Polly or a Kipps reborn in 1929, if less sunny and innocent than Wells was. Osborne adds to the rich tradition of English low comedy, which draws on the snobberies and vulgarities of lower-middle-class life, with its guts, its profligate will to survive despite its maudlin or self-pitying streak. He calls his people Edwardian, for manners drag on long after their presumed historical death; really his family were on the bohemian verges. Both the Welsh and the Cockney sides—the latter known in the family folklore as "the Tottenham Crowd," with some sniffing of the nose—had a racy leaning towards pubs, music halls, and theatre. (All, except his sad father, lived to a tremendous age.) His two grandfathers were well-established if secretive rakes; one was the manager of a once famous London pub in the theatre district and had an early-morning spat with the lavishly seductive Marie Lloyd. Osborne's Welsh father was a self-taught pianist who could sing a song. He earned his living as an advertising copywriter of sorts until his health collapsed. He first met Nellie Beatrice Grove, who was to be the playwright's mother, when she was a barmaid in the Strand. She had left school at twelve to scrub floors in an orphanage, had quickly bettered herself as a cashier in a Lyons Corner House, and eventually went on to the bar of a suburban hotel. She resented her sister Queenie putting on airs because she had, by some family accident, been "educated" and worked in a milliner's. (The class struggle has its nuances.) If one uncle was a stoker in the Navy, another had an admired connection with Abdulla cigarettes. Was he a director? Goodness knows, but he smoked the expensive things all day. Bids for gentility were natural in a family that, on both sides, took some pride in having "come down in the world." Osborne writes:

> ... the Groves seemed to feel less sense of grievance, looking on it as the justified price of profligate living or getting above yourself, rather than as a cruel trick of destiny . . . They had a litany of elliptical sayings, almost biblical in their complexity, which, to the meanest mind or intelligence, combined accessibility and authority. Revealed family wisdom was expressed in sayings like, "One door opens and another one always shuts" (the optimistic version—rare—was the same in reverse). "I think I can say I've had my share of sorrows." Like Jesus they were all acquainted with grief. "I can always read him like a book"; "I've never owed anyone anything" (almost the Family Motto this); "You can't get round him, he's like a Jew and his cash box"; "Look at him, like Lockhart's elephant."

The last was a characteristic piece of poetic fancy by which the Londoner draws on local history. The words meant that someone was relating the young Osborne to times before his own; he was "clumsy." The elephant evoked a popular large bun sold at a cheap and now extinct eating-house in the Strand. I believe the American equivalent would be Child's.

Osborne was an only child, and for long years he was too sickly to be sent to school. No adult spoke to him much, so he listened, puzzling his way through the family babble. Religion was remote. Comfort in the discomfort of others, he remarks, was the abiding family recreation. "Disappointment," Osborne adds, "was oxygen to them." The Family Row at Christmas was an institution, the Groves shouting, the Osbornes calmer and more bitter in their sense of having been cheated at birth. Nellie Beatrice, the barmaid mother, mangled the language with her Tottenham mispronunciations— very upsetting to the precise and eloquent Welsh. As she complained, they "passed looks" when she spoke. Her genius shone at the bar:

> Quick, anticipative with a lightning head for mental arithmetic, she was, as she put it, a very smart "licensed victualler's assistant" indeed. "I'm not a barmaid I'm a victualler's assistant—if you please." I have seen none better. No one could draw a pint with a more perfect head on it or pour out four glasses of beer at the same time, throwing bottles up in the air and catching them as she did so.

She was known as Bobby, and was noted for shouting out her wartime catch phrases: "Get up them stairs"; "The second thing he did when he come home was to take his pack off"; or "I couldn't laugh if I was crafty." At home, her energies were restless. She was a relentless cleaner, whether she lived in digs in dreary Fulham or in a snobby suburb, and never stopped stripping and cleaning the few rooms they lived in, taking up all the carpets and taking down all curtains once a week. She loved moving house. Meals, such as they were, were made to be washed up rather than to be eaten. She was a mistress of the black look. She was hungry for glamour, not for bringing up children, and certainly not a sickly boy who caught every illness going. Her ideal—after the father died and the war filled her purse with wartime tips— was to "go Up West," walk round the big London stores without buying anything, complaining of her feet, and have a lunch at the gaudy Trocadero, where she could look suitably stand-offish. She was deeply respectable. This is the half-cruel portrait by her son, who was to become a "better class of person." He confesses to a struggle against a shame of her:

My mother's hair was very dark, occasionally hennaed. Her face was a floury dark mask, her eyes were an irritable brown, her ears small, so unlike her father's ("He's got Satan's ears, he has"), her nose surprisingly fine. Her remaining front teeth were large, yellow, and strong. Her lips were a scarlet-black sliver covered in some sticky slime named Tahiti or Tattoo, which she bought with all her other make-up from Woolworth's. She wore it, or something like it, from the beginning of the First World War onwards. She had a cream base called Crème Simone, always covered up with a face powder called Tokalon, which she dabbed all over so that it almost showered off in little avalanches when she leant forward over her food. This was all topped off by a kind of knicker-bocker glory of rouge, which came in rather pretty little blue and white boxes—again from Woolworth's—and looked like a mixture of blackcurrant juice and brick dust. The final coup was an overgenerous dab of California Poppy, known to schoolboys as "fleur de dustbins."

What froze him was that she was incurious about him.

The frail short-lived father had been white-haired since his twenties. His skin was extremely pale, almost transparent. He had the whitest hands I think I have ever seen; Shalimar hands he called them. ("Pale hands I love beside the Lethe waters," of Shalimar. It was one of his favourite Sunday ballads.)

But his long fingers were stained by nicotine. His clothes were unpressed and his bowler hat and mac were greasy, but he was particular about his cuffs and collars and his highly polished, papery shoes. A gentle, sad creature, he is oddly described as being like a "Welsh-sounding prurient, reticent investigator of sorts from a small provincial town." For some reason unknown—not only because of his long spells in hospital—the couple were mostly apart.

For the only child, schools were places of pain and humiliation. Certainly they were often rough. He had to discover cunning. At one mixed school, the adolescent girls turned out to be the thumping bullies of the smaller boys, preparing them for the sex war. Still, in the suburbs, there were sympathetic, literate families who helped the backward autodidact. He was nothing more than a nuisance to his energetic mother, and by now they almost hated one another. He was luckier than he thinks to be sent to a third-rate boarding school, for he did at least read a lot and did pretty well with his belated education. But he was laughed at for saying he wanted to be a historian and go to a university. All he was fit for, he was told, was journalism. He was sacked for hitting a master who had slapped him and for writing love-letters to a girl there. Schools took a stern line on that. The sexual revolution, though rife elsewhere, did not easily penetrate the semi-genteel regions of provincial life. So journalism it was. The Benevolent Society to which his father had subscribed and which had paid for his schooling completed its obligations by getting him introduced to a publisher who produced trade journals like the Gas World. He had to prepare himself for this by going to typing and shorthand classes.

Folly is often a salvation in such dreary circumstances. Osborne was eighteen, spotty, shy, and longing for friends, especially girls. It occurred to him that a course of dancing lessons at a school that put on amateur theatricals was a likely chance. He became a dim star and sent his photograph to a theatrical agent; the bohemian traits of his upbringing sprang up in his sullen, slightly flashy being. He had first to disentangle himself from the usual sentimental suburban engagement to a nice enough girl who took her reluctant boyfriend (earning two pounds a week) to the windows of furniture shops. The warning was clear. He jilted her, wrote her remorseful, high-minded letters, was tormented by guilt and by threats and denunciations from the parents. But he was soon out on tour with a third-rate company and learned about theatre without training from the bottom, starting with the job of assistant stage-manager and understudying the five actors, aged between twenty-five and seventy. What is clear from the long picaresque experiences with this down-at-heel and hungry company is that he was really a writer and, despite poetising ambitions, had a marvellous ear for real speech. The book is punctuated by passages from his plays that hark back to what he heard "on the road." The "real" life is in fact the overflow of theatrical life evoking people outside. On that first long tour, sexually starved, he simpered after a fluttering actress called Sheila but soon had the simper knocked out of him by a formidable actress called Stella, an aggressive thirty-year-old, with "the shoulders of a Channel swimmer" and a body that "looked capable of snapping up an intruder in a jawbone of flesh." She was "arrogantly lubricious" and had "an almost masculine, stalking power." She was not put off by his sickly appearance and his acne; she expertly detected the writer in him, and was after him to revise his first attempt as a collaborator, on a play that she and her husband wanted to put on. When she and Osborne became lovers, they quarrelled incessantly about dramatic construction; she was out for the commercial success of another *Autumn Crocus* or *Dinner at Eight*—what he calls "a Nice Play" about middle-class gatherings. She in fact woke up his independent intelligence. He discovered he had his own ideas about the theatre. She said he was a lazy, arrogant, dishonest amateur—not only that but ungrateful to her complaisant husband, who tolerantly rescued them when the company's run stopped and the money ran out. She had to take a job as a waitress and Osborne became a dishwasher. She eventually left him for a job in the north, and he admits that he spitefully left her door unlocked and her electricity turned on when he left the flat she had lent him. Rightly, she never forgave him. Years later, the play did run for a week, with Osborne trying to recognise some lines of his own in it.

The knockabout theatrical chapters tend to be repetitive, but they are rich in sharp, short portraits, especially of the theatrical landladies. They end with his runaway marriage with one Pamela, a capable young actress. He was tactless enough to carry on this passion when the company got to her own home town, in the face of her hostile family. They were well-established drapers. The correlative scripture of what went on in real life will be seen in the quotations from *Look Back in Anger*, notably Jimmy Porter's speech about the wedding:

> Mummy was slumped over her pew in a heap—the noble, female rhino, pole-axed at last! And Daddy sat beside her, upright and unafraid, dreaming of his days among the Indian Princes, and unable to believe he'd left his horsewhip at home.

Osborne says that this is a fairly accurate account of the wedding, except for the references to the Indian Princes. They seem unlikely in the life of a local draper. Daddy has in fact been elevated socially by the "angry" exposer of class consciousness. Osborne is safer as a guide to congealed suburban or theatrical snobberies. He now writes about the episode:

> I was aware that I had left behind the sophistication and tolerance of the true provinces. Sprung from Fulham and Stoneleigh, where feelings rarely rose higher than a black look, the power of place, family, and generation in small towns was new to me. In the suburbs, allegiances are lost or discarded on

dutifully paid visits. The present kept itself to itself. In such a life there was no common graveyard for memory or future. The suburb has no graveyard.

Just before the end of the book there is a collection of extracts from Nellie Beatrice's letters. Years have passed, but she's still on the move, saving up gift stamps for a new carpet-shampoo cleaner, washing down the ceiling, though "I never did like Housework." She just wanted things clean. And then comes her crushing phrase:

I'll say that for him—he's never been *ashamed* of me. He's always let me meet his friends—and they're all theatrical people, a good class all of them, they speak nicely.

And to his notebook Osborne groans:

I am ashamed of her as part of myself that can't be cast out, my own conflict, the disease which I suffer and have inherited, what I am and never could be whole.

About that time, 1955, George Devine rowed out to Osborne, who was living on a barge on the Thames, and offered him a twenty-pound option on *Look Back in Anger*. English theatre changed in a night. I look forward to Volume Two.

(1990)

SALMAN RUSHDIE

MIDNIGHT'S CHILDREN

In Salman Rushdie, the author of *Midnight's Children* (Jonathan Cape, 1981), India has produced a great novelist—one with startling imaginative and intellectual resources, a master of perpetual story-telling. Like García Márquez in *One Hundred Years of Solitude*, he weaves a whole people's capacity for carrying its inherited myths—and new ones that it goes on generating—into a kind of magic carpet. The human swarm swarms in every man and woman as they make their bid for life and vanish into the passion or hallucination that hangs about them like the smell of India itself. Yet at the same time there are Western echoes, particularly of the irony of Sterne in *Tristram Shandy*—that early non-linear writer—in Rushdie's readiness to tease by breaking off or digressing in the gravest moments. This is very odd in an Indian novel! The book is really about the mystery of being born. Rushdie's realism is that of the conjuror who, in a flash, draws an incident out of the air and then makes it vanish and laughs at his cleverness. A pregnant woman, the narrator's mother, goes to a fortune-teller in the Delhi slum:

> And my mother's face, rabbit-startled, watching the prophet in the check shirt as he began to circle, his eyes still egglike in the softness of his face; and suddenly a shudder passing through him and again that strange high voice as the words issued through his lips (I must describe those lips, too—but later, because now . . .) "A son."
>
> Silent cousins—monkeys on leashes, ceasing their chatter—cobras coiled in baskets—and the circling fortune-teller, finding history speaking through his

lips.

And the fortune-teller goes on, sing-songing:

"Washing will hide him—voices will guide him! Friends mutilate him—blood
will betray him . . . jungle will claim him . . . tyrants will fry him . . . He will have
sons without having sons! He will be old before he is old! *And he will die . . . before
he is dead*."

Outside the room, monkeys are throwing down stones on the street from
a ruined building.

This is pure *Arabian Nights* intrigue—for that son, Saleem Sinai, now
thirty-one, is writing about what he is making up about his birth; he is
dramatising his past life as a prophecy, even universalising his history as a
mingling of farce and horror and matching it with thirty years of the Indian
crowd's collective political history. The strength of a book that might
otherwise be a string of picaresque tales lies in its strong sense of design.
Saleem claims that it is he who has created modern India in the years that
followed Indian independence—has dreamed into being the civil strife and
the wars—as a teller of stories, true or untrue, conniving at events and
united with them. Central to this is the fantasy that the children born at
midnight on the day of liberation, as he was, have a destiny. The Prime
Minister himself pronounces this: "They are the seed of a future that would
genuinely differ from anything that the world had seen at that time."
Children born a few seconds before the hour of what Saleem calls
Mountbatten's "tick-tock" are likely to join the revelling band of conjurors
and circus freaks and street singers; those born a few seconds after midnight,
like Parvati, the witch, whom Saleem eventually marries, will be genuine
sorcerers. Saleem himself, born on the stroke of the hour, will be amazingly
gifted but will also embody the disasters of the country. The novel is an
autobiography, dictated by a ruined man to a simple but shrewd working
girl in a pickle factory—to this Saleem's fortunes have fallen. (She is
addressed from time to time as if she were Sterne's "dear Eliza.") The
fortune-teller's words "washing will hide him" point to Fate. The prophecy
was not a joke.

The rich Delhi Muslims who raise him are not his parents: he is a
changeling, and not their son. The wrong ticket has been tied to his toe by
a poor Goanese nurse, who, demented by the infidelity of her husband, a
common street singer, had allowed herself to be seduced by a departing
English sahib. Saleem is ugly, dwarfish, with a huge snotty nose, and is
brought up rich; the real son is Shiva, brought up poor. Years will pass
before the nurse confesses. The point of the political allegory becomes

clear. Shiva, like the god, will become the man of action, riot, and war—the bully, cunning in getting to the top. Saleem's gift will be the passive intellectual's who claims the artist's powers of travelling into the minds of people. The rival traits will show in their school days. Proud of being midnight's children, the boys form a privileged gang. Saleem sees the gang as a gathering of equals in which every one has the right to his own voice. Shiva, brought up on the streets and refusing to be a whining beggar, rejects Saleem's democratic dream:

> "Yah, little rich boy: one rule. Everybody does what I say or I squeeze the shit outa them ... Rich kid, you don't know one damn thing! ... Where's the reason in starving, man? ... You got to get what you can, do what you can with it, and then you got to die."

The effect of Indian independence on the rich family is to give them the opportunity to buy up the property of the departing British cheaply, and speculation drives Saleem's "father" to delusion. When he ages, he shuts himself up to fret about getting the words of the Koran in the right order. Then the riots of partition begin; there is the war in Kashmir; identifying himself with mass-consciousness, Saleem declares the war occurred because he dreamed it; Gandhi is assassinated; there is the war between India and Pakistan. In Bombay, where Saleem's family have migrated to make money, the bombing smashes their houses and kills off several of them. These events are evoked in parodies of news-flashes from All India Radio. Saleem, indeed, sees himself as a private radio sending out his satirical reports; once they are issued, the narrative returns to his story. He has a strange sister—a delightfully mischievous girl, known as the Brass Monkey, whose main sport is setting fire to the family's shoes. When Saleem discovers the truth about his birth, he falls in love with her; she turns him down and becomes pious, and Saleem henceforth believes all his failures in love are due to the sin of a metaphysical incest. The girl eventually becomes a superb cold-hearted singer and is "the darling of the troops" in the war. Failure in sexual love haunts all the family. The more his "parents" disappoint each other sexually, the more they apply themselves to loving each other. Saleem grows up to be something of a voyeur or vicarious lover.

In his attitude to love, Saleem is very much the ever wilful, inventive, teasing Scheherazade, prolonging the dreams of his people and puncturing them at the point of success. For example, his Aunt Pia, notorious for making emotional scenes, may be seen wantonly going through the motions of seducing Saleem—who is only ten at the time—but the act is physical charade: her extreme sexual provocation is put on as a "scene" in which she rids herself of a private grief. Love is a need and custom, sexuality is play-acting. Towards the end of the book, Saleem will refuse to consummate his marriage to the witch Parvati (who has saved his life and who loves him), but not because she is pregnant by another man—in fact, his brother and opposite, the womanising Shiva. Saleem pretends he is impotent. Why this self-love? Is it possible that—too entranced by his fantastic powers of invention—he is the artist in love with storytelling itself? Or do such episodes spring from a fundamental sense that India is a chaos in which no norm can be realised? What a Westerner would call Saleem's self-pity is the egoist's devious and somehow energising passivity and resignation. It is, at any rate, the obverse of Shiva's grossly self-seeking attitude to life. Shiva is not a man to spend himself in a breathless stream of words.

All this is brought to life by Rushdie's delight in ironies of detail, which is entirely beguiling, because the smallest things, comic or horrible, are made phenomenal. But when we come to the war in East Pakistan the narrative takes on a new kind of visionary power. Saleem is a soldier, and in defeat and flight he leads a tiny group of men into the jungle—see the sorcerer's prophecy!—where he sometimes calls himself "I," sometimes "he" or "buddha," and maybe also Ayooba, as if desperation had become a fever that burns out his identity. The soldiers are diminished by the rain forest, which has become a phantom personage who arouses in them all the guilt they have hidden, and punishes them for the horrors they have committed.

But one night Ayooba awoke in the dark to find the translucent figure of a peasant with a bullet-hole in his heart and a scythe in his hand staring mournfully down at him . . . After this first apparition, they fell into a state of mind in which they would have believed the forest capable of anything; each night it sent them new punishments, the accusing eyes of the wives of men they had tracked down and seized, the screaming and monkey-gibbering of children left fatherless by their work—and in this first time, the time of punishment, even the impassive buddha with his citified voice was obliged to confess that he, too, had taken to waking up at night to find the forest closing in upon him like a vice, so that he felt unable to breathe.

The forest permitted a "double-edged" nostalgia for childhood, strange visions of mothers and fathers; Ayooba, for example, sees his mother offering her breasts, when she suddenly turns into a white monkey swinging by her tail high up in a tree. Another lad hears his father telling his brother that their father had sold his soul for a loan from his landlord, who charged three hundred per cent—"so it seemed that the magical jungle, having tormented them with their misdeeds, was leading them by the hand towards a new adulthood." But there are worse tests to come: in a ruined temple the soldiers are deluded by lascivious dreams of houris, evoked by a statue of a savage multi-limbed Kali. The men wake up discovering the meaninglessness of life, the pointless boredom of the desire to survive.

The experience of these very ordinary men is a purgation but not a salvation. As in an opera—and perhaps that is what *Midnight's Children* really is—the next grand scene is of comic magic. The conquering armies enter Dacca, led by a vast company of ghetto minstrels, conjurors, magic men. Marching with the troops come the entertainers:

> . . . There were acrobats forming human pyramids on moving carts drawn by white bullocks; there were extraordinary female contortionists who could swallow their legs up to their knees; there were jugglers who operated outside the laws of gravity, so that they could draw oohs and aahs from the delighted crowd as they juggled with toy grenades, keeping four hundred and twenty in the air at a time . . . And there was Picture Singh himself, a seven-foot giant who weighed two hundred and forty pounds and was known as the Most Charming Man In The World because of his unsurpassable skills as a snake charmer . . . he strode through the happily shrieking crowds, twined from head to foot with deadly cobras, mambas and kraits, all with their poison-sacs intact . . . Picture Singh, who would be the last in the line of men who have been willing to become my fathers . . . and immediately behind him came Parvati-the-witch.

She was rolling her magic basket along as she marched, and—would you believe it?—eventually helped Saleem to escape by popping him into it. After her magic, the allegory: it is Shiva who seduces Parvati and deserts her, and Picture Singh who makes Saleem marry her, in the ghetto where Picture Singh draws the crowd with his snakes while Saleem, the man of conscience, shouts political propaganda. (Mr Rushdie has already told us that the magicians are all Communists of every known hue and schism.) This episode, like so many others in the book, is almost delicately touching, but, of course, there is disaster in the next act. Back in India, Saleem is a political prisoner and is forced to submit to vasectomy. The man who lied to Parvati when he said he was impotent is now truly impotent as he dictates this long story to Padma, the working girl, who has got him a job in the pickle factory. He loves inventing chutneys—they have the power of bringing back memories.

The novel is, in part, a powerful political satire in its savaging of both political and military leaders. The narrator's hatred of Mrs Gandhi—the Widow (that is to say, the guillotine)—is deep. But I think that as satire the novel is at variance with Mr Rushdie's self-absorption and his pursuit of poetic symbols: the magic basket in which one can hide secret thoughts, and so save oneself, is an example; another is "the hole," which recurs, and suggests that we see experience falsely, because in a little over-excited peep at a time. These symbols are rather too knowing; he is playing tricks with free association. Padma, the not-so-simple factory girl to whom the ruined Saleem dictates the book, pities his wretchedness but often suggests that he is piling it on, and is suspicious of his evasiveness. So much conjuring going on in Saleem's imagination does bewilder us. But as a *tour de force* his fantasy is irresistible.

(1990)

Also available in Vintage

V.S. Pritchett

THE LADY FROM GUATEMALA

'The great master of the short story in our time'
Margaret Drabble

'One of the century's most distinguished short story writers
in English'
James Wood, *Guardian*

'V.S. Pritchett catches something about the English character that no writer since Dickens has seen: its obsessive and
excitable nature, its exoticism in love and melancholy'
Claire Tomalin, *Sunday Times*

'Pritchett's stories invite and merit re-reading, and, what is
more important, they encourage us to look again at those
parts of life we like to think are settled'
Robert Kiely, *New York Times Book Review*

VINTAGE

John Cheever

THE WAPSHOT SCANDAL

'A master American storyteller'
TIME

Once upon a time the Wapshots of St. Botolphs were distinguished for their unshakeable good opinion of themselves. But
in John Cheever's simultaneously poignant and hilarious
companion volume to *The Wapshot Chronicle*, the family
members drift far from their New England Village – and into
the demented caprices of the mighty, the bad graces of the IRS,
and the humiliating abyss of adulterous passion.

'I read *The Wapshot Scandal* with pure delight – in the characters, in the firm and deceptively simple style, and most of all in
the continual power of invention'
Malcolm Cowley

VINTAGE

Also available in Vintage

William Faulkner

THE SOUND AND THE FURY

'Faulkner has inexhaustible invention, powerful imagination, and he writes, generally like an angel'
Arnold Bennett

Ever since the first furore was created on publication day in 1929, *The Sound and the Fury* has been considered one of the key novels of this century. In essence this is a novel about lovelessness – 'only an idiot has no grief; only a fool would forget it. What else is there in this world sharp enough to stick to your guts?' It is a novel about intense passionate family relationships wherein there is no love, only self-centredness.

'Faulkner at his best – even sometimes at his worst – has a power, a richness of life, an intensity to be found in no other American writer of our time'
Malcolm Cowley

VINTAGE

Ernest Hemingway

THE OLD MAN AND THE SEA

'The best story Hemingway has written…no page of this
beautiful master-work could have been done better or
differently'
Sunday Times

'It is unsurpassed in Hemingway's *oeuvre*. Every word tells and
there is not a word too many'
Anthony Burgess

Set in the Gulf Stream off the coast of Havana, Hemingway's
magnificent fable is the story of an old man, a young boy and
a giant fish. It was *The Old Man and the Sea* that won for
Hemingway the Nobel Prize for Literature. Here, in a perfectly
crafted story is a unique and timeless vision of the beauty and
grief of man's challenge to the elements in which he lives.

'A quite wonderful example of narrative art. The writing is as
taut, and at the same time as lithe and cunningly played out, as
the line on which the old man plays the fish'
Guardian

VINTAGE

Also available in Vintage

Elizabeth Bowen

THE HOUSE IN PARIS

With an introduction by A.S. Byatt

'Her most atmospheric book...very eerie
and richly descriptive'
Daily Telegraph

To the stuffy, French *bourgeois* house, with the evil old
woman in her sickroom upstairs, come two children who
have never met before to spend a few hours in the care of
Mme Fisher's daughter before going on their separate ways.
Henrietta, conventionally English but not unfeeling, is on
her way to stay with relations at Mentone; Leopold, with his
disconcerting manner and precocious slyness, is there
because events in the lives of other grown-up characters are
moving towards some sort of tragic climax. It is as if the
whole of the past has led up to this gloomy afternoon, which
also holds within it the seeds of a no less tragic future.

'If there is anything to the catch phrase, "life felt", it is
here – in Elizabeth Bowen's munificence of detail, the fine
closeness of the atmosphere which she creates'
Peter Ackroyd, *Sunday Times*

'Her most moving novel...all Miss Bowen's most brilliant
qualities are here in evidence – her wit, her descriptive
power, above all her sense of the tragic'
Jocelyn Brooke

VINTAGE

Angela Carter

WISE CHILDREN

'Inventive and brilliant'
Victoria Glendinning, *The Times*

A richly comic tale of the tangled fortunes of two theatrical
families, the Hazards and the Chances, Angela Carter's
witty and bawdy novel is populated with as many sets of
twins and mistaken identities as any Shakespeare comedy,
and celebrates the magic of over a century of showbusiness.

'Wonderful writing...there is not much fiction around that is
as good as this'
Ruth Rendell, *Telegraph*

'A funny, funny book. *Wise Children* is even better than
Nights at the Circus. It deserves all the bouquets, diamonds
and stage-door Johnnies it can get'
Salman Rushdie, *Independent on Sunday*

VINTAGE

A SELECTED LIST OF CLASSICS
AVAILABLE IN VINTAGE

☐	THE DEATH OF THE HEART	Elizabeth Bowen	£6.99
☐	THE HEAT OF THE DAY	Elizabeth Bowen	£6.99
☐	THE HOUSE IN PARIS	Elizabeth Bowen	£6.99
☐	THE PATH TO THE SPIDERS' NESTS	Italo Calvino	£5.99
☐	THE WAPSHOT SCANDAL	John Cheever	£6.99
☐	ABSALOM, ABSALOM!	William Faulkner	£6.99
☐	THE SOUND AND THE FURY	William Faulkner	£6.99
☐	THE OLD MAN AND THE SEA	Ernest Hemingway	£6.99
☐	THE TRIAL	Franz Kafka	£6.99
☐	DARKNESS AT NOON	Arthur Koestler	£6.99
☐	SONG OF SOLOMON	Toni Morrison	£6.99
☐	SULA	Toni Morrison	£6.99
☐	LADY FROM GUATEMALA	V.S. Pritchett	£7.99
☐	FLAWS IN THE GLASS	Patrick White	£6.99

- All Vintage books are available through mail order or from your local bookshop.

- Please send cheque/eurocheque/postal order (sterling only), Access, Visa, Mastercard, Diners Card, Switch or Amex:

☐☐☐☐☐☐☐☐☐☐☐☐☐☐☐☐

Expiry Date:_____Signature:_____

Please allow 75 pence per book for post and packing U.K.
Overseas customers please allow £1.00 per copy for post and packing.

ALL ORDERS TO:

Vintage Books, Books by Post, TBS Limited, The Book Service,
Colchester Road, Frating Green, Colchester, Essex CO7 7DW

NAME:_____

ADDRESS:_____

_____

_____

Please allow 28 days for delivery. Please tick box if you do not
wish to receive any additional information ☐

Prices and availability subject to change without notice.